LEADER DEVELOPMENT FOR TRANSFORMING ORGANIZATIONS

Growing Leaders for Tomorrow

Gregory Bedny and David Meister
The Russian Theory of Activity: Current Applications to Design and Learning

Michael T. Brannick, Eduardo Salas, and Carolyn Prince
Team Performance Assessment and Measurement: Theory, Research, and Applications

Jeanette N. Cleveland, Margaret Stockdale, and Kevin R. Murphy
Women and Men in Organizations: Sex and Gender Issues at Work

Aaron Cohen
Multiple Commitments in the Workplace: An Integrative Approach

Russell Cropanzano
Justice in the Workplace: Approaching Fairness in Human Resource Management, Volume 1

Russell Cropanzano
Justice in the Workplace: From Theory to Practice, Volume 2

David V. Day, Stephen J. Zaccaro, Stanley M. Halpin
Leader Development for Transforming Organizations: Growing Leaders for Tomorrow

James E. Driskell and Eduardo Salas
Stress and Human Performance

Sidney A. Fine and Steven F. Cronshaw
Functional Job Analysis: A Foundation for Human Resources Management

Sidney A. Fine and Maury Getkate
Benchmark Tasks for Job Analysis: A Guide for Functional Job Analysis (FJA) Scales

J. Kevin Ford, Steve W. J. Kozlowski, Kurt Kraiger, Eduardo Salas, and Mark S. Teachout
Improving Training Effectiveness in Work Organizations

Jerald Greenberg
Organizational Behavior: The State of the Science, Second Edition

Uwe E. Kleinbeck, Hans-Henning Quast, Henk Thierry, and Hartmut Häcker
Work Motivation

Martin I. Kurke and Ellen M. Scrivner
Police Psychology into the 21st Century

Joel Lefkowitz
Ethics and Values in Industrial and Organizational Psychology

Manuel London
Job Feedback: Giving, Seeking, and Using Feedback for Performance Improvement, Second Edition

Manuel London
How People Evaluate Others in Organizations

Manuel London
Leadership Development: Paths to Self-Insight and Professional Growth

Robert F. Morrison and Jerome Adams
Contemporary Career Development Issues

Michael D. Mumford, Garnett Stokes, and William A. Owens
Patterns of Life History: The Ecology of Human Individuality

Kevin R. Murphy
Validity Generalization: A Critical Review

Kevin R. Murphy and Frank E. Saal
Psychology and Organizations: Integrating Science and Practice

Susan E. Murphy and Ronald E. Riggio
The Future of Leadership Development

Erich P. Prien, Jeffery S. Schippmann and Kristin O. Prien
Individual Assessment: As Practiced in Industry and Consulting

Ned Rosen
Teamwork and Bottom Line: Groups Make a Difference

Heinz Schuler, James L. Farr, and Mike Smith
Personnel Selection and Assessment: Individual and Organizational Perspectives

John W. Senders and Neville P. Moray
Human Error: Cause, Prediction, and Reduction

Frank J. Smith
Organizational Surveys: The Diagnosis and Betterment of Organizations Through Their Members

George C. Thornton III and Rose Mueller-Hanson
Developing Organizational Simulations: A Guide for Practitioners and Students

Yoav Vardi and Ely Weitz
Misbehavior in Organizations: Theory, Research and Management

---

For more information on LEA titles, please contact Lawrence Erlbaum Associates, Publishers, at www.erlbaum.com.

LEADER DEVELOPMENT FOR TRANSFORMING ORGANIZATIONS

Growing Leaders for Tomorrow

Edited by

David V. Day
Pennsylvania State University

Stephen J. Zaccaro
George Mason University

Stanley M. Halpin
U.S. Army Research Institute

Ψ Psychology Press
Taylor & Francis Group
NEW YORK AND HOVE

Senior Acquisitions Editor:	Anne Duffy
Editorial Assistant:	Kristin Duch
Cover Design:	Sean Trane Sciarrone
Textbook Production Manager:	Paul Smolenski
Full-Service Compositor:	TechBooks
Text and Cover Printer:	Sheridan Books, Inc.

This book was typeset in 10/12 pt. Times Roman, Bold, and Italic.
The heads were typeset in Americana, Americana Bold, and Americana Bold Italic

First published by Lawrence Erlbaum Associates, Inc., Publishers
10 Industrial Avenue
Mahwah, New Jersey 07430

This edition published 2012 by Psychology Press

Psychology Press
Taylor & Francis Group
711 Third Avenue
New York, NY 10017

Psychology Press
Taylor & Francis Group
27 Church Road, Hove,
East Sussex, BN3 2FA

Psychology Press is an imprint of the Taylor & Francis Group, an informa business

Library of Congress Cataloging-in-Publication Data

Leader development for transforming organizations : growing leaders for
   tomorrow / edited by David V. Day, Stephen J. Zaccaro, Stanley M.
   Halpin.
      p.   cm. — (Series in applied psychology)
      ISBN 0-8058-4585-2 (casebound : alk. paper)—ISBN 0-8058-4586-0
   (pbk. : alk. paper)
      1. Leadership—Study and teaching.   2. Executives—Training of.
   I. Day, David V., 1956–   II. Zaccaro, Stephen J.   III. Halpin, Stanley M.
   IV. Series.

HD57.7.L415   2004
658.4'092—dc22   2003021748

10 9 8 7 6 5 4 3 2

Contents

Series Foreword   ix
Jeanette N. Cleveland and Edwin A. Fleishman

Preface   xi

Acknowledgments   xii

About the Authors   xiii

I: BACKGROUND AND OVERVIEW

1 Growing Leaders for Tomorrow: An Introduction   3
David V. Day and Stanley M. Halpin

2 Leadership Challenges for the Future   23
Maj. Gen. (Ret.) Lon E. Maggart

II: ACCELERATING LEADER DEVELOPMENT

3 Understanding the Development of Leadership Complexity
Through Latent Growth Modeling   41
David V. Day and Charles E. Lance

4 Examining the Full Range Model of Leadership: Looking Back
to Transform Forward   71
Bruce J. Avolio

5 A Technology to Support Leader Development:
Computer Games   99
Harold O'Neil and Yuan-Chung Fisher

III: COGNITIVE SKILLS DEVELOPMENT

6 The Development of Adult Cognition: Understanding Constancy
and Change in Adult Learning   125
Diane F. Halpern

7   Self-Awareness, Identity, and Leader Development   153
    Douglas T. Hall

8   Leadership as the Orchestration and Improvisation of Dialogue:
    Cognitive and Communicative Skills in Conversations Among
    Leaders and Subordinates   177
    Marvin S. Cohen

IV: DEVELOPING PRACTICAL AND EMOTIONAL
     INTELLIGENCE

9   Practical Intelligence and Leadership: Using Experience
    as a "Mentor"   211
    Anna T. Cianciolo, John Antonakis, and Robert J. Sternberg

10 Emotional Intelligence and Leadership Development   237
    David R. Caruso and Charles J. Wolfe

V: ENHANCING TEAM SKILLS

11 Leadership in Virtual Teams   267
    Stephen J. Zaccaro, Sharon D. Ardison, and Kara L. Orvis

12 Promoting Effective Leadership Within Multicultural Teams: An
    Event-Based Approach   293
    *Eduardo Salas, C. Shawn Burke, Katherine A. Wilson-Donnelly,
    and Jennifer E. Fowlkes*

13 Developing Teams and Team Leaders: Strategies and Principles   325
    Eduardo Salas, C. Shawn Burke, and Kevin C. Stagl

VI: CONCLUSIONS AND IMPLICATIONS

14 Leader Development and Change Over Time: A Conceptual
    Integration and Exploration of Research Challenges   359
    Katherine J. Klein and Jonathan C. Ziegert

15 Toward a Science of Leader Development   383
    David V. Day and Stephen J. Zaccaro

Author Index   401

Subject Index   415

Series Foreword

Jeanette N. Cleveland
Pennsylvania State University

Edwin A. Fleishman
George Mason University
Series Editors

There is a compelling need for innovative approaches to the solution of many pressing problems involving human relationships in today's society. Such approaches are more likely to be successful when they are based on sound research and applications. The Series in Applied Psychology offers publications which emphasize state-of-the-art research and its application to important issues regarding human behavior in a variety of work and social settings. The objective of the series is to bridge both academic and applied interests.

We are pleased to welcome this book into our Series in Applied Psychology. The book deals with the development of leaders within organizations. Although leader development has been discussed in the past, the emphasis has been on training methods and practices. The focus of this book is on 'what gets developed' in leader development: the cognitive, socio-emotional and behavioral skills, abilities, and knowledge required by leaders. Further, there is an exciting paradigm shift articulated among the chapters: rather than seeking to identify leaders and draw them into the organizations, leaders can be developed within the organizations.

The authors discuss the 'growing' of leaders within organizations (Day and Halpin). Specifically the approach emphasizes that all employees are potential leaders and that the major role of a leader is to develop leader skills among employees at all levels of the organization in order to transform their organizations.

The book addresses the following questions: 1) What do we mean by leadership? 2) What characterizes transformation in organizations? 3) How can leader development transform organizations?

Throughout the book are chapters that present theoretical frameworks for leader development including lifespan (Avolio), developmental theories (Day and Halpin), cognitive development and theory (Halpern,), notions of developmental readiness (Hall), and leader complexity (Day and Lance). Interspersed throughout the book are chapters specifically linking scientifically developed theoretical frameworks with their practical application to a number of organizational settings, including military settings (Maggart, O'Neill, etc). Further, the developmental lifespan and complexity issues raised have a number of implications for how leader development is assessed.

The chapter by Day and Lance discusses current measurement models and ways to extend them to facilitate the assessment of the complexities associated with leader development and change. These newer more complex models are necessary given the lifespan approach to leader development. The role of leaders as primary developers of other leaders is presented by Avolio in his full range leadership model. O'Neill and Fisher draw from research conducted within the military to describe ways in which technology (specifically computer games) can be used to develop appropriate leader skills.

Three chapters address the development of cognitive skills. In their respective chapters, Halpern draws from the adult development research and Hall draws from the career literature to describe the interactive developmental process involved in both cognitive and identity growth. The richness of research methodologies presented in this book is exemplified in the Cohen chapter on the analysis of both verbal and nonverbal interaction among people in conversation.

The discussion of the development of leader cognitive skills includes developing practical cognitive skills (Cianciolo, Antonakis, and Sternberg) and emotional intelligence (Caruso and Wolfe). In addition, three chapters are devoted to enhancing team skills. Zaccaro, Ardison, and Orvis discuss the roles of swift trust, motivation, and affect necessary for leadership in virtual teams. Salas, Burke, Fowlkes, and Wilson explore leadership in multi-cultural teams and assert a number of propositions for the application of research to such teams. The actual process and strategies for developing team leaders are presented by Salas, Burke, and Stagl.

In the two concluding chapters, Klein and Ziegert discuss the pace at which leaders develop over time; and Day and Zaccaro summarize the key issues and themes throughout the book with the goal of moving the topic of leader development toward a more scientific endeavor.

This book is on the cutting edge of the field of organizational behavior. The ongoing, dynamic perspective reflected across these chapters represents a shift in research and practice paradigms in the area of leader development. The book is a critical read for graduate students in applied psychology, organizational behavior, and management. It should be of interest to researchers, consultants, and thoughtful executives concerned with leader development in organizations.

Preface

Organizations in countries around the world and across a broad array of domains—industry, government, health care, not-for-profit, education, and military—are looking to leadership as a way of building a sustained competitive advantage. Building competitive advantage around leadership involves considerable investment of resources over an extended time period; thus, it should also involve judicious investment. Strategy in any form entails making difficult choices, and to be strategic about leadership development requires tough choices about the what, the where, and the how of investment.

This book examines numerous topics that are considered especially relevant for making a strategic leader development investment. The topics covered have theoretical and empirical connections to important aspects of growth, change, adult development, and underlying abilities, skills, and competencies needed to lead effectively in times of great complexity. In addition, these are investment areas identified by the U.S. Army—a world-class organization faced with the need for radical transformation—as particularly relevant for future success and survival. Another consideration is that the topics discussed are those needed in organizations that are changing and developing—as well as the kinds of skills, competencies, and perspectives that are needed for transforming those organizations. Development can and should involve organizational change. This book identifies key concerns in developing leaders and leadership and in transforming organizations to better meet the challenges of a complex world.

Two aspects of this book in particular distinguish it from the numerous volumes on leadership in the scholarly and popular literatures. Most importantly, the overarching focus is on development. There are many offerings on the topic of leadership, but relatively few that focus on leader development, especially from a scholarly, academic perspective. Of those books that do address leadership development, either their orientation is toward the practicing manager, or their emphasis is on leadership development practices (e.g., 360-degree feedback, mentoring, executive coaching). This book has a unique perspective in examining those underlying psychological competencies and processes that are viewed as especially relevant for leader development. These are the theoretically grounded causal explanations for the what, the why, and the how of leader development as a developmental process (highlighted in Part II, Accelerating Leader Development). Understanding these issues will help provide a theoretical foundation for better appreciating what needs to be developed (i.e., cognitive skills, practical and emotional intelligence, and team skills) to guide the specific practices chosen for leader development.

The chapters collected in this volume are based on "white papers" originally commissioned by the U.S. Army Research Institute to better help Army officers and researchers understand important issues in leader development. A workshop was held from May 30 to June 1, 2002, which included the editors and authors as well as invited participants from the military and research communities. The purpose of the workshop was to develop, hone, and integrate ideas and themes both within and across the chapters. Workshop discussions (and hence this collection of chapters), focused on four central themes (a) accelerating leader development, (b) cognitive skills development, (c) developing practical and emotional intelligence, and (d) enhancing team skills. We have added an introductory section that contributes contextual background and relevance to the core chapters, and a conclusions section that summarizes the scholarly contributions of the collection.

Although this book is about leader development and was sponsored by the U.S. Army Research Institute, it does not focus on any individual exemplar leaders from the Army or any other domain. Rather, the book is about developing the science to form the basis of principles that can guide the Army and other organizations to grow their future generations of leaders. Those readers who will likely find the book of interest are those who share our interest in developing a science of leader development. That includes students, scholars, and practitioners in the fields of leadership and development. We hope that this book provides an impetus for building a scientific understanding of how to develop leaders and transform organizations.

Acknowledgments

Support for the work represented in this book was provided in part by the U.S. Army Research Institute for the Behavioral and Social Sciences. However, the views, opinions, and findings contained in the book are the authors' and do not necessarily represent those of the Department of the Army or the Department of Defense.

The editors wish to thank Debora Mitchell and Doug Spiegel for their many contributions to this project. We also thank Anne Duffy of Lawrence Erlbaum Associates, Inc., and the Editors in its' Series in Applied Psychology, Jan Cleveland and Ed Fleishman, for their invaluable support.

About the Authors

John Antonakis is Assistant Professor of Human Resources Management at the Faculty of Economics and Business Administration (Ecole des Hautes Etudes Commerciales) of the University of Lausanne, Switzerland. He received his Ph.D. in Applied Management and Decision Sciences from Walden University, where he was awarded the Frank Dilley Best Dissertation Award for his work on the contextual nature of the Multifactor Leadership Questionnaire. Previously, Dr. Antonakis was a Postdoctoral Associate in the Department of Psychology at Yale University. His research interests include individual-difference antecedents of effective leadership, the measurement of leadership, and the links between context and leadership as applied to neocharismatic and transformational leadership models. He is also interested in cross-cultural organizational behavior.

Sharon D. Ardison is a research psychologist with the U.S. Army Research Institute for the Behavioral and Social Sciences. Her research focuses on Army leader development, training, quality personnel, doctrine, equipment, force mix, and climate/environment. Her current projects include evaluation of Army training and leader development of civilians, and commissioned, noncommissioned, and warrant officers. She has also been involved in assessment of human relations, battalion/brigade stabilization, deployment, and retention. Her expertise is in survey development and testing, data collection, and database management. As contracting officer representative on a number of outside contracts, she is currently examining teams (composition and behaviors), especially as they relate to the current high-tech virtual environments and multinational settings. During her career with the Army, Dr. Ardison has been assigned to a number of task forces and projects under the direction of the Secretary of the Army and the Army Chief of Staff.

Bruce J. Avolio holds the Donald and Shirley Clifton Chair in Leadership at the University of Nebraska in the College of Business Administration. He is the Director of the Gallup Leadership Institute and is a Gallup Senior Scientist. Professor Avolio has an international reputation as a researcher in leadership, having published over 80 articles and 5 books. He consults with a large number of public and private organizations in North America, South America, Africa, Europe, Southeast Asia, Australia, New Zealand, and Israel. His research and consulting also includes work with the militaries of the United States, Singapore, Sweden, Finland, Israel, and South Africa. His most recent books are *Transformational and Charismatic Leadership: The Road Ahead* (coedited with Francis J. Yammarino; Oxford: Elsevier Science, 2002) and *Made/Born: Leadership Development in Balance* (Mahwah; NJ: Lawrence Erlbaum Associates, Inc., forthcoming). His other books include *Full Leadership Development: Building the Vital Forces in Organizations* (Thousand Oaks, CA: Sage, 1999) and *Developing Potential Across a Full Range of Leadership: Cases on Transactional and Transformational Leadership* (coedited with Bernard M. Bass; Mahwah, NJ: Lawrence Erlbaum Associates, Inc., 2000).

C. Shawn Burke is a research associate at the University of Central Florida, Institute for Simulation and Training. Her primary research interests include teams, team leadership, team training and measurement, and team adaptability. Most recently, her research has focused on understanding and training for team adaptability. Within this line of research, she is investigating the impact of stress, leadership, and multicultural teams. She has presented work at numerous peer-reviewed conferences, has published in several scientific journals on the topics of teams and team training, and serves as an ad hoc reviewer for the journal *Human Factors*. She holds a Ph.D. in Industrial/Organizational Psychology from George Mason University.

David R. Caruso is a research affiliate in the Department of Psychology at Yale University, as well as a Vice President of Harris McCully Associates, a New York City-based human resources consulting firm. He was a National Institute of Child Health and Human Development predoctoral fellow and received a Ph.D. in Psychology from Case Western Reserve University. Upon graduation, he was awarded a National Institute of Mental Health fellowship and spent 2 years as a postdoctoral fellow in Developmental Psychology at Yale University. His consulting practice provides executive assessment, leadership development, executive coaching, and team development services. He is the coauthor of the Mayer, Salovey, Caruso Emotional Intelligence Test (MSCEIT), has published a number of journal articles and book chapters, and is coauthoring a book on emotionally intelligent management.

Anna T. Cianciolo is a postdoctoral research associate at the Center for the Psychology of Abilities, Competencies, and Expertise at Yale University. She received her B.A. from the University of Michigan in Psychology, and her M.A. in Cognitive and Biological Psychology from the University of Minnesota. She received her Ph.D. in 2001 in Engineering Psychology from the Georgia Institute of Technology, under the direction of Dr. Phillip L. Ackerman. Dr. Cianciolo's research centers on the exploration of individual differences in human performance from a cognitive perspective. Her interests lie in taking a step outside of traditional assessment methodologies in order to reconceptualize performance not only as a function of human capabilities, but as an interaction between personal characteristics (e.g., knowledge) and environmental constraints (e.g., task demands). Her work has appeared in the *Journal of Experimental Psychology: Applied* and *Human Performance.*

Marvin S. Cohen received his Ph.D. from Harvard University in 1980 and founded Cognitive Technologies, Inc., in 1990, where he is president and chief scientist. Dr. Cohen's recent research has focused on understanding and training critical thinking and leadership, through the integration of dialogue theory and cognitive models of thinking and decision making. He is also designing decision aids that support critical thinking and decision making in time-constrained and uncertain environments. His other work involves development and testing of methods for cognitive task analysis, modeling real-time decision making in a variety of domains (based on data from experiments, interviews, and naturalistic observation), training and evaluating critical thinking performance, computer simulation of real-time decision making, decision aids that adapt to users, training users to assess appropriate trust in decision aid outputs, and knowledge-based collaborative information management.

David V. Day is Professor of Psychology at Pennsylvania State University and a fellow of the American Psychological Association. He received a B.A. degree in Psychology from Baldwin-Wallace College, and M.A. and Ph.D. degrees in Industrial/Organizational Psychology from the University of Akron. Dr. Day has published more than 40 journal articles and book chapters, many pertaining to the topic of leadership. He serves on the editorial board of the *Journal of Management* and is an associate editor of *Leadership Quarterly.* From 2000 to 2002, he served as a civilian member of the U.S. Army Panels for Training and Leader Development, which reported to the Chief of Staff on the state of the Army's practices in the areas of training and leader development for officers, noncommissioned officers, and civilians.

Yuan-Chung Fisher is a Ph.D. student in the Rossier School of Education at the University of Southern California. Her research interest is on communication media and educational technology. She is studying educational computer games and computer-assisted learning. Within the foreseeable future, she expects to work more with computer games with the guidance of her academic adviser, Dr. Harry O'Neil. She received her B.A. in Journalism at National Cheng Chi University in Taiwan and her M.A. in Telecommunications at Michigan State University. For 7 years, before her Ph.D. study, Joan worked as a television news reporter and news anchorwoman for three television companies in Taipei, Taiwan. Her last job was a reporter and anchor at Taiwan Television Company, one of the four TV networks in Taiwan. She lives with her husband, Tom, and their young daughter in Alhambra, California.

Jennifer E. Fowlkes has over 15 years of experience in areas of human factors and training, which includes team training and performance, training effectiveness evaluations, simulator sickness research, and performance test battery development. Most recently, her research has focused on training and assessment of adaptive team performance in distributed training environments. Dr. Fowlkes is a senior cognitive engineer at CHI Systems, Inc. She holds a Ph.D. in Experimental Psychology from the University of Georgia.

Douglas T. Hall is Professor of Organizational Behavior in the School of Management at Boston University. He is also the Director of the Executive Development Roundtable and a core faculty member of the Human Resources Policy Institute. He has also served as Acting Dean and Associate Dean of Faculty Development and Faculty Director for Masters Programs at the School of Management. He has held faculty positions at Yale, York, Michigan State, and Northwestern Universities, as well as visiting positions at Columbia University, the University of Minnesota, and the U.S. Military Academy at West Point. At Northwestern he held the Earl Dean Howard Chair in Organizational Behavior and served as Department Chair. He has recently served as a Visiting Erskine Fellow at the University of Canterbury in Christchurch, New Zealand. He is the author of numerous books and scholarly articles on careers and management. He is a recipient of the American Psychological Association's Ghiselli Award for research design and the Walter Storey Professional Practice Award from the American Society for Training and Development. He is a fellow of the American Psychological Association and a fellow of the Academy of Management.

Diane F. Halpern is Professor of Psychology and Director of the Berger Institute for Work, Family, and Children at Claremont McKenna College. Prior to her appointment at Claremont McKenna, she was a professor in the psychology department at California State University, San Bernardino. She has won many awards for her teaching and research, including the 2002 Outstanding Professor Award from the Western Psychological Association, the 1999 American Psychological Foundation Award for Distinguished Teaching, and the Outstanding Alumna Award from the University of Cincinnati. She is the author of many journal articles and several books on critical thinking, sex differences in cognitive abilities, and work–life balance. She has served as president of the Western Psychological Association, the Society for the Teaching of Psychology, and the Division of General Psychology of the American Psychological Association. She is the current (2004) president of the American Psychological Association.

Stanley M. Halpin is a senior member of the federal civil service, and has worked for the Department of the Army for 33 years. For the last 20 years, he has served as the Chief of the U.S. Army Research Institute's group at Fort Leavenworth, Kansas. The Leader Development Research Unit at Fort Leavenworth has conducted research on the U.S. Army's tactical decision-making processes, including development of procedures to improve staff performance, and development of training techniques for decision makers and decision-making groups. Over the last few years the research unit has broadened its focus and extended its research program to address interpersonal and team skills as well as cognitive skills. He has a B.S. in Industrial and Labor Relations from Cornell University (1965) and an M.S. and Ph.D. in Social Psychology from Purdue University (1970).

Katherine J. Klein is Associate Professor of Industrial and Organizational Psychology in the Department of Psychology at the University of Maryland. She earned her B.A. from Yale University and her Ph.D. from the University of Texas. Her research and writing focus on three interrelated topics: multilevel theory and methods, organizational innovation (especially employee stock ownership and computerized technology implementation), and work teams (including team diversity, leadership, network structure, and effectiveness). She is an Associate Editor of the *Journal of Applied Psychology* and has served on the editorial boards of *Academy of Management Review, Academy of Management Journal*, and *Leadership Quarterly,* among others. Her research has been funded by the National Science Foundation, the Army Research Institute, the Bureau of Labor Statistics, private foundations, and corporations. She is a Fellow of the Society for Industrial and Organizational Psychology and the American Psychological Association.

Charles E. Lance received his Ph.D. in Psychology from the Georgia Institute of Technology and is now Professor of Industrial/Organizational psychology and Chair of the Applied Psychology Program at the University of Georgia. His research interests are in the areas of measurement and prediction of performance, research methods, and structural equation modeling. Dr. Lance is a fellow of the Society of Industrial and Organizational Psychology and the American Psychological Association, serves on the editorial boards of *Organizational Research Methods, Personnel Psychology, Group & Organization Management,* and *Human Resource Management Review.*

Maj. Gen. (Ret.) Lon E. Maggart has more than 36 years of leadership experience in leading both small groups and very large, complex organizations. He is an experienced speaker and author on leadership including expertise in critical thinking and thinking models. He completed his military career as the Commanding General at Fort Knox, Kentucky. Since his retirement from the military, he has held responsible leadership positions in the civilian sector, including Director, Center for Semiconductor Research; Interim Senior Vice President, Engineering; and (his current position) Chief of Staff, RTI International. As the Chief of Staff, he is responsible for the day-to-day operations of the organization and for advising the Chief Executive Officer. He received a B.A. in Political Science at Kansas State University in 1966 and an M.S. in Human Resource Management from the University of Utah in 1974. His military education included the Center for Creative Leadership in Greensboro, North Carolina, the Army War College at Carlisle Barracks, Pennsylvania, the U.S. Army Command and General Staff College at Fort Leavenworth, Kansas.

Harold F. O'Neil is a professor of learning and instruction at the University of Southern California's Rossier School of Education and a project director at the Center for Research on Evaluation, Standards, and Student Testing. His research interests include the computer-based assessment of workforce readiness, particularly problem-solving and collaboration skills, the teaching and measurement of self-regulation skills, the role of motivation in testing, and the training effectiveness of computer games. He has conducted cross-cultural research in Japan on the role of test anxiety and performance, and in Taiwan and Korea on the role of self-regulation and achievement. He has also conducted research on the role of financial incentives on low-stakes tests such as the National Assessment of Educational Progress and the Third International Mathematics and Science Study. In all of these research areas, he is interested in technology applications.

Kara L. Orvis is a doctoral candidate in the Industrial/Organizational Psychology program at George Mason University and currently employed as a senior research fellow at the U.S. Army Research Institute in Alexandria, Virginia. She received her M.A. in Industrial/Organizational Psychology from George Mason University in 1999 and her B.A. degree from Ohio Wesleyan University. Her main research interests have been in the realms of teams, multiteam systems, and leadership, concentrating on team training and leadership development. Her dissertation research is investigating the impact of leadership processes on team process and performance in colocated and distributed team environments. While at Army Research Institute she is concluding a series of evaluations and controlled experiments on the training effectiveness of distance learning technology.

Eduardo Salas is a Professor of Industrial/Organizational and Human Factors Psychology at the University of Central Florida. Previously, he was a senior research psychologist and head of the Training Technology Development Branch of the Naval Air Warfare Center Training Systems Division for 15 years. He has coauthored over 200 journal articles and book chapters and has coedited 11 books. He is or was on the editorial boards of *Journal of Applied Psychology*, *Personnel Psychology*, *Military Psychology*, *Group Dynamics*, *International Journal of Aviation Psychology*, and *Journal of Organizational Behavior*. He is the editor of *Human Factors* and is currently the series editor for the Professional Practice Book Series and has served on numerous Society for Industrial and Organizational Psychology (SIOP) committees throughout the years. He is a fellow of the American Psychological Association, SIOP, and the Human Factors and Ergonomics Society.

Kevin C. Stagl is a graduate student in the Industrial and Organizational Psychology Ph.D. program at the University of Central Florida (UCF). He is currently employed as a research assistant at UCF's Institute for Simulation and Training (IST). At IST his theoretical and empirical research addresses the full spectrum of team effectiveness issues including staffing, training, and facilitating adaptive team performance. Prior to joining UCF and IST, Kevin spent 5 years as a researcher in an organizational consultancy. In his former role, Kevin worked with an international team of psychologists to design, develop, deliver, and maintain selection, development, and promotional systems.

Robert J. Sternberg is IBM Professor of Psychology and Education and Director of the Center for the Psychology of Abilities, Competencies, and Expertise at Yale. The Center is dedicated to the advancement of theory, research, practice, and policy advancing the notion of intelligence as developing expertise that is modifiable and capable of development throughout the life span. He received his Ph.D. from Stanford University in 1975 and his B.A. summa cum laude, Phi Beta Kappa, from Yale University in 1972. He also holds honorary doctorates from the Complutense University of Madrid, Spain; the University of Leuven, Belgium; the University of Cyprus; and the University of Paris V, France. He is the author of over 900 journal articles, book chapters, and books, and has received over $15 million in government and other grants and contracts for his research. He was the 2003 president of the American Psychological Association.

Charles J. Wolfe is president of Charles J. Wolfe Associates, LLC, a results-driven consulting firm. He is a keynote speaker, consultant to *Fortune* 500 companies, and author. His expertise includes applying emotional intelligence to leadership development, executive coaching, performance management, teams, and change management. Prior to founding his own company, he was Director of Management Development at Hartford Insurance, Director of Organization Development at Exxon, and Organizational Behavior Research Associate in the Executive Program for Management Development at Harvard. He also created and hosted a radio talk show called "Family Education and Understanding." He frequently guest lectures at the Massachusetts Institute of Technology's Sloan School. His consulting is prominently featured in CRM's "Learning Video on Emotional Intelligence." In 2003 he presented two live audio broadcasts on emotional intelligence and performance management to over 100 companies worldwide. His publications include articles on emotional intelligence, corporate culture change, and the the Ford–Iacocca case for Harvard Business School.

Katherine A. Wilson-Donnelly is a graduate student in the Applied Experimental and Human Factors Psychology Ph.D. program at the University of Central Florida in Orlando, Florida. She earned a B.S. degree in Aerospace Studies from Embry-Riddle Aeronautical University in 1998 and an M.S. degree in Modeling and Simulation from the University of Central Florida in 2002. She is also a research assistant at the Institute for Simulation and Training. Her primary research interests include team training, safety, diversity, and human performance. She has numerous publications and has presented work at several national conferences. In addition, she is a student affiliate of the Human Factors and Ergonomics Society, the American Psychological Association, and the Society for Industrial and Organizational Psychology.

Stephen J. Zaccaro is Professor of Psychology at George Mason University, Fairfax, Virginia. He has been studying, teaching, and consulting about leadership for almost 20 years. He has written over 80 articles, book chapters, and technical reports on leadership, as well as on group dynamics, team performance, and work attitudes. He has written *The Nature of Executive Leadership: A Conceptual and Empirical Analysis of Success* (Washington, DC: American Psychological Association, 2001) and coedited *Occupational Stress and Organizational Effectiveness* (coedited with Anne W. Riley; Westport, CT: Praeger, 1987) and *The Nature of Organizational Leadership: Understanding the Performance Imperatives Confronting Today's Leaders* (coedited with Richard J. Klimoski, San Francisco: Jossey-Bass/Pfeiffer, 2001). He has also directed funded research projects in the areas of team performance and shared mental models, leadership training, cognitive and metacognitive leadership capacities, and executive leadership.

Jonathan C. Ziegert is a doctoral student in the Industrial/Organizational Psychology program at the University of Maryland. His research interests include the topics of leadership, group processes, and implicit attitudes and biases.

I
Background and Overview

1

Growing Leaders for Tomorrow: An Introduction

David V. Day
Pennsylvania State University

Stanley M. Halpin
U.S. Army Research Institute

There are indications that our nation's leadership is in crisis. Financial and other scandals, bankruptcies, and forced resignations afflict our corporate, religious, educational, and political institutions. Although the so-called newsworthy stories that dominate the headlines may exaggerate the true extent of any leadership problem, there is reason to believe that organizations may not be prepared for the leadership challenges of the future. Recent (proprietary) survey data indicate that only about one fifth of the chief executive officers surveyed believed that they and their colleagues are prepared to lead their respective firms in the future. An issue contributing to this feeling of a leadership gap is the profound transformation that continues in business, education, and the military—basically in every domain.

The challenges faced by organizations have become increasingly complex. As a result, businesses and other organizations are changing their structures, reducing layers of management control, and striving to become more agile and responsive to their environments. The result of these ongoing transformations is that there is a pervasive need for people at every level to participate in the leadership process. No single leader can possibly have all the answers to every problem, especially if those problems are in the form of adaptive challenges—those problems for which an organization has no preexisting resources, tools, solutions, or even sensemaking strategies for accurately naming and describing the challenge (Heifetz, 1994). Consequently, all organizational members need to be leaders and all leaders need to be better prepared to participate in leadership. The full extent of a current leadership "crisis" may be arguable; however, there is little arguing that there is an acute need to develop leadership more comprehensively across all organizational levels and to do so as quickly as possible. This will require considerable attention from today's leaders and the willingness to commit significant resources to leadership development. It will also require greater responsibility on the part of those being developed to be active and intentional experiential learners. Organizations can only do so much; most of the really meaningful developmental experiences occur in the context of ongoing work (McCall, Lombardo, & Morrison, 1988).

What is it about leadership that makes it worth the hefty investment? Why is leadership so important to organizations? Rather than purely an illusory effect or attribution artifact, leadership is associated with distinct tasks, duties, functions, and responsibilities. These have been conceptualized in many different ways, including task orientation and socioemotional orientation (Bales, 1958); consideration and initiating structure (Stogdill & Coons, 1957); influence, motivation, consideration, and intellectual stimulation (Bass & Avolio, 1994); and setting direction, building commitment, and facing adaptive challenges (Drath, 2001). As Avolio (chap. 4, this volume) argues, the relevant point is not which particular tasks are most important for leadership. It is instead more important to recognize that there are discernible leadership functions that contribute to organizational adaptability and effectiveness. Put simply, accomplishing these leadership tasks adds value to organizations. The purpose of this book is to focus on the components of leader development that can help individuals better participate in the leadership tasks of their respective organizations. It is our contention that this type of leadership participation can be enhanced regardless of one's particular position in the hierarchy or whether an individual is in a formal leadership position or not.

Our approach to leadership does not begin with a traditional job analysis to identify definitive leadership tasks or leader knowledge, skills, and abilities. It is probably impossible for any single job analysis to be successful in this endeavor given the wide range of missions, domains, and environments that characterize modern organizations. Furthermore, research on implicit leadership theories (e.g., Eden & Leviathan, 1975) has found a diversity of perspectives on the meaning of leadership. These differing implicit theories are important because they determine the perceived relevance of various types of leader behavior in an organization (Lord & Maher, 1991). Because the role of leader is susceptible to influence not only from external factors (e.g., factors affecting an organizational mission), but also from intraorganizational perspectives, we focus on those attributes or characteristics that contribute to an overall ability to participate in leadership responsibilities (broadly defined) and that can also be developed in individuals. Despite the voluminous leadership literature, relatively little is known about exactly what gets developed in leader development.

Highhouse (2000) pointed out that the grooming of executives prior to World War II consisted mainly of job rotations and mentoring (Dooher & Marquis, 1952). Highhouse reviewed what he calls the first major attempt at management development—the widespread use in U.S. business and industry of sensitivity training (often called T-groups or encounter groups) for executives. The approach involved small unstructured groups of managers struggling to deal with lack of structure, to develop an atmosphere of self-examinations, mutual trust, openness to change in their views, overcoming their own resistance to change, and acceptance of feedback about their behavior (see Bradford, 1974; Schein & Bennis, 1965). Thousands of U.S. managers participated in this movement, which peaked in the 1960's and whose outcomes were never subjected to systematic evaluation of their subsequent leadership performance.

Perhaps the first systematic evaluation of a leadership development program was carried out at the International Harvester Company (Fleishman, 1953; Fleishman, Harris, & Burtt, 1955) as part of the Ohio State Leadership Studies. The company had developed a central school to which managers were sent for several weeks. This was one of the first programs of its type aimed at the "broader development" of managers. Subjects included team building, human relations, planning and organizing, and logical thinking. Methods included role playing, group discussions, and workshops.

The major findings still have relevance to today's leadership development efforts. First, these interventions resulted in changes in leadership attitudes and behavior (leader consideration and initiating structure) when trainees were evaluated before and after training as compared with control groups of comparable managers. However, these effects did not persist when managers returned to their plants. The most critical variable in enhancing this transfer of leadership training was the "leadership climate" in the plant. This led to a change in policy, focusing on development of more senior managers prior to training of subordinate managers in organizations.

More recently, the focus of leader development efforts have been mainly on the various methods used to develop leaders (e.g., Conger & Benjamin, 1999; McCauley, Moxley, & Van Velsor, 1998; Vicere & Fulmer, 1998) than about the actual target of those efforts in terms of what is developed. The purpose of the present book is to address this lapse directly. It brings together the perspectives of a number of researchers interested in the *what* as much as the *how* of leader development, in addition to the *why*.

To promote a better understanding of the intended approach and contribution of this book, we first address three questions: (a) What do we mean by leader development? (b) What characterizes transforming organizations? And (c) How can leader development transform organizations? These questions help to frame the subsequent contributions in this book.

LEADER DEVELOPMENT

What do we mean by leader development? What kinds of things represent leader development? How is leader development different from leader*ship* development? These are all reasonable questions that deserve careful attention. The designation of leader—rather than leader*ship*—development was chosen purposefully. Day (2000) argued that there is a fundamental difference between leader and leadership development. What many organizations term a leadership development effort should more accurately be labeled as leader development. This difference is more than mere semantics.

Most development approaches focus exclusively on the individual and ignore the social context. It is presumed that developing individual leaders will result in better leadership; however, this is at best a tenuous assumption. That approach is equivalent to teaching someone better communication skills but not considering the roles of others in the communication process. If someone speaks and there is no one around to listen or respond (or no one can understand the language), has communication occurred? Most would say no. Who has received the communication? The speaker has spoken but has not necessarily communicated. If I develop individual-level knowledge, skills, and abilities (i.e., "human capital") that are relevant for leadership, but do not use these skills or do not find them useful in creating and developing relationships with others (i.e., "social capital"), can it be said that leadership was developed? Again, most would say no. How can someone lead without others to follow? Leadership is a complex interaction involving leaders, followers, and situations (Fiedler, 1996). It is a function of the relationships that are created and maintained with others (i.e., social capital) and the resulting interpersonal context. Nonetheless, developing individual leaders is critically important to leadership development. Without the individual preparation for the demands and challenges of leadership, many will find themselves in over their heads in such situations. Our primary purpose in this book is to bring together a coherent and comprehensive treatment of what to focus on in leader development and how such efforts can be used to transform individuals, teams, and organizations.

Whereas leader development focuses on individuals, leadership development must attend to the social and interpersonal nature of the phenomenon. Leadership requires a social context, and therefore cannot be directly developed unless groups of people are brought together over time. This is because leadership development depends on fostering social relations among individuals in a group, team, or organization (Day, 2000). However, leadership can develop naturally (i.e., without direct intervention) as a result of people participating in shared work together. One way we may support and accelerate leadership development is to help individuals learn how to learn from their experiences so that leader development becomes one part of ongoing self-development. In other words, leadership can be seen as an outcome of mutual commitments, interpersonal relationships, and social processes; leader development is the preparation of the individual to work within that social context. Rather than an input to a particular situation, leadership is more appropriately conceptualized as an outcome of effective social structures and processes (Salancik, Calder, Rowland, Leblebici, & Conway, 1975). Thus, leadership is drawn from social structures and processes in an organization rather than added to them. These structures and processes, however, are at least partly a function of the development of individual leaders. The knowledge, skills, and abilities that compose the basics of human capital can be developed and used as inputs to enhance group functioning. Put simply, the quality of a social process is heavily dependent on the quality and sophistication of the individuals participating in the process.

Instead of debating whether leader development or leadership development is more appropriate for an organization, what deserves greater attention is how to bridge individual leader development with more collective leadership development efforts. Strategies are needed to better link individual leader inputs with the outcomes of group processes. Despite this important need, the focus of this book is primarily on individual leader development with additional focused attention on leader development and leadership within team contexts. It is worth mentioning again that developing individual leaders is not the same as leadership development nor does it guarantee that better leadership will follow. However, both are necessary for high-performing, healthy, and adaptive organizations. We are starting with leader development because we see it as the foundation on which to build and bridge with other efforts.

The U.S. Army leadership doctrine (1999; FM22-100) speaks of leader development in terms of technical, tactical, conceptual, and leadership competencies. More broadly, it may be argued that leaders must have the fundamental skills to accomplish their job (technical skills), they must be able to understand how to employ their own talents and those of others to achieve organizational goals (tactical and conceptual skills), and they must know how to work with and through others to accomplish those goals (leadership skills). The focus and the value-added nature of leader development may vary across this range of skills. Leader development could enhance the cognitive and behavioral complexity of leaders, contributing to greater adaptability and self-awareness. Leader development efforts could increase individual emotional intelligence or the ability to learn from experience and result in enhanced tacit knowledge. Dialogue skills could be developed leading to better critical thinking. These are examples of the kinds of attributes that can be targeted in leader development. Organizational needs and individuals' personal goals interact to determine what change actually occurs as a result of leader development efforts. This intersection between organizational needs and individual development is explored more fully in the next section.

TRANSFORMING ORGANIZATIONS

Organizations are rarely, if ever, at complete stasis. They undergo continuous change—whether it is barely perceptible incremental or the kind of radical, discontinuous change that can rock an organization to its foundation. In this manner, organizations experience continuous ongoing transformation. There have been recent suggestions, however, that organizations must be more purposeful and even radical in their efforts at transformation. The suggestion is that those organizations that do not radically transform by destroying the old are fated to be destroyed by their competition (Thurow, 1999).

The reasons behind this bold statement are clear. There is unprecedented unpredictability and uncertainty (i.e., turbulence) in virtually every industry and organizational domain. Nothing is certain any longer but uncertainty. Even reputable corporate firms have seen their value rise and drop precipitously within a matter of days or weeks (not months or years). In the educational domain, institutions are faced with serious competition from for-profit universities and online education providers, coupled with dramatic reductions in state appropriations and steep declines in endowment portfolios associated with value losses in the stock market. In primary and secondary education, charter schools have emerged as legitimate competition for students and government funding. Military organizations are perhaps facing the greatest set of challenges ever to their core mission of protecting the nation. Terrorism threats epitomize unpredictability. Military organizations must somehow counter these threats while also continuing to prepare for more traditional (i.e., Cold War-type) missions. Details of the U.S. Army's efforts regarding transformation are the focus of Maj. Gen. (Ret.) Lon Maggart's chapter in this book (chap. 2, this volume). As Gen. Maggart attests, the transformation toward an Objective Force is a complex undertaking involving changes in doctrine, organization, and equipment, and, in many ways, fundamental changes to the Army culture, most especially in leadership. For this reason, the Army is examining and rethinking the ways in which it conducts training and leader development (http://www.army.mil/features/ATLD/ATLD.htm) with the goal of leveraging leader development initiatives as a catalyst for transformation. Although the impetus behind this book can be found in the Army's transformation, it is by no means pertinent only to the Army or even just the military. The evidence is compelling that transformation is a ubiquitous and pervasive need across every type of organization.

It is difficult to identify any contemporary organizational domain that is stable, is predictable, and requires little if any transformation. We live in a dynamic and turbulent world that is better characterized by a fast pace of change as opposed to slow and steady growth. This type of rapid transformation is not inherently natural to people. We have perhaps hard-wired tendencies to prefer stability and predictability to uncertainty and change. It has been argued that individuals, groups, and organizations are likely to respond to perceived threats with habituated, over-learned (i.e., rigid) responses (Staw, Sandelands, & Dutton, 1981). It is exactly this entrenched threat–rigidity pattern that must be overcome if organizations are to transform effectively and quickly.

Organizations that are facing major changes usually must adapt or transform with the managers already in place rather than selecting a new cadre with every new change effort. Thus, there is a premium on the ability to develop managers who are able to cope with change more effectively (Judge, Thorensen, Pucik, & Welbourne, 1999). Leader development efforts can contribute to building the capacity for rapid transformation. One thing that impedes effective change is being locked into rigid or restricted approaches to leadership. The ability of individual leaders to conceptualize and enact multiple leadership strategies in a given situation is a primary mechanism for building leadership capacity in organizations (Day, 2001). This capacity offers the potential for greater adaptability in the face of uncertainty and possibly mitigates threat–rigidity tendencies. However, there are no easy answers to the question of how to develop individuals willing and able to embrace constant change instead of fearing and resisting it.

An issue related to the changing nature of work in many organizations is a shift from experiencing mainly closed types of problems to increasing exposure to open problems. There is a distinction made in problem-solving research regarding the degree to which a problem has been formulated and structured before an individual begins the process. Specifically, there is a proposed continuum of problem types, from closed to open problems (Getels & Csikszentmihalyi, 1967, 1976). A closed problem is one that is presented to an individual for which there is a known solution and problem-solving method. A good example of a closed problem is a basic algebra problem. There is a verifiable and correct solution to this type of problem; furthermore, there are also proven methods for effectively and efficiently solving the problem. At the other end of the continuum is an open problem, in which an individual is required to find, invent, or discover the problem, and for which there is not a known solution or problem-solving method. Most artistic and other creative endeavors are characterized by open problems. Whereas both types of problems require some degree of creativity to solve, they may require very different kinds of creativity (Unsworth, 2001). Leaders at top organizational levels have most often been exposed to open problems, and those at middle and lower levels have been exposed primarily to closed problems; however, this configuration may be changing. Due to sophisticated technology, greater interdependence in the nature of organizational work, greater problem complexity, and a whole host of additional factors, organizations need leaders at all levels to deal with open and otherwise ill-structured problems. Leader development efforts can help in developing individuals who can handle this kind of complexity.

One thing seems certain: A traditional training emphasis will unlikely be completely successful in developing leaders of the future, especially leaders that are faced with open problems. Training is characterized by the basic approach of providing individuals with proven solutions to known problems. Training is therefore most appropriate for situations in which closed problems are the norm. However, how does one train people to discover problems and handle situations that cannot even be envisioned, let alone attempt to provide them with proven solutions? Instead of a pure training focus, transformation efforts require greater attention to development.

A fundamental difference between training and development is that development efforts focus on preparing individuals to quickly make sense of their environments and to learn their way out of problems (Dixon, 1993). In this manner, there is a premium on individuals who can create innovative solutions and improvise with limited resources. Karl Weick (1993) referred to this ability as "bricolage," and it is not something that is especially amenable to training, at least training as it is conventionally viewed (i.e., bounded, short-term programs). Rather, there is a need for more long-term investment strategies that help people envision multiple possibilities to every situation, think creatively, improvise, and move toward change instead of away from it. Whereas certain knowledge, skills, and abilities can and should be trained (e.g., they contribute to enhanced adaptability), there needs to be a recognized demarcation between the kinds of attributes that can be improved or acquired through training and those requiring the use of more complex and comprehensive developmental interventions.

Although there is a need to differentiate between those skills that can be acquired through training and those better suited for development efforts, ultimately there is a blurry line between training and development in most applications. Those interventions designed to enhance complex skills usually maintain aspects of both approaches. The choice is rarely as simple as whether to provide training or provide development. Rather, the challenge is in how to link both approaches, thereby more efficiently and effectively bringing about the desired changes in individuals. When is a pure training approach appropriate? The answer is probably when there are definitive skills that must be acquired and known procedures for delivering the desired content to facilitate the acquisition of those skills. When is development the appropriate type of intervention? Probably when the ultimate goal is some relatively macro or global (and less concrete) change such as general coping, adaptation, identity, or leadership. For example, it does not make much sense to try to *train* identity; however, there is a rich literature on identity *development*. The time frame also is much longer with development than training, and the interventions generally are less bounded and less structured. It is our position that leadership is more likely to be enhanced through development efforts than by traditional training. However, as mentioned, it is possible (and even desirable) to link training with development. Unfortunately, there are few examples of how to do this effectively in organizations.

Comprehensive, organization-wide leader development efforts require a long-term perspective. The payoffs from leader development investment strategies can contribute to organizational success, but are rarely immediate. However, there may be ways to accelerate the process. One means could be through the use of advanced technology, such as simulations or other kinds of games that allow individuals to try out different behaviors or ways of thinking under relatively safe conditions. O'Neil and Fisher (chap. 5, this volume) review a number of these approaches and how the Army and other organizations use them to promote the leader development process. Another strategy for accelerating the development process is to target those cognitive, socioemotional, and behavioral attributes that are most desired.

The present approach to leader development also is based on the premise that developing leaders at all organizational levels is an appropriate and effective means of transforming organizations. Transforming individuals through leader development efforts also transforms organizations. This is because—as some scholars have proposed—the "people make the place" (Schneider, 1987). The approach is similar to developing shared mental models about power across organizational levels (Fiol, O'Connor, & Aguinis, 2001). The difference is that power is the ability or potential to influence (French & Raven, 1959), whereas leadership can take alternative forms including dialogue and collective sensemaking (Drath & Palus, 1994). In this manner, leadership transcends power; however, there is an inherent commonality in that both leadership and power are social constructions. Just as changing the power mental models of organizational members can potentially lead to the effective development and transfer of power across organizational levels, changing the predominant ways of thinking about leadership (i.e., changing the mental models or implicit theories) can alter the way in which leadership is perceived and enacted.

Why is it that everyone needs to be developed as a leader? It might be argued that this is likely to invite problems if everyone wants to lead and no one wants to follow. This argument assumes that the primary function of leaders is to tell others what to do. However, that is a relatively narrow perspective on the nature of leadership, that is, that it has to do mainly with providing structure, setting direction, or creating a vision. This is overly narrow because any organization must have many leaders beyond those who happen to be in leadership positions. Those who have developed as leaders will have the knowledge, skills, and abilities to understand, interpret, structure, imagine, take initiative, and provide direction. Those in formal leadership positions may have final authority, but others, within their own more constrained domains, will still need to draw on virtually the same set of leader attributes. These "other" leaders support the organizational leadership and extend the reach of those in formal leadership positions. Their leadership is manifest through their ability to work effectively with others, derive consensus, take initiative, question, and propose. These forms of participation in leadership are rarely considered as leadership per se, especially from traditional (i.e., narrow) perspectives.

Rather than viewing leadership as the province of a few elites that have formal leadership role designations, an alternative perspective views leadership as an outcome of effective social structures and processes (Salancik et al., 1975). It is the aggregate ability to create shared work that is meaningful to people and to add value to an organization. From this latter perspective, everyone can and should participate in leadership. Thus, there is an organizational imperative to help prepare everyone for this participation. The preparation is what we are calling leader development.

The foundation of leader development is based on the development of cognitive, socioemotional, and behavioral skills. These skills, supported by leader attributes such as self-awareness, openness, trust, creativity, and practical, social, and general intelligence, provide the basis of leadership. The combination and interaction of these foundational skills and attributes enhance the overall level of leader complexity (Hooijberg, Hunt, & Dodge, 1997). In essence, leader complexity creates the potential to envision and enact multiple leadership strategies in a given situation. As such, it is especially valuable in contexts in which open problems are experienced (i.e., those problems that need to be discovered and have no ready-made solution). The kinds of cognitive skills that contribute to enhanced complexity include problem recognition, problem solving, and critical thinking. Although general mental ability and practical intelligence are also important considerations, they are less amenable to development through training or other interventions. However, other forms of adult cognition may be developed successfully (Halpern, chap. 6, this volume). Socioemotional or interpersonal skills include such things as communication, understanding, and mentoring. Behavioral or team skills include key aspects of transformational leadership and leading in virtual environments. All of these various leader skills—in addition to issues related to modeling leader growth and development, technologies to support leader development, and developing teams and team leaders—are discussed in greater detail in the subsequent chapters of this book. One remaining issue to address more fully in this chapter is our view on how leader development can help transform organizations.

TRANSFORMING ORGANIZATIONS THROUGH LEADER DEVELOPMENT

Much of what has been written about leader development (including what has been written here so far) assumes that development initiatives are implemented primarily in response to environmental and organizational change (e.g., Judge et al., 1999). From this perspective, leader development efforts are conceptualized at least implicitly as reactive in nature. A particular type of change is experienced or predicted, and developmental initiatives are introduced as a means of responding to the change. An alternative perspective is that leader development can be a proactive mechanism for transforming organizations. Indeed, it could be argued that once leader development initiatives have been implemented and have begun to take root, the results of those efforts inherently change the social fabric of an organization, beginning with fundamental changes in the expectations (i.e., norms and beliefs) of leaders across all levels.

It is worth reiterating the important notion that the people make the place (Schneider, 1987). People are attracted to and selected into and out of an organization based on their fit with the prevailing values, beliefs, and personality characteristics of other people in that organization (Schneider, Goldstein, & Smith, 1995; Schneider, Smith, Taylor, & Fleenor, 1998). Organizations are comprised of people and their relationships, not the buildings or the services or the products. Therefore, if the people are developed and transformed, it is a logical conclusion that the organization is also transformed. But transformed in what way? More specifically, in what ways can individual change contribute to organizational development?

It is not always known what kind or type of change will be necessary. Despite the emphasis that organizations place on strategic planning, they are notoriously poor at predicting the future (who isn't?). Implementing training or development initiatives in response to immediate, pressing change runs the distinct risk of reacting too late. It is analogous to a football coach putting in a defensive scheme for the play that has just occurred. It is possible that the defense will be effective (especially if a similar offensive play is run again), but this type of reactive measure usually is not very effective over the long term. In organizations, by the time the implemented training programs or other initiatives can have an impact on the intended developmental target, some other—perhaps completely different—type of change is likely to be pressing. In this fashion, organizations are always at least one step behind the change, trying desperately to catch up in a futile race against a constantly moving target. Because of this elusive goal, organizations not only are unprepared for the future, but are also largely unprepared for the present. Leader development efforts can help prepare individuals and organizations to better manage change that occurs regardless of its nature. This also applies to the need to initiate desired change, and not just react to it.

Developing cognitive, social, and behavioral complexity (i.e., differentiation and integration) builds capacity for conceptualizing and responding in multiple ways in leadership situations (Day & Lance, chap. 3, this volume; Hooijberg et al., 1997). Instead of a limited and perhaps rigid means of thinking and acting, developing complex leaders is likely to change the way in which key leadership functions are performed in organizations. This creates opportunities for creative and adaptive strategies for identifying potential problems and figuring out how to deal with them. Another example is the full range model of leadership (Avolio, 1999; Avolio, chap. 4, this volume), which seeks primarily to develop components of transformational leadership (i.e., idealized influence, inspirational motivation, intellectual stimulation, and individualized consideration). Recent empirical evidence suggests that leaders who were rated higher on transformational leadership also scored higher on a test of moral reasoning (Turner, Barling, Epitropaki, Butcher, & Milner, 2002). Developing transformational leaders through the implementation of the full range model might therefore be expected to transform the aggregate level of moral reasoning in an organization, potentially enhancing the overall ethical foundation of a firm.

The preceding are two specific examples of how leader development can be used as a proactive agent to transform organizations. It is also possible that when leader development efforts are implemented across a broad range of organizational levels—and not reserved exclusively for only those at or near the top—greater potential is created for organizational transformation. In particular, such efforts begin to change the fundamental beliefs and expectations (i.e., culture) about the responsibility for leadership. If everyone has clear expectations regarding their responsibility for participating in leadership and understants that the organization is investing in them as individual leaders to help promote effective leadership participation, then it is likely that different attitudes, values, and ways of thinking and behaving will follow. There will be cultural transformation. This does not mean that everyone is now the chief executive officer, or even that everyone is equally accountable for organizational outcomes. However, these efforts symbolize an important step toward more fully sharing leadership responsibility. These kinds of expectations can be potent forces for transformation, and in this manner, leader development can drive organizational transformation.

In his book subtitled *Rethinking the Source of Leadership*, Drath (2001) made the provocative assertion that all leadership is shared leadership. Even the most autocratic, dictatorial, command-and-control style of leadership requires followers who see this as leadership and respond appropriately by allowing influence, direction, commitment, or other leadership processes to occur. If followers do not share in this perception of leadership (or what Drath called a leadership principle), then leadership does not happen. Drath also argued that more complex kinds of leadership that take on interpersonal and relational aspects require different (i.e., more complex or sophisticated) leadership principles. His proposed central leadership tasks—setting direction, building commitment, and facing adaptive challenges— require these more sophisticated, though less-commonly recognized, forms of leadership.

More complex leadership principles are needed because there are distinct limitations with the simpler, personal forms of leadership. For example, in simpler forms of leadership, if a leader cannot recognize a problem or identify a solution in a given situation, the entire team or organization flounders. There is no other way to provide leadership than to have the person in the leadership position figure it all out and convey to followers what to do. The leadership principle being followed assumes that leadership is something that a leader possesses and is brought forth when a leader expresses this leadership toward followers (Drath, 2001). In organizations where more sophisticated ways of leadership have been developed, there are additional resources to be tapped when a formal leader gets stuck. The first leadership principle based on personal dominance does not go away completely because it is one that is apparently firmly entrenched in the human experience.

However, more sophisticated leadership principles can transcend the simpler principles, thus enhancing adaptability across a wider range of challenges.

Many of the kinds of problems being faced by today's organizations are what can be termed adaptive challenges—situations that have not been previously experienced and have no standard resources for making sense of them or responding adaptively. There are no known solutions to such problems, and it may not even be obvious how to identify or construct the problem (i.e., it is an open rather than closed problem). Weick (1993) referred to a sense of *vu jàdé* (the opposite of déjà vu), which can paralyze people when faced with adaptive challenges: "I have never been here before . . . I have no idea where I am . . . I don't know what to do . . . I don't know who can help me" (pp. 633–634). In such cases, organizations need people at all levels who are prepared to share in more complex forms of leadership. To do so, however, they first need to be prepared to think about and enact different ways of participating in leadership. A basic tenet of social psychology teaches that "thinking is for doing" (Fiske, 1992), that is, people must be able to first think about complex forms of leadership before being able to recognize, enact, or participate in them. A corollary of this principle is that doing causes further thinking (Carlston, 1994). The various leader development components discussed in this book—from critical thinking to cultural awareness—are all potentially important in developing more complex ways of thinking and acting, which can enhance the ability to better participate in leadership.

Changing the level of individuals' self-concepts may be a critical first step in developing more complex leaders (and leadership principles) in organizations. Research and theory have suggested that self-identities can be organized into at least three separate levels: individual, interpersonal, and group or collective (Brewer & Gardner, 1996). In moving beyond a traditional and personal approach to leadership (in which the leader is thought to take care of all leadership functions personally) to one in which everyone is expected to participate in leadership processes, it may be necessary to first redefine the level at which the self is identified—from an individual level to a broader group or collective level. This is particularly important because the evidence suggests that there are inhibitory processes among identity levels, such that activating the collective level makes it unlikely that the interpersonal or individual levels will be accessed concurrently (Lord, Brown, & Freiberg, 1999). Intervening on the identity levels of leaders might sound extreme; however, enhancing self-awareness (Hall, chap. 7, this volume) would likely evolve toward understanding more complex interrelationships between oneself and others. In this manner, enhancing self-awareness inherently involves a shift to more inclusive levels of self-identification.

The choices that are made regarding what to address in leader development initiatives can have a profound impact on the resulting transformation. Choosing to emphasize the development of emotional intelligence (Caruso & Wolfe, chap. 10, this volume) will likely result in leaders who pay close attention to their own and others' emotions, and also legitimize (as opposed to deny) the role of emotions in organizational life. Focusing more closely on developing dialogue skills in leader development (Cohen, chap. 8, this volume) would likely have a very different transformational effect on individuals and, ultimately, the organization. The point of relevance is that the nature of what it "looks like" to participate in leadership (across all organizational levels) will vary partly as a function of what is emphasized in the development process. Following the open systems principle of equifinality (Katz & Kahn, 1978), the transformational outcomes of leader development efforts will be reached from different initial conditions and by a variety of paths.

It has been observed that the basic nature and structure of organizations is in the midst of great change (Drucker, 1995). Many past and present organizations were and are structured based mainly on formal rank and power. If flexibility is required of organizations (and most signs indicate that it is), then the way in which organizations are structured needs to change drastically. According to Drucker, what is needed is a structure based on mutual understanding and responsibility. One place to begin with regard to this desired change is in promoting the shared understanding and responsibility for participating in leadership. It is our contention that leader development efforts can transform present structures to those that are more solidly grounded in these desired ends.

SUMMARY

A basic premise of this book is that there is an acute need to develop leadership more comprehensively across all organizational levels and to accelerate the leader development process. The kinds of challenges that organizations in every feasible domain are facing require a broad capacity for leadership if they are to transform themselves effectively. Given the novelty and complexity of many of these challenges, it is unlikely that any single leader can hold all of the answers. Successful adaptation to such challenges is likely to require a broad participation in leadership; however, individuals need to be prepared to take on such responsibility. Leader development is not only necessary for organizations currently undergoing transformation; such efforts can also contribute significantly to future organizational transformation.

THIS BOOK'S PLAN

The chapters in this book address different aspects of leader development for transforming organizations. After this section on relevant background and overview perspectives (Part I), several approaches are proposed (e.g., using sophisticated modeling techniques for tracking growth and development, basing efforts on a sound and empirically supported theoretical model, and using technologies to support leader development) that are thought to accelerate the leader development process (Part II). Other sections are devoted to particular aspects of leader development, such as cognitive skills development (Part III), the development of practical and emotional intelligence (Part IV), and enhancing team leader skills (Part V).

In the second chapter of Part I, Maj. Gen. (Ret.) Lon E. Maggart provides an overview on how the U.S. Army is aggressively pursuing transformation. The working assumption is that the fundamental ways in which the Army will be called upon to defend the nation and serve the interests of the United States will change. Simply put, the lingering Cold War model of expected conflict is dangerously inappropriate for the realities of today and tomorrow. This intentional transformation process makes the Army an excellent organizational backdrop for an examination of leader development. In the U.S. Army, as in many other organizations, it is imperative that attention be given now to the needs of the future. This chapter provides an overview of the ongoing Army transformation process and uses that as the context for a discussion of the requirements for leader development.

The chapter by David V. Day and Charles E. Lance explores the concept of growth, and links growth with the meaning and modeling of leader development. They argue that fundamental to growth are changes in the complexity of thinking, acting, and interacting with others (i.e., cognitive, behavioral, and social complexity, respectively). Research and theory converge across numerous domains to suggest *differentiation* and *integration* as core components of complexity. Theoretical work in the area of adult development generally, and leader development specifically, is reviewed for examples of how complexity is treated as a central component of development. More technical concerns associated with the conceptualization and measurement of change are then addressed, with a particular emphasis on latent growth modeling as a powerful statistical tool that can be used to model most if not all forms of change. The chapter concludes with example applications of latent growth modeling (feedback, distance learning, mentoring, and simulations) to the potential study of leader development. Research is encouraged in these and other related areas to better understand the investments that organizations make in their leaders with an eye toward improving and accelerating the overall leader development process.

Bruce J. Avolio reviews the literature that has examined the full range model in terms of measuring and validating its constructs, as well as the model's applications to predicting individual and group processes and performance. A little over ten years ago, Avolio and Bass launched the "full range" model of leadership to provide a hierarchical model that included constructs ranging from highly passive and ineffective to those that were highly proactive, idealized, and effective. Avolio's chapter also examines how the full range model of leadership can be used as a general heuristic for examining leadership assessment and development at individual, team, and organizational levels.

The purpose of the chapter by Harold F. O'Neil and Yuan-Chung Fisher is to cover various technological means for teaching and assessing leadership. Technology is defined broadly and viewed as consisting of hardware and software systems as well as systematic procedures used to facilitate learning and assessment. Individual and team learning and assessment contexts are discussed. A framework of collaborative problem solving is then used to describe group aspects of leadership. For individual leadership, an example of the use of formative evaluation designs for computer-based games, both console and personal computer, is discussed.

In the first chapter of Part II, Diane F. Halpern reviews empirical studies from applied and experimental settings to provide an overview of what is known about adult learning. The need for lifelong learning has become increasingly urgent as the world has become increasingly complex. The rate at which knowledge has been growing is exponential and the most valued asset of any society in the coming decades is a knowledgeable thinking workforce. The best preparation for this unknown and rapidly changing future is the twin abilities to learn efficiently and think critically. Because of the escalating rate at which new knowledge is replacing old, lifelong learning has become a necessary reality and not just a slogan. Everyone will need to play the student role at repeated points in his or her life. Thus, the enhancement of adult learning is critical for the workforce of the 21st century and for the economic and military health of our country and the planet. A practical issue for the increasing number of adult learners is how the theories and research from the science of learning can be applied to design effective learning activities that build on older learners' lifetime of experiences and take into account their special learning needs.

Douglas T. Hall argues that in today's complex, turbulent organizations, a critical competency for successful individuals is the ability to learn; specifically, how to deal with the changing demands of the environment and how to develop the appropriate new skills. There are two overarching personal capabilities that help people "learn how to learn" new skills and competencies: *self-awareness* (or identity) and *adaptability*. Because of the superordinate power of these two capabilities in helping the person to grow new competencies, they have been termed "metacompetencies." Hall's chapter provides a detailed examination of the self-awareness metacompetency, because relatively little consideration has previously been given to its organizational implications. The purpose of the chapter is to examine the nature of self-awareness, the different theoretical perspectives that have been used to study the concept, what role it plays in adult and leadership development, and what organizations might do to create cultures that promote the development of self-awareness.

The purpose of Marvin S. Cohen's chapter is to review relevant concepts from communications theory and describe how they can be applied to the area of leader development. Leadership skill is exemplified in the use of different types of dialogue to achieve organizational objectives. The chapter uses examples to explore how different types of dialogues emerge in conversations—the shared knowledge they depend on, strategies participants use to trade off task efficiency and interpersonal consideration, devices that manage the flow of conversation, and different types of initiative and dominance. Critical thinking is a dialogue with oneself or others in which a claim is challenged by raising questions about alternative possibilities. These concepts can guide further research and help organizations identify objectives for leader development, design appropriate training scenarios and exercises, provide meaningful feedback, and measure success. Through the application of dialogue theory, leadership development can become more than the development of individual thinking skills, but may include the development of skills to understand and guide others. In this way, critical thinking and dialogue theory can serve as a bridge between individual cognitive skills development and team development.

Part III examines the relevance of two alternative forms of "intelligence"— practical and emotional—to leadership and leader development. The theory of practical intelligence presented by Anna T. Cianciolo, John Antonakis, and Robert J. Sternberg provides an explanation for how people seem to know just what to do in particular situations. They discuss the critical characteristics of the theory of practical intelligence that distinguish it from other attempts to understand leadership, and examine the measurement issues inherent in assessing such a complex phenomenon as practical problem solving. Recent research findings are shared that indicate the utility of such assessments for understanding common sense. The chapter concludes with a discussion of the potential role of measuring practical intelligence in facilitating experience-based learning and enhancing leadership capability.

David R. Caruso and Charles J. Wolfe address the role of emotional intelligence in leading and developing leaders. They define emotional intelligence as the ability to perceive emotions, access and generate emotions so as to assist thought, understand emotions and emotional knowledge, and reflectively regulate emotions so as to promote emotional and intellectual growth. Thus, the authors suggest that emotional intelligence might be a key requirement for the development of effective leaders. As a type of intelligence, can emotional intelligence be objectively measured and can emotional knowledge be learned? In this chapter, these issues are discussed and an ability model of emotional intelligence is presented. Research questions regarding the measurement of emotional intelligence and what it predicts are reviewed.

Part IV changes focus to leaders within a team context. Future leaders of organizations, regardless of context, will be managing increasingly complex types of teams. Organizational teams are quickly becoming global, with geographically dispersed members working temporally dispersed schedules. Furthermore, the rapid tempo of change in today's operating environments, coupled with shifting demands and requirements from key stakeholders, has placed a premium on the use of temporary teams in which members come together temporarily and then disband. Stephen J. Zaccaro, Sharon D. Ardison, and Kara L. Orvis examine the notion of swift trust and the influence of leadership on its development in geographically dispersed teams. Their chapter summarizes the ideas and models in the current literature, offers some conclusions and conceptual principles derived from this summary, and provides some prescriptions for leadership research. The chapter also provides a framework adapted from existing team research for defining the dimensions of team virtuality. Finally, the authors describe a model for leader–team dynamics that is used to review and interpret the literature on leadership and virtual team processes, including the role of swift trust.

Globalization and technological advances are causing teams to become increasingly diverse in many ways. Perhaps one of the most prominent and least understood of these diversity variables is national culture. Research on the effects of national culture on leadership in terms of individual competencies as well as on how leadership style interacts with national culture has been conducted quite extensively within the past 20 years. However, most of the conceptual and empirical work that has been conducted has not focused on multiculturalism in teams. The purpose of the chapter by Eduardo Salas, C. Shawn Burke, Jennifer E. Fowlkes, and Katherine A. Wilson-Donnelly is to address the challenges presented in leading multicultural teams, such as those found within military environments. It also reviews how these challenges may be turned into opportunities by extracting lessons learned from those currently using multinational teams.

Although the military has long used teams within mission-critical, high-impact environments, strategic complexity and technological advances are causing an increased awareness of the adaptive capabilities afforded by effective teams across all organizational domains. The ability of the military to use teams where members are distributed in time and space, as well as teams where members are co-located, has provided additional adaptive capabilities. The military has invested much money into understanding the requisite training tools, strategies, and methodologies used for building and maintaining effective team performance. This understanding is relevant to myriad organizational contexts, not just the military. Therefore, the purpose of the chapter by Eduardo Salas, C. Shawn Burke, and Kevin C. Stagl is to review the literature on teams to extract a representative sample of the competencies needed for effective team performance. Based on these competencies, an outline is proposed of what is known regarding the instructional strategies that can be used to train the targeted competencies. The chapter also examines the limited literature on training team leaders in order to extract principles and guidelines from this literature.

Part V offers two concluding chapters, by Katherine J. Klein and Jonathan C. Ziegert and by David V. Day and Stephen J. Zaccaro, respectively. These chapters review the key contributions of the preceding chapters and also provide integrative perspectives in terms of new understandings, implications, and remaining research needs.

REFERENCES

Avolio, B. J. (1999). *Full leadership development: Building the vital forces in organizations.* Thousand Oaks, CA: Sage.

Bales, R. F. (1958). Task roles and social roles in problem-solving groups. In E. E. Maccoby, T. M. Newcomb, & E. L. Hartley (Eds.), *Readings in social psychology* (3rd ed., pp. 437–447). New York: Holt, Rinehart & Winston.

Bass, B. M., & Avolio, B. J. (1994). *Transformational leadership: Improving organizational effectiveness.* Thousand Oaks, CA: Sage.

Bradford, L. P. (1974). *National Training Laboratories: Its history, 1947–1970.* Bethel, ME: National Institute for Applied Behavioral Science.

Brewer, M. B., & Gardner, W. (1996). Who is this "we"? Levels of collective identity and self representations. *Journal of Personality and Social Psychology, 71,* 83–93.

Carlston, D. E. (1994). Associated systems theory: A systematic approach to cognitive representations of persons. *Advances in Social Cognition, 7,* 1–78.

Conger, J. A., & Benjamin, B. (1999). *Building leaders: How successful companies develop the next generation.* San Francisco: Jossey-Bass.

Day, D. V. (2000). Leadership development: A review in context. *Leadership Quarterly, 11,* 581–613.

Day, D. V. (2001, April). *Understanding systems forces for sustainable leadership capacity.* Paper presented at the 16th annual conference of the Society for Industrial and Organizational Psychology, San Diego, CA.

Dixon, N. M. (1993). Developing managers for the learning organization. *Human Resource Management Review, 3,* 243–254.

Doohar, M. S., & Marquis, V. (Eds.). (1952). *The development of executive talent: A handbook of management development techniques and case studies.* New York: American Management Association.

Drath, W. (2001). *The deep blue sea: Rethinking the source of leadership.* San Francisco: Jossey-Bass.

Drath, W. H., & Palus, C. J. (1994). *Making common sense: Leadership as meaning-making in a community of practice.* Greensboro, NC: Center for Creative Leadership.

Drucker, P. F. (1995). *Managing in a time of great change.* New York: Truman Talley/Dutton.

Eden, D., & Leviathan, U. (1975). Implicit leadership theory as a determinant of the factor structure underlying supervisory behavior scales. *Journal of Applied Psychology, 60,* 736–741.

Fiedler, F. E. (1996). Research on leadership selection and training: One view of the future. *Administrative Science Quarterly, 41,* 241–250.

Fiol, C. M., O'Connor, E. J., & Aguinis, H. (2001). All for one and one for all? The development and transfer of power across organizational levels. *Academy of Management Review, 26,* 224–242.

Fiske, S. T. (1992). Thinking is for doing: Portraits of social cognition from daguerreotype to laserphoto. *Journal of Personality and Social Psychology, 63,* 877–889.

Fleishman, E. A. (1953). Leadership climate, human relations training, and supervisory behavior. *Personnel Psychology, 6,* 205–222.

French, J. R., & Raven, B. H. (1959). The bases of social power. In D. Cartwright (Ed.), *Studies in social power* (pp. 150–167). Ann Arbor: University of Michigan, Institute for Social Research.

Getels, J. W., & Csikszentmihalyi, M. (1967). Scientific creativity. *Science Journal, 3,* 80–84.

Getels, J. W., & Csikszentmihalyi, M. (1976). *The creative vision: A longitudinal study of problem-finding in art.* New York: Wiley.

Heifetz, R. (1994). *Leadership without easy answers.* Cambridge, MA: Harvard University.

Highhouse, S. (2002). A history of the T-group and its early applications in management development. *Group Dynamics: Theory, Research, Practice, 6,* 277–290.

Hooijberg, R., Hunt, J. G., & Dodge, G. E. (1997). Leadership complexity and development of the Leaderplex model. *Journal of Management, 23,* 375–408.

Judge, T. A., Thoresen, C. J., Pucik, V., & Welbourne, T. M. (1999). Managerial coping with organizational change: A dispositional perspective. *Journal of Applied Psychology, 84,* 107–122.

Katz, D., & Kahn, R. L. (1978). *The social psychology of organizations* (2nd ed.). New York: Wiley.

Lord, R. G., Brown, D. J., & Freiberg, S. J. (1999). Understanding the dynamics of leadership: The role of follower self-concepts in the leader/follower relationship. *Organizational Behavior and Human Decision Processes, 78*, 167–203.

Lord, R. G., & Maher, K. J. (1991). *Leadership and information processing: Linking perceptions and performance.* Boston: Unwin Hyman.

McCall, M. W., Lombardo, M. M., & Morrison, A. M. (1988). *The lessons of experience: How successful executives develop on the job.* Lexington, MA: Lexington.

McCauley, C. D., Moxley, R. S., & Van Velsor, E. (Eds.). (1998). *The Center for Creative Leadership handbook of leadership development.* San Francisco: Jossey-Bass.

Salancik, G. R., Calder, B. J., Rowland, K. M., Leblebici, H., & Conway, M. (1975). Leadership as an outcome of social structure and process: A multidimensional analysis. In J. G. Hunt & L. L. Larson (Eds.), *Leadership frontiers* (pp. 81–101). Kent, OH: Kent State University.

Schein, E. H., & Bennis, W. G. (1965). *Personal and organizational change: The laboratory approach.* New York: Wiley.

Schneider, B. (1987). The people make the place. *Personnel Psychology, 40*, 437–453.

Schneider, B., Goldstein, H. W., & Smith, B. D. (1995). The ASA framework: An update. *Personnel Psychology, 48*(4), 747–773.

Schneider, B., Smith, B. D., Taylor, S., & Fleenor, J. (1998). Personality and organizations: A test of the homogeneity of personality hypothesis. *Journal of Applied Psychology, 83*, 462–470.

Staw, B. M., Sandelands, L. E., & Dutton, J. E. (1981). Threat–rigidity effects in organizational behavior: A multilevel analysis. *Administrative Science Quarterly, 26*, 501–524.

Stogdill, R. M., & Coons, A. E. (Eds.). (1957). *Leader behavior: Its description and measurement.* Columbus: Ohio State University, Bureau of Business Research.

Thurow, L. C. (1999). *Building wealth: The new rules for individuals, companies, and nations in a knowledge-based economy.* New York: HarperCollins.

Turner, N., Barling, J., Epitropaki, O., Butcher, V., & Milner, C. (2002). Transformational leadership and moral reasoning. *Journal of Applied Psychology, 87*, 304–311.

Unsworth, K. (2001). Unpacking creativity. *Academy of Management Review, 26*(2), 289–297.

U.S. Army (1999). *FM22-100: Army Leadership.* Washington, D.C.: Author.

Vicere, A. A., & Fulmer, R. M. (1998). *Leadership by design.* Boston: Harvard Business School.

Weick, K. E. (1993). The collapse of sensemaking in organizations: The Mann Gulch disaster. *Administrative Science Quarterly, 38*, 628–652.

2

Leadership Challenges for the Future

Maj. Gen. (Ret.) Lon E. Maggart
RTI International

The Army is currently in the throes of transforming from a heavy, cold war force to its stated Objective Force of the future. The Objective Force is a concept that describes how the Army can evolve into a light and deployable force with sufficient firepower to sustain itself against a variety of threats. This transformation is a complex undertaking involving changes in doctrine, organization, and equipment, and, in many ways, fundamental changes to the Army culture, most especially in leadership. Most certainly, these changes will be difficult. However, equally as certain, the leadership and training demands necessary to transform the Army will require a fundamental cultural change significantly more complex than the other issues, especially given the mounting emphasis on high technology.

How the Army deals with the manifold leadership challenges involved in this transformation will be particularly instructive for corporate business organizations faced with similar challenges. Academic institutions that study and teach leadership development will also find this process worthy of study, as the concept of combining leadership and high technology is an area abundant in possibility. Clearly, the downturn in the world economy, the events of September 11, 2001, and the demise of several prestigious companies in the United States due to failures in ethical leadership have produced a significantly different work environment in which both the Army and commercial businesses must operate. At the least, change and growth will take place in a heretofore-undefined environment. This chapter shows that the same issues with which military leaders must contend—rapid deployment, knowledge versus practice, seeing and understanding the battlefield, change, and logistics—all apply to corporate businesses as well.

The concept of applying knowledge learned from observing change in the Army to corporate business ventures might seem odd at first. After all, the Army does not earn revenue, return dividends, or produce goods. However, practitioners in both environments and students of leadership understand that the similarities in leadership between corporate businesses and the Army are far greater than the differences. The idea that the Army and big business are more alike than not is supported by the well-known organizational consultant Margaret Wheatley. In an article in *Fortune*, Wheatley is credited with pointing out to the Army that leaders in business or in uniform must learn to adapt to that uncertain environment. While they cannot control the random and ambiguous changes that affect their organizations, they can identify the cohesive corporate mission or competency and make sure it is imprinted on every worker or soldier (Smith, 1994, p. 212). The lead-in statement to the article announced in bold type, "the [Army] is now a learning organization that's way ahead of business in retraining senior managers and keeping the [chief executive officer's] attention fixed on the future" (p. 203). The article further pointed out that "The Army is striving to become everything the modern organization is supposed to be—adaptive, flexible, a learning enterprise, even getting closer to the ... needs of the customer" (p. 203). In fact, for years, the Army has been the progenitor of innovative leadership, leadership training, and leadership development processes.

The randomness and uncertainty to which Margaret Wheatley referred has become even more ominous in the years since the article was published. The uncertainty created by international terrorism, the implications of numerous ethical failures on the part of senior leaders in business and accounting firms, and the imponderable, massive infusion of multifaceted and complex technologies describe a future in which most established leadership and management practices no longer apply.

An anecdotal review of the tactical results from tank and infantry battalion training rotations at the National Training Center (NTC), Fort Irwin, California, over the past 20-plus years serves as a credible way to compare current leadership capabilities with those expected of the Objective Force. The NTC provides realistic joint and combined arms training focused on developing leaders and units. It does this by using an instrumented battlefield that can accurately locate and visually portray the position and movement of units to assist highly trained observer-controllers who observe, analyze, train, and provide feedback to rotating units during the planning, mission preparation, and execution phases of tactical operations.

Observer-controllers also coach and mentor training units on maneuver warfare, battle command, and combined-arms war fighting while the unit attempts to demonstrate tactical competence in these areas against a resident "world-class" opposing force. The opposing force provides an extremely competent, ruthless, thinking enemy that is more highly skilled and more relentless than any anticipated present or future enemy the Army might have to confront.

Training units go through a series of sequential operations against the opposing force that are systematically reviewed and critiqued using a process called the after-action review. The observer-controllers facilitate self-discovery using the after-action review to teach, train, and improve performance among the leaders and soldiers of the training unit. The NTC and the after-action review process are generally regarded as the most important reasons for the success of Army forces in the 1991 Gulf War.

The NTC is not only a powerful training tool; it also provides an accurate picture of how well Army units are trained. In fact, the NTC provides an important way of comparing current sequential tactical operations and conventional leadership capabilities with the intricate, distributed, simultaneous, and successive operations expected of the Objective Force. I believe most observers would agree that commanders at the NTC find it difficult to cope with the modest demands of transition between tactical events under the existing tough, but not overtaxing, requirements imposed upon them during a 2-week training rotation. The idea of moving through ever more complex operations in succession over an extended period of time will place extraordinary demands on intellect and leadership that are not currently addressed in Army training programs and cannot be eliminated or even greatly simplified by the application of more technology.

The term *technology* appears frequently in the text that follows for two primary reasons. First, technology has invaded virtually every aspect of our lives from cell phones to computers. The world economy runs on technology. We have to live with it and deal with it whether we want to or not. Second, technology is an essential enabler for the Objective Force. The Army simply will not be able to communicate the information necessary to fight in the future without the assistance of very specialized high-technology equipment and software. However, technology is a two-edged sword. It creates as many problems as it solves, and some of them are so subtle that they are barely understood and rarely addressed. For example, in Army applications, technology primarily attacks the information problem—more precisely, the situational awareness problem—on modern battlefields. It does not address the leadership, intellectual, and training issues associated with *performing* convoluted operations. This is a long-standing problem of enormous proportions that has not been thoroughly addressed during the transition process.

I have used the term *situational awareness* rather than *situational understanding* to illustrate the point that understanding the situation does not equate to understanding how to solve the problems the situation presents. Execution requires far more than knowledge of where enemy and friendly units are located, what they are doing, or which buttons to push and when to push them. Execution requires mastery of complicated tactical issues and leadership that inspires others to perform dangerous tasks. Execution on the battlefield of the future will require very highly tuned tacit knowledge and some sense of how to transfer that knowledge to others. At the same time, it is leadership and not technology that instills courage and confidence in ordinary soldiers to perform extraordinary deeds under seemingly hopeless circumstances.

Commanders will never know or understand everything about the battlefield, no matter how sophisticated sensors become. Situational awareness and situational understanding are worthy concepts against which to establish equipment and doctrinal requirements and are necessary though not sufficient prerequisites for achieving battlefield dominance. This is because battlefield dominance means more than being able to see, detect, and target. Battlefield dominance means that the product of these efforts achieves the desired intent. For example, the stated purpose of the recent effort in Afghanistan was to find, surround, and kill or capture Osama bin Ladin and other important al Qaeda leaders. If the military effort there accomplished some of these outcomes but did not result in the killing or capture of even a single significant leader, can we say we dominated the battlefield? Of course not!

The point about stated outcomes is significant in another way. The commander must clearly understand what he or she wants as an outcome of battle and must clearly transmit that intent to every soldier and leader in the organization. If the intent is not clear, then nothing will be dominated beyond fuel, ammunition, and mess operations. Even without perfect knowledge of the battlefield, the commander can drive ambiguity to zero and dominance into the 90s if the intent is clear. Perturbations caused by the enemy then become short-term distractions to the eventual and inevitable achievement of the commander's intent and at least a defined degree of dominance.

Battlefield dominance in this sense requires practice in formulating and transmitting intent, practice in receiving and understanding intent, the ability to recognize and adapt to changes that occur during execution, and the courage and ability to conduct independent, decentralized operations in response to these changes. The ability to do these things will only develop in an organization that encourages independent thinking and decentralized execution.

Leadership is the essential ingredient in developing the trust necessary for building cohesion in an organization and the only source I know of for heart, grit, determination, endless hope, and tenacity. The leader is the only one who can lead subordinates past mere understanding into the realm of doing. It is leadership, not technology, that needs the most attention in the Army as it moves inexorably toward the Objective Force. The section titles that follow roughly capture the major precepts of the Objective Force. These titles are not particularly descriptive of comparable civilian business challenges; however, the requirements to accomplish them are, so I have included what might be appropriate subtitles for corporate businesses.

DEPLOYMENT AND COMBAT OPERATIONS ON ENTRY OR CHALLENGES ON ENTERING INTO A NEW BUSINESS OR MARKET ARENA

In my more than 30 years on active duty, I have had the opportunity to undergo the transition from peace to war on two occasions. The first was during the Vietnam War, in which I served as an advisor with the Vietnamese Regional and Popular Forces near the Cambodian border. The second was during the Gulf War, where I commanded a tank brigade in the First Infantry Division organized with two tank battalions, a mechanized infantry battalion, an artillery battalion, and a support battalion. This brigade fought all 4 days of the war. By the time we arrived in Saudi Arabia, I had 25 years of experience, roughly half of which was in tactical units. I had multiple return of forces to Germany (REFORGER) rotations and multiple National Training Center rotations, nearly 6 years of teaching experience, and been responsible for writing or editing the original versions of the most relevant tactical field manuals in service at the time. It is in this context that the following considered opinions are offered.

The notion of rapidly deploying into a hostile environment and quickly springing into action against the enemy requires, in addition to understanding the situation electronically, the ability of leaders to make a rapid transition from a peacetime environment filled with bureaucratic requirements to a war environment filled with chaos and urgent demands for decisions and rapid execution. It is difficult, if not impossible, to evolve quickly from the "inside-the-box," convergent thinking processes required in peacetime to the "out-of-the-box," divergent thinking processes required in combat, particularly if the peacetime environment is one characterized by a zero-defect mentality. Tactical decisions are difficult enough to make with all the associated possibilities and ramifications without adding the career implications of making a poor or incorrect decision.

Even though the Gulf War was conventional in nature and the only real advanced technology we had in the First Infantry Division was a global positioning system (GPS), we did come to understand the nature of the transition between rapidly moving operations, each with different characteristics and each executed with little or no information on the enemy or adjacent forces. With little more than 45 min of respite between operations over a 4-day period, all the leaders in my brigade were taxed. They were not taxed by the imponderables of the operation, nor with the lack of information, but with the complexities associated with thousands of minute details necessary to manage the constant, brain-numbing changes required during each phase of the attack. We expended enormous amounts of energy to keep personnel and machines focused on the mission while engaging the enemy, avoiding friendly fires, and navigating while bouncing over bone-breaking terrain in the dead of night in horrible weather. Clearly, technology could help solve some of these issues. However, in the final analysis, it was the superb leadership of my subordinate commanders that created success.

The commanders in the brigade were effective in large part because we built a cohesive team long before we deployed to Saudi Arabia. We also had the time to practice the range of operations we expected to encounter later in combat before we were committed. These two assets—cohesion and practice—enabled our leaders to expand their frames of reference and adapt to the realities of combat that are not currently replicated in the field at the NTC or explained in textbooks or classroom instruction.

The six battalion commanders in my brigade and my executive officer were extraordinary men. Each had great intellect and each had spent years at the battalion level learning how to command. Each of them had multiple combat training center rotations, REFORGER exercises, and experience in large-scale maneuvers in Europe. One was a combat infantryman from the Vietnam era. They could adapt because they had the experience to do so and they operated in an environment that permitted innovation and independent action. They were also innovative, creative, imaginative, perceptive and had great vision. For virtually their entire careers, they spent time thinking about and executing combat operations. They were not distracted by peace-keeping duties or other important but not combat-oriented activities. More importantly, we had developed a shared frame of reference. We each worked hard to build a cohesive team. My job was to establish the framework within which they could operate independently and to give them the guidance, encouragement, and permission to command their organizations as they saw fit. My job was to run the brigade. Their jobs were to run the battalions. We did not confuse the two roles.

Even with all of this, adapting was not easy. This was the first time any of us had seen a fully deployed combat brigade on the ground. Even at the NTC, there is insufficient space to employ an entire brigade with its fire support, engineers, and combat service support. Only REFORGER exercises offered something similar, and even these were a stretch of the imagination, as units just lined up and drove down the highways instead of deploying across the terrain in tactical formations. The adaptability necessary for success with the Objective Force will be difficult to achieve for battalion commanders of the future who currently get only 2 years of total experience at that level before taking command.

There is one last point about leading with respect to instant deployment worldwide. The successful commander knows the enemy and makes sure his or her soldiers do as well. In preparation for the Gulf War, we read about and were briefed extensively on Iraqi tactics, techniques, and equipment. We understood how Sadaam fought against the Iranians and against his own people. We knew the capabilities of his T72M1 main battle tank; we understood the fire trenches, Iraqi strong points, and how defensive positions were prepared. We also understood the culture of the region, including with which hand to shake and with which hand to take food. Rapid-entry operations of the future may come at the expense of being versed in enemy culture, order of battle, and tactics. Technology may bring knowledge but will not ensure the understanding necessary to coordinate the tactical agenda and the realities of how a particular enemy fights. In practical term, this means taking a more balanced approach between rapid response and regional focus. As the Army moves toward a force projection capability based in the United States, more emphasis will be necessary in establishing and maintaining habitual relationships internally and abroad in order to ensure unit cohesion and regional expertise.

KNOWLEDGE AND UNDERSTANDING VERSUS DOING OR GETTING THE JOB DONE IN AN AMBIGUOUS ENVIRONMENT

The topic of knowledge versus understanding is an issue that has been discussed since the original small digital experiments were conducted at Fort Knox, Kentucky, in the early 1990s. At the heart of the argument are questions that remain unanswered. Is it possible to devise and execute a tactical operation electronically? Does this system work in contact with the enemy? Can the commander really understand the situation, particularly the human dimension, expressed by the symbols that appear on a screen? Can the commander really trust that the symbols represent reality? These are knowledge-versus-understanding issues. Clearly technology will simplify the volume and complexity of battlefield tasks for the commander and staff, but in order for technology to enhance understanding, users at all levels must be clear about the potential dangers as well.

The problem with "symbology" is that it is shorthand for a more complex reality. A symbol on a screen may display a unit of action's size and location, perhaps even activity, but a symbol, even if represented in three dimensions, cannot convey vehicle arrays, dispersion, use of terrain except in the most general nature, the state of readiness of the equipment and soldiers, the mental attitude of the leaders, and a host of other essential information. It is difficult even when viewing a symbol displaying appropriate equipment and personnel strengths, fuel and ammunition status, and activity codes to avoid thinking of the unit on the ground as anything other than full up, rested, and ready to go in spite of the fact that in reality the unit may be only two vehicles that are partially operable and nearly out of fuel.

Is it possible for a commander to convey to his or her subordinate commanders intent, passion, persistence, hope, and a range of other emotions using only symbols? Imagine trying to do this with successive, rapidly occurring, but totally different types of operations conducted over a short period of time but over a great distance in space. Can the commander hope to determine emotional inputs from his or her subordinates with enough clarity to understand their states of mind, capacities to fight, and levels of fear, using electronic means? If the commander has to default to voice communications to get this understanding, then all the advantage of speed found in technologically advanced systems is lost. And even if it were technologically possible to use avatars that looked like each subordinate commander and that could replicate the facial expressions, voice inflections, and hand and arm movements appropriate to the emotional state being transmitted, the time consumed would be equivalent to an interpersonal encounter.

There are many dimensions to understanding the situation. Symbols portray one of those dimensions—the physical dimension. However, leadership is an emotional business gripping the heart, soul, and imagination of those being led. Soldiers respond to the inspiration of their commander, not to a collection of symbols, no matter how skillfully represented on a screen. Understanding intent is totally different from understanding the situation. Symbology may help communicate intent, but it does not equate to understanding the intent.

There is no substitute for looking into the eye of subordinates to see whether they really understand what their commander wants them to do. The written word transmitted electrically to a screen is a poor substitute for backbriefing the commander to demonstrate understanding. Even with voice recognition software, using a screen to gain understanding would be time consuming and difficult to perform while on the move.

The patterns formed by symbols may also be misleading. If several units report the same enemy unit from different vantage points and they appear on a screen somewhere as three different units, what is the impact on the commander's perception of the battle? In such an event, even sophisticated software will take time to register that only one enemy unit is in question, not three.

A worse problem with patterns is that they can be interpreted differently depending on one's frame of reference. Even if everyone in an organization is looking at the same common relevant picture of the battlefield, they may perceive it in a completely different way. Clearly the information portrayed from various sensors will be interpreted differently depending on the frame of reference and experience of the person doing the interpretation. When this information is fused with other data, the resulting picture of the battlefield very likely will be perceived in unintended ways. There is a vast chasm between situational awareness and situational understanding. The worst possible tactical outcome is the belief that one understands a battlefield situation when in fact one does not.

Unfortunately, Objective Force leaders will have to lead from a distance using technology. This raises some challenging questions for future leadership development beyond those identified earlier in the text, which include the following:

- How will leaders identify feelings through symbols on a display screen?
- How will a leader's decision making based on intuition and identification of emotions gained from close and personal contact with battle be affected when those intangibles must now be derived from looking at a symbolic display?
- How will we train Objective Force leaders to identify, use, understand, and manage emotions?

Assuming some understanding of the situation, the issue is then transformed from knowing and understanding to doing. Even if technology is not perfect, and even if all the training support information is limited or nonexistent, the commander must still transcend these deficiencies to execute and win. This can be done if leaders devise tactical concepts that are easily understood and transmitted and if they find innovative ways to ascertain that the intended concepts are in fact understood and are being executed as envisioned.

This will be difficult in an environment in which complex successive generic operations that differ in nature and intent are the norm. To execute such operations, the commander must practice formulating solid, easy-to-understand statements of tactical intent and have subordinate commanders who are expert in executing that intent in a decentralized manner. However, it will be impossible for the commander to use the existing decision processes to do this on the fly. An entirely new set of standards will be necessary if the Objective Force is to execute as previously described. It will also be very difficult to formulate training to do this unless some basic tactical guidelines are established to provide a standard context to focus the training.

In the transition period between the World War II field manuals and the "How to Fight" manuals of the late 1970s, a great doctrinal debate centered on how much detail to provide in field manuals. One side supported the notion that field manuals should provide only the conceptual framework within which to select and apply a tool bag of tactics and techniques. The opposing side supported the notion that every possible detail about how to conduct tactical operations should be written into the manuals. The Objective Force will require more of the former than the latter. Decentralized execution will not be realized if it has to follow some prescribed solution. Commanders conducting rapidly successive, disparate operations will need to have the latitude to apply their best judgment on how to execute.

In existing doctrine, the various tactical operations of movement to contact, hasty attack, hasty defense, and so on have been around for decades, and the tasks, conditions, and standards for each have been examined ad nauseum. If the

Objective Force is to use generic operations such as attack, defense, and so on with no specified type distinction such as hasty attack, deliberate attack, or counterattack, then it will be possible for these types of operations to be performed expertly only if the commander has the latitude (and over the expressed requirement) in training to set the conditions on which to practice his or her ability to provide clear intent and the context for how he or she wants subordinates to execute.

The object is for the commander to gain skill in describing the intent and expected outcomes and for subordinates to use all the available tools in imaginative ways that satisfy the requirement envisioned by the commander. The training process will require focused, no-nonsense after-action reviews, but over time it should be possible for subordinate commanders to learn how to function together to achieve the stated intent. The real trick is for the commander to be comfortable with subordinates executing in a decentralized manner. Centralized leaders are not usually comfortable with mission-type orders and decentralized execution.

From our experience in the Gulf War, and after hours of practice, our execution of traditional operations such as breaching, defile drills, hasty attacks, and movements to contact in a decentralized manner became second nature. This ability translated into success later in the campaign when operations became generic and there was no time for detailed plans and orders. In many instances, my commanders simply executed what needed to be done and told me about it afterward. I relied on the judgment of my subordinate commanders and did not waste time trying to find out how they were executing my order. It was enough for me to know that they could and would devise ways of accomplishing the mission. We had built an organization and a leadership climate where subordinate commanders could freely operate within a very large framework that I had established. This permitted enormous fluidity to the battle and empowered those in charge of executing to take whatever measures seemed appropriate. All Objective Force leaders must be capable of independent action to successfully cope with the rapidly changing nature of the combat operations they will conduct.

The trick to doing this lies in the ability of commanders to visualize the sequence of events of a battle in their mind's eye. By the time we executed the breach of the Iraqi defense line, the operation was laid out in each of our minds as a mental map of the breach site. In fact, we had no operations overlay, no boundaries, no way of identifying from looking at our operational graphic what the concept of operation was. We used a graphical layout of the Iraqi positions over which was transposed a novel way of identifying objectives and artillery groups using the same designator. When fires were called or an objective cleared, the simple transmission that "Objective 10A" had been taken allowed everyone in the brigade to achieve instant understanding of what was actually happening on the battlefield.

This capability is achieved only by trust, cohesion, and constant practice reinforced by honest after-action reviews. Even 10 years after the war, I can still see each battle clearly in my mind. I cannot describe in detail what each battalion did, but in a general sense, I can retrace every move that subordinate battalions made. Interestingly, my understanding of the battles was based solely on listening to the radio and watching with my eyes. Clearly, technology would have helped, but it would not have been better than the understanding I achieved after months of working on a close and continual basis with each battalion individually and then collectively as a six-battalion brigade.

SEEING AND UNDERSTANDING THE BATTLEFIELD OR APPRECIATING THE BUSINESS ENVIRONMENT

Objective Force commanders must understand that where they have been on the battlefield is as important as where they are going. They must make provisions to see this aspect of battle as clearly. Noncontiguous, successive, generic operations over extended distances will inevitably result in bypassed enemy forces and intermingled friendly forces. Both pose dangers for follow and support forces and especially for combat service support organizations moving forward. The deadliest enemy on the battlefield is often a friendly unit, and with speeds of munitions exceeding 6,000 ft/sec, there will not be much "checking the situational awareness monitor" when these unexpected direct fire encounters arise.

The intellectual ability to understand how all the battlefield pieces fit, along with the possible outcomes of action, is one of the most difficult tasks for the leader. Technology will help, but the innate ability to make sense of multiple, disparate, complex facts is a mandatory leadership skill for the future. This skill is especially important if the Objective Force is to achieve the ability to maneuver unencumbered by boundaries. It may be that the only way around a flank or to outdistance and reposition behind enemy forces is to retrace ground covered earlier in the fight.

If the Objective Force is to truly achieve maneuver dominance, then it must do so on a battlefield free from all but the most essential boundaries and other restrictive control measures. Until the Army achieves the technological capability to operate without boundaries and restrictive measures, it must use conventional graphical representations that are generated and updated manually. Although it is possible to update graphical representations with voice interaction, the Army is a long way from reaching this point. Therefore, direct fire battles will have to be controlled by frequency-modulated radios using voice communications or through totally decentralized operations that go with the flow. This reinforces the notion that commanders have to rely on subordinates, build a mental map of the battle to execute, and use technology that is available to ensure that fires and maneuvers do not conflict with or affect adjacent units. Pattern recognition is an essential skill for accomplishing this and commanders will have to become expert at recognizing existing and emerging patterns quickly enough to understand and, if necessary, alter the course of battle. The training implications are enormous.

CHANGING PATTERNS OF OPERATIONS OR ADJUSTING TO MARKET AND BUSINESS CHANGES

The ability of Objective Force organizations to rapidly change missions and orders is also associated with the ability to rapidly change their pattern of operations. The words roll off the lips, but the leadership challenge is how to effect such changes. In the existing doctrine, for better or worse, most practitioners understand, at least superficially, what is required to conduct any of the various forms of maneuver. The graphics are more or less standardized, as are the orders and commands to initiate them. Although I never supported enumerating the distinction between various types of attacks and defenses precisely because doing so limits rapid transition between the two, being able to do so makes sense from the perspective of teaching and evaluating the execution of said tactics.

The challenge for commanders using current doctrine is to modify these basic maneuvers to accommodate the realities of the battlefield. Improvising in this manner comes with years of practice and a thorough understanding of second- and third-order tactical effects. As Gen. Gordon Sullivan said many times, "You can't play jazz like Dave Brubeck until you have learned the basics." Unfortunately, until a unit has progressed to the improvisation level, standardized forms of maneuver will continue to be boxes within which creative thinking and maneuver are restricted. Objective Force operations will require Dave Brubeck-like improvisation to be successful.

Objective Force leaders will have to learn how to unleash the powerful innovative spirit of subordinates in ways that are standardized enough to be described, drawn, executed, and changed easily. Changing patterns of operations is easier said than done if the patterns are not defined well enough to allow for specific training programs. The more permutations there are in improvised patterns, the more complex the intellectual processes become. Clearly the commander cannot just transmit the word "attack" to achieve the desired result.

The Objective Force commander must be able to improvise, but this can be achieved only through constant practice both in live and virtual simulations and, more importantly, constant work in perfecting the art of achieving a clear understanding of intent by every soldier in the organization. The challenge for Objective Force commanders will be in training new leaders and soldiers who join the unit and, then integrating units who are attached during combat to improvise in concert with those already trained to do so.

LOGISTICS OR PROVIDING ADEQUATE SUPPORT TO ONGOING OPERATIONS

The Objective Force calls for operations to be sustained internally for 3 days. This is an achievable concept, but the challenge comes on the evening of the third day when resupply must take place. During the Gulf War, at the time I needed resupply the most, my thin-skinned, wheeled vehicles had to negotiate slowly through a hail of exploding Iraqi ammunition trucks, burning T72s, random Iraqi soldiers who still wanted to fight, and literally tons of shrapnel and twisted metal strewn over the battlefield. I could not continue the attack without fuel and ammunition, and even resupply vehicles with tracks would have found the going tough through the smoking remnants of the Tawakalna Division the morning after our night attack.

I found that my most difficult task during the Gulf War, beyond preventing fratricide, was sustaining the force while moving quickly over long distances, particularly during foul weather and hours of darkness. The fact is that logistics is far too important to be left to staff planners. The Objective Force commander will have to plan for logistics in even more meticulous detail than tactical operations. To fix this, commander training for the Objective Force must include a large measure of logistics, including how to conduct effective logistical rehearsals. Logistics is a complex undertaking with lots of moving parts, and none of the units is armed with anything more substantial than a 50-caliber machine gun. The planning required to protect logistical forces on a dispersed battlefield moving forward to resupply on day 3 will be a daunting undertaking and is work unsuited for amateurs.

Finally, and most importantly, in addition to the obvious planning and execution challenges, Objective Force commanders will have to find ways to integrate support units into the same cohesive relationship that organic units enjoy. If it works out that logistical units are organic to the units of action, the task becomes easier. Logistical operations cannot be an adjunct to the tactical scheme. Logistics must be an integral part of the operation with the same status that the basic tactical operations of maneuver and fires enjoy.

SUMMARY

Combat is a significant emotional event and leaders who command Objective Force units must develop training programs to ensure that no soldier is exposed to complex situations in which the stakes are high, the risks considerable, and the consequences of failure devastating without first experiencing them in a training environment. Soldiers and leaders must have an appreciation for the emotional challenges that they, and those for whom they are responsible, will experience during the course of difficult, sometimes life-threatening tasks. Developing a comprehensive training program that uses live, virtual, and constructive simulations to train soldiers and leaders in these complicated areas is a massive undertaking. We never quite got there with the existing force, a fact that all must be mindful of, as the battlefield demands on the Objective Force will be even greater and will require even more sophisticated training methodologies than we currently have.

The Objective Force will be executed based on the intellect of the leaders, not from the pedantic performance of tasks from a mission training plan (a training document that provides units a clear description of "what and how" to train critical collective tactical tasks). We will not get to the Objective Force with existing formal sequential training and educational experiences. Leaders of the Objective Force must be men and women who, in addition to possessing traditional leadership skills, must be imaginative, creative, innovative, courageous, intuitive, adaptive, versatile, undaunted by ambiguity, decisive, compassionate, tenacious, technologically literate, and able to think conceptually and act with only the good of this country in mind. We teach very few of these skills in the Army today, yet without these skills, there simply will not be any leaders who can meet the demands of the Objective Force. We must transform the schoolhouses to address these new skills and accommodate the more rigorous training methodologies required to prepare the Objective Force to execute the way it is intended.

Finally, success will depend even more on the ability of leaders to establish an environment of trust that permits everyone in the organization, within bounds, to express their opinions openly and without fear of embarrassment or reprisal. It is impossible to achieve the out-of-the-box divergent thought necessary to execute Objective Force operations without open, honest communications throughout each organization that must execute them. Equally important, trust is the first step toward cohesion. Cohesion is the catalyst that will enable the Objective Force to gain information superiority; execute fire, maneuver, close combat, and assault in a dynamic battle of action–reaction–counteraction; present the enemy with multiple dilemmas, causing the enemy to act ineffectively; and gain lethal overmatch to destroy, dislocate, and disintegrate enemy forces, finishing the enemy decisively at a time and place of our choosing.

The purpose of this chapter is to provoke thought on some of the leadership requirements for the Objective Force. The follow-up is to answer the knotty issues posed and seek ways to begin finding methodologies for eliminating these shortcomings through training. This will not be easy. We never totally figured out how to train the existing conventional force. We rushed to implement improvements before we had clearly defined all of the critical actions and activities necessary to employ these improvements effectively. We never identified all of the commander and staff processes necessary for command and control, so we could never build the training support packages necessary to train leaders and soldiers properly. We never made the transition from what we did have into understandable digital processes with appropriate training mechanisms.

We missed the mark because we were in too much of a hurry to move into the future. We did not dedicate the time and effort to do the research necessary to identify the interactive, analytical, decision, and execution processes that exist between and among commanders, staffs, and soldiers. We did not commit to completing the boring, grinding work of sorting through and relating tasks, activities, and functions with missions. We did not spend enough time understanding complex processes, tactics, and procedures using simulations. There were a lot of things we did not do that we should have done.

We now have a chance to do all of these things before we field the Objective Force. From my perspective, there are several important areas that the Army must address if the Objective Force is going to be successful. These include the following:

• Recognize and make the significant cultural changes required to reward peacetime divergent thinking at all levels. This includes a change in focus from "doing things right" to "doing the right thing." It also means that the Army must establish as the norm leaders at all levels who are highly flexible, able to adapt to constant change, and who can tolerate decentralized operations, open communication, divergent thought—and the truth, regardless of how painful. We also need to develop leaders who can establish climates of command that foster such activities.

• Expedite the research necessary to find ways to teach leaders advanced intellectual skills like creativity, innovation, imagination, visioning, adaptability, and the flexibility to adapt to constant and dramatic battlefield change.

• Dramatically increase the opportunities for practicing decentralized operations, beginning with a change in the way we write doctrine, think about boundaries, use simulations in the schoolhouse, and define what constitutes success in tactical operations, both in units and at the combat training centers.

• Find ways to educate and train that instill and reward the ability for autonomy in executing independent action within a broad commander's intent. To do this, commanders must be rewarded for learning how to give broad intent and then allowing subordinates find the best solutions.

• Conduct the education and training necessary to ensure that combat leaders are as conversant with complex logistics as they are with fires and maneuver.

• Commit the resources necessary to define and record the interactive, analytical, decision, and execution processes that exist or should exist between and among commanders, staffs, and soldiers for conventional, digital, and then Objective Force units.

The message to take away from this chapter is that leadership and leadership development are key considerations in transforming organizations. Both must be included in the vision for change and both are tools necessary to drive the vision to a successful conclusion.

ACKNOWLEDGMENTS

The helpful suggestions of Kathy Quinkert, Brian Zahn, Mike Shaler, Pat Ritter, Jeanette James, Jill Miller-Denning, David Day, Chuck Wolfe, and others transformed this chapter from an interesting intellectual exercise into a (hopefully) useful document. I am constantly reminded of the significant intellect that resides with in these special colleagues and have found that with their input, the quality of my work improves dramatically. I thank them for taking the time to make my words meaningful and my intent clear.

REFERENCE

Smith, L. (1994, September 19). New ideas from the Army (really). *Fortune, 130*, 203–212.

II

Accelerating Leader Development

3

Understanding the Development of Leadership Complexity Through Latent Growth Modeling

David V. Day
Pennsylvania State University

Charles E. Lance
University of Georgia

Growth... change... development. These concepts are fundamental for much of the thinking and writing about leadership. However, little attention has been given to explicitly describing or explaining the leadership growth process. This is surprising because growth is endemic to life. All living organisms grow from birth through maturity. Humans even demonstrate cognitive gains and improvements well into adulthood and old age (Baltes, 1987). However, what is meant by the term *growth*? How is growth related to development? What is known about how to conceptualize and model growth? Furthermore, what is the relevance of growth and development to enhancing organizational leadership? These are key questions that this chapter will address. The overarching purpose is to expound on the concept of growth and to link it to the meaning, measurement, and modeling of leadership development. The chapter concludes with three specific examples of how sophisticated modeling efforts could be used to understand and evaluate the leader development process.

Inherent to the concept of growth is *change*. As an organism grows, it changes. One type of growth-related change is quantitative in nature: Something gets taller, larger, or heavier. In other words, there are growth-related attributes that can be readily measured and quantified. However, most types of growth processes involve more than just a quantitative change in state. As living beings grow, for example, greater numbers of cells are created, which are organized into various muscles, organs, and connective tissue. Growth is therefore characterized by more than just quantitative cell change; there is also a qualitative change in state. Qualitative change is more difficult to conceptualize and measure than quantitative change, but the issue is complicated by their interrelated nature. A means of understanding the interrelationship of qualitative and quantitative change associated with growth is through the concept of *complexity*.

Increased complexity is a direct function of the number and type of interrelated connections among the component attributes of a system (Gharajedaghi, 1999). As a result of increased complexity, a system and its attributes become more difficult to separate, analyze, and understand. Another implication of viewing growth in terms of increased complexity is that the change from a relatively simple state to a complex one is not always simple and linear. Greater complexity is thought to involve a number of underlying processes, with *differentiation* and *integration* providing a typical common foundation for understanding complexity (Hooijberg, Hunt, & Dodge, 1997; Schroder, Driver, & Streufert, 1967). Furthermore, differentiation and integration complement each other in a reciprocal manner.

All open systems (i.e., systems with boundaries permeable to the environment) move in the direction of differentiation and elaboration, as well as integration and coordination (Katz & Kahn, 1978). The complementary processes of differentiation and integration are defining features of system growth. One way to conceptualize the differentiation process is in terms of specialization. For example, the sense organs evolve as highly differentiated structures from primitive nervous tissues; personality changes from a relatively simple organization of mental functions to an elaborate but highly organized system of beliefs and emotions (Harvey, Hunt, & Schroder, 1961). Forces that integrate and coordinate the system for unified functioning augment differentiation processes. Effective system functioning requires both the specialization that occurs through differentiation and the coordination of these specialized attributes by means of integration. *Development* of any system (biological, social, or other) is therefore defined as the purposeful simultaneous transformation toward higher levels of differentiation and integration (Gharajedaghi, 1999).

There is an implicit causal ordering in the patterning of differentiation and integration. Specifically, differentiation always precedes integration (Kegan, 1994). Before something can be internalized, integrated, or reconnected to a broader system, it first must be distinguished from other aspects of that system. Human development has been conceptualized as an ongoing cycle of differentiation and integration, moving toward ever-increasing levels of system (i.e., cognitive, behavioral, social) complexity. The constructive–developmental framework of Robert Kegan (1982, 1994) exemplifies this cyclical process. It is also a recognized model that describes growth as increased complexity throughout the human life span.

KEGAN'S DEVELOPMENTAL FRAMEWORK

The foundation of Kegan's (1982, 1994) model is based on the supposition that humans construct a subjective understanding of the world, which shapes their experiences. Accordingly, two individuals can construct different meanings from an identical event (e.g., a leadership episode) depending on their respective developmental level. Individuals at higher levels of development are able to use a greater number of knowledge principles to construct their experiences (differentiation) and to make more interconnections among these principles (integration). This results in a broader perspective on how things are interrelated (inclusiveness). A simpler way of stating this is that more advanced developmental levels are associated with a broader repertoire of knowledge principles and more of a "big picture" orientation toward the world.

The notion of continuous growth and change is central to Kegan's (1994) developmental framework. Individuals are thought to be continuously involved in a process of being embedded in a certain knowledge principle (i.e., way of knowing) and simultaneously attempting to disembed themselves from that principle to a higher level of complexity. Movement to a higher developmental level (i.e., growth) occurs when an individual can disembed himself or herself from a given principle that is held as "subject." A principle that is subject is something that one *sees with* implicitly, whereas a principle that is "object" is used to *see through* experience explicitly. Something that is subject is so basic to functioning that one is unaware of it. A principle that can be held as object is something that can be directly reflected on, taken control of, or otherwise operated on; it is distinct and differentiated from other principles. What is subject at a specific developmental level becomes object at the next higher level. What one sees *with* and takes for granted at one level becomes something one sees *through* and analyzes explicitly at the next.

An example of this subject–object distinction is race. At early stages of development, a White person (especially in many parts of the United States) may not see himself or herself as having a race. Race is implicit to thinking at early levels as something that defines someone. Race is what other people are, not something that other people have. When a person is embedded in the knowledge principle of race, there is little ability for that person to reflect on how race shapes one's experiences or worldview. However, experiences in which being a White person becomes salient to that individual are impetus for the transition to considering race as object.

Once a knowledge principle can be considered explicitly as object, it is then possible to integrate it with a broader knowledge system; however, that principle can always be extracted from the knowledge system and considered separately. A different way of stating this is that individual self-awareness is enhanced through adding knowledge principles that can be held as object. Principles that are subject for an individual cannot be differentiated from other elements of a knowledge system; they cannot be reflected on or acted on in a purposeful manner. Thus, there is no opportunity for development in terms of self-awareness. Complexity is enhanced by the gradual development of a broader, more inclusive knowledge system containing qualitatively different levels of both differentiation and integration. As explained by Kegan (1994), "Each successive principle subsumes or encompasses the prior principle. That which was subject becomes object to the next principle. The new principle is a higher order principle (more complex, more inclusive) that makes the prior principle into an element or tool of its system" (p. 33).

Kegan's model can be quite complex and difficult to summarize. A more concrete, applied example might help illustrate the concepts of growth and development from Kegan's perspective. In the domain of leadership, Drath and his associates (Drath, 2001; Drath & Palus, 1994) have proposed that individuals construct and enact (i.e., "make sense" of) leadership in different ways, depending on their respective levels of developmental complexity. A relatively simple way of constructing leadership is in terms of personal *dominance*. According to this knowledge principle, leaders are defined by their inner qualities, personal strength, or integrity. This is not a wrong way to construct leadership, but it is inherently limiting because an individual leader is expected to act as a sort of hero—to solve all of the group's problems or to rescue people in trouble. When problems arise that the individual leader cannot solve, there is no way to draw on other problem-solving resources in the group. There is an inability to construct leadership in a more complex manner, which puts the success and survival of the group at risk.

A more sophisticated or complex way of constructing leadership is through interpersonal *influence*. This knowledge principle does not replace dominance, but transcends it through greater inclusion of other voices and viewpoints. There are still those situations in which a dominant construction of leadership is best (e.g., emergencies); however, adding interpersonal influence to a leader's world view allows for other kinds of possible responses to a given situation. Nonetheless, there are situations in which influencing others to embrace a shared vision is insufficient because the situation, problem, or environment is so novel or complex that there is a need for a collective crafting of possibilities.

At this even more sophisticated level is the principle of relational *dialogue*. Again, this principle transcends but does not replace the others. Rather than looking to a strong individual leader or granting influence to the collective vision, relational dialogue constructs all persons as leaders and sees that influence emerges as people make commitments to one another and allow others to make claims on them. The fundamental question at this level of complexity is not so much "who is the leader?" as it is "how can I participate in this leadership process effectively?" (Drath & Palus, 1994). Individuals who can construct leadership in terms of relational dialogue can also construct it (i.e., hold it as object) as interpersonal influence or personal dominance; however, someone who constructs leadership only as personal dominance cannot take a more complex world view. The influence and dialogue approaches to leadership are subject in their dominance world view.

COMPLEXITY AS A DEVELOPMENTAL IMPERATIVE

An important question to consider is why complexity is a developmental imperative: What (if any) advantage is there to being relatively complex as compared with being relatively simple? Most scholars have argued that complex behavior is critical to adaptation and survival (Denison, Hooijberg, & Quinn, 1995). Individuals (as well as organizations) are healthy and thrive when they are capable of many responses to a given situation; they become brittle and vulnerable to changing conditions when they are uniform and specialized (Sale, 1982). However, complex human behavior flows from a foundation of complex thought. A fundamental principle of social psychology is that thinking is for doing (Fiske, 1992); however, a corollary of this principle is that doing causes thinking (Carlston, 1994). Cognition and behavior are reciprocally related—both are necessary for an extensive repertoire of possible adaptive responses to a given situation.

There is also evidence to suggest that the world is becoming increasingly complex. The mental demands of modern life often create situations in which people find themselves in over their heads (Kegan, 1994). It is widely accepted that the complexity of challenges faced in a role increases as one progresses up the organizational hierarchy. More recently, however, the need for handling greater complexity is being pushed further and further down the organizational chart. Ambiguous and unpredictable strategic environments require leaders at all levels who can respond to the challenges presented by a variety of missions. To meet these and other unforeseeable challenges, leader development in the form of purposeful transformation toward higher levels of cognitive, behavioral, and even social complexity are needed. Investments in this type of individual transformation typically are viewed in terms of leadership development.

Leadership development has been defined as the expansion of a person's capacity to be effective in leadership roles and processes, which are those things that enable groups of people to work together in productive and meaningful ways (McCauley, Moxley, & Van Velsor, 1998). There is a tight connection between expanding individual leadership capacity and enhancing complexity. Capacity is the overall potential of an individual, team, or organization to conceptualize and enact different leadership strategies in a given situation (Day, 2001). Thus, capacity comes about through the development of cognitive, behavioral, and social complexity, which in turn are based primarily in differentiation and integration.

LEADERPLEX MODEL

A recently proposed leadership framework attempts to integrate the cognitive, behavioral, and social elements of complexity. The leaderplex model (Hooijberg et al., 1997) consists of a causal framework in which cognitive and social complexity (each comprising differentiation and integration) directly influence behavioral complexity (defined as behavioral repertoire and differentiation), which ultimately is proposed to enhance leader and organizational effectiveness, respectively. Research supports the general assertion that behavioral complexity is positively associated with leader effectiveness (Denison et al., 1995). Thus, a more detailed treatment of the various components in the model is warranted, including how they might be the focus of intentional developmental efforts.

Cognitive complexity has a rich history, extending back to the work of George Kelly, who defined it in terms of the number and variety of the personal constructs held by an individual (Kelly, 1955). In a similar vein, the leaderplex model defines *cognitive differentiation* in terms of the number of dimensions and categories within dimensions used in the perception of the physical and social environment. *Cognitive integration* refers to the extent that independent dimensions can be combined in ways that enhance an individual's ability to meet the demands of a given situation (Hooijberg et al., 1997). The advantage of greater cognitive complexity is that it is associated with more sophisticated information processing, including the tendency to search for more information and to conduct a more thorough analysis of available information. However, cognitive complexity is not the same thing as general mental ability or intelligence, although there is likely to be a positive correlation between the constructs as a function of a third variable such as maturation.

The leaderplex model places social complexity as antecedent to behavioral complexity. The conceptual foundation of social complexity is the general acknowledgment that leaders are enmeshed in an interpersonal environment; thus, complexity with regard to the demands and intricacies of various social situations is required in order to develop appropriate situation-based behaviors (Zaccaro, 1999). *Social differentiation* is thought to consist of a number of facets, including an enhanced understanding of social relationships and networks, the ability to regulate one's own emotions and recognize emotions in others, and the level of self-complexity in an individual. The self-complexity facet refers to organizing self-knowledge in terms of a greater number of attributes that are relatively independent of one another (Linville, 1985), which may have particular relevance to the concept of leader self-awareness. *Social integration* pertains to an individual's capacity to synthesize the various components of a social situation for enhanced understanding and unified system functioning in social contexts.

Behavioral complexity is of key importance to leadership effectiveness because leadership inevitably involves action. For this reason, the leaderplex model proposes that complexity causally mediates the relationship between cognitive and social complexity and leader effectiveness. The components of behavioral complexity are behavioral repertoire and differentiation. *Behavioral repertoire* refers to the number of different leadership roles that can be performed, whereas *behavioral differentiation* is thought to be the extent to which these roles can be performed differently across situations (Hooijberg et al., 1997). There is abundant research (see Yukl, 2002, for a review) indicating that adapting leadership roles to situational characteristics tends to be more effective than rigid leadership role performance. Nonetheless, there are a number of unresolved questions about the leaderplex model, including what constitutes the content of complexity, how to best measure the various aspects of complexity,[1] the appropriate causal relationship among the various concepts, and the types of purposeful strategies for developing cognitive, social, and behavioral complexity.

RECONCEPTUALIZING LEADERSHIP COMPLEXITY

Despite the apparent value of the leaderplex model for understanding the growth of leaders and the antecedents of leadership effectiveness, the model does not specify the respective content of behavioral, cognitive, or social complexity. This may seem like a reasonable shortcoming given that different types of complexity may be needed in different leadership domains. However, recent work in the area of leader "metacompetencies"—or those attributes of continuous learning that help leaders learn how to learn (Briscoe & Hall, 1999)—can help to provide an understanding of how to develop and enhance complexity. Those key learning metacompetencies are identity (self-awareness) and adaptability.

Organizations need leaders who are self-aware and adaptive. One without the other is insufficient. Leaders who are adaptive without being self-aware will change simply for the sake of change. This is a particularly undesirable attribute because

---

[1] An extended treatment of measurement issues is beyond the scope of this chapter primarily because there are no universally agreed-upon measures of the different types of complexity. There also is little agreement about whether complexity can be assessed directly or whether it is best to measure various aspects of differentiation and integration separately as composites of complexity. However, there is a general acknowledgement that complexity and its components must be measured in context (Hooijberg et al., 1997). Measures should be designed to assess constructs in specific situations that challenge or otherwise encourage complexity. Some possible measurement examples include Kelly's (1955) Role Concept Repertoire Test for estimating cognitive complexity in interpersonal perception domains, social network analysis for measuring the structure of an individual's social relationships as an indicator of social complexity, and 360-degree leadership ratings for measuring others' perceptions of a leader's level of behavioral complexity. These examples are just a few of the many possible measures that could be used in leader development research. There is a distinct need for a more comprehensive taxonomy of complexity measures as well as additional empirical studies to assess their adequacy (i.e., construct validity) in leadership domains.

LEADER DEVELOPMENT

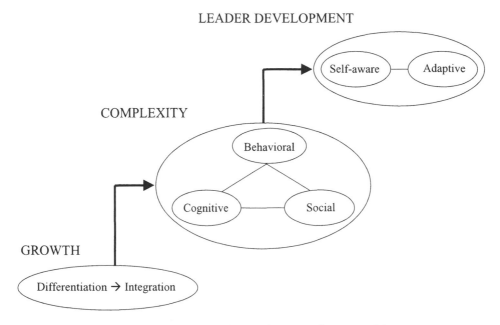

FIG. 3.1. Proposed leadership complexity model.

change for its own sake has no grounding based on internalized values and an awareness of individual strengths and limitations. In a related vein, a self-aware leader who is not adaptive will fail to change when necessary for meeting critical, new, environmental challenges. Thus, there is a reciprocal relationship between the self-awareness and the adaptability of an effective leader. A question that needs to be addressed concerns the most appropriate ways of conceptualizing, measuring, and ultimately developing self-awareness and adaptability in all leaders.

What does it take to be self-aware and adaptive? What are the kinds of things that compose these "metacompetencies?" It might appear on the surface that self-awareness is a type of cognitive or social complexity (e.g., self-complexity; Linville, 1985) and that adaptability is a form of behavioral complexity (e.g., executive flexibility; Zaccaro, 1999). However, a more careful scrutiny of these constructs indicates that there are aspects of behavioral, cognitive, and social complexity associated with each. Thus, the leaderplex model needs to be modified and extended to be suitable for understanding how the growth of complexity helps to develop self-aware and adaptive leaders (see Fig. 3.1).

Self-Awareness

Self-awareness is an important capacity for leaders in every domain. It involves a personal understanding of one's strengths and weaknesses, how these strengths and weaknesses influence others, and the life experiences and situational factors that have shaped these strengths and weaknesses (McCauley et al., 1998). In this way, self-awareness allows leaders to recognize and develop opportunities for other individuals. Broader self-awareness also helps leaders understand (a) how best to carry out their roles and responsibilities, (b) how to maximize their contributions to a group, and (c) what personal shortcomings they need to avoid or change.

Underlying broad self-awareness is a large number of differentiated and integrated categories that are used to characterize the self (cognitive complexity). Self-aware leaders are able to process a wide variety of self-relevant information, integrate across a large number of cognitive categories, and construct multifaceted identities. Self-awareness also incorporates an understanding of the extent to which social situations can be differentiated and that extensive integration and synthesis of the underlying situational components can be conducted to promote an understanding of self in interpersonal domains (social complexity). Self-aware leaders are active and accurate perceivers of interpersonal contexts. Self-awareness also involves a heightened awareness of the strengths and limitations of one's behavioral tendencies across different situations and how the roles one plays can be differentiated across leadership situations (behavioral complexity). Thus, developing leaders who are self-aware requires paying attention to all of the various components of cognitive, social, and behavioral complexity.

Adaptability

Leaders who are highly adaptive are able to thrive in uncertainty, quickly make sense of complex environments, provide creative solutions in ambiguous situations, and help others do the same (Weick, 1993). Adaptability also involves the capacity to quickly learn one's way out of problems and not to expect previous situations or solutions to be generalizable (Dixon, 1993). Adaptability in a leader's behavior, however, is grounded in those cognitive skills needed to rapidly make sense of a wide range of social situations (both familiar and unfamiliar) and to choose what actions are most appropriate (Zaccaro, 1999; Zaccaro, Gilbert, Thor, & Mumford, 1991). Research has demonstrated that individuals develop and store cognitive representations of their micro, reaching movements (Rosenbaum, Loukopoulos, Meulenbroek, Vaughan, & Engelbrecht, 1995); thus, it is sensible to assume that more macro movement sequences (i.e., leadership behaviors) have a cognitive trace as well.

With respect to the cognitive component of adaptability, greater numbers of stored and integrated categories of behavior are associated with greater levels of cognitive complexity for enhancing adaptability. Because thinking is for doing (Fiske, 1992), having stored in memory a wide variety of behavior options should enhance adaptability. Social differentiation and integration (social complexity) involve an awareness and understanding of the types of various leadership situations that are likely to be encountered. Because leadership is primarily enacted in interpersonal (i.e., social) environments, having relatively complex organizing principles (Kegan, 1994) for the social aspects of leadership will help improve overall leader functioning and effectiveness. A leader's behavioral repertoire and behavior differentiation (i.e., behavioral complexity) may be the touchstone of adaptability, but, as noted by Zaccaro et al. (1991; Zaccaro, 1999), it rests on a foundation of cognitive and social complexity. The growth and development of adaptability involve a reciprocal cycle of thinking and doing.

DEVELOPING LEADERSHIP COMPLEXITY

There are a number of formal programs and practices that have been used to develop leaders; however, the state of the art is to embed development in the context of ongoing work initiatives that are tied to key strategic imperatives (Day, 2000). The goal is to help people learn and develop better from their work, rather than take them away from their work to develop. Indeed, leadership development is ongoing and can be part of one's everyday experience. There need not be a formal, structured program for development to occur; rather, the individual leader must be reflective and intentional about learning from every experience, especially those with implications for developing better self-awareness and adaptability. However, one area in need of greater conceptual clarity is the causal connection between the development of cognitive and behavioral complexity. Does a leader need to *think* in more complex ways before he or she can *act* in more complex ways? A consideration of how job assignments are used for development might help shed light on this question.

One of the most effective means of developing greater complexity of thinking or action is to take on situations that require a more complex organizing system. Kegan (1994) referred to this as being "in over our heads." Researchers in the domain of leadership development refer to similar work-related situations as "stretch" assignments (McCauley & Brutus, 1998). Key to any developmental job assignment is that there is a challenge. However, also key for maximizing the benefits of such assignments is that they are appropriate—not too much or the wrong kind of stretch—and that there is an intentional learning component associated with the assignment. Thus, a developmental stretch assignment can be any challenging job, task, or role that requires thinking and acting in more complex ways. Underlying the choice of such an assignment should be the purposeful transformation of the individual to a more complex level of leadership functioning.

It usually is not possible to prepare people completely for a stretch assignment. In fact, some organizations are intentional about putting people into jobs for which they are only partially prepared as a means of developing leaders in the context of ongoing work (Day & Halpin, 2001). Thus, complexity develops as a function of being in a challenging job assignment that requires greater complexity in order to be effective. Although cognitive and social complexity may temporally precede behavioral complexity in such assignments, there are certainly circumstances in which doing causes thinking. Enacting a new set of behaviors can be a catalyst for thinking about leadership in new ways.

Another typical means of trying to promote leadership development is through feedback interventions. The content of the feedback can take the form of results of written assessments (e.g., personality inventories) or the impressions of those around the leader both within and across organizational levels (e.g., 360-degree assessment). It is interesting to note that feedback interventions have been shown to result in performance decrements in approximately one third of the studies that were reviewed (Kluger & DeNisi, 1996). However, evaluation efforts with regard to the effects of feedback on leadership development are almost nonexistent in the published literature (Day & Halpin, 2001). One reason may be that leadership development is a difficult concept to operationalize and model over time. This chapter may help provide clarity to this issue by helping researchers better link the type of feedback with the relevant type of complexity to be enhanced. For example, written feedback may be most useful for enhancing the cognitive complexity component of self-awareness or adaptability. Informal verbal feedback that is offered close in time to when a particular behavior is enacted may help to further behavioral complexity. Coaching or mentoring may provide the type of feedback that is especially helpful for enhancing social complexity through advice on how to make sense of complicated interpersonal situations or for seeing social networks in a broader context. Thus, the present emerging framework of leadership complexity might be useful in focusing predictions of what exactly changes as a result of leadership development initiatives.

One of the key questions posed previously concerned the meaning and measurement of growth. As a means of furthering an understanding of how leaders grow and develop over time and how leadership complexity is enhanced, it is necessary to provide an overview of the conceptual, measurement, and modeling issues associated with change. This overview provides the basis for identifying procedures that will allow for sound longitudinal modeling of leadership development. It will also help to suggest how best to examine the causal links among cognitive, social, and behavioral complexity and the developmental outcomes of self-awareness and adaptability. We first outline the general underlying issues associated with the conceptualization and measurement of change, and then provide several examples of how the recommended modeling technique (latent growth modeling) can be used to examine issues related to leader development.

ISSUES IN THE CONCEPTUALIZATION AND MEASUREMENT OF CHANGE

Theories and models of "growth" and "development" necessarily imply *change*. Historically, the measurement of change has been a large and controversial topic. Because of the complexities in the conceptualization and measurement of change, it was questioned whether psychologists should even attempt to measure change

TABLE 3.1
Issues in the Conceptualization and Measurement of Change (e.g., Leader
Cognitive Complexity)

1. **Random versus systematic change**. Do changes in leader cognitive complexity represent true, systematic changes or merely random fluctuations over time? Are measured changes due to actual changes in leader cognitive complexity or fluctuations due to measurement error?

2. **Reversible versus irreversible change**. Is change strictly unidirectional and monotonic or reversible so that leaders' cognitive complexity could return to previous levels? Is the form of change linear, an inverted U, or some more complex function?

3. **Unitary versus multipath change**. Are there individual differences in the ways in which leaders undergo transitions from one state of leader cognitive complexity to another (e.g., linear vs. quadratic change)? Can subgroups of individuals who follow different forms of change be identified?

4. **Continuous versus discontinuous change**. Is change continuous and monotonic or discontinuous and "catastrophic?" Is change gradual or does it follow a "step" function associated with transition between discrete stages?

5. **Qualitative versus quantitative change**. Do changes in leader cognitive complexity simply reflect greater or lesser complexity or are there qualitatively different shifts in leader cognitive complexity? Do changes in leader cognitive complexity lead to fundamentally different interpretations of what leader cognitive complexity is?

6. **Individual- versus group-level change**. Is change appropriately conceptualized and measured at the individual or group level of analysis? Is the phenomenon individual-specific or shared?

7. **Individual differences in change**. If leaders *do* share a common form of change (e.g., linear), are there individual differences in their starting points (initial status) and rates of change (slope) over time?

8. **Concomitant change**. Is change over time in leader cognitive complexity associated with change in other factors, for example, leader social complexity?

9. **Between-groups differences in change**. Is change invariant across groups, for example, leaders who undergo one form of leader development program versus another, or an "experimental" group versus a "control" group?

Note. From "The Conceptualization and Analysis of Change Over Time: An Integrative Approach Incorporating Longitudinal Mean and Covariance Structure Analysis (LMACS) and Multiple Indicator Latent Growth Modeling (MLGLM)," by D. Chan, 1998, *Organizational Reasearch Methods, 1,* pp. 468–469. Copyright 1998 by Sage. Adapted with permission. And from "We Should Measure Change—And Here's How," by C. E. Lance, A. W. Mead, and G. M. Williamson, in *Physical Illness and Depression in Older Adults: A Handbook of Theory, Research, and Practice* (p. 209), edited by G. M. Williamson, D. R. Shaffer, and P. A. Parmalee, 2000, New York: Plenum. Copyright 2000 by Kluwer Academic/Plenum Publisher. Adapted with permission.

(Cronbach & Furby, 1971). The answer now seems to be yes, we can, and we should (Lance, Meade, & Williamson, 2000). Nevertheless, conceptual and methodological issues concerning change remain complex.

Table 3.1 lists several issues in the conceptualization and measurement of change that were identified in two recent comprehensive reviews in the psychological literature (Chan, 1998a; Lance, Meade, & Williamson, 2000). Note that these issues concern both the theoretical treatment of change, or how the psychological construct in question should or should not change, and the operationalization of change, or how change over time is measured. These are different issues, and the former logically precedes the latter. The link between how change is measured and its particular conceptualization is critical. Each of the issues in Table 3.1 is discussed briefly using leader cognitive complexity as a domain in which change might be investigated.

1. Change in leader cognitive complexity could be *random* or *systematic*. Conceptually, leader cognitive complexity may fluctuate nonsystematically, or may be so prone to situation-specific influences that no systematic change is expected theoretically or discernible empirically. In this scenario, leader cognitive complexity might be determined exclusively by "random shocks" (James, Mulaik, & Brett, 1982) and no systematic change should be expected or detected. On the other hand, change in leader cognitive complexity may be systematic. In this case, leader cognitive complexity follows some organized, systematic developmental trajectory. It is desirable that change in leader cognitive complexity be modeled on the basis of *true* leader cognitive complexity scores (or estimates) rather than on fallible scores that contain substantial measurement error. This is a concern because leadership constructs are often operationalized using observed measures (e.g., multi-item composite scores) that contain nonsystematic measurement error and possibly systematic response bias (e.g., halo, leniency) in addition to their true score components. As such, use of unreliable or biased measures of leader cognitive complexity can obscure true change in leader cognitive complexity and reduce the likelihood of detecting actual change in leaders' cognitive complexity.

2. Change in leader cognitive complexity may be *reversible* or *irreversible*. Head trauma from an automobile accident could result in irreversible deficits in cognitive functioning. On the other hand, leaders might revert or relapse (Marx, 1982) to less complex cognition if steps (e.g., refresher training) are not taken to sustain leader cognitive complexity (Lance et al., 1998). A desirable characteristic of any approach to the measurement of change is that it be capable of detecting reversible as well as irreversible change.

3. Change in leader cognitive complexity may be *unitary* or *multipath*. Leaders may change from one level of leader cognitive complexity to another, but the ways they get to higher complexity levels may be quite different. For example, one leader may follow a gradual, linear path toward greater complexity. Another leader may initially increase complexity rapidly, then asymptote later in a negatively accelerated quadratic growth pattern. Yet another leader may increase complexity slowly at first, then increase more rapidly later in a positively accelerated nonlinear pattern. Two key issues are whether or not a given approach to change measurement permits the identification of subgroups (clusters) of individuals who share similar functional forms of change, which is a desirable property and a measurement issue, and whether subgroup (cluster) membership is predictable on the basis of salient psychological characteristics, which is both a theoretical and a measurement issue.

4. Change in leader cognitive complexity could be *continuous* or *discontinuous*. Changes on most psychological characteristics are assumed to be continuous, and

probably appropriately so. However, dramatic, abrupt, "catastrophic" changes have been discussed in areas such as organizational change (e.g., Nadler & Tushman, 1995), figure perception (e.g., Stewart & Peregoy, 1983), employee turnover (e.g., Sheridan, 1985), and employee motivation (e.g., Guastello, 1987). It is conceivable that leader cognitive complexity or other variables related to leader effectiveness might also change discontinuously. For now, the important points are that discontinuous change, if present, should be predictable theoretically and detectable empirically.

5. Change may be *qualitative* or *quantitative*. The alpha, beta, and gamma change typology (Golembiewski, Billingsley, & Yeager, 1976) is of particular relevance here. *Alpha* change is defined in terms of change in level on some constantly calibrated instrument in some conceptually constant domain such as increases in children's knowledge of science through middle school or decreases in cognitive functioning with progression of dementia in the elderly. *Beta* change refers to a recalibration of some measurement scale in a constant conceptual domain and is usually interpreted as a change in response threshold or shift in leniency or severity over time or as a function of some intervention. For example, employees might describe their coworkers in more favorable terms following sensitivity training, not because their coworkers have changed, but because standards for judging coworkers' behaviors have changed. *Gamma* change involves a qualitative redefinition of some conceptual domain. For example, leaders may take a more differentiated view of what constitutes "leader effectiveness" following a leader development intervention aimed at enhancing leader cognitive complexity so that leader effectiveness is defined qualitatively differently following the intervention, perhaps as a more differentiated concept following training than it was before. Of key concern is that tests for beta and gamma change be conducted as a prerequisite to assessing longitudinal alpha change or researchers run the risk of comparing "apples to schnitzels to touchdowns" (Lance, Vandenberg, & Self, 2000, p. 135) instead of apples to apples over time. Another issue is that some leader development efforts may be geared specifically to engender beta or gamma changes, and, if so, these should be measured. Thus, it is important that all three types of changes be detectable.

6. It is also important that change can be assessed at both the *individual* and the *group* level of analysis. Some constructs like leader cognitive complexity may be meaningful theoretically only at the individual level of analysis. Other constructs may be meaningful at both the individual and group levels (e.g., individual-level job satisfaction and group-level morale; individual-level psychological climate and aggregate-level organizational climate). Either way, any approach to measurement should be adaptable to assessing change at multiple levels of analysis.

7. Often there are *individual differences in change* over time even though the functional *form* of change is homogeneous across individuals. For example, given a linear growth trajectory, individuals can differ both in their *initial status* and *rate of change*. For example, school children may start the school year with different levels of readiness to benefit from instruction (i.e., their initial status) as a function

of their previous education or differences in parental relationships. They may also differ in the rate at which they learn during the school year (rate of change) as a function of nutrition, motivation, and familial support. It is important to be able to measure the extent of individual differences in initial status and change over time, and to identify other exogenous variables that are responsible for differential growth patterns.

8. *Concomitant change* may be routinely expected in some domains. For example, children gain height, weight, and intellect in tandem. In other areas, questions of concomitant change are of much greater theoretical interest. For example, the issue of concomitant change relates to the following: (a) As leaders develop, do leader cognitive complexity and leader social complexity develop in parallel? (b) Does development in leader cognitive complexity *lead* development in leader social complexity such that leader cognitive complexity may be a prerequisite for leader social complexity? (c) Is development in leader cognitive complexity independent of development in leader social complexity? An effective strategy for change assessment should provide the means for addressing questions such as these.

9. Finally, *between-groups differences in change* may or may not be expected. For example, different approaches to leader development may be differentially effective in realizing their goals and may have an impact on different aspects of leader development. For example, highly realistic simulations (e.g., virtual reality) may enhance leader cognitive complexity to a greater extent than social complexity, whereas coaching may have just the opposite effects. It is important that an effective strategy for assessing change can model differential change across groups, such as those who have undergone alternative leader development programs, leaders of differing (cognitive) abilities and experience, and leaders from different cultural orientations.

In summary, the issues listed in Table 3.1 represent points that researchers should consider in the theoretical conceptualization of change as it applies to the substantive domain in which they are working. That is, what are the particular characteristics of change that are expected within a given substantive domain? Table 3.1 also highlights desirable characteristics of a general approach to the assessment of longitudinal change. In the next section we evaluate several popular approaches to the measurement of change using these criteria. We then discuss in detail one approach, latent growth modeling, which has particular promise.

RELATIVE EFFICACY OF VARIOUS APPROACHES TO THE MEASUREMENT OF CHANGE

Table 3.2 summarizes our assessment of the relative efficacy of a number of popularly adopted approaches to the assessment of longitudinal change according to the issues summarized in Table 3.1. With one exception (multiple-indicator latent

TABLE 3.2

Relative Efficacy of Various Approaches to the Measurement of Longitudinal Change

	Descriptive Statistics	Change Scores	t Tests	ANOVA	MANOVA	Lagged Regression	LGM	MLGM
1. Control for random measurement error?	No	No	No	No	No	No	Ltd	Yes
2. Reversible and irreversible change?	Ltd	Ltd	Ltd	Yes	Yes	Ltd	Yes	Yes
3. Unitary and multipath change?	No	Ltd	No	No	No	No	Yes	Yes
4. Continuous and discontinuous change?	Ltd	Ltd	Ltd	Ltd	Ltd	Ltd	Ltd	Yes
5. Qualitative and quantitative change?	No	No	No	No	No	No	No	Yes
6. Individual- and group-level change?	No	Yes	No	No	No	No	Yes	Yes
7. Individual differences in change?	No	Yes	No	No	No	Ltd	Yes	Yes
8. Concomitant change?	Ltd	Yes	No	No	Yes	No	Yes	Yes
9. Between-groups differences in change?	Ltd	Ltd	Ltd	Ltd	Ltd	Ltd	Yes	Yes

Note. LGM, Latent growth model; MLGM, multiple-indicator latent growth model; Ltd, limited. From "The Conceptualization and Analysis of Change Over Time: An Integrative Approach Incorporating Longitudinal Mean and Covariance Structure Analysis (LMACS) and Multiple Indicator Latent Growth Modeling (MLGLM)," by D. Chan, 1998, *Organizational Research Methods*,1, pp. 468–469. Copyright 1998 by Sage. Reprinted by permission of Sage Publications, Inc. And from "We Should Measure Change—And Here's How," by C. E. Lance, A. W. Meade, and G. M. Williamson, in *Physical Illness and Depression in Older Adults: A Handbook of Theory, Research, and Practice* (p. 209), edited by G. M. Williamson, D. R. Shaffer, and P. A. Parmalee, 2000, New York: Plenum. Copyright 2000 by Kluwer Academic/Plenum Publishers. Adapted with permission.

growth modeling, MLGM), these approaches were identified by Lance, Meade, and Williamson (2000) as those that were most often used to assess longitudinal change in the literature they reviewed.[2]

Our assessment of each of the techniques listed across the top of Table 3.2 for each of the criteria listed along the left of the table indicates whether (a) the technique addresses the issue listed (Yes), for example, change (i.e., difference) scores can be calculated at either the individual or group level of analysis; (b) the technique addresses the issue, but only in a limited way (Ltd., limited), for example, descriptive statistics *can* be used to assess both reversible and irreversible change, but their analysis is subjective and primitive; or (c) the technique does not address the issue listed (No), for example, use of descriptive statistics and change scores (at least in their typical application) do not correct for random measurement error. As is clear from Table 3.2, our assessments of the most popularly invoked procedures for assessing longitudinal change indicate that most of these procedures fare poorly according to the criteria listed here. This is illuminating in that the vast majority of studies reviewed by Lance, Meade, and Williamson (2000) used some form of ANOVA or regression-based model, which is not efficacious according to the criteria in Table 3.2. Although used far less frequently, LGM and MLGM fulfill most, or all, of the criteria for an effective approach to the measurement of longitudinal change.

LATENT GROWTH MODELS
OF LONGITUDINAL CHANGE

Although the development of LGM dates back over 40 years (Rao, 1958), it received little attention until the 1980s (e.g., McArdle, 1986, 1988; Meredith & Tisak, 1990), and is only now being introduced into the applied psychology literature (e.g., Chan, 1998a; Lance, Vandenberg, & Self, 2000). For interested readers, there are excellent, and more thorough, introductions to LGM (e.g., Duncan & Duncan,1995; Duncan, Duncan, & Stoolmiller, 1994; Lance, Vandenberg, & Self, 2000; Willett & Sayer, 1994).

Conceptually, LGM begins with measures on characteristics of a single individual obtained on multiple occasions. In Fig. 3.2, a plot of measures of a single hypothetical leader's cognitive complexity scores obtained at four times of measurement (T1–T4) show an irregular, but generally increasing pattern. Fitting a

---

[2]We recognize that there are other, more specialized approaches to assessing change, such as survival analysis, time series analysis, catastrophe theory, and chaos theory, but we do not consider them here. Each of those approaches is designed to assess a particular type of change and is not intended as a general analytic model for longitudinal change assessment, and their use in the literature is very infrequent. We also acknowledge hierarchical linear modeling (HLM) as a viable approach to longitudinal change assessment, but under most conditions HLMs can be estimated as latent growth models, which are generally more powerful and flexible than HLMs.

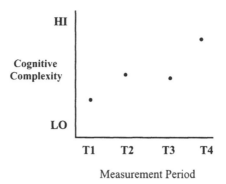

FIG. 3.2. Plot of one hypothetical leader's cognitive complexity scores over four equally spaced measurement periods.

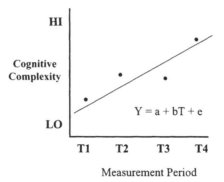

FIG. 3.3. Fitted linear growth trajectory for one hypothetical leader's longitudinal development in cognitive complexity.

linear regression line to the leader's data as is shown in Fig. 3.3 summarizes this growth trajectory. Note that the regression equation (a) summarizes the *linear* relation between leader cognitive complexity and time, so that the growth curve fitted is a "straight-line growth curve"; (b) is fitted for a *single individual*; and (c) is *purely descriptive*, that is, inferential statistics are of no interest. Fitting the straight-line growth curve for the hypothetical leader in Fig. 3.3 provides information relating to the leader's *initial status*, or the intercept parameter a, which indicates the level of the leader's cognitive complexity at the beginning of the measurement process (i.e., T1); and *rate of change*, or the slope parameter b, which indicates the rate of linear change on leader cognitive complexity over the course of the measurement process (T1–T4). The initial status parameter a indicates where a leader "starts out" in terms of his or her level of cognitive complexity and the slope parameter b indicates relatively how slowly or rapidly the leader's cognitive complexity changes over time.

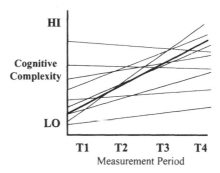

FIG. 3.4. Plot of linear growth trajectories for several hypothetical leaders' longitudinal development in cognitive complexity.

However, a single person is not a study. LGM involves the analysis of multiple individuals' growth curves. Figure 3.4 shows, for example, our original leader's straight-line growth curve (in bold) along with several other hypothetical leaders' growth curves. *These individual-level growth curves are the basic units of analysis for LGM.* Note that each individual has a unique set of initial status and slope (or growth) parameters corresponding to his or her particular growth trajectory. Normally, the means of the *a* and *b* parameters are calculated to characterize the average initial status and slope in the sample. Note that the hypothetical leaders represented in Fig. 3.4 have quite different starting points for their growth curves, that is, there is substantial variability in individuals' initial status. Although most leaders' cognitive complexity trends are increasing, the rates of change differ from leader to leader, that is, there is also substantial variability in leaders' slopes or rates of change. These parameters are the basic building blocks for LGM: (a) *growth curves*, which are estimated at the individual level of analysis, (b) estimated mean *initial status and change* for the sample, and (c) estimated *variance* of the initial status and change parameters for the sample.

LGMs are implemented using confirmatory factor analysis (CFA; Bollen, 1989; Lance & Vandenberg, 2002). Figure 3.5 shows a basic CFA implementation of a LGM for a model with three measurement periods (minimum recommended number to assess change), where (a) Y_1 to Y_3 indicate measures for the same variable (e.g., leader cognitive complexity) over three measurement waves, (b) η_1 and η_2 are latent variables (common factors), which represent initial status and change, respectively, (c) ζ_1 and ζ_2, normally referring to latent residuals, are included to model variances of and covariances among the ηs (the LISREL program does not define a parameter matrix for covariances among ηs, so the Ψ matrix, which is defined as the covariances among ζs is used for this purpose), (d) ψ_{12} represents the covariance between η_1 and η_2, and (e) the εs represent error terms (technically, "uniquenesses"). The single-headed arrows connecting the ηs to the Ys represent factor loadings of the Ys on the η factors. Note, however,

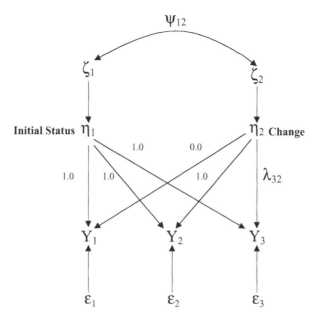

FIG. 3.5. Basic linear growth model.

that unlike more traditional applications of CFA, the factor loadings in LGM are almost entirely fixed parameters. This is done to link the observed Y scores to the underlying initial status and change scores for each individual. For the ith individual,

$$Y_{i1} = 1.0 * \eta_{i1} + 0.0 * \eta_{i2} + \varepsilon_{i1} \qquad \text{This returns a score for initial status only}$$

$$Y_{i2} = 1.0 * \eta_{i1} + 1.0 * \eta_{i2} + \varepsilon_{i2} \qquad \text{Initial status plus one unit of change}$$

$$Y_{i3} = 1.0 * \eta_{i1} + 2.0 * \eta_{i2} + \varepsilon_{i3} \qquad \text{Initial status plus two units of change}$$

for a "straight line" LGM (i.e., the factor loading λ_{32} shown in Fig. 3.5 is set equal to 2.0 for a linear change model). Thus, unlike more traditional applications of CFA in which latent variables are accorded some substantive interpretation (e.g., latent "job satisfaction"), the latent variables in LGM are *chronometric factors*, which model change parameters associated with the focal variable (e.g., leader cognitive complexity).

At this point we note that LGM satisfies three important criteria in Table 3.2. First, LGM *controls for random measurement error* (Criterion 1), as change is modeled at the level of latent variables or common factors, which are perfectly reliable at least in theory (Mulaik, 1972). Second, because LGM estimates individual-level growth curves, the extent of *individual differences in change* (Criterion 7) is estimable as the variance of the a and b parameters in Fig. 3.4 or, equivalently, the variance of the η_1 and η_2 parameters in Fig. 3.5. Finally, because mean growth parameters are estimable for the sample, change can be assessed both at the *individual and the group level* of analysis (Criterion 6).

Extensions to the Basic LGM

Table 3.3 lists several extensions to the basic LGM discussed so far. The first of these is the specification of higher order curves (e.g., quadratic, cubic) or other functional forms that may be of interest. Returning to Fig. 3.5, this would be accomplished by adding another change latent variable and choosing appropriate factor loading coefficients to model the desired function. Recall that in the earlier example, η_2 was designed to measure *linear* change with factor loading coefficients of 0, 1, and 2 for measurement waves T1, T2, and T3, respectively. *Quadratic* change could be modeled by adding an η_3 factor with coefficients 0, 1, and 4 (i.e., by squaring the coefficients for the linear change function). Alternately, an inverted-V function could be modeled with coefficients -1, 2, and -1 for an η_3 factor. If there are four or more measurement waves, a cubic function could be modeled with the addition of an η_4 factor and choice of appropriate factor loading coefficients. Other, irregular (e.g., step) functions could also be modeled. This extension permits the modeling of both *continuous and discontinuous change* (Criterion 4 in Table 3.2).

Second, "unspecified" or "optimal" change functions can be modeled. This is the case that is actually shown in Fig. 3.5, where λ_{32} is shown as a freely estimated parameter. Statistically, at least two of the factor loadings for the η_2 latent variable in Fig. 3.5 must be fixed (i.e., specified a priori) for identification purposes, but the remaining factor loadings may be freely estimated. These are thought of as "optimal" change functions because (a) they may take whatever form that best describes the type of change that is occurring in the sample and (b) they often provide a better description of the data than, for example, strict linear change. "Unspecified" or "optimal" change functions can also easily identify situations in which individuals return to their initial status after some period of growth. As such, optimal change functions permit the estimation of *reversible and irreversible change* (Criterion 2 in Table 3.2).

TABLE 3.3

Extensions to the Basic Latent Growth Model

1. Higher order (e.g., quadratic, cubic) and other a priori specified growth functions
2. Unspecified or "optimal" change functions
3. Assessment of change in multiple domains
4. Assessment of change in multiple groups
5. Latent class analysis
6. Multiple indicator latent growth models

Third, the basic LGM can be extended to examine change in multiple domains simultaneously (Willett & Sayer, 1996). For example, a model such as depicted in Fig. 3.5 could be estimated simultaneously for both leader cognitive complexity and leader social complexity. This is a powerful extension, as it allows researchers to address questions such as whether initial status on leader cognitive complexity is associated with initial status on leader social complexity (do leaders who have higher leader cognitive complexity in the beginning also have higher leader social complexity?). More interesting, it can also address whether change in leader cognitive complexity is associated with change in leader social complexity (do leaders who increase on leader cognitive complexity over time also increase on leader social complexity?). With at least four measurement waves it can be investigated whether change in one domain leads or lags change in another domain (do leader cognitive complexity and leader social complexity change simultaneously— a generalized growth pattern—or does change in leader cognitive complexity *lead* change in leader social complexity?). If the latter, it could be concluded that development in leader cognitive complexity may be necessary for the development of leader social complexity. This extension allows researchers to address critical questions pertaining to *concomitant change* (Criterion 8 in Table 3.2).

Fourth, LGMs can be estimated simultaneously in multiple groups. An LGM such as shown in Fig. 3.5 could be estimated simultaneously for a group of leaders who have undergone simulation training on leader social complexity and a control group for whom leader social complexity measures were obtained at the same time but who underwent no training. A key question would be whether the patterns of development—not simply posttest scores—in the training group were similar to those in the control group (it would be expected that they were not). Thus, this extension supports the analysis of *between-groups differences in change* (Criterion 9 in Table 3.2).

Fifth, Muthén (2001; Muthén & Shedden, 1999) developed a variant of latent class analysis that identifies subgroups of individuals who share similar developmental trajectories. The procedure uses latent variable mixture modeling and clustering techniques to identify the most likely number of (overlapping) groups of individuals who differ *across* groups in terms of their growth trajectories, but share similar growth trajectories *within* groups. Conceptually, the approach clusters similar growth curves such as those shown in Fig. 3.4. This extension allows the researcher to test whether there exists *unitary and multipath change* within a sample (Criterion 3 in Table 3.2).

Finally, the basic LGM can be extended to include multiple manifest indicators for each measurement wave. In the case of leader cognitive complexity, these might be (a) different measures, developed separately, to measure leader cognitive complexity, (b) individual items from a single leader cognitive complexity measure, or (c) subtests or subsections from a single leader cognitive complexity measure. This type of model has been referred to as a curve-of-factors model (McArdle, 1988), a multiple indicator LGM (MLGM; Chan, 1998a), and a second-order

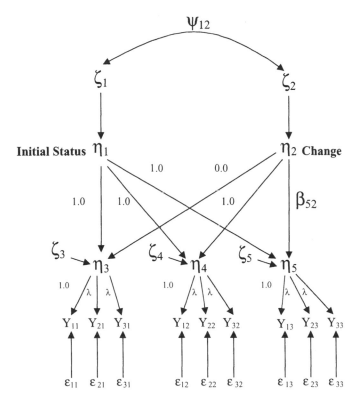

FIG. 3.6. Multiple-indicator linear growth model.

factor LGM (Lance, Vandenberg, & Self, 2000). We use Chan's (1998a) terminology. An example of a MLGM is shown in Fig. 3.6. Note that it is identical in form to the model in Fig. 3.5 except that three measures (the Ys) are included for the construct at each measurement period (i.e., η_3–η_5). Including multiple indicators (multiple measures) accomplishes three important goals. First, it operationalizes the measurement of the focal variable at each time period as a latent variable, which controls for random measurement error (this is related to Criterion 1 in Table 3.2). Second, the MLGM model disentangles nonsystematic measurement error (contained in the εs in Fig. 3.6) from systematic time-specific effects (contained in ζ_3–ζ_5 in Fig. 3.6), which are otherwise confounded in the in the εs in Fig. 3.5. Perhaps most important, it permits assessment of longitudinal measurement equivalence and invariance (Vandenberg & Lance, 2000), which concerns whether the relationships between observed measures (the Ys in Fig. 3.6) and the constructs they are intended to represent (η_3–η_5 in Fig. 3.5) are constant over time. If beta or gamma change has occurred over time, they will not be. Use of MLGM models permits assessment of measurement *ine*quivalence (Horn & McArdle, 1992; Vandenberg & Lance, 2000), or possible beta or gamma changes as a prerequisite to assessing longitudinal change. Thus the MLGM supports the analysis of both *qualitative* (i.e., beta and gamma) *and quantitative change* (alpha change, or change in level over time, Criterion 5 in Table 3.2).

Summary

Any review of LGM is necessarily complex because of the technical nature of its content, and this review is no exception. However, there are a few important "take-away" points from the previous section:

- Historically, change has been difficult to measure and model.
- Part of the difficulty has been that change is not a unitary phenomenon—there are many different types of change.
- Recent advances in modeling and statistical estimation procedures have solved many of the key problems in change measurement that have nagged researchers over the years.
- LGM, as one of these recent advances, is a powerful statistical tool, which can be used to model most if not all of the various forms of change.

With these points in mind, we can better understand, describe, and influence the growth of future leaders if we approach the development process with LGM concepts (and with notions of the growth in complexity) in mind.

The concluding section of this chapter provides three specific examples of how to capitalize on the power of LGM in examining key aspects of leader development. These examples underscore the fact that nearly every experience tied to ongoing organizational work can contribute to leader development. However, this has both positive and negative implications. On the positive side, leader development is occurring every day in an ongoing manner in organizations. On the negative side, little is known about the kinds of initiatives, experiences, or processes that contribute the most to leader development. Research using methods designed to model change over time can contribute to a better understanding of how different experiences and processes develop leaders.

EXAMPLE APPLICATIONS OF LGM TO UNDERSTANDING LEADER DEVELOPMENT

Feedback

It is widely acknowledged that feedback is important to individual growth and development. Much of the increased use of multisource or 360-degree feedback is attributable to the central role that different perspectives on individual performance can play in building a comprehensive picture of an individual's impact on others. Nonetheless, there is little empirically based understanding of how multisource feedback enhances leader development. An underlying assumption regarding the use of feedback in organizations is that it builds deeper self-awareness in leaders (Day, 2000). However, it is unclear exactly how this feedback process results in greater self-awareness. Is it the availability of more information about oneself (i.e., cognitive differentiation) or how the information is used to integrate across a larger number of cognitive categories (i.e., integration) that drives development? Because differentiation precedes integration (Kegan, 1994), there is an implicit causal order in the differentiation–integration distinction, but it has not been examined formally in leadership contexts. Thus, it is proposed that to the extent that feedback enhances both cognitive differentiation and integration, the greater are the levels of cognitive complexity and self-awareness that are developed.

Another potentially important aspect of feedback is the relationship between cognitive, social, and behavioral complexity. Given that self-awareness comprises all three of these complexity components, a feedback process that provides explicit means for linking cognitive, social, and behavioral components of complexity should result in greater self-awareness than a feedback process that does not try to link these aspects of complexity. A causal change model could be introduced and examined using LGM to enhance leader development by forging explicit relationships between the various complexity components over time.

Distance Learning

Technological advances in computing and the Internet have made the delivery of instructional content widely available to many audiences. This is an attractive development for many organizations because it can potentially make instructional materials available to a wider audience and can help reduce the costs associated with residential instruction. However, with this opportunity for greater employee access through electronic media is the potential loss to development associated with the sharing of experiences that occur in a typical residential class. The opportunity to build relationships and connections with others in different parts of an organization is a valuable component of residential instruction. However, how valuable is this relationship-building aspect in terms of leader development? Are the employees who access the same instructional content through distance learning somehow disadvantaged by not being involved in the residential aspect of learning?

At issue in this debate over the relative advantages and disadvantages of distance learning is the role that social complexity plays in development. The opportunity to interact face to face with others over the course of a week or two of residential instruction may play a key role in the development of social complexity for self-awareness and adaptability. It is proposed that both the within-person and the between-groups development of social complexity enhance learning and leader development. Specific interventions could be designed to enhance the social complexity of those who undertake training and development through distance learning. Thus, distance learning could be more often used as an effective complement of—or even replacement for—residential instruction without any serious disadvantages to leader development.

Simulations

Simulations and other types of synthetic environments can be potent developmental tools. In particular, they allow participants to try out new behaviors and ways of thinking without the risks associated with similar experiences in the field. Simulations serve as micro-worlds (Senge, 1990) for stretch assignments that are potentially dangerous or career limiting. To maximize the effectiveness of simulations for leader development, attention must be given to the desired learning and growth processes. What needs to be developed in a leader and how will the simulation help to accomplish this developmental goal? These are critical questions to address; otherwise development becomes an ad hoc as opposed to an intentional process.

Simulations provide ideal training and evaluation venues because they are realistic, yet also allow for the control over confounding factors that affect the intervention. The relative challenge associated with a simulated experience can be systematically varied and tied to the measurement of cognitive, social, and behavioral complexity. Additional variables such as personality, cognitive ability, or experience can be incorporated into the research design to more closely examine between-individual differences in development. Simulations should be tied to research in order to answer important questions around who benefits most from a particular experience and how the experience contributes to the development of self-aware and adaptive leaders.

Conclusion

These examples are intended to illustrate how critical leader development issues can be addressed through LGM. The development of leaders is something that takes place on an ongoing and daily basis. It is also a long-term investment. Indeed, Gen. Fred Franks (Ret.) noted that the longest development process in the U.S. Army is the development of a commander (i.e., top-level leader), which takes from 22 to 25 years. This is a longer developmental cycle than that associated with developing a new tank, helicopter, or other weapon. For this reason alone, it makes sense to develop and implement empirically grounded interventions and evaluate them using state-of-the-art procedures such as LGM. Such efforts could be a catalyst to the ongoing investments that any organization makes in its leaders with an eye toward improving and accelerating the overall leader development process.

REFERENCES

Baltes, P. B. (1987). Theoretical propositions of life-span developmental psychology: On the dynamics between growth and decline. *Developmental Psychology, 23*, 611–626.

Bollen, K. A. (1989). *Structural equations with latent variables.* New York: Wiley.

Briscoe, J. P., & Hall, D. T. (1999). Grooming and picking leaders using competency frameworks: Do they work? An alternative approach and new guidelines for practice. *Organizational Dynamics, 28*(2), 37–52.

Carlston, D. E. (1994). Associated systems theory: A systematic approach to cognitive representations of persons. *Advances in Social Cognition, 7*, 1–78.

Chan, D. (1998a). The conceptualization and analysis of change over time: An integrative approach incorporating longitudinal mean and covariance structure analysis (LMACS) and multiple indicator latent growth modeling (MLGM). *Organizational Research Methods, 1*, 421–483.

Cronbach, L. J., & Furby, L. (1971). How should we measure "change"—Or should we? *Psychological Bulletin, 74*, 68–80.

Day, D. V. (2000). Leadership development: A review in context. *Leadership Quarterly, 11*, 581–613.

Day, D. V. (April, 2001). *Understanding systems forces for sustainable leadership capacity.* Paper presented at the 16th annual conference of the Society for Industrial and Organizational Psychology, San Diego, CA.

Day, D. V., & Halpin, S. M. (2001). *Leadership development: A review of industry best practices* (Technical Report No. 1111). Fort Leavenworth, KS: Army Research Institute.

Denison, D. R., Hooijberg, R., & Quinn, R. E. (1995). Paradox and performance: Toward a theory of behavioral complexity in managerial leadership. *Organization Science, 6*, 524–540.

Dixon, N. M. (1993). Developing managers for the learning organization. *Human Resource Management Review, 3*, 243–254.

Drath, W. (2001). *The deep blue sea: Rethinking the source of leadership.* San Francisco: Jossey-Bass.

Drath, W. H., & Palus, C. J. (1994). *Making common sense: Leadership as meaning-making in a community of practice.* Greensboro, NC: Center for Creative Leadership.

Duncan, T. E., & Duncan, S. E. (1995). Modeling the processes of development via latent variable growth curve methodology. *Structural Equation Modeling, 2*, 178–213.

Duncan, T. E., Duncan, S. C., & Stoolmiller, M. (1994). Modeling developmental processes using latent growth structural equation modeling. *Applied Psychological Measurement, 18*, 343–354.

Fiske, S. T. (1992). Thinking is for doing: Portraits of social cognition from daguerreotype to laserphoto. *Journal of Personality and Social Psychology, 63*, 877–889.

Gharajedaghi, J. (1999). *Systems thinking: Managing chaos and complexity.* Boston: Butterworth Heinemann.

Golembiewski, R. T., Billingsley, K., & Yeager, S. (1976). Measuring change and persistence in human affairs: Types of change generated by OD designs. *Journal of Applied Behavioral Science, 12*, 133–157.

Guastello, S. J. (1987). A butterfly catastrophe model of motivation in organizations: Academic performance. *Journal of Applied Psychology, 72*, 165–182.

Harvey, O. J., Hunt, D. E., & Schroder, H. M. (1961). *Conceptual systems and personality organization.* New York: Wiley.

Hooijberg, R., Hunt, J. G., & Dodge, G. E. (1997). Leadership complexity and development of the leaderplex model. *Journal of Management, 23*, 375–408.

Horn, J. L., & McArdle, J. J. (1992). A practical and theoretical guide to measurement invariance in aging research. *Experimental Aging Research, 18*, 117–144.

James, L. R., Mulaik, S. A., & Brett, J. M. (1982). *Causal analysis: Models, assumptions, and data.* Beverly Hills, CA: Sage.

Katz, D., & Kahn, R. L. (1978). *The social psychology of organizations* (2nd ed.). New York: Wiley.

Kegan, R. (1982). *The evolving self: Problem and process in human development.* Cambridge, MA: Harvard University.

Kegan, R. (1994). *In over our heads: The mental demands of modern life.* Cambridge, MA: Harvard University.

Kelly, G. (1955). *The psychology of personal constructs.* New York: Norton.

Kluger, A. N., & DeNisi, A. (1996). The effects of feedback on performance: A historical review, a meta-analysis, and a preliminary feedback intervention. *Psychological Bulletin, 119*, 254–284.

Lance, C. E., Meade, A. W., & Williamson, G. M. (2000). We should measure change—And here's how. In G. M. Williamson, D. R. Shaffer, & P. A. Parmalee (Eds.), *Physical illness and depression in older adults: A handbook of theory, research, and practice* (pp. 201–235). New York: Plenum.

Lance, C. E., Parisi, A. G., Bennett, W. R., Teachout, M. S., Harville, D. L., & Welles, M. L. (1998). Moderators of skill retention interval/performance decrement relationships in eight U.S. Air Force enlisted specialties. *Human Performance, 11*, 103–123.

Lance, C. E., & Vandenberg, R. J. (2002). Confirmatory factor analysis. In F. Drasgow & N. Schmitt (Eds.), *Advances in measurement and data analysis* (pp. 221–254). San Francisco: Jossey-Bass.

Lance, C. E., Vandenberg, R. J., & Self, R. M. (2000). Latent growth models of individual change: The case of newcomer adjustment. *Organizational Behavior and Human Decision Processes, 83*, 107–140.

Linville, P. W. (1985). Self-complexity and affective extremity: Don't put all of your eggs in one cognitive basket. *Social Cognition, 3*, 94–120.

Marx, R. D. (1982). Relapse prevention for managerial training: A model for maintenance of behavior change. *Academy of Management Journal, 30*, 433–441.

McArdle, J. J. (1986). Latent variable growth within behavior genetic models. *Behavior Genetics, 16*, 163–200.

McArdle, J. J. (1988). Dynamic but structural equation modeling of repeated measures data. In J. R. Nessleroade & R. B. Cattell (Eds.), *Handbook of multivariate experimental psychology* (2nd ed., pp. 561–614). New York: Plenum.

McCauley, C. D., & Brutus, S. (1998). *Management development through job experiences: An annotated bibliography.* Greensboro, NC: Center for Creative Leadership.

McCauley, C. D., Moxley, R. S., & Van Velsor, E. (Eds.). (1998). *The Center for Creative Leadership handbook of leadership development.* San Francisco: Jossey-Bass.

Meredith, W., & Tisak, J. (1990). Latent curve analysis. *Psychometrika, 55*, 107–122.

Mulaik, S. A. (1972) *Foundations of factor analysis.* New York: McGraw-Hill.

Muthén, B. O. (2001). Latent variable mixture modeling. In G. A. Marcoulides & R. E. Schumacker (Eds.), *New developments and techniques in structural equation modeling* (pp. 1–33). Mahwah, NJ: Lawrence Erlbaum Associates.

Muthén, B. O., & Shedden, K. (1999). Finite mixture modeling with mixture outcomes using the EM algorithm. *Biometrics, 55*, 463–469.

Nadler, D. A., & Tushman, M. L. (1995). Types of organizational change: From incremental improvement to discontinuous transformation. In D. A. Nadler, R. B. Shaw, A. E. Walton, & Associates (Eds.), *Discontinuous change: Leading organizational transformation* (pp. 15–34). San Francisco: Jossey-Bass.

Rao, C. R. (1958). Some statistical methods for the comparison of growth curves. *Biometrics, 14*, 1–17.

Rosenbaum, D. A., Loukopoulos, L. D., Meulenbroek, R. G. J., Vaughan, J., & Engelbrecht, S. E. (1995). Planning reaches by evaluating stored postures. *Psychological Review, 102*, 28–67.

Sale, K. (1982). *Human scale* (2nd ed.). New York: Putnam.

Schroder, H. M., Driver, M. J., & Streufert, S. (1967). *Human information processing: Individuals and groups functioning in complex social situations.* New York: Holt, Rinehart, & Winston.

Senge, P. M. (1990). *The fifth discipline: The art and practice of the learning organization.* New York: Doubleday.

Sheridan, J. E. (1985). A catastrophe model of employee withdrawal leading to low job performance, high absenteeism and job turnover during the first year of employment. *Academy of Management Journal, 28*, 88–109.

Stewart, I. N., & Peregoy, P. L. (1983). Catastrophe theory modeling in psychology. *Psychological Bulletin, 94*, 336–362.

Vandenberg, R. J., & Lance, C. E. (2000). A review and synthesis of the measurement invariance literature: Suggestions, practices, and recommendations for organizational research. *Organizational Research Methods, 3*, 4–69.

Weick, K. E. (1993). The collapse of sensemaking in organizations: The Mann Gulch disaster. *Administrative Science Quarterly, 38*, 628–652.

Willett, J. B., & Sayer, A. G. (1994). Using covariance structure analysis to detect correlates and predictors of individual change over time. *Psychological Bulletin, 116*, 363–381.

Willett, J. B., & Sayer, A. G. (1996). Cross-domain analyses of change over time: Combining growth modeling and covariance structure analysis. In G. A. Marcoulides & R. E. Schumacker (Eds.), *Advanced structural equation modeling: Issues and techniques* (pp. 125–157). Mahwah, NJ: Lawrence Erlbaum Associates, Inc.

Yukl, G. (2002). *Leadership in organizations* (5th ed.). Upper Saddle River, NJ: Prentice-Hall.

Zaccaro, S. J. (1999). Social complexity and the competencies required for effective military leadership. In J. G. Hunt, G. E. Dodge, & L. Wong (Eds.), *Out-of-the-box leadership: Transforming the twenty-first-century army and other top-performing organizations* (pp. 131–151). Stamford, CT: JAI.

Zaccaro, S. J., Gilbert, J. A., Thor, K. K., & Mumford, M. D. (1991). Leadership and social intelligence: Linking social perceptiveness to behavioral flexibility. *Leadership Quarterly, 2*, 317–347.

4

Examining the Full Range Model of Leadership: Looking Back to Transform Forward

Bruce J. Avolio
University of Nebraska–Lincoln

INTRODUCTION

Since Avolio and Bass first launched the full range leadership model (FRL) in 1990, considerable attention has been given to testing its validity across a broad spectrum of organizational settings and national cultures (Avolio, 1999; Bass, 1998). In this chapter, I lay the groundwork for using the full range model as one of the scaffolds upon which we can build a more complete model for individual, team, and strategic leadership development. I begin by briefly reviewing the model and then discuss aspects of its measurement and how it relates to performance, followed by a discussion of how it can be used to interpret leadership development.

Defining Full Range Leadership (FRL) Development

In line with the core definition for leadership development used in this book, I view full range leadership development as a comprehensive life-span process that involves the accumulation of unstructured and structured experiences and

71

their impact on the maturation of both leaders and followers. One key aspect that differentiates the FRL model from other models is that leadership development involves building leaders of higher moral character.

The core of the FRL model is centered on the concept of developing oneself to develop others. Specifically, as leaders mature and gain moral perspective, they invest more time and energy in promoting the development of others versus satisfying their own needs. As Day and Lance note (chap. 3, this volume), through the accumulation of developmental experiences the moral structure of an individual can be enhanced providing sufficient structure to assess complex moral challenges. This basic premise is at the core of what drives transformational leadership to the highest end of the full range of leadership.

A Brief Retrospective Look at the Conceptualization of the FRL Model

Arguably, the main contribution made by Bass (1985) was the inclusion of transformational leadership in his model and the attention he gave to discussing charismatic leadership. Building on Burns (1978), Bass provided a renewed focus on high-impact leadership. Certainly, political scientists such as Burns (1978) and Downton (1973) had discussed charisma as part of transforming leadership, using Weber's (1924/47) work as a basis for developing their models. Yet, most prior discussions inferred that charismatic leadership was an "untouchable" construct, probably not measurable and certainly not something one could develop.

Avolio and Bass (1987) began to discuss charisma as a component of transformational leadership. They demonstrated that it was observable at all organizational levels. Avolio and Gibbons (1988) then extended Bass' model by discussing ways transformational leadership could be developed in life and through structured training interventions. In the latter part of the 1980s, the field of leadership began moving away from focusing just on transactional models of leadership, such as House and Mitchell's (1975) path–goal theory, to more colorful aspects of leadership, such as charisma.

At the same time that Bass' model was emerging in the literature, suggestions were made to relax assumptions that Weber articulated in his theory of charismatic leadership. This marked the starting point of a decade-long discussion, which involved Beyer (1999), Klein and House (1995), and Yukl (1999), among others, addressing what constituted the emergence of charismatic leadership. One of the critical issues that emerged from these early discussions about charisma, and remains a concern for scholars in the leadership field, was whether charismatic and transformational leadership were distinct and could be measured. This led to another concern: If we can measure it, can the higher end of the full range be developed?

Conceptual and Measurement Ideals

It is important to make a distinction between what is currentlymeasurable and what is in theory possible. In leadership research, if two constructs are too highly correlated, many authors conclude they do not exist independently. Let me offer an example with respect to the FRL model. Some authors have argued that there is little if any distinction between consideration and individualized consideration, which Bass (1985) introduced when he distinguished transactional and transformational leadership. Their conclusions are based on research showing high correlations between scales representing these two constructs (Bass, 1998). I would suggest that such conclusions are, at best, hasty; at worst, false. Managers who are considerate are probably more attuned to people, to people's needs, to individual concerns, and to addressing those concerns. It is certainly possible to make a clear distinction between being considerate to others and being focused on individual needs, challenging those needs, and elevating them to higher levels.

Leaders must get to know their followers' needs, capabilities, and aspirations to challenge them and develop them into leaders. This is a fundamental assumption of the FRL model and of the development of both leaders and followers. To systematically and reliably transform followers into leaders requires an understanding of how to challenge their needs and raise their capabilities to their full potential. So, part of the transforming process that occurs is in the individual as he or she reshapes and reprioritizes his or her needs, as Bass discussed when referring to the shift from lower maintenance transactional to higher level transformational needs. In the operational model of leadership development presented later in this chapter, the intended "trigger events" a leader chooses for his or her follower do require individualized consideration.

Measurement concerns were also raised regarding the distinction between transactional contingent reward and individualized consideration leadership. Generally, the two scales that represent each of these constructs correlate in the .6 to .7 range. Here again, there is no doubt that transactional leadership represents a different form or construct than transformational leadership, even if the measures do not always make this distinction, which has not always been the case (e.g., Antonakis, 2001, and Avolio, Bass, & Jung, 1999). The important point is that the finer the distinctions we can make with respect to construct validation, the better leadership theories become as a basis for comprehensive leadership development.

Components of FRL Model

At the low end of the FRL, Bass and Avolio (1994) referred to the construct of leadership as nontransactional leadership. Laissez-faire leaders do not enter into agreements, nor do they clarify the path that helps followers move toward the desired goals and objectives. They are comfortable with leaving followers to their own devices and not having any disagreements cloud their relationship. They do not develop themselves and they certainly do not develop followers.

The second construct of leadership is managing by exception passively, or passive–avoidant leadership. Such leaders are activated when things go wrong, accepting fairly wide deviations for what goes wrong before responding. Their developmental focus creates a fear of making mistakes, which typically stifles innovation and development.

Moving to a more active style, leaders who manage by exception actively pay closer attention to details about not only things that have gone wrong, but also things that can potentially go wrong. This leadership construct represents an active monitoring of deviations from performance standards that might disrupt the status quo.

The leader who actively focuses on what is wrong specifies boundaries that must be adhered to and what will happen if they are not. Managing by exception is no less of a transaction than using contingent reward-type leadership with followers. However, there are fundamental differences in the types of exchanges that occur between leader and follower. The more constructive form of transactional leadership represented in the literature as contingent reward can be described as follows: If you perform this task, then you will receive this outcome or reward. Downton (1973) referred to transactional leadership as "a process of exchange that is analogous to contractual relations in economic life [and] contingent on the good faith of the participants" (p. 75). Downton also described transactional leadership as representing the fulfillment of contractual obligations, which over time creates trust and establishes a stable relationship where mutual benefits can be exchanged between leaders and followers.

The shift to transactional contingent reward leadership corresponds to a shift into the present and the not-so-distant future. Yet, when Bass (1985) originally chose the term *contingent reward* for transactional leadership, he pretty much meant contingent reward. Today, the notion of what constitutes transactional leadership goes beyond simple contingent reward exchanges and has implications for leadership development. Executing transactions reliably builds trust and respect, which provides a solid base for transformational leadership. Developing leadership perspective in this part of the range requires leaders to understand how to build such exchanges with followers and how to execute those exchanges reliably.

From a measurement point of view, the current items that make up the contingent reward scale no longer sufficiently measure what Bass (1985) and Burns (1978) described as transactional leadership. The revised scale now contains items that measure what Yammarino and Bass (1990) referred to as *recognition type* versus *reward type* items. Goodwin, Wofford, and Whittington (2001) addressed this problem directly. They reported that four of the original items that tapped into external contracts and/or extrinsic rewards related modestly to transformational leadership, for example, "Tells me what to do to be rewarded for my efforts" (explicit contract) versus "Expresses his/her satisfaction when I do a good job" (implicit contract). Goodwin et al. (2001) reported the average correlation between the *explicit type* contingent reward scale and four scales of transformational leadership was .49 versus .71 for the *implicit* type items, and concluded, "these data provide a basis for extending the transformational leadership construct to include a reward dimension.... The fact that... do not include reward-for-performance contracts into their leadership scheme, does not prevent them from providing appropriate social, monetary, and other forms of rewards" (pp. 771–772).

With the addition of explicit to implicit contracting, it is now easier to argue for a conceptual bridge between the constructs that represent transactional and transformational leadership. Implicit contracting involves recognition-based rewards, intrinsic motivation, and satisfaction. We can extend such implicit contracting to each individual, and by adding in his or her unique needs and expectations, we end up at *individualized* consideration. At the higher end of individualized consideration, leaders not only understand and satisfy individual needs and expectations, they challenge and motivate those individuals to higher levels—and that is part of the "transformation" that occurs in both leaders and followers. As Bass (1985) noted, transformational leaders move followers from focusing on their "self-interests" to considering the "collective interests" of their group. Stretched to the extreme, the leader must develop followers to fulfill leadership roles, which could be viewed as being part of the leader's "possible selves" or mental model of what constitutes his or her leadership (Markus and Nurius, 1986, as discussed later).

The remaining three components of transformational leadership represent what Bass and his colleagues referred to as higher level constructs of leadership. The higher level comes from the higher order effects, for example, aiding the development of people, changing the way people think, and developing identification with whatever cause the leaders and followers are pursuing. Intellectual stimulation is the component that facilitates the transformation of thinking in followers. It challenges basic core assumptions and models of work and life by challenging "how things work." Through such challenges and reframing, people come to think differently and respond differently, which constitutes part of the transformational effects. For example, leaders may challenge followers to think about whether they can lead, thereby elevating their self–efficacy or ways of thinking about their own self-concepts of leadership.

Inspirational leadership—the third component—is quite difficult to separate from charismatic leadership (or what has been called "idealized" leadership) of transformational leadership—the fourth component of transformational leadership. Inspiring leadership is elevating in the sense that it energizes people to go beyond what is expected or contracted. It is this construct that provided the basis for Bass' (1985) book title, *Leadership and Performance* **Beyond** *Expectations* (emphasis added).

Shamir, House, and Arthur (1993) made an important connection between motivation and leadership that has implications for leadership development. They argued that an inspiring leader knows how to link a follower's self-concept to what that leader represents in his or her vision. Higher levels of identification motivate people to go beyond contracts and exchanges in terms of both their own development and their performance. The intriguing question is how to develop such high levels of identification in leader and follower relationships. What types of trigger events cause leaders to follow a particular path, and what mechanisms help them develop their followers' identification with the vision? How does each contribute to self-awareness, self-regulation, and self-development?

The sort of identification process described here evolves from linking individuals' self identifies to their leaders' (and organization's) values and beliefs. The development process begins with self-awareness and evolves to a heightened level of awareness of what constitutes the future direction for both leaders and followers. However, as Yukl (1998) concluded after reviewing research on this topic, "a variety of different influence processes may be involved in transformational leadership, and different transformational behaviors may involve different influence processes" (p. 328).

Kark and Shamir (2003) discussed how there might be a *dual effect* with respect to the influence of identification processes on follower motivation and performance. They suggested that transformational leaders can have a dual effect, by influencing followers both through personal identification with the leader and through social identification with the work unit. They argued that these different forms of identification can result in different outcomes. They pointed to how an individual's self-concept becomes connected to the collective concept of a group, and how that collective concept builds a sense of alignment in organizations around a common purpose, vision, or mission (Shamir, Zakay, Breinin, & Popper, 1998). With this in mind, leadership development must include how leaders create such individual and collective identification.

The last component is idealized leadership, often referred to as socialized charisma in some articles. Howell (1992) drew a distinction between good and bad charismatic leader and used McClelland's need motivation theory as a basis for calling the bad ones *personalized* charismatic leaders and the good ones *socialized*. The personalized leaders were described as concerned about satisfying their own needs at the expense of their group, organization, or community. The socialized leaders focused on leading for the "good of the community" even when sacrifices were required. This distinction has led to an emerging line of research distinguishing two types of charismatic leaders (O'Connor, Mumford, Clifton, Gessner, & Connelly, 1995).

To fully understand the distinction between personalized and socialized charismatic leaders necessitates the inclusion of moral reasoning. Kuhnert and Lewis (1987) and Avolio and Gibbons (1988) both addressed this distinction by including Kegan's (1982) work on moral perspective-taking capacity or reasoning to describe authentic transformational leadership. In effect, to be transformational and to have transformational effects involves a higher level of moral perspective and reasoning, or as Day and Lance (chap. 3, this volume), note, moral complexity.

Recent evidence reported by Turner, Barling, Epitropaki, Butcher, and Milner (2002) shows that leaders who were rated higher on transformational leadership also scored higher on moral reasoning. The "holy grail" of leadership seems within reach, and once fully understood in terms of its influence on transformational leadership, we can begin to develop higher levels of moral reasoning in our emerging and current leaders. This kind of leadership development could be based on the trigger events to which we expose them and the nature of self-awareness created through reflection. For example, the individual may be exposed to events that show how his or her decisions affect individuals who are far removed from the leader. Such scenarios help the leader to understand that sometimes decisions have far greater impact than he or she initially conceived, and that some trade-offs may need to be considered before making the decision.

In sum, I have taken some time to describe the full range model in a way that prepares for a discussion of the following three major topics: Can we measure these components? What is their impact? How can they be developed?

MEASURING THE FRL COMPONENTS: MORE IS USUALLY BETTER

Over the past 15 years, the Multi-factor Leadership Questionnaire (MLQ) has become the most widely used survey for measuring Bass' multi-factor theory of leadership (Hunt, 1999). Starting with the original MLQ survey, there has been criticism for failing to reproduce the original factor structure proposed by Bass (1985): Charisma/Inspirational, Intellectual Stimulation, Individualized Consideration, Contingent Reward, Management-by-Exception, and Laissez-faire. Bycio, Hackett, and Allen (1995) suggested that researchers using the MLQ should consider using simpler factor structures to represent the component factors. I would like to argue against using a simpler factor structure, and advocate a more "complex" hierarchical model of leadership, which is reproduced in Fig. 4.1. My reason for proposing a more complex model is not just based on measurement concerns, but is also intended to facilitate the development of leadership in more exacting ways.

The hierarchy presented in Fig. 4.1 includes all of the first-and second-order factors that have been associated with the FRL model. Along the top are four higher order constructs of transformational, transactional, management-by-exception, and passive or avoidant leadership. At the next level are more specific factors, which break out even further at the third level. The highlighted factors in the model represent what constitutes the nine factors that make up the FRL model.

Several observations on this hierarchical model are worth noting. First, highlighted factors cut across all three levels of constructs represented in the model presented in Fig. 4.1. For example, I have highlighted the transactional exchange construct because two recent studies testing the nine-factor model did not partition

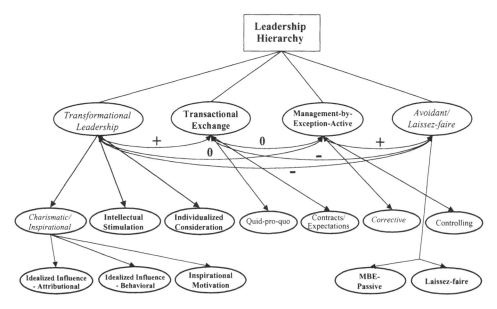

FIG. 4.1.   A hierachical model of leadership.

this construct into the two subconstructs discussed by Goodwin et al. (2001). The constructs designated in italics have been examined in other models representing the FRL model.

Examining a Hierarchical Model of Leadership for Development

The components of transformational and transactional leadership and their meaning have been identified in a variety of ways including factor analyses, observations, interviews, and descriptions of a follower's ideal leader. Using the Multi-factor Leadership Questionnaire (Bass, 1985), Avolio et al. (1999) Antonakis (2001) and Antonakis, Avolio and Sivasubramaniam (in press) identified and reaffirmed four *distinct* components of transformational leadership, which included Idealized, Inspiring, Intellectually Stimulating, and Individualized Consideration. By keeping these components separate, we can guide our developmental efforts, because each component likely necessitates different developmental strategies.

Following Bass' (1988) proposal to examine a six-factor model of leadership that combined charismatic and inspirational leadership, Avolio et al. (1999) reported the best-fitting model for the MLQ survey were those six factors. Avolio et al. (1999) also conducted *post hoc* tests of several higher order factor models, including two correlated higher order factors representing transformational and contingent reward leadership. Their results produced better discriminant validity among the six lower order factors when they included these higher order factors in the overall model.

Avolio (1999) extended earlier work by providing a nine-factor model, which included Idealized (Attributed and Behavioral), Inspiring, Intellectually Stimulating, Individualized Consideration, Contingent Reward, Active and Passive Management-by-Exception, and Laissez-faire leadership. Strong empirical support for this nine-factor model comes from findings reported by Antonakis (2001) and Antonakis et al. (in press). Antonakis (2001) reviewed the literature on transformational and transactional leadership and identified any study that reported correlations among the nine factors described here. His results provided consistent support for the nine-factor model, as compared to eight other models of leadership. All of these comparative models had been cited in the leadership literature as potential alternative models underlying the MLQ survey. Antonakis (2001) reported that the nine-factor model held up across all of the moderating conditions including high risk, low risk, majority male leaders, majority female leaders, low-level leaders, middle-level leaders, and so on.

Extending the work of Antonakis (2001), Antonakis et al. (in press) examined the nine-factor model by testing it at the item versus the scale level examined by Antonakis (2001). Antonakis had access to scale score correlations in his study, not item-level data. In two separate large sample studies, evidence supported the nine-factor model.

Demonstrating the distinction between the various higher and lower order factors composing the full range is certainly important to validating the model itself. However, making what might appear to be fine distinctions between these respective constructs also has relevance to leadership development. As Day (2000) pointed out, there has been relatively little systematic work done on building a comprehensive theory of leadership development. At the core of effective leadership development is a well-validated leadership model.

DEMONSTRATING THE EFFICACY
OF A WELL-VALIDATED MODEL

If someone is going to develop leadership, there must be a model to guide the selection of what areas need to be developed and ways to measure those areas to see if any positive change occurred. Most leadership development programs do not have such theoretical models underlying their developmental framework. Thus, if we use the full range model as a starting point for leadership development, beyond establishing our ability to measure it, the next obvious question is whether exhibiting its components will have predictable effects on motivation and performance. Stated differently, why learn a model that has not proven to be valid? The validity of the model is in part motivation for learning it. Basing leadership development on a construct valid model is a way of testing the model in terms of its predicted impact on performance. How? If the model predicts that transformational leaders will develop followers who are more critically independent in their thinking, then training leaders to be transformational should result in followers being more critically independent.

A Hierarchical Model of Leadership and Performance Impact

In describing the full range leadership model, I first discussed the x axis, which represents each of the leadership styles in terms of a range that includes highly inactive to proactive. The y axis is whatever criterion measure one chooses to include, but let us for the sake of argument use performance effectiveness, because one should not use a model of leadership to guide development if it does not have some relevance to performance. When Avolio and Bass developed the full range model, they presented not only the constructs composing the model along the activity range just described, but also how each construct was expected to relate to performance effectiveness. This strategy built on Bass' (1985) notion that transformational leadership would augment transactional leadership in predicting performance.

Since Bass' (1985) book, there have been four quantitative reviews of his model (DeGroot, Kiker & Cross, 2000; Dumdum, Lowe, & Avolio, 2003; Gaspar, 1992; Lowe, Kroeck, and Sivasubramaniam, 1996). Gasper's (1992) work focused primarily on educational settings, in which he aggregated a number of study variables later shown to be important moderators of leadership style and effectiveness. Lowe et al. (1996) used an earlier five-factor model of leadership to guide their meta-analysis. They examined the relationship between transformational and transactional leadership with individual and organizational-level measures of effectiveness. They also included three different moderators of the transformational leadership and effectiveness relationship—type of criterion, level of leader, and type of organization—demonstrating how each moderated the relationship between leadership and performance. Both meta analyses provided support for the full range model, with transformational leadership demonstrating the highest positive relationship with performance.

DeGroot et al. (2000) completed a third meta-analysis of this literature, producing a positive relationship between ratings of charismatic leadership and performance. They reported that the relationship between charismatic leadership and performance varied when leadership and performance were examined at an *individual* versus *group* level, concluding that "results show an effect size at the group level of analysis that is double in magnitude relative to the effect size at the individual level" (p. 363).

A recent meta-analysis extended the work of Lowe et al. (1996) by examining 12 scales making up the MLQ versus the 5 reported in their study. The 12 scales included the 9 leadership constructs as well as 3 outcome measures: Satisfaction, Extra Effort, and Effectiveness. This meta-analysis reported by Dumdum et al. (2003) included an examination of the relationship between leadership style and satisfaction. Satisfaction in this analysis included measures of personal satisfaction and satisfaction with one's job.

Results of this fourth meta-analysis and an examination of moderators confirmed what was reported in earlier meta-analyses. This consistent pattern of results is encouraging, suggesting these relationships are enduring and not tied to one period, a particular version of the MLQ, or other artifacts such as the cohort of raters or outcomes evaluated. For example, the corrected correlations reported for rated effectiveness with various transformational scales produced by Lowe et al. (1996) versus the latest results are as follows: .68 (.73) for Idealized, .59 (.62) for Individualized Consideration, and .57 (.60) for Intellectual Stimulation. Contingent Reward was somewhat different .56 (.41), but would lead to the same conclusion as reported by Lowe et al. (1996).

Causal Links for Leadership Development and Performance

There has not been a complete test of the FRL model in terms of causally linking its components to performance effectiveness. Nevertheless, sufficient groundwork has been developed to lend confidence to using the components of the FRL model in leadership development interventions. Dvir, Eden, Avolio, and Shamir (2002) set out to conduct a true field experiment in which they "created" the construct of transformational leadership using a training program based on the full range model. Participants were platoon commanders in the Israeli Defense Force. The more positive impact of the experimental versus the control group leaders (who were also trained in transformational leadership but not using the FRL model) on direct follower development and on indirect follower performance confirmed key causal propositions in Bass' (1985) transformational leadership theory. The experimental platoon commanders had a positive impact on their indirect followers' performance after 6 months had elapsed, where indirect followers were below squad leaders. They also had a direct positive impact on squad leader's self-efficacy, level of extra effort, critical-independent thinking, and collectivistic orientation, the latter being marginally significant ($p < .06$). The impact on the squad leaders' development provides preliminary evidence in support of the basic idea that transformational leaders develop followers into leaders.

Similar support for such training interventions was provided by Barling, Weber, and Kelloway (1996). They reported positive changes in MLQ ratings of transformational leadership following a 1-day training and coaching intervention program based on the full range model. Barling et al. (1996) were able to produce significant changes in follower ratings on several components of transformational leadership.

In sum, I have presented a broad summary of research providing relatively strong confirmation for the construct validity of key components of the FRL model. Clearly, not all of the components have been tested as extensively as others. Moreover, one might argue that the "right" criterion measure has not been included in many of the studies linking transformational leadership to performance. For instance, many studies included measures of performance, but not measures of extraordinary performance, nor measures of either the leader's or the follower's development. There is a need to focus on what gets developed in others due to developing the leader's transformational leadership. Nevertheless, most of the main propositions put forth by Bass (1985) have been confirmed. These results provide a basis for moving toward using the model as part of a broader unified theory of leadership development.

DEVELOPING A FULL RANGE OF LEADERSHIP POTENTIAL

One central issue concerning development involves what is actually changed or transformed due to leadership training. For example, has leadership development occurred because a leader is more aware of a new model of leadership? Has it occurred when the leader takes that model and in some way changes his or her implicit model of leadership? Has it occurred when the leader exhibits new behaviors? Or is leadership development simply reflected in the nature and qualities of followers' ways of thinking, behaving, and performing? House and Aditya (1997) stated,

> There is little evidence that charismatic, transformational, or visionary leadership does indeed transform individuals, groups, large divisions of organizations, or total organizations, despite claims that they do so. . . . There is no evidence demonstrating stable and long-term effects of leaders on follower self-esteem, motives, desires, preferences, or values." (p. 443)

One could argue that if transformational leadership was developed, it would be reflected in all of the criterion measures mentioned by House and Aditya (1997).

A MULTILEVEL MODEL OF SELF-LEADERSHIP DEVELOPMENT

The beginning point of developing leadership in any individual starts with an enhanced sense of awareness, which leads to behaviors or ways of thinking that are new, sustained over time, and become part of the individual's repertoire.

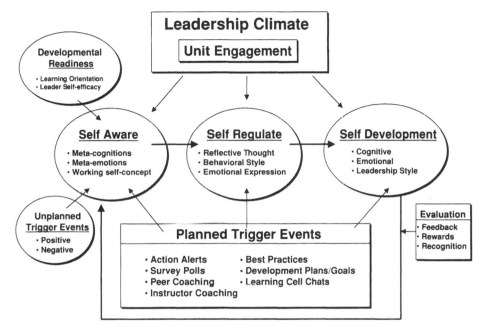

FIG. 4.2. A multilevel model of self-leadership development. This model is based on earlier published work by Luthans & Avolio (2003).

Figure 4.2 shows the central elements of self awareness → self-regulation → self-development. The antecedents to self-awareness include the person's developmental readiness and the events that cause such awareness to come to the foreground.

Developmental Readiness

To optimize the validity of leadership development, the interventions must be customized to the target individual's *developmental readiness*. This focus represents individualized consideration in that by knowing an individual we are better able to enhance his or her awareness and leadership potential. Developmental readiness is a function of how the individual views himself or herself, based on personality predispositions such as level of openness, prior experience, cognitive and emotional capacity, and other events or challenges that are currently attracting the individual's attention (Avolio, 1999).

Emotional self-awareness is one core component of emotional intelligence (Goleman, 1998; Salovey & Mayer, 1990). Emotional self-awareness refers to knowing and understanding one's own range of emotion and the knowledge of effects these emotional states have on others. Emotional self-awareness has been considered an important missing component in the self-development leadership process and relates to the broader category of enhancing interpersonal competence in terms of social awareness and social skills.

Another important component of self-awareness relates to being aware of one's cognitive resources and limitations, how they influence one's choice of behaviors, and how those choices affect others. Just as leaders have various strengths and weaknesses in the area of emotional intelligence, they also have strengths and weaknesses in the area of cognitive abilities. Metacognition refers to one's knowledge of strengths and weaknesses and the ability to monitor cognitive functioning for improvement (Hertzog & Hultsch, 2000).

Developmental readiness relates to an individual's level of moral reasoning. For instance, individuals with lower levels of moral reasoning will have difficulty critically evaluating how they come across as leaders with followers based only on self-reflection. They are typically incapable of stepping back and seeing how their actions affect others. They can take actions that hurt others emotionally without realizing the impact of their choices. Conversely, someone at a higher level of moral reasoning is capable of stepping back to understand how his or her behavior affects others. It is through the reflective process that he or she is able to re-evaluate leadership and the relationships that are built with others.

Related to an individual's developmental awareness and how he or she responds to certain events is the individual's goal orientation. Dweck (1986) identified two broad orientations toward goals, a *learning goal orientation* and a *performance goal orientation*. Individuals who have a learning goal orientation are likely to derive greater self-awareness from both positive and negative feedback (Brett & Atwater, 2001). Creating an environment or culture that supports a learning goal orientation focus could contribute to generating greater self-awareness, self-regulation, and self-development. This is exactly the type of environment that transformational leaders create for their followers.

Leaders who are intellectually stimulating create the conditions in which followers and associates are more willing to learn. Such leaders expand boundaries of what is "safe" to challenge, and therefore encourage followers to dig deeper into their core assumptions and models that frame their thinking and awareness. Transformational leaders encourage followers to revisit their normative assumptions or values, question them, and broaden their perspective. To do so, followers must be aware of assumptions, working self-concept, and mental models that guide their choices, so that over time, they can impart their knowledge to followers and develop them into leaders. Such self-knowledge falls into the range of metacognitions. As Maj. Gen. Maggart notes (chap. 2, this volume), for this type of exchange to occur, the leader must create an environment where such openness is reinforced to support "out-of-the-box" thinking.

Developmental Trigger Events

How prior developmental experiences have been reinforced can positively or negatively contribute to an individual's level of developmental readiness. Specifically, the type of experiences or "trigger events" and how they have been utilized to support self-leadership development can enhance or inhibit one's readiness to try something new. Building on past successful developmental experiences can prepare an individual to take on more difficult and challenging experiences because his or her efficacy for leadership and its development is likely to be higher. Conversely, if past experiences have not been reinforced, the individual may see little utility in engaging in further development triggered by similar events.

One way to enhance self-awareness and development is to place the individual in crisis, thereby highlighting areas for further development. Negative experiences tend to enhance learning and promote self-reflection (Moxley, 1998). The problem with this approach is that we cannot ethically simulate the type of life events that trigger fundamental developmental change. There is also relatively little theoretical guidance on how to conceptualize and arrange work and life experiences that contribute to optimal leadership development (Day, 2000).

Trigger events that enhance self-awareness do, however, naturally occur. Trainers or coaches need to prepare learners to reflect on these events and derive deeper interpretations. Discussions of transformational leadership emphasize stepping back and revisiting events and situations as a way of capitalizing on such natural trigger events. The "life-span" leadership development strategy being recommended here involves using unplanned life events and challenges to enhance self-awareness, regulation, and development. Alternatively, we could develop a contextual model of trigger events to systematically examine their impact on leadership development. Specifically, if we pursued introducing certain events at key developmental points in time, the developmental trajectories created might not be as abrupt or even as dramatic as ones caused by natural trigger events. Nevertheless, we may still be able to enhance self-awareness, and ultimately leadership development, but with less risk and disruption to the target learner.

This whole approach suggests to both the learner and the trainer that leadership development is *both* made and born. Challenging the notion that leadership development cannot occur across the entire life span goes against some very strong working self-concepts of many leaders and followers. However, emerging evidence points to the fact that leadership development does indeed occur throughout the life span, based on a positive incremental model of development. These findings run counter to the crisis-based models of development pervading the leadership literature (London, 2002).

Transformational leaders learn the needs and capacities of followers and then challenge them in order to develop followers into leaders. Trainers must take on the same role to develop an individual's full leadership potential. This involves not only the specific interactions between leader (trainer) and learner, but also the conditions established in the context of promoting development. If we can compress and replicate key "growth" events enhancing leadership potential in training, we will have successfully shown how to optimize leadership development. Unfortunately, life is a sloppier program for developing leadership. This program happens to work in some situations, whereas in others it either does not work at all or it may even diminish an individual's capacity to lead.

THE CONTEXT FOR LEADER AND LEADERSHIP DEVELOPMENT

Self-Awareness

Throughout this discussion of enhancing self-awareness, it should be clear that leadership development must be examined in context by viewing it as dynamic and emerging (Day, 2000). In terms of the model presented in Fig. 4.2, the context includes the previous context and the one emerging. This leads to the question of how we can leverage the context to enhance self-leadership development. Leaders set the conditions to engage followers and themselves in the process of raising awareness about their development. They also facilitate the regulation of development by giving feedback to followers pointing out areas for further improvement, reinforcing followers for trying, and reinforcing followers' peers for reinforcing the target learners' efforts to develop their leadership potential. Atwater, Waldman, Atwater, and Cartier (2000) reported that individuals who were more cynical about their organization and who did not believe positive change was possible were less likely to improve in terms of leader development following feedback. Those individuals who were more positive about the feedback process were more likely to change following feedback.

Inspiring leaders create a sense of purpose that all members of the unit fully identify with over time. That sense of purpose can also include a positive "can do" attitude toward change and development. By creating such high levels of identification and purpose, leaders and followers are more likely to work to enhance each other's potential because they are all working toward a common goal. Within a highly engaged unit, the leader can facilitate the development process directly or indirectly through the peers of the target leader. Peers observe the target leader more frequently, and therefore have more opportunity to support the leadership development of their colleagues. By role modeling and through continuous reinforcement, the individually considerate leader can develop peers of a target leader to operate in the same manner, creating a climate in which peers exhibit the same type of leadership development emphasis with each other. The level of organizational support for leadership development can provide a supportive culture for learning that can enhance the use of feedback to increase self-awareness (Facteau, Facteau, Schoel, Russell, & Poteet, 1998) as well as provide support for self-regulation to practice ways to lead others.

Transformational leaders engage themselves and others in creating a sense of self-awareness that involves a continuous accumulation of information about the self and others' perceptions in terms of both strengths and weaknesses. Self-awareness is therefore closely linked to self-leadership development and needs to be reinforced more over an extended period of time to have a positive impact on development. It also suggests that leadership development must be ubiquitous.

Self-Regulation

In terms of reinforcing the self-regulation link, over 90% of leadership training involves little if any follow-up interventions to "upgrade" or boost an individual's self-awareness (Avolio, 1999; London, 2002) or to reinforce self-regulation behavior during critical periods of transferring what was learned into practice. Without proper alerts, reinforcement, reflection, and support for self-regulated change, it is unlikely that any attempts at leadership development will be sustained in an operational context. To sustain self-development we need to transform the context to support development at the point when leaders are trying to execute tasks. The changes in the context must make it possible for individuals to feel they can provide transparent feedback to the target leader to support self-leadership development.

In Fig. 4.2, the planned trigger events are very much geared toward enhancing self-regulatory behavior. For example, the peer or coach can contract with the target learner to periodically discuss objectives or changes the learner has agreed to pursue in his or her leadership development plan. Part of the agreement may be for the peer or coach to intellectually stimulate or challenge the target learner to step back and question basic assumptions after he or she has had a difficult interaction with a follower. Such coaching may also take the form of inspirational leadership, using appropriately timed encouragements to reinforce a change in behavior or style. It can also be at the idealized level in terms of being a role model for the behavior.

All coaching and learning can be geared toward behavioral self-regulation, including emotional or cognitive development. For instance, doing random check-ins with a target learner each week following training might involve simply asking, "Have I thought about positive ways of developing the most challenging follower; have I commented positively on someone's work; have I tried to take the other person's position on an issue?"

The changes we expect in the learner, or, as, noted earlier, in the follower, can occur in terms of cognitions, emotions, or behaviors. Finally, whether or not these changes actually stick depends on what the organization does to evaluate the desired change, reinforce it, and reward it over time.

SUMMARIZING FOUR COMPONENTS SUPPORTING SELF-LEADERSHIP DEVELOPMENT

The overall focus that I have taken in this chapter on self-leadership development addresses four distinct components. The first dimension deals with the model of oneself or what Markus and Nurius (1986) called the "possible self," "actual or real self," and "feared self." These various selves can be represented as being part of an individual's working self-concept (Ruvolo & Markus, 1992). The working self-concept represents a dynamic repository of information about oneself and provides the structure for regulating one's future learning and performance. Possible selves represent what individuals would like to become and offer a link between what people think, feel, and desire. Thus if I consider leadership as solely getting performance results, then my possible self will not likely change in terms of the developmental components of transformational leadership.

In terms of the trigger events mentioned earlier, how one's possible self is created depends on the feedback he or she receives from significant others and the interpretation of life events as they have been experienced. Family members, managers, coaches, and teachers provide different frames of reference, which make an individual aware of different possible self-identities. Such input often creates tension between what the individual sees as his or her actual self and the possible self that could emerge. Transformational leaders intentionally create such tension for their followers, inviting them to challenge the important roles they need to assume and the self-identity they need to develop.

The second dimension contributing to self-development relates to how an individual models behavior and then how that modeling translates into self-beliefs and efficacies about that individual's capabilities. By knowing more about what constitutes the model of oneself and what one believes in, the individual can translate those views into what he or she estimates as the chances of succeeding at a particular task or challenge.

The third dimension relates to the individual's behavior. It represents what he or she exhibits based on the first two dimensions and is linked to what the individual chooses to self-regulate.

The fourth dimension involves examining the context in which the "self" is made more aware. The context contains the trigger events that initiate what an individual thinks is possible, what he or she fears trying, and the support he or she receives to reduce the gap between what is possible and what is feared. Over time the developmental process changes how the person defines his or her "actual" self.

Creating the Conditions to Sustain Leadership Development

The time when a learner is most vulnerable is right after he or she returns from a leadership development workshop. The person's level of awareness has been raised, and now he or she *simply* has to translate implicit knowledge into explicit knowledge and action. Ironically, this is typically where the least support is provided for development.

One strategy to explore for future institutional leadership development workshops is to train participants to reflect and learn when the learning opportunities present themselves or when they are created in line with some strategic development planning process. I am not suggesting that training programs focus on theory and then deal with practice in the operational environment. To the contrary, I am suggesting that training workshops focus on teaching participants how to translate theory into practice, so that when they need the theory in practice, they will know how to best utilize it for enhancing self-awareness, self-regulation, and self-development.

Transformational leaders are characterized as idealized, inspiring, intellectually stimulating, and individually considerate. Taking one construct, we know that intellectually stimulating leaders get followers to challenge basic assumptions about solving problems, thereby energizing their followers to come up with unique ways of solving those problems. In a training workshop, participants can learn what constitutes intellectual stimulation by working on scenarios and cases relevant to the challenges they will be confronting in the operational context. They could learn the importance of being intellectually stimulating in terms of engaging the full thinking capacity of their followers and how it can affect their adaptability to handle dynamic and unanticipated events. What the training workshop can provide is a deep conceptual understanding of intellectual stimulation—what it looks like, how it can be applied, and where the leader is in terms of being intellectual stimulating with others. At the boundary of the workshop and on into the operational environment, sustaining self-awareness in terms of how an individual goes about being intellectually stimulating is one critical component of enhancing leadership development.

A second critical component is reinforcing self-regulation, especially in the early phases of trying on a new way of thinking and behaving as a leader. Specifically, a leader may choose to engage followers in the decision-making process not to improve the decision outcome, but rather to enhance follower development. This leader's self-reflection on how he or she approached the problem differently is a critical component in the self-awareness process and ultimately in terms of what the leader chooses to change, the regulation of change, and ultimately the impact on self-leadership development. All of these actions on the part of the leader acting as a role model can show his or her followers how to intellectually stimulate each other and their respective followers.

To sustain self-development, the learner must be reinforced for trying new approaches and strategies, as well as taking time to reflect on what worked, what needs to be tried again, improved on, and changed. Both structured and unstructured reflection must occur for learners to derive the best learning experience from their work. Ubiquitous leadership development involves stimulating such self-reflection at the point when learning is most needed—when executing critical leadership tasks.

Schon (1983) described "reflection in action" as a fundamental component of the learning process, which can occur in both structured and unstructured ways within an operational context. Using a structured format, the intervention is designed specifically to create a review of the "experience," similar to the after-action review or debriefing process. In the unstructured mode, the experience is unplanned, but the individual is still offered some opportunity and support to make sense of what happened. What supports such reflective learning is having time to reflect, having access to others who have had similar experiences, and receiving feedback from others who think differently about these experiences.

Essentially, through reflection and enhanced self-awareness people learn how to reorganize the world around them and make better sense of interactions and events (Drath, 2001). Individuals learn to construct and make sense of events in different ways, which results in them developing a broader perspective about how to adapt to new, unanticipated events. By definition, when a learner is confronted with a new challenge, he or she must figure out how to organize that experience to lead followers through it. To the extent that we can take advantage of the learning derived from a broad range of complex experiences, we can continuously enhance leadership development at work as opposed to taking learners away from work to develop their leadership potential. This process can create more self-aware leaders who are able to process a wider variety of self-relevant information and use that information to enhance their leadership in real time, minimizing any transfer of training issues (Day & Lance, chap. 3, this volume).

NEXT STEPS IN ADVANCING LEADERSHIP DEVELOPMENT

I began this chapter discussing the evolution of a leadership model in terms of the constructs, how accurately they were measured, evidence for the model's construct validity, and how the model can be applied to development. I indicated that perhaps the best test of a leadership model is to demonstrate its impact on development. The range examined in the full range model is not all inclusive, nor was it intended to be from the outset. Nevertheless, there is still a need to refine the constructs that compose the model and examine how they operate at all levels of analysis across different types of organizations and cultures. Moreover, as more managers work at a distance from their followers, a vast new area for leadership research has opened up with respect to leading at a distance, indirectly and through technology.

I introduced a model of leadership for development after there was evidence for its construct validity and tested its impact on leadership development. The field of leadership development must first establish the construct validity of its models and measures and then design impact studies to examine optimal ways to transfer theory into leadership practice. This has generally not been the way leadership development has evolved and it represents the weakest domain of research in the field.

The time is propitious to change the state of leadership development research in that the field has matured a great deal over the past 20 years. The models and methods to measure leadership are getting better. The field has gotten beyond the "how to define leadership" question and has come to accept that it is a complex social influence process. The field has never been better prepared to validate leadership development models and methods, given its base.

NEW DIRECTIONS AND CONSIDERATIONS

As people in organizations have become more of what constitutes "the organizational system," the need to look at leadership and organizational development simultaneously has become obvious. Discussions by accountants such as Baruch Lev (2001) about the "intangible" assets in organizations point to the fact that the value of many organizations rests in their people, their knowledge, how well that knowledge is stored and transferred, and how quickly new knowledge is developed. As organizations have standardized around the same basic information technology and more organizations connect up through the same enterprise resource program (ERP) systems, what constitutes an organization has become how its people are developed, linked together, and supported.

Let me provide some examples to support these points and then turn to why leadership development is not simply about an individual, but about developing a total system. From 60% to 70% of technology implementations such as ERP systems fail—similar to the number the of failures in the merger and acquisition process (Schmidt, 2001). Merging technology systems into an existing organization is as disruptive (Avolio, Kahai, & Dodge, 2000), as merging two distinct organizations. Technology changes the flow of information thereby changing the nature of decision making, power bases, and organizational structure. DeSanctis and Poole (1994) suggested, in what they referred to as adaptive structuration theory, that people do not *use* technology, they *appropriate* it, and through the process of appropriation, they adapt their structures and processes to take advantage of the new technology. Alternatively, they may not appropriate the new technology at all, and none of the adaptation and change described earlier occurs. I would argue the same is true for leadership models in that they may or may not be fully appropriated.

What all these processes have in common is that people in the organizations undergoing change were being asked to relate to each other differently; to transform their relationships, often in profound ways, to adapt to the new system; and in some significant ways to change their possible selves. I believe the same is true when we attempt to develop leadership, and by including the total system on our radar screen during its implementation and follow-up phases, we have a better chance of making it stick.

Although we are moving in the right direction in terms of supporting self-regulation, it simply is not enough to make these change efforts stick. The typical cultural forces in organizations will overwhelm the 5-day "wonder" programs on leadership development, most of which are *not* based on well-validated models and methods. For example, take the best of leadership development programs and take a high-potential manager and put her through that program. Now place that manager back in an organization that has a highly disengaged workforce and let her go to work developing her leadership. Even if she is a very senior manager, the forces against the *appropriation* of new leadership approaches will likely wear down the best graduate of any world-class leadership development program.

To the degree organizations are knowledge-based systems that focus human assets and capital toward some targeted goal, then leadership development interventions must be examined as being part of a total system change process. Otherwise, what we are in effect doing is developing a leadership model in the working self-concept of participants that is at odds with the collective working self-concept in the organization, and inevitably those models will clash. The avid historian might ask, "Is that not true of all great leaders who have transformed organizations if not entire nations, including Lenin, Mandela, Kennedy, Ghandi, and Joan of Arc?" Yes, but many of those great leaders were killed and imprisoned. When we send our "enlightened" leaders back to their respective organizations, they are often seen as going against the flow of the organization, and unless they are pretty clever revolutionaries, it is likely that what was learned will not be translated into practice.

The opportunity confronting us is that people in organizations have never been more connected with the potential of being aligned around a common mission and purpose. Witness what happens when a virus gets into a company's network and how quickly that virus gets transmitted to every individual system. Because we are so highly connected, it is difficult if not impossible to poke one part of the system without being concerned about interactions in some other part. The same can be said for the stock market and why a governor has been placed on how far and fast it can fall. To be totally successful in leadership development, we must now consider how the leadership development system co-evolves with the existing organizational system, changing along the way elements in that system that keep people from achieving their full potential.

I have now come to the point where it is safe to say that leadership development is also organizational development. Transforming individuals for self-leadership development necessitates that we take the organizational context into account in every aspect of designing the leadership intervention. As noted earlier, a context in which people support development (versus on which fosters cynicism) will help to facilitate the acceleration of development over time. This represents a nontrivial task for the complex, globally based organization, which spans many cultures, time zones, and settings. It suggests when we choose to implement a leadership development program we must be very clear with people in terms of its purpose and intended impact on the organization. As noted by Maj. Gen. Maggart (chap. 2, this volume), there is a need to clarify the intent of what we are attempting to accomplish in terms of leadership development. The leader must show how leadership development is essential to achieving the overall mission of the organization. Indeed, the clarity of what needs to be developed must be reinforced through dialogue, evaluation, feedback, and reflection. Consequently, after deciding which leadership model to use as the basis for a leadership development program, the very next step is developing the evaluation system.

Evaluating leadership development interventions, is essentially testing the construct validity of the model that underlies leadership development. Taking the full range model as an example, there is an expectation that transformational leadership transforms followers into leaders. Having a valid theoretical model to guide leadership development efforts is fundamental to understanding how this "black box" works. For example, transformational leaders identify the needs of followers and then work to elevate their needs to higher levels of potential. Such leaders change the way followers construct problems. Transformational leaders also change the way they energize their followers. Thus we must measure the working self-concept of the leader and follower prior to intervention, during intervention, and some time afterward to see whether the change in thinking sticks. "Would that which constitutes their possible selves change over time?" would be a reasonable standard by which to measure a leadership development program targeted towards empowering an entire workforce. Specifically, we can assess what they believe constitutes their roles as leaders prior to intervention to see whether training alters their working self-concept. Lord, Brown, and Frieberg (1999) also discussed the role of the follower's self-concept in the leadership development process. To the extent that a follower's self-concept changes, one could deduce that the leadership development process had transformed the follower.

Changing the way we think about others or how we work problems is interesting, but does it change behavior, and does it change the interactions among people? For example, one of goals of the leadership development intervention might be to enhance workforce engagement (Harter, Schmidt, & Hayes, 2002). Harter et al. (2002) defined employee engagement as "the individual's involvement and satisfaction with as well as enthusiasm for work" (p. 269). Teaching leaders about transformational leadership helps them understand that attending to each member's needs, while also finding a way to align those needs around a common purpose, constitutes much of what successful leaders do in organizations.

To assess impact, we need to assess the learner's view of individual needs, how to align those needs, the change in behavior that signals followers that the leader cares for each follower's development, the change in engagement levels, the change in network configurations as some groups become linked that were never previously linked, and ultimately the impact this all has on employee–client relationships and firm performance.

Every leadership development intervention involves the creation of a new causal model, which I argue must include a multilevel systems view of leadership. Relevant to the developmental model described here, we would want to (at the least) examine engagement levels prior to our leadership intervention because this is one force that can significantly derail our best efforts to align employees around a common purpose. Engagement may be affected by a host of factors such as the structure of the organization, the overall culture, how well connected people are to each other, the reinforcements for being engaged, and so on.

What should now be clear from this discussion is that leadership development is *always* a multilevel development process. The safe bet is to look at least two levels up in desiging and conceptualizing a comprehensive model of leadership development. The first level is the individual leader, the second constitutes relationships with followers, peers, and superiors, and the third is unit and organizational culture and climate. Taking into account the second and the third levels becomes critical to sustaining the self-regulation process and continuously advancing self-development. Leadership development *never* occurs alone.

Without a construct valid model at the core of leadership development efforts, we have no road map to follow. Without validated instruments, our "GPS" system is broken and we cannot determine whether we are on track. We also cannot provide feedback and offer opportunities for reflection and reinforcing ubiquitous leadership development. Failing to take the next two levels up into consideration when designing a leadership development intervention sets up a weak force (our new learner) against a strong force (the organizational context), and the results are, as I have discussed, likely to hit up against the 30% success ceiling.

MOVING TOWARD UBIQUITOUS
LEADERSHIP DEVELOPMENT
STRATEGIES

We are moving into an age of ubiquitous communications. Never before have we been so connected via technology, such that wherever we go, our information systems follow. We are designing smart systems for transportation that adjust and accommodate to our individual needs. Smart supply chain systems have helped global retailers supply and resupply stores anytime and anywhere in real time. Walking down the street, I can pull up a map of the area on my cell phone and view alternative routes to my destination. I am alerted at my desk top to upcoming meetings. Sitting in the middle of a canteen in Singapore, I can pull up my e-mail, respond, and go back to eating my lunch, without being plugged into the wall.

Let me lay out what I envision constitutes a ubiquitous leadership development system and how such a system would facilitate self-awareness, self-regulation, and self-development. My assumptions are that we first build on a well-validated model and have methods for measuring it and that we have applied the three-level rule in terms of levels of analysis.

In some of my previous work (Avolio, 1999), I have suggested that ubiquitous leadership development can be viewed in terms of being part of a "life stream." Each person has his or her own life stream, in which they accumulate events, experiences, challenges, and catastrophes. These trigger events shape the individual before he or she gets to the trigger mechanism we have described as a leadership development intervention. They help shape and form an individual's "developmental readiness" or capability and motivation to take on the next developmental challenge—and the next, and the next.

Learning can now occur literally anytime and anywhere with the support of advanced information technology. Soldiers can go to www.company.com and pull in real time information about what other company commanders have done in circumstances similar to those the learner is confronting. Soon we will be able to "push" information that coincides with events learners need additional data or information to address. Such "pushing" of information will occur as "intelligent agents" gather information from the Web and send it to the learner based on a profile of needs, capabilities, and goals.

Leaving leadership development workshops with a pocket personal computer, will allow coaches to interact in real time with learners as they go back into their organization to implement changes. The coach can send alerts through the calendar to remind the learner to reflect on key learning opportunities. Similar alerts can be sent to followers and associates to motivate them to challenge this leader. A link can be provided to a helpful article or chat, depending on the learner's goals or expectations. The learner can signal the coach with questions, which the coach can discuss anytime and anywhere. All of this is possible in terms of current technology. However, the question is whether people are ready for such ubiquitous leadership development. The other question that must be asked is whether learning and leadership development theories are up to the task.

SUMMARY AND CONCLUSIONS

We are at a point where leadership and its development has never been more prominently on organizational leaders' radar screens. To meet these high expectations for leadership development we must begin to build our models of leadership to include a multilevel perspective. Leadership development involves systemic change, even when focused on one individual. Evaluation is sorely needed to validate leadership development efforts and, perhaps more importantly, sustain these efforts over time. I am advocating evaluation as a way of learning what is working, what is still needed, and how far downstream we have come in leadership development. I am also advocating evaluation for another reason. Throughout history, there has been no greater force for achieving good or evil than leadership. If we accept the responsibility for developing it, then we ought to accept the responsibility for evaluating what we are doing. No leadership development program should be deployed without a comprehensive evaluation plan.

REFERENCES

Antonakis, J. (2001). *The validity of the transformational, transactional, and laissez-faire leadership model as measured by the Multi-factor Leadership Questionnaire (MLQ 5X)*. Unpublished doctoral dissertation, Walden University, Minneapolis, MN.

Antonakis, J., Avolio, B. J., & Sivasubramaniam, N. (in press). Examining the contextual nature of the nine factor full range theory using the multi-factor leadership questionnaire. *Leadership Quarterly*.

Atwater, L. A., Waldman, D. A., Atwater, D., & Cartier, F. (2000). An upward feedback field experiment: Supervisor's cynicism, follow-up and commitment to subordinates. *Personnel Psychology, 53*, 275–297.

Avolio, B. J. (1999). *Full leadership development: Building the vital forces in organizations*. Thousand Oaks, CA: Sage.

Avolio, B. J., & Bass, B. M. (1987). Transformational leadership, charisma and beyond. In J. G. Hunt, B. R. Balaga, H. P. Dachler, & C. Schriesheim (Eds.), *Emerging leadership vistas* (pp. 29–50). Elmsford, NY: Pergamon.

Avolio, B. J., Bass, B. M., & Jung, D. I. (1999). Re-examining the components of transformational and transactional leadership using the Multifactor Leadership Questionnaire. *Journal of Occupational and Organizational Psychology, 72*, 441–462.

Avolio, B. J., & Gibbons, T. C. (1988). Developing transformational leaders: A life span approach. In J. A. Conger & R. N. Kanungo (Eds.), *Charismatic leadership: The elusive factor in organizational effectiveness* (pp. 276–308). San Francisco: Jossey-Bass.

Avolio, B. J., Kahai, S. S., & Dodge, G. (2000). E-leading in organizations and its implications for theory, research and practice. *Leadership Quarterly, 11*, 615–668.

Barling, J., Weber, T., & Kelloway, E. K. (1996). Effects of transformational leadership training on attitudinal and financial outcomes. *Journal of Applied Psychology, 81*, 827–832.

Bass, B. M. (1985). *Leadership and performance beyond expectations*. New York: Free Press.

Bass, B. M. (1988). The inspirational process of leadership. *Journal of Management Development, 7*, 21–31.

Bass, B. M. (1998). *Transformational leadership: Industrial, military and educational impact*. Mahwah, NJ: Lawrence Erlbaum Associates, Inc.

Bass, B. M., & Avolio, B. J. (1994). *Transformational leadership: Improving organizational effectiveness*. Thousand Oaks, CA: Sage.

Beyer, J. M. (1999). Taming and promoting charisma to change organizations. *Leadership Quarterly, 10*, 307–330.

Brett, J., & Atwater, L. A. (2001). 360 degree feedback: Accuracy, reactions and perceptions of usefulness. *Journal of Applied Psychology, 86*, 1–13.

Burns, J. M. (1978). *Leadership*. New York: Harper & Row.

Bycio, P., Hackett, R. D., & Allen, J. S. (1995). Further assessments of Bass' conceptualization of transactional and transformational leadership. *Journal of Applied Psychology, 80*, 468–478.

Day, D. V. (2000). Leadership development: A review in context. *Leadership Quarterly, 11*, 581–614.

DeGroot, T., Kiker, D. S., & Cross, T. C. (2000). A meta-analysis to review organizational outcomes related to charismatic leadership. *Canadian Journal of Administrative Sciences, 17*, 356–371.

DeSanctis, G., & Poole, M. S. (1994). Capturing the complexity in advanced technology use: Adaptive Structuration Theory. *Organization Science, 5*, 121–147.

Downton, J. V. (1973). *Rebel leadership: Commitment and charisma in the revolutionary process*. New York: Free Press.

Drath, W. (2001). *The deep blue sea: Rethinking the source of leadership.* San Francisco: Jossey-Bass.

Dumdum, R., Lowe, K., & Avolio, B. J. (2003). A meta-analysis of transformational and transactional leadership correlates of effectiveness and satisfaction: An update and extension. In B. J. Avolio & F. J. Yammarino (Eds.), *Transformational and charismatic leadership: The road ahead* (pp. 35–66). Oxford: Elsevier Science.

Dvir, T., Eden, D., Avolio, B. J., & Shamir, B. (2002). Impact of transformational leadership on follower development and performance: A field experiment. *Academy of Management Journal, 45,* 735–744.

Dweck, C. S. (1986). Motivational processes affecting learning. *American Psychologist, 41,* 1040–1048.

Facteau, C. L., Facteau, J. D., Schoel, L. C., Russell, J. E., & Poteet, M. L. (1998). Reactions of leaders to 360-degree feedback from subordinates and peers. *Leadership Quarterly, 9,* 427–448.

Gaspar, R. (1992). *Transformational leadership: An integrative review of the literature.* Unpublished doctoral dissertation, Western Michigan University, Kalamazoo.

Goleman, D. (1998). *Working with emotional intelligence.* New York: Bantam.

Goodwin, V. L., Wofford, J. C., & Whittington, J. L. (2001). A theoretical and empirical extension of the transformational leadership construct. *Journal of Organizational Behavior, 22,* 759–776.

Harter, J. K., Schmidt, F. L., & Hayes, T. L. (2002). Business-unit level relationship between employee satisfaction, employee engagement, and business outcomes: A meta-analysis. *Journal of Applied Psychology, 87,* 268–279.

Hertzog, C., & Hultsch, D. (2000). Metacognition in adulthood and old age. In I. M. Craik and T. A. Salthouse (Eds.), *The handbook of aging and cognition* (2nd ed. pp. 417–466). Mahwah, NJ: Lawrence Erlbaum Associates, Inc.

House, R. J., & Aditya, R. N., (1997). The social scientific study of leadership: Quo vadis? *Journal of Management, 23,* 409–473.

House, R. J., & Mitchell, T. R. (1975). Path–goal theory of leadership. *Journal of Contemporary Business, 3,* 81–97.

Howell, J. P. (1992). Two faces of charisma: Socialized and personalized leadership in organizations. In J. A. Conger & R. N. Kanungo (Eds.), *Charismatic leadership: The elusive factor in organizational effectiveness* (pp. 213–236). San Francisco: Jossey-Bass.

Hunt, J. G. (1999). Transformational/charismatic leadership's transformation of the field: An historical essay. *Leadership Quarterly, 10,* 129–144.

Kegan, J. (1982). *The evolving self: Problem and process in human development.* Cambridge, MA: Harvard University Press.

Kark, R., & Shamir, B. (2003). The dual effect of transformational leadership: Priming relational and collective selves and further effects on followers. In B. J. Avolio & F. J. Yammarino (Eds.), *Transformational and charismatic leadership: The road ahead* (pp. 67–94). Oxford: Elsevier Science.

Klein, K. J., & House, R. J. (1995). On fire: Charismatic leadership and levels of analysis. *Leadership Quarterly, 6,* 183–198.

Kuhnert, K.W., & Lewis, P. (1987). Transactional and transformational leadership: A constructive/developmental analysis. *Academy of Management Review, 12,* 648–657.

Lev, B. (2001). *Intangibles: Management, measurement, and reporting.* Washington, DC. Brookings Institute.

London, M. (2002). *Leadership development: Paths to self-insight and professional growth.* Mahwah, NJ: Lawrence Erlbaum Associates, Inc.

Lord, R. G., Brown, D. J., & Freiberg, S. J. (1999). Understanding the dynamics of leadership: The role of follower self-concepts in the leader/follower relationship. *Organizational Behavior and Human Decision Processes, 78,* 167–203.

Lowe, K. B., Kroeck, K. G., & Sivasubramaniam, N. (1996). Effectiveness correlates of transformational and transactional leadership: A meta-analytic review. *Leadership Quarterly, 7,* 385–425.

Luthans, F., & Avolio, B. J. (in press). Authentic leadership: A positive developmental approach. In Cameron, K. S., Dutton, J. E., & Quinn, R. E. (Eds), *Positive organizational scholarship*. San Francisco: Berrett-Kochler.

Markus, H., & Nurius, P. (1986). Possible selves. *American Psychologist, 41*, 954–969.

Moxley, R. S. (1998). Hardships. In C. D. McCauley, R. S., Moxley, & E. Van Velsor (Eds.), *The Center for Creative Leadership handbook of leadership development* (pp. 194–213). San Francisco: Jossey-Bass.

O'Connor, J., Mumford, M. D., Clifton, T. C., Gessner, T. L., & Connelly, M. S. (1995). Charismatic leaders and destructiveness: A historiometric study. *Leadership Quarterly, 6*, 529–558.

Ruvolo, A. P., & Markus, H. R. (1992). Possible selves and performance: The power of self-relevant imagery. *Social Cognition, 10*, 95–124.

Salovey, P., & Mayer, J. D. (1990). Emotional intelligence. *Imagination, Cognition, and Personality, 9*, 185–211.

Schmidt, J. A. (2002). *Making mergers work: The strategic importance of people.* Washington, DC: Towers Perrin/SHRM Foundation.

Schon, D. (1983). *The reflective practitioner.* NY: Basic Books.

Shamir, B., House, R. J., & Arthur, M. (1993). The motivational effects of charismatic leadership: A self-concept based theory. *Organization Science, 4*, 1–17.

Shamir, B., Zakay, E., Breinin, E., & Popper, M. (1998). Correlates of charismatic leader behavior in military units: Subordinates' attitudes, unit characteristics, and superiors' appraisals of leader. *Academy of Management Journal, 41*, 384–409.

Turner, N., Barling, J., Epitropaki, O., Butcher, V., & Milner, C. (2002). Transformational leadership and moral reasoning. *Journal of Applied Psychology, 87*, 304–311.

Weber, M. (1924/1947). *The theory of social organizations.* New York: Free Press.

Yammarino, F. J., & Bass, B. M. (1990). Long-term forecasting of transformational leadership and its effects among naval officers. In K. E. Clark & M. B. Clark (Eds.), *Measures of leadership* (pp. 151–170). West Orange, NJ: Leadership Library of America.

Yukl, G. (1998). *Leadership in organizations* (4th ed). Englewood Cliffs, NJ: Prentice-Hall.

Yukl, G. (1999). An evaluation of conceptual weaknesses in transformational and charismatic leadership theories. *Leadership Quarterly, 10*, 285–306.

5

A Technology to Support Leader Development: Computer Games

Harold O'Neil and Yuan-Chung Fisher
University of Southern California

In this chapter we suggest one promising technological means for teaching and assessing leader development. We define technology broadly and view it as consisting of hardware and software systems as well as systematic procedures used to facilitate learning and assessment. We discuss an example of the use of computer-based games for teaching and assessing individual leadership. The chapter closes with some suggestions for future research.

WHAT IS LEADERSHIP?

There are multiple views of leadership in the civilian and military sectors. For example, as indicated by the American Society for Training and Development (Sindell & Hoang, 2001), with leadership one practices specific behaviors and qualities, such as knowledge acquisition, strategic thinking, communication skills, self-awareness, and developing others (Sindell & Hoang, 2001, p. 1). As indicated by Goleman (2000), there are also different leadership styles—for example, coercive, authoritative, affiliative, democratic, pace setting, and coaching. Moore and Diamond (2000) defined academic leadership as the capacity to release and engage human potential in the pursuit of a common cause (p. 2). Their model of leadership includes the following dimensions: Leadership is purposeful, leadership empowers people to act, and leadership is not about one's own high individual performance. It is about evoking high individual performance in others. Thus, one's conception of leadership requires some specification in regard to which aspects of leadership are being developed and for what context. In this chapter, leadership is contextualized in the U.S. Army, as the game application example is for Army leadership training, and thus the Army's definition of leadership is used.

With respect to leadership, a recent Army definition is as follows: "Leadership is influencing people—by providing purpose, direction, and motivation—while operating to accomplish the mission and improving the organization" (U.S. Department of the Army, 1999). This definition was refined in the following manner. "Leaders inspire Soldiers to behave professionally and to accomplish missions effectively. Therefore, the Army grows leaders with the character, competence, commitment, and courage to take action when and where required. Leadership requires imagination and initiative" (U.S. Department of the Army, 2001b, p. 12). Furthermore, the operational environment puts a premium on self-awareness and adaptability:

> Self-aware leaders understand their operational environment, can assess their own capabilities, determine their own strengths and weaknesses, and actively learn to overcome their weaknesses. Adaptive leaders must first be self-aware—they have the additional ability to recognize change in their operating environment, identify those changes, and learn how to adapt to succeed in their new environment. (p. 12)

The processes of awareness and adaptation in the educational psychology literature are labeled self-regulation (Hong, O'Neil, & Feldon in press; O'Neil & Abedi, 1996).

As can be seen in Fig. 5.1, from the Army's *Field Manual 22–100* on leadership (U.S. Department of the Army, 1999), leadership has many facets. Which ones might be developed using technology? Our hypothesis is that attributes, skills, and actions are productive areas. Values could probably be developed through a combination of selection, training, and education. For example, the Army does not permit individuals with felony records to enlist.

An additional critical leadership issue is the time frame being targeted for development (e.g., now vs. 2020). For this discussion, we focus on 2020. In the Army, the Objective Force (U.S. Department of the Army, 2001a) will be fully implemented in this time frame.

What attributes, skills, and actions are required in the Objective Force? There has been analytic work by the Army Science Board (Miller & O'Neil, 2001), the Defense Science Board, and the Institute for Defense Analyses (F. Brown, 2000) on this topic. In the area of a leader's challenges in the exercise of command for the Objective Force, there are several issues in common with today's Army: making complex, multicomponent decisions in dynamic environments, severe time

FIG. 5.1. Army leadership definition and Army leadership doctrine. From *Army Field Manual No. 22-100* (p. 1–3), U.S. Department of the Army, 1999. Washington, DC: U.S. Department of the Army Headquarters. Copyright 1999 by U.S. Department of the Army.

pressures, severe consequences and little tolerance for error, demanding physical conditions, performance and command pressure, sustained operations and fatigue, and distributed, multioperator problems.

What will be new in the 2020 time frame are the implications for leader development, that is, a need to compress and accelerate development of maturity, experience, and expertise for leaders through practice in either operational environments or synthetic environments, teaching and assessing the following: quick adaptive thinking, rapid decision making, efficient knowledge use and appropriate exploitation of information technology, more capable ways of thinking and problem solving, confidence in one's own conceptual abilities, and increasing mental and physical endurance. In summary, although most apparent in a military organization, the need to compress and accelerate leader development is an important issue that many other organizations are facing as well.

WHAT IS LEADER DEVELOPMENT?

For this chapter, we have adopted the U.S. Army's definition of leader development: "Leader Development is [a] continuous, progressive, and sequential process through which leaders acquire the skills, knowledge, and behavior necessary to maintain a trained and ready Army in peace-time to deter war" (U.S. Department of the Army, 1994, p. 48).

As can be seen in Fig. 5.2, the Army's leader development model consists of three activities (seen as pillars) that support leader development: institutional training and education, operational assignments, and self-development. These activities are organized in a career ladder for Army personnel. Although the Army is in the process of updating its approach, as of the writing of this chapter, the model in Fig. 5.2 is current Army doctrine in leadership development. Alternative views of leader development in industry can be found in Day and Halpin (2001) and Yearout and Miles (2001).

WHAT TECHNOLOGIES WOULD BE APPROPRIATE FOR LEADER DEVELOPMENT IN THE MILITARY?

There are multiple possible technologies to support institutional training and education and self-development. We define technology broadly and view it as consisting of hardware and software systems as well as systematic procedures used to facilitate learning and assessment.

A critical issue is which technology to select to support which aspects of leader development. However, there is no research to serve as best evidence to match a

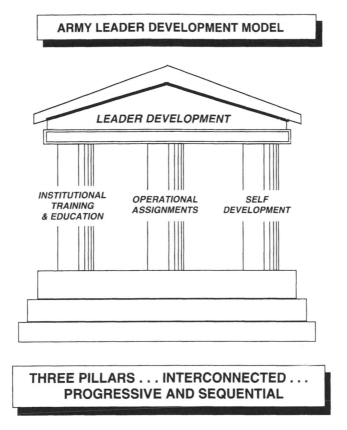

FIG. 5.2. Army leader development model. From *The Enduring Legacy. Leader Development for America's Army* (Pamphlet 350–58, p. 2), U.S. Department of the Army, Washington, DC: U.S. Department of the Army Headquarters. Copyright 1994 by U.S. Department of the Army.

leader development requirement with a specific technology solution. How, then, can one choose? One could view this problem as a media selection problem (Clark, 1994; Sugrue & Clark, 2000). However, in this research area there is little evidence that a specific medium is uniquely suited for a specific learning objective. Clark, Bewley, O'Neil, and Kosman (2002) generated four criteria to resolve this particular media selection issue. Their analysis, for an analogous issue of what existing U.S. Navy courses should be selected for distance learning delivery, indicated that the first selection criterion is whether the media can simulate all necessary conditions of the job setting; the second is provision of necessary sensory-mode information to achieve all objectives; the third is feedback to support instructional goals; and the fourth is cost. Our back-of-the-envelope calculations for this chapter indicate that computer games would be cost-effective for many leader development applications and could offer sufficient practice and feedback opportunities if designed appropriately.

WHAT ROLE DO GAMES HAVE IN THE MILITARY AND CIVILIAN SECTORS?

Educators and trainers began to take notice of the power and potential of computer games for education and training in the 1970s and 1980s (Donchin, 1989; Malone, 1981; Malone & Lepper, 1987; Ramsberger, Hopwood, Hargan, & Underhill, 1983; Ruben, 1999; Thomas & Macredie, 1994). Computer games were potentially useful for instructional purposes and were hypothesized to provide multiple benefits: (a) complex and diverse approaches to learning processes and outcomes, (b) interactivity, (c) ability to address cognitive as well as affective learning issues, and, perhaps most importantly, (d) motivation for learning.

The major application, of course, is for entertainment. During the past three decades, vast numbers of people have embraced game technology for entertainment. However, the popularity of computer games has not been restricted to the entertainment sector. The business sector has long used games and simulations to train staff members in developing fiscal and economic skills (Adams, 1998; Faria, 1998; Washbush & Gosen, 2001). The military sector also uses simulation-based games in flight and combat training (O'Neil & Andrews, 2000). The Army has also used games for recruiting purposes (Chambers, Sherlock, & Kucik, 2002).

WHAT ARE THE CHARACTERISTICS OF COMPUTER GAMES?

Computer games, often called video games, typically require a screen (television, monitor, or liquid crystal display) on which the game is viewed and any of a number of input devices (such as a controller, joystick, keyboard, or keypad) through which one interacts with the game. The types of computer games include arcade video games (often found in shopping malls), home-TV video games (e.g., Xbox), hand-held video games (e.g., Game Boy), and computer video games (such as those played on a PC or Macintosh computer). Games have been classified into the following seven genres by Laird and van Lent (2001): action, role playing, adventure, strategy games, god games, team sports, and individual sports. Game use may include game playing (the use of ready-made games; Alessi & Trollip, 2001) or game designing (the act of building a game; Alessi, 2000a).

Most computer games can be viewed as simulations of some form or another. Simulation games model a process or mechanism relating task-relevant input changes to outcomes in a simplified reality that may not have a definite endpoint. A simulation game consists of four key components: (a) settings that are real, but not necessarily realistic, (b) roles or agendas for the participants, (c) rules, and (d) scoring, recording, monitoring, or other kinds of systematic measurement (Christopher, 1999). Realism-based simulations include contemporary car racing games, business simulations, sports, combats, and civilization development games. More abstract simulations involve adventure, fantasy, and space battle games. Simulations are not games, however, except in that they are specifically designed to allow learning through interaction with an underlying model and have all the characteristics of a game, including competition, rules, and winning and losing (Faria, 1998). For this chapter, a computer game will be defined as a rule-governed, goal-focused, microcomputer-driven activity incorporating principles of gaming and computer-assisted instruction (Driskell & Dwyer, 1984).

DO GAMES TRAIN? EVIDENCE FROM THE CIVILIAN AND MILITARY SECTORS

Unfortunately, there is limited evidence as to the training effectiveness of games for adults. We conducted several literature searches to find such empirical evidence. We searched the Psychological Abstracts Information Services (PsycINFO) and the Educational Resources Information Center (ERIC) databases to find journal articles published between 1990 and 2002. Multiple searches were performed on each database (for journal articles only, in English) using the following keywords: *game, computer game, PC game, computer video game,* and *video game.*

The results from the PsycINFO search are presented in Table 5.1. For the term *game,* in PsycINFO there were 2,199 hits in the 1990 through 2002 time frame. To reduce the magnitude of this review, we used AND operators to tailor the review to computer and video games. For example, using "computer AND game," we considered 33 of 402 hits relevant based on the PsycINFO abstracts. Each abstract was reviewed to determine its relevance to the topic (e.g., adult learners, empirical, focus on evaluation or the instructional strategies of feedback

TABLE 5.1
Literature Search in PsycINFO (1990–2002 Time Frame)

	Hits	Relevant Hits (Relevant Abstracts)	Relevant Articles (Nonempirical)	Relevant Articles (Empirical)	Relevant Articles (Military)
Game	2199				
Computer game	402	33	20	4	2
PC game	7	0	0		
Computer video game	106	8	1	1	0
Video game	192	6	2	1	0

and practice). The articles for these 33 abstracts were retrieved and read. Twenty articles were considered possibly relevant (e.g., the articles focused on topics such as adults). Of these 20 articles, 4 had empirical data. Thus, there were 4 relevant articles from 402 hits for "computer AND game." The remaining key words, shown in Table 5.1, yielded an additional 2 unique relevant articles. Thus, there were 6 relevant articles from PsycINFO that we used in our review. We conducted a similar search in ERIC/Journals. There were 2 additional relevant empirical articles in ERIC.

We expanded our search through the Internet to locate additional relevant articles. This search produced 2 new articles that were considered relevant. Thus, there were only 10 articles that we found relevant (e.g., that included empirical evidence for use of game technology in education or training). In summary, the recent scientific base is very limited regarding the training effectiveness of gaming technology in training and education for adults in both the civilian and the military sectors.

We then classified this limited game literature into five major categories: promotion of motivation (e.g., fun), enhancement of thinking skills, facilitation of metacognition, improvement of knowledge and skills, and building of attitude. Halpern (2002) discussed the categories and their role in adult learning in more detail, particularly for long-term retention and transfer.

Promotion of Motivation

According to Woolfolk (2001), "motivation is usually defined as an internal state that arouses, directs, and maintains behavior" (p. 366). Internal promotion of motivation can be viewed from two perspectives, intrinsic and extrinsic. Intrinsic motivation refers to behaviors that are engaged in for their own sake, meaning that tasks are performed for internal reasons, such as joy and satisfaction (Woolfolk, 2001). Extrinsic motivation, on the other hand, refers to behaviors that are performed for external reasons, such as reward, obligation, or threat of punishment (Deci, Vallerand, Pelletier, & Ryan, 1991). Games, in general, appear to inherently motivate users by stimulating their curiosity (Thomas & Macredie, 1994). The motivation comes from the challenge, elements of fantasy, novelty, and complexity of games (Malone, 1981; Malone & Lepper, 1987). A few recent studies have provided empirical results that suggest increased motivation as one of the positive side effects of games for learning.

A study by Amory, Naicker, Vincent, and Adams (1999) showed that the majority of the undergraduate students participating in the study appeared to be intrinsically motivated playing a computer game. It was suggested that the students who enjoyed playing the educationally based game appeared to be motivated by the "fun" aspects of computer technology and as a result gained knowledge. A study by Ricci, Salas, and Cannon-Bowers (1996) found a significant positive correlation between a student's level of enjoyment during training and his or her test score. Participants who perceived their learning method (a computer game, in this case) as enjoyable were more likely to score significantly higher on a test than participants who did not like using the computer game.

Enhancement of Thinking Skills

Thinking skills encompass skills of information processing, reasoning, enquiry, creation, and learning strategies (O'Neil, 1978). Researchers have asserted that computer games help improve students' skills in practical reasoning (Wood & Stewart, 1987), complex problem solving (Hayes, 1981), transfer of learning (Crisafulli & Antonietti, 1993), making inferences and engaging in inductive reasoning (Mayer & Sims, 1994), and using metaphorical maps to generate alternative solution paths (Quinn, 1996). Such use of computer games may help enhance different ways of thinking about problems (differentiation), which can lead to new insights or strategies for cognitively making sense of a problem situation. This line of theory is captured well by Day and Lance (chap. 3, this volume).

There is evidence to suggest that in playing computer games, cognitive processes are enhanced. Doolittle (1995) found that individuals who play computer games showed flexibility in the internal representations of their thinking. These individuals were able to increase their ability to overcome "functional fixedness" (inability to move beyond the usual functions of an object), had greater creative ability, and established the ability to generate a number of alternative hypotheses in problem situations. A study by Greenfield, DeWinstanley, Kilpatrick, and Kaye (1994) used response time to targets shown at different locations on a computer screen to measure divided attention and found that video game experience is a factor in improving strategies of divided attention. The study implied that such skills practiced with computer games can be transferred to a new task that requires monitoring of multiple visual locations, for example, instrument flying, military activities, and air traffic control. Another study, by Okagaki and Frensch (1994), found that spatial-oriented video games have the potential to improve late adolescents' mental rotation and spatial visualization skills.

Facilitation of Metacognition

Metacognition is a thinking skill that refers to "thinking about thinking" (Paris & Paris, 2001). It generally includes two dimensions of thinking: (a) the knowledge one has about one's own thinking and (b) one's ability to use this awareness to regulate one's own cognitive processes. O'Neil and Abedi (1996) defined metacognition to consist of planning and self-assessment. In a way, metacognition is like the "mission control" of the cognitive system, enabling students to coordinate the use of knowledge and a combination of many separate strategies to accomplish a single goal (Bruning, Schraw, & Ronning, 1999). Metacognitive skills can be potentially increased as a result of playing computer games, along with learning various kinds of thinking skills. For example, Bruning et al. (1999) and Pillay,

Brownlee, and Wilss (1999) in their qualitative studies found that game playing allowed players a chance to use metacognitive skills. It was observed that game players perceptively monitored their moves, made inferences, and generated and validated hypotheses. The studies concluded that the constant monitoring of their thinking by game players is evidence of a metacognitive approach. However, if one is claiming that games increase metacognition, then these skills would have to be measured.

Improvement of Knowledge and Skills

Knowledge includes declarative knowledge and procedural knowledge. Skills are defined as proficiency, facility, or dexterity that is acquired or developed through training or experience. Several studies have shown evidence that computer games can enhance learning and retention of knowledge. A study by Ricci et al. (1996) on military trainees found that participants assigned to the game condition scored significantly higher on a retention test than did participants assigned to test (paper-based question-and-answer form) and text (paper-based prose form) conditions. In another study, Betz (1995–1996) used examination scores to demonstrate that students who used the computer simulator together with reading a text learned more than students who only read the text in engineering and technology fields. Westbrook and Braithwaite (2001) provided strong evidence that a health care game was an effective tool in improving learning outcomes (e.g., factual knowledge and information-seeking skills).

Through visualization, experimentation, and the creativity involved in game playing (Betz, 1995–1996), computer games not only enhance learning but also can lead to improvement in complex real-world motor skills such as driving on highways or flying airplanes (Arthur et al., 1995). The beneficial effect of such training is based on the fact that, as learners are exposed to various situations, they develop knowledge of the different domains (i.e., knowing "what to do") (Magill, 1993), which, in turn, gives rise to better and faster decisions (Starkes & Lindley, 1994). For example, Fery and Ponserre (2001) found evidence that experience in golf video game playing can be transferred to actual real-life putting skills.

Another example is found in a computer game used to train cadets at an Israeli Air Force flight school (Gopher, Weil, & Bareket, 1994). The game chosen for the study was Space Fortress II and the task required in the game was to control a moving spaceship in a hostile environment. To achieve a maximum score, cadets had to destroy a threatening space fortress and all mines and avoid being hit by either the fortress or the mines. Transfer effects from game training to actual flying were tested during eight flights (45–60 min each) in the transition stage to the high-performance jet trainer. Results showed that the game group performed significantly better than the no-game group in the subsequent test flights.

Gopher et al. (1994) concluded that, although the elements and parameters of the computer game were physically remote from those of the flight situation, the game provided a useful training context for developing flight-relevant skills, particularly those related to the control of attention and coping with high cognitive load. Cadets who played the game were assumed to have learned the value of exploring alternative response modes and developing attention strategies in a context that bears general relevance to a real flight situation. However, neither of these variables was explicitly measured.

Improving Attitudes

Attitudes are commonly viewed as summary evaluations of objects (e.g., oneself, other people, issues, etc.) along a dimension ranging from positive to negative (e.g., Petty, Priester, & Wegener, 1994). A study by Adams (1998) showed that the most important learning associated with using computer games is not the learning of facts, but rather the development of certain attitudes acquired through interaction with software (e.g., becoming aware of the complexity of a task, developing respect for decision makers in the real world, and developing humility toward accomplishing the task).

IN WHAT CONTEXT WILL THE USE
OF GAMES FOR LEADER DEVELOPMENT
BE EXPRESSED?

The example context for this chapter is Battle-Command (U.S. Department of the Army, 2001c). Battle-Command is the leadership element of combat power; that is, commanders, assisted by the staff, visualize the operation, describe it in terms of intent and guidance, and direct the actions of subordinates. Commanders direct operations in terms of the battlefield operating system (BOS), which consists of intelligence, maneuver, fire support, air defense; mobility, countermobility, and survivability; combat service support; and command and control (U.S. Department of the Army, 2001c, p. 5–15). Commanders directly influence operations by personal presence, supported by their command and control (C2) system (adapted from U.S. Department of the Army, 2001c, p. 5–1). There have been games developed for Battle-Command and for recruiting by the Army (Chambers et al., 2002).

What Are Some Example Games Designed
for Battle-Command?

The Institute for Creative Technologies (ICT) is developing several such games. The ICT was established on August 18, 1999, by the U.S. Army in collaboration with the University of Southern California (USC) to enlist the entertainment and game industry talent to work collaboratively with USC faculty and staff and the

TABLE 5.2
Game Evaluation Specifications

	Full Spectrum Command	Full Spectrum Warrior	Full Spectrum Command Board Game
Purpose and domain	Battle-Command with the focus on visualization, description, and directing	Squad leadership, battle drills	Battle-Command with focus on directing
Type of game platform	PC/CD ROM	Microsoft Xbox, CD ROM	Board game with miniatures
Analogous game	None	Rainbow 6, Ghost Recon (Tom Clancy)	None
Commercialization intent	Secondary	Secondary	Secondary
Contractor	Quicksilver Software	Sony Imageworks, Pandemic Studios	Legless Productions
Genre[a]	Real-time strategy game	Real-time strategy game	Turn-based strategy game
Length of contract	1 June 2001 + 18 months	1 June 2001 + 2 years	Completed 1 June 2001– 1 March 2002
Training use	Integrated into course	Supplemental	Integrated into course
Length of game	60 min (including after-action review)	15–20 min	45 min–1.5 hr
Terminal learning objectives[b]	To be determined	To be determined	To be determined
Players and learners	Captains, first lieutenants	Squad leaders	Captains, first lieutenants
Type of learning[c]	Problem solving	Problem solving	Problem solving
AI entity roles[d]	Not applicable	Not applicable	Not applicable
Domain knowledge	Battle command at company level with a focus on directing	Squad management, battle drills	Fire and movement, some battle planning
Type of play	Tactical understanding, information management, resource allocation	Resource management	Tactical understanding
Time frame	Now–2020	Now–2020	Now–2020
Time to learn game rules[e]	4hr + homework + practice games	1 hr + 2 hr practice games	4 hr + homework + practice games

Availability of tutorial	No	No	No
Manual	Yes	Yes	Yes
User perspective	Remote third person, or first person	Over-the-shoulder third person	Top down (see everything)
Play value (it is fun[f])	Secondary	Secondary	Secondary
Plan of instruction	Yes	No	Yes
Feedback in game	Implicit feedback	Implicit feedback	Implicit feedback
After-action review[g]	Yes	Yes	None
Nature of practice	One scenario per game play	One scenario per game play	One scenario per game play
Single vs. multiple user	Single user	Single user	Multiple user
2020 technology	RISTA	RISTA	RISTA
Type of training supported[h]	Walk	Crawl	Walk
Scenarios (number, type)	Type (patrol, deliberate attack, defend) × context (McKenna, mini McKenna, McKenna town, McKenna village) × time of day (early, mid, late)	Type (patrol, deliberate, attack, defend) × time of day (early vs. late)	Type (patrol, deliberate, attack, defend) × time of day (early vs. late)
Key milestones	Alpha October 2002, final January 2003	Alpha February 2003, final June 2003	Completed

Note. RISTA = reconaissance, intelligence, surveillance, targeting, and acquisition.

[a] Action, role planning, adventure, strategy games, goal games, team sports, individual sports (Laird & van Lent, 2001).

[b] Action, conditions, standards.

[c] Domain knowledge, problem solving, collaboration or teamwork, self-regulation, communication (Baker & Mayer, 1999; see also Anderson & Krathwohl, 2001, for an alternative model of learning).

[d] Laird and van Lent (2001). Tactical enemies, partners, support characters, story directors, strategic opponents, units, commentators.

[e] Basic game play, that is, an educated user, not winning strategies.

[f] Challenge, fantasy, novelty, complexity.

[g] Planned, explainable artificial intelligence.

[h] Crawl versus walk versus run.

111

U.S. Army to conduct research and development on immersive training simulations. The logic for such a center can be found in the National Research Council (1997) report on modeling and simulation linking environment and defense.

One long-range ICT goal is to help design the next generation of Army simulators and games. One of the major research areas of ICT is computer games whose major purpose is training, not entertainment. Three games have been designed; development has been completed on one of them, and the two remaining games will be completed in 2003 (Institute for Creative Technologies, 2001a, 2001b, 2001c, 2001d; Legless Productions, 2001a, 2001b; Pandemic Studios, 2002; Quicksilver Software, 2001). The specifications for the three games can be found in Table 5.2. These specifications were reviewed by the ICT program manager and were accurate as of the time of writing this chapter.

As can be seen in Table 5.2, the three games are labeled Full Spectrum Command, Full Spectrum Warrior, and Full Spectrum Command Board Game. A game is often characterized by game developers in terms of the following key specifications: type of platform that supports the game, type of players using the game, contractor, genre, purpose/domain, and key milestones. For example, Full Spectrum Command is supported by a PC with CD-ROM, for captains and first lieutenants, and was developed by Quicksilver Software, Inc., as a real-time strategy game whose domain is Battle-Command at the company level. The key milestone was October 2002, when full functionality was expected to be present with some programming errors (or buggy form) in the game.

From a trainer's point of view, a game is often characterized in terms of the following key specifications regarding domain knowledge to be learned: learning objectives (tasks, conditions, and standards), training use, learners, practice, and feedback. The different mental models of game developers versus trainers drive these differences in the characterization of games. For example, as can be seen in Table 5.2, for Full Spectrum Command, the domain knowledge is Battle-Command at the company level with a focus on visualizing, describing, and directing. However, for training purposes, this set of knowledge and skills needs to be further analyzed (e.g., is the focus on planning, situational awareness, tactical decision making, etc.?). Each of the skills or kinds of knowledge would require different instructional strategies and different assessment measures.

As can be seen in Table 5.2, as of the writing of this chapter, terminal learning objectives still need to be determined. The learners will be captains and first lieutenants in the Captain Career Course at Fort Benning, Georgia. As indicated in Fort Benning documentation, the mission of this course is to train captains in the art and science of combined-arms battle command and battle staff leadership across the full spectrum of operations within contemporary operational environments. The Full Spectrum Command focus is a subset of this mission; that is, it will train and assess battle command in an infantry company within a peace-keeping mission in an urban environment. The training will be integrated into the Captain Career Course, consistent with the program of instruction (POI). The feedback will be implicit in the game itself, as the after-action review (AAR) is planned, but was not implemented as of the writing of this chapter. The specific AAR for Future Spectrum was to be implemented in September 2002. Future versions of the AAR will have an explainable AI function (van Lent, 2002).

KEY ISSUES IN TRAINING GAME DESIGN

A key issue in training/education game design is the specification of what particular construct one is teaching using a game (Alessi, 2000b). Initially, one must have a definition of the construct, and then some sort of instructional system design (ISD) process (e.g., Dick, Carey, & Carey, 2001; Mayer, 2001, 2002; Tennyson & Foshay, 2000) must be applied. The Army's version of ISD is called Systems Approach to Training. Common to all ISD models is a clear specification of the goal or objective of learning. From this goal or objective, the instructional strategies follow (e.g., nature of feedback, timing of feedback, etc.) and assessment issues are defined (e.g., how do we know that individuals have more of outcome X after a training or educational activity?). Different Xs [e.g., leadership (O'Neil, Baker, & Fisher, 2002), situational awareness (Endsley & Garland, 2000; Endsley et al., 2000; Graham & Matthews, 1999), and decision making (Cohen, Freeman, & Thompson, 1998; Klein, 1997; Phillips et al., 2001; Strater, Endsley, Pleban, & Matthews, 2001)] require different instructional strategies, assessment measures, after-action reviews, and homework assignments.

For example, if the game is conceptualized as teaching tactical problem solving, then the work of O'Neil (1999) on problem solving would be appropriate. His view of problem solving is based on Mayer and Wittrock's (1996) conceptualization: "Problem solving is cognitive processing directed at achieving a goal when no solution method is obvious to the problem solver" (p. 47). This definition is further analyzed into components suggested by the expertise literature: content understanding or domain knowledge, domain-specific problem-solving strategies, and self-regulation (see, e.g., O'Neil, 1999). Self-regulation is composed of metacognition (planning and self-checking) and motivation (effort and self-efficacy). Thus, in specifying the construct of problem solving, to be a successful problem solver, one must know something (content knowledge), possess intellectual tricks (problem-solving strategies), be able to plan and monitor one's progress toward solving the problem (metacognition), and be motivated to perform (effort and self-efficacy) (O'Neil, 1999, pp. 255–256). Each of these problem-solving elements would have to be taught and assessed in the game context.

Finally, for training games, there must be an after-action review (Morrison & Meliza, 1999). Such a technique is the way the Army provides feedback for simulations and provides the context for learning (Morrison & Meliza, 1999). Such a feature would be expected from a game used in training. Critical, of course, is to decide what one is teaching (e.g., tactical decision making vs. situational awareness). The content of the AAR varies depending on the goal or objective of the simulation or game. The process is described as follows (B. R. Brown, Nordyke, Gerlock, Begley, & Meliza, 1998):

> AAR aids display the unit's plan (what was supposed to happen), identify "what happened" during the execution, and stimulate player discussions on "why it happened." During these discussions . . . players learn from their mistakes and benefit from the lessons learned by other players. The AAR, in effect, becomes the bridge between the completed training event and the next training event, providing post-exercise learning on "how to improve" that enables leaders to fix training weaknesses. (p. 12)

This AAR should be supported by game software that would collect necessary information on the topic being taught during the game play. For example, for a tactical decision game (implying that the goal of the training is improved decision making), there would be multiple levels of information for the AAR. The elements of performance that are scored and reported (e.g., loss exchange ratios, hits and misses, rounds expended, etc.) would be a subset of the AAR information, not the major focus of the AAR. The next level, beyond the player's actions, would probably be the tactical lessons learned (e.g., use of covering fire in an urban environment fighting asymmetric forces). The final level of AAR information would be how both sets of data (elements of performance and tactical lessons learned) provide information on the training goal (e.g., improved decision making).

DISCUSSION

A useful place to start in leadership training or education using game technology is to generally define the goals and objectives of the expected learning. This first step is seldom explicit for game research in training and education. In particular, the lack of specific training goals and objectives was also true for the ICT games. Why was this so? Quite simply, game developers have mental models very different from training researchers. Much of the game research involves a technology-push approach—that is, build the state-of-the-art game (mainly fun, some training), then the customer will generate the training applications, which in turn will also be evaluated by the customer. This implicit mental model drove the process that resulted in the ICT contracts awarded to the game developers on June 1, 2001.

Following the award of the contracts, the Army characterized the ICT games as training devices (i.e., a requirements-pull approach). The games (mainly training, some fun) would be driven by training requirements, and evaluation would be done by the ICT. Because the training device approach was the Army's expectation, training requirements and assessment should have been a major influence on concept development and software production. Resources for training analysis and assessment would have to have been applied to these processes initially.

Developers would have needed to change their mental models of how to conceptual and develop the games. Contracts would have been renegotiated. Such changes would have been done soon after the initiation of a training game project, because, at some point, the process would be irreversible due to time or money expenditure.

Such changes did not occur in budget or schedule. Like mythical man-months (Brooks, 1975) in software development, adding more people to a game project to make it a training game would not have speeded the process up and would have cost more money. Furthermore, additional money was not available from the Army for a planned evaluation (O'Neil, Baker, & Fisher, 2002). The execution of the planned formative evaluation would also have provided feedback in terms of lessons learned, and thus would have been useful for specification of future research and development activities in the use of gaming for leadership development.

Suggestions for Future Research

There is a need for research on formative evaluation of games. Although the concept of formative evaluation is foreign to game developers, a few evaluation plans have been developed (e.g., O'Neil et al., 2002; ThoughtLink, 2000). None of these plans was executed, due to lack of funding. However, there is some hope in this area. The Army has plans in fiscal year 2003 (October 1, 2002–September 20, 2003) to fund a limited evaluation of the ICT games. This evaluation is to be conducted by the Army Research Institute.

The expense of such work would be reduced if an assessment tool kit for evaluation of individual and team proficiency in leader development games existed. We believe the research base is robust enough in the following areas to reduce the risk of such tool development; for example, in problem solving (O'Neil, 1999, 2002), situational awareness (e.g., Endsley, 1995; Endsley & Garland, 2000; Graham & Matthews, 1999; Strater et al., 2001), and tactical decision making (e.g., Cohen et al., 1998; Klein, 1997; Phillips et al., 2001).

Three additional areas would also profit from investment: (a) Development of assessment tools for evaluation in distance learning leadership development gaming applications; for example, issues in Table 5.2 would be a good starting point. (b) Investigation of the role of feedback and practice in games; for example, a theory of hints is needed. One resource common to the gaming community is books of hints and solutions for specific games (e.g., *Riven*; see Keith & Barton, 1997). In these books, hints and tactical solutions are given with increasing levels of specification, for example, first, a general overview of game mechanics, followed by general hints, then specific hints, then specific solutions in the form of specific procedures to solve specific tactical problems. Such a resource should be created for the leader development gaming community, based on research. (c) The results of such feedback research during the game would also funnel into new research in AAR processes.

For example, at a formative evaluation meeting at Pandemic (one of the game developers) an interesting idea emerged. Since the AAR for their squad-level action game will be without instructor support (see Table 5.2), the data displays of success and failure (the AAR) must be organized to facilitate learning. The following process could be used: First, the goal of the game (e.g., situation awareness or tactical problem solving) would be under the control of the student. Second, after a goal is chosen by the student, then data would be generated and formatted to indicate the amount of learning consistent with that chosen goal. To implement this idea, a matrix (type of goals × type of learning × type of assessment) would be generated by the developers. For example, if situation awareness were chosen as a goal, then in the game, the problem-solving scenario would require the players to provide status reports to headquarters. At the AAR, a discrepancy score between the student's knowledge (what he or she reported) and ground truth (i.e., what the game "knows") would be calculated. Then, a measure of situation awareness would be generated with cut scores (e.g., low discrepancy scores equal good situation awareness). Finally, feedback would be generated consistent with being above or below the cut score.

In summary, in this chapter we suggested a technology that can support both institutional training and education activities; and self-development activities; that is, the use of games for training purposes. A defining characteristic of games is that they are motivating, and such motivation is very important in self-development. Obviously, games could also be used in institutional training and education. Following a review of the literature, we provided examples of games the Army plans to test in an institutional leadership training course and their formative evaluation. We closed with a discussion of evaluation challenges and suggested research and development in the application of games to training.

ACKNOWLEDGMENTS

This research was supported in part by the U.S. Army Simulation, Training and Instrumentation Command (STRICOM) and in part by the Army Research Institute for Behavioral and Social Sciences. However, the findings and opinions expressed in this work do not reflect the positions or policies of STRICOM or the Army Research Institute.

Thanks for intellectual support go to Jim Korris, Creative Director, ICT; Rob Sears, Program Manager for Game Development, Legless Productions; Drs. Jim Black and Alesya Paschal of STRICOM, who monitored the ICT contract for the government; and to the following developers, who were willing to share information and ideas: Mike Mancuso of Quicksilver Software, Inc., and Josh Resnick of Pandemic Studios. Finally, the contributions of the Army subject matter experts should be acknowledged: Captains Brent Cummings and Lance Oskey and SFC Jack Batten gave consistent good advice and accurate Army information.

REFERENCES

Adams, P. C. (1998). Teaching and learning with SimCity 2000. *Journal of Geography, 97*(2), 47–55.

Alessi, S. M. (2000a). Building versus using simulations. In J. M. Spector & T. M. Anderson (Eds.), *Integrated and holistic perspectives on learning, instruction and technology: Improving understanding in complex domains* (pp. 175–196). Dordrecht, the Netherlands: Kluwer.

Alessi, S. M. (2000b). Simulation design for training and assessment. In H. F. O'Neil, Jr., & D. H. Andrews (Eds.), *Aircrew training and assessment* (pp. 197–222). Mahwah, NJ: Lawrence Erlbaum Associates, Inc.

Alessi, S. M., & Trollip, S. R. (2001). *Multimedia for learning. Methods and development* (3rd ed.). Boston: Allyn & Bacon.

Amory, A., Naicker, K., Vincent, J., & Adams, C. (1999). Computer games as a learning resource. *British Journal of Educational Technology, 30,* 311–321.

Anderson, L. W., & Krathwhol, D. R. (Eds.) (With Airasian, P. W., Cruikshank, K. A., Mayer, R. E., Pintrich, P. R., Raths, J., & Wittrock, M. C.). (2001). *A taxonomy for learning, teaching, and assessing.* New York: Longman.

Arthur, W., Jr., Strong, M. H., Jordan, J. A., Williamson, J. E., Shebilske, W. L., & Regian, J. W. (1995). Visual attention: Individual differences in training and predicting complex task performance, *Acta Psychologica, 88,* 3–23.

Baker, E. L., & Mayer, R. E. (1999). Computer-based assessment of problem solving. *Computers in Human Behavior, 15,* 269–282.

Betz, J. A. (1995–1996). Computer games: Increase learning in an interactive multidisciplinary environment. *Journal of Educational Technology Systems, 24,* 195–205.

Brooks, F. P., Jr. (1975). *The mythical man-month: Essays on software engineering.* Reading, MA: Addison-Wesley.

Brown, B. R., Nordyke, J. W., Gerlock, D. L., Begley, I. J., & Meliza, L. L. (1998, May). *Training Analysis and Feedback Aids (TAAF Aids) study for live training support* (Study Report, Army Project No. 2O665803D730). Alexandria, VA: U.S. Army Research Institute for the Behavioral and Social Sciences.

Brown, F. (2000, January). *Preparation of leaders* (Document D-2382). Alexandria, VA: Institute for Defense Analyses.

Bruning, R. H., Schraw, G. J., & Ronning, R. R. (1999). *Cognitive psychology and instruction* (3rd ed.). Upper Saddle River, NJ: Merrill.

Chambers, C., Sherlock, T. D., & Kucik III, P. (2002). The Army Game Project. *Army, 52*(6), 59–62.

Christopher, E. M. (1999). Simulations and games as subversive activities. *Simulation and Gaming, 30,* 442.

Clark, R. E. (1994). Media will never influence learning. *Educational Technology Research and Development, 42*(2), 21–29.

Clark, R. E., Bewley, W., O'Neil, H. F., Jr., & Kosman, G. (2002). *Heuristics for selecting distance learning courses.* Unpublished manuscript, University of California, Los Angeles, National Center for Research on Evaluation, Standards, and Student Testing (CRESST).

Cohen, M. S., Freeman, J. T., & Thompson, B. (1998). Critical thinking skills in tactical decision making: A model and a training strategy. In J. A. Cannon-Bowers & E. Salas (Eds.), *Making decisions under stress. Implications for individual and team training* (pp. 155–189). Washington, DC: American Psychological Association.

Crisafulli, L., & Antonietti, A. (1993). Videogames and transfer: An experiment on analogical problem solving. *Ricerche di Psicologia, 17,* 51–63.

Day, D., & Halpin, S. M. (2001). *Leadership development: A review of industry best practices* (Technical Report 1111). Alexandria, VA: U.S. Army Research Institute for the Behavioral and Social Sciences.

Deci, E. L., Vallerand, R. J., Pelletier, L. G., & Ryan, R. M. (1991). Motivation and education: The self-determination perspective. *Educational Psychologist, 26,* 325–346.

Dick, W., Carey, L., & Carey, J. O. (2001). *The systematic design of instruction* (5th ed.). New York: Addison Wesley Longman.

Donchin, E. (1989). The learning strategies project. *Acta Psychologica, 71,* 1–15.

Doolittle, J. H. (1995). Using riddles and interactive computer games to teach problem-solving skills. *Teaching of Psychology. Special Issue: Psychologists teach critical thinking, 22,* 33–36.

Driskell, J. E., & Dwyer, D. J. (1984, February). Microcomputer videogame based training. *Educational Technology, 24*(2), 11–17.

Endsley, M. R. (1995). Measurement of situation awareness in dynamic systems. *Human Factors, 37,* 65–84.

Endsley, M. R., & Garland, D. J. (Eds.). (2000). *Situation awareness. Analysis and measurement.* Mahwah, NJ: Lawrence Erlbaum Associates, Inc.

Endsley, M. R., Holder, L. D., Leibrecht, B. C., Garland, D. J., Wampler, R. L., & Matthews, M. D. (2000). *Modeling and measuring situation awareness in the infantry operational environment* (Research Report 1753). Alexandria, VA: U.S. Army Research Institute for the Behavioral and Social Sciences.

Faria, A. J. (1998). Business simulation games: Current usage levels—An update. *Simulation and Gaming, 29,* 295–308.

Fery, Y. A., & Ponserre, S. (2001). Enhancing the control of force in putting by video game training. *Ergonomics, 44,* 1025–1037.

Goleman, D. (2000). Leadership that gets results. *Harvard Business Review, 78,* 78–90.

Gopher, D., Weil, M., & Bareket, T. (1994). Transfer of skill from a computer game trainer to flight. *Human Factors, 36,* 387–405.

Graham, S. E., & Matthews, M. D. (Eds.). (1999). *Infantry situation awareness. Papers from the 1998 Infantry Situation Awareness Workshop.* Alexandria, VA: U.S. Army Research Institute for the Behavioral and Social Sciences.

Greenfield, P. M., DeWinstanley, P., Kilpatrick, H., & Kaye, D. (1994). Action video games and informal education: Effects on strategies for dividing visual attention. *Journal of Applied Developmental Psychology, 15,* 105–123.

Halpern, D. F. (2002, May). *The development of adult cognition: Understanding constancy and change in adult learning* (Report to the U.S. Army Research Institute). Claremont, CA: Claremont McKenna College, Berger Institute for Work, Family, and Children.

Hayes, J. R. (1981). *The complete problem solver.* Philadelphia, PA: The Franklin Institute Press.

Hong, E., O'Neil, H. F., Jr., & Feldon, D. (in press). Gender effects on mathematics achievement: Mediating role of state and trait self-regulation. In A. M. Gallagher & J. C. Kaufman (Eds.), *Mind the gap: Gender differences in mathematics.* Cambridge: Cambridge University Press.

Institute for Creative Technologies. (2001a). *C-FORCE—Fire team leader level. Training aid: Future infantry tactics and command in year 2020—Modeling of the integration of information technology into a U.S. Army light infantry company* (Research proposal, July 2001). Los Angeles: University of Southern California, Institute for Creative Technologies.

Institute for Creative Technologies. (2001b). *CS XII—Company commander level. Training aid: Future infantry tactics and command in year 2020—Modeling of the integration of information technology into a U.S. Army light infantry company* (Research proposal, July 2001). Los Angeles: University of Southern California, Institute for Creative Technologies.

Institute for Creative Technologies. (2001c). *CS XII—Company commander level. Training aid: Future infantry tactics and command in year 2020—Modeling of the integration of information technology into a U.S. Army light infantry company* (Research proposal, August 2001). Los Angeles: University of Southern California, Institute for Creative Technologies.

Institute for Creative Technologies. (2001d). *C-FORCE preliminary design document. Version 2.1* (Future Combat Systems, LLC). Los Angeles: University of Southern California, Institute for Creative Technologies.

Keith, W. H., Jr., & Barton, N. (1997). *Riven: The sequel to Myst, hints and solutions.* Indianapolis, IN: Brandy.

Klein, G. (1997). Developing expertise in decision making. *Thinking and Reasoning, 3,* 337–352.

Laird, J. E., & van Lent, M. (2001). Human-level AI's killer application: Interactive computer games. *AI Magazine, 22*(2), 15–25.

Legless Productions. (2001a). Introduction and overview. In *U.S. Army transformation: FCS Project. The integration of information technology and robotic sensors into a standard U.S. Army light infantry rifle company in the year 2020. Concept book for the CS XII and C-FORCE projects.* Los Angeles: University of Southern California, Institute for Creative Technologies.

Legless Productions. (2001b). *U.S. Army transformation: FCS Project. The integration of information technology and robotic sensors into a standard U.S. Army light infantry rifle company in the year 2020. Concept book for the CS XII and C-FORCE projects.* Los Angeles: University of Southern California, Institute for Creative Technologies.

Magill, R. A. (1993). *Motor learning: Concepts and applications* (4th ed.). San Francisco, CA: Freeman.

Malone, T. W. (1981). Toward a theory of intrinsically motivating instruction. *Cognitive Science, 4,* 333–369.

Malone, T. W., & Lepper, M. R. (1987). *Aptitude, learning and instruction III: Cognitive and affective process analysis.* Hillsdale, NJ: Lawrence Erlbaum Associates, Inc.

Mayer, R. E. (2001). *Multimedia learning.* New York: Cambridge University Press.

Mayer, R. E. (2002). A taxonomy for computer-based assessment of problem solving. *Computers in Human Behavior, 18,* 623–632.

Mayer, R. E., & Sims, V. K. (1994). For whom is a picture worth a thousand words? Extensions of a dual-coding theory of multimedia learning. *Journal of Educational Psychology, 86,* 389–401.

Mayer, R. E., & Wittrock, M. C. (1996). Problem-solving transfer. In D. C. Berliner & R. C. Calfee (Eds.), *Handbook of educational psychology* (pp. 47–62). New York: Simon & Schuster Macmillan.

Miller, J., & O'Neil, H. F., Jr. (2001, February). *Leader (leadership) development Independent Review Team findings and recommendations.* Report of the Independent Review Team for Dr. A. Michael Andrews, Deputy Assistant Secretary of the Army (Research & Technology), Washington, DC.

Moore, M. R., & Diamond, M. A. (2000). *Academic leadership: Turning vision into reality.* New York: Ernst & Young.

Morrison, J. E., & Meliza, L. L. (1999). *Foundations of the after action review process* (Special Report 42). Alexandria, VA: U.S. Army Research Institute for the Behavioral and Social Sciences.

National Research Council. (1997). *Modeling and simulation linking entertainment and defense.* Washington, DC: National Academy Press.

Okagaki, L., & Frensch, P. A. (1994). Effects of video game playing on measures of spatial performance: Gender effects in late adolescence. *Journal of Applied Developmental Psychology, 15,* 33–58.

O'Neil, H. F., Jr. (Ed.). (1978). *Learning strategies.* New York: Academic.

O'Neil, H. F., Jr. (1999). Perspectives on computer-based performance assessment of problem solving: Editor's introduction. *Computers in Human Behavior, 15,* 255–268.

O'Neil, H. F., Jr. (Ed.). (2002). Computer-based assessment of problem solving [Special issue]. *Computers in Human Behavior, 18*(6).

O'Neil, H. F., Jr., & Abedi, J. (1996). Reliability and validity of a state metacognitive inventory: Potential for alternative assessment. *Journal of Educational Research, 89,* 234–245.

O'Neil, H. F., Jr., & Andrews, D. (Eds.). (2000). *Aircrew training and assessment.* Mahwah, NJ: Lawrence Erlbaum Associates, Inc.

O'Neil, H. F., Jr., Baker, E. L., & Fisher, J. Y. C. (2002). *A formative evaluation of ICT games* (Report to Institute for Creative Technologies, University of Southern California). Los Angeles: University of Southern California and UCLA/National Center for Research on Evaluation, Standards, and Student Testing (CRESST).

Pandemic Studios. (2002, August). *C4 United States Army. Version 3.0.* Santa Monica, CA: Author.

Paris, S. G., & Paris, A. H. (2001). Classroom applications of research on self-regulated learning. *Educational Psychologist, 36,* 89–101.

Petty, R. E., Priester, J. R., & Wegener, D. T. (1994). *Handbook of social cognition.* Hillsdale, NJ: Lawrence Erlbaum Associates, Inc.

Phillips, J., McCloskey, M. J., McDermott, P. L., Wiggins, S. L., Battaglia, D. A., Thordsen, M. L., & Klein, G. (2001). *Decision-centered MOUT training for small unit leaders* (Research Report 1776). Alexandria, VA: U.S. Army Research Institute for the Behavioral and Social Sciences.

Pillay, H. K., Brownlee, J., & Wilss, L. (1999). Cognition and recreational computer games: Implications for educational technology. *Journal of Research on Computing in Education, 32,* 203–216.

Quicksilver Software. (2001, November). *CS XII. An infantry company command simulator. Simulation design document. Milestone 6 submission copy.* Available at www.quicksilver.com.

Quinn, C. N. (1996). Designing an instructional game: Reflections on "Quest for Independence." *Education and Information Technologies, 1,* 251–269.

Ramsberger, P. F., Hopwood, D., Hargan, C. S., & Underhill, W. G. (1983). *Evaluation of a spatial data management system for basic skills education. Final phase I report for period 7 October 1980–30 April 1983* (HumRRO FR-PRD-83-23). Alexandria, VA: Human Resources Research Organization.

Ricci, K. E., Salas, E., & Cannon-Bowers, J. A. (1996). Do computer-based games facilitate knowledge acquisition and retention? *Military Psychology, 8,* 295–307.

Sindell, M., & Hoang, T. (2001). *Leadership development. Management development* (Info-line). Alexandria, VA: American Society for Training and Development.

Ruben, B. D. (1999). Simulations, games, and experience-based learning: The quest for a new paradigm for teaching and learning. *Simulations and Gaming, 30,* 498–505.

Starkes, J. L., & Lindley, S. (1994). Can we hasten expertise by video simulations? *Quest, 46,* 211–222.

Strater, L. D., Endsley, M. R., Pleban, R. J., & Matthews, M. D. (2001). *Measures of platoon leader situation awareness in virtual decision-making exercises* (Research Report 1770). Alexandria, VA: U.S. Army Research Institute for the Behavioral and Social Sciences.

Sugrue, B., & Clark, R. E. (2000). Media selections for training. In S. Tobias & J. D. Fletcher (Eds.), *Training and retraining: A handbook for business, industry, government, and military* (pp. 208–233). New York: Macmillan.

Tennyson, R. D., & Foshay, W. R. (2000). Instructional systems development. In S. Tobias & J. D. Fletcher (Eds.), *Training and retraining: A handbook for business, industry, government, and the military* (pp. 111–147). New York: Macmillan.

Thomas, P., & Macredie, R. (1994). Games and the design of human–computer interfaces. *Educational Technology, 31,* 134–142.

ThoughtLink. (2000, September). *Effect of Spearhead II in AC3 DL—Experiment plan* (Draft). Vienna, VA: Author.

U.S. Department of the Army. (1994). *The enduring legacy. Leader development for America's Army* (Pamphlet 350–58). Washington, DC: U.S. Department of the Army Headquarters.

U.S. Department of the Army. (1999). *Army field manual no. 22-100.* Washington, DC: U.S. Department of the Army Headquarters.

U.S. Department of the Army. (2001a). *Concepts for the Objective Force* (White Paper). Washington, DC: U.S. Department of the Army Headquarters. Retrieved December 21, 2002, from http://www.army.mil/features/WhitePaper/ObjectiveForceWhitePaper.pdf.

U.S. Department of the Army. (2001b). *The Army: FM 1.* Washington, DC: U.S. Department of the Army Headquarters.

U.S. Department of the Army. (2001c, June). *Operations (FM 3-0), Battle Command.* Washington, DC: U.S. Department of the Army Headquarters.

van Lent, M. (2002, March). *Explainable AI. Preliminary technical design.* Unpublished manuscript, University of Southern California, Institute for Creative Technologies.

Washbush, J., & Gosen, J. (2001). An exploration of game-derived learning in total enterprise simulations. *Simulation and Gaming, 32,* 281–296.

Westbrook, J. I., & Braithwaite, J. (2001). The health care game: An evaluation of a heuristic, web-based simulation. *Journal of Interactive Learning Research, 12,* 89–104.

Wood, L. W., & Stewart, R. W. (1987). Improvement of practical reasoning skills with computer skills. *Journal of Computer-Based Instruction, 14*(2), 49–53.

Woolfolk, A. E. (2001). *Educational psychology* (8th ed.). Needham Heights, MA: Allyn & Bacon.

Yearout, S., & Miles, G. (2001). *Growing leaders. A leader-builder handbook.* Alexandria, VA: American Society for Training and Development.

III

Cognitive Skills Development

6

The Development of Adult Cognition: Understanding Constancy and Change in Adult Learning

Diane F. Halpern
Claremont McKenna College

For much of the history of psychology, adulthood was treated as though it were a relatively uninteresting developmental plateau that followed the rapid rise in physical and cognitive development of adolescence and preceded the steady decline that led to old age and death. The most influential developmental psychologists of the 20th century must have believed that psychological development was halted before most people reached their adult height. For the eminent Swiss developmental psychologist Jean Piaget (1952), final stages of cognitive development were achieved before the adult years were reached.

Several events have come together to create a new interest in adult development, especially in cognitive and emotional domains. Perhaps the most important impetus for making adult development a critical research topic is the phenomenal increase in expected life spans. In the last 100 years or so, life expectancies have increased by several decades (from age 47 at the start of the 20th century to approximately 77 at the start of the 21st century) in most, but not all, regions of the world. The large number of people living well into adulthood and old age has created a need for a better understanding of this stage of life. As John Horn (2001), a psychologist who specializes in adult cognition, recently reminded us that learning and cognitive development do not end on entry into the adult years.

THE NEED FOR LIFELONG LEARNING

There is a riddle that goes something like this: "What do you call a secretary who has not learned new job skills in the last 10 years?" The reader can probably guess the answer—"unemployed." The same answer would be correct for almost any job category above menial labor that can be named. The need for lifelong learning has become more urgent over the last two to three generations as the world has become increasingly complex. The future of our country and our planet requires that a greater proportion of the population achieve an advanced education. Adults who only a generation or two ago may have wondered if they should complete high school now need to continue to learn new and complex cognitive skills throughout their adult years, and this learning needs to build upon a solid foundation of knowledge and thinking skills. The rate at which knowledge has been growing is exponential and the most valued asset of any society in the coming decades is a knowledgeable, thinking workforce.

The need for lifelong learning can clearly be understood by considering the problems and needs of the military, although any other large organization would provide the same rationale. Modern warfare will never again consist of two armies facing off against each other across a battlefield. Large-scale victories will not be won with arm-to-arm combat where physical strength determines the outcome. The tragic events of September 11, 2001, and the horrors like the deaths on the USS Cole have clearly shown that today's wars are wars of intelligence—both in the sense of acquiring and recognizing information and in the intelligent use of information. The best preparation for this unknown and rapidly changing future is the twin abilities to learn efficiently and think critically. Lifelong learning is a necessary reality, not just a slogan. Everyone will need to play the student role at repeated points in his or her life. Adult students will need to return to school periodically throughout their lifetimes to update skills and learn wholly new content areas, and informal on-the-job learning will take on new significance as the nature of jobs changes. Rapid changes in knowledge require new kinds of leadership—leaders who have the necessary knowledge to achieve a goal and leaders who can manage amid the uncertainty of nonstop change. Thus, understanding and enhancing adult learning and thinking skills may be the primary means of developing effective leaders for an ever-changing, knowledge-based world.

If readers are still not persuaded that understanding how adults learn is a central concept for developing leadership, Kiel, Rimmer, Williams, and Dolye (1996) provided a succinct conclusion from their studies on the development of leadership among top-level executives that should convince even the most skeptical: "We have found that a majority of weaknesses in leadership effectiveness are the result of required skills that have never been learned" (68). Regardless of one's view of leadership development as a "developed ability," "learned skill or trait," or "emergent quality," some basic concepts in adult learning are important in the design of effective leadership programs: how to enhance near and far transfer; rote versus higher conceptual learning; the importance of teacher and learner expectations; recognizing cues that signal when specific knowledge, skills, or abilities are needed; and metacognitive monitoring. The principles of adult development and learning are as critical in the design of leadership programs as they are in fostering any other learning outcome. An integral component of quality leadership is the ability to help others learn. Thus, good leaders need to understand how to enhance their own learning and how to design meaningful learning experiences for those they are leading.

THE UNEVEN COURSE OF HUMAN DEVELOPMENT

It is misleading to think about human development as a single variable. There is no single curve that can represent the way humans change over time, because different abilities have different developmental trajectories. There are also important individual differences in the rate at which abilities grow and decline and multiple ways that learning and other accommodations alter the rate of change. It is clear that older models of adulthood as a "plateau" sandwiched between years of growth that preceded adulthood and years of decline that followed adulthood do not present an accurate depiction of the multiple processes undergoing change.

DEFINITIONS

The focus of this chapter is adult learning and cognition. Unlike the other chapters in this volume, it does not focus on leadership per se. It is included in the belief that by understanding and applying general principles of how people learn and think, more effective leadership programs will be designed. *Learning is defined as a relatively permanent change in behavior as a result of experience.* The use of the phrase "relatively permanent" is included to differentiate learning from temporary changes that might be caused by fatigue, hunger, or extremes in temperatures, for example. The inclusion of the phrase "result of experience" is included to differentiate learning from maturational changes such as slowing in response times or the inability to recall names and other proper nouns, which commonly occur as people age.

Cognition refers to the ability to think, learn, and remember. Cognitive psychology has eclipsed traditional learning theories, which were focused on stimulus–response relationships. The cognitive approach assumes that learners are not just passive recipients of information from their environment. They actively seek information and process the information in pursuit of goals (e.g., finding one's way through space).

Development refers to changes that occur over time due to both maturational processes and learning. It is not possible to separate biological contributions to development from environmental contributions. The age-old nature–nurture tug of war is rejected in favor of a new model—a psychobiosocial model in which biological and learning processes have mutually reciprocal effects and, thus, are inextricably related. To clarify the intent of this model, consider, for example, a recent study in which the brains of living (intact) healthy taxi drivers in London showed enlarged portions of their right posterior hippocampus relative to a control group of adults whose employment required less frequent use of spatial skills. The cab drivers showed a positive correlation between the size of the region of the hippocampus that is activated during the recall of complex routes and the number of years they worked in this occupation (Maguire, Frackowiak, & Frith, 1997; Maguire et al., 2000). The finding that size of the hippocampus varied as a function of years spent driving taxis makes it likely that it was a lifetime of complex way-finding that caused the brain structures used in certain visuospatial tasks to increase in size. Studies like this one and others show that it is impossible to separate environmental influences from biological ones because they are mutually dependent.

Adult cognitive development occurs in a social context, which influences rates of cognitive change, motivation, attitudes toward learning and using new knowledge and skills, and health-related variables such as diet and exercise, which can also influence cognition. Outside of the laboratory, individuals' willingness and ability to learn vary as a function of their social role (e.g., parenting an infant, young child, or teen; having novice or expert status in a field), beliefs in their ability to learn, age-related deadlines (e.g., likelihood of a promotion at their current age, years to retirement), opportunities for learning, the interplay of opportunities for formal learning and informal learning, self-development, and virtually every other psychological variable that can be named.

MENTAL AGING IN ADULTHOOD

Traditional texts in adult developmental psychology have always claimed that there are no obvious indicators of mental aging for most people until they are well into their 60s, and that for most people, the effects are minor and easily compensated with the wisdom accumulated by adults in their sixth decade of life. Although this reassuring fact has held up to strict scrutiny and refined experimental methods, we now know that mental declines begin at a surprisingly young age, but the decreases in cognitive ability are not discernible until (approximately) age 60 because younger adults have an excess of "cognitive capital." This excess capital means that earlier declines are not noticeable in everyday contexts. Recent

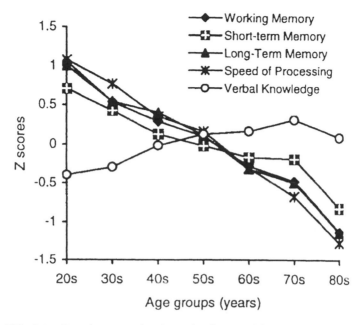

FIG. 6.1. Developmental trajectories for cognitive components—working memory, short-term memory, long-term memory, speed of processing, and verbal knowledge. From Park, D. C., Lautenschlager, G., Hedden, T., Davidson, N. S., Smith, A. D., & Smith, P. K. (2002). Models of visuospatial and verbal memory across the adult life span. *Psychology and Aging, 17,* 299–320. Copyright © 2002 by the American Psychological Association. Reprinted with permission.

research by Denise Park and her colleagues (University of Michigan, 2001) shows that cognitive capacity begins to decline in adults who are in their 20s, with no noticeable loss "even though they are declining at the same rate as people in their 60s and 70s because they have more capital than they need."

As seen in Fig. 6.1, from a news release (University of Michigan, 2001) describing Park's recent research, different cognitive components (or abilities) show different rates of decline. The rate of decline for the memory components is fairly stable beginning at age 20, but verbal knowledge continues to increase through the 70s, and only shows a relatively slight decline into the 80s and beyond. The increase in accumulated knowledge—experience—compensates, in part, for the earlier declines. Although this may seem like depressing news, the more optimistic message is that the decline in memory components is not noticeable in most everyday interactions (but can be documented in laboratory settings) until age 60.

Paul B. Baltes and his colleagues at the Max Planck Institute in Germany (Baltes, Staudinger, & Lindenberger, 1999) have conducted one of the longest

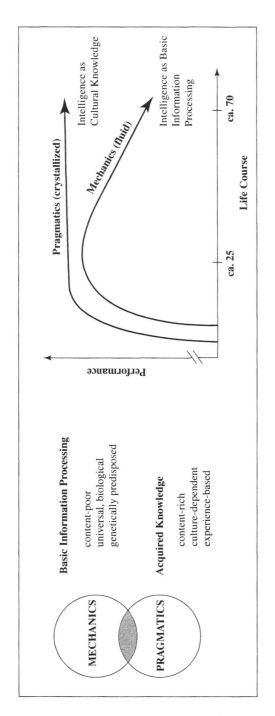

FIG. 6.2. Developmental trajectories for crystallized (pragmatic) and fluid (mechanic) abilities. Reprinted with permission from the *Annual Review of Psychology*, Volume 50 © 1999 by Annual Reviews. www.annualreviews.org

running longitudinal studies of cognitive aging. Like Park, he also differentiated rates of cognitive decline, but he used the distinction between *fluid abilities*, which are used in solving novel problems, and *crystallized abilities*, which require the recall or application of a well-learned task or information. Baltes et al. made a distinction between the basic information processing tasks that are more often studied in laboratory settings (e.g., identifying words that are flashed on a screen for a brief exposure or reacting as quickly as possible—usually with a key press—to some category of stimuli) and those that are pragmatic or used to accomplish a real-world task (e.g., reading a text, solving a real-life problem). Pragmatic tasks benefit more from experience and accumulated wisdom and therefore show fewer signs of cognitive decline than basic tasks. Laboratory studies of basic tasks may present a view of adult cognition that is unnecessarily pessimistic given that performance on pragmatic tasks reveals fewer signs of cognitive aging. For virtually all real-life tasks expected of leaders, performance remains high well into the sixth decade of life (or beyond) under normal aging conditions.

As seen in Fig. 6.2, from Baltes et al.'s (1999) review of life-span intellectual functioning, the growth and steady state of pragmatic or crystallized knowledge over the life course proceeds with a steep growth curve until around age 25, followed by decades of constancy. By contrast, mechanics or fluid abilities show steady growth until around age 25, followed by a constant rate of decline into old age. It is interesting to note that although Park and Baltes et al. used different cognitive measures and parsed cognitive components differently (i.e., Park separated cognition into different memory components and Baltes et al. separated cognition into fluid and crystallized components), the two reported similar scenarios of mental aging. Speed and capacity components begin a steady trajectory of decline in the 20s, verbal and pragmatic components remain constant until old age.

UNDERSTANDING DEVELOPMENTAL TRAJECTORIES

Each of the cognitive trajectories produced by Park and Baltes et al. shows the change of cognitive components as a function of age. The implications of these trajectories are less clear than the general principles that some cognitive components show steady decline beginning in the 20s and others stay constant into old age. It is important to remember that these are descriptions of normal aging. One implication of these graphic depictions is that developmental change is a constant and gradual process—there are no sudden declines, so there should not be any single age where cognitive capacities are "suddenly" diminished. Mental aging can be conceptualized as a steady slope, with no abrupt precipices or "falling off" stages. These data suggest that small accommodations over the life span are a better strategy for offsetting cognitive aging effects than are any plans for change in cognitive strategies at a specific age.

Learning continues through the adult life span, but component processes like working memory—the ability to hold "bits" of information in an actively aware state while transforming them in some way (e.g., imagining what a map would look like if it were held in a different orientation)—slows, and the ability to simultaneously perform multiple novel tasks declines. However, multiple well-known tasks would show little change because crystallized intelligence remains fairly steady. There are also age-related declines in the ability to ignore irrelevant information (e.g., irrelevant movement on a screen) and declines in the ability to inhibit a response (e.g., not press a lever when the response of pressing a lever is well learned). Fortunately, most adults show good adjustment to multiple transitions in adulthood. Often without conscious awareness, they select developmentally appropriate goals, use compensatory mechanisms (e.g., use a written list to compensate for memory decline), and often take preventive actions like improving their diet and increasing cardiovascular exercise (Heckhausen, 1997).

INTELLIGENCE AS DEVELOPED EXPERTISE

An important dimension of adult cognition is missing from the mainstream models of adult intelligence—the idea that we develop expertise in specialized areas and maintain the ability to perform at a high level in our area of expertise can be conceptualized as a type of intelligence. Cognitive tasks are often categorized into multiple categories that depend on the length of the memory system being used (e.g., short-term or long-term), the type of information being processed (e.g., visuospatial or verbal), modality of input (e.g., visual working memory, auditory working memory), and speed of decision making across a variety of cognitive tasks. Each of these combinations of length of memory, type of information, modality, and speed at a decision task has a somewhat different developmental trajectory through adulthood and all decline at a steady rate through adulthood, except for well-learned and well-practiced "assemblies." Adults seem to maintain a fairly high and consistent level of functioning for declarative knowledge in those areas where they have their greatest expertise. Adult thinking and problem solving in the area of one's expertise is the age-related compensation that we achieve with advancing years. However, extant tests are not measuring these important aspects of thinking and problem solving, and thus may be providing a far too gloomy picture of adult cognition. Older adults demonstrate high levels of reasoning, memory, and cognitive speed in their areas of expertise (e.g., playing bridge, flying planes), yet score lower than their younger colleagues on cognitive tests. The accumulated wisdom that is manifested in one's area of expertise can often more than compensate for the greater ease of learning of younger adults.

MOTIVATION TO LEARN

Most people tend to talk about learning as though it were a single process; however, learning is a multifaceted phenomenon. There can be no simple or single law of learning because there are many types of "learnings," each with somewhat specialized law. Some types of learning are effortless; others require considerable effort. There are large individual differences in people's willingness to engage in new learning experiences. There is a huge literature on this topic, and increasingly, research on motivation to learn is differentiating between the adult learner in settings that involve learning new skills and knowledge and in continuous learning situations where the goal is to make gradual additions to one's knowledge and skills—a more usual paradigm for informal and on-the-job learning (e.g., Colquitt & Simmering, 1998).

The motivation to learn also depends, in part, on the characteristics of the work environment and the consequences for success and failure at the newly learned task. Consider a hypothetical chief executive officer (CEO) who is expert in a known technology. She may lack the background of some of the people who report to her that will make learning a new technology easier for them, or she may just fear that she will look less competent if a new and unfamiliar technology is adopted. This hypothetical CEO is not likely to embrace the benefits of the new technology unless learning proceeds in a way that allows her to conceal her difficulties with the new task (i.e., protect her image as an intelligent person) and will not threaten her position of leadership in the group. Organizational rewards and messages about the need for new learning and the consequences of failing to learn need to be carefully considered or motivation to learn can be a major impediment at a time when continuous and lifelong learning needs to be a reality.

The U.S. Department of Labor, Bureau of Labor Statistics (1995) estimated that 70% of learning through the workplace is informal (also called "experiential"), meaning that learning takes place outside a classroom setting or with pedagogy that is closer to modeling or coaching than formalized instruction. The "need to know" is often more obvious in informal job settings because the information being learned is more likely to be used immediately to complete a task. Correspondingly, the motive to learn may be higher than in classroom settings where the link between the information to be learned and its use is harder to discern. Given that most on-the-job training is self-directed and informal, it is imperative that organizational leaders understand how people learn so they can incorporate principles for good learning into the design of workplaces.

Expectancy Models

Albert Bandura (1986, 2001) proposed a causal model that was designed to explain self-efficacy, an individual's own belief in his or her ability to learn or succeed at a task. The large body of research on self-efficacy that has accumulated over the past 25 years suggests that people who are high on measures of self-efficacy will volunteer for new learning opportunities and take more responsibility for monitoring and furthering their own learning than individuals who score low on self-efficacy measures (Bandura, 1986). High self-efficacy is (arguably) an indirect measure of motivation to learn. It is used to explain the origins and operations of self-confidence in the ability to achieve a goal—in this case, to learn a task. Self-efficacy models have been used successfully in many studies to explain individual differences in learning attitudes.

Recent advances in expectancy models have suggested that the extent to which a person believes in his or her ability to achieve a goal needs to be divided into two distinct parts. One part is concerned with learning; the other, performance. An individual might, for example, have high confidence in his or her ability to learn something, but not be confident in his or her ability to demonstrate that learning by meeting some normed standard. Similarly, a person might feel confident that he or she can learn a new type of technology, but not at all confident about performing well on a test where he or she has to demonstrate the ability to use the technology to a panel of judges. The distinction between beliefs about one's ability to learn and one's ability to demonstrate or perform a task as evidence of learning can explain some of the learning goals that people choose for themselves (Colquitt & Simmering, 1998; Dweck, 1986). When designing a learning program for adults, it is important to focus on the way learning and performance are assessed. Will the performance be graded, which now adds the possibility of failure, or will assessment be incorporated without a rating in the learning cycle? Will there be some cut point below which the individual "fails?" Of course, there are some tasks and knowledge where "fail points" are necessary (e.g., pilot training), but they are not necessary in every learning setting. Careful thought should be given to the way learning is assessed.

The Effects of Feedback

Standard learning texts always emphasized the need for feedback or knowledge of results as an essential component for enhancing learning, but more recent reviews have shown that feedback is a complex variable that sometimes hinders learning (Kluger & DeNisi, 1996; Quinones, 1995). When data from many studies were combined in a meta-analysis, the overall effect size for feedback was a healthy $d = .41$, but this sizable effect masks the fact that more than one third of the studies showed that feedback depressed learning and performance. Feedback is important in that it provides information to the learner about his or her performance, but the learner still has to derive meaning from it. What does good or poor performance really mean to a learner? Is successful learning indicative of the intelligence or skill of the learner, the difficulty of the learning task, the way learning performance is assessed, or the amount of effort expended? Additionally, how will the feedback be used? Do salary and other types of advancement depend on the assessment? Is there a competition that is being gauged with the feedback? Learning settings need to be designed so that the type of feedback is matched to the intended reason for the learning task. Even a formerly simple concept like feedback needs to be understood in terms of its intended use.

Feedback provides recipients with information about how the person or organization providing the feedback feels about their performance. If the feedback is part of a performance review that will be used in determining raises, promotions, and other types of compensation, it signals positive or negative consequences for the future, and it goes beyond information that can be *used* by the learner to judgments *about* the learner. On the other hand, if feedback is private and its intended use is to improve performance, then the recipients are more likely to accept it and use it for this purpose.

The Importance of Errors

Errors play an important, but often overlooked, role in training and performance. An intolerance for errors can have unintended detrimental effects (Gully, Payne, Koles, & Whiteman, 2002). Errors provide more information about learners' understanding and cognitive structures than correct responses, and thus can be used to diagnose and correct faulty understanding or other variables that contribute to poor performance (e.g., performance variables). Of course, it is desirable to avoid errors for well-learned behaviors, but when the behavior is exploratory and especially during the training phase, errors need to be perceived as an opportunity for further learning. Creative responses, especially when they are in response to novel situations, will be reduced if there is little or no tolerance for errors (Smith, Ford, & Kozlowski, 1997).

INDIVIDUAL DIFFERENCES

Models designed to explain the "motivation to learn" are useful for understanding group outcomes, but individual people differ along multiple dimensions. Psychologists may be able to use models of individual differences to predict average group performance, but predictions at the level of the individual will always be more problematic and error-prone. The psychological literature on personality is vast, so only some of the most relevant personality variables are included here.

Research on adult cognition has focused on selected personality factors as a way of understanding their mutual influences of cognition and personality. A leading model of personality focuses on only five basic factors—neuroticism, agreeableness, extraversion, openness to experience, and conscientiousness (Mc-Crae & Costa, 1997). This model is commonly known as the "Big Five" theory of personality. Of these five factors, conscientiousness and openness to experience have the most obvious connection to adult learning. Conscientiousness is usually defined as being diligent, concerned with accuracy, and punctual. It is often associated with higher levels of productivity in a variety of occupations and has the most generalizability of the personality factors (Hochwarter, Witt, & Kacmar, 2000). Theoretically, it would be expected that anyone who is conscientious will be concerned with accuracy and will work to a higher level (higher criterion) than a less conscientious person, but there may be a cost associated with this trait in that a highly conscientious person may complete less work than a person who is less concerned with accuracy. Openness to experience is implicated in the willingness or motivation to learn because learning leads to new ways of thinking or new ways of performing tasks. Although these generalizations about conscientiousness and openness to experience may be broadly true, people are influenced by many situational variables (what is being learned, prior learning histories, how they are being assessed), and thus, considered in isolation, the personality traits do not offer much promise in understanding the most important variables that influence learning.

Recent research designed to test a theoretical model of "motivation to lead" found that conscientiousness loaded onto relevant factors in the proposed model—leadership self-efficacy (belief in one's ability to lead effectively), past leadership experience, and social-normative motivation to lead (sense of duty or responsibility to lead)—and openness to experience loaded onto leadership self-efficacy and past leadership experience (Chan & Drasgow, 2001). Thus, the same personality factors that are theoretically associated with learning motivation are also associated with the motivation to lead. It seems that good leaders and good learners share some similar personality traits.

There are several reasons to believe that what some researchers call a *need for cognition* may be a more useful personality variable for understanding the way people approach learning tasks (Cacioppo, Petty, Feinstein, & Jarvis, 1996). This need for cognition is defined as an individual's tendency to engage in and enjoy effortful cognitive endeavors and has been examined in well over 100 empirical studies. The construct is positively related to the amount of information recalled, the number of thoughts generated, higher levels of knowledge, better performance on college coursework, the likelihood of correcting an initial judgment if it is deemed incorrect, and a host of other variables that are important in high-level learning and performance. It may be that need for cognition is conceptually similar to motivation for learning and can be used as a proxy variable for motivation to lead. Taken together, these constructs may be the critical drivers of effective leader self-development.

Relationship Among Personality Variables, Interests, Motivational Traits, and Cognitive Abilities

In a large-scale study using college students as participants, Ackerman, Bowen, Beier, and Kanfer (2001) administered a broad battery of tests including ability tests, self-report interest scales, personality assessments, and activity and experience questionnaires. Although these authors were specifically addressing the question of sex differences in tests that load on crystallized and fluid intelligence scales, their work has larger significance for the entire field of individual differences. They found that knowledge in "supportive domains" can have large influences on knowledge in a target domain (e.g., knowledge of calculus has a large effect on knowledge of physics). In examining the relationship among interests, personality, and abilities, Ackerman et al. (2001) used clusters of traits, including several different measures of personality, abilities, motivation, interests, and self-concepts that influence the ability or willingness to invest one's cognitive resources in developing a domain of knowledge. Ackerman believed that a major determining factor in domain knowledge can be related to a small number of trait complexes, which either support or hinder cognitive development in an area of knowledge. Research on trait complexes suggests that providing experiences with a wide range of activities where individuals can experience success may be a useful way of creating interests that support cognitive abilities, although this possibility remains speculative.

HOW WE LEARN

Psychologists already have a substantial body of research that could be used to inform programs designed to foster learning for leadership. Unfortunately, the research literature is usually ignored as the stakeholders in education and leadership development grasp for the ephemeral "magic" of quick fixes. Anyone involved in leadership development has probably received countless glossy brochures advertising leadership scales (with no indicators of validity, reliability, or any psychometric property), training programs, games, and simulations that have no empirical support as to their effectiveness, and a variety of "feel good" materials that vaguely look like something we would want leaders to know. Far too many leadership training and development programs are atheoretical, not grounded in what we know about adult learning, and nonempirical. Perhaps an appreciation for including assessment in any learning program is an indicator of a leader who will seek and use information when making decisions. What follows are some basic principles that could be applied in any adult learning situation, including distance education with online components; learning from text, laboratory, and classroom instruction; and learning in informal learning settings. An extensive list of references supporting these conclusions can be found in Halpern and Hakel (2002).

Basic Principles

1. What and how much is learned in any situation depends heavily on prior knowledge and experience. Psychologists use the term "construction of knowledge" because each learner builds meaning using what is already known. For example, in an explanation of this principle in *How People Learn* (Bransford, Brown, & Cocking, 1999), we are told about a fish who learns about the dry world from a bird. When the bird describes beings who can walk upright and breathe air, the fish imagines fish-looking people walking on their tails, with both gills surrounded with water and lungs filled with air. The best predictor of what is learned at the completion of a lesson, course, or informal learning experience is what the learner thinks and knows at the start of the lesson, course, or informal learning experience. Unfortunately, prior beliefs and earlier learning opportunities, especially when the learning is informal, are usually ignored in the design of learning programs. Even adults are treated as though they were tabula rasa.

Applications for Education and Training. Assess learner knowledge and understanding at the start of instruction, probing for (unstated) underlying assumptions and beliefs that may influence the knowledge, skills, and abilities to be learned and test for changes in knowledge structures as learning progresses. Look for postlearning drifts, as learner understanding may drift toward what it was at the start of instruction.

2. We maintain mental models (beliefs) for a wide variety of complex phenomena including those we encounter in the physical world (e.g., moving objects) and social world (e.g., stereotypes about members of groups) because, for the most part, they make sense to us. To assess learning we need to understand how our conceptual models have changed or resisted change. Our models of the world "work," and are therefore difficult to change. Individuals' beliefs about the world are organized into mental models that make sense and work, that is, models that do a reasonably good job in their day-to-day life. These models or schema represent connected understanding that influences the way we know many related concepts. Because these models are often implicit, that is, not consciously known, it can be difficult to identify their influences.

Applications for Education and Training. Be aware of ways in which learners are acquiring knowledge that conflicts with or replaces the desired learning. For example, a learner may have an implicit model of good leadership that was acquired from many years of watching Captain Kirk on *Star Trek*. From the learner's perspective, these implicit models work well, a fact that could make it more difficult to learn the leadership skills being taught if the skills to be learned are different from those modeled by Captain Kirk.

3. Learning is influenced by learners' and instructors' epistemologies (theories about learning). Academic motivation is related to beliefs about learning. Many adults believe that they cannot "do math," or understand science, or write poetry, or succeed in some other academic discipline or at some task. When one asks them about this belief, one finds that what they are really saying is that they believe that learning should be easy, but when they learn in these disciplines, it is effortful. What they do not know is that learning and remembering involve multiple, interdependent processes. Some types of learning occur implicitly, that is, without conscious awareness. Other types of learning are very easy, whereas still others are effortful, perhaps even painful and aversive. It is only after individuals invest in the hard work of learning that they find additional learning in these fields becomes easy and more automatic.

Many people maintain fixed beliefs about the nature of learning and these beliefs guide how they explain good learning and learning failures and, as predicted by expectancy theory, the willingness to engage in learning tasks (Dweck, 1986). Beliefs about learning tend to be invariant across learning tasks and contexts, but there is no single set of learning principles that will always work or all-purpose explanation of success and failure. The best way to learn and recall something will depend, in part, on what it is one wants learners to learn and recall, as well as what they already know, and the learners' own beliefs about the nature of learning.

Applications for Education and Training. Have learners articulate their implicit beliefs about learning so they can be examined, and if desired, include in the learning task the learning of a new model of how people learn.

4. Experience alone is a poor teacher. There are countless examples where what people learn from experience is, in fact, systematically wrong. For example, a therapist may believe that a particular intervention worked when a client improves after that intervention; of course, if most clients enter therapy at times of crisis, then improvement is likely no matter what intervention is taken because of the ubiquitous effect of regression to the mean. If a client does not improve, then therapists reason that he or she was too sick to benefit from the good treatment. There are countless examples of this sort of erroneous thinking, where beliefs about the world are maintained and strengthened despite the fact that they are wrong. People end up with great confidence in their erroneous beliefs. Confidence is not a reliable indictor of depth or veracity of learning. In fact, research in metacognition has shown that most people are poor judges of how well they comprehend a complex topic (Maki, 1998). What is missing from most real-life situations is systematic and corrective feedback about the consequences of various actions. In the absence of reliable and regular feedback, we tend to believe that our interpretations of social events are accurate or the reasoning behind a political belief system is valid when it may not be.

Although experience alone is a poor teacher, guided learning or learning with an experiential component is the primary mode of on-the-job learning. Skills and knowledge may develop best when a combination of formal and informal learning experiences are used (Grolnic, 2000). If informal (or experiential) learning is planned, the relevant workplace activities that develop the targeted skills and abilities need to be identified. There also needs to be sufficient time and practice allowed for a beneficial outcome.

Applications for Education and Training.   Plan deliberate instruction of the to-be-learned knowledge, skills, and abilities to complement informal on-the-job learning. Incorporate systematic informational feedback in instructional design.

5. Lectures are a satisfactory arrangement for learning if the desired outcome is to produce learners who can repeat or recognize the information presented, but one of the worst arrangements for the promotion of in-depth understanding.   There are two related points in this statement—the problem that lecturing is not optimal for deep learning and the reliance on recognition tests, which most often provide evidence of shallow learning, as an index of learning. These two problems feed on each other because large-lecture learning is often assessed with multiple-choice tests, especially when the number of learners is large. Large lecture classes where learning is assessed with multiple-choice tests is a relatively low-cost way of teaching and assessing learning, so it is easy to understand the widespread use of this pedagogical model.

As deWinstanley and Bjork (2002) recognized, learning is not like recording a verbatim account of something that was heard or read—it is an interpretive process where students are active participants. Learners need "cues" that trigger the interpretation and cause them to engage the material actively, even if they are sitting silently in a large lecture. It is possible to get learners to elaborate information that is presented in lectures by relating the new information to information that is already well known, using imagery, asking probing questions that test for understanding, or applying other methods of discourse analysis (Graesser, Person, & Hu, 2002).

Graesser et al. (2002) argued that "deep" comprehension occurs when learners generate their own explanations about the causes and consequences of events and the logical "derivatives" of the information they learned. They developed a software program that asks questions learners need for a deep understanding of the information to be learned. The model of discourse processing they used in their software program is based on a hypothetical interchange in which a teacher asks a question, the student responds, and the teacher evaluates the response, with the main departure from this model being the substitution of the computer program for the role of the teacher. Their program incorporates assessment into a learning cycle so that students learn from the evaluation of their responses.

Applications for Education and Training. Break long periods of lecture into shorter segments with periods that require active learning. Test for conceptual learning, not simply recognition.

6. The process of remembering influences what learners will and will not remember at different times in the future. Asking learners to recall some information leads to selective "forgetting" for other related information that they were not asked to recall, and when tested soon after the initial learning, students often perform less well on a later test than when the initial test is given after a longer retention interval. Principles of learning are difficult to discuss in isolation, because activities that occur at the time of the initial learning, during the retention interval, and at recall are interdependent, working together to determine what is remembered at some time after the first recall test. According to standard "memory trace" theories of how we remember, the act of remembering strengthens some memory traces and weakens—or perhaps fails to strengthen—others, a fact that should influence how we test students (Druckman & Bjork, 1994). Another variable that is often ignored in pedagogical design is the length of the retention interval between the initial learning and the first test. Students who are tested frequently receive higher scores than students who are tested infrequently, which creates the impression that frequent testing is a sound educational practice. However, frequent testing also leads to overconfidence in learners who erroneously believe that their long-term retention for the information will be better than it actually is, a belief that should lead them to put less time and effort into studying the material for future recall (Benjamin, Bjork, & Schwartz, 1998). The detrimental effect of testing soon after information is learned is another example where the short-term benefits of an educational practice mask the long-term detriments associated with it. Assessment is a critical determinant of what is retained and cannot be thought of as an "add-on" or external component in the design of effective training programs.

Applications for Education and Training. Plan tests so that the information that is sampled at recall is the information considered to be most important. Use multiple tests so that more information gets recalled. Do not test immediately after learning, even though it may appear that learners are learning better with immediate tests.

7. Less is more, especially with regard to long-term retention and transfer. Repair manuals for complex machinery or user manuals for many computer programs can be mammoth. Instructional programs need to consider the balance between how much and how well something is learned. Instructional designers need to make careful choices. An emphasis on in-depth understanding of basic principles is often a better instructional design than a more encyclopedic coverage of topics. If cursory knowledge of a broad area is desirable, then learners and instructors should share this goal so that they can learn and teach in ways that will achieve a more cursory knowledge of the information to be learned. However, if a deep understanding of basic principles is the desired outcome, then teaching and learning will proceed differently toward this goal. Instructors and learners should have clearly articulated goal statements at the start of instruction that guide instructional design and learning activities.

Applications for Education and Training.   Consider depth and breadth of knowledge that is needed when planning learning activities and communicate these objectives to learners.

8. The single most important variable in promoting long-term retention and transfer is "practice at retrieval"—learners need to generate responses, with minimal retrieval cues, repeatedly, over time and with varied applications, so that recall becomes more fluent and more likely to occur across a variety of contexts and domains of knowledge.   Practice at retrieval necessarily occurs over time and within a context. Transfer of training can be facilitated by altering the context for retrieval. Thus, practice at retrieval, the length of time between learning and retrieval and subsequence tests of retrieval, and retrieval context are interdependent variables that jointly determine what and how much is remembered.

Practice at Retrieval.   Simply stated, information that gets retrieved becomes more retrievable. In the jargon of cognitive psychology, the strength of the memory trace for the information that was retrieved grows stronger with each retrieval. Practice at retrieval facilitates recall at a later time more than additional practice without retrieval or more time expended in the learning phase. For example, the *testing effect* is a term used for the oft-repeated finding that taking a test can facilitate subsequent test performance, but only for the items that were recalled on the first test (Wheeler & Roediger, 1992). It is interesting to note that practice at retrieval may be a particularly good technique for learning second-language vocabulary, face–name associations, and technical terms. The benefits of retrieving (information that was learned earlier) and generating (producing answers in response to new questions) information are among the most robust findings in the learning literature (Cull, 2000; Lawson & Chinnappan, 1994; Wittrock, 1990).

Spacing of Retrieval Intervals.   The effect of practice at retrieval is necessarily tied to a second robust finding in the learning literature—spaced practice is preferable to massed practice. Bjork and his coauthors (e.g., Druckman & Bjork, 1994) suggested spacing the retrieval intervals (also known as tests or tests of retrieval) such that the interval between each test becomes increasingly longer, with the actual time between intervals chosen such that retrieval accuracy remains high. For example, consider learning new vocabulary in a second language. The first test could be 1 day after the initial learning, the second test, 3 days after the first, the third test, 1 week after the second, and a fourth test, 1 month after the third. The intervals for each succeeding test are determined by the level of accuracy on the preceding test.

The Effect of Retrieval Context. Most often, knowledge, skills, and abilities that are learned in one context are needed in multiple and varied contexts. The problem in getting knowledge, skills, and abilities to transfer—that is, to be spontaneously retrieved and used—is that there are no obvious cues to trigger recall in contexts that are different from the one in which the learning was achieved. This is a particular problem when the information to be learned is a critical thinking skill because critical thinking skills are transcontextual (needed in many different contexts). Critical thinkers need to create the recall cues from the structural aspects of the problem or argument, so that when the structural aspects are present, they can serve as cues for retrieval. When critical thinking skills are learned so that they transfer appropriately and spontaneously, critical thinkers can focus on the structure of a problem or argument so the underlying characteristics become salient instead of the domain-specific surface characteristics.

Applications for Education and Training. Use repeated retrieval trials, spaced over time with increasing intervals between the trials, and teach and test with varied examples so that the information that is learned will transfer across contexts and domains of knowledge.

9. Variable conditions at learning can make the learning more effortful and less fun, but they also result in better learning (long-term retrieval). "Presenting key concepts from more than one standpoint and demonstrating the relevance of key ideas in multiple contexts" will encourage variability in learning (deWinstanley & Bjork, 2002, p. 24). In the jargon of cognitive psychology, key ideas will have multiple retrieval cues and thus be more "available" in memory— that is, easier to remember. Lovett and Greenhouse (2000) found that when students learned to solve multiple problems using varied problem sets during learning, the initial learning took significantly longer, but the students who learned with a variety of examples performed better on transfer problem sets than students who practiced only on similar problems. Thus, it seems that complex information is learned best and is most likely to transfer to novel situations when it is taught using a variety of different examples, even though the initial learning make take longer and be more effortful.

Principles derived from empirical studies show the successful transfer of complex skills can serve as a model for instructional design. Blocking and massed practice can give a false sense of mastery, whereas variability at learning shows learning deficiencies and allows for earlier remediation. Some misalignment of text and class materials will require that students do the work of integrating the information. Variability at learning is a basic principle, which like practice at retrieval, is associated with higher effort and less favorable student ratings. However, like practice at retrieval, it pays high dividends for the effort exerted.

As in previous examples, the match between the way the information is intended to be used and the way it is learned is critical. If the goal is to create "deep" knowledge structures that can be used to solve novel problems in multiple contexts (as opposed to recognition memory), then the additional effort of variable learning conditions will pay off in enhanced memory.

Applications for Education and Training.   Vary learning conditions, even though it will increase the time and effort needed to learn as a way of increasing conceptual learning and long-term retention.

10. Re-representing: When learners are required to take information that is presented in one format (e.g., words) and translate it to an alternative format (e.g., a schematic diagram), learning is generally enhanced.   It is commonly accepted that humans process information via two distinct channels— one for visuospatial information and one for auditory–verbal information (Baddeley, 1999; Halpern & Collaer, in press). It seems that active learning is even more effective when learners integrate information from both visuospatial and verbal representations (Mayer, 1999, 2001, 2002). The underlying idea in re-representing is that learners required to draw visuospatial "concept maps" need to create an organization for information and need to communicate their organization via a "map" or "network" of ideas—two activities that enhance learning. Complex concepts can be related to each other in numerous ways, and it is the depiction of the correct relationship among concepts that is central to all graphic organizing techniques.

Networks are graphic organizers in which several different types of relationships are made explicit. Dansereau and his colleagues have conducted much of the work in this area. He developed a training manual and program for counselors in substance abuse programs where concept maps (he called them *guide* maps) were used to create treatment plans and assess progress in the program (Dees & Dansereau, 2000). He found that these maps promote organized thinking in the messy real world of drug treatment and that they can be guides for organizing future learning.

Students report that concept mapping is a more effortful learning experience, but it pays off in longer term gains—a common theme for many of the techniques that are beneficial for long-term retention. Similarly, requiring writing (explaining in words) in a mathematics or schematic learning task takes advantage of dual coding strategies in memory. Mayer (2002) applied the idea of dual-processing channels for processing information to the design of educationally effective multimedia. He reported large gains in student understanding and retention when multimedia are designed to take advantage of both channels. Verbal explanations and animated scenarios were used either alone or together in scientific lessons. He found that verbal narration combined with animation yielded the greatest educational gains. It is also true that adults often have preferred modes of learning—verbal or visual. By requiring both types of information processing in learning, the two can support an enhanced understanding better than reliance on one mode. (Readers familiar with dual coding theories of memory and cognition will recognize re-representing as an application of that theory.)

Applications for Education and Training. Have learners draw concept maps for material that is primarily verbal and write verbal descriptions, conclusions, and summaries for information that is primarily visuospatial. Use both verbal and visuospatial processing for all learning tasks.

HOW TO ACCELERATE LEARNING: TEACHING FOR TRANSFER AND LONG-TERM RETENTION

Everyday technology is becoming increasingly complex. Many automobiles now come equipped with global positioning systems that are designed to help us move through space, we have new word processing programs to help us handle "paper" work, and data forecasting programs to help us plan our money are a necessary pain for almost anyone who invests their money. The number of new technologies we need to learn continues to increase at a rapid rate. Large numbers of adults are looking for ways to learn these complex systems more quickly and with less effort. Instructional designs need to place greater emphasis on teaching for transfer so that adult learners can adjust to emerging technologies quickly— not needing to relearn the technology every time they use it. With these goals in mind, new learning can be accelerated because it can build on a solid base of prior learning. To remain competitive, modern organizations must become learning organizations, and successful leaders need to understand and incorporate learning opportunities into the day-to-day operations of their organizations or risk becoming obsolete.

A learning program that incorporates several of the previously discussed "ways we learn" would be expected to show superior gains in learning, regardless of whether the objective is enhancing leadership skills or helping leaders acquire necessary knowledge for their organization. However, instructional design is a time-consuming process, and is usually given little attention, when in fact it should be the engine that drives all learning programs.

RECOMMENDATIONS FOR FUTURE
RESEARCH

To begin designing learning programs around these basic principles, we already have a sufficient body of knowledge about how adults learn. But there are many research questions that need to be addressed.

1. We know how to assess learning, but how do we assess the intelligent use of learned information? In other words, how do we know if the learned information will be used in thoughtful ways and not applied in a rote fashion in situations where other responses might have been better? If most adult learning is, in fact, informally achieved in the course of doing one's job (U.S. Department of Labor, Bureau of Labor Statistics, 1995), how can we assess the quality of that learning and compare it to more formal (classroom type) learning? As the demands of contemporary life become increasingly complicated, we need adults who can learn and think critically. There are no good tests of critical thinking for adults, yet the development of critical thinking is the most often mentioned outcome from an advanced education, and surely a main goal for a quality military—or any organization. We cannot gauge the success of an educational intervention if there are no good ways to measure gains. The absence of a quality measure of critical thinking makes it likely that we are missing an important dimension of adult cognitive functioning—one that is more closely aligned with expertise than with subcomponents of intelligence, such as using data appropriately, demonstrating causal reasoning, thinking with numbers, and recognizing bias (Halpern, 2003).

2. How can we design research that can "scale up," that is, research designs for large and diverse groups of learners, multiple researchers, and teachers, with at least a quasi-randomized design that will allow stronger causal inferences than most educational research designs? Learning research needs to be funded for longer periods of time so that long-term retention and transfer can be assessed using strong research designs that permit causal conclusions (e.g., random assignment of participants to conditions). Long-term retention and transfer are the reasons for education, but we cannot determine the effectiveness of any educational application or intervention if the funding runs out before learners leap the many educational gaps that often signal the end of a learning assessment.

3. How does an individual's model of how people learn influence the nature of his or her own learning? Some research has suggested that the success of Asian cultures in advancing learning is, at least in part, attributable to the Asian belief that intelligence is not a fixed quantity, but that it can be modified with hard work (Peng & Nisbett, 1999). What would happen if educational programs were designed to change beliefs about learning such that more people believed in the "effort-exerted" model of learning and intelligence? Would we produce better learners who understand the need for hard work as a component to developing one's abilities instead of the belief that ability is a fixed quantity that cannot be expanded? Expectancy models predict that by changing fundamental beliefs about the nature of learning, we could improve learning itself, but this hypothesis has not been studied on a large scale and not with adults, whose beliefs may be less malleable than those of children. There are many people who believe that they cannot be effective leaders. We do not know if changing this fundamental belief about one's abilities would, in fact, help them learn necessary skills of leadership.

4. How do different types of feedback influence learning, including the willingness to learn a complex task? We know a great deal about schedules of feedback, but much less about the way feedback will be used and interpreted as a variable affecting learning. In an extensive series of studies, Amabile (1996) showed that evaluative feedback is detrimental to the creative process. When feedback is used in ways that can result in loss of self-esteem, status, or rank, it may hinder learners with low self-efficacy (people who do not expect to be successful at the learning task), but help learners with high self-efficacy (people who believe they will be successful at the learning task). A better understanding of the conditions under which feedback enhances or reduces learning is needed, especially as it pertains to leaders, where negative feedback about one's performance may be inherent in some leadership positions.

5. The motivation to learn is increasingly important as adults need to make learning choices throughout their adult years. When will someone readily engage in a learning task and when will the same person avoid new learning? Many adults are deciding for themselves what they want to learn and when and how they want to learn it. We know very little about the variables that contribute to learner-directed learning. How do other social roles (parent, spouse, commander) influence one's willingness to assume the role of learner? How can we make learning an exciting and desirable activity? What are we doing that causes some people to avoid new learning? There are unlimited hypotheses, but few have been tested in laboratory settings.

6. How can we assess intelligent thinking in adults in their areas of expertise? It is unfortunate that this area of human cognition is not well recognized. We may be losing high-quality talent by relying on measures that are easier to administer and score, but do not present a valid picture of adult cognition. Consider a hypothetical mechanic who is highly skilled in engine repair and has decades of experience on one type of engine. When a major change in the design of engines is made, supervisory personnel may need to determine who should train to work on the new type of engine. A general test of intelligence, a multiple-choice test with questions that are not specific to the engine he or she knows, a speeded test of some type of repair, or a test of his or her ability to learn some new component of engine repair might underestimate his or her true potential. It may take this person a little longer to make the change to the new engine than it would a younger person or someone with a different type of background, but after the initial period of learning, he or she could perform at a high level. We need to know more about the nature of expertise and the ways it offsets the effects of aging.

7. Can adults learn to be more accurate in their judgments of learning and knowing, and, if so, would these gains translate into better learning, given that most people cannot accurately assess the quality of their own knowledge and understanding of complex topics? The general inability to make accurate assessments of one's knowledge and comprehension is made worse because most people erroneously believe that they can accurately make such assessments. Two examples from this large literature are a study by Pressley and Ghatala (1988), which found that students were as confident in the accuracy of their answers to questions they answered incorrectly as they were to questions they answered correctly, and a study by Rawson, Dunlosky, and Thiede (2000), which found that judgments about metacomprehension tended to be quite poor. We do not know if people can be trained to provide more accurate self-assessments, and, if so, whether improved metacognition will lead to better learning. This is an area ripe for research, especially with older adults.

8. How can we assess gains in critical thinking given that there is a large research literature showing that people can become better thinkers when they receive specific instruction designed to improve critical thinking? A strong case for critical thinking instruction comes from several different studies by Nisbett and his colleagues (Nisbett, 1993). For example, in one study, Nisbett and his coauthors phoned students at their home after the coursework was completed, under the guise of conducting a survey. They found that students spontaneously applied the thinking skills that they had been taught in school when they encountered novel problems, even when the school-related context cues were absent (Fong, Krantz, & Nisbett, 1986). In a different study, college students learned inductive reasoning tasks using realistic scenarios from many different domains. Unfortunately, research where critical thinking was taught to adults in the middle adult years is seriously lacking. On-the-job training programs that teach critical thinking need to look at objective measures of their effectiveness. Research based on college students (and graduate and law students, who are often in their late 20s and early 30s on average) all concluded that critical thinking is "a skill" and that "it is transferable" (Jepson, Krantz, & Nisbett, 1993, p. 82). Despite the fact that there is a vast research literature all pointing to the same conclusion—that adults can learn to be better thinkers—there have been no high-quality, large-scale studies to investigate the extent to which thinking can be improved, the real-world implications of this fact, and the best ways to achieve the important goal of improving critical thinking (for all ability levels). This is an important area for future research, especially in leadership training because of the critical necessity for leaders who can think critically.

9. What are the critical differences that underlie informal learning when compared with learning that occurs in formal educational settings? Modeling, either through a formal mentoring program or without a formalized structure (Johnson, 2002), coaching (Kiel et al., 1996), and on-the-job learning (McCauley, Ruderman, Ohlott, & Morrow, 1994) are important contexts for learning. Intuitively, it seems that a major portion of "what we know" is learned in informal settings—estimates from the U.S. Department of Labor, Bureau of Labor Statistics (1995) support this theory—but we do not know what sorts of informal experiences lead to good learning, and we do not have good assessment techniques to identify the effectiveness of different types of learning (e.g., interpersonal skills, job-specific skills, general cognitive enhancement) in informal settings. Valid and reliable measures are difficult to obtain in informal settings where much of the learning is "incidental" or not planned in advance. Experience plays a key role in learning, especially for practical skills and in jobs where skills and knowledge develop over time, but the identification of quality "learning opportunities" remains more elusive, especially when considering opportunities to learn about leadership (McCauley et al., 1994).

10. How can we effectively disseminate learning principles from the science of learning so that they are used in applied settings? We need to invest in dissemination projects with as much care and planning as we put into the research itself. There need to be rewards for good educational practices along with positive outcomes for researchers and teachers who are willing to take risks, even when the knowledge gained from those risks is that some method did not work as hoped. How can we disseminate research findings so that they translate into practice? How can we inform the design and execution of educational programs with findings from the science of learning? In other words, how can we apply the science of learning to adult education (Halpern & Hakel, 2002)? Effective dissemination is an important research question in its own right.

There are, of course, numerous other examples showing that knowledge of how people learn, think, and remember should be at the heart of any education program, including, and perhaps most importantly, leadership training programs. One conclusion is clearly warranted: With appropriate instruction, we can improve how people learn, remember, and think. The basic principles of how adults learn should be guiding the design of training programs in general, and more specifically for the topic of this book, the design of leadership training programs.

The enhancement of learning is the most important task we face as a technological society. Workplace and citizenship skills are more complex than ever before; a thinking, educated military, workforce, and citizenry is our best hope for the future. The rate at which knowledge has been growing is exponential and the most valuable (and valued) asset of any society in the coming decades will be an educated, thinking populace—human capital is our wisest investment. Recent tragic events have shown that more than ever, we need to prepare adult learners to learn efficiently, think critically, and lead effectively so that the United States can remain competitive and cooperative in the 21st century. We need leaders for the new challenges; the ideas in this chapter should be valuable in designing programs for leadership and change.

REFERENCES

Ackerman, P. L., Bowen, K. R., Beier, M. E., & Kanfer, R. (2001). Determinants of individual differences and gender differences in knowledge. *Journal of Educational Psychology, 93,* 797–825.

Amabile, T. (1996). *Creativity in context.* Boulder, CO: Westview.

Baddeley, A. D. (1999). *Working memory.* Needham Heights, MA: Allyn & Bacon.

Baltes, P. B., Staudinger, U. M., & Lindenberger, U. (1999). Lifespan psychology: Theory and application to intellectual functioning. *Annual Review of Psychology, 50,* 471–507.

Bandura, A. (1986). *Social foundations of thought and action: A social–cognitive theory.* Englewood Cliffs, NJ: Prentice-Hall.

Bandura, A. (2001). Social cognitive theory: An agentic perspective. *Annual Reviews in Psychology, 52,* 1–26.

Benjamin, A. S., Bjork, R. A., & Schwartz, B. L. (1998). The mismeasure of memory: When retrieval fluency is misleading as a metamnemonic index. *Journal of Experimental Psychology: General, 127,* 55–68.

Bransford, J., Brown, A., & Cocking, R. (Eds.). (1999). *How people learn: Brain, mind, experience, and schooling.* Washington, DC: National Research Council.

Cacioppo, J. T., Petty, R. E., Feinstein, J. A., & Jarvis, W. B. G. (1996). Dispositional differences in cognitive motivation: The life and times of individuals varying the need for cognition. *Psychological Bulletin, 119,* 197–253.

Chan, K.-Y., & Drasgow, F. (2001). Toward a theory of individual differences and leadership: Understanding the motivation to lead. *Journal of Applied Psychology, 86,* 481–498.

Colquitt, J. A., & Simmering, M. J. (1998). Conscientiousness, goal orientation, and motivation to learn during the learning process: A longitudinal study. *Journal of Applied Psychology, 83,* 654–665.

Cull, W. L. (2000). Untangling the benefits of multiple study opportunities and repeated testing for cued recall. *Applied Cognitive Psychology, 14,* 215–235.

Dees, S. M., & Dansereau, D. F. (2000). *TCU guide maps: A resource for counselors.* Fort Worth, TX: Texas Christian University, Institute of Behavioral Research.

deWinstanley, P. A., & Bjork, R. A. (2002). Successful lecturing: Presenting information in ways that engage effective processing. In D. F. Halpern & M. D. Hakel (Eds.), *New directions in teaching and learning: No. 89. Applying the science of learning to university teaching* (pp. 19–32). San Francisco: Jossey-Bass.

Druckman, D., & Bjork, R. A. (Eds.). (1994).*Learning, Remembering, Believing: Enhancing Human Performance.* Washington, DC: National Academy Press.

Dweck, C. S. (1986). Motivational processes affecting learning. In A. Lesgold & R. Glaser (Eds.), *Foundations for a psychology of education* (pp. 87–136). Hillsdale, NJ: Lawrence Erlbaum Associates, Inc.

Fong, G. T., Krantz, D. H., & Nisbett, R. E. (1986). The effects of statistical training on thinking about everyday problems. *Cognitive Psychology, 18,* 253–292.

Graesser, A. C., Person, N. K., & Hu, X. (2002). Improving comprehension through discourse processing. In D. F. Halpern & M. D. Hakel (Eds.), *New directions in teaching and learning: No. 89. Applying the science of learning to university teaching* (pp. 33–44). San Francisco: Jossey-Bass.

Grolnic, S. (2000). Informal learning in the workplace: What educators can learn. *CAEL Forum and News: Learning Policy in the New Economy, 2000* (Fall), 1618.

Gully, S. M., Payne, S. C., Koles, K. L. K., & Whiteman, J.-A. K. (2002). The impact of error training and individual differences on training outcomes: An attribute–treatment interaction perspective. *Journal of Applied Psychology, 87,* 143–155.

Halpern, D. F. (2003). *Thought and knowledge: An introduction to critical thinking* (4th ed.). Mahwah, NJ: Lawrence Erlbaum Associates, Inc.

Halpern, D. F., & Collaer, M. L. (in press). Sex differences in visuospatial abilities: More than meets the eye. In P. Shah & A. Miyake (Eds.), *Higher-level visuospatial thinking and cognition.* Cambridge, MA: Cambridge University Press.

Halpern, D. F., & Hakel, M. (Eds.). (2002). *From theory to practice: Applying the science of learning to the university and beyond.* San Francisco: Jossey-Bass.

Heckhausen, J. (1997). Developmental regulation across adulthood: Primary and secondary control of age-related challenges. *Developmental Psychology, 33,* 176–187.

Hochwarter, W. A., Witt, L. A., & Kacmar, K. M. (2000). Perceptions of organizational politics as a moderator of the relationship between conscientiousness and job performance. *Journal of Applied Psychology, 85,* 472–478.

Horn, J. L. (2001, November). *Crawling out of the g rut; Creeping on to an expertise wagon.* Paper presented at the Third International Spearman Seminar, Sydney, Australia.

Jepson, C., Krantz, D. H., & Nisbett, R. E. (1993). Inductive reasoning: Competence or skill? In R. E. Nisbett (Ed.), *Rules for reasoning* (pp. 70–89). Hillsdale, NJ: Lawrence Erlbaum Associates, Inc.

Johnson, W. B. (2002). The intentional mentor: Strategies and guidelines for the practice of mentoring. *Professional Psychology: Research and Practice, 33,* 88–96.

Kiel, F., Rimmer, E., Williams, K., & Dolye, M. (1996). Coaching at the top. *Consulting Psychology Journal: Practice and Research, 48,* 67–77.

Kluger, A. N., & DeNisi, A. (1996). Effects of feedback intervention on performance: A historical review, a meta-analysis, and a preliminary feedback intervention theory. *Psychological Bulletin, 119,* 254–284.

Lawson, M. J., & Chinnappan, M. (1994). Generative activity during geometry problem solving. *Cognition and Instruction, 12,* 61–93.

Lovett, M. C., & Greenhouse, J. B. (2000). Applying cognitive theory to statistics instruction. *American Statistician, 54,* 196–209.

Maguire, E. A., Frackowiak, R. S. J., & Frith, C. D. (1997). Recalling routes around London: Activation of the right hippocampus in taxi drivers. *Journal of Neuroscience, 17,* 7103–7110.

Maguire, E. A., Gadian, D. G., Johnsrude, I. S., Good, C. D., Ashburner, J., Frackowiak, R. S., & Frith, C. D. (2000). Navigation-related structural change in the hippocampi of taxi drivers. *Proceedings of the National Academy of Sciences, 97,* 4398–4403.

Maki, R. H. (1998). Testing predictions over text material. In D. J. Hacker, J. Dunlosky, & H. C. Graesser (Eds.), *Metacognition in educational theory and practice* (pp. 117–144). Mahwah, NJ: Lawrence Earlbaum, Associates, Inc.

Mayer, R. E. (1999). *The promise of educational psychology.* Upper Saddle River, NJ: Prentice-Hall.

Mayer, R. E. (2001). *Multimedia learning.* Cambridge: Cambridge University Press.

Mayer, R. E. (2002). Cognitive theory and the design of multimedia instruction. In D. F. Halpern & M. D. Hakel (Eds.), *New directions in teaching and learning: No. 89. Applying the science of learning to university teaching* (pp. 55–71). San Francisco: Jossey-Bass.

McCauley, C. D., Ruderman, M. N., Ohlott, P. J., & Morrow, J. E. (1994). Assessing the developmental components of managerial jobs. *Journal of Applied Psychology, 79,* 544–560.

McCrae, R. R., & Costa, P. T., Jr. (1997). Personality trait structure as a human universal. *American Psychologist, 52,* 509–516.

Nisbett, R. E. (1993). *Rules for reasoning.* Hillsdale, NJ: Lawrence Erlbaum Associates, Inc.

Peng, K., & Nisbett, R. E. (1999). Culture, dialectics, and reasoning about contradiction. *American Psychologist, 54,* 741–754.

Piaget, J. (1952). *The origins of intelligence in children.* New York: International Universities Press.

Pressley, M., & Ghatala, E. S. (1988). Delusions about performance on multiple-choice comprehension tests. *Reading Research Quarterly, 23,* 454–464.

Quinones, M. A. (1995). Pretraining context effects: Training assignments as feedback. *Journal of Applied Psychology, 80,* 226–238.

Rawson, K. A., Dunlosky, J., & Thiede, K. W. (2000). The rereading effect: Metacomprehension accuracy improves across reading trials. *Memory and Cognition, 28,* 1004–1010.

Smith, E. M., Ford, J. K., & Kozlowski, S. W. J. (1997). Building adaptive expertise: Implications for training design. In M. A. Quinines & A. Ehrenstein (Eds.), *Training for a rapidly changing workplace: Applications for psychological research* (pp. 89–118). Washington, DC: American Psychological Association.

University of Michigan. (2001). *Studies show that memory starts to decline in our mid-20s.* University of Michigan News Release, 13 August 2001 [Online]. Retrieved 30 November 2001 from http://www.umich.edu/~newsinfo/Releases/2001

U.S. Department of Labor, Bureau of Labor Statistics. (1995). *Survey of employer provided training—Employee results.* Washington DC: Author.

Wheeler, M. A., & Roediger, H. L. (1992). Disparate effects of repeated testing: Reconciling Ballard's (1913) and Bartlett's (1932) result. *Psychological Sciences, 3,* 240–245.

Wittrock, M. C. (1990). Generative processes of comprehension. *Educational Psychologist, 24,* 345–376.

7

Self-Awareness, Identity, and Leader Development

Douglas T. Hall
Boston University

In today's complex, turbulent organizations, a critical competency for success-ful leaders is the ability to learn how to deal with the changing demands of the environment and develop the appropriate new skills. There are two overarching personal capabilities that help leaders "learn how to learn" new skills and com-petencies: *self-awareness* (or identity) and *adaptability* (Briscoe and Hall, 1999; Hall, 1986a, 1986b, 2002; Hall and Associates, 1996). Because of the superor-dinate power of these two personal capabilities in helping the person grow new competencies, I refer to them as "metacompetencies." This chapter is a detailed examination of one of these metacompetencies: self-awareness. Much less is known about self-awareness in organizations than is known about adaptabil-ity.[1] I examine the nature of self-awareness, the different theoretical perspectives that have been used to study the concept, what role it plays in leadership de-velopment, and what organizations might do to create cultures that promote its development.

---

[1] For a detailed literature review of adaptability in work organizations, see Morrison and Hall (2002).

IDENTITY

Leader development is largely personal development. A major aspect of personal development is the process of becoming more aware of one's self. Regarding personality characteristics of the leader, *identity*[2] is probably the most important aspect of leader and career development, going back to the pioneering work of Donald Super (1957), who described the work career as the implementation of one's conception of the self. It is the person's sense of identity that, by definition, helps her evaluate herself. It tells her how she fits into her social environment and it tells her about her uniqueness.

Identity is a complex and multifaceted construct, which relates to the way an individual perceives himself or herself in relation to "others" in the environment. (Identity is one type of cognition; cognition about the self, or "metacognition," and thus many of the notions of cognitive development discussed by Halpern, chap. 6, this volume, can also be used to understand identity development.) The "others" in the person's environment can be people, groups, organizations, the physical environment, or any other entity with which the person has a relationship (Kegan, 1982). Baumeister (1986) defined a person's identity as a way of seeing the self, a personal construction or interpretation of the self. Ashforth and Mael (1989) discussed in detail the functioning of identity in the context of organizations, listing the critical antecedents and outcomes of organizational identity. Important antecedents include the social prestige of the organization and the distinctiveness of the organization's values and practices. Important outcomes include loyalty and commitment as well as pride in being a member.

SELF-AWARENESS

A person may not be fully conscious of all of the components of his or her identity. Some components may be so deeply embedded that they may not be salient as self-descriptions. An example might be race for White Americans who have spent all of their lives in White environments.

Self-awareness, on the other hand, refers to the extent to which people are conscious of various aspects of their identities and the extent to which their self-perceptions are internally integrated and congruent with the way others perceive them. Thus, the identity is more a description of what the sense of self *is*, whereas self-awareness contains more of an evaluative component, referring to the *quality* and *accuracy* (i.e., agreement with "others") of those self-perceptions. Self-awareness, then, is a measure of the person's ability to be truly conscious of the components of the self and to observe it accurately and objectively.

---

[2]For the purposes of this analysis, the terms self, self-concept, and identity are be used synonymously. Self and identity, as used in the psychology literature, are reflexive concepts, meaning that they refer to the person's image or view of himself or herself.

Daniel Goleman (1998) referred to self-awareness as "the first component of emotional intelligence—which makes sense when one considers that the Delphic oracle gave the advice to 'know thyself' thousands of years ago" (p. 95). Goleman defined self-awareness at "the ability to recognize and understand your moods, emotions, and drives, as well as their effect on others" (p. 95). Caruso and Wolfe (chap. 10, this volume) also stress the importance of leaders' ability to be aware of their emotions and those of others and to recognize the impact of their own emotions on their thinking and decisions. Thus, we see the two facets of self-awareness, the internal (recognizing one's own inner state) and the external (recognizing one's impact on others.) Self-awareness is one element in the *development* of the person's identity.

This issue of awareness of the self is made even more explicit in the theory of identity development proposed by Robert Kegan (1982). In Kegan's model, growth of the identity involves the person's ability to see the self with some objectivity, and to take perspective on the self and observe it as if from a distance. This is in contrast to the less-developed state, where the self is more embedded (i.e., the "subject"), that is, where the person *is* the self and is not able to observe and reflect upon it.

Thus, leader development can be viewed as the process of increasing the *fit* between the leader's role requirements and personal identity. From this viewpoint, leader growth is a synthesizing process, integrating (or aligning) the leader with his or her work environment (Hall, 2002; Super, 1992).

PERSONAL IDENTITY
AND SOCIAL IDENTITY

In the sections that follow, I examine two different facets of the person's overall sense of self: personal identity and social identity. Personal identity refers to those qualities in the leader's self-perceptions that are unique to him or her. Social identity describes that portion of the overall identity that derives from the person's membership in a particular social group, such as a gender group or a racial or ethnic group. Although both facets feed in to affect one's overall self-concept, the dynamics of each are so strong and so important that specialized areas of literature have grown up around each one. Most of the early work on identity dealt with personal identity, whereas the area of social identity theory (often referred to as SIT) became recognized as a distinct area of academic inquiry in the 1980s.

PERSONAL IDENTITY
AND SUBIDENTITIES

A strong sense of identity is a prerequisite for pursuing a successful leadership career. If the leaders were not clear on their needs, motivations, abilities, values, interests, and other important personal elements of self-definition, it would be very

difficult for them to know where to head in life. This concept is put into words by
David Campbell (1974) in the title of his classic book, *If You Don't Know Where
You're Going, You'll Probably End Up Somewhere Else*, and also in the biblical
saying, "For if the trumpet give an uncertain sound, who shall prepare himself for
battle?" (1. Cor. 14:8). The identity has several components. For each social role
that a person occupies, there is a *subidentity*, or a part of the identity, which is
evoked by that role. Thus, I see myself in one way when I am with my children
(through my subidentity as father) but my self-perceptions are somewhat different
when I am with a former college roommate—this is my subidentity as an old friend.
For me, other subidentities would include husband, professor (which can be further

Lower Level of Leader Development

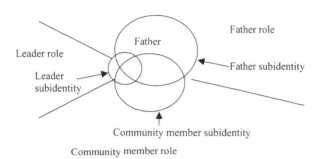

Higher Level of Leader Development

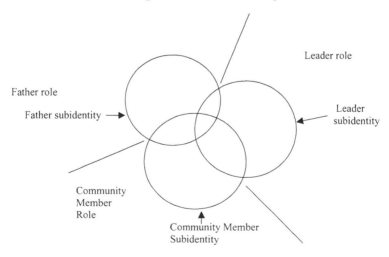

FIG. 7.1.   Leader subidentity growth: sample subidentities of two
hypothetical leaders.

subdivided), neighbor and community member, brother, son-in-law, hobbyist, and yard worker. The role represents a position in social space (Ashforth, 2001), with its concomitant expectations of behavior, whereas the subidentity represents self-perceptions as one responds to these role expectations (Hall, 1971, 1972; Hall & Associates, 1996).

As shown by Day and Lance (chap. 3, this volume), leader development occurs as the person's leader subidentity grows more complex and becomes more differentiated. A healthy and authentic identity is one in which the component subidentities are integrated. Thus, leader development is, in fact, the creation of new aspects of the self that relate to the leader role (i.e., growth in the leader subidentity). To illustrate these concepts, the sample career subidentities of two hypothetical people are shown in Fig. 7.1. The top part represents a person with low career involvement (i.e., a small portion of the identity engaged in the career role), and the bottom part depicts a person with a higher level of involvement in the career.

SOCIAL IDENTITY THEORY (INCLUDING RACE, ETHNICITY, AND GENDER)

Before discussing the impact of career processes upon identity, I briefly touch on one other source of influence—background factors—that also have a bearing on identity development. Social identity theory (SIT) describes the ways that gender, ethnicity, race, national background, and other aspects of social group membership all can affect the type of identity a person develops and the way in which it develops. Minority-group members in any setting are often discriminated against, with the result that they often must be "super-people" to attain equal opportunities for a good job and advancement. These extra obstacles can lead to identity perceptions that life's rewards are beyond the person's control, leading to feelings of helplessness, dependency, apathy, anger, and self-hate, which have sometimes been reported as part of the identity "baggage" of underrepresented members of any society.

Minority-group membership can also add to the difficulty of resolving identity issues. Erik Erikson (1966) in a classic early paper on the concept of identity in race relations made an eloquent statement of the interconnection between the identity of a person and the communal identity of a people. Similarly, identity development has "two kinds of time: a *developmental stage* in the life of the individual and a *period* in history" (Erikson, 1966, p. 160). Therefore, a member of a minority group must in a sense do double identity work, resolving what it means to be a mature human being and what it means to be a member of a particular group. Thomas and Alderfer (1989) discussed how members of racial minority groups "often feel caught in a struggle between two distinct cultural worlds" (p. 135).

Ella Bell (1986) pointed out that because of this identity duality, Black Americans are necessarily *bicultural*. She defined biculturalism as the "sociocultural repertoire of [racial minorities], as they move back and forth between the Black community and dominant culture" (p. 21).

IDENTITY CHANGES IN THE LEADER'S CAREER: WHAT AFFECTS CHANGES IN SELF-AWARENESS?

Now that I have given a sense of what identity is, I can consider the question of what facilitates the development of the growth of the leader's identity. As just shown, race, culture, and history are part of the answer, but what else needs to be considered? This question can be examined in terms of two different time periods in the person's career. The first is when he or she is making an initial career choice, usually in high school or college. The focus here is on the later years, following the initial choice (i.e., the duration of the leader's career). Unfortunately, we know far less about identity changes during the adult, working years than we know about adolescent changes as related to career choice.

Of the various factors that predict career and leader development (such as background and education, cognitive factors, skills, personality, career experiences, and person–organization fit), the one that seems to be the most useful in understanding the growth of self-awareness is key *experiences* in the person's career (McCall, 1998; McCall, Lombardo, & Morrison, 1988). It appears that critical events and role transitions may alter a person's identity, or at least trigger personal explorations, which later lead to changes in self-awareness. In particular, failures and other career setbacks have a powerful ability to make the person more self-reflective and more open to feedback from others.

I now turn to the changes in identity that are stimulated by events in the process of the leader's career. As is known from work on career stages (Hall, 2002), the person's life history may be viewed as a series of passages from one role to another: high school student, college student, company trainee, engineer, manager, and so on.

Status Passage

The activities denoting these stages have been termed "rites of passage" (Van Gennep, 1960). It is generally possible to identify three major phases: *separation* of the person from his customary environment, *initiation* from the old role into the new one, and *incorporation or reintegration* into the original or a new environment.

In a more contemporary setting, William Bridges (1994) discussed a similar view of change and transition. He described change as a shift in one's external world. A transition, on the other hand, is the internal process, the identity change, that people go through as a result of that external shift. Like Van Gennep, Bridges saw this identity change happening in three stages. The first step is an *ending*, in which the person loses the old status; followed by a *neutral zone*, in which the person feels thrown into the chaos of change but does not yet see something else to replace the loss; and finally *beginnings*, where the person has achieved a sense of a new identity, with its new understandings, attitudes, and values.

The initiation phase is a highly visible component of institutionalized role transition. In it, personal changes are focused in a fairly short, intense time period. During the initiation, the holders of the desired role test the newcomers to determine whether they are up to the standards of the group. A positive evaluation leads to public certification of group membership. Because of this certification, the newcomers begin to feel more like they belong, that is, their identity has changed so that they now see themselves as part of the new group. Perhaps the clearest and most familiar example of this phase is the fraternity or sorority initiation, which can cause changes in a person's attitudes.

Although there are obviously few, if any, formal initiation rites in the work career, there are nevertheless many role transitions and turning points that serve the function of mini-initiations. For example, the recruitment and interviewing process is an important test of the candidate's abilities; the more difficult obtaining a job offer from a particular organization is perceived to be, the more the candidate might identify with that organization, once hired. Training programs and probationary periods, especially in firms with "up or out" policies, contain elements of initiation rites. Indeed, some initial job experiences, such as the audit function in accounting firms, are so routine and unsatisfying that they are often experienced as a form of hazing. A newcomer to a particular job may be tested by the boss, peers, or subordinates and may be very much aware of the particular point at which their confidence was won and group membership was granted. In addition, induction into a career-related organization such as a management club or a million-dollar roundtable in life insurance, which denotes promotion to a particular level or a certain level of performance, is often treated quite ceremoniously and helps newcomers accept this advancement or achievement more readily into their sense of identity.

Military organizations are probably more likely to use formal ceremonies to mark these status changes than most other types of systems. Commissioning is obviously a major event in an officer's career, and the date of commission (which includes class rank as a differentiator for members of a class that is commissioned on the same day) is a marker of seniority that follows the officer throughout his or her career. Other important ceremonies to recognize individual career achievements include promotions (with the pinning on of the new rank), award of medals and special citations, completion of an assignment, and retirement. When groups of individuals are so honored, the ceremonies may include music, parades, speeches by high-ranking officers and other dignitaries, and formal and informal parties. I remember with great fondness from my year as a visiting professor at the U.S. Military Academy at West Point several department and Academy functions observing a variety of individual achievements (including the visitor's "crossing the bar" and attaining the age of 40!) These symbolic observances serve the dual function of helping to change a person's awareness of self and to promote the cohesion of the community.

Effects of Role Transitions on Self-Awareness

Movement (either a transfer, a job change, or a promotion) into a new role can also induce considerable identity change, regardless of whether a form of initiation is present. Thus, another way to look at identity change is to examine the *transition* that occurs as one moves into a role—that is, not passages between roles, but movement within a role. Nicholson and West (1988, 1989) identified a process of phases through which a person makes a transition into a role. First is a period of *preparation*, which happens before entering the role, where the person develops initial expectations and then creates an orientation and attitudes toward the change. Next comes the *encounter* with the new role—the initial entry process, which involves exploration and sense making about the new role. Third comes *adjustment*, where the individual changes in response to the role, shapes the role, and develops a network of relationships related to the role. In the final phase of the role transition (i.e., *stabilization*), a person achieves a level of personal and organizational effectiveness in the role.

There are certain predictable changes in identities that occur as the individual makes certain status or role changes over the course of a career. For example, when the recently graduated MBA becomes a manager, the expectations that the new manager and other people associate with that role induce new self-perceptions and feelings of responsibility. The more time spent in the organization and the higher the level attained in the hierarchy, the more investments are made in the organization and thus the stronger is the tendency to identify with the it (Hall, Schneider, & Nygren, 1970; Whetten & Godfrey, 1998).

In the case of leaders, the more they advance in a leadership hierarchy and experience success, the greater their self-confidence and awareness of their personal authority tends to be (Hollenbeck & Hall, 2002).

Socialization Effects on Identity

The process of influence that results in these identity changes over time is called socialization. For example, based on work by Fisher (1986) and Van Maanen (1976), Ashforth and Saks (1996, p. 149) described socialization as a process that "focuses on how individuals learn the beliefs, values, orientations, behaviors, skills, and so forth necessary to fulfill their new roles and function effectively within an organization's milieu . . . . Thus, socialization facilitates the adjustment of newcomers to organizations."

Orville Brim (1966) originally developed the model of socialization that has been most frequently applied to organizations. Brim's model consists of five methods that organizations employ to modify the identities of new recruits. One dimension describes whether the socialization is (a) *individual* or *collective*. That is, are new recruits processed by themselves or as part of a group? A second dimension describes whether the socialization is (b) *formal* or *informal*, that is, whether the newcomer is explicitly defined as a new member and set apart in some way from more experienced members. A third aspect is (c) *sequential versus random*, which describes whether there is a prescribed set of status passages in the process or a more emergent process. Of great relevance in contemporary organizations is the (d) *serial versus dysjunctive* dimension. Serial means that a current new member can learn from previous cohorts of new members, whereas dysjunctive reflects a process of discontinuous change, such that current newcomers cannot learn from the experiences of previous generations. Finally, (e) *investiture versus divestiture* describes whether the change process involves adding new elements to the person's identity or stripping away elements of the old identity.

ADULT DEVELOPMENT AND STAGES OF IDENTITY EVOLUTION

Another lens for viewing identity change over the course of the career is provided by theories of adult development. The most important of the adult development models as they relate to identity change and career growth are those of Daniel Levinson, (1997; Levinson, Darrow, Klein, Levinson, & McKee, 1978) and Robert Kegan (1982, 1994).

Daniel Levinson

Levinson sees the life course as a series of periods, called *stages*, which build the structure of the self, separated by structure-changing periods (*transitions*). In the structure-building periods, the person's developmental task is to build a life structure that is appropriate for that era in the person's life. For example, the task in the 20s is to create an initial independent adult life structure, after the person has left the parents and has entered the adult world for the first time. This task is quite different from that of the 40s, when an early structure has been created but one's roles are changing, requiring that a new structure be created to fit the roles and responsibilities of midlife. A life structure is an underlying pattern or design in one's life, and it is based primarily on one's total set of relationships. As these new structures are successively created, the developmental task includes not just engaging in new behaviors, but also working through a new definition of self that is congruent with these behaviors. If one is to be a whole person, one's attitudes and perspectives toward life must change and be brought into alignment as well.

A driving force in the person's life, according to Levinson, is the person's life *dream*, the ideal view of what kind of person he or she hopes to become. Movement in relation to the dream takes place in the transitional periods, where much of the structure of the previous stage is undone, views of the self and of one's world are reexamined, and choices are made that will lead to a new life structure. Some of this change is self-initiated and some is forced on the person by the environment, new roles such as work roles or the loss of same, other people, changes in one's body and health, and so forth. Levinson reported that transitions generally last about 5 years, and he identifies specific ages at which people go through the various stages and transitions that he identified. He also pointed out that no single life stage is permanent, and he computed that about half of our adult lives are spent in transitions (Levinson, 1986). Thus, in this view, life is a constant process of change and development. Each transition serves both as the ending of the previous stage and the beginning of the next.

Thus, we can see how the sociologists' and the social psychologists' theories of roles and role transitions and the developmental psychologists' models complement each other nicely to help us understand role transitions. The role transition literature focuses on old and new roles, their interface with a person's identity, and the dynamics of the change process as the person moves out of, into, and through each role. The adult development literature, on the other hand, adds the idea that most adults in a given culture tend to go through particular life roles in a predictable order and in predictable time periods in life. Although the developmental theorists also have an interactionist view (i.e., the interaction between the social environment and the individual), the primary focus moves inside, to the identity of the person and how that develops in predictable ways.

Robert Kegan

Another developmental model that is becoming increasingly important in organizational behavior was originally proposed by Robert Kegan (1982, 1994; see the review by Day and Lance, chap. 3, this volume). In his view, development occurs not so much in an age-driven manner as from the person's encountering new situations that contain increasingly greater complexity. In Kegan's view, the self *evolves* in a process of increasing maturation and ability to comprehend complexity in the environment. As the person increases his or her capacity to deal with this complexity, the identity grows in its capacity to take in complexity and to integrate it in a way that permits committed action. Influenced by Piaget, the Kegan model proposes a series of levels of identity, as the person moves from being very dependent and self-focused to being both autonomous and interdependent and able to comprehend a very complex system of relationships in which he or she operates.

A driving force in Kegan's model is the person's interactions with various levels of self–other relationships, where other means not just people, but sources of influence, such as jobs, communities, and challenging tasks. Development is seen as a process of successive differentiation of the self and reintegration at higher levels of complexity.

This differentiation and integration is played out through a process of *subject–object relations*, where what is "subject" is a deeply ingrained part of the self, so much so that the person is not conscious of it. The object is that which the person is moving to become distinct or separate from. This movement toward separateness is the process of development or growth. An example is a person who is being controlled by impulses that are clearly in conflict with his or her own interests, needs, or values (subject, i.e., that which the person is aware of). As the person develops, he or she moves from a less evolved state where the person *is* his or her impulses (i.e., where they are subject) to one where the person is aware that he or she *has* those impulses (where they are object, something the person can observe and reflect on). As the person becomes more differentiated from his or her impulses, being able to "get up on the balcony" and observe those impulses, the person is able to control (integrate) them better.

This theory of this interindividual stage helps us understand why people in work settings can be so resistant to feedback about the self. If they are operating at the interpersonal stage, where they are their relationships, or at the institutional stage, where they are their careers in that organization, feedback about personal behavior and performance is threatening to those relationships and to those careers. It is only when the person is functioning at the interindividual stage that there is enough psychological distance from the relationships and organizational membership that he or she is truly free to hear or take in this feedback about the self. Thus, the reason that it is hard to use feedback constructively to increase self-awareness and improve personal effectiveness is that it requires a developmental shift (psychological growth, if you will) to develop this capacity.

How can the person achieve this psychological development to enable an increase in self-awareness in this way? According to Kegan, an important source of developmental support is the *holding environment*, a setting containing relationships where the person can be safe, vulnerable, step back and reflect on the self, and experiment with new behaviors. Kegan and Lahey (2000) provided a guidebook for good developmental conversations that can hold people and help them deal successfully with developmental tasks.

Occupational Studies of Identity Development

The Chicago School

A body of research growing out of a tradition that originated among sociologists at the University of Chicago focused on regularized changes in a person's self-awareness that were driven by moving into and out of specific roles. Classic works include Anselm Strauss' (1970) *Mirrors and Masks: The Search for Identity* and Howard Becker, Blanche Geer, Everett Hughes, and Anselm Strauss' (1961) study of medical student socialization, *Boys in White*. An overview of this work was reported by Barley (1989). An excellent discussion of more recent research on identity changes can be found in Ashforth (2001).

Hill's Research on Managerial Identity Development

Linda Hill (1992) conducted one of the most detailed studies of identity changes in the early career experiences of managers. She followed 19 managers (14 men and 5 women) through their first year as sales and marketing managers. Before their promotion, all of these people were individual contributors (called specialists, producers, or professionals).

Hill found that there were two key ways in which these managers' identities were transformed as they moved into their new roles. First, they moved from specialists and doers to generalists and agenda setters. That is, rather than directly performing technical tasks themselves, they orchestrated diverse tasks and people. Psychologically, they had to switch their identification with their individual specialist tasks to identification with the business or with the role of manager.

A related identity transformation for these emerging managers was moving from seeing themselves as individual actors to seeing themselves as a network builders. Psychologically, this meant switching from defining success through their independent task accomplishment to valuing the accomplishments of others and to valuing interdependence.

To make this transformation work, Hill found that these managers had to master four key tasks: learning what it means to be a manager, developing interpersonal judgment, gaining self-knowledge, and coping with stress and emotion (Hill, 1992, p. 6). Much of this learning, then, is identity learning, or learning about oneself, and some is learning more about what the role requires. Interestingly, only one of these tasks relates to a specific competency area (interpersonal judgment). As Hill (1992) found, most of this learning did not happen intellectually; it happened experientially:

> The lessons were learned as the managers confronted the daily litany of interactions and problems in their new assignments. And they were learned incrementally, gradually. Sometimes the managers were aware that they were learning, but most often they were not. The learning consisted principally of "gradual and tacit chang"; with the accumulation of evidence and experience came the erosion of one set of beliefs, attitudes, and values and buildup of another. (pp. 7–8)

Ibarra's Research on Identity Change

Related to Hill's work is that of Herminia Ibarra (2003). In an in-depth study of 23 professionals and managers who made successful transitions from "just a career" to something experienced as more creative or spiritual, Ibarra examined the process by which people go through changes in their identities.

One of the important contributions of Ibarra's work is identifying the period between identities as an important period in its own right. It is important for people to "name" this period and give importance and meaning to it. Most people, however, think of this transition time as "nonbeing," or just a way station between one identity and the next, and they want to get past it as quickly as possible. Ibarra's research shows the value and creative possibilities of this period of growth.

Ibarra also found that the process of identity change is often one marked by a series of small changes. It is often initiated by an exploratory period in which the person tries on a number of "possible selves." This may be done at a fantasy level or through small experiments in which the person actually tries some activities related to a new identity. Examples are taking on side projects or temporary assignments or going back to school. Thus, a major change can be reduced to a series of small steps that make it a safer and easier process.

As a result of this study, Ibarra identified three ways of "working identity." One is through this process of experimenting with new professional identities. Another useful step is finding and interacting with new networks of people. This is consistent with Higgins and Kram's (2001) argument that much of contemporary mentoring and developmental relationship activity takes place through career networks. The third way is "making sense," which entails reframing key life experiences—"interpreting what is happening today, reinterpreting past events, and creating compelling stories that link the two" (Ibarra, 2003, p. 133).

Schein's Research on Career Anchors

Research by Edgar Schein developed the concept of *career anchors*, a central organizing force in a person's identity. Schein (1996) defined the career anchor as follows: "A person's career anchor is his or her self-concept, consisting of 1) self-perceived talents and abilities, 2) basic values, and, most important, 3) the evolved sense of motives and needs as they pertain to the career" (p. 80).

Schein's initial research in the mid-1970s identified five anchors: (a) autonomy and independence, (b) security and stability, (c) technical–functional competence, (d) general management competence, and (e) entrepreneurial creativity. Studies in the 1980s found three additional categories: (f) service or dedication to a cause, (g) pure challenge, and (h) lifestyle. Schein argued that these anchors evolve over time through an accumulation of career experiences. Once the career identity has been formed, they serve to help ground the person, anchoring him or her in the same way that basic values and motives do. Schein also pointed out that most people are not aware of their career anchors until they come to critical decision points in their careers or personal life. Because of that, he advocated that people develop self-awareness about these anchors so that they will be prepared in advance for making these critical career decisions.

Schein's (1996) prediction about the career world of the future was as follows: "The only reliable prediction is that we will have to become perpetual learners, more self-reliant, and more capable than ever in dealing with surprises of all sorts. It should be a field day for those anchored in pure challenge" (p. 88). This conclusion, of course, fits perfectly with my main point, stated at the outset of this chapter, of the need for organizations to find ways to help members develop their learning metacompetencies for dealing with a turbulent complex environment.

Schein developed an instrument (Schein, 1998) to help an individual assess his or her career anchors, and this is commercially available. This career-anchors measure is thus an excellent tool an organization could use to help individuals increase their self-awareness around their career motivation. Because these career anchors are so job and organization related, they represent a useful facet of identity to be used in a formal organizational career or leadership development program.

Relational Influences on Development

Many of the processes that enhance self-awareness that I have discussed, such as socialization, role transitions, and adult development processes, are inherently relational. That is, they all, by their nature, posit a process of development that is based on a series of interactions over time between the person and others in the work environment. However, because these relationships are so deeply woven into the texture of the process, they may not be immediately obvious to the observer. Before I move on, it is important to stop and make explicit this relational component of the development of identity as a "front and center" form of influence.

In recent years, the relational aspect of career development has been more widely recognized (Fletcher, 1998; Hall & Associates, 1996; Higgins & Kram, 2001). Because processes like leadership and self-awareness are intrinsically interactional (i.e., leaders need followers, and the best way to test the accuracy of one's self-awareness is against the perceptions of others), relationships play a powerful role in the growth of a leader's self-awareness.

I would argue that these relational competencies play a dual role in the development of a leader's self-awareness. On one hand, as these competencies grow, the person's leadership capacities are correspondingly enhanced. That is, these competencies are part of the leader's development. On the other hand, the more the leader possesses these qualities, the better able he or she is to learn from experiences and formal education and training. That is, by having effective relationships with competent others in the work environment, a person has access to their knowledge and experience, feedback, challenges, coaching, support, networks, encouragement, reinforcement, and all other developmental resources that they represent.

Some of the more common ways that relational influences on development are played out in organizations are through traditional mentoring, peer mentoring, networking, support groups, coaching, counseling, developmental supervision, and strong leadership. As the diversity in the workforce and the turbulence and complexity of the work environment increase, there is a corresponding increase in the diversity of types of developmental relationships in people's careers (Kram & Hall, 1996).

As one indication, through its absence, of the importance of relational support for self-awareness and leader development, consider the case of Sears' attempt to accelerate the development of its store managers (Hall, 1999). Traditionally, it was understood that it took 14 or 15 years to "grow" a store manager in a promotion-from-within leader development system. Then, utilizing research that showed how a well-selected progression of assignments could promote rapid development (Berlew & Hall, 1966), Sears designed new career paths with a strategic sequence of assignments that would grow key skills faster. In fact, they were able to advance people to the position of store manager within 7 years, with good performance results. However, over a period of years, the head of leadership development at Sears noticed that the turnover of these new store managers was higher than usual. In fact, at that time (the 1970s) the store manager role was a mark of great career success in the Sears organization, and, traditionally, store managers rarely left the organization. What was happening here?

Subsequent research determined that many of these accelerated developers had derailed over a longer period of time. Why? Most important was that, because of their rapid advancement, they had not developed a personal network that would provide them with relational support. In fact, because they had moved up so quickly and had developed a feeling that they were "solo acts," they had alienated many people along the way. Also, because of their fast movement and rapid successes, they had not had opportunities to experience failures and setbacks from which to learn. Thus, they had not developed resilience and the ability to ask for help and learn from others, all critical qualities in the development of identity (as well as adaptability, although that is not my topic here).

From this case, Hall (1999) drew the following conclusion:

> These relational qualities [that these accelerated developers did not develop] are in marked contrast to the notions of individual mastery and achievement in the traditional model of career success. For most people, and particularly for most men, learning these relational skills and becoming comfortable incorporating them as part of one's identity would represent significant personal development. However, it is precisely these new skills that the new protean career model demands. (p. 238)

DIMENSIONS OF IDENTITY

Unlike most other constructs that have been used in social, industrial, or organizational psychology, identity has not traditionally been thought of in terms of discrete dimensions. Rather, it has been used generally as a global clinical concept.

However, if one were attempting to describe a person's identity, these are some of the aspects that one might want to capture:

- *Social identity.* There are two subdimensions here: (a) How strongly (or weakly) does the person identify himself or herself as a member of a specific social group (i.e., gender, racial, ethnic, nationality, ability, sexual orientation, socioeconomic). (b) What group(s) constitute this social identity?
- *Organizational identity.* How strongly does the person identify with the employing organization? There could be multiple organizational identities here if the person had salient memberships in religious, community, educational, professional, and other organizations.
- *Family identity.* How strongly is the person identified with his or her family?
- *Work and career identity.* How does the individual perceive his or her particular set of skills, experiences, competencies, interests, and values that are brought to the workplace?
- *Values.* In addition to the previous dimensions, which refer to specific *content* of the identity, an additional characteristic of the identity is the extent to which the person values the specific aspects of these categories of content as well as how much the person values each component within each category.
- *Personal identity.* This is a very broad concept, and here it is probably best to ask the individual to provide the specific dimensions that he or she uses to perceive himself or herself. For example, one person might have a personal identity of someone who is warm, friendly, open, smart, creative, and hard working, whereas another might self-identify as a good athlete, well read, curious, tall, and energetic. However, two general personal constructs might be (a) self-confidence, or self-efficacy (which describes the strength of a person's beliefs that he or she is capable of successfully performing certain specific tasks) and (b) self-esteem (the generalized self-evaluative feeling that a person has).
- *Personal identity clarity.* This is a measure of how clear or certain the person is about who he or she is and what are his or her core values, needs, and interests. This would also include having what career theorists call "career maturity." However, the adult developmental theorists, such as Daniel Levinson, remind us that this sense of identity clarity is never "won" once and for all. Rather, it ebbs and flows as the person encounters each new stage or season of life.
- *Accuracy of self-perceptions.* This is a measure of the fit between the individual's self-perceptions and the perceptions of him or her that are held by significant others. In work organizations, feedback processes such as 360-degree feedback are an attempt to increase this self-perceptual accuracy.
- *Identity learning ability.* This dimension taps the person's skills in gathering and utilizing new information about the self. Feedback seeking is one important aspect of this identity learning ability and this activity has been well-studied in the

organizational behavior literature. However, it is not enough just to get feedback—if the person does not use it to make the appropriate changes, it is of little value. This ability to learn about the self is a key ingredient of the more general competency that has come to be called "learning agility."

WAYS OF PROMOTING IDENTITY CLARITY AND SELF-AWARENESS

Throughout this discussion, I have made various references to ways that organizations can help a person change his or her identity and degree of self-awareness. I summarize them here.

1. *Use formal ceremonies to mark identity passages.* As I said earlier, military organizations do this quite well, and the leadership literature stresses the need for celebrations of major achievements in all types of organizations (Kouzes and Posner, 1995). This is probably one of the most underutilized resources for human development in today's work world.

2. *Consciously use developmental relationships.* The best-known type of developmental relationship is mentoring, but a much wider range of relationships can promote growth: peers, subordinates, bosses, clients and customers, family, community, educators, coaches, and so on. It appears that informal processes work better than formal programs for developmental relationships, which makes it difficult to form precise prescriptions about what organizations should do in this area. My recommendation would be to take a two-pronged approach: (a) *Create conditions* to promote the formation of good developmental relationships, such as gatherings of like-minded people, networking events, social events, formal processes to introduce new arrivals to experienced members of a unit, and so on, and (b) *identify and recognize* good developmental relationships when they happen naturally. Create award programs to provide recognition for leaders who are great developers of other leaders.

3. *Create organizational holding environments to facilitate self-awareness.* As we know from the work of Kegan (1982, 1994) it is important to create sources of support, or "holding environments," containing psychological safety, acceptance, and challenge, to nudge the person along in his or her development. The effects of developmental relationships can be multiplied if a whole environment of support can be created. Some examples of holding environment groups would be support groups of various kinds (e.g., men's groups, women's groups, recovery groups, job-search and career-change groups), "alumni groups" from organizational training and education programs that contract to keep meeting periodically to reinforce and support new work behaviors, off-site retreats of coworkers or project teams to work on long-term improvement, and facilitated team

360-degree feedback retreats. The idea here is to create a "container" for development that operates away from the stresses of the everyday work environment, where the focus is on development and learning about the self as opposed to current performance. We need to learn more about the different forms that support groups might take and how they can be better incorporated into the life of employing organizations.

4. *Use self-assessment tools to promote greater self-awareness.* A variety of instruments and processes are available to provide an opportunity for leaders to engage in self-reflection and deepen understanding of the self. Particularly useful self-assessment tools include the Career Values Card Sort for clarifying career values; the Career Success Map and Career Anchors to identify work themes and work and family orientations; the Myers–Briggs Type Inventory, the Learning Tactics Inventory, and the Learning Styles Inventory to get at ways of taking in information and solving problems; and the Leadership Practices Inventory, to identify five key dimensions of effective leader behavior. These and other forms of self-assessment can be usefully combined with assessments from other people (see next item).

5. *Use 360-degree feedback and performance feedback for development.* These types of feedback have become familiar technologies in today's organizations, but they have been used primarily to enhance performance. Ironically, however, I would argue that they the better when they are used for the person's development and are separated from performance management. The concept of feedback purely for development is another rich area of untapped human potential. Because identity is a social construct involving self–other relations, feedback from relevant others in the environment is critical to identity development.

6. *Use reflection techniques.* In recent years we have also developed strong yet simple technology for using reflection on experience as a way of capturing the lessons of experience (Hall, 2002; Seibert & Daudelin, 1999). Journals, learning logs, after-action reviews, and end-of-assignment transition reports are all effective ways of helping people build on past experience and recognize changes in themselves that these experiences have produced.

7. *Encourage variety of experience in the assignment process.* Recent work on careers and learning has shown that variety and novel experiences are powerful stimuli for triggering self-exploration and learning about the self (Karaevli & Hall, in press). When a person is given a new assignment that is similar to the previous one, the person is not motivated to avoid routine modes of behavior, but when the new assignment is clearly different from anything previously done, there is greater openness to change and learning. Unfortunately, organizations tend to prefer to put the person in an assignment that is related to the person's past experience, to maximize the chances for success. Thus, organizations tend to opt for high performance rather than development. The antidote for this phenomenon is to use variety and development as explicit criteria in making assignments.

LITERATURE GAPS AND RESEARCH
QUESTIONS CONCERNING IDENTITY

Despite all of the work reviewed here, there is still much that we do not know about identity and self-awareness in work settings. Some of the more important gaps in our knowledge are the following:

• *Unstudied links between identity and motivation.* Although the research on motivation at work has been huge, there has been virtually no examination of the relationship between identity and motivation, as Batista (1996) pointed out. Deaux (1992) called for more attention to identity-motivated behavior, and Rosenberg (1979) similarly urged researchers to move beyond self-esteem to understand better the connection between the self-concept and its underlying motives.

• *Lack of longitudinal research.* There is (still!) a need for more longitudinal research on the time-based process of identity change. Because self-awareness is inherently such a time-dependent phenomenon (in the sense that self-awareness takes a period of time to grow), this concept stands in particularly great need of longitudinal inquiry. There was significant research on identity changes during occupational role transitions in the heyday of the Chicago School of sociology in the 1950s and 1960s, but little of this sort of work has been done in contemporary work organizations. The work of Hill (1992) and Ashforth (2001), as well as Pratt's (2000) study of identity development in Amway distributors, and Howard and Bray's (1998) longitudinal study of A.T.&T. managers, would be good models here for future work.

• *Measurement: Self-awareness is a "messy" variable to operationalize.* The measurement issues re identity are significant. It is inherently a clinical concept and has typically been studied with qualitative, clinical measurement methods. We need to develop more and better quantitative approaches to the study of identity issues.

• *How do rapid role changes drive identity changes?* How does identity change as specific roles change over time? Most research on identity change has assumed that the role is stable, whereas the person's identity is labile. However, because speed is so prevalent in today's work environments, roles change as fast as people do. What are the mutually interactive processes by which roles and identities affect each other?

• *Unclear links between personal identity and social identity.* How can we track changes in personal identity and social identity as well as their mutual inter-dependences? In much the same way as roles are changing rapidly, so are social group roles and identifications, as Bell and Nkomo's (2001) research indicates. What does it mean to be a member of a particular minority group today versus 10 or 15 years ago? What does it mean to have been raised as part of a majority group and then have that group turn into a minority group? Or, as in the case in certain parts of Eastern Europe or Africa, what does it mean to be socialized as part of a dominant group and then have that group become a nondominant (and perhaps severely oppressed) group? How is the development of one's personal identity affected by these changes in social identity? As suggested earlier in this chapter, helping a person become more self-aware around race, gender, or some other aspect of social identity may be a promising intervention strategy for raising self-awareness around personal identity.

  • *How can better holding environments for enhancing self-awareness be created in contemporary organizations?* We know that developmental relationships and supportive environments play a major role in the development of self-awareness, but there has been little research on planned interventions to create such environments. Questions we need to learn more about include (a) what are the critical features of a good holding environment and (b) what are some creative, new, and practical types of holding environments that can be utilized in the context of a turbulent, time-pressured contemporary work environment (Hall and Hall, 1976)?

  • *How does the protean career contract affect development of self-awareness?* More specifically, in the era of the protean career, how does the protean career identity act as a causal agent (Hall and Mirvis, 1996)? That is, how does self-efficacy affect career effort and subsequent success (Bandura, 1986)? Is there, in fact, a success spiral (Hall and Foster, 1977)? When is the protean sense of self a causal agent, and when is it an outcome of some concrete experience?

  • *How do quick, everyday changes in self-awareness occur?* We need more research on short-cycle career processes. Some examples are identity changes resulting from role transitions, identity changes resulting from career learning cycles (downsides as well as positive effects), and identity changes during daily role transitions (i.e., transitions from home to work and back, as described by Hall and Richter, 1988).

  • *How do objective (or external) career changes affective subjective career changes?* How can we trace the mutual impacts of the objective career (e.g., role) and the subjective career (e.g., identity)? As objective careers become more boundary-less, how does the person "track" these changes onto his or her identity? If there is less sense of boundary or status passage in the career today, does that mean that there is less sense of career "progress" or growth?

  • *What is career growth?* Regarding the previous point, in a larger sense, *how do we define and measure growth in the career?* In conversation with people I would regard as having a protean career, it seems clear that a major issue for them is the lack of the traditional yardsticks by which to measure career success. They do not have the traditional progressions of jobs and titles by which to mark their progress. Although it is clear to them when they are learning and expanding their capacities, they worry that these accomplishments are not visible to others. They certainly cannot be put on one's resume. Although we do have skill-based or functional resumes, the growth of skills still does not have universal currency. We need fresh new ideas for framing, extracting, communicating, and valuing protean identity growth in the career.

CONCLUSIONS

Although it is generally well understood that a primary component of leader development is personal development (McCall, 1998), exactly what we mean by "personal development" has not been as well understood. We have devoted more energy to learning what kinds of experiences lead to development than to understanding development itself. This chapter has been an attempt to put a microscope on this process by examining the person's awareness of self and how it grows.

There are good reasons why research on self-awareness has been limited. Self-awareness and the closely related concept of identity are difficult to define and even harder to measure. Ironically, this may be one of the few instances in science in which it is easier to change something than it is to understand it. In this chapter, I discussed how personal identity is affected by social identity as well as by status passages, role transitions, socialization, adult development, and career changes. I also proposed some basic dimensions of organizational identity and some areas for further research.

My goal in this work is to raise the concepts of identity and self-awareness to make them more visible and salient for research and practice. The way people see themselves is so basic to how they behave and yet so "invisible" because it is such an internal and often privately held process. Yet many of the activities of individuals in organizations—and certainly of leaders in organizations—are motivated by how people perceive themselves and how they hope to have others perceive them. Thus, a person's level of self-awareness can be a limitation or a facilitator of personal learning. We need to learn more about how self-awareness can lead to the greater tapping of human potential in contemporary organizations.

REFERENCES

Ashforth, B. (2001). *Role transitions in organizational life: An identity-based perspective.* Hillsdale, NJ: Lawrence Erlbaum Associates, Inc.

Ashforth, B., & Mael, F. (1989). Social identity theory and the organization. *Academy of Management Review, 14,* 20–39.

Ashforth, B., & Saks, A. M. (1996). Socialization tactics: Longitudinal effects on newcomer adjustment. *Academy of Management Journal, 39,* 149–178.

Bandura, A. (1986). *Social foundations of thought and action.* Englewood Cliffs, NJ: Prentice-Hall.

Barley, S. (1989). Careers, identities, and institutions: The legacy of the Chicago School of sociology. In M. B. Arthur, D. T. Hall, & B. S. Lawrence (Eds.), *The handbook of career theory* (pp. 41–65). New York: Cambridge University Press.

Becker, H., Geer, B., Hughes, E., & Strauss, A. (1961). *Boys in white.* Chicago: University of Chicago Press.

Battista, M. (1996). *Motivation for reemployment: The role of self-efficacy and identity.* Unpublished doctoral dissertation, City University of New York.

Baumeister, R. F. (1986). *Identity: Cultural change and the struggle for the self.* New York: Oxford University Press.

Bell, E. L. (1986). *The power within: Bicultural life structures and stress among Black women.* Unpublished doctoral dissertation, Case Western Reserve University.

Bell, E. L., & Nkomo, S. M. (2001). *Our separate ways: Black and White women and the struggle for professional identity.* Boston: Harvard Business School Press.

Berlew, D. E., & Hall, D. T. (1966). The socialization of managers: Effects of expectations on performance. *Administrative Science Quarterly, 11,* 207–223.

Bridges, W. (1994). *Jobshift: How to prosper in a workplace without jobs.* Reading, MA: Addison-Wesley.

Brim, O. (1966). Socialization through the life cycle. In O. G. Brim & S. G. Wheeler (Eds.), *Socialization after childhood* (pp. 3–49) New York: Wiley.

Briscoe, J. P., and Hall, D. T. (1999). Grooming and picking leaders using competency frameworks: Do they work? An alternative approach and new guidelines for practice. *Organizational Dynamics, 28*(2), 37–52.

Campbell, D. P. (1974). *If you don't know where you're going, you'll probably end up somewhere else.* Allen, TX: More.

Deaux, K. (1992). Personalizing identity and socializing self. In G. Breakwell (Ed.), *Social psychology of identity and the self-concept.* London: Academic.

Erikson, E. H. (1966). The concept of identity in race relations: Notes and queries. *Daedalus, 95,* 145–171.

Fisher, C. D. (1986). Organizational socialization: An integrative review. *Research in Personnel and Human Resources Management, 4,* 101–145.

Fletcher, J. (1998). *Disappearing acts: Gender, power, and relational practice at work.* Cambridge, MA: MIT Press.

Goleman, D. (1998). What makes a leader? *Harvard Business Review, 1998*(November–December), 93–102.

Hall, D. T. (1971). A theoretical model of career subidentity development in organizational settings. *Organizational Behavior and Human Performance, 6,* 50–76.

Hall, D. T. (1972). A model of coping with role conflict: The role behavior of college educated women. *Administrative Science Quarterly, 17,* 471–486.

Hall, D. T. (1986a). Dilemmas in linking succession planning to individual executive learning. *Human Resource Management, 25,* 235–265.

Hall, D. T. (1986b). Breaking career routines: Midcareer choice and identity development. In D. T. Hall & Associates (Eds.), *Career development in organizations* (pp. 120–159). San Francisco: Jossey-Bass.

Hall, D. T. (1999). Accelerate career development—at your peril! *Career Development International, 4,* 237–239.

Hall, D. T. (2002). *Careers in and out of organizations.* Thousand Oaks, CA: Sage.

Hall, D. T., & Associates. (1996). *The career is dead—Long live the career: A relational approach to careers.* San Francisco: Jossey-Bass.

Hall, D. T., & Foster, L. W. (1977). A psychological success cycle and goal setting: Goals, performance, and attitudes. *Academy of Management Journal, 20,* 282–290.

Hall, D. T., & Hall, F. S. (1976). The relationship between goals, performance, success, self-image, and involvement under different organization climates. *Journal of Vocational Behavior, 9,* 267–278.

Hall, D. T., & Mirvis, P. H. (1996). The new protean career: Psychological success and the path with a heart. In D. T. Hall & Associates (Eds.), *The career is dead—long live the career: A relational approach to careers* (pp. 15–45). San Francisco: Jossey-Bass.

Hall, D. T., & Richter, J. (1988). Balancing work life and home life: What can organizations do to help? *Academy of Management Executive, 2,* 213–223.

Hall, D. T., Schneider, B., & Nygren, H. T. (1970). Personal factors in organizational identification. *Administrative Science Quarterly, 15,* 176–190.

Higgins, M. C., & Kram, K. E. (2001). Reconceptualizing mentoring at work: A developmental network perspective. *Academy of Management Review, 26,* 264–288.

Hill, L. A. (1992). *Becoming a manager: Mastery of a new identity.* Boston: Harvard Business School Press.

Hollenbeck, G. P., & Hall, D. T. (2002). *Self confidence and leadership development* (Tech. Rep.). Boston: Boston University School of Management.

Ibarra, H. (2003). *Working identity: Unconventional strategies for reinventing your career.* Boston: Harvard Business School Press.

Kegan, R. (1982). *The evolving self: Problem and process in human development.* Cambridge, MA: Harvard University Press.

Kegan, R. (1994). *In over our heads: The mental demands of modern life.* Cambridge, MA: Harvard University Press.

Kegan, R., & Lahey, L. L. (2000). *How the way we talk can change the way we work: Seven languages for transformation.* San Francisco: Jossey-Bass.

Kouzes, J. M., & Posner, B. Z. (1995). *The leadership challenge: How to keep getting extraordinary things done in organizations* (2nd ed.). San Francisco: Jossey-Bass.

Kram, K. E., & Hall, D. T. (1996). Mentoring in a context of diversity and turbulence. In E. E. Kossek & S. A. Lobel (Eds.), *Managing diversity: Human resource strategies for transforming the workplace* (pp. 108–136). Cambridge, MA: Blackwell.

Levinson, D. J. (with Levinson, J. D.). (1997). *The seasons of A woman's life.* New York: Ballantine.

Levinson, D. J. (1986). A conception of adult development. *American Psychologist, 41,* 3–13.

Levinson, D. J., Darrow, C. N., Klein, E. B., Levinson, M. H., & McKee, B. (1978). *The seasons of a man's life.* New York: Knopf.

McCall, M. W., Jr. (1998). *High flyers.* Boston: Harvard Business School Press.

McCall, M. W., Jr., Lombardo, M., & Morrison, A. (1988). *Lessons of experience: How successful executives develop on the job.* New York: Lexington.

Morrison, R. H., & Hall, D. T. (2002). *Adaptability and adaptation: Toward a conceptual model* (Tech. Rep.). Boston University School of Management, Boston: Executive Development Roundtable.

Nicholson, N., & West, M. A. (1988). *Managerial job change.* London: Cambridge University Press.

Nicholson, N., & West, M. A. (1989). Transitions, work histories, and careers. In M. B. Arthur, D. T. Hall, & B. S. Lawrence (Eds.), *Handbook of career theory* (pp. 133–201). New York: Cambridge University Press.

Pratt, M. G. (2000). The good, the bad, and the ambivalent: Managing identification among Amway distributors. *Administrative Science Quarterly, 45,* 456–493.

Rosenberg, M. (1979). *Conceiving the self.* New York: Basic Books.

Schein, E. H. (1978). *Career dynamics.* Reading, MA: Addison-Wesley.

Schein, E. H. (1996). Career anchors revisited: Implications for career development in the 21st century. *Academy of Management Executive, 10,* 80–88.

Schein, E. H. (1998). *Career anchors: Discovering your real values.* San Francisco: Jossey-Bass/Pfeiffer.

Seibert, K. W., & Daudelin, M. W. (1999). *The role of reflection in managerial learning: Theory, research, and practice.* Westport, CT: Quorum.

Strauss, A. (1970). *Mirrors and masks: The search for identity.* San Francisco: Sociology Press.

Super, D. E. (1957). *The psychology of careers.* New York: Harper.

Super, D. E. (1992). Toward a comprehensive theory of career development. In D. H. Montross & C. J. Shinkman (Eds.), *Career development. Theory and practice* (pp. 35–64). Springfield, IL: Thomas.

Thomas, D. A., & Alderfer, C. P. (1989). The influence of race on career dynamics: Theory and research on minority career experiences. In M. B. Arthur, D. T. Hall, & B. S. Lawrence (Eds.), *Handbook of career theory* (pp. 133–158). New York: Cambridge University Press.

Van Gennep, A. (1960). *The rites of passage.* Chicago: University of Chicago Press.

Van Maanen, J. (1976). Breaking in: Socialization to work. In R. Dubin (Ed.), *Handbook of work organization, and society.* Chicago: Rand Mc Nally (pp. 67–130).

Whetten, D. A., & Godfrey, P. A. (Eds.). (1998). *Identity in organizations: Building theory through conversations.* Thousand Oaks, CA: Sage.

8

Leadership as the Orchestration and Improvisation of Dialogue: Cognitive and Communicative Skills in Conversations Among Leaders and Subordinates

Marvin S. Cohen
Cognitive Technologies, Inc.

LEADERSHIP AS COGNITIVE–COMMUNICATIVE INTERACTION

Communication is not simply a medium through which leadership happens to be exercised; it is part of its substance. Leaders must communicate—and be seen to communicate—in order to influence the beliefs, actions, and emotions of others in pursuit of organizational goals. Even when communication is not an objective, leader actions often lead to expectations and commitments for both the leader and others in the organization to whom the action becomes known (Weick, 2001). Nevertheless, most theories of leadership pay little explicit attention to communication (Bass, 1990; Yukl, 1998), and communication specialists have not systematically studied features of everyday discourse that might characterize effective leadership (e.g., Drew & Heritage, 1992; van Dijk, 1997). The strategy in leadership theory has been to hypothesize broad leadership traits (e.g., intelligence, sociability, self-confidence) or leadership styles (e.g., directive, participative, transformational) and the conditions under which the traits or styles tend to be effective (e.g., subordinates with high vs. low motivation or competence). This macro level of analysis tells us little about the expression of traits or styles in concrete social action, how they affect team performance in real-world contexts, or the underlying cognitive skills (Barge, 1994; Northouse, 2001). Measures of traits or styles are usually based on global subjective impressions averaged across subordinates rather than observed behaviors in specific situations. Relatively static traits and styles distract attention from the cognitive processes that are responsible for flexibility, improvisation, and tradeoffs in dynamic situations (Barge, 1994). The measures rely on prior identification of leaders by their formal position in a hierarchy rather than by their actual behavior and influence or by their knowledge and mastery of specific cognitive skills and communicative strategies. Not surprisingly, findings are often too general and ill defined to provide the concrete guidance we need for leader development.

The purpose of this chapter is to investigate what an approach to leadership might look like that is based on the cognitive and communicative skills underlying leaders' interactive behavior. It focuses on a specific approach, *cognitive dialogue theory*, whose fundamental data are real-world sequences of communicative actions in interactive exchanges among participants (or potential participants) in group activity. The theory characterizes the cognitive competencies (e.g., knowledge representations, processing strategies, and preferences) that enable individuals to adapt their individual actions to the intentions of others, develop shared intentions, and thereby participate in and lead collective action (Blumer, 1969, pp. 109–110). Cognitive dialogue theory integrates three sources of concepts from the study of communication—transaction knowledge structures (or dialogues), relationship-oriented strategies, and conversational devices: (a) Individuals in the same culture or organization create, adapt, and share knowledge structures that represent the goals and essential components of communicative exchanges. These structures serve as plans for different types of *dialogues*, that is, characteristic, recognizable, multiperson conversational transactions such as negotiation, deliberation, information exchange, expert consultation, or resolution of disagreement, which leaders use to orchestrate group activity. (b) Participants must often improvise during a dialogue in order to accomplish their objectives under conditions of social risk. In constructing and navigating a dialogue, leaders use strategies that balance task efficiency against the need to protect themselves and their interlocutors against encroachments on privacy and positive regard. (c) A language community makes available a variety of conversational devices that dialogue participants can use to control the flow of talk. Skilled communicators creatively exploit such techniques to anticipate, influence, and respond to others' speech, both to increase efficiency and to minimize social risk.

A leadership paradigm centered on cognitive and communicative skills has methodological, theoretical, and practical implications: (a) Methodologically, it can provide descriptive tools for a more bottom-up, data-driven approach to complement the top-down strategy that currently prevails. It invites existing theories to spell out more precisely how traits and styles are embodied in knowledge structures, cognitive processes, and behavior and allows theories to be tested by means of careful and precise naturalistic observation (Barge, 1994). (b) It should also help us progress beyond current theories. Cognitive analysis of discourse among leaders, subordinates, and others is consistent with an emerging view of the way cognitive and social processes shape one another on evolutionary (Whitten & Byrne, 1997), cultural (Sperber, 1996), developmental (Rogoff & Lave, 1999), and adult practioner (Hutchins, 1995) time scales. A cognitive–communicative framework for leadership should draw from and contribute to an emerging cognitive–social paradigm (Turner, 2001). (c) The approach should have an immediate practical payoff in the development of better leaders. For example, cognitive dialogue theory defines leadership as (in large part) *the skillful adaptation and implementation of different types of dialogue to achieve group objectives.* Precise characterization of cognitive competencies associated with dialogue roles, interactive strategies, and conversational devices helps trainers identify objectives in leader development, design appropriate training exercises, and provide meaningful feedback. There is already evidence that methods of this kind are effective in training leadership and critical thinking by battlefield officers (Cohen et al., 2003). Recipients of such training acquire reflective awareness and control over skills that are ordinarily left to chance (Day & Lance, chap. 3, this volume). Training enables them to practice, adapt, and create communicative transactions that bring leadership into being.

LEADERSHIP IN (INTER)ACTION: AN EXAMPLE

This chapter uses examples to explore the application to leadership of some core concepts and methods of a cognitive–communicative framework. Table 8.1 contains a conversation with a superior that occurred while Robert Mason (1983) was on an aircraft carrier headed for his first deployment in Vietnam as an Army helicopter pilot. Although this is a military example, the ideas developed in this chapter draw significantly from work in other domains, such as business, government, counseling, education, and everyday conversation.

The exchange in Table 8.1 is deceptively simple. It exemplifies a process by which participants *negotiate* the type of dialogue transaction that is to be conducted and the roles that are to be played while protecting one another's freedom of action and self-regard (Brown & Levinson, 1987). I will take a line by line tour of this exchange to discover both the basic competencies and the more subtle leadership

TABLE 8.1
A Conversation That Illustrates Leadership Skills

1	L:	(Leese sat next to me at breakfast.) I've assigned you to fly a [helicopter gun] ship off the carrier when we get to Qui Nhon. (He smiled.)
2	M:	Really? (I smiled back weakly....)
3	L:	Something wrong?
4		You look kind of sick.
5		This chow getting to you?
6	M:	No, the chow's okay.
7		I'm not too sure about my ability to fly a Huey off a carrier.
8	L:	It says here (he produced a penciled note) that you're checked out in Hueys. All four models. (He looked back at me.)
9	M:	Well, I *have* flown them,
10		but it was mostly time under the hood at altitude.
11		I had about ten hours of contact-flying instruction in them.
12	L:	How long have you been out of flight school? (I noticed smile wrinkles around his eyes as he looked at the front of his paper and then at the back.)
13	M:	I graduated in the middle of May.
14	L:	So you don't feel too confident flying off the ship?
15	M:	That's right.
16	L:	Okay. (He put his notes on the plastic tablecloth next to his food tray.)
17		I've just reassigned you to fly with me.
18	M:	Thanks.
19		I'd rather not end my tour just getting off the boat.
20	L:	Oh, I'm sure you wouldn't have any trouble,
21		but I need a copilot,
22		and from what you say you need the practice.

Note. The speakers are Leese (L) and Mason (M). Parentheses enclose comments by Mason. From *Chickenhawk* (pp. 54–55), by R. Mason, 1983, New York: Penguin. Copyright 1983 by Robert C. Mason. Adapted with permission.

skills that it displays. Table 8.2 is a less successful exchange that gives us a glimpse of what can happen when such skills are not employed.

SOURCES OF COGNITIVE
DIALOGUE THEORY

Cognitive dialogue theory draws on and integrates three approaches to the analysis of communicative interaction.

Pragmatics. Pragmatics starts from the premise that speech is a form of action. Like other actions, utterances must be understood in terms of the intentions of the agent; unlike other actions, part of the intention of a communicative act is that its intention be recognized (Levinson, 1983). These intentions need not be visibly displayed by the content or structure of a sentence but may depend on

TABLE 8.2

A Conversation in Which Expectations Are Violated

1	M	What [are you] trying to do, kill us? (We had just got back from our marathon mission with Grunt Six just two hours before. Shaker knew we had already put in eight hours of flight time today and twenty hours the day before.)
2	S	No, I'm not trying to kill you...
3		Mason, you're new to our unit
4		and fresh out of flight school,
5		and I'm responsible for your training.
6		You need all the night flying you can get.
7	M	But—
8	S	You got some sleep last night, right?
9	M	Yes.
10	S	So be ready to go at 2000 hours.

Note. The speakers are Shaker (S) and Mason (M). Parentheses enclose comments by Mason. From *Chickenhawk* (p. 188), by R. Mason, 1983, New York: Penguin. Copyright 1983 by Robert C. Mason. Adapted with permission.

knowledge of the context and speaker. Unlike traditional *syntax* (how words combine to make a sentence) and traditional *semantics* (how word meanings combine to determine the truth conditions of a sentence), pragmatic concepts apply in principle to nonlinguistic gestures, intonations, pictures, and sounds. Pragmatics has produced elegant and useful theoretical concepts that explain how shared assumptions about rational cooperation and mutual knowledge are used to convey intent (e.g., Brown & Levinson, 1987; Sperber & Wilson, 1995). It has been flawed, however, by its focus on individual utterances rather than multiperson extended exchanges, reliance on hypothetical examples rather than empirical data, emphasis on the linguistic form of sentences rather than background knowledge and context, and overemphasis on deliberative cognitive processes rather than more rapid recognition-based processes. Recent work in pragmatics, however, has begun to take account of findings from conversation analysis and from cognitive psychology (e.g., Brown & Levinson, 1987; Geis, 1995; Sperber & Wilson, 1995).

Conversation Analysis. This work, like pragmatics, emphasizes what people *do* in conversational interaction, but it is intensely empirical in its focus on real-world data. An individual utterance is never analyzed by itself, but always in the context of utterances that come before and after. A conclusion about the use of a communicative device to achieve a specific effect must be based on regularities in multiperson interactive behavior that are observed across many instances in a large corpus of transcribed exchanges (Pomerantz & Fehr, 1997; Sacks, 1995). Conversation analysts resist premature macro-level theorizing common in many branches of social science (e.g., about the role of power and status), cognitive presuppositions (e.g., that deliberative reasoning underlies the use of conversational devices), and prior assumptions about the features of real-world conversations that will turn out to be significant. Despite or because of these constraints, conversation analysis has proven to be an extremely productive research paradigm (Silverman, 1998). Conversation analysis ultimately may supply a body of well-substantiated empirical generalizations that call for theoretical explanation. Like the work of Geis (1995), cognitive dialogue theory extends cognitive concepts from pragmatics to help organize, explain, and clarify empirical findings and concepts in conversation analysis.

Dialogue Theory. Work on dialogues originated in logic but has been influenced by both pragmatics and conversation analysis. As a result, it is distinctive in having both a normative and a descriptive motivation. Dialogue theory studies reasoning and decision making as they actually occur in multiperson interactions rather than as a static set of logically related premises and conclusions (Hamblin, 1970; Rescher, 1977; van Eemeren & Grootendorst, 1983; van Eemeren et al., 1993). It seeks to identify the different types of argumentation (i.e., the dynamic exchange of reasons for and against a conclusion) that are observed in conversation, when such exchanges are correctly accomplished, and the kinds of errors to which they are subject. Walton (1995, 1998) extended dialogue theory beyond argumentation to an array of other dialogue types, such as negotiation, deliberation, inquiry, information seeking, and even quarreling. The method is to start with observed types of interactive exchange as in conversation analysis but to build idealized models based on concepts from pragmatics. The idealized models show how each type of transaction should be conducted based on a mutual assumption that the participants will cooperate to achieve the goal of that particular type of dialogue. Dialogue theory promises an evaluative framework that directly maps descriptive and cognitive analyses of actual exchanges onto normative process models to identify where they diverge. If leadership skill is manifested through communicative transactions, then prescriptions for improving leadership must also be couched in transactional terms. Dialogue theory allows us to do this.

In the following sections, I show how concepts from these areas combine in increasingly sophisticated ways to account not only for basic communicative competencies, but also for the more advanced interactive skills needed for leadership.

SHOWING FACTS

A company sergeant wants to alert the commander that the enemy is setting up positions on the next hill. To do so, the sergeant looks in that direction while she has the commander's attention. The commander follows her gaze and sees the enemy activity for himself. The sergeant could have *told* the commander about the enemy activity, but she was able to *show* him direct evidence instead (Sperber & Wilson, 1995, pp. 50–51). People often take action (which may be a mix of telling and showing) in order to produce cognitive responses in other people. The intended cognitive responses may include acquiring new *beliefs* (e.g., about enemy activity), forming *intentions* to do actions (e.g., to give the appropriate orders), or experiencing *emotions* (such as gratitude, alarm, anger, or amusement). I call the intent to produce such a response a *cognitive intention* (generalizing the definition in Sperber & Wilson, 1995, pp. 54–60).

Communicative situations vary in the *accessibility* of the intended cognitive effects, that is, the degree to which the desired responses are primed by the context and shared background knowledge. Accessible cognitive responses may be successfully elicited even if the person in whom they are produced does not recognize the other person's intent to elicit them. In the example in the previous paragraph, because the enemy activity was visible and the sergeant's intent was simply to convey that information, the commander might have followed the sergeant's gaze and acquired the desired beliefs without realizing that the sergeant intended for him to do so. By contrast, when relatively inaccessible cognitive effects are intended, they typically depend for their success on more explicit linguistic encoding. For example, the sergeant would have had to say more if her intent was to produce a more complex belief based on nonshared knowledge, for example, "The intel officer was wrong again about what the enemy would do."

Recognition of cognitive intent might be useful even when it is not necessary for success of the intent. For example, the manner of the sergeant's action might have indicated to the commander that she *meant* him to look in the same direction; such recognition might help focus the commander's attention and make the relevant facts more salient. Recognition of intent might be also be desirable as a sign that the relevant information is not simply known by each individual but is mutually known. Future interaction and coordination can proceed with the assurance that each knows that the other knows it. In fully communicative interactions, the agent not only intends to produce a cognitive response, but also intends for the recipient to become aware of that intent (Grice, 1989). The intent to make one's cognitive intent known is called a *communicative intent* (Sperber & Wilson, 1995, p. 61).

There are situations in which recognition of a cognitive intent tends to work against success of the cognitive intent. Leaders sometimes take advantage of highly accessible information to keep their cognitive intent under wraps. For example, it is useless to tell others that one is courageous, decisive, intelligent, honest, or empathetic. To have credibility, these things must be shown. Both leaders and subordinates may sometimes engage in behaviors that have a natural association with various traits not (only) because they have such traits, but so that others can see that they do. Such a cognitive intent may be undermined if recognized, suggesting that the behavior is "only for show." In other cases, recognition of intent might threaten the intended audience with loss of face. For example, a type of communication that is sometimes face threatening is *instruction* (Keppler & Luckmann, 1991; Knoblauch, 1991). Superiors who wish to help subordinates perform a procedure correctly might let subordinates see them modeling the procedure but do so in such a way that the subordinates are unaware of the instructional intent.

Leese's sitting next to Mason at breakfast (line 1, Table 8.1) provided direct evidence of Leese's accessibility and willingness to talk with subordinates, whether or not sending such a message was recognized by Mason as Leese's intention. Sometimes, as will be shown, a leader can exploit ambiguity of cognitive intent in order to avoid premature commitment or to test the intentions of others.

EXPRESSING EMOTION

The exchange of smiles between Leese and Mason in lines 1 and 2 (Table 8.1) illustrates how recognition of intent can interact with more accessible natural meaning. Although smiling is naturally associated with positive affect, there is no guarantee that it will always have its natural meaning because adults can smile or refrain from smiling voluntarily. Rather than intending to deceive, however, smilers may intentionally exploit a smile's natural meaning to signal that they are pleased with something (or in more complex cases, to communicate ironically that they are not pleased). Even when no irony is intended, smilers may be counting on recognition of the intent underlying a voluntary smile to make the natural message more salient. This account of *social smiling* probably fits Leese's smile in line 1 (Table 8.1), which functions as both a greeting and a signal that the business at hand is not expected to be unpleasant.

The preferred response to the first part of a greeting is a second greeting that echoes the first in style (Sacks, 1995, vol. 1, pp. 3–11). In line 2, Mason indicates that he "smiled back *weakly*" at Leese. Any deviation from an expected response draws attention to itself because it may be a clue pointing toward a more complex cognitive intent. Leese may infer that Mason's intended message is something like, *I'm glad to see you too (hence, smile), but there is something else that I am not pleased about (hence, weak smile)*. Evidence that this was Leese's conclusion appears in his follow-up question in line 3, "Something wrong?" Understanding Mason's weak smile depends on a process that takes into account both natural meaning and less accessible intentional deviations from customary patterns. The ability both to show and to recognize emotion requires sensitivity to the moment-by-moment dynamics of cognitive intent in everyday interactions. Caruso and Wolfe (chap. 10, this volume) give a fuller picture of how people identify, understand, and attempt to influence the emotions of others. Emotional intelligence, for both leaders and subordinates, is intertwined with conversational skill.

COMMUNICATING INTENT

Communicative intent is often essential for achieving the desired cognitive effect (Grice, 1989, chaps. 5, 14, and 18). Speakers are not likely to get a question answered, have an order obeyed, or convince someone of a claim unless recipients recognize their intent to ask a question, give an order, or defend a claim, respectively. Communicative intentions (e.g., to ask questions, give orders, and defend claims) define what Austin (1965) and Searle (1969, 1979) called *speech acts*.

For example, in line 7 (Table 8.1), Mason did a number of things in addition to uttering a sequence of sounds. First, Mason made an *assertion*. This counts as a type of speech act because he accomplished it simply by getting Leese to *understand* that his cognitive intent was to convey information (rather than have an order obeyed, a question answered, etc.). A speech act is successful when its communicative intent is accomplished, that is, when the cognitive intent is recognized by the recipient (whether or not it is successful). Of course, Mason's intent in line 7 was not merely to make an assertion. He also wanted to change Leese's mind about his ability to fly off the carrier (the cognitive intent). Success of the communicative intent may be necessary for achieving the desired cognitive effect but is seldom sufficient. Success of the cognitive intent depends on many other factors in addition to recognition of that intent, such as the listener's prior views, trust in the speaker's credibility, and further information that the listener may obtain. For example, the discussion in lines 8 through 15 (Table 8.1) provided Leese with additional information bearing on the truth of Mason's assertion in line 7.

Line 7 is also an indirect *request* by Mason to be released from the flying assignment mentioned in line 1. A request, like an assertion, counts as a speech act because it is accomplished by getting the recipient to recognize the relevant cognitive intent (in this case, to get the recipient to do something) whether or not the cognitive intent is successful. Note that the assertion in line 7 is regarded as a *direct* speech act because it uses a linguistic form (declarative sentence) that is conventionally associated with asserting, whereas the request in line 7 is an *indirect* speech act because it does not (e.g., Mason did not say, "Please reassign me" or "I request that you reassign me"). Cognitive dialogue theory shifts the emphasis from individual communicative actions to the more extended transactions to which they contribute. Emphasis on transactions will provide a better insight into the leadership skills required for initiating, recognizing, and implementing cognitive and communicative intentions.

RELYING ON COOPERATION

If people did not understand indirect communication, they could not participate in real-life conversations. But how are people able to do so? Two basic answers have been offered to this question. One lays out normative principles for conversational cooperation that could be used in deliberative reasoning about the intent of a speaker. The other approach attempts to identify cognitive processes that under most circumstances satisfy the normative principles relatively automatically without any explicit reasoning at all. Both are important for a full understanding of what conversational interaction is and should be.

According to Grice (1989, chaps. 2, 7, and 17), the hearer *infers* the speaker's intent through reasoning that is based on (a) the literal, conventional meaning of the uttered sentence, (b) mutual knowledge about the background and the context, and (c) mutual assumptions about cooperation. One of Grice's major contributions was to lay out a general normative framework for communication that spells out assumptions about cooperation that make communication work. Grice introduced his overarching cooperative principle as follows: "Make your conversational contribution such as is required, at the stage at which it occurs, by the accepted purpose or direction of the talk exchange in which you are engaged" (p. 26). Grice's idea is at the heart of what we mean by a *dialogue*: A dialogue corresponds to a mutually recognized purpose in a talk exchange and a set of constraints that participants impose on themselves as to what counts as a suitable contribution at each point in the exchange.

Could Leese and Mason have used the cooperative principle and the specific maxims that Grice derived from it to infer the identity of the indirect speech acts in their exchange? Take Mason's response "Really?" in line 2 as an example. The inference process, which Searle (1979, pp. 46–47) believed must largely be unconscious, takes place in two stages: (a) Apparent violation of the cooperative principle triggers awareness of a problem in interpreting Mason's utterance. Taken literally, "Really?" implies disbelief. Disbelief seems unlikely, however, because Mason and Leese both know, and know that the other knows, that Leese has the authority to make the assignment and is unlikely to have forgotten or lied about it. So Mason could not have meant "Really?" literally as a question about the truth of the assignment. (b) The problem is solved by showing that the violation of the cooperative principle is only apparent. If Mason meant to make a cooperative contribution to the conversation, he must have had some other intent. "Really?" may suggest that Mason had a good reason not to expect the assignment. If so, a decision contrary to that reason might make him uncomfortable, and this is something worth communicating. If Mason anticipated that Leese would reason in this way, he intended to perform the speech act of *expressing discomfort with the assignment*.

The Gricean inference model remains an important source of insight into normative constraints on conversation. However, it has problems as a model of actual cognitive processes because it requires explicit representation of, and reasoning with, maxims of cooperation and assumptions about mutual knowledge. Sperber and Wilson (1995) proposed a more cognitively plausible account, which they called *relevance theory*, according to which maxims of cooperation and assumptions about mutual knowledge are implicit in the operation of cognitive mechanisms. According to that theory, recognition that an action probably has some communicative intent causes the recipient to attend to the action, thereby linking it in working memory with contextual information that is currently accessible to both the recipient and the action's originator. The combination of this information and the communicative action may generate cognitive effects (such as strengthening or weakening beliefs, intentions, and affect) through rapid and relatively automatic processes. If no relevant effects are generated, the recipient accesses more information from long-term memory or the external environment to combine with the original stimuli. The longer the process goes on, the less accessible the information becomes to which the recipient shifts attention and the more costly it becomes to obtain (i.e., it requires more steps of retrieval from long-term memory or examination of a larger area of the external environment). The degree of relevance of the communication depends on the magnitude of change in the recipient's cognitive state (beliefs, actions, and affect) relative to the cognitive effort required to generate it. The process stops as soon as the expected additional gain in cognitive effects is exceeded by the expected additional costs (Sperber & Wilson, 1995, pp. 137–142) (for a similar process in decision making, see Cohen & Thompson, 2001). The threshold of relevance can be adjusted up or down based on experience with particular communicators (e.g., how useful has their information been in the past?) or judgments about what they are able or willing to deliver on the current occasion (e.g., do they have a reason to be vague or to lie?). On this view, recognition of intent for indirect communications may occur rapidly and relatively automatically without necessarily passing through a stage of literal interpretation. Mason's "Really?" in line 2 might combine in Leese's working memory with Leese's own statement in line 1 and with associated contextual and background information to activate the explanation that Mason is uncomfortable with the assignment. Basic communicative competence includes a repertoire of interactive patterns that can be quickly recognized and implemented. Leadership skill may involve a wider repertoire of patterns, better understanding of their conditions of use, more effective strategies that can be used for search and retrieval from long-term memory when familiar patterns do not fit, and the ability to blend and modify existing patterns to communicate in novel situations.

TRANSACTING CONVERSATIONAL BUSINESS

According to relevance theory, rapid identification of a speaker's intent depends on the accessibility of appropriate knowledge in long-term memory. This knowledge appears to include structures specialized for communicative interaction. There are two broad approaches to those structures. Speech act theory implies that the recognition of intent is the matching of *individual* utterances to models of speech acts. Cognitive dialogue theory, by contrast, focuses on matching *sequences* of utterances to mental models of dialogue. *Dialogues* are multiturn, multiperson exchanges that participants jointly create and recognize by acting within the constraints of dialogue-specific roles. From the dialogue point of view, the pragmatic meaning of an individual utterance is the contribution it makes to the overall interactive exchange in which it occurs (Geis, 1995). Such contributions are of two kinds, one joint and the other role specific: (a) Individual utterances help the participants collaboratively understand and construct the type of transaction that they are conducting (the communicative intent) and (b) individual utterances help a participant achieve the goals associated with his or her specific role in the transaction by affecting the beliefs, actions, or affect of other participants (the cognitive intent). Thus, parties to an exchange use utterances associated with particular roles to construct recognizable dialogues in which they wish to play those roles. Cognitive dialogue theory suggests that leadership competence includes the ability to determine which types of dialogue are appropriate under which conditions, produce or heighten the salience of stimuli that enable others to recognize the intended type of dialogue, and recognize and respond appropriately to the transactional intentions of others.

Different kinds of interactive business (e.g., requesting–promising, asking–telling, challenging–justifying) are associated with different dialogue models in long-term memory. Figure 8.1 is a dialogue mental model for a *request–offer* transaction. Most of the elements of Fig. 8.1 resemble speech act conditions proposed by Searle and others for individual speech acts of requesting and promising. Thus,

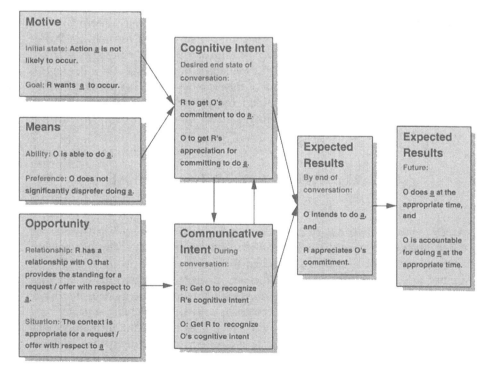

FIG. 8.1. Dialogue mental model for *request–offer* transaction. R = *requesting* role, O = *offering* role, a = an action or set of actions. Arrows signify *is a reason for* or *is a precondition of*.

Fig. 8.1 inherits all the support provided by linguistic data (e.g., regarding indirect requests and promises) that is cited in support of speech act theory (Geis, 1995; Searle, 1969, 1979). In addition, it accounts for facts about observed conversations that speech act theory leaves unexplained, such as symmetries between requesting and offering and the collaboration that is often required for their accomplishment (Geis, 1995; van Eemeren & Grootendorst, 1983). (For example, line 14 by Leese and line 15 by Mason in Table 8.1 work together to convey the same information as line 7, and can therefore be counted as an indirect request by Mason even though Leese plays an essential role. The same two lines simultaneously count as an indirect offer by Leese even though Mason plays an essential role!) Cognitive dialogue theory is more in the spirit of Grice's initial conception: The cooperation necessary to execute a request or an offer manifests itself in the relationships among utterances by different parties as they contribute to the overall direction of the conversation. Dialogue structures also have an advantage from the point of view of relevance theory as patterns to be recognized. A dialogue structure can be matched and its activation strengthened by multiple utterances in an ongoing interaction, whereas a speech act structure may have only one chance to be triggered, by a single utterance. Cognitive dialogue theory also builds on work by Bratman (1999, pp. 93–161), Grosz and Sidner (1990), and Searle (1990) on shared intentions and shared plans in both discourse and domains of practice. Finally, there is independent evidence that people use causal models of this kind (i.e., "stories") to predict and explain one another's actions (Cohen, Freeman, & Thompson, 1998; Pennington & Hastie, 1993; Schank, 1990).

Cognitive dialogue theory implies that four things must happen if any transaction is to be successful: (a) One or more persons must (recognizably) intend to engage in a particular type of transaction; (b) all the parties must (recognizably) accept the type of transaction they are to conduct and the roles they are to play in it; (c) optionally, the parties may elicit relevant information from each other about the satisfaction of conditions for accomplishing the transaction goals; and (d) the parties must recognize whether the conditions are satisfied and whether the transaction has been successful. Figure 8.1 contributes to the achievement of each of these items in three different ways: (a) as a partial plan for achieving collaborative and role-specific objectives, (b) as a source of stimuli that enable others to recognize the intended transaction and its current status, and (c) as a source of normative expectations and obligations that govern the conduct of the transaction. Depending on the richness of the shared context, an entire transaction may be accomplished by one or two words, a quick exchange of glances, a simple question and answer, or a discussion lasting hours, days, or weeks.

As a plan, Fig. 8.1 implies that an initial *motive* together with a possible *means* to fulfill it leads one or more of the parties to adopt a *cognitive intent*. The cognitive intent together with an *opportunity* (an appropriate situation for broaching the issue and appropriate relationships with other parties) leads in turn to a *communicative intent* to make the cognitive intent known to others. The communicative intent is successful in a narrow sense (comparable to the performance of a speech act like requesting or offering) if the other parties recognize the intended transaction and the intended role (requester or offerer) of the speaker. The communicative intent successfully initiates a transaction if the parties *share* the communicative intent from the perspective of complementary roles, that is, if they recognizably accept the transaction structure as a plan for the exchange. The transaction ends successfully if all parties share the cognitive intent, because they agree implicitly or explicitly that the conditions (motive and means) specified in the plan for adopting that intent are satisfied. The *expected results* of a successful transaction include achievement of the end state specified by the cognitive intent (commitment by the offerer to do the action, reciprocated by the requester's appreciation) and fulfillment of the motive (the requested action is performed by the offerer at the appropriate time). If the parties do not arrive at a shared cognitive intent, the transaction will continue, be temporarily suspended, or end without success.

The communicative intent is implemented by producing or drawing attention to verbal or nonverbal stimuli that match components of the appropriate dialogue structure. An utterance matches the structure if it asks for, provides, or otherwise activates information that fills a slot in the structure. The structure itself does not impose rigid constraints on what kinds of communicative actions might do the job or in what order they need to occur. To the extent that the parties already share relevant knowledge and know that they share it, they may have to say or do very little to achieve mutual recognition of the intended transaction and of their respective roles in it. A plausible structure will generally be activated rapidly by pattern matching to features of the actions and the situation (Sperber & Wilson, 1995). However, if a ready match is not found or if utterances do not fit any familiar transaction type very well, participants may have to draw on less immediately accessible background knowledge to construct more novel explanations and plans for their exchange (Cohen et al., 1998; Cohen & Thompson, 2001).

There is a positive relationship between *actually* producing utterances that match a dialogue structure and being *normatively* obligated to do so. The clearer the match between a speaker's utterances and a particular structure, the stronger are the expectations formed by other participants that the speaker will continue to adhere to the norms associated with that structure and the greater is the obligation felt by the speaker to do so. Highly ambiguous utterances, such as line 2 ("Really?"), and irrelevant utterances, such as lines 4 through 5, are less likely to generate mutually recognized commitments.

The initiator of a dialogue is the first to communicate commitment to the relevant cognitive intent. Cognitive dialogue theory makes no assumptions as to which role initiates a transaction. For example, R (the requester) may initiate a transaction by asking, "Can you help me change this tire?" or, more indirectly, "Did you happen to bring your jack?" (both of which match the means condition in Fig. 8.1). O (the offerer) may initiate a transaction by asking, "Do you want some help with that tire?" or, more indirectly, "Is that tire giving you trouble?" (both of which match the motive condition). They may, of course, have different reasons for initiating or participating in this transaction, for example, R to get back on the road and O to earn R's gratitude and indebtedness. A request–offer transaction may thus begin with "speech acts" of requesting or offering. There are cases, however, in which it is difficult to determine which person, if either, has taken the initiative. Requests and offers sometimes emerge in parallel through an exchange of utterances that provides a progressively better match to the structure:

R: Boy, today just isn't my day.
O: Is that a flat tire you've got there?
R: Yep.
O: Well, I've changed a lot of flats in my day.
R: Thanks, I could use a hand.

Here, the requester (R) may have been fishing for an offer of help but relies on the potential offerer (O) to improve the match to the request–offer structure. As a result, R enjoys a degree of deniability regarding the intent to *request* help. Analysis in terms of individual speech acts obscures the way communicative and cognitive intentions emerge collaboratively, gradually, and in parallel. One party is the initiator only if his or her utterances recognizably match the intended structure at an earlier point in time.

Mason's "Really?" in line 2 (Table 8.1) weakly matches the motive condition in Fig. 8.1 because it suggests that he is uncomfortable with the assignment. Figure 8.1, however, does not easily account for Leese's remarks in lines 3 through 5. Their apparent irrelevance suggests either that Leese has failed to recognize the intended request–offer transaction or declines, at least for now, to participate. Mason's line 7 is more explicit and provides a much better match, making him the initiator of the transaction. By far the best explanation of line 7 in the context of line 1 is that Mason wants Leese to recognize his intention to get Leese to change his assignment. Leese directly addresses Mason's complaint in line 8, suggesting that he has recognized the intended request and moreover has agreed to play the role of a potential offerer in a request–offer dialogue.

By engaging in a mutually recognized transaction of a given type, the participants become subject to the normative constraints associated with that type of transaction. First, they implicitly accept the recognized structure as a criterion of relevance (hence, of cooperation) for the rest of the exchange. Further utterances are expected to match conditions in the dialogue structure. For example, each utterance in lines 8 to 15 either elicits or provides information pertaining to Mason's motive for his request. Second, by engaging in a transaction (and accepting Fig. 8.1 as a plan for the exchange), participants implicitly agree to accept the cognitive intent if relevant conditions are satisfied. From a Gricean point of view, a cooperative transaction requires that both parties at least *conditionally* accept the relevant cognitive intent, subject to verification of motive and means; that is, they must at least be *potential* offerers or requesters. If they are in doubt about motive or means conditions, they are expected to reflect on or verify them. For example, the recipient of an offer may refuse to accept it until assured by the offerer that he or she can fulfill the request without too much inconvenience (i.e., the means condition in Fig. 8.1 is satisfied). By the same token, the recipient of a request may want to make sure that the requester has a good reason for the request (that is, the motive condition is satisfied). The critical discussion in lines 8 through 15 in Table 8.1 reflects Leese's interest in further verifying the motive conditions of Mason's request.

If the parties to a transaction agree that motive and means conditions are satisfied, the transaction concludes successfully with a shared *unconditional* cognitive intent (i.e., the request is granted or the offer accepted). Like recognition and sharing of communicative intent, however, recognition and sharing of cognitive intent can emerge gradually rather than all at once; there need not be a single "moment of decision." The accumulation of positive matches in lines 8 through 15, by means of Leese's questions and Mason's answers, moves Leese farther into the gravitational orbit of commitment to a shared cognitive intent; it would be more and more surprising and awkward if he did finally refuse to change the assignment. Still, line 17, in which Leese explicitly grants Mason's request, is not wholly redundant.

Figure 8.1 is only one element in a much larger nexus of knowledge and goals, variation in which accounts for variability in content across different instances of the same dialogue type. Variation is also contributed by the different strategies and conversational devices that people may adopt to conduct a dialogue. However, Fig. 8.1 captures an important invariant structure underlying very diverse exchanges that traditional speech act theory fails to describe. Cognitive dialogue training helps leaders learn to understand the purposes and elements of different types of dialogue, initiate them when appropriate, recognize them when initiated by others, and understand and respect the constraints and expectations associated with dialogue roles at each stage of the transaction (Cohen et al., 2003).

NEGOTIATING DIALOGUE ROLES

How a transaction is accomplished is as important as the transaction itself for understanding and training leadership skills. For example, in one case the participants may be slow to provide clues regarding the type of exchange they intend or what they wish to achieve by it, whereas in another case they may be straightforward. Participants may prefer some ambiguity in order to create space for implicit negotiation about the type of discussion and the roles that are to be played. One or both parties may want to keep their cognitive intentions hidden until they have a better read on what the other participants want or will accept. Implicit negotiation can establish the terms for future interactions between the same parties, and a suitable outcome may facilitate efficient future coordination. The difference between what is minimally required for the accomplishment of a transaction (e.g., lines 1, 7, and 17 in Table 8.1) and what actually happens (e.g., lines 1 through 22) is one indication of the importance of interpersonal goals in an exchange relative to immediate task goals. When well managed, this extra effort may be an astute investment in the success of future transactions (Hutchins, 1990, p. 218).

The most ambiguous part of Leese and Mason's conversation occurs in lines 1 to 7. There are two major approaches that can help us figure out what is happening here, pragmatics (Brown & Levinson, 1987) and conversation analysis (Sacks, 1995), and they dovetail nicely. In combination, they provide an account of how interpersonal or team-building goals are manifested in real-world conversational exchanges between leaders and subordinates.

Protecting Face

The basic idea of Brown and Levinson's (1987) *politeness theory* is that participants in conversational exchanges are concerned with protecting the *face* of themselves and their partners. There are two varieties of face threats (pp. 59–68). *Negative face threats* involve restricting freedom of action or invading privacy. A request virtually automatically counts as a negative face threat to the recipient of the request. *Positive face threats* involve not being highly regarded or valued by others. Blatant noncooperation and negative affect addressed to a specific person are obvious positive face threats. More subtly, criticism and disagreement often count as positive face threats by implying that their targets should have known better. Having a request rejected is also a positive face threat because it may imply that the requester's merits or needs are insufficiently valued. Politeness theory predicts that transactions associated with face threats (such as request–offer dialogues) will tend to be accompanied by strategies for mitigating those threats. Negative politeness strategies typically involve steering gingerly around the edges of the relevant dialogue mental model (p. 131). In general, the more imperfect the match between an utterance and a structure and the more distant the match is from the cognitive intent component, the less threatening is an utterance to the recipient's freedom of action (i.e., his or her negative face). Thus, negative politeness strategies work directly *against* efficiency in getting the request done by increasing ambiguity about what transaction is taking place (communicative intent) and throwing roadblocks in the way of accomplishing it (cognitive intent). Positive politeness strategies (p. 102) also reduce efficiency because they impose extraneous demands on the interaction, such as taking time to show concern for the other party's interests. Brown and Levinson (1987, pp. 71–84, 250) proposed a cost–benefit tradeoff mechanism for choosing interactive strategies, in which efficiency in the transaction is traded off against the perceived seriousness of the face threat implicit in the transaction, the power or authority of the target of the threat, and the social distance between the two parties.

These observations suggest a method that analysts can use to uncover relationship goals in a conversational interaction: Look for alternative sequences of utterances that could have been used in place of the actual one and would have been more efficient in accomplishing the same transactional goal. Then ask why those alternatives were not used. This method is consistent with the research methodology pursued by conversation analysts (e.g., Sacks, 1995, vol. 2, pp. 538–541). For example, the exchange between Leese and Mason begins in line 1 when Leese sits down and tells Mason about his assignment. Consider some of the alternatives available to Leese at this point. Leese could have simply said, "You're going to fly a ship off the carrier." The effect of this direct order would be to discourage a counter-request by Mason. Instead, Leese referred explicitly to his own role in making the assignment ("I've assigned you"). These words would be irrelevant and redundant if Leese's goal was only to communicate an order. Both the formulation of line 1 and the choice of a private setting may be clues pointing toward a more complex cognitive intent, namely, to inform Mason that Leese is open to questions about the assignment (matching the opportunity condition for a request–offer transaction, as shown in Fig. 8.1). However, this interpretation runs into problems: It conflicts with Grice's cooperative principle, which prescribes that communicators be clear and unambiguous. Why didn't Leese ask Mason a direct question, such as, "How do you feel about flying a ship off the carrier?" Moreover, in lines 3 through 5, Leese passes up another chance to ask Mason directly whether there was a problem with the assignment, instead commenting on Mason's appearance and asking about his reaction to the food. In other words, Leese *chooses* to respond to the half smile (which expresses discomfort, but has an unclear target) and to ignore "Really?" (which clearly refers to the assignment), thus prolonging the ambiguity for another turn.

A possible explanation is that Leese was concerned with face, both his own and Mason's. Asking Mason directly how he felt about an order might suggest that obedience was up to the subordinate, threatening Leese's negative face (i.e., his freedom to make assignments as he sees fit) and his positive face (i.e., his image as a decisive and respected leader, whom subordinates do not challenge). Second, an explicit question would suggest that Leese had doubts about Mason's ability, and such doubts would threaten Mason's positive face. (Leese's later remark in line 20, "I'm sure you wouldn't have any trouble," confirms that Mason's positive face was a concern to Leese.) In another words, if Leese had asked Mason point blank, "Are you capable of flying a ship off the carrier?," he would have been showing *less* rather than more "individual consideration." Line 1 nicely finesses these problems because it can be construed as an assertion, an order, or a indirect question. It is conducive to discussion (contributing to the success of that cognitive intent) without revealing that discussion *was* Leese's cognitive intent.

Politeness strategies, especially ambiguity, enable a leader to maintain a decisive posture while at the same time leaving a perceptible opening for subordinates to raise questions. Politeness strategies enable subordinates to take small, measured steps toward a risky transaction, such as request–offer. In training based on cognitive dialogue concepts, leaders are taught to recognize the social risks associated with different types of dialogue, consider the degree of indirectness or directness that might be appropriate on a given occasion, and recognize and correct misunderstandings both of their own intent and that of other dialogue participants (Cohen et al., 2003).

Nevertheless, politeness theory is not the whole story. In the course of this exchange, Mason's role is gradually transformed from cautious recipient of an order to someone who claims the right to *question* the order and make a *counter-request* of his own. Politeness theory does not explain the evolution of Mason's position. What was it about Leese's responses—which, after all, remained studiously noncommittal—that encouraged Mason in this progression and made the request–offer transaction possible? What, if anything, suggested to Mason that he might succeed in this implicit negotiation?

Controlling the Floor

Whereas pragmatists explain utterances in terms of individual and shared goals, conversation analysts look at the general functions that communicative devices serve in a system of conversation as shown by examination of a large corpus of exchanges. The devices they examine typically involve sequences of utterances and are characterized abstractly so as to capture the most general possible rules of conversation. One such conversational mechanism involves *adjacency pairs*, which help regulate turn taking in conversation (Sacks, 1995, vol. 2, pp. 521–541). Adjacency pairs are such that when the first part occurs, the person to whom it is addressed is obligated (by mutual expectations of cooperation) to perform the second part. This class includes greetings or goodbyes followed by greetings or goodbyes, questions followed by answers, requests and offers followed by acceptances or rejections, assertions or claims followed by agreements or disagreements, complaints or accusations followed by denials or excuses or apologies, and compliments followed by acceptances of a compliment. Usually, only one of the allowable second parts of an adjacency pair is *preferred* by the initiator, for example, acceptance of a request and agreement with a claim. Mason's half smile and "Really?" in line 2 are each allowable but dispreferred responses to adjacency-pair first parts in line 1, the former to Leese's smile and the latter to Leese's statement of the assignment. When the preferred response does not occur, the responder is *accountable*: It is perceived as reasonable for the first speaker to ask for an explanation, and so it is not surprising that Leese does so (lines 3–5). The request for an explanation is itself the first part of another adjacency pair, which obligates the responder to produce an appropriate second part. This chain of expectations can be exploited by an individual, like Mason, who has a limited perceived *right to speak*. The nonprivileged party may produce a dispreferred response as a way to induce the first speaker to demand an explanation. That demand, in turn, serves as an invitation to the responder to say things that he or she wanted to say in the first place. If it works, the responder is obligated (by mutual expectation) to say what he or she did not originally have the right to bring up. Thus, Mason's "Really?" functions to set Leese up as the questioner and Mason as the *answerer* in the remainder of the conversation. A more primitive version is a child's saying to a parent, "You know what, Mom?" When the adult responds by asking, "What?," the child has an unambiguous right to speak (Sacks, 1995, vol. 1, pp. 256–257). From the point of view of pragmatics, Mason's response in line 2 was a transactionally inefficient response to the flying assignment, driven by the need to protect face. This is true as far as it goes, but conversation analysis supplies a positive function for Mason's line 2 response, as part of a negotiation for floor time in order to initiate a request–offer transaction. In *this* aim it was entirely successful.

By the same token, pragmatics sees Leese's response in lines 3 through 5 as transactionally inefficient because Leese did not use more direct alternatives (e.g., asking Mason about his feelings about the assignment). Does it follow that Leese did nothing to facilitate such a transaction? To answer that, we need to imagine that Leese did want to preclude a discussion of the assignment (i.e., to negate the opportunity condition in Fig. 8.1) and ask whether more efficient tactics might have been available for him to accomplish that. For example, Leese could have responded to Mason's "Really?" with "Yes" or the equivalent and gone on to another topic. Leese had yet another efficient alternative: a general query (e.g., "Something wrong?") without mentioning the food. What, if anything, did "This chow getting to you?" accomplish? It turns out that lines 3 through 5 are an example of another frequently used conversational device, a *correction invitation*, which in this particular context has precisely the function of accepting Mason's implicit request for floor time (Sacks, 1995, vol. 1, pp. 21–25). A correction invitation is a question (in this case, "Something wrong?") accompanied by a sample answer ("This chow getting to you?"). The expected response, that is, the second part of this adjacency pair, is not a simple *yes* or *no*, but *yes* or *no plus an explanation* (Sacks, 1995, vol. 2, p. 414). The aim of a correction invitation is to induce the responder to speak the truth by obliging him or her to correct the questioner's mistake. After this correction invitation, cooperation obliges Mason to initiate the request–offer transaction, and Mason gets right to the point in his next utterance (line 7, Table 8.1). In sum, Mason has asked for the floor in line 2, and Leese has granted it to him in lines 3 to 5 (matching the opportunity condition of the request–offer transaction), with the additional face benefits that Mason is not personally accountable for questioning the assignment and Leese is not accountable for asking Mason how he felt about the assignment. Politeness theory explains the ambiguity of lines 1 through 6, conversation analysis explains the interactive work that is accomplished despite that ambiguity, and dialogue theory explains the transaction roles that emerge as a result.

Initiative is often recognized when subordinates take on nonobligatory tasks that they know will win the leader's approval. In this interaction, by contrast, Mason has no such assurance. He must decide whether to take an initiative (i.e., make a request about the flying assignment) that presents a significant social risk. Dialogue, politeness, and conversation-analytic perspectives highlight the skill that both parties used to maneuver their way to a protected space where Mason could express his concerns without transgressing face boundaries. This also suggests another, quite speculative explanation of Leese's ambiguity in lines 1 and 3 to 5, in addition to mitigating threats against face. Leaders may sometimes use ambiguity about their own intent to create opportunities for subordinate initiative under conditions of real uncertainty. The leader can observe the subordinate's willingness to act when the subordinate cannot fully anticipate the superior's reaction. In this way, leaders can assess the ability of subordinates to identify appropriate initiatives and avoid inappropriate ones.

THINKING CRITICALLY

There is a distinct change in the tone and structure of the conversation between Leese and Mason after line 7. Leese has just become aware of Mason's indirect request to change the assignment. He does not respond immediately because he does not agree with the reason Mason gives for the request, that he is unable to fly off the carrier. The conversation suddenly focuses like a laser on this claim. Argumentation—the exchange of reasons for and against a claim—typically begins in this way, as an *insertion sequence* in some other ongoing activity such as a request–offer dialogue (Sacks, 1995, vol. 2, p. 529). Van Eemeren and Grootendorst (1983; van Eemeren et al., 1993) pioneered the use of concepts from pragmatics to analyze argumentation. They regarded a conversation in which argumentation takes place, that is, a *critical discussion*, as a loosely structured discourse *genre*, like television interviews, business meetings, and sermons, in which various individual-utterance speech acts occur. An alternative account of argument in terms of dialogue mental models and relevance theory is simpler and explains more of its structure, including the roles that both challenger and defender play at each stage of dialogue. We have successfully used this model to train leadership skill in collaborative critical thinking (Cohen et al., 2003).

Figure 8.2 is a dialogue mental model for the transaction *challenge–defend*. It is used when two parties disagree about a hypothesis and at least one of them is *motivated* to resolve their disagreement. The relevant *means* is that one of the individuals (the defender) has reasons that might persuade the other (the challenger) to accept the hypothesis. Given the appropriate *opportunity*, a challenger can start the exchange by raising specific objections or general doubts about a claim to which the other party appears committed (matching the motive component of the model in Fig. 8.2). Alternatively, a defender can start the exchange by volunteering reasons that anticipate a challenger's potential objections to the defender's point of view (matching the means component of the model). The transaction begins when both parties accept the challenge–defend transaction as a criterion of relevance for the rest of the exchange and adopt at least a conditional shared cognitive intent. Challengers intend to accept the claim *if and only if* it can be properly justified, and their motivation for challenging is precisely to elicit such a justification from

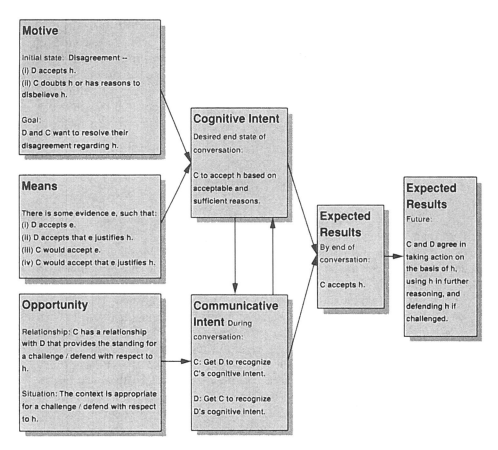

FIG. 8.2. Dialogue mental model for *challenge–defend* transaction. D = *defending* role, C = *challenging* role, h = a set of hypotheses or claims, e = a set of statements that may serve as reasons for believing h. Arrows signify *is a reason for* or *is a precondition of.*

defenders (or else conclude that none exists). In other words, by accepting the norms of this kind of dialogue, cooperative challengers agree to be open-minded; they are sincerely prepared to be persuaded by defenders. Defenders begin with an unconditional intent to persuade challengers yet must be prepared to suspend advocacy for the claim if the defense turns out to be unsuccessful.

Challengers and defenders work together to determine whether there is an adequate justification of the claim. The challenger's job is to envisage mental models of the situation in which the claim is false, whereas the defender's job is to plausibly exclude such possibilities. In doing so, each introduces new factors into their mental models corresponding to reasons to doubt the claim and reasons to accept it, respectively (Cohen, Salas, & Riedel, 2002; Johnson-Laird, 1983).

If the defender succeeds, the parties agree to accept the hypothesis because the most plausible surviving mental models include it. Whether or not the disagreement is resolved, however, the parties emerge with better understanding of their own views (Walton, 1998, pp. 57–60), in particular, a more complete situation model, more finely discriminated alternative mental models for aspects of the situation that remain uncertain, and awareness of assumptions that are not shared by others. The process of argumentation also provides insight into other parties' views. Finally, it is likely in many contexts to expand the sphere of mutual knowledge (beliefs that each party knows that the other holds) and thereby provide an improved basis for further interaction and coordination.

The benefits of a challenge–defend dialogue—in resolving conflicting views, promoting situation understanding, identifying uncertainty, and surfacing shared beliefs—are counterbalanced by the face threat that it poses to the participants. Every line from 8 to 15 in Table 8.1 is shaped partly by politeness, despite the fact that the more powerful individual, Leese, was challenging the less powerful one, Mason. For example, Leese did not state outright that he doubted line 7; he simply gave a reason for doubting without labeling it as such. Mason's response starts in line 9 with "Well," which is a conversational device that prepares the recipient for an upcoming dispreferred response. This effort to mitigate surprise is followed by emphasis on something Mason and Leese agree on ("I *have* flown them"), which provides a reassuring counterbalance to the upcoming disagreement (Sacks, 1995, vol. 1, p. 736). In lines 10 and 11 Mason finally gets to the disagreement ("but . . ."). These tactics reduce positive face threats by blurring the disagreement while still allowing the participants to recognize it and to continue challenging and defending efficiently.

Critical thinking training based on cognitive dialogue theory (Cohen et al., 2003) focuses on skills in recognizing and explicitly acknowledging disagreement, prioritizing issues on which disagreement exists, determining what type of dialogue will take place, recognizing different types of uncertainty that call for different kinds of argument, identifying hidden assumptions, and evaluating the overall plausibility of alternative mental models or stories.

SHARING CONTROL

Leese allowed a subordinate to question a decision and defend a reason for retracting it, and resolved the issue in the subordinate's favor. A leader needs a distinctive set of skills to do this while avoiding face threats to his own authority and image. To appreciate this, let us take a broader view of the issue of control in conversation and the different levels at which it can be exercised by both leaders and subordinates. In doing so, we are not directly concerned with the "power" of Leese over Mason due to their positions in an organizational hierarchy. The most "powerful" individual need not dominate a conversation at all times or in all respects. External variables like power, sociability, intelligence, and expertise (or any other purported traits or styles of leadership) may be among the determinants of conversational asymmetry on a particular occasion, and conversational asymmetry may shape and maintain the importance of those variables over longer spans of time. However, the role of external factors should not be presupposed during the analysis of the conversation itself.

Several different observable levels of conversational dominance can be identified (Linell & Luckmann, 1991). At the most basic level is *quantitative dominance*, measured crudely by the number of words produced by each party in the exchange. In this instance, Leese has 90 words to Mason's 65. This measure is not particularly meaningful unless analysis of the conversation turns up evidence that one speaker was directly responsible for reducing the participation of the other, for example, by interrupting or by ignoring what the other party says (Kasermann, 1991). We will look at an example where this did occur between a leader and a subordinate (Table 8.2), but there are no signs that Leese exercised that kind of dominance over Mason.

The next level in the analysis of conversational asymmetries is *interactional dominance*, the relative balance between reaction and initiative on a turn-by-turn basis. The basic assumption of *initiative–response analysis* (Rommetveit, 1991) is that each turn sets conditions of relevance for the turn that follows. Thus, each turn may contribute to a conversation in either or both of two ways: (a) by creating new conditions of relevance for the next turn, for example, as the first part of an adjacency pair such as a question or a request and (b) by complying with the conditions defined by the previous turn, for example, as the second part of an adjacency pair like the answer to a question or the response to a request. The balance between the proactive score and the reactive score averaged over the turns taken by a participant is the participant's initiative–response (IR) index. The difference between the IR indices of two participants in a conversation measures the asymmetry between influencing and being influenced for those participants in that conversation. It is clear that Leese dominated Mason in terms of IR measures. Leese used turns that demanded a response from Mason on three of seven occasions (i.e., the three explicit questions in turns beginning at lines 3, 12, and 14). All of Leese's other turns contained assertions that added information to the exchange, thus inviting a response from Mason though not demanding one. Mason, by contrast, did not use any turns to demand a response from Leese. Moreover, Mason had two turns that were purely reactive, adding no new information at all and thus returning the initiative to Leese (turns at lines 2 and 15). At the turn-by-turn level, therefore, Leese was very much in charge of the exchange. *Semantic dominance* reflects the degree to which one party or the other controls the topic of discussion. Leese was dominant here also because he introduced the topic that occupied their attention throughout (Mason's flying assignment). The exchange was semantically cooperative, however, in the sense that every turn by either party (except, of course, line 1) was topically relevant to the turn before.

These measures do not capture the influence that Mason exercised through active participation in two dialogue transactions. Mason initiated a request–offer transaction that Leese agreed to participate in and was its potential beneficiary in the role of requester. He became its actual beneficiary when Leese granted his request. Although Leese was responsible for the initiation of a challenge–defend dialogue, Mason was the potential beneficiary in the role of defender and as beneficiary of the superordinate request–offer dialogue. Although it is not clear whether Mason's defense actually changed Leese's mind, it was successful in getting Leese to drop his challenge. Dialogue mental models thus capture influence in collaborative transactions that IR measures miss, based on conversational data that are ignored by macro-theories of power.

FAILING TO COOPERATE

Mason and Leese each used conversational devices to overcome obstacles posed by face threats to a successful transaction. By contrast, the conversation between Mason and another superior (Shaker) presented in Table 8.2 has a very different dominance profile and a very different outcome (Mason, 1983, p. 188). By the time of this conversation, Mason has been flying missions in Vietnam for 3 months and is considerably more experienced than in the earlier conversation. After less than 2 hours of sleep in 2 days of nonstop flying and with a sense of a job well done, Mason and his partner are stunned to hear Shaker assign them an unexpected new flying mission. Mason is certain that Shaker is aware of their exhaustion and suspects bad faith in the assignment decision. Mason catches up with Shaker as he walks out of the briefing and initiates the exchange in Table 8.2.

In terms of quantitative dominance, this conversation is extreme: 49 words for Shaker and only 10 for Mason. Moreover, the word-count evidence is strengthened by direct evidence of suppression, such as Shaker's interruption of Mason (lines 7 through 8) and Mason's failure to take a full turn after the interruption (line 9) (Kasermann, 1991). IR analysis gives the same verdict. Mason and Shaker had one turn each in the high-initiative category (lines 1 and 8, respectively), but both of Shaker's other two turns either demanded a response or introduced new information, whereas neither of Mason's did. What about dominance at the dialogue level? It might be supposed that Mason performed better at this level because he initiated an indirect request to change his assignment (line 1) even though the request was not granted (line 10). Closer examination of the exchange reveals, to the contrary, that Mason and Shaker never achieved the shared acceptance and agreement on relevance criteria necessary for a transaction. Because this was due in large part to active violation of expectations by Shaker, a dialogue-based analysis supports the conclusion that Shaker was dominant.

Mason begins the exchange (line 1 of Table 8.2) with an utterance that is ambiguous regarding its transactional intent. It hints at the existence of a reason for changing the assignment but is several steps removed from matching the request–offer structure. In this case, Mason has chosen ambiguity not to *avoid* a face threat to Shaker, as in Table 8.1, but to create one (even if taken as an exaggeration, "trying to kill us" is a serious accusation). In addition, Mason lays a trap for Shaker. If Shaker agrees to change the assignment in response to the highly indirect request in line 1, it can only be because he is already aware of the reason (Mason's exhaustion) and therefore it amounts to a confession of bad faith in the original assignment (another threat to Shaker's positive regard). If line 1 was intended to be a request, Mason has provided a disincentive for the preferred response (a change in assignment).

Shaker denies the accusation (line 2, Table 8.2) and defends his denial (lines 3–6) by giving an alternative explanation for the assignment (namely, that Mason needs practice flying at night), which does double duty as a reason for rejecting a reassignment request. In these moves, Shaker evokes expectations associated with the roles of defender in challenge–defend (Fig. 8.2) and potential offerer in request–offer (Fig. 8.1). Unfortunately he violates both sets of norms. The reasons Shaker provides (lines 3–6) in defense of line 2 fail to match the means conditions of a challenge–defend dialogue. First, they do not supply reasons that the potential challenger (Mason) would ever be likely to accept; both Shaker and Mason knew that Mason had plenty of night-flying experience. Second, they are not an adequate defense of the conclusion (line 2) even if true because they fail to address the exhaustion that Shaker certainly recognized as the point of line 1. Shaker has taken advantage of Mason's ambiguity in line 1 to pretend that Mason had no reason at all for uttering it. It is clear that the ostensible defender (Shaker) has no real desire to resolve the disagreement, a violation of the motive condition of challenge–defend. Moreover, as a response to Mason's indirect request, lines 3 to 6 violate a key expectation imposed by Fig. 8.1, that a request will be granted if it is strongly motivated (e.g., by extreme exhaustion) and the offerer has no compelling reason to disprefer granting it (Shaker has provided no such reason). Finally, both the instructional tone of lines 2 through 6 and the claim that Mason needs more night-flying experience are attacks against Mason's positive face. In sum, lines 2 through 6 are an aggressively noncooperative response at the dialogue level despite their surface civility.

Mason is probably trying to raise the issue of exhaustion explicitly in line 7 ("But—"). By interrupting him (line 8), Shaker violates Mason's legitimate expectation of being allowed to challenge the reasons that Shaker presented in lines 3 to 6. Shaker shows his unwillingness to continue in the role of defender and shifts the defender's burden of proof to Mason (another violation of mutual expectations associated with challenge–defend). In line 8, Shaker challenges Mason's implicit claim to be exhausted, thereby revealing that he had been aware of it from the start. Shaker's challenge, moreover, depends on an unacceptable assumption (that any amount of sleep is enough, no matter how little) and therefore counts as another violation of the motive condition (a genuine desire to resolve disagreement). Viewed as a conversational device, the question in line 8, "You got some sleep last night, right?," presupposes a specific answer (because it is declaratively phrased) and discourages any elaboration or objection (because it is brusque). Finally, line 10 unilaterally ends the discussion, making clear that the decision will not take Mason's input into account.

At each turn, Shaker mimicked acceptance of a dialogue role, raising expectations associated with defender, potential offerer, and challenger. In each case, however, he proceeded to violate the relevant constraints. Although Shaker's tactics may have begun as retaliation for Mason's initial misstep in line 1, the exchange probably exacerbated Mason's original suspicion of unfairness in the assignment. Punishment for raising questions in discussion is consistent with vindictive motives in the assignment decision itself. The consequences of unfair assignments (in particular, favoring some subordinates over others) can be severe, involving deadly risk in combat and stalled careers in business, and are of intense concern to subordinates. They should also be of concern to leaders because perceived unfairness may cause a breakdown in the mutual trust necessary for collective action (Shay, 1995, pp. 10–14). Shaker never addressed those concerns.

Leadership training based on cognitive dialogue theory teaches leaders how to manage and stay in control of interactive exchanges without transgressing norms that maintain trust. They learn to recognize the expectations that their own actions elicit in others and to avoid implicit commitments that they do not intend to keep. In particular, they learn to turn down a proffered dialogue role when they judge that it is inappropriate without closing off the possibility of a more appropriate dialogue at a later time.

SENSE MAKING

Cognitive dialogue theory has an interesting corollary. The meaning of a transaction and the utterances within it may change retrospectively as the participants' understanding of the enterprise evolves. As the type of activity being conducted becomes more overt and less ambiguous, changes direction, or is viewed in retrospect, the contribution of earlier utterances may be seen in a different light. The Leese–Mason exchange (Table 8.1) has several examples of retrospective meaning that become accessible only after the request–offer structure is recognized as the appropriate match at line 7: (a) Leese's sitting down next to Mason may be seen in hindsight as showing an intent to permit and even invite discussion with subordinates. (b) Line 1 can be taken to describe the situation that Mason wanted to change. (c) Mason's "Really?" in line 2 can be seen as expressing a desire to change the assignment. In these cases, the meaning of previous events is clarified as a byproduct of the transaction itself. In other cases, however, dialogue participants may intentionally make statements that modify the contents of the transaction structure or its mapping to previous actions and thus retroactively change the meanings of earlier events.

For example, lines 14 and 15 (Table 8.1) appear to be a puzzling redundancy in which Leese elicits a repetition of line 7 just before he announces his decision to grant Mason's reassignment request. The effect is to reconstruct the conversation *as if* the challenging and defending in lines 8 through 13 had never taken place at all. This can be explained, therefore, as retroactive sense making designed to simulate the immediate acceptance of Mason's request in line 7 and mitigate the positive face threat that the entire critical dialogue posed to Mason.

The conversation might have ended with Mason's expression of appreciation ("Thanks") in line 18 of Table 8.1 (matching the expected results component of Fig. 8.1). However, it continues for a few more lines even *after* the work of the request–offer and challenge–defend transactions are completed. This part of the exchange allows the parties to disclose and revise their understandings of what has just occurred. In lines 18 and 19, Mason implies that Leese's reason for agreement to the reassignment was avoidance of disaster (motive). Mason thus sees the request–offer dialogue as one in which he had nothing positive to offer Leese in exchange for disrupting the flying schedule. Leese subtly but firmly rejects this understanding of their conversation. In line 20, Leese indicates that he is not convinced of Mason's inability to fly off the carrier, implicitly redefining the claim that was settled in the challenge–defend dialogue (the sincerity of Mason's worry rather than its validity). Leese goes on in lines 21 and 22 to supply an entirely new context for the request–offer dialogue. As for motive, Mason will get some practice, alleviating his worry about his flying ability (line 22). At the same time, Leese will get a copilot that he needed anyway (line 21), so the effect is not to degrade the performance of the unit but to enhance it (means). Leese encourages Mason to see the entire exchange as a plus–plus negotiation in which everyone, including the organization itself, comes out ahead. In these few lines at the end of the conversation, Leese redirects Mason's attention from self- to group-centered objectives. Cognitive dialogue theory explains how leaders can use conversational exchanges to accomplish on a micro level the retrospective sense making that Weick (2001) identified as a major contributor to the development of organizational purpose and meaning.

CONCLUSION: COGNITIVE DIALOGUE THEORY AND LEADER DEVELOPMENT

This chapter focused on two hypotheses. The first is that leadership skills are manifested in the interactions that leaders have with subordinates and others. The second is that those interactions can be illuminated by an integration of cognitive and communicative concepts, methods, and findings. The purpose of the chapter was to illustrate one such integration, cognitive dialogue theory, and show how dialogue mental models, politeness strategies, and conversational devices can be combined for naturalistic description, theoretical understanding, and practical measurement of conversations between leaders and subordinates. A third hypothesis was that understanding leadership behavior in terms of the cognitive skills underlying dialogue can contribute to the development of better leaders. To fully develop and test this idea, it will be necessary to (a) identify patterns of individual differences and situational contingencies in the use of dialogue models, politeness strategies, and conversational devices in conversations among leaders, subordinates, and others, (b) incorporate findings into the curricula of leader development programs, and (c) measure the outcomes.

The chapter identified an important set of skills to be included among the objectives of a cognitive and communicative approach to leader development. Dialogue mental models figure prominently in such leadership skills as learning how to recognize different types of transactions (e.g., negotiation, inquiry, deliberation, request–offer, and challenge–defend), determining when they are appropriate and when not, and mastering the associated expectations and roles. Politeness strategies capture complementary aspects of leadership skill, such as identifying negative threats to freedom of action, identifying positive threats to self-regard, learning how such threats can obstruct dialogue transactions, and adopting appropriate strategies for mitigating threats while accomplishing the business at hand. Skill in the use of conversational devices enables leaders to put dialogue skills into practice. They include learning to detect and handle conversational control tactics by others, learning to predict the responses of others, negotiating demands for attention and floor time with subordinates, and being able to control conversation when necessary without violating trust.

There are many obstacles to successful conduct of collaborative transactions such as request–offer and challenge–defend. Among them are (a) tendencies to disguise requests and disagreements because of face threats (the problem that Mason and Leese tackled successfully in Table 8.1), (b) unwillingness to generate and consider alternative possibilities (part of Mason's problem in line 1 of Table 8.2), and (c) adoption of actively noncooperative attitudes in response to face threats (Shaker's problem in Table 8.2). These difficulties are sometimes camouflaged by other, more legitimate reasons for declining such transactions: for example, fleeting opportunities that call for quick decisions, time lags between planning and implementation that impose a cost on revisiting and revising plans, low-stakes decisions which do not warrant additional deliberation, and occasional inappropriate challenges to authority. It is no small accomplishment for leaders to plot a safe path for themselves and subordinates through these opposing dangers and opportunities.

Popular "dialogue" approaches address such problems by explicitly declaring a safe setting where authority hierarchies, organizational practices and exigencies, interpersonal conflicts, and time constraints are to be held in suspension

(Bohm, 1996; Isaacs, 1999; Yankelovich, 1999). This is a special *type* of dialogue that concentrates on relationship goals and excludes immediate task goals. Like request–offer or challenge–defend, "dialoguing" has its own characteristic motives (to remove fundamental long-term obstacles to effectively working together), means (an ability to reflect on deeply rooted assumptions in a nonjudgmental manner), opportunity (a license to regard all participants as equal and to suspend task work for the duration of the dialogue), and cognitive intent (to develop a deeper mutual understanding). In most cases, however, participants in group activity have no choice but to tend to task and relationship issues simultaneously, as in Tables 8.1 and 8.2. Dialogues are an essential part of everyday activity, along with the complications of time stress, differences in rank, social risk, and the inertia of habitual practices. Leadership training in real-world contexts should emphasize (a) skill in judging *when* it is desirable to spend time in a particular type of dialogue transaction and when it is not (Cohen et al., 1998; Cohen & Thompson, 2001), (b) skill in translating such judgments into effective conversation management by means of politeness strategies and conversational devices without threats to the positive regard of subordinates and without undermining group cohesion, and (c) collaborative techniques that are not personally threatening to either leaders or subordinates for presenting, challenging, and defending requests and claims to both improve task performance and encourage "buy-in" by subordinates.

Early work on leadership tried to identify distinct *behaviors* corresponding to task and relationship concerns. The problem this work encountered is that a single behavior often reflects both kinds of concern at once (Yukl, 1998, p. 56). Theories that focus on leadership styles rather than behavior bypass this difficulty by obtaining subjective judgments that average over behaviors and situations, permitting high overall scores in both categories. As a result, however, style theories supply little concrete understanding of how and why subjectively assessed styles manifest themselves in action. The practical guidance provided by such theories is not always as general as "show concern for both tasks and people," but it is far from specific.

One important contribution of cognitive dialogue theory is its demonstration of just how closely intertwined task and relationship concerns can be in leadership while allowing us to understand and measure them separately. The task of leaders is to strike a balance that is right for the situation. The way to understand how leaders succeed or fail in striking this balance is to analyze real conversations and the cognitive skills they draw on. The way to improve their chances of success is to instruct, demonstrate, practice, and reward skills of dialogue.

REFERENCES

Austin, J. (1965). *How to do things with words.* Oxford: Oxford University Press.
Barge, J. K. (1994). *Leadership: Communication skills for organizations and groups.* New York: St. Martin's.

Bass, B. M. (1990). *Bass and Stodgill's handbook of leadership: Theory, research, and managerial applications.* New York: Free Press.

Blumer, R. (1969). *Symbolic interactionism.* Berkeley: University of California Press.

Bohm, D. (1996). On dialogue. In L. Nichol (Ed.), *On dialogue* (pp. 6–47). London: Routledge.

Bratman, M. E. (1999). *Faces of intention.* Cambridge: Cambridge University Press.

Brown, P., & Levinson, S. C. (1987). *Politeness: Some universals in language usage.* Cambridge: Cambridge University Press.

Cohen, M. S., Adelman, L., Bresnick, T., Marvin, F., Salas, E., & Riedel, S. (2003). *Using dialogue methods to teach critical thinking in Army battlefield tactics.* Manuscript in preparation.

Cohen, M., Freeman, J. T., & Thompson, B. B. (1998). Critical thinking skills in tactical decision making: A model and a training method. In J. Cannon-Bowers & E. Salas (Eds.), *Decision-making under stress: Implications for training and simulation* (pp. 155–189). Washington, DC: American Psychological Association.

Cohen, M. S., Salas, E., & Riedel, S. (2002). *Critical thinking: Challenges, possibilities, and purpose.* Arlington, VA: Cognitive Technologies.

Cohen, M. S., & Thompson, B. B. (2001). Training teams to take initiative: Critical thinking in novel situations. In E. Salas (Ed.), *Advances in cognitive engineering and human performance research* (pp. 251–291). Amsterdam: JAI.

Drew, P., & Heritage, J. (1992). *Talk at work.* Cambridge: Cambridge University Press.

Geis, M. (1995). *Speech acts and conversational interaction.* Cambridge: Cambridge University Press.

Grice, P. (1989). *Studies in the way of words.* Cambridge, MA: Harvard University Press.

Grosz, B. J., & Sidner, C. L. (1990). Plans for discourse. In P. R. Cohen, J. Morgan, & M. F. Pollack (Eds.), *Intentions in Communication* (pp. 417–444). Cambridge, MA: MIT Press.

Hamblin, C. H. (1970). *Fallacies.* Newport News, VA: Vale.

Hutchins, E. (1990). The technology of team navigation. In J. Galegher, R. E. Kraut, & C. Egido (Eds.), *Intellectual teamwork: Social and technological foundations of cooperative work* (pp. 191–220). Hillsdale, NJ: Lawrence Erlbaum Associates, Inc.

Hutchins, E. (1995). *Cognition in the wild.* Cambridge, MA: MIT Press.

Isaacs, W. (1999). *Dialogue and the art of thinking together.* New York: Currency.

Johnson-Laird, P. N. (1983). *Mental models.* Cambridge, MA: Harvard University Press.

Kasermann, M. (1991). Obstruction and dominance: Uncooperative moves and their effect on the course of conversation. In I. Markova & K. Foppa (Eds.), *Asymmetries in dialogue* (pp. 101–123). Savage, MD: Barnes & Noble.

Keppler, A., & Luckmann, T. (1991). 'Teaching': Conversational transmission of knowledge. In I. Markova & K. Foppa (Eds.), *Asymmetries in dialogue* (pp. 143–165). Savage, MD: Barnes & Noble.

Knoblauch, H. (1991). The taming of foes: The avoidance of symmetry in informal discussions. In I. Markova & K. Foppa (Eds.), *Asymmetries in dialogue* (pp. 166–194). Savage, MD: Barnes & Noble.

Levinson, S. C. (1983). *Pragmatics.* Cambridge: Cambridge University Press.

Linell, P., & Luckmann, T. (1991). Asymmetries in dialogue: Some conceptual preliminaries. In I. Markova & K. Foppa (Eds.), *Asymmetries in dialogue* (pp. 1–20). Savage, MD: Barnes & Noble.

Mason, R. (1983). *Chickenhawk.* New York: Penguin.

Northouse, P. G. (2001). *Leadership: Theory and practice.* Thousand Oaks, CA: Sage.

Pennington, N., & Hastie, R. (1993). A theory of explanation-based decision making. In G. Klein, J. Orasanu, & C. Zsambok (Eds.), *Decision making in action: Models and methods* (pp. 188–201). Norwood, NJ: Ablex.

Pomerantz, A., & Fehr, B. (1997). Conversation analysis: An approach to the study of social action as sense making practices. In T. A. van Dijk (Ed.), *Discourse as social interaction* (pp. 64–91). Thousand Oaks, CA: Sage.

Rescher, N. (1977). *Dialectics: A controversy-oriented approach to the theory of knowledge*. Albany: State University of New York Press.

Rogoff, B., & Lave, J. (1999). *Everyday cognition: Development in social context*. Cambridge, MA: Harvard University Press.

Rommetveit, R. (1991). Dominance and asymmetries in *A Doll's House*. In I. Markova & K. Foppa (Eds.), *Asymmetries in dialogue* (pp. 195–220). Savage, MD: Barnes & Noble.

Sacks, H. (1995). *Lectures on conversation*. Malden, MA: Blackwell.

Schank, R. C. (1990). *Tell me a story: Narrative and intelligence*. Evanston, IL: Northwestern University Press.

Searle, J. R. (1969). *Speech acts: An essay in the philosophy of language*. Cambridge: Cambridge University Press.

Searle, J. R. (1979). *Expression and meaning: Studies in the theory of speech acts*. Cambridge: Cambridge University Press.

Searle, J. R. (1990). Collective intentions and actions. In P. R. Cohen, J. Morgan, & M. E. Pollack (Eds.), *Intentions in communication* (pp. 401–416). Cambridge, MA: MIT Press.

Shay, J. (1995). *Achilles in Vietnam: Combat trauma and the undoing of character*. New York: Simon & Schuster.

Silverman, D. (1998). *Harvey Sacks: Social science and conversation analysis*. New York: Oxford University Press.

Sperber, D. (1996). *Explaining culture: A naturalistic approach*. Oxford: Blackwell.

Sperber, D., & Wilson, D. A. (1995). *Relevance: Communication and cognition*. Oxford: Blackwell.

Turner, M. (2001). *Cognitive dimensions of social science*. Oxford: Oxford University Press.

van Dijk, T. A. (1997) *Discourse as social interaction*. London: Sage.

van Eemeren, F. H., & Grootendorst, R. (1983). *Speech acts in argumentative discussions*. Dordrecht, Holland: Foris.

van Eemeren, F. H., Grootendorst, R., Jackson, S., & Jacobs, S. (1993). *Reconstructing argumentative discourse*. Tuscaloosa: University of Alabama.

Walton, D. N. (1995). *A pragmatic theory of fallacy*. Tuscaloosa: University of Alabama.

Walton, D. N. (1998). *The new dialectic: Conversational contexts of argument*. Toronto: University of Toronto.

Weick, K. (2001). *Making sense of organizations*. Oxford: Blackwell.

Whitten, A., & Byrne, R. W. (1997). *Machiavellian intelligence II*. Cambridge: Cambridge University Press.

Yankelovich, D. (1999). *The magic of dialogue: Transforming conflict into cooperation*. New York: Simon & Schuster.

Yukl, G. (1998). *Leadership in organizations* (4th ed.). Upper Saddle River, NJ: Prentice-Hall.

IV

Developing Practical and Emotional Intelligence

9

Practical Intelligence and Leadership: Using Experience as a "Mentor"

Anna T. Cianciolo, John Antonakis, and Robert J. Sternberg

Yale University

The descriptors "complex" and "rapidly changing" are frequently used to characterize today's organizations, referring both to private-sector companies and to the U.S. military. These descriptors reflect general agreement that the swift rate of information change, the proliferation of technology in workplace environments, the globalization of work teams and communication networks, and the increased impact of occupational decisions are requiring organizational agility like never before. Leaders are expected to set the standard for the foresight and swift decision making required for organizational agility and ultimate success. The far-reaching, even global, consequences that high-profile corporate failures can have illustrate the potential impact of leadership decisions. Recent shifts in the mission of the U.S. Army from conventional war fighting to peacekeeping and combating terrorism provide an example of the extent to which leadership must effect organization-wide change under considerable time pressure.

The frenetic turnover rate within leadership positions, combined with limitations on the number of people who can guide an organization from its highest ranks, requires an accelerated pace of leadership development in promising, lower ranking leaders. Rapid leader development refers to preparing future leaders quickly for leadership roles as well as producing leaders who can move swiftly up the ranks within an organization. Because much of what successful leaders know is learned informally on the job (McCall, Lombardo, & Morrison, 1988; Yukl, 1999), it is critical that rapid leadership development enhances leaders' ability to learn from their on-the-job experiences. Scientific research can inform rapid leadership development by identifying the characteristics of individuals who learn quickly from their experiences and exploring ways in which experience-based learning can be facilitated. Yet, it is not generally understood how experience-based learning occurs or why individuals have ease or difficulty with this type of learning.

Although the status of leadership research indicates remarkable advance in our understanding of such a complex phenomenon as leadership, leadership research has generally not sought to explain the cognitive skills and knowledge that leaders use to determine what to do in a given situation and learn from their experiences. Notable exceptions can be found in the work of such scholars as Hooijberg, Hunt, and Dodge (1997), Sashkin (1988), and Zaccaro (1999). Sashkin (1988), for example, noted that in order to generate vision and align the members of an organization, leaders must understand the systemic nature of their work environment. However, Sashkin did not address the cognitive processes through which leaders gain the necessary knowledge to form an effective understanding and how the leader regulates his or her knowledge acquisition. Other notable exceptions include the skills-based approach to understanding leadership put forth by Mumford, Zaccaro, Harding, Jacobs, and Fleishman (2000). Mumford and his colleagues (Connelly et al., 2000; Zaccaro, Mumford, Connelly, Marks, & Gilbert, 2000) have attempted to identify and assess the general-level knowledge and metacognitive skills possessed by successful leaders and have examined their relation to leadership performance in both civilian and military settings. The initial results of this work seem promising, although neither the role of richer, more complex knowledge structures in leadership problem solving or the ways through which such knowledge is acquired were investigated.

Understanding leadership in complex, rapidly changing organizations therefore calls for an approach that supplements current leadership theory by identifying and describing the cognitive skills involved in acquiring and applying experience-based knowledge. By taking a knowledge-based approach to understanding expertise, the theory of practical intelligence—part of the broader theory of successful intelligence (Sternberg, 1997)—provides a scientific method for exploring knowledge-acquisition and application processes and how these processes relate to leadership performance (Sternberg, 2002). Such an approach would complement advances already being made in leadership research by providing insight into how the general behavioral repertoires of successful leaders described in the literature actually play out in specific situations.

Successful intelligence is defined as the balance of one's strengths and weaknesses toward the achievement of desired goals, given a particular sociocultural context. Individual differences in analytical (i.e., traditional) intelligence, practical intelligence, and creative intelligence determine, in part, the relative cognitive strengths and weaknesses a person has. Practical intelligence supports everyday problem solving in situations where problems must be defined before a solution can be reached and the information necessary to determine a solution strategy is often incomplete. Leaders typically encounter such ill-defined problem-solving situations as they work to impart their vision and guide their organization. Everyday problems are solved in three ways: (a) adaptation of the self to the environment in which the problem occurred, (b) modification (shaping) of the environment to better support the self, and (c) selection of a new environment in which the problem does not occur.

Consider the unpromising academic records of such widely known successful leaders as Bill Gates and Gen. George Patton. The theory of successful intelligence can account for the, to many, counterintuitive relationship between the academic performance of these individuals and their performance as leaders by acknowledging that there is more to success than academic, or traditional, notions of intelligence. According to the theory of successful intelligence, these leaders knew how to capitalize on their strengths, especially their practical intelligence, in order to achieve success. The particular problem-solving strategies employed by these leaders have not been scientifically analyzed; however, the theory of successful intelligence would suggest that they seemed to know just what to do to solve particular problems because they knew when to adapt to their situation and when to play an active role in determining their situation, either by making modifications to the situation or choosing a new situation altogether. The theory of successful intelligence would not suggest that these leaders relied on practical intelligence alone. Of course, analytical intelligence, analogous to intelligence as traditionally defined, certainly plays a role (House & Aditya, 1997; Lord, De Vader, & Alliger, 1986; Smith & Foti, 1998), as does creative intelligence and wisdom (Sternberg & Vroom, 2002).

Given the vast amount of time and money already devoted to leader selection and leadership education, it is important to consider what the theory of practical intelligence really has to offer. That is, what implications for leadership theory and for human resources management does this theory have? How would a scientific theory of experience-based learning buttress rapid leadership development efforts in specific?

Organizational selection and development practices provide ample evidence that experience-based learning is considered an important part of a leader's capability. The use of assessments of job-related decision making and knowledge—situational judgment tests (SJTs)—to select and train managers in diverse job domains is effective and widely accepted (McDaniel & Nguyen, 2001) (also called low-fidelity simulations; Motowidlo, Hanson, & Crafts, 1997). Identifying and measuring experience-based knowledge is especially important for understanding successful leadership more completely because traits and behaviors identified as important to successful leadership still fail to account completely for individual differences in leadership capability (Sternberg, 2002; Sternberg et al., 2000). However, there does not exist a consensus regarding what SJTs measure (McDaniel,

Morgeson, Finnegan, Campion, & Braverman, 2001; McDaniel & Nguyen, 2001; Weekley & Jones, 1999). With a scientific understanding of experience-based learning and on-the-job problem solving, reliable and valid SJTs can be created because they are based on theory (McDaniel & Nguyen, 2001). Our research has shown that SJTs based on the theory of practical intelligence are reliable and valid and show a substantial relation to managerial performance (Wagner & Sternberg, 1985, 1990a) and military leadership (Sternberg et al., 2000), even when considered along with measures of general cognitive ability.

Formal leadership education, though based on theory, falls short of fully developing in junior leaders the practical knowledge necessary to lead and the cognitive skills that can be used to acquire this knowledge rapidly on the job. Decades of leadership research have informed formal leadership education by outlining the broad dispositional characteristics and describing the general-level behaviors of successful leaders (e.g., Bass, 1998; House & Aditya, 1997; Zaccaro, Foti, & Kenny, 1991). The focus of this research, however, has been to explain the process by which the traits and behaviors of successful leaders have an impact on individuals, groups, or organizations. This research does not shed light on what a leader must know in order to demonstrate such general leader behaviors as "empowering subordinates" or "providing individualized consideration." An understanding of how experience-based knowledge is acquired and applied to making leadership decisions makes it possible to develop leader-training methodologies that target the specific cognitive processes and knowledge structures that must be enhanced through intervention.

In this chapter, we describe in greater detail the theory of practical intelligence and how it relates to rapid leader development. Our discussion includes an overview of the construct of practical intelligence, the measurement issues associated with creating assessments of practical intelligence, and a broad sketch of our research findings. We conclude with a presentation of our ongoing leader development research and planned future research directions.

THE THEORY OF PRACTICAL INTELLIGENCE—WHAT IS IT?

Practical intelligence is defined as a general ability to learn from experience and to apply experience-based, or tacit, knowledge to novel everyday problem situations. We use the term *tacit* to refer to experience-based knowledge because such knowledge is not explicitly taught and it often is difficult to articulate. A critical distinguishing characteristic of tacit knowledge is that it is an active form of knowledge, specifying the particular action that must be taken, given a particular condition, rather than a list of facts that can be memorized and assessed with discrete test items. Someone who is practically intelligent acquires tacit knowledge more readily than others and knows how to apply it in novel situations. An implication of the theory of practical intelligence is that someone who has high practical intelligence will develop leadership expertise more quickly than will someone who has lower practical intelligence because successful leadership is theorized to depend not only on academic knowledge, but on experience-based learning as well. In order for tacit knowledge to be acquired, however, an individual must have been exposed to the knowledge via experience. The theory and its related measurement techniques described here represent an attempt to capture the interaction of experience and ability.

The theory of practical intelligence was developed in response to traditional conceptions of intelligence based on conventional ability testing. The theory has sought to broaden traditional conceptions by proposing a basic ability—practical intelligence—coupled with a cognitive explanation for how ability facilitates performance in particular environments—through tacit knowledge acquisition and application. It is the attempt to incorporate environmental demands into an understanding of basic intellectual functioning that sets the theory of practical intelligence apart from most theories of intelligence and of expertise, including theories of successful leadership. This theory differs from modern contingency theories of leadership (e.g., House, 1996) in that it does not focus on the behaviors associated with effective leadership in certain situations, but describes the cognitive processes and knowledge that allow leaders to adjust their style flexibly to particular problem situations. This theory is related to cognitive complexity approaches to leadership (Hooijberg et al., 1997) in that the distinction between practical intelligence and tacit knowledge on one hand and general cognitive ability on the other is analogous to the distinction made by Day and Lance (chap. 3, this volume) between cognitive complexity and general cognitive ability. Cognitive complexity, as well as practical intelligence and tacit knowledge, is posited to contribute to more complex and flexible behavioral repertoires independently of general cognitive ability.

According to the theory of practical intelligence, to identify an expert in a particular domain is to identify a person who has, through experience, gained an acute sensitivity to the important information in a given situation and the knowledge of what to do in response to this information. This expert has developed a rich set of condition–action procedures that permits skilled performance in the domain in which he or she has invested time and therefore had experience and the opportunity to acquire tacit knowledge. The key characteristic of this theory—defining expertise in terms of environmental demands and intellectual capability—makes it particularly useful for supplementing current leadership theory because it explains how the personality traits and behaviors of successful leaders actually work in a particular context. A theory that links the demands of the environment to the capability of the individual is well situated to enhance leadership development in ways that current leadership theory cannot because the theory demystifies how experts seem to know exactly what to do in particular situations. Furthermore, the theory of practical intelligence is linked to a wide-ranging theory of intelligence that has been extensively tested and therefore allows for the operationalization of psychological constructs in a way that supports measurement (Antonakis, Hedlund, Pretz, & Sternberg, 2002; Hedlund et al., 1998; Wagner, 1987; Wagner & Sternberg, 1985, 1990b; Wagner, Sujan, Sujan, Rashotte, & Sternberg, 1999).

For the purposes of connecting the theory of practical intelligence to rapid leadership development, we present the following questions we have tried to answer through our research:

1. What cognitive skills underlie individual differences in experience-based learning? There are clearly individual differences in the ability to acquire knowledge from experience. Indeed, we have watched our colleagues and perhaps observed ourselves make the same mistakes over and over again while only slowly gaining the critical insights that would terminate the cycle of error. Sternberg's (1997) theory of practical intelligence describes the cognitive processes and problem-solving skills of the practically intelligent individual that give rise to this ability and can be enhanced through intervention. According to the theory, there are three cognitive processes through which knowledge acquisition occurs: (a) selective encoding, (b) selective combination, and (c) selective comparison.

In any given situation, a person is bombarded with bits of information, only some of which is relevant to accomplishing a particular purpose. *Selective encoding* is the successful targeting of only the relevant information for the purposes of problem solving and learning. *Selective combination* is the integration of multiple pieces of selectively encoded information into a unified whole that creates a meaningful pattern and, eventually, a knowledge structure. *Selective comparison* is the integration of a newly developed pattern of information or knowledge structure with previously existing knowledge structures. Past knowledge, through comparison with newly acquired information, is brought to bear on problem solving, resulting in the development of a more complex body of knowledge to bring to new situations. The practically intelligent person experiencing a new problem exercises these three cognitive processes through reflection. They allow him or her to develop a sensitivity to the information present in the environment and in previous experiences that guides problem solving and behavior. The increased behavioral complexity made possible by the development of these discriminatory and integrative knowledge-acquisition processes has direct implications for leadership effectiveness through enhancing the flexibility of a leader's behavioral repertoire (Day & Lance, chap. 3, this volume).

Consider as an example archers trying to improve their respective targeting skills. In order to diagnose the causes of targeting errors and learn how to improve, practically intelligent archers will devote attention to the tension likely present in their shoulders, arms, and hands or to the tightness in their breathing, as opposed to the kind of shoes they are wearing (selective encoding). The archers will also devote attention to how the information coming from their bodies covaries with the visual cues they use for targeting (selective combination). Tightened shoulders, for example, may systematically offset the edge of the bow to the left or right, which causes the arrow to go astray. Finally, the archers will actively discern how the meaningful patterns of information present in the environment (e.g., direction and strength of wind) compare to previous experiences in which the arrow went astray or landed on target (selective comparison). This comparison will help the archers determine how the pattern of kinesthetic sensations they receive ultimately results in a hit or missed target. In the skilled archer who is practically intelligent, these cognitive processes are automatic and effortless. These cognitive processes must be carefully articulated for and practiced by individuals attempting to develop them.

2. We know that knowledge based in experience is important, but how does this knowledge actually work when someone is solving a difficult problem? The facilitative effect of experience-based knowledge is understood by recognizing that the environment serves as a gateway to demonstrating that knowledge. Ecological psychologists have long recognized that performance is a function of the fit between the capability of the individual to complete some task and the environmental support for completing that same task (Gibson, 1979/1986). For example, these psychologists recognized that a person's swimming performance depends on two things: (a) that the person is capable of swimming and (b) that the person is in a medium that is "swim-in-able." Findings from cross-cultural research support the use of an ecological approach to understanding intellectual functioning. This research reveals that knowledge and environmental context interact to determine demonstrated expertise (Sternberg & Grigorenko, 1997; Sternberg et al., 2001). In this research, it was demonstrated that conventional tests of intelligence widely administered in the United States showed little relation to the kind of practical knowledge about medicine required for survival in a disease-troubled rural Kenyan village. As formal Western schooling was not a critical antecedent of success in this environment, neither was performance on the tests that reflect the outcomes of such schooling.

An implication of this work is that when trying to understand individual differences in performance, one cannot consider the intellectual capabilities of the individuals independently of the environment in which they are asked to perform. Provided that new experiences are similar in nature to previous ones, experience-based knowledge creates the critical link between what a person knows and the demands made by the environment. Experience-based knowledge facilitates performance by allowing the individual to define the novel problems being faced in an environment that is functionally similar to the one in which the knowledge was acquired. Problem definition has been determined to be an important aspect of expert performance (Antonakis, Hedlund, Pretz, Cianciolo, & Sternberg, 2002; Sternberg, 1977, 1981).

3. How is experience-based knowledge applied by the practically intelligent? A person who has a well-developed set of problem-solving skills, such as defining the problem correctly when several alternative problem definitions exist, developing an effective strategy for solving the problem, and monitoring progress toward problem solution, is the best equipped to apply tacit knowledge to practical problem solving. Problem-solving skills are widely known and described in detail in the literature and so will not be given additional attention here.

4. Can we, through training, develop knowledge-acquisition processes in people who do not already possess them? Can practical intelligence be improved? The answer to this question stems from an understanding of both knowledge-acquisition processes and practical problem solving. Once the knowledge critical to expert performance is determined and the cognitive processes of people who are particularly adept at acquiring this knowledge are identified, the insight is available for developing training interventions geared toward building expert performance. Put another way, the tacit knowledge of expert performers can be made explicit and shared. Alternatively, the cognitive processes and problem-solving skills that experts use to gain experience-based knowledge can be developed in less expert individuals. Current on-the-job leadership development efforts, such as executive coaching, mentoring, action learning, and communities of practice (see Day, 2000, for a summary), may help make tacit knowledge held by experts in an organization explicit. The relatively delayed delivery of feedback in these sorts of development activities, however, may preclude the enhancement of knowledge-acquisition processes.

The following sections briefly describe the theory of practical intelligence as it pertains to the development of measures of practical intelligence and tacit knowledge. The necessary differences between such measures and traditional measures of intelligence are highlighted, and the measurement properties of the developed measures are discussed. In addition, the potential role of measuring practical intelligence in facilitating experience-based learning and enhancing leadership capability are described.

PRACTICAL INTELLIGENCE AND TACIT KNOWLEDGE—A COGNITIVE EXPLANATION FOR ABILITY

The theory of practical intelligence provides a testable explanation for how experience-based knowledge is acquired and how it facilitates performance when people encounter a problem situation. A simple, conceptual depiction of this explanation is provided in Fig. 9.1, which illustrates the process of acquiring new tacit knowledge and applying this knowledge to everyday problem-solving situations. Immediately apparent in the figure is the interdependence of tacit knowledge and

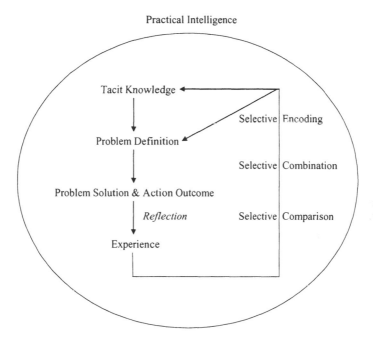

FIG. 9.1. A conceptual model of tacit knowledge and practical intelligence.

practical intelligence. Through the three knowledge-acquisition processes, practical intelligence allows for the acquisition of tacit knowledge, knowledge that is not explicitly taught, but rather acquired through experience. Tacit knowledge and knowledge-acquisition processes aid in both defining a complex, ill-defined problem situation and, by extension, determining the action to take to solve the problem. Practical intelligence plays an additional role in determining a problem solution and the corresponding action that should be taken after the application of tacit knowledge and knowledge acquisition processes. Reflection on the problem solution and action outcome—which can occur consciously when solving novel problems or unconsciously when dealing with routine problems—creates an experience that can be used as a "mentor," an experience in which tacitly held beliefs and their influence on the problem-solving process can be changed through the application of the three knowledge-acquisition processes, selective encoding, selective combination, and selective comparison.

A more detailed depiction of how practical intelligence and tacit knowledge facilitate performance is provided in Fig. 9.2, which features an example familiar to all working adults. The example involves a subordinate who is not performing as well as is expected. Figure 9.2 illustrates the process through which tacit knowledge is acquired and applied to solving the leadership problem in this example.

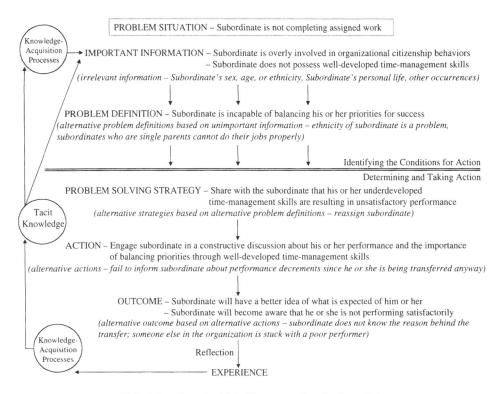

FIG. 9.2.   Practical intelligence—detailed model.

Identifying the Conditions for Action

As shown in Fig. 9.2, a hypothetical manager has encountered a new problem situation; a subordinate is failing to complete assigned work. As stated previously, typical leadership-problem situations present the leader with a multitude of information, much of it irrelevant to actually defining the problem, but yet potentially salient to the leader who lacks experience or has failed to learn from experience. Selective encoding helps the practically intelligent leader determine what information is relevant for solving the problem and what is not. In the case of the hypothetical manager, the relevant information includes the facts that the subordinate is overly involved in organizational citizenship behaviors and that the subordinate does not possess the kind of time-management skills necessary to balance organizational citizenship behaviors with job-specific tasks. Irrelevant information in the example might be the sex, age, or ethnicity of the subordinate, details about the subordinate's personal life, or other events that become spuriously linked to the problem. Selective combination helps the hypothetical manager determine that the subordinate is failing to complete assigned work because the ability to balance priorities is lacking. Inability to integrate this information may lead one to incorrectly determine the nature of the problem. By engaging in selective comparison, the manager in this example could determine the similarity of the current situation with tacit knowledge acquired from past experiences in order to more completely define the problem.

Together, the identification of important information in a problem situation, the combination of this information into a meaningful pattern, and the comparison of this information with tacit knowledge from past experience allows the problem solver to define exactly the problem being faced. In this example, the hypothetical manager defined the problem as one in which the subordinate was incapable of balancing his or her priorities for success.

As shown italicized in Fig. 9.2, alternative problem definitions based on the selection of irrelevant information in the problem situation and incorrect tacit knowledge base are possible. A simplified depiction of *incorrect* tacit knowledge leading to the selection of incorrect information might look, for example, like this: If a subordinate is a single parent (condition), the subordinate will demonstrate inferior work performance and should be reassigned (action). This incorrect tacit knowledge may guide the hypothetical manager to select details about the subordinate's personal life as important information in the problem situation. The alternative, incorrect, problem definition might then be that the subordinate's single parenthood is a problem (i.e., the problem would not exist if the subordinate was married or childless).

Determining and Taking Action

After defining the problem, the problem solver must devise a strategy to solve the problem. This strategy, based on how the problem was defined, determines the action that must be taken to solve the problem. One's tacit knowledge assists in the development of solution strategies not only by aiding in the selection of the conditions for action, but also by coupling particular actions with specific conditions. In the case of the manager in this example, the strategy for dealing with the subordinate having trouble juggling priorities is to share with the subordinate that his or her underdeveloped time-management skills are resulting in unsatisfactory performance. The manager takes action by engaging the subordinate in a constructive discussion about his or her performance and the importance of balancing priorities through well-developed time-management skills. It is critical that action be taken so that the appropriateness of the conditions used as triggers for action can be tested and learning can occur (Schön, 1983).

As shown by the italicized material in Fig. 9.2, having incorrect tacit knowledge or inefficient knowledge-acquisition processes influences the entire problem-solving cycle because problem-solving strategies, corresponding actions, and resulting outcomes are based on one's having (a) focused on irrelevant information in the problem situation and (b) defined the problem erroneously. A manager who defined the problem as one of single parenthood may request that the subordinate be reassigned. This manager would then take action to remove the problem subordinate, resulting in a failure to improve the actual problem situation.

Learning from experience based on action outcomes occurs only after action is taken and the individual reflects on the desirability of the action outcomes and the steps that led up to taking action. Reflection on the outcome of action taken allows the problem solver to determine whether the problem solution has been reached or whether a re-evaluation of problem-solving strategies or even problem definition is necessary in order to reach the desired outcome. When desired outcomes occur, new tacit knowledge containing links between conditions and actions is formed, learning from experience has happened, and subsequent performance is enhanced. When undesired outcomes occur, prior tacit knowledge must be re-evaluated through reflection, tested in action, and then updated. Through reflection, experience then becomes a "mentor," as individuals learn to treat desired outcomes as support for particular pieces of tacit knowledge and to treat undesired outcomes as informational sources for improving their knowledge and skill.

MEASURING TACIT KNOWLEDGE AND PRACTICAL INTELLIGENCE

Early research and measurement development efforts based on the theory of practical intelligence took place within particular occupational domains (e.g., management) in which the goal was to provide an explanation of expert performance in terms of an ability–experience interaction. Although practical intelligence is theorized to be a general ability, therefore facilitating tacit-knowledge acquisition across domains, domain-independent tests of cognitive processing were not expected to test the theory or enhance the explanation of expertise because tacit knowledge was theorized to be a critical aspect of ability and performance. Explaining expert performance in terms of the acquisition and application of tacit knowledge required the development of innovative ways of assessing such knowledge using reliable and valid measures. Tacit knowledge, as defined in the previous section, is a rich set of internalizations of the links between particular conditions in a problem situation and the corresponding actions that should be taken. Practical intelligence is the ability to acquire correct tacit knowledge and apply it to novel problem situations. Therefore, assessments of tacit knowledge and practical intelligence must require the individual to possess tacit knowledge important to a particular problem situation and apply this knowledge to solve the problem presented.

Situational judgment testing, an assessment method used in occupational research and personnel selection for decades (McDaniel & Nguyen, 2001), provides a particularly useful method for measuring tacit knowledge and practical intelligence. As reported in the literature, situational judgment tests (SJTs) may be used to assess a variety of personal characteristics, including personality, integrity, motivation, and cognitive skills, although little research has been done to determine what SJTs measure or how well SJTs can be used to measure a single construct (McDaniel et al., 2001; McDaniel & Nguyen, 2001; Weekley & Jones, 1999). Our research indicates that using SJTs to assess tacit knowledge and practical intelligence is useful and valid for certain purposes. The details of the developmental process of our tacit-knowledge and practical-intelligence assessments for military leaders have been discussed in detail elsewhere (Antonakis, Hedlund, Pretz, & Sternberg, 2002; Sternberg et al., 2000), and therefore only the aspects relevant to construct validity and predictive validity will be highlighted here.

Broadly speaking, we have created two types of tacit-knowledge inventories. As with traditional SJTs, both types of tacit-knowledge inventory present the individual with scenarios that depict problems typically encountered by a leader. In the case of military leadership, the problems might involve dealing with an insubordinate soldier or delivering bad news to a commanding officer who "shoots the messenger." The scenarios are based on stories of tacit-knowledge acquisition shared by expert leaders and require application of the implicit "rule," or condition–action link, that the experts felt they had learned from their experience in order to solve the problem. The primary difference between these two types of tacit-knowledge inventory developed to date lies in the degree to which responding to the problem in the scenario requires participants to articulate the cognitive processes they used to determine how to solve the problem as opposed to rating the quality of various problem-solving strategies. The first type of measure assesses the outcome of having tacit knowledge and practical intelligence—that complex practical problems are adequately solved. The second type of measure assesses not only the outcome of possessing and applying tacit knowledge, but also the cognitive processes employed by the individual during the acquisition and application of tacit knowledge.

Figure 9.3 features a representative problem scenario from the Tacit Knowledge Inventory for Managers (TKIM; Wagner & Sternberg, 1990b). It is an example of the first type of tacit-knowledge measure described in the preceding paragraph. As shown in the figure, a practical problem typically faced by managers is presented and the individual must rate, on a scale from 1 to 7, the quality of each in a set of problem solving strategies corresponding to the problem scenario. A similar inventory for assessing tacit knowledge for military leadership (TKML; Hedlund et al., 1998) at varying levels of rank has also been developed. Although there are multiple ways of computing "scores" on the assessment, performance on the inventory is measured by determining the amount of discrepancy between or agreement with the ratings of the individual taking the inventory and the average ratings given by a target group, typically experts. In some cases scoring is consensually based (Sternberg et al., 2000).

Figure 9.4 features some elements of the second type of measure, an extended case study, which is more akin to an in-basket assessment or a low-fidelity simulation (Motowidlo, Dunnette, & Carter, 1990) and is used in our research of military

You and a co-worker jointly are responsible for completing a report on a new product by the end of the week. You are uneasy about this assignment because he has a reputation for not meeting deadlines. The problem does not appear to be lack of effort. Rather, he seems to lack certain organizational skills necessary to meet a deadline and also is quite a perfectionist. As a result, too much time is wasted coming up with the "perfect" idea, product, or report. Your goal is to produce the best possible report by the deadline at the end of the week. Rate the quality of the following strategies for meeting your goal on a 1-to 7-point scale.

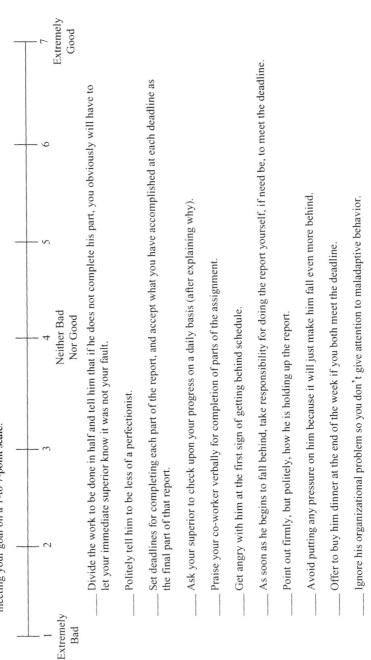

1	2	3	4	5	6	7
Extremely Bad			Neither Bad Nor Good			Extremely Good

___ Divide the work to be done in half and tell him that if he does not complete his part, you obviously will have to let your immediate superior know it was not your fault.

___ Politely tell him to be less of a perfectionist.

___ Set deadlines for completing each part of the report, and accept what you have accomplished at each deadline as the final part of that report.

___ Ask your superior to check upon your progress on a daily basis (after explaining why).

___ Praise your co-worker verbally for completion of parts of the assignment.

___ Get angry with him at the first sign of getting behind schedule.

___ As soon as he begins to fall behind, take responsibility for doing the report yourself, if need be, to meet the deadline.

___ Point out firmly, but politely, how he is holding up the report.

___ Avoid putting any pressure on him because it will just make him fall even more behind.

___ Offer to buy him dinner at the end of the week if you both meet the deadline.

___ Ignore his organizational problem so you don't give attention to maladaptive behavior.

FIG. 9.3. Example of a Tacit Knowledge Inventory for Managers (TKIM) scenario.

SCENARIO OVERVIEW

You are 2nd LT, Pete Quandry, and have recently taken over an infantry platoon with 30 soldiers and 4 Bradleys. Because you have just come on board as a platoon leader, you need to learn a lot about weapon systems and procedures. The former PL left nothing on paper to get you oriented. The platoon is currently in a state of flux because Platoon SGT, Joe Forte, just left. SSG Ed Newell, a squad leader, has been promoted from among his peers without a change in rank to replace him. Apparently, your company commander, CPT Powers, was very dissatisfied with the previous PL but had a lot of respect for the former PSG because he kept the soldiers in line. He clearly has high expectations of you and the platoon and has already given you responsibility for a new tactical mission. You and the CPT agree that this will be a great opportunity for you to develop your technical skills. You also hope it will be an opportunity to show him that you are competent.

BACKGROUND

Apparently, CPT Powers found it so frustrating to work with the former PL that he often communicated directly with PSG Forte. PSG Forte had the reputation for being highly demanding and directive with the platoon. (See attachment 1) PSG Newell knows a lot about weapon systems and procedures. You are pleased that he seems interested and willing to share his expertise. You will need to rely heavily on him to successfully accomplish the mission next week. The Platoon has a mix of experienced and newly enlisted soldiers. Several were in combat together. Attachment 2 is an early interaction with PSG Newell about the platoon. The training records indicate that all of the soldiers are current in their PT and weapons qualifications and Newell reports that the platoon has consistently met training standards. However, you have some serious concern about platoon performance because during recent FTX, you observed that the soldiers piled out of the vehicles and lit cigarettes rather than setting up a secure perimeter as their battle drill dictated. You made an on-the-spot correction and later counseled Newell about this.

ONE WEEK BEFORE THE MISSION

On Monday morning this week you discovered that one of the leader books was not up to date in the garrison. You addressed this immediately with the appropriate squad leader and emphasized the importance of knowing the whereabouts of soldiers at all times. Later in the day you discussed the issue with PSG Newell who expressed a great deal of frustration because he had addressed this and other issues with the squad leaders previously and they seemed to "yes" him without following through.

On Tuesday, there was an accident with one of the Bradleys in a training exercise. PSG Newell verbally reprimanded the soldier and squad leader who were directly involved. See attached accident report.

This morning (Wednesday) you met with PSG Newell to discuss details of the upcoming mission and your concerns about platoon performance. During the meeting he informed you that CPT Powers contacted him late in the day yesterday to inquire about how things were going with the mission. You were stunned to hear this because CPT Powers could have easily reached you yesterday at that time of day.

You have only a few days left to motivate your troops and prepare for the mission.

Attached:
1) An interaction with one of the NCOs.
2) An interaction with PSG Newell about the platoon
3) An accident report

Questions:

1. What are the problems that need to be addressed in this situation?
2. What do you believe is the single most important problem?
3. Which of the problems you have identified must be dealt with (a) in the short term and (b) in the long term?
4. In light of this situation what course of action would you take?
5. Are there any courses of action that might at first look appealing that you would avoid?
6. List any additional information/resources you would need to optimally address the problem.
7. List any past experiences you drew upon in choosing your course of action. Why were these experiences helpful?
8. What specific outcome do you hope will result from the action you have chosen?
9. What obstacles, if any, do you anticipate to obtaining this outcome? How would you know that this outcome has been achieved?

FIG. 9.4. Elements from a Tacit Knowledge for Military Leadership (TKML) extended case study.

leadership. As is evident in the figure, a more in-depth description of the problem scenario is provided as well as additional information on which problem solutions may be based. Although space does not permit illustration of them here, attachments presenting bits of conversations and an accident report are included as part of the extended case study, which depicts a complex problem and a dilemma. In addition, there are open-ended questions following the problem scenario rather than a to-be-rated list of possible problem-solving strategies. Two such pilot measures have been created and tested thus far, one appropriate to platoon leaders and the other appropriate to company commanders (Antonakis, Hedlund, Pretz, & Sternberg, 2002). Work is being devoted to developing and validating more of these case studies at varying levels of rank.

Assessments featuring rich, complex problem situations differ substantially from traditional assessments of intelligence and complex cognition, which are designed to control the information available in the test items or to minimize the degree to which prior knowledge can assist in arriving at correct answers. For example, in such tests of analogical reasoning as the Cattell Culture Fair Test of g, test items are designed to minimize the influence of enculturation on test performance by not requiring language for item completion. The items on this test comprise a set of figures in which all of the information necessary to reach the answer to the problem is provided, extraneous information is minimized, and there is only one correct answer. [This said, it should be noted that even so-called "culture fair" tests require knowledge for their solution—generally fairly abstract knowledge that is learned in school (Neisser, 1976).] More complex tests of aptitude and achievement, such as the Armed Services Vocational Aptitude Battery (ASVAB), require a greater contribution of acquired knowledge, but still involve relatively well-defined problems with one correct answer. For this reason, items on traditional tests of aptitude and achievement place a great deal of emphasis on decision making typical of academic environments rather than on the complex problem solving more typical of nonacademic environments, such as leadership.

In contrast, assessments of tacit knowledge and practical intelligence are designed to capture the complexity of everyday problems in which the information necessary for solving the problem is not complete and there is no definitive "correct" answer. Nevertheless, individuals completing tacit-knowledge and other practical-intelligence assessments must still solve problems that result in a quantified representation of performance that is expected to have measurement characteristics comparable to that of traditional intelligence tests. The items on conventional intelligence tests and practical-intelligence assessments differ, however, in that items on practical-intelligence assessments require the individual to define the problem that must be solved by identifying the important concrete information in the problem situation and determining the specific actions that should be taken based on that information. Therefore, it is expected that scores on the tacit-knowledge and practical-intelligence measures will show only a modest relation to conventional intelligence tests. Note, however, that practical-intelligence tests are not intended to and do not replace conventional academic-intelligence tests. Rather, the former tests are intended to supplement the latter in explaining and predicting expert performance.

RESEARCH SUPPORT FOR PRACTICAL INTELLIGENCE AND ITS MEASUREMENT

Several years of research, development, and testing of our tacit-knowledge and practical-intelligence measures indicate that the TKIM and TKML, as well as other occupation-specific tacit-knowledge measures, are relatively valid measures of their associated theoretical constructs (Antonakis, Hedlund, Pretz, & Sternberg, 2002; Hedlund et al., 1998; Wagner, 1987; Wagner & Sternberg, 1985, 1990b; Wagner et al., 1999). First, confirmatory factor analysis has indicated that the covariance among problem scenarios in tacit-knowledge measures can be accounted for by a hierarchical set of factors (Cianciolo, Grigorenko, Jarvin, Gil, Drebot, & Sternberg, 2002). Lower order factors represent the tacit-knowledge domain shared by the problem scenarios within a particular measure and a single higher order factor represents practical intelligence, the ability that allows for tacit-knowledge acquisition across knowledge domains. Because performance on tacit-knowledge scenarios requires both the possession of specific tacit knowledge and the efficient application of this tacit knowledge, the finding that performance on each scenario requires some contribution of scenario-specific capability but also general mental functioning is expected. Evidence indicating the lack of correspondence between tacit-knowledge measures and tests of verbal reasoning indicates that the commonality among the problem scenarios is not based simply on the shared demands they make on reading skills (Sternberg et al., 2000; Sternberg, Wagner, & Okagaki, 1993; Wagner, 1987; Wagner & Sternberg, 1985, 1990a; Wagner et al., 1999).

Second, as expected, tacit-knowledge measures generally have a small ($r < .20$), typically nonsignificant correlation with conventional intelligence tests, including, as already mentioned, tests of verbal reasoning (Sternberg et al., 2000; Wagner, 1987; Wagner & Sternberg, 1985, 1990a; Wagner et al., 1999). In some cases, the correlation is even negative (Sternberg et al., 2001). For example, scores on a verbal-reasoning test exhibited small ($r = .18$) to moderate ($r = .25$) correlations with the TKML (Sternberg et al., 2000). The moderate correlations that were found in that study were not surprising, given that SJTs have shown such correlations with general cognitive ability in other research (McDaniel & Nguyen, 2001).

Finally, tacit-knowledge measures have been shown to be valid and useful predictors of workplace performance and leadership effectiveness even when examined together with traditional measures. Scores on tacit-knowledge measures have shown significant bivariate correlations with salary and merit-based increases (Wagner, 1987; Wagner & Sternberg, 1985), performance ratings for bank managers (Wagner & Sternberg, 1985), ratings of leadership effectiveness (Sternberg et al., 2000), sales volume and sales awards (Wagner et al., 1999), and performance evaluations in a broad sample of workers in the United States and Spain (Cianciolo et al., 2002).

Recent research investigating the validity of tacit-knowledge extended case studies has shown initial support for assessing tacit knowledge and practical intelligence using an open-ended question approach (Antonakis, Hedlund, Pretz, & Sternberg, 2002a). First, as expected, confirmatory factor analysis has indicated that performance on these measures could best be accounted for by four metacognitive problem-solving factors comprising problem identification, solution generation, information representation, and outcome monitoring (Antonakis, Hedlund, Pretz, Cianciolo, & Sternberg, 2002). These findings directly support the theory of successful intelligence (Sternberg, 1997), which asserts the importance of these problem-solving skills as a mechanism for tacit knowledge application and practical problem solving. Using a similar conceptualization of metacognitive skills, Marshall-Mies et al. (2000) demonstrated that metacognitive abilities predict independently measured leadership outcomes.

Second, Antonakis, Hedlund, Pretz, Cianciolo, and Sternberg (2002) demonstrated that the relation between problem identification and scores on the TKML was strongest of all the relations of the TKML with problem-solving factors, independent of the effects of military rank. (Performance on the TKML did increase, however, with military rank, supporting previous findings.) This finding complements findings from other research investigating differences in the problem solving of experts versus less skilled individuals, which has shown that of the total time spent on problem solving, experts spend more time on problem diagnosis than any other aspect of problem solving, whereas less skilled individuals spend relatively little time on problem diagnosis before attempting to determine a problem solution (e.g., Sternberg, 1977, 1981). In addition, this finding builds on our previous research by indicating a relation between problem identification and the tacit knowledge that is used in problem solving. These results do not indicate that knowledge is a necessary and sufficient condition for expertise. Rather, these results indicate the importance of the ability to acquire, organize, and apply knowledge above and beyond simply possessing it.

Together, these findings indicate that tacit knowledge and the cognitive problem-solving processes involved in practical intelligence exist and can be measured in a valid way using a situational judgment testing methodology. The commonality among these measures cannot be explained by their shared demand on reading capability or general intelligence, but instead can be explained by their shared demand on general practical intelligence, the acquisition and application of tacit knowledge. These measures also show consistent relations to measures of workplace performance and leadership effectiveness.

IMPLICATIONS FOR RAPID LEADER DEVELOPMENT

The practical application of this research to leadership selection is immediately apparent. By applying the theory of practical intelligence to the situational judgment testing methodology, we have developed reliable, theory-based assessments that can be used to predict leader performance both in management and in the military. These assessments capture what a leader must know in order to do his or her job effectively and whether or not a particular individual has gained that knowledge from his or her experiences. As discussed in more detail in the next section, we are seeking to increase the practical utility of the tacit-knowledge inventory through the development of inventories that assess tacit knowledge at a more general level and so can be used across job domains (Cianciolo et al., 2002). Investigation of the relation between practical intelligence and such constructs as emotional intelligence (Caruso & Wolfe, chap. 10, this volume) could shed light on ways in which the theory of practical intelligence can be incorporated into leader development efforts already practiced in corporate settings.

Our other ongoing research is devoted to understanding how practical intelligence can be improved. As stated in the theory, practical intelligence is believed to be a form of developing expertise (Sternberg, 1998), an ability that is not largely immutable, but can be improved with intervention and practice. It remains an empirical question, however, whether we can enhance the ability to learn from experience. The increased complexity and rapid rate of change in modern leadership environments require that individuals constantly expand their knowledge about their occupational domains. Failure to keep up to date on the technological innovations that streamline logistical processes or the cultural changes influencing target market, for example, would prevent corporate leaders from developing in their organization the competitive edge critical for profit growth and investor confidence. Leaders who are capable of developing a flexible knowledge base that is responsive to changes in technology, personnel, culture, and mission of their organization will be better equipped to deal with leadership-related problems in their dynamic work environment. For this reason, understanding practical intelligence and how it can be facilitated has far-reaching implications for enhancing the knowledge that leaders acquire on the job.

Two approaches to enhancing expertise through improving practical intelligence and tacit knowledge have been discussed in the literature (Wagner & Sternberg, 1990a). The first approach is direct and involves making the tacit knowledge that experts possess explicit. In direct instruction, experts share rules of thumb—procedures indicating what to do given particular environmental conditions—with people having less expertise. The problem-solving scenarios present in tacit-knowledge measures—both the short vignette versions and the extended case studies—could provide a useful forum for imparting tacit knowledge. Indeed, selected scenarios from the TKML have been used extensively by the military through the Web site www.companycommand.com, which is geared toward providing leaders at the company level with resources, including expert advice, for enhancing leadership capability. Interested leaders can read the scenarios and select a preferred response strategy or read the comments of other leaders regarding the various response strategy options. The following is one such comment:

> It would be better to take input from your grassroots soldiers.... This lets the leadership assess attitudes and viewpoints that the troops are sharing. This is also a good measurement of how good your command communications structure is working. Nobody says you have to take any input to heart, but to pontificate from on high without feedback is a surefire way to obsolescence. (MSG. W., 2001)

Comments such as these, which are fueled by the scenarios and the anonymous chat environment, reveal the otherwise unspoken knowledge that successful leaders share.

A similar, experimental forum for sharing tacit knowledge, called Knowledge Post, is being developed through our collaboration with Knowledge Analysis Technologies and the Army Research Institute. Like www.companycommand.com, this forum presents soldiers with scenarios depicting problems typically experienced by military leaders. In contrast to www.companycommand.com, Knowledge Post features scenarios that are more complex and are appropriate to varying levels of rank. Furthermore, it allows soldiers to provide their own solutions to the problems presented in the scenarios rather than rating possible solutions that have been provided. Discussion among the networked soldiers who use Knowledge Post will be used to provided feedback and train soldiers for on-the-job duties in an environment that is intermediate between institutional education and actual occupational experience. Data pertaining to the actual learning outcomes associated with using the direct approach to impart tacit knowledge have not yet been collected, however.

The first approach is limited in inducing learning that has a "short" shelf-life. That is, if the environment changes, the knowledge gained may become obsolete. The second approach to improving practical intelligence and tacit knowledge is indirect and involves imparting strategies for extracting information from experience and improving problem solving. In other words, the indirect approach discussed here is a method based on the theory of practical intelligence for teaching people how to improve their knowledge-acquisition and application processes. This approach has long-term learning implications because one develops one's ability to obtain knowledge in different environmental conditions. Contrary to acquired knowledge, the ability to learn from experience can never become obsolete.

The findings from initial work in educational settings suggest that the indirect approach can be fruitful. For example, Sternberg et al. (1993) tested a tacit-knowledge training intervention in which they attempted to enhance the effectiveness of trainees' ability to identify (selectively encode), integrate (selectively combine), and compare (selectively compare) the important information in a private-sector management problem situation by evaluating the transcripts of potential (fictional) applicants and making a hiring decision. In the experiment, three groups of trainees each received instruction in a method of information use: extracting important information about the applicants from their transcripts, integrating the diverse pieces of information in the transcripts to form a unified impression of the applicants, or comparing the information in the transcripts to previously acquired knowledge. Two additional groups served as controls and did not receive an intervention. Sternberg et al. (1993) found that participants who were trained to extract important information or to compare new with previous information performed better than did the people in the control groups.

Because the U.S. Army recognizes the importance of acquiring knowledge from experience (U.S. Department of the Army, 1999; Yukl, 1999), our ongoing research for the Army Research Institute involves the development and testing of an indirect training methodology using the TKML and the extended case studies. In this research, we are testing competing training interventions for improving the experience-based acquisition of tacit knowledge about military leadership. The training interventions are distinguishable by their target of intervention. One intervention, for example, emphasizes the condition aspect of tacit knowledge, drawing attention to the assumptions trainees used to define the problems they solved. Trainees will complete a tacit-knowledge pretest featuring selected TKML items and an extended case study; then will they participate in guided practice during which they analyze what information they used to define the problems in the pretest. In this intervention, trainees will share their thoughts about statements such as the following: "Describe the factors you considered when you chose your goal and identified the most important problem in the case study (e.g., doctrine, personal values, assumptions about army culture, procedures, and personnel, knowledge based on previous experiences)" and "Imagine you had identified one of the secondary problems as the main problem. What goal would you accomplish by solving this problem as if it was the most critical?"

A second intervention emphasizes the action aspect of tacit knowledge, providing methods for reflecting on action outcomes. In this condition, trainees will receive feedback regarding how military experts solved the problems present in the pretest scenarios. Trainees will then participate in guided reflection on how the expected outcomes of their actions might differ from those outcomes corresponding to the actions of experts and what this discrepancy might indicate about the accuracy of their tacit knowledge. During the reflection, they will share their responses to such questions as "What outcome do you feel your actions would achieve?" and "What outcome do you feel the experts' actions would achieve?"

A third intervention targets both the condition and action aspects of tacit knowledge, involving exercises focused on both problem definition skills and reflection practices. In this research, we will compare the learning outcomes of each intervention—measured via the difference between tacit knowledge pretest and posttest performance and changes in leadership behaviors in the field—to each other as well as to a nonintervention control condition.

We do not intend to develop these interventions as a substitute for experience, but rather as a method for furthering the theoretical as well as practical understanding of how knowledge is acquired from experience. Practically speaking, the interventions are designed to develop awareness in trainees that the information they are using to solve problems and to evaluate the quality of problem solutions comes from their experiences. It is expected that awareness of how to use experience as a "mentor" will have a long-term positive effect on experience-based learning in motivated trainees, thus improving practical intelligence. The interventions are also designed to provide personal reflection techniques that draw attention to the incorrect tacit knowledge that can lead to undesirable action outcomes. Improving self-awareness in this manner is often difficult, but is critical for enhancing leadership capabilities and requires experience to develop (Argyris, 1999). Indeed, our own previous research indicated that in the absence of experience, tacitly held beliefs are resistant to change through brief, discussion-oriented interventions (Antonakis, Hedlund, Pretz, & Sternberg, 2002).

FUTURE RESEARCH DIRECTIONS

There are several interesting directions that future research using the theory of practical intelligence may take. We are devoting part of our continuing research to further exploration of the construct of practical intelligence as a basic ability and to its measurement. Our published measures of practical intelligence have featured tacit knowledge that is highly relevant to the job domains in which we examined the relation between practical intelligence and occupational performance (e.g., management, sales, military leadership). Although there is evidence indicating that performance on tacit-knowledge inventories is more general than was expected (Sternberg et al., 2000; Wagner, 1987), the congruence between the knowledge required by the inventories and required by the jobs investigated has led some scholars to doubt that practical intelligence is a unique construct, different from job knowledge (Schmidt & Hunter, 1993).

We believe that practical intelligence is a basic ability to learn from experience and that it is general across the domains in which tacit knowledge is required, and we are developing and testing measures of tacit knowledge that are much more general in nature than those developed in our previous research. Initial evidence provided by this work supports previous research suggesting that performance on a tacit-knowledge inventory can be accounted for by a single factor (Sternberg et al., 2000; Wagner, 1987). The current research extends these findings by indicating via confirmatory factor analysis that a hierarchical model specifying multiple lower order "inventory" (tacit knowledge) factors and a single, higher order practical intelligence factor has good fit to the data (Cianciolo et al., 2002). We have also found that measures of general tacit knowledge assess a construct distinct from general mental ability, even when examined in less range-restricted populations than Yale University students (Cianciolo et al., 2002). Although it has not yet been tested, we expect that such measures will show comparable validities to those of conventional intelligence tests and more job-specific tacit knowledge inventories and provide evidence that situational judgment tests can be used to assess a unique construct, practical intelligence. Another potential approach for assessing practical intelligence that we have not yet tried would involve dynamic testing in which an individual is exposed to a somewhat novel experience and is then exposed to a follow-up experience that requires the application of similar knowledge. Individual differences in the successful acquisition and application of knowledge in such a testing environment and across multiple types of experiences would provide important insight into the nature of practical intelligence.

Future research with interesting practical applications for training involves investigating how to develop simulations that present problem scenarios that develop in real time and must be handled within the time constraints characteristic of many leadership problem situations. This research would be particularly useful in aiding such high-stakes leadership decisions as conflict negotiation, combat tactics, and emergency procedures. The theory of practical intelligence and tacit knowledge in particular is well suited to aid the development of such simulations because it provides guidance for determining what skills and knowledge must be developed via training simulation. Another research direction of particular importance for training involves investigation of the dimensions along which two environments must be similar in order for tacit knowledge to be applicable to both. Taxonomies of "experiences" relevant to particular training objectives (i.e., the acquisition of particular pieces of tacit knowledge) could be created via case studies or training simulations. This would require not only an in-depth exploration of the condition aspect of tacit knowledge in particular environments, but an investigation into how actions become linked or fail to become linked with particular conditions.

CONCLUSIONS

Successful leadership in complex, rapidly changing organizations depends on the ability to learn quickly from experience and apply experience-based knowledge to solving problems swiftly and effectively. Leadership research has achieved a great deal with regard to illuminating the dispositional characteristics and behavioral patterns that successful leaders share (Avolio, chap. 4, this volume; Yukl, 1999), but has not yet provided insight into what is learned from experience and why some people acquire more experience-based knowledge than others. Without this insight, efforts devoted to rapid leadership development cannot produce leaders who have optimized their ability to learn quickly on the job and can develop this ability in their team members.

The theory of practical intelligence provides insight into experience-based learning by explaining the cognitive processes used to acquire tacit knowledge as well as characterizing what exactly is being learned when tacit knowledge is acquired. Although measuring practical intelligence and tacit knowledge is a difficult endeavor, reliable measures have been created and have served as practical tools for illuminating individual differences in work performance and leadership effectiveness. Such tools also provide an important method for enhancing leadership capabilities by providing a forum through which specific tacit knowledge can be discussed and shared or by providing low-fidelity training simulations through which trainees can practice problem solving and knowledge acquisition—skills leaders must use in the field.

ACKNOWLEDGMENTS

Preparation of this chapter was supported by the U.S. Army Research Institute (contracts DASW01-99-K-0004 and DASW01-00-K-0014). We are grateful to these agencies for their support. The ideas expressed in this chapter are solely those of the authors and do not represent any official position or policy on the part of these agencies. We are also grateful to the reviewers of earlier drafts of the chapter for their helpful comments and criticisms, which have made this chapter much more successful than it would have been as a solitary effort. Send correspondence to Anna T. Cianciolo, Global Information Systems Technology, Inc., Trade Centre South, Suite 301, 100 Trade Centre Drive, Champaign, IL 61820.

REFERENCES

Antonakis, J., Hedlund, J., Pretz, J. E., & Sternberg, R. J. (2002). *Exploring the nature and acquisition of tacit knowledge for military leadership.* (Res. Note No. 2002-04). Alexandria, VA: U.S. Army Research Institute for the Behavioral and Social Sciences.

Antonakis, J., Hedlund J., Pretz, J. E., Cianciolo, A. T., & Sternberg, R. J. (2002). *Metacognitive problem-solving abilities and tacit knowledge of leaders: A preliminary validation.* Manuscript in preparation.

Argyris, C. (1999). Tacit knowledge and management. In R. J. Sternberg & J. A. Horvath (Eds.), *Tacit knowledge in professional practice* (pp. 123–140). Mahwah, NJ: Lawrence Erlbaum Associates.

Bass, B. M. (1998). *Transformational leadership: Industrial, military, and educational impact.* Mahwah, NJ: Lawrence Erlbaum Associates, Inc.

Cianciolo, A. T., Grigorenko, E. L., Jarvin, L., Gil, G., Drebot, M., & Sternberg, R. J. (2002). *Tacit knowledge and practical intelligence: Advancements in measurement and construct validity.* Under Review. Submitted to: Intelligence.

Connelly, M. S., Gilbert, J. A., Zaccaro, S. J., Threlfall, K. V., Marks, M. A., & Mumford, M. D. (2000). Exploring the relationship of leadership skills and knowledge to leadership performance. *Leadership Quarterly, 11*(1), 65–86.

Day, D. V. (2000). Leadership development: A review in context. *Leadership Quarterly, 11*, 581–613.

Gibson, J. J. (1986). *The ecological approach to visual perception.* (Original work published 1979). Hillsdale, NJ: Lawrence Erlbaum Associates, Inc.

Hedlund, J., Horvath, J. A., Forsythe, G. B., Snook, S., Williams, W. M., Bullis, R. C., Dennis, M., & Sternberg, R. J. (1998). *Tacit knowledge in military leadership: Evidence of construct validity* (Tech. Rep. 1080). Alexandria, VA: U.S. Army Research Institute for the Behavioral and Social Sciences.

Hooijberg, R., Hunt, J. G., & Dodge, G. E. (1997). Leadership complexity and development of the leaderplex model. *Journal of Management, 23*(3), 375–408.

House, R. J. (1996). Path–goal theory of leadership: Lessons, legacy, and a reformulated theory. *Leadership Quarterly, 7*(3), 323–352.

House, R. J., & Aditya, R. N. (1997). The social scientific study of leadership: Quo vadis? *Journal of Management, 23*(3), 409–474.

Lord, R. G., De Vader, C. L., & Alliger G. M. (1986). A meta-analysis of the relation between personality traits and leadership perceptions. An application of validity generalization procedures. *Journal of Applied Psychology, 71*(3), 402–410.

Marshall-Mies, J. C., Fleishman, E. A., Martin, J. A., Zaccaro, S. J., Baughman, W. A., & McGee, M. L. (2000). Development and evaluation of cognitive and metacognitive measures for predicting leadership potential. *Leadership Quarterly, 11*(1), 135–153.

McCall, M. W., Lombardo, M. M., & Morrison, A. M. (1988). *The lessons of experience: How successful executives develop on the job.* Lexington, MA: Lexington.

McDaniel, M. A., Morgeson, F. P., Finnegan, E. B., Campion, M. A., & Braverman, E. P. (2001). Use of situational judgment tests to predict job performance: A clarification of the literature. *Journal of Applied Psychology, 86*(4), 730–740.

McDaniel, M. A., & Nguyen, N. T. (2001). Situational judgment tests: A review of practice and constructs assessed. *International Journal of Selection and Assessment, 9*(1/2), 103–113.

Motowidlo, S. J., Dunnette, M. D., & Carter, G. W. (1990). An alternative selection procedure: The low-fidelity simulation. *Journal of Applied Psychology, 75*(6), 640–647.

Motowidlo, S. J., Hanson, M. A., & Crafts, J. L. (1997). Low-fidelity simulations. In D. L. Whetzel & G. R. Wheaton (Eds.), *Applied measurement methods in industrial psychology* (pp. 241–260). Palo Alto, CA: Davies-Black.

MSG. W. (2001, October 26). RE: #1: New People. Message posted to http://www.companycommand. com/htdocs/dcforum/DCForumID37/1.html

Mumford, M. D., Zaccaro, S. J., Harding, F. D., Jacobs, T. O., & Fleishman, E. A. (2000). Leadership skills for a changing world: Solving complex problems. *Leadership Quarterly, 11*(1), 11–35.

Neisser, U. (1976). General, academic, and artificial intelligence. In L. Resnick (Ed.), *The nature of intelligence* (pp. 135–144). Hillsdale, NJ: Lawrence Erlbaum Associates, Inc.

Sashkin, M. (1988). The visionary learner. In J. A. Conger & R. N. Kanugo (Eds.), *Charismatic leadership: The elusive factor in organizational effectives* (pp. 122–160). San Francisco: Jossey-Bass.

Schmidt, F. L., & Hunter, J. E. (1993). Tacit knowledge, practical intelligence, general mental ability, and job knowledge. *Current Directions in Psychological Science, 2*, 8–9.

Schön, D. A. (1983). *The reflective practitioner: How professionals think in action.* New York: Basic Books.

Smith, J. A., & Foti, R. J. (1998). A pattern approach to the study of leader emergence. *Leadership Quarterly, 9*(2), 147–160.

Sternberg, R. J. (1977). *Intelligence, information processing, and analogical reasoning: The componential analysis of human abilities.* Hillsdale, NJ: Lawrence Erlbaum Associates, Inc.

Sternberg, R. J. (1981). Intelligence and nonentrenchment. *Journal of Educational Psychology, 73*(1), 1–16.

Sternberg, R. J. (1997). *Successful intelligence.* New York: Plume.

Sternberg, R. J. (1998). Abilities are forms of developing expertise. *Educational Researcher, 27*(3), 11–20.

Sternberg, R. J. (2002). Successful intelligence: A new approach to leadership. In R. E. Riggio, S. E. Murphy, & F. J. Pirozzolo (Eds.), *Multiple intelligences and leadership* (pp. 9–28). Hillsdale, NJ: Lawrence Erlbaum Associates, Inc.

Sternberg, R. J., Forsythe, G. B., Hedlund, J., Horvath, J. A., Wagner, R. K., Williams, W. M., Snook, S. A., & Grigorenko, E. L. (2000). *Practical intelligence in everyday life.* Cambridge: Cambridge University Press.

Sternberg, R. J., & Grigorenko, E. L. (Eds.) (1997). *Intelligence, heredity, and environment.* New York: Cambridge University Press.

Sternberg, R. J., Nokes, C., Geissler, P. W., Prince, R., Okatcha, F., Bundy, D. A, & Grigorenko, E. L. (2001). The relationship between academic and practical intelligence: A case study in Kenya. *Intelligence, 29*(5), 401–418.

Sternberg, R. J., & Vroom, V. (2002). The person versus the situation in leadership. *Leadership Quarterly, 13*, 301–323.

Sternberg, R. J., Wagner, R. K., & Okagaki, L. (1993). Practical intelligence: The nature and role of tacit knowledge in work and at school. In J. M. Puckett & H. W. Reese (Eds.), *Mechanisms of everyday cognition* (pp. 205–223). Hillsdale, NJ: Lawrence Erlbaum Associates, Inc.

U.S. Department of the Army (1999). *Military leadership (FM 22-100).* Washington, DC: Headquarters, Department of the Army.

Wagner, R. K. (1987). Tacit knowledge in everyday intelligent behavior. *Journal of Personality and Social Psychology, 52*(6), 1236–1247.

Wagner, R. K., & Sternberg, R. J. (1985). Practical intelligence in real-world pursuits: The role of tacit knowledge. *Journal of Personality and Social Psychology, 49*(2), 436–458.

Wagner, R. K., & Sternberg, R. J. (1990a). Street smarts. In K. E. Clark & M. B. Clark (Eds.), *Measures of leadership* (pp. 493–504). West Orange, NJ: Leadership Library of America.

Wagner, R. K., & Sternberg, R. J. (1990b). *Tacit Knowledge Inventory for Managers.* San Antonio: Psychological Corporation.

Wagner, R. K., Sujan, H., Sujan, M., Rashotte, C. A., & Sternberg, R. J. (1999). Tacit knowledge in sales. In R. J. Sternberg & J. A. Horvath (Eds.), *Tacit knowledge in professional practice* (pp. 155–182). Mahwah, NJ: Lawrence Erlbaum Associates, Inc.

Weekley, J. A., & Jones, C. (1999). Further studies of situational tests. *Personnel Psychology, 52*(3), 679–700.

Yukl, G. (1999). Leadership competencies required for the new army and approaches for developing them. In J. G. Hunt, G. E. Dodge, & L. Wong (Eds.), *Out-of-the-box leadership: Transforming the twenty-first-century army and other top-performing organizations* (pp. 255–276). Stamford, CT: JAI.

Zaccaro, S. J. (1999). Social complexity and the competencies required for effective military leadership. In J. G. Hunt, G. E. Dodge, & L. Wong (Eds.), *Out-of-the-box leadership: Transforming the twenty-first-century army and other top-performing organizations* (pp. 131–151). Stamford, CT: JAI.

Zaccaro, S. J., Foti, R. J., & Kenny, D. A. (1991). Self-monitoring and trait-based variance in leadership: An investigation of leader flexibility across multiple situations. *Journal of Applied Psychology, 76*, 308–315.

Zaccaro, S. J., Mumford, M. D., Connelly, M. S., Marks, M. A., & Gilbert, J. A. (2000). Assessment of leader problem-solving capabilities. *Leadership Quarterly, 11*(1), 37–64.

10

Emotional Intelligence and Leadership Development

David R. Caruso
Yale University

Charles J. Wolfe
Charles J. Wolfe Associates, LLC

Major General (Ret.) Maggart's (chap. 2, this volume) view of leadership places emotion front and center: "Leadership is an emotional business that grips the heart, soul, and imagination of those being led." Perhaps that is understandable, for, as Maj. Gen. Maggart also notes, "Combat is a significant emotional event and leaders ... must develop training programs that ensure no soldier is exposed to the horrors of war without first experiencing them in a training environment." The job of the military, especially during times of war, will clearly have a large emotional component. But what about the *corporate* soldiers and their leaders? The business environment, no matter how competitive, is not a battlefield. Although business leaders do not have to lead their troops into physical battle, shrinking markets, globalization, recession, and heightened competition have caused leaders to engage in innovative strategies such as flatter organization structures, quality circles, reengineering, self-managed teams, downsizing or rightsizing, outsourcing, and lean manufacturing. Each new initiative that represents major change in a company represents an opportunity to transform the company. To be successful in implementing and creating transformational change in a company requires leaders who recognize the emotional impact significant change creates among organizational members and who understand how to minimize resistance to change. Business leaders must know how to generate excitement and a sense of opportunity associated

237

with change. The emotional business of leadership is illustrated by a case study of two team leaders responsible for new product development.

Ken was one of the more positive and enthusiastic division heads in the company. At the start of a recent product development review meeting, the team members appeared to be somewhat disheartened and low in spirits. Ken, with his dynamic and enthusiastic style, was able to generate a sense of hope and excitement. With the meeting now in full swing, team members reported a good deal of progress, and Ken predicted that the product effort would come in under, or at, budget and on time.

The product development review meeting facilitated by Roberta, another division head in the same company, was much different. The group was initially excited by the progress made to date, but as the meeting progressed, Roberta's negative style caused the team to focus on minutiae and details. Feeling down, the team members started to focus on problems relating to product quality and timing.

Asked which leader is the more effective of the two, it is likely that most people would select Ken. However, Ken's project failed miserably and Roberta's project succeeded. Apparently, there were serious quality problems with Ken's development effort that went undetected until production began. The problems that Roberta's team discovered were addressed much sooner in the development cycle, and although their launch was delayed by a few weeks, the product performed up to and beyond original specifications.

Certainly the emotion and optimism of a leader like Ken is not always enough to result in success. Other, often external and uncontrollable factors play a role in the success or failure of an idea, a project, or a team. In this case, though, the failure was a direct result of Ken's consistently positive and optimistic leadership style. Ken created a positive mood in himself and in others. In doing so, he and his team generated new and creative ideas, but they were not focused on the details, and the hints that there were quality issues were not attended to.

After Ken and his team failed, Roberta was charged with reconfiguring the entire product line and coming up with next-generation concepts. Her mandate was to resolve the quality issues and bring the project budget back into line. The team and project that she inherited had serious problems. She began her new role on a Monday morning and immediately called a series of debriefing meetings with her entire staff. Roberta kept her eye on the details in her serious and analytical way. She focused on what was wrong with existing concepts and guided her talented team along the same lines. During the first four days of her tenure as project leader, Roberta had seemingly managed to make a bad situation worse. She did nothing to enhance the team's morale and the team meetings were negatively charged. Throughout that first round of meetings, Roberta seemed to passively encourage the negativity, and merely jotted down notes whenever people pointed out a problem.

Rumors of worsening problems reached William, the division's chief operating officer, and he called Roberta to his office to demand an explanation. He was surprised when Roberta did not deny that there was a negative atmosphere, but he was shocked when Roberta told him that this was just what she had planned. She showed William her set of detailed meeting notes and pointed out that the team had identified dozens of product, quality, and marketing issues. She noted, "Before we can fix this thing, we have to know what is broken. Now is the time for action and energy, but not before." She laid out her plan of attack to William, who was not merely satisfied by the explanation, but visibly impressed.

Roberta demanded that all staff attend Friday's team meeting. She had used her meeting notes to outline the key problem areas, and she opened the meeting by enumerating the various issues. Roberta looked around the room at the hang-dog faces, smiled, and then quietly, but resolutely, told them, "This is great news and terrific progress. You folks have done some difficult analysis work here and I want to commend all of you for your efforts." Quizzical looks were exchanged around the room. "I'm not saying I am pleased with the problems. I am pleased that you were able to quickly and efficiently identify the problems." Although she spoke softly, her words seemed to hit each person right between the eyes: "Now, it is up to us to figure out just what we can do about these problems. This team has the brains and the talent and the spirit to accomplish this objective." Roberta continued in this way for quite a few minutes, and as she did so the energy level in the room began to rise. People stirred in their seats and leaned forward. Heads nodded in agreement. With the hard work of problem diagnosis behind them, the team began the real work of creative idea generation and problem resolution.

It was all according to plan, and the situation was resolved to the satisfaction of all parties. In achieving this objective, Roberta displayed a set of sophisticated information processing abilities. Roberta correctly identified how the team felt. She reasoned that the earlier project problems had led the team to become disappointed and the continuing problems caused them to feel frustrated. She understood that these feelings of guilt and worry were focusing the team on the negative details of the project. However, such feelings facilitated the work of the team: to identify as many problems as possible in order to uncover the underlying product issues. It was not her job, she reasoned, to make the team happy, and in fact, to have done so would have proved disastrous. The upbeat team would be moving forward in their thinking without ever having diagnosed the cause of their problems. Roberta understood that once the problems were diagnosed, it would become necessary for the team to change gears and become reinvested in the project. By itself, optimism or pessimism is neither adaptive nor maladaptive. Rather, it is the intelligent and flexible use of these, and other, emotions that may facilitate effective leadership.

It is our contention that a better understanding of leadership can be obtained through the inclusion of such emotion-based abilities in leadership models. Specifically, a view of emotionality that is integrated with rationality, along with broadening our definition of intelligent behavior to include reasoning about and reasoning with emotion, offers new insights into what makes for an effective leader and how such leaders can be developed. In this chapter, we propose that an ability approach to emotional intelligence provides a useful framework for better understanding the role of emotion in leadership performance and in leader and leadership development (see Day, 2000, for a discussion of the distinction between leader and leadership development). Specifically, we describe this model of emotional intelligence and how these emotional skills can be objectively measured, developed, and applied.

EMOTIONS AT WORK

Historically, the role of emotions in effective business leadership has largely been ignored. When emotion was addressed at all, it was to examine the ways in which unregulated emotion, or negative affect, can damage an individual leader or an organization. Generally, although workers will experience strong emotions at work, they have learned that it is inappropriate to express these feelings (Gibson, 1997). Emotions have also been viewed by psychologists as either irrelevant to human thought or, at times, a negative influence on thinking, rationality, and judgment (e.g., Woodworth, 1940; Young, 1936, 1943).

However, there is another point of view on emotions and the role that they can play in adaptation and success. Neuroscientists now suggest that rationality is well served by emotionality and, in fact, that emotions are *necessary* for effective judgment and decision making (Damasio, 1994). Affect may also have an increasingly important role as processing involves greater complexity, ambiguity, uncertainty, new information sources, and a need for accurate, sound decisions (see, e.g., Forgas, 1995). Specific moods are known to influence cognition in different ways. Positive moods facilitate certain inductive reasoning processes (Isen, 1987) and negative moods can facilitate certain deductive reasoning processes (Sinclair & Mark, 1995). People in a negative mood may make more pessimistic judgments than those in a positive mood (Bower, 1981; Salovey & Birnbaum, 1989).

ABOUT EMOTIONAL INTELLIGENCE

The abilities displayed by Roberta center around her ability to reason about emotion and to reason with emotion. It has been known for some time that emotional abilities, such as emotion perception and emotional knowledge, exist. For decades, researchers have examined these abilities and created ways to measure them. Individual differences in these abilities also exist and seem to have an impact on important life outcomes. Furthermore, it has been observed that these abilities develop with age. Intelligence researchers and intelligence test creators such as Binet, Kaufman, Spearman, Thorndike, and Wechsler also actively investigated the role of emotion in intelligence, even creating tasks that attempt to objectively measure emotional abilities (Matarazzo, 1972). That emotions can inform thinking and thought can influence emotion is the foundation of the ability-based model of emotional intelligence.

WHAT IS EMOTIONAL INTELLIGENCE?

The ability concept of emotional intelligence was initially defined as "the ability to monitor one's own and others' feelings and emotions, to discriminate among them, and to use this information to guide one's thinking and action" (Salovey & Mayer, 1990). Elements of both emotion knowledge and emotion perception were clearly embedded within this model, but the model's inclusion of the facilitation ability added a somewhat unique component to the mix. The model grouped together a set of abilities and provocatively labeled them a standard intelligence, similar to verbal or spatial intelligence.

A few years after the initial scientific publications on this topic, the term "emotional intelligence" (EI) was given a much broader meaning by the popular press and came to mean many different things than what the term was originally intended to convey. These popularized definitions appear to consist more of implicit theories of personality or competencies than as a form of intelligence. Most people are familiar with the EI construct as described by Goleman (1995). Goleman based his initial description on the Salovey and Mayer (1990) model, but broadened the concept quite a bit. Goleman indicated that emotional intelligence consists of five dimensions: (a) knowing one's emotions, (b) managing emotions, (c) motivating oneself, (d) recognizing emotions in others, and (e) handling relationships. The stretching of this modest intelligence model is apparent later in Goleman's (1995) book when he notes, "There is an old-fashioned word for the body of skills that emotional intelligence represents: character" (p. 285).

The concept of emotional intelligence was also made popular in measurement circles after the release of the BarOn EQ-i in 1997. According to Bar-On (1997), emotional intelligence is "an array of noncognitive capabilities, competencies, and skills that influence one's ability to succeed in coping with environmental demands and pressures" (p. 14).

Goleman (1998) revised his notion of EI, and although the overall definition appears to be relatively similar to the previous one, this new workplace-focused EI model bears a striking resemblance to traditional leadership competency models. Emotional intelligence, operationalized by a 360-degree measure (Emotional Competence Inventory, or ECI), was defined as the "capacity for recognizing our own feelings and those of others, for motivating ourselves, and for managing emotions well in ourselves and in our relationships" (Boyatzis, Goleman, & Rhee, 2000). The ECI has measures of four aspects of emotional intelligence. The first, *Self-Awareness*, includes measures of emotional self-awareness, accurate self-assessment, and self-confidence. The second, *Self-Management*, measures self-control, trustworthiness, conscientiousness, adaptability, achievement orientation, and initiative. The third, *Social Awareness,* measures empathy, organizational awareness, and service orientation. The fourth, *Social Skills,* includes measures related to developing others: leadership, influence, communication, change catalyst, conflict management, building bonds, and teamwork and collaboration.

Mayer and Salovey later revised their model in 1997 to suggest that emotional intelligence could best be described as consisting of four related abilities: the ability to accurately identify emotions, the ability to generate emotions and use emotions to help with thinking, understanding the causes of emotion, and being able to manage emotional and rational information in ways that led to effective and adaptive outcomes.

The theory of an ability-based approach to emotional intelligence as a standard intelligence serves as a foundation for our work in leader development. Although other models may serve a useful purpose for applied leadership development, the ability-based approach clearly places emotional intelligence within an intelligence framework (for more about this distinction see Mayer, Salovey, & Caruso, 2000a, 2000b). The ability model contributes a unique dimension that does not appear in any other existing model of emotional intelligence or leader development.

IS EMOTIONAL INTELLIGENCE A FORM OF INTELLIGENCE?

How does one identify a new intelligence? We have argued that to be considered a form of intelligence, emotional intelligence must meet three criteria. The first is conceptual in nature and addresses whether a form of intelligence can be described and operationalized as a mental ability rather than as a dispositional trait or behavior. The second criterion is that a form of intelligence must be related to, but distinguishable from, other intelligences (Carroll, 1993; Neisser et al., 1996). The third criterion is developmental and requires that a form of intelligence develops with age and through experience.

Gardner (1999) listed eight criteria for intelligence forms. In brief, these are (a) potential isolation by brain damage, (b) the existence of individuals with exceptional ability, (c) a core set of operations, (d) a distinctive developmental history, (e) an evolutionary basis, (f) evidence from experimental tasks, (g) psychometric support, and (h) encoding of information in a symbol system. Research has addressed, some, but not all, of these criteria.

There has been a suggestion that if emotional intelligence simply reflects cognitive processing of emotion information, then it should not be considered as a separate intelligence. Critical to the existence of a separate, emotional intelligence is the idea that emotions are unique. As Izard (2002) so well put it:

"If emotions had no unique functions and no capacity to operate independently, theorists could relegate them to the domain of cognition and deal with them as any other type of information. Emotions do contain information, but they also have subjectively experienced feeling and motivational states like no other type of information. Emotion feelings are the primitives of awareness, capable of influencing mind before they register in self-reflective consciousness. They have preemptory access to channels serving imagery, decision-making, and instrumental action. Emotion information can translate ordinary cognition into creative thought, trigger a courageous act of altruism, or power impulsive violence." (p. 797)

While the debate over the existence of emotional intelligence has raged, much of the debate has stemmed from the different approaches to defining emotional intelligence. Discussion of the ability model of emotional intelligence has moved from a question of does it exist to those of how can it be measured reliably and what does it predict? (for in-depth discussion of this topic see Mayer, Caruso & Salovey, 1999; Mayer, Salovey, Caruso, & Sitarenios, 2001, 2003).

THE ABILITY MODEL
OF EMOTIONAL INTELLIGENCE

Figure 10.1 presents a pictorial representation of the ability model and shows that the four abilities are separate, but related. First, emotional information enters the cognitive system and is identified. Next, cognition is influenced according to certain rules. The emotional data are cognitively processed and analyzed. Finally, the emotion data are integrated into our thinking. This approach to emotional intelligence assumes that each ability, or branch, develops from the other. Thus, it is a hierarchical model.

The Model

The first branch of the ability model is *identifying emotions*. This branch includes a number of skills, such as the ability to identify feelings in one's self and in others, to express emotions accurately, and to differentiate between real and phony emotional expressions.

In order to accurately judge how a subordinate feels, a leader may have to rely upon his or her ability to read nonverbal cues, as most workers do not express their feelings to their boss (Gibson, 1997). The one exception to the no-expression rule is that a feeling of *acceptance* appears to be a normative emotional experience and thus is expressed. Retrospective reports indicate that anger is the emotion that is most commonly expressed, whereas fear and sadness are expressed at much lower levels. Of eight emotions examined in this study, joy was expressed the least, with just 19% of people reporting that they expressed their feeling of joy. Furthermore, workers are less likely to express emotion to their superiors than they are to peers or to subordinates (Gibson, 1997).

The second branch of the ability model is *using emotions to facilitate thought*. This branch includes the ability to use emotions to redirect attention to important

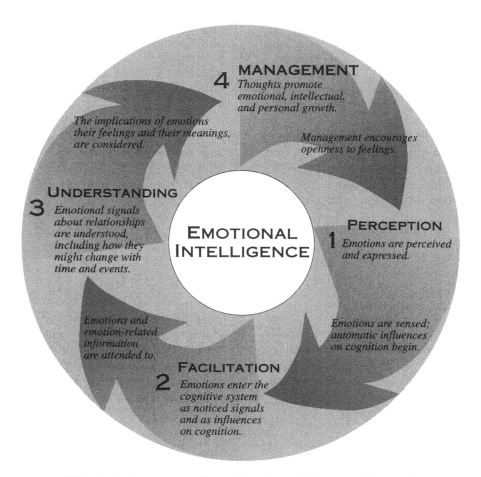

FIG. 10.1. A representation of the Mayer–Salovey ability model of emotional intelligence.

events, generate emotions that facilitate decision making, use mood swings as a means to consider multiple points of view, and use different emotions to encourage different approaches to problem solving (e.g., to use a happy mood to assist in generating creative, new ideas). Although the case of Roberta illustrates the *strategic* use of a negative mood (matching the mood to the task in order to enhance performance), the work performance of employees who are *consistently* in a negative mood tends to be lower than the performance of employees who are positive (Ashby, Isen & Turken, 1999). Moods that may result from the use of humor can enhance creative problem solving (Morreall, 1991).

The third branch is *understanding emotions*. This is the ability to understand complex emotions and emotional "chains," understand how emotions undergo transitions from one stage to another, recognize the causes of emotions, and understand relationships among emotions.

Being able to understand the chain of emotions that arise from our perceptions of a situation is one key to managing emotion, especially negative emotion (Mischel & DeSmet, 2000).

The fourth branch of the ability model is *managing emotions*. Managing emotions includes the ability to stay aware of one's emotions, even those that are unpleasant, the ability to determine whether an emotion is clear or typical, and the ability to solve emotion-laden problems without necessarily suppressing negative emotions. One can manage one's emotions internally or can manage and regulate the emotions of others. In a study of bill collectors, for instance, Sutton (1991) found that managers directed their emotion-regulation actions to assist their employees to regulate their feelings when handling an angry customer.

Hochschild's (1983) ground-breaking work in emotional labor brought to light the need for many service workers to carefully monitor and regulate their emotions. Data have not completely supported the notion that emotional labor necessarily has negative consequences for workers. For example, surface acting, in which a person modifies their facial expressions, may be more stressful and reduce service delivery quality relative to deep acting, in which a person modifies his or her underlying feelings (Grandey, 2003).

A detailed discussion of the psychological processes that underlie each of these four abilities is found in Barrett and Salovey (2002).

A Model of Leader or Leadership Development? The ability model includes abilities of both self-awareness and management as well as awareness and management of others. Therefore, the intrapersonal competencies addressed in leader development are addressed by the model, as are the interpersonal competencies of leadership development (Day, 2000).

MEASURING EMOTIONAL INTELLIGENCE

Emotional skills and abilities can be measured a number of different ways: via self-report, through observation, or through a performance test. We quickly examine the first two of these methods and their suitability for measuring emotional intelligence before we focus on the third measurement approach.

Self-Report

Self-report measures ask a person to read a series of statements and indicate the extent to which the statement describes the person or the extent to which he or she agrees with the statement. Questions of this sort that might measure emotional intelligence include those such as "I am aware of my emotions," "I have a good understanding of emotions," and so forth. The self-report of abilities and traits relies upon the individual's self-understanding. If a person's self-concept is accurate, then it is possible that these types of measures can serve as an accurate measure of the actual ability or trait. If the person's self-concept is inaccurate, which is often the case (e.g., Taylor & Brown, 1988), then self-report measures yield information only concerning the person's self-concept rather than the actual ability or trait. In general, however, people are not very good at estimating their level of ability. In fact, self-reported intelligence correlates with actual measured intelligence modestly, below $r = .30$ or so (Paulhus, Lysy, & Yik, 1998). Such associations indicate that people's self-reports of their mental abilities are quite independent of their actual abilities.

Informants

Another common measurement methodology employed by many organizations is the use of observers or informants. Known as 360-degree feedback, this method provides information regarding how a group of people view a selected target person. An informant approach to measuring emotional intelligence might include asking a person's clients, peers, and boss a series of questions such as "Is X aware of emotions?" and "Does X understand how people feel?".

If our goal is to measure behaviors, then this method makes a good deal of sense. However, more internal cognitive styles and capacities are judged much less accurately by others (Funder & Dobroth, 1987). Consider the case of the project team leaders, Ken and Roberta. Despite the fact that Roberta demonstrated effective emotional intelligence in her approach to leading her department whereas Ken did not, it is very likely that she would not have been rated as highly as Ken in a 360-degree measure.

Such an approach, therefore, remains a step removed from actual abilities. When observers are asked to evaluate the ability of videotaped targets, the correlations top out at about .30. Therefore, as a method of estimating a person's ability, this approach seems to be lacking.

Ability or Performance Measures

The third method to measure an ability is to use a performance measure. In this approach, a person solves problems, and the speed, accuracy, or both with which they solve these problems are measured. Ability measures attempt to quantify a person's actual capacity to perform specified tasks, not just one's beliefs about such capacities (Carroll, 1993; Mayer & Salovey, 1993; Neisser et al. 1996; Scarr, 1989). For instance, if we want to measure spatial ability, we might ask a person to reproduce a block model. In the case of emotional ability, if we want to understand how well people perceive emotion, we can show them a sad face, for example, and see if they recognize the facial expression. If we want to understand how well they reason about emotions, we can provide an emotional problem and assess the quality of their reasoning in response.

Mayer, Salovey, Caruso Emotional Intelligence Test

The Mayer, Salovey, Caruso Emotional Intelligence Test (MSCEIT) is just such a performance or ability test (see Mayer, Salovey, & Caruso, 2002, for details). It poses a series of eight types of emotion problems, and the test taker attempts to solve the problems (Fig.10.2). Two tasks measure each of the four emotional abilities or branches. One MSCEIT task, Faces, presents a color photograph of a person, and the test taker indicates how that person is feeling, using a set of emotion rating scales. The Pictures task presents a set of color photos of natural environments or computer-generated designs, and the test taker indicates the extent to which specified emotions are expressed in each, or by each, photo or design. The Faces and Pictures tasks measure the person's identifying or perceiving emotions ability.

Using emotions to facilitate thought is measured by the Facilitation and Sensations tasks. The Facilitation task asks the test taker to indicate how effective different moods are in solving a certain problem. The Sensations task asks the person to generate a mild emotion and then compare this emotion to a series of sensations such as color, taste, and temperature.

Understanding emotions is measured with multiple-choice questions. The Blends task is similar to an emotional vocabulary test in which the test taker selects the best definition for complex emotion terms. The Changes task presents an initial emotional state and then asks what would happen if that emotion were to decrease or intensify.

The Emotion Management task measures managing emotions. A brief scenario is presented and an outcome specified. The effectiveness of a set of strategies is then evaluated based on how well the strategy will meet the objective. These scenarios are about self-management or managing mood and emotion in oneself. The Emotional Relationships task is identical, only the scenarios here are about interpersonal interactions.

Scoring the MSCEIT. Emotional intelligence ability tests have a problem that initially seems somewhat unique to this type of ability measure: how to score the test questions. The MSCEIT employs two different scoring methods: general and expert consensus. General consensus scoring relies upon the results of a large group of people. Results are pooled, and test scores reflect the degree to which the test taker agrees with the general consensus.

The MSCEIT is also scored according to expert consensus. The use of expert panels to score intelligence test responses is common. Consider, for example, the Wechsler scales of intelligence, in which many of the subtests employed an expert panel to derive correct answers. The MSCEIT employed a group of 21 emotions

Branch 1 - Identifying Emotions

How much of each emotion is expressed by this face?

a) No Happiness	1	2	3	4	5	Extreme Happiness
b) No Fear	1	2	3	4	5	Extreme Fear

Branch 2 - Facilitating Thought

What mood(s) might be helpful to feel when meeting in-laws for the very first time?

	Not Useful			Useful	
a) Tension	1	2	3	4	5
b) Surprise	1	2	3	4	5
c) Joy	1	2	3	4	5

Branch 3 - Understanding Emotions

Tom felt anxious, and became a bit stressed when he thought about all the work he needed to do. When his supervisor brought him an additional project, he felt _____. (Select the best choice.)

a) Overwhelmed   d) Self Conscious
b) Depressed   e) Jittery
c) Ashamed

Branch 4 - Managing Emotions

1. Debbie just came back from vacation. She was feeling peaceful and content. How effective would each action be in preserving her mood?

Action 1: She started to make a list of things at home that she needed to do.
Very Ineffective   1..........2...........3..........4..........5 Very Effective

Action 2: She began thinking about where and when she would go on her next vacation.
Very Ineffective   1..........2...........3..........4..........5 Very Effective

Action 3: She decided it was best to ignore the feeling since it wouldn't last anyway.
Very Ineffective   1..........2...........3..........4..........5 Very Effective

FIG. 10.2. Example of test items from the Mayer, Salovey, Caruso Emotional Intelligence Test (MSCEIT).

experts, drawn from the ranks of the International Society for Research on Emotions (ISRE). The correlation between these two scoring methods (general consensus and expert consensus) is well above .90 for the MSCEIT. The greatest differences between the two scoring methods occur for identifying and understanding emotions, areas where emotion theory and expertise have been institutionalized in manuals, textbooks, and research reports. That is, our expert knowledge of emotion is most advanced in the areas of emotion recognition and emotion theory.

Reliability and Validity. Split-half reliability estimates for the MSCEIT at the total score and four branch levels range from .79 to .93. Unlike self-report measures of emotional intelligence, the MSCEIT is relatively independent of traditional measures of personality traits or dispositional traits. Correlations between the MSCEIT and traditional measures of cognitive intelligence are in the moderate range, around .30. There is as yet little research using the MSCEIT in leadership settings, but what data do exist show promise. In one study of nurse leaders, leaders scoring higher on the MSCEIT tended to employ a participatory, consensus-based leadership style (Vitello-Cicciu, 2001). In another study, managers who were most teamlike in orientation on the Blake and Mouton Managerial Style Grid scored significantly higher on emotional intelligence than did managers who were classified as nonteam managers (Moss, 2001).

EMOTIONAL INTELLIGENCE AND ITS ROLE IN LEADERSHIP

We do not propose the concept of emotional intelligence as a replacement for leadership theories or models of effective leadership. Instead, we believe that emotional intelligence can enhance existing models of leadership development in two ways. First, trait-based approaches to leadership can simply add another dimension or set of skills to their list of important variables. Second, our approach to emotional intelligence can overlay onto existing process-based leadership development models.

How Would Emotionally Intelligent Leaders Lead?

What sort of leadership behaviors should emotional intelligence result in? Unlike the popular conception of emotional intelligence, which suggests that emotional intelligence is the key to success, the Mayer–Salovey ability model indicates that emotional intelligence may play a significant role in leader development and leadership.

We also assume that the differences between emotionally intelligent leaders and less emotionally intelligent leaders will not necessarily show up in a specific situation or outcome. These differences will play out on a large canvas, across situations, and across a span of time. Although these differences may not always result in a positive difference in leadership effectiveness, emotionally intelligent leaders should tend to behave in ways that engender better and more effective communications with followers. The interpersonal connections they develop and the quality of such connections will likely take a great deal of time to emerge and then to be observed.

Emotional Intelligence Within the Framework of Leadership

We next examine how the ability model of emotional intelligence informs discussions regarding leadership competencies. A classic definition of the functions of management includes planning, motivating staff, making decisions, facilitating creative thinking, being socially effective, and influencing others in order to achieve a goal (Yukl, Wall, & Lepsinger, 1990). One set of leadership competencies is drawn from the definition of leadership as outlined by the U.S. Department of the Army (2001):

> Leaders inspire Soldiers to behave professionally and to accomplish missions effectively. Therefore, The Army grows leaders with the character, competence, commitment, and courage to take action when and where required. Leadership requires imagination and initiative. Sometimes that means taking action without orders; sometimes it means standing fast until new orders arrive. At all times, leadership requires sound judgment." (p. 11)

More recently, Yukl (1998) updated his view of leader activities to include five actions of leaders: (a) develop collective goals, (b) create a sense of importance and meaning, (c) generate enthusiasm, (d) promote flexible thinking and decision making, and (e) create an organizational identity. We use this set of leadership skills to hypothesize about how emotionally unintelligent and emotionally intelligent leaders might act. The results of our analysis are listed in Table 10.1. As can be seen, the ability model of emotional intelligence does not replace existing leadership frameworks, but instead seeks to provide a clearer understanding of the emotional processes that underlie certain aspects of leadership.

How Emotional Intelligence Abilities Are Displayed by Leaders

The second way that emotional intelligence can inform work on leadership development is to examine how the four skills or abilities composing this intelligence can be leveraged by effective leaders. Next, we hypothesize how leaders may enhance their effectiveness through the use of these four abilities (see Caruso, Mayer, & Salovey, 2001, and George, 2000, for detailed discussion).

TABLE 10.1

Emotional Intelligence Processes and Leadership Functions

Leader Function	Emotional Intelligence Ability			
	Identify	*Facilitate*	*Understand*	*Manage*
Develop collective goals	Begin by assessing the feelings of the organization	Generate moods to create openness and sharing	Recognize stages of team development	Address emotional needs of team members
Create a sense of meaning		Generate mood-congruent thoughts	Understand how people will respond to initiatives	Attract talented people to the organization
Generate enthusiasm		Develop an inspirational vision		Maintain a positive tone
Promote flexible thinking		Alter moods to influence thinking		Reward adaptive behavior
Create organizational identity	Identify the strength of group cohesiveness			Create feelings of group cohesion and enhance morale

How Leaders May Employ the Ability
to Identify Emotions

A leader who accurately identifies that his or her staff is confused or has clearly not bought into the new strategy can alter his or her approach. It is the clueless leader who issues orders and commands without observing how the staff reacts. The ability to identify emotions also includes identifying internal states, that is, a leader must also be able to accurately identify his or her own feelings. This skill may be termed self-awareness, and it is believed that greater self-awareness influences managerial performance. One recent study found that managers whose self-ratings were more congruent with their direct reports' ratings tended to be high-performing managers (Church, 1997). This study concluded that manager self-awareness leads to greater management performance.

How Leaders May Employ the Ability to Use
Emotions to Facilitate Thought

"Leadership, which embraces the emotional side of directing organizations, pumps life and meaning into management structures, bringing them to full life" (Barach & Eckhardt, 1996, p. 4). As our case studies illustrate, how people feel influences their judgment and decision making. It is the effective leader who knows this and employs this ability to create an emotional tone that will facilitate the team's performance. Perhaps this ability is most evident in athletic leadership. The coach of the underdog team infuses the team with energy and positive thinking. In this positive mood, they generate new ideas and enthusiasm to help them win the game. The coach of the top-seeded, undefeated team knows that his team must dampen their ebullient mood just enough to stay focused on executing their game plan. In essence, effective leadership generates and communicates emotions among the group, a phenomenon known as emotional contagion (Barsade & Gibson, 1998). Positive emotional contagion is thought to enhance group cooperation and reduce group conflict (Barsade, 2002).

It is this emotional intelligence ability that likely underlies symbolic management. Symbolic management employs symbols such as myths and stories to direct people's attention toward a common goal. Symbols may include corporate logos or a powerful vision statement that sends a message that is both understood and felt by employees. "Symbolic management is effective because it draws on the qualities of the heart and of the head—and, at times, it entirely bypasses the latter for the former" (Ashforth & Humphreys, 1995, p. 111).

How Leaders May Employ the Ability to Understand Emotions

Strategic and marketing plans must include a competitive analysis and an in-depth understanding of market trends. Although no leader has a perfectly accurate crystal ball, leaders must be able to understand the impact of major economic or political events on their lines of business. Similarly, effective leadership will most likely involve an in-depth understanding of followers' feelings and emotions. Leaders who understand the impact of an event on the morale of their team will be better equipped to handle the resulting frustration or leverage the resulting excitement.

Understanding emotions is the ability to recognize how feelings change and why they change. This ability also provides a leader with a cognitive understanding of the feelings of followers, or cognitive-based empathy. Understanding emotions may operationalize the social ability of leaders that has been defined as the "ability and judgment in working with and through people, including an understanding of motivation and an application of effective leadership" (Hersey & Blanchard, 1988, p. 7).

How Leaders May Employ the Ability to Manage Emotions

Emotionality in the workplace is often viewed as unprofessional. However, the ability to manage emotions does not mean that emotions are kept on a tight rein for fear that they will leak out in inappropriate ways. Instead, this ability allows a leader to stay open to feelings, whether they are comfortable or uncomfortable, and to integrate these emotions into his or her thinking. That emotions contain data is one of the basic underlying principles of the ability model of emotional intelligence. To ignore an important source of data or information is to risk making an uninformed decision. Indeed, effective coping strategies often directly address the underlying cause of an emotion rather than focus on the emotion itself (Weiss & Cropanzano, 1996).

Because managerial mood affects employee work performance (George, 1995), it is likely that the ability to manage one's own and other's emotions is one of the skills that allow leaders to create beneficial moods. Similarly, charisma, the regulation of the emotions of team members by its leader (Friedman, Riggio, & Casella, 1988; Wasielewski, 1985), appears to require the ability to enhance pleasant emotions and de-emphasize unpleasant emotions in others. Charismatic leadership, a form of transformational leadership (Bass, 1985, 1997; Bass, Avolio, & Goodheim, 1987), may also have its roots in managing emotions (Ashkanasy & Tse, 1998).

THE ROLE OF EMOTIONAL INTELLIGENCE IN LEADERSHIP DEVELOPMENT

The model of emotional intelligence that we are describing can be applied directly to leadership development in a number of ways.

Social and Behavioral Complexity

Leadership development has been characterized, in part, as the development of the capacity to handle greater complexity, including social and behavioral complexity through the processes of social differentiation and social integration (Day & Lance, chap. 3, this volume). The abilities that constitute emotional intelligence, such as emotional identification and emotional regulation, are an explicit part of this complexity model. The ability model of emotional intelligence as described in this chapter provides a framework for the understanding, measurement, and development of a set of core leadership development competencies. By describing and teaching the ability model, we take emotions from background to foreground, from subject to object, thereby enabling leaders to develop these abilities (Day & Lance, chap. 3, this volume).

Development of Two Social Leadership Behaviors

We next examine two qualities of effective leaders in the context of emotional intelligence. These two social abilities are given a good deal of attention, but are often believed to be the result of innate talent or the province of "born" leaders. These are the development of *morale* and *empathy*.

Morale

Morale has been oft-studied and its importance is hard to exaggerate:

> Morale is the human dimension's most important intangible element. It's a measure of how people feel about themselves, their team, and their leaders. High morale comes from good leadership, shared hardship, and mutual respect. It's an emotional bond that springs from common values like loyalty to fellow soldiers and a belief that the organization will care for families. High morale results in a cohesive team that enthusiastically strives to achieve common goals. Leaders know that morale, the essential human element, holds the team together and keeps it going in the face of the terrifying and dispiriting things that occur in war. (U.S. Department of the Army, 1999, p. 3–3)

The ability model of emotional intelligence, with its explicit focus on emotion and its impact on thinking, may provide a means to better understand the mechanisms of morale and its development.

The ability model may be able to provide a process map that can be applied to the understanding and development of morale. Leaders first must identify the state of their subordinate's feelings to determine the morale, or emotional tone, of the organization. These feelings influence the perceptions and cognitions of the organization. The leader must analyze the situation in order to understand the cause of the group's emotions and how these feelings may change over time. Finally, for example, if morale is low, the leader can initiate a series of emotion management projects in order to change the emotional tone of the organization.

Empathy

Often viewed as a "soft skill" that is best left to psychologists to develop, the ability to empathize with others plays an important role in leadership. Consider what Lieut. Gen. William G. Pagonis (U.S. Army) said about this quality: "Empathy was an absolutely vital quality in the context of the Gulf War. We asked ourselves constantly: What do the other people on our team need? Why do they think they need it, and how can we give it to them?" (Pagonis, 2001, p. 110). Pagonis went on to talk about how the need for empathy operates on many different levels. He referred to his relationship with the Saudis, who

> were inclined to avoid conflict with their 550,000 guests. . . . It was our responsibility therefore, to anticipate their needs and avoid crises. One day several months after the war ended, I realized that our two inactivated firing ranges were still littered with unexploded ordnance and that the Bedouins would soon be traversing these areas again. We put ourselves in the shoes of the Bedouins and of the Saudi officials who had to protect the interests of these desert wanderers. We cleaned up the ranges well before the Saudi Arabians had to put pressure on us to do so. With that we earned their continued respect and cooperation. (pp. 111–112)

Periodically, great tragedies strike, and can range from an act of war to a great flood or earthquake that devastates thousands and causes great pain among those who survive. Tragedies occur on a much smaller level more frequently, such as the loss of a loved one, the loss of a job, or finding out a colleague, friend, or child has been diagnosed with cancer. Whether small or large, tragic circumstances and the emotions that surround them spill over into the workplace. Research at the University of Michigan and the University of British Columbia's CompassionLab has demonstrated that some organizations suppress compassion, whereas others create an environment in which compassion is expressed and spreads: "We've found that a leader's ability to enable a compassionate response throughout a company directly affects the organization's ability to maintain a high performance in difficult times. It fosters a company's capacity to heal, to learn, to adapt, and to excel" (Dutton, Frost, Worline, Lilius, & Kanov, 2002, p. 56).

Case studies suggest that employees will reward companies that demonstrate caring and empathy. There is the noteworthy example of Aaron Feurstein, whose Malden Mills manufacturing plant in Massachusetts burned down on December 11, 1995. Instead of taking his insurance settlement of $300 million and relocating or retiring, he decided to rebuild. He announced in December that he would pay the payroll for his employees through the end of the month. He paid them again in January and in February: "His generosity made quite an impact on his employees: Productivity at the plant nearly doubled once it reopened" (Dutton et al., 2002, p. 61). The debt that Malden Mills took on to reopen eventually forced it into bankruptcy, but even in this case, Feuerstein made every attempt to minimize job cuts and maintain benefits.

Such a sense of compassion may arise from feeling what others feel. Research using the MSCEIT suggests that those who score higher on this test of emotional intelligence tend to be more emotionally empathetic than low-scoring individuals.

Teaching Emotional Knowledge and Skills

Can emotional intelligence be increased? There are not enough data to answer the question with any degree of confidence. On one hand, we view EI similarly to other abilities or aptitudes, and thus as a measure of one's potential, as "displayed under favorable conditions" (Carroll, 1993, p. 8).

On the other hand, retrospective reports of how one was parented and other self-reports of environmental differences are related to one's measured emotional intelligence (see, e.g., Mayer et al., 1999). No matter whether one's "emotional IQ" or potential can be altered, there are sufficient data to support the idea of teaching emotional skills and emotional knowledge (see, e.g., Salovey & Sluyter, 1997). Although it is hypothesized that one's level of emotional intelligence may influence the rate of acquiring new emotional skills and the ultimate level of one's emotional knowledge, such skills and knowledge can be taught and enhanced.

Teaching the Ability to Identify Emotions

If nonverbal communication and the identification of emotions can be taught to autistic children, then certainly we should be able to enhance the ability of adults to attend to and accurately perceive emotional states in themselves and in others. The work of Ekman (1973) and others clearly shows that such skills can be developed.

Teaching the Ability to Use Emotions to Facilitate Thought

It is relatively straightforward to demonstrate how emotions and cognitions are linked and to teach leaders which moods facilitate which types of problem solving (Palfai & Salovey, 1993; Schwarz, 1990). Creative thinking can be enhanced through such training as well (Goodwin & Jamison, 1990).

Teaching the Ability to Understand Emotions

Emotion terms and families have been developed to the extent that it is relatively straightforward to develop a curriculum to teach *about* emotions. Various emotion taxonomies and theories exist and most leaders should find that these formal models match closely their own thinking on the subject (Ortony, Clore, & Collins, 1988).

Teaching the Ability to Manage Emotions

Teaching these skills must start with the understanding that minimizing emotion is not the goal of leadership development, nor is the goal the artificial enhancement or exaggeration of emotion. Regulating our own and other's emotions may require a balance between thinking and feeling, so that the quality of emotional data is not degraded. Teaching emotion management strategies can be based on our database of techniques that work (Gross, 1998; Thayer, Newman, and McClain (1994). The skillful disclosure of emotion has also been trained and taught with great success (Pennebaker, 1993, 1997).

Providing a Framework for Leadership Development

The ability model of EI and the MSCEIT measurement based on it provide us with a model of leadership and its development.

Blueprint for Development

The ability model of emotional intelligence provides leaders with a blueprint for development. As a simple process model, the four-ability model can be overlaid on top of existing development programs in order to provide a structured way to

TABLE 10.2

Ability Model of Emotional Intelligence as a Framework for Development

Step	What To Do
Identify emotions	Listen, ask questions, and paraphrase to ensure understanding. How am I feeling? How is he, she, or the others feeling?
Use emotions to facilitate thought	Determine how these feelings influence our thinking. Change the tone if necessary. What feelings are in play now, and are they the feelings most appropriate to the situation? If not, what feelings would be more appropriate and why?
Understand emotions	Examine the causes of these feelings and what may happen next. What might happen to the existing feelings without any attention to them or attempt to change them? If we want to create different feelings, what might we do?
Manage emotions	Include the rational, logical information with the emotional data to make an optimal decision. Based on the answers to the questions above, what do we need to do to manage our and others' existing emotions? If we choose to change emotions for ourselves and others, how will we make that happen?

develop the emotional skills of leaders. We have taught the model to a number of managers and leaders. Although we have yet to assess systematically the efficacy of such training, there is great intuitive appeal to such an approach (e.g., Wolfe, 2001). Table 10.2 illustrates how we present and teach executives to understand and utilize this model.

It is likely that many effective leaders already have some sort of informal process in place to help them understand situations and make effective decisions. The emotional intelligence ability model can help leaders by providing a structure or framework for complex intra- and interpersonal problem-solving skills that have an impact on the ability to lead effectively. An effective leadership development tool is the case study approach. Case studies also provide an effective technique for the development of the emotional intelligence abilities described in this chapter. Consider the case of Gene Cattabiani, a Westinghouse Steam Turbine Division executive in the 1970s, who was known as a good engineer as well as a "people person" (Peace, 2001, p. 102). We take this case and place it within the ability model of emotional intelligence framework.

When Cattabiani took over the division, there was little or no trust between management and union leaders. He identified that both managers and union members were angry and distrusting of one another ("identifying emotions"). Cattabiani noted that both sides were focused on fault finding and details as a result of their anger and fear and that there was little interest in creative problem identification or resolution ("using emotion to facilitate thought"). Whereas managers viewed shop floor workers as lazy and greedy, union members viewed managers as incompetent, overpaid, and more or less unnecessary ("understanding emotions").

There was a compelling need to cut costs and improve productivity, but the animosity between labor and management made it seem unlikely that cooperative negotiations could take place. "Gene decided it was up to him to break this impasse and begin to change attitudes on both sides by treating union leaders and the workforce with respect, honesty and openness. To me this made a great deal of sense. If managers began treating union members with dignity and worth, they might just respond by treating us the same way" (Peace, 2001, p. 102).

Cattabiani decided that he needed to instill a sense of fear to change the tone of the relationship between the union and management ("using emotion to facilitate thought"). For the fear to be useful, it had to be fear of the possible financial failure of the organization so that both union and management were threatened by a common enemy, motivating both sides to begin developing collective goals to address the situation. As Yukl (1998) indicated, developing collective goals is one of the key competencies of leadership. To develop collective goals, it is necessary to identify emotions that are barriers between groups and change the emotions to something that works toward mutual goal development.

Cattabiani realized that the union had viewed the business as highly profitable and that they wanted a larger slice of the pie. Because senior management in the past had chosen not to share financial information with the union, the union did not realize that profits had been shrinking and that the pie had gotten smaller ("understanding emotions").

Cattabiani decided to change that. As long as the union felt that management was lying to it to keep more of the profits for themselves, the union was not likely to change its adversarial position ("understanding emotions"). He wanted people in the union to understand they were partners in this venture, that times were tough, and that they needed to fear the consequences of continuing internal confrontation. He felt the best way to engender cooperation and trust was to share information and treat people with respect ("managing emotions").

Cattabiani called a meeting of the entire workforce, not just the union leaders, for the first time in the division's history. Despite the fact that the rank and file viewed Cattabiani and his colleagues as the enemy, he was committed to his idea. His first presentation was a nightmare. Participants heckled him and shouted abuse and threats. However, Cattabiani rose to the challenge. Cattabiani's abilities and perseverance generated a sense of openness and vulnerability. He did not become confrontational or defensive ("managing emotions"). He continued to make his presentations until every worker was made aware of the current state of the business.

Cattabiani next started going out on the factory floor, a first for someone at his level, and he talked with the workers. Peace (2001) noted that "people began to offer a nod of recognition—a radical change from the way they used to spit on the floor as he walked by. Even more remarkable was his interchange with hecklers. Whenever he spotted one he would walk over and engage them in conversation" (p. 103).

These exchanges, however, led to meaningful and candid dialogue and the people on the shop floor began to trust Cattabiani. By avoiding defensiveness and being open to criticism he became more credible in the eyes of the union members ("managing emotions"). He gave employees broader, more flexible assignments. He also imposed layoffs, and he raised standards in both throughput and quality control. This all led to greatly improved financial performance, productivity improvements, and broader, more flexible assignments for employees along with a promotion to executive vice president for Cattabiani. Employees also had greater opportunity for growth and promotion. In addition, the plant remained open and those employees who performed were rewarded with steady employment.

As Peace (2001) observed,

> Whenever I'm tempted to insulate myself from the painful consequences of some business decision, Gene's experience reminds me that it's more productive to listen to objections and complaints, to understand what subordinates are thinking and feeling, to open up to their arguments and their displeasure. It was this kind of vulnerability that made Gene credible to the people whose help he most needed in order to succeed. (p. 104)

The nature of the interactions that Peace described and his view of management was not popular in the 1980s, but it sounds remarkably similar to Yukl's (1998) leadership model. This leadership model describes *what* a leader such as Cattabiani did. The emotional intelligence ability model framework provides us with a better understanding of *how* Cattabiani achieved these objectives.

CONCLUSIONS

Research Needs

The popularity of the concept of emotional intelligence has outpaced the science behind it. It is our hope that researchers will focus their attention on the ability model of emotional intelligence as they examine its role in leadership effectiveness.

The relationship of emotional intelligence to other abilities and intelligences also needs to be explored. It will be particularly interesting to examine the interplay of emotional and practical intelligence (Sternberg, 1997). Some of the many questions that must be addressed include the relationship between these two intelligences, their relative contribution to our understanding of leadership development, and whether certain aspects of emotional knowledge are a form of tacit knowledge. (For a discussion of practical intelligence, see Cianciolo, Antonakis, & Sternberg, chap. 9, this volume.)

Practical Implications

Although the study of emotional intelligence is relatively new, the ability model appears to hold promise for leadership development research and practice.

Certainly, however, we need to remind ourselves that no single set of abilities will be able to adequately encompass all of the skills that effective leaders must possess. There are many variables that must be added to the leadership equation, including skills, competencies, and dispositional traits. It might also be advisable to understand that not all outcomes can be predicted based upon leadership variables: "When I asked a station commander what strengthens the resolve of his pilots he answers 'leadership' and then after a pause often adds 'and the quality of their equipment'" (Moran, 1967, p. 98). The best leadership development programs will give our leaders a decided advantage, but let us remember that there are variables beyond the scope of our control.

Given the importance of emotion and its central place in leadership effectiveness, leadership development programs must take the development of emotional skills more seriously. Leaders cannot be allowed to dismiss emotion as irrelevant or to define their role in purely rational terms.

Developing effective leaders for today means that we must equip them with the latest training and skills, but developing leaders who can be effective tomorrow may require developing leaders who can think and feel, remain open to various sources of information, and can effectively integrate these data sources. We have always known that leaders at all levels, especially at the highest levels, need to learn how to lead using skills beyond those that come from hierarchical authority.

The model of emotional intelligence described in this chapter can inform leadership development programs. Existing programs can be enhanced and new programs developed. It is our hope and belief that such an approach to leadership development will provide all leaders with the critical emotional skills they need to succeed. Although the ability-based model of emotional intelligence does not answer every question about human behavior, research indicates that it is measuring a unique piece of the puzzle not measured by other concepts. We believe the inclusion of this model as an addition to leadership development research, theory, and practice will have a significant impact on our ability to teach people how to create inspired performance.

REFERENCES

Ashby, F. G., Isen, A. M., & Turken, A. U. (1999). A neuropsychological theory of positive affect and its influence on cognition. *Psychological Review, 106,* 529–550.

Ashkanasy, N. M., & Tse, B. (1998, August). *Transformational leadership as management of emotion: A conceptual review.* Paper presented at the First Conference on Emotions and Organizational Life, San Diego, CA.

Ashforth, B. E., & Humphreys, R. H. (1995). Emotion in the workplace: A reappraisal. *Human Relations, 48,* 97–125.

Barach, J. A., & Eckhardt, D. R. (1996). *Leadership and the job of the executive.* Westport, CT: Quorum.

Barrett, L. F., & Salovey, P. (2002). *The wisdom in feeling: Psychological processes in emotional intelligence.* New York: Guilford.

Bar-On, R. (1997). *Bar-On Emotional Quotient Inventory: A measure of emotional intelligence.* Toronto, Canada: Multi-Health Systems.

Barsade, S. G. (2002). The ripple effect: emotional contagion and its influence on group behavior. *Administrative Science Quarterly, 47,* 644–675.

Barsade, S. G., & Gibson, D. E. (1998). Group emotion: A view from top and bottom. *Research on managing groups and teams* (Vol. 1, pp. 81–102). Westport, CT: JAI.

Bass, B. M. (1985). *Leadership and performance beyond expectations.* New York: Free Press.

Bass, B. M. (1997). Does the transactional–transformational leadership paradigm transcend organizational and national boundaries? *American Psychologist, 52,* 130–139.

Bass, B. M., Avolio, B. J., & Goodheim, L. (1987). Biography and the assessment of transformational leadership at the world class level. *Journal of Management, 13,* 7–20.

Bower, G. H. (1981). Mood and memory. *American Psychologist, 36,* 129–148.

Boyatzis, R. E., Goleman, D., & Rhee, K. S. (2000). Clustering competence in emotional intelligence: Insights from the Emotional Competence Inventory. In R. Bar-On & J. D. A. Parker (Eds.), *The handbook of emotional intelligence: Theory, development, assessment, and application at home, school, and in the workplace.* San Francisco: Jossey-Bass.

Carroll, J. B. (1993). *Human cognitive abilities: A survey of factor-analytic studies.* New York: Cambridge University Press.

Caruso, D. R., Mayer, J. D., & Salovey, P. (2001). Emotional intelligence and emotional leadership. In R. Riggio & S. Murphy (Eds.), *Multiple intelligences and leadership* (pp. 55–74). Mahwah, NJ: Lawrence Erlbaum Associates, Inc.

Church, A. H. (1997). Managerial self-awareness in high-performing individuals in organizations. *Journal of Applied Psychology, 82,* 281–292.

Damasio, A. R. (1994). *Descartes' error: Emotion, reason, and the human brain.* New York: Avon.

Day, D. V. (2000). Leadership development: A review in context. *Leadership Quarterly, 11,* 581–613.

Dutton, J. E., Frost, P. J., Worline, M. C., Lilius, J. M., & Kanov, J. M. (2002). Leading in times of trauma. *Harvard Business Review, 2002* (January), 54–61.

Ekman, P. (1973). *Darwin and facial expression: A century of research in review.* New York: Academic.

Forgas, J. P. (1995). Mood and judgment: The affect infusion model (AIM). *Psychological Bulletin, 117,* 39–66.

Friedman, H. S., Riggio, R. E., & Casella, D. F. (1988). Nonverbal skill, personal charisma, and initial attraction. *Personality and Social Psychology Bulletin, 14,* 203–211.

Funder, D. C., & Dobroth, K. M. (1987). Differences between traits: Properties associated with inter-judge agreement. *Journal of Personality and Social Psychology, 52,* 409–418.

Gardner, H. (1999). *Intelligence reframed.* New York: BasicBooks.

George, J. M. (1995). Leader positive mood and group performance: The case of customer service. *Journal of Applied Social Psychology, 25,* 778–794.

George, J. M. (2000). Emotions and leadership: The role of emotional intelligence. *Human Relations, 53,* 1027–1055.

Gibson, D. E. (1997). The struggle for reason: The sociology of emotions in organizations. *Social Perspectives on Emotion, 4,* 211–256.

Goleman, D. (1995). *Emotional intelligence.* New York: Bantam.

Goleman, D. (1998). *Working with emotional intelligence.* New York: Bantam.

Goodwin, F. K., & Jamison, K. R. (1990). *Manic-depressive illness.* New York: Oxford University Press.

Grandey, A. A. (2003). When the "show must go on": Surface acting and deep acting as determinants of emotional exhaustion and peer-rated service delivery. *Academy of Management Journal, 46,* 86–96.

Gross, J. J. (1998). Antecedent- and response-focused emotion regulation: Divergent consequences for experience, expression, and physiology. *Journal of Personality and Social Psychology, 74,* 224–237.

Hersey, P., & Blanchard, K. H. (1988). *Management of organizational behavior.* Englewood Cliffs, NJ: Prentice-Hall.

Hochschild, A. R. (1983). *The managed heart: The commercialization of human feeling.* Berkeley, CA: University of California Press.

Isen, A. M. (1987). Positive affect, cognitive processes, and social behavior. *Advances in Experimental Social Psychology, 20,* 203–253.

Izard, C. E. (2002). Translating emotion theory and research into preventive interventions. *Psychological Bulletin, 128,* 796–824.

Matarazzo, J. D. (1972). *Wechsler's measurement and appraisal of adult intelligence* (5th ed.). New York: Oxford University Press.

Mayer, J. D., Caruso, D. R., & Salovey, P. (1999). Emotional intelligence meets standards for a traditional intelligence. *Intelligence, 27,* 267–298.

Mayer, J. D., & Salovey, P. (1993). The intelligence of emotional intelligence. *Intelligence, 17,* 433–442.

Mayer, J. D., & Salovey, P. (1997). What is emotional intelligence? In P. Salovey & D. Sluyter (Eds.), *Emotional development and emotional intelligence: Implications for educators* (pp. 3–31). New York: Basic Books.

Mayer, J. D., Salovey, P., & Caruso, D. R. (2000a). Emotional intelligence as zeitgeist, as personality, and as a mental ability. In R. Bar-On & J. D. A. Parker (Eds.), *The handbook of emotional intelligence* (pp. 92–117). San Francisco: Jossey-Bass.

Mayer, J. D., Salovey, P., & Caruso, D. R. (2000b). Selecting a measure of emotional intelligence: The case for ability scales. In R. Bar-On & J. D. A. Parker (Eds.), *The handbook of emotional intelligence* (pp. 320–342). San Francisco: Jossey-Bass.

Mayer, J. D., Salovey, P., & Caruso, D. R. (2002). *Manual for the MSCEIT.* Toronto, Canada: Multi-Health Systems.

Mayer, J. D., Salovey, P., Caruso, D. R., & Sitarenios, G. (2001). Emotional intelligence as a standard intelligence: A Reply. *Emotion, 1,* 232–242.

Mayer, J. D., Salovey, P., Caruso, D. R., & Sitarenios, G. (2001). Measuring emotional intelligence with the MSCEIT V2.0. *Emotion, 3,* 97–105.

Mischel, W., & DeSmet, A. L. (2000). Self-regulation in the service of conflict resolution. In M. Deutsch & P. T. Coleman (Eds.), *The handbook of conflict resolution: Theory and practice* (pp. 256–275). San Francisco: Jossey-Bass.

Moran, L. (1967). *The anatomy of courage.* Boston: Houghton Mifflin.

Morreall, J. (1991). Humor and work. *Humor: International Journal of Humor Research, 4,* 359–373.

Moss, M. T. (2001). *Emotional determinants in health care executive leadership styles.* Unpublished doctoral dissertation, Medical University of South Carolina, Charleston.

Neisser, U., Boodoo, G., Bouchard, T. J., Boykin, A. W., Brody, N., Ceci, S. J., Halpern, D. F., Loehlin, J. C., Perloff, R., Sternberg, R. J., & Urbina, S. (1996). Intelligence: Knowns and unknowns. *American Psychologist, 51,* 77–101.

Ortony, A., Clore, G. L., & Collins, A. (1988). *The cognitive structure of emotions.* Cambridge: Cambridge University Press.

Palfai, T. P., & Salovey, P. (1993). The influence of depressed and elated mood on deductive and inductive reasoning. *Imagination, Cognition, and Personality, 13,* 57–71.

Pagonis, W. G. (2001). Leadership in a combat zone. *Harvard Business Review, 2002* (December), 107–116.

Paulhus, D. L., Lysy, D. C., & Yik, M. S. M. (1998). Self-report measures of intelligence: Are they useful as proxy IQ tests? *Journal of Personality, 66,* 525–554.

Peace, W. H. (2001). The hardwork of being a soft manager. *Harvard Business Review, 2001* (December), 99–106.

Pennebaker, J. W. (1993). Putting stress into words: Health, linguistic, and therapeutic implications. *Behavior Research and Therapy, 31,* 539–548.

Pennebaker, J. W. (1997). Writing about emotional experiences as a therapeutic process. *Psychological Science, 9,* 162–166.

Salovey, P., & Birnbaum, D. (1989). Influence of mood on health-relevant cognitions. *Journal of Personality and Social Psychology, 57,* 539–551.

Salovey, P., & Mayer, J. D. (1990). Emotional intelligence. *Imagination, Cognition, and Personality, 9,* 185–211.

Salovey, P., & Sluyter, D. (Eds.), (1997). *Emotional development and emotional intelligence: Implications for educators.* New York: Basic Books.

Scarr, S. (1989). Protecting general intelligence: Constructs and consequences for intervention. In R. L. Linn (Ed.), *Intelligence: Measurement, theory, and public policy.* Urbana: University of Illinois Press.

Schwarz, N. (1990). Feelings as information: Informational and motivational functions of affective states. In E. T. Higgins & E. M. Sorrentino (Eds.), *Handbook of motivation and cognition* (Vol. 2, pp. 527–561). New York: Guilford.

Sinclair, R. C., & Mark, M. M. (1995). The effects of mood state on judgmental accuracy: Processing strategy as a mechanism. *Cognition and Emotion, 9,* 417–438.

Sutton, R. I. (1991). Maintaining norms about expressed emotions: The case of bill collectors. *Administrative Science Quarterly, 36,* 245–268.

Sternberg, R. J. (1997). *Successful intelligence.* New York: Plume.

Taylor, S. F., & Brown, J. D. (1988). Illusion and well-being: A social psychological perspective on mental health. *Psychological Bulletin, 103,* 193–210.

Thayer, R. E., Newman, J. R., & McClain, T. M. (1994). Self-regulation of mood: Strategies for changing a bad mood, raising energy, and reducing tension. *Journal of Personality and Social Psychology, 67,* 910–925.

U.S. Department of the Army. (1999). *Army field manual 22-100.* Washington, DC: Headquarters, Department of the Army.

U.S. Department of the Army. (2001). *Army field manual FM 1.* Washington, DC: Headquarters, Department of the Army.

Vitello-Cicciu, J. M. (2001). *Leadership practices and emotional intelligence of nurse leaders.* Unpublished doctoral dissertation, The Fielding Institute. Santa Barbara, CA.

Wasielewski, P. L. (1985). The emotional basis of charisma. *Symbolic Interaction, 8,* 207–222.

Weiss, H. A., & Cropanzano, R. (1996). Affective events theory: A theoretical discussion of the structure, causes, and consequences of affective experiences at work. *Research in Organizational Behavior, 18,* 1–74.

Wolfe, C. J. (2001). Results of emotionally intelligent actions at Kaiser Permanente. *Competency and Emotional Intelligence Quarterly, 8,* 25–26.

Woodworth, R. S. (1940). *Psychology* (4th ed.). New York: Holt.

Young, P. T. (1936). *Motivation of behavior.* New York: Wiley.

Young, P. T. (1943). *Emotion in man and animal: Its nature and relation to attitude and motive.* New York: Wiley.

Yukl, G. A. (1998). *Leadership in organizations* (4th ed.). Upper Saddle River, NJ: Prentice-Hall.

Yukl, G. A., Wall, S., & Lepsinger, R (1990). Preliminary report on the validation of the management practices survey. In K. E. Clark & M. B. Clark (Eds.), *Measures of leadership* (pp. 223–238). West Orange, NJ: Leadership Library of America.

V

Enhancing Team Skills

11

Leadership in Virtual Teams

Stephen J. Zaccaro
George Mason University

Sharon D. Ardison
U.S. Army Research Institute

Kara L. Orvis
George Mason University

Today, leaders in organizations need to manage increasingly complex forms of teams. Team members can span the world, as global networks of constituencies, stakeholders, and partners commonly characterize organizations in the 21st century. Such global networks have emerged in response to the rapid pace of operating environments and the need for multiple work units to adapt quickly to changes. Work across these networks has become more highly interdependent, and growth in information and communication technology has provided the means for doing such work more efficiently. Within organizations, more workers are telecommuting, working from home offices or sites away from home offices. To accommodate different worker needs, many companies operate on various flextime schedules. These factors have fueled growth in virtual, geographically, and temporally dispersed teams and organizations.

These changes have significant implications for the practice of organizational leadership. Yet, the current literature contains sparse amounts of *systematic* theory on leading virtual teams in today's organizations. This chapter provides a framework, adapted from previous team research, for defining the dimensions of team virtuality. It also describes a model for leaderteam dynamics, which is then used to review and interpret the literature on leadership and virtual team processes. In essence, the framework to be presented describes fundamental leader performance requirements for successfully leading virtual teams. Accordingly, in the final section of this chapter, we describe some leader competencies that promote virtual team leadership and offer some leader development prescriptions.

WHAT ARE VIRTUAL TEAMS?

Defining virtual teams requires first defining the nature of teams (see Fleishman & Zaccaro, 1992). Salas, Dickinson, Converse, and Tannenbaum (1992) provided a good working definition of a "team" as "a distinguishable set of two or more people who interact, dynamically, interdependently, and adaptively toward a common and valued goal/objective/mission, who have been assigned specific roles or functions to perform, and who have a limited life-span of membership" (p. 4).

This definition highlights several features that apply also to virtual teams. First, team members typically have different and unique roles, with each role being critical for collective success. Successful team action requires that individual member strengths, resources, and contributions be identified and a plan developed for how best to integrate and utilize these contributions (Hinsz, Tindale, & Vollrath, 1997). In virtual teams, where members may be geographically dispersed, requisite resource may become exponentially more complex.

A second feature of teams is that team processes and dynamics should fit environmental contingencies and adapt when those contingencies change. Zaccaro, Rittman, and Marks (2001) argued, "Truly effective teams are those that are able to maintain high levels of collective performance, even as team and environmental circumstances become decidedly adverse" (p. 457). This feature pertains particularly to virtual teams, which often form in response to dynamic environmental conditions and are intended to be especially adaptive structures.

Finally, Salas et al. (1992) emphasized that teams have a limited life span of membership. Although this aspect is not commonly found in other definitions of teams (e.g., Nieva, Fleishman, & Rieck, 1978), it has been suggested as a significant feature of virtual teams by several researchers (Jarvenpaa & Leidner, 1999; Townsend, DeMarie, & Hendrickson, 1998).

Although virtual teams are a relatively new organizational form, they share fundamental characteristics with traditional teams: They are composed of two or more members who have specific roles and are required to act interdependently. Several central features of virtual teams are present in more traditional organizational structures (e.g., communication over a distance, dispersed team members; Sessa, Hansen, Prestridge, & Kossler, 1999). Recent definitions have highlighted key characteristics. Table 11.1 summarizes several definitions of virtual teams in the current literature.

Griffith and Neale (2001) offered a model of team virtualness that reflects two dimensions identified across the definitions in Table 11.1, (a) percentage of time spent working apart (or team dispersion) and (b) level of technological enablement

TABLE 11.1

Sample Definitions of "Virtual Team"

A virtual team [is] a self-managed knowledge work team, with distributed expertise that forms and disbands to address specific organizational goals. (Kristof, Brown, Sims, & Smith, 1995, p. 230)

A virtual team, like every team, is a group of people who interact through interdependent tasks guided by common purpose. Unlike conventional teams, a virtual team works across space, time, and organizational boundaries with links strengthened by webs of communication technologies. (Lipnack & Stamps, 1997, pp. 6–7)

A global virtual team is an example of a new organizational form, where a *temporary team* is assembled on an as-needed basis for the duration of a task, and staffed by members from the far corners of the world (Jarvenpaa & Ives, 1994; Lipnack & Stamps, 1997; Miles & Snow, 1986). In such a team, members (1) physically remain on different continents and in different countries, (2) interact primarily through the use of computer-mediated communication technologies (electronic mail, videoconferencing, etc), and (3) rarely or never see each other in person (Knoll & Jarvenpaa, 1995; Ohara-Devereaux & Johansen, 1994). (Jarvenpaa, Knoll, & Leidner, 1998, p. 30)

Teams identified as virtual teams usually fall under a more expansive definition of a project or task-focused team that can include interorganizational membership and physical dispersion that is bridged primarily by new communication technologies such as the internet, faxes, videoconferencing and groupware, which allow for real-time meetings from almost any location. (Oakley, 1998, p. 4)

Virtual teams are groups of geographically and/or organizationally dispersed coworkers that are assembled using a combination of telecommunications and information technologies to accomplish an organizational task. Virtual teams rarely, if ever, meet in a face-to-face setting. They may be set up as temporary structures, existing only to accomplish a specific task, or may be more permanent structures, used to address ongoing issues, such as strategic planning. Further, membership is often fluid, evolving according to changing task requirements. (Townsend, DeMarie, & Hendrickson, 1998, p. 18)

Virtual teams, composed of geographically dispersed members who communicate and carry out their activities using technologies such as e-mail and videoconferencing depend upon effective collaborations for their success. (Cohen & Mankin, 1999, p. 105)

A virtual team is an evolutionary form of a network organization (Miles & Snow, 1986) enabled by advances in information and communication technology (Davidow & Malone, 1992; Jarvenpaa & Ives, 1994). The concept of virtual implies permeable interfaces and boundaries: project teams that rapidly form, reorganize, and dissolve when the needs of a dynamic marketplace change: and individuals with differing competencies who are located across time and cultures (Mowshowitz, 1997; Kristof et al., 1995). (Jarvenpaa & Leidner, 1999, p. 791)

(ranging from no technology, meaning all face-to-face interaction, to use of a broad range of communication technology). They argued that the vast majority of organizational teams fall somewhere along these two dimensions.

The literature on virtual teams makes a further distinction about team members working apart. Team dispersion is defined in terms of both geographic and temporal space. Thus, Mittleman and Briggs (1999) described five types of team interaction dispersion:

1. *Same time, same place.* This is the traditional team format, and corresponds to the more face-to-face end of Griffith and Neale's team dispersion

dimension. Such teams tend to make minimal use of communication technology or use various computer-based group decision support systems in their face-to-face interactions.

2. *Same time, different place.* Here, team members interact in the same temporal space, but are located elsewhere geographically. Communication technologies, such as teleconferencing, videoconferencing, and real-time computer networks, mediate these interactions.

3. *Different time, same place.* Team members may be in a similar geographic location, but move in and out of that space at different time intervals. Such teams may have members who work different shifts, are on different flextime schedules, or travel frequently. Communication bulletin boards and e-mail enable the interactions of these teams.

4. *Different time, different place.* In this form, different team members are both geographically and temporally dispersed. Team interactions are mostly asynchronous and likely to be completely mediated through technology.

5. *Anytime, anyplace.* Mittleman and Briggs (1999) used this form to describe team members who are constantly on the move and interact entirely through communication technology. Such members may not have an office, but rather travel from site to site.

These distinctions extend Griffith and Neale's dimension of team interaction dispersion. However, the literature also cites an additional feature of virtual teams, not covered by Griffith and Neale's model, which is the relative permanence of the team. Jarvenpaa and Leidner (1999), in defining types of global teams, argued that virtual teams were temporary forms, where "members may have never worked together before, and who may not expect to work together again as a group" (p. 792). Thus, team membership is temporary and dependent on transient organizational needs. Several other researchers have argued for impermanence as a key feature of virtual teams (Kristof, Brown, Sims, & Smith, 1995; Miles & Snow, 1986; Oakley, 1998). However, Townsend et al. (1998) define virtual teams as being "temporary, existing only to accomplish a specific task, or more permanent structures, used to address ongoing issues, such as strategic planning" (p. 18). Integrating this property of virtual teams with the definitions and dimensions offered by Griffith and Neale (2001) suggests that virtual teams can vary not only on technological enablement and interaction dispersion, but also on their relative permanence (see Figure 11.1).

Virtual teams and organizations, thus, are *organizational forms in which member interactions are often constrained by geographic and/or temporal dispersion, are mostly mediated through electronic communication technology, and whose permanence varies according to task and mission demands.* A critical implication of this definition for leadership is that leader performance requirements will vary not only along a dimension of face-to-face versus distant team interactions, but

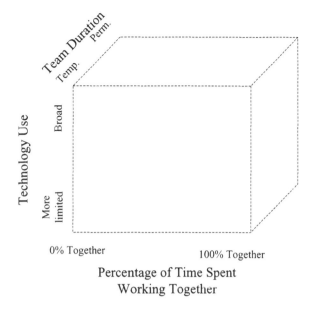

FIG. 11.1. Dimensions of virtual teams. (Adapted from Griffith & Neale, 2001).

also on the degree of technological empowerment and team permanence. For example, highly sophisticated video technology can moderate the effects of distance on leader–team communications and information processing. Also, a lack of team permanence would create the need for leadership strategies to develop quick trust.

Although research on virtual teams has emphasized these main features of dispersion, communication technology, and impermanence, other features can moderate virtual team processes, just as they do traditional team processes. These include the characteristics of team boundaries (open vs. closed), role structure (flexible vs. rigid), and intrateam relationship structure (vertical vs. horizontal, or self-managing). By their very nature of spatial and temporal dispersion, virtual teams may, on average, exhibit more open boundaries, flexible role structures, and self-managing qualities than traditional face-to-face teams. However, further research will be necessary to document these distinctions and explore their meaning for virtual team processes.

A MODEL OF LEADERSHIP AND VIRTUAL TEAM PROCESSES

Zaccaro, Rittman, and Marks (2001) argued that leaders contribute to team effectiveness by influencing five team processes: *motivational, affective, cognitive, coordination,* and *boundary spanning.* Motivational processes refer to team members' choices to engage in tasks and the amount of resources they allocate to task accomplishment (Kanfer and Ackerman, 1989). Affective processes refer to the expression and modulation of emotion and affect among team members. Cognitive processes include collective information processing (Hinsz et al., 1997) as well as the generation of shared knowledge and transactive memory. Coordination processes occur when team members integrate and synchronize their activities in concerted action. Boundary-spanning processes refer to outreach and environmental scanning activities by team members. Leaders influence team performance by shaping, directing, encouraging, and managing these processes.

Virtual teams need to engage in similar sets of processes to achieve success. Yet, the degree of dispersion and permanence of the team as well as its communication technology can greatly alter how effectively, or even whether, these processes occur. They also change which processes are more functional for team success. Likewise, these features of virtual teams moderate how leadership processes influence team dynamics. These relationships are shown in Fig. 11.2.

Team Motivational Processes

Team effectiveness is grounded in members being motivated to work hard on behalf of the team. This collective motivation derives from the *cohesion* of the team, from its sense of *collective efficacy,* and from the *trust* engendered among

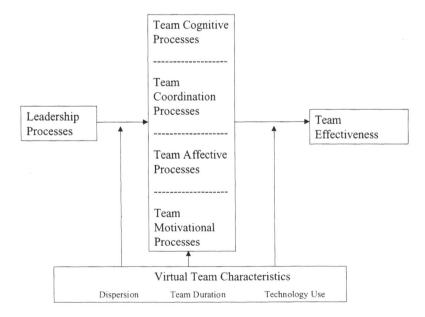

FIG. 11.2. Virtual team characteristics and leader-team relations.

team members. It is useful to note that highly motivated individuals may come together and, by virtue of their common interests, already exhibit higher degrees of trust, cohesion, and efficacy at the onset of team formation (Jarvenpaa, Knoll, & Leidner, 1998). However, these team qualities can quickly be dissipated by early team miscues and disappointments, with resulting negative consequences for team motivation.

In cohesive groups, members care about the success of other group members because their own goal attainment is often inextricably bound to collective achievement. They will exert strong effort on behalf of the group and their fellow members to facilitate group success. When faced with adversity or possible failure, members of highly cohesive groups (a) are likely to be more committed to the task and devote more effort to its accomplishment, (b) set and enforce more stringent performance norms that compel such effort (Zaccaro & McCoy, 1988), (c) plan more efficiently and develop more appropriate performance strategies (Hackman, 1976; Hackman & Morris, 1975), and (d) persist at task accomplishment.

High cohesiveness is likely to be a function of members' beliefs that, together, they can effectively accomplish the tasks they need to accomplish for their team to be successful. Such beliefs have been labeled *collective efficacy* (Bandura, 1986) and defined as a team property that reflects the members' confidence that collectively they can perform a particular task or mission well (Zaccaro, Blair, Peterson, & Zazanis, 1995). As members feel more confident of their team's capabilities, they are more motivated to work hard for the team, persist in the face of collective obstacles, and are willing to accept more difficult challenges. Such teams also set more difficult goals and are more committed to these goals (Weldon & Weingart, 1993).

Successful cooperative relationships are grounded fundamentally in trust. In essence, team members are more likely to contribute more of their individual efforts to collective action when they trust one another. Trust follows from "the expectation that others will behave as expected" (Jarvenpaa et al., 1998, p. 31). Team members trust the team as a whole when it "(a) makes a good-faith effort to behave in accordance with any commitments both explicit and implicit, (b) is honest in whatever negotiations preceded such commitments, and (c) does not take excessive advantage of another, even when the opportunity is available" (Cummings & Bromiley, 1996, p. 303). Thus, team trust resides in the expectations team members have of and for each other.

Lipnick and Stamps (1999) offered three targets of team trust. The first refers to trusting the competence and integrity of fellow team members. This form of trust reflects beliefs that fellow members can and will accomplish their tasks and missions. Note the parallel to collective efficacy. However, team trust includes not just competence beliefs, but also expectations that members intend to act accordingly. The second target refers to team purpose and the belief that personnel and material resources will be available to accomplish the team's mission. Likewise, such trust reflects perceived fairness and justice in team and organizational policies.

Information links and channels represent a third target of team trust. Members need to rely on consistent and reliable sources of information both within the team (i.e., other team members) and outside of the team. Such trust grows when a large amount of high-quality information, relevant to team functioning, is available to all team members.

How does trust develop in teams? Lewicki and Bunker (1996) proposed a three-stage model, incorporating three types of trust specified by Shapiro, Sheppard, and Cheraskin (1992). The first stage involves the development of *calculus-based trust*, where team members trust fellow workers to behave consistently. The motivation for such consistency is both fear of punishment, if consistent behavior does not occur, and the perceived value in having trust. The second stage reflects the emergence of *knowledge-based trust*, where team members know one another well enough that their behaviors can be more easily "anticipatable." Such knowledge and trust develops from repeated interactions and communications across a variety of different situations. The third stage of trust development occurs when *identification-based trust* emerges among team members. Here, trust emerges when team members understand and share each other's values, needs, goals, and preferences. Thus, each member is trusted to act as an agent for other members and for the team as a whole. Lewicki and Bunker (1996) argued that each form of trust builds upon the type of trust successfully established at earlier stages and that considerable time and interactions are necessary to develop the latter stages of trust.

A key point, though, for virtual teams is that trust, particularly knowledge-based and identification-based trust, evolves from a long period of face-to-face interactions (Lewicki & Bunker, 1996; Mayer, Davis, & Schoorman, 1995; Shapiro et al., 1992). Members of virtual teams that are characterized by impermanence, where team tenure is relatively short, and high geographic dispersion, where face-to-face interactions are rare, may struggle to develop such forms of collective trust.

Team Motivational Processes and Leadership in Virtual Teams

Trust. The three dimensions of virtuality, permanence of team tenure, percentage of face-to-face interaction, and degree of technological sophistication can adversely influence team trust and team member motivation. As noted earlier, if a virtual team is not expected to exist for very long, coming together only for the duration of a particular task, team members cannot gain the knowledge and shared experiences that foster knowledge-based and identification-based trust. Thus, only calculus-based trust can exist in the team. However, low anticipation of future interactions also undercuts such trust because it minimizes the risks and penalties for unreliability and behavioral inconsistency.

Greater physical distance among team members also impairs the development of trust. Jarvenpaa and Leidner (1999, p. 792) noted, "face-to-face encounters are considered irreplaceable for both building trust and repairing shattered trust (Nohria & Eccles, 1992; O'Hara-Devreaux & Johansen, 1994)." Such encounters provide a greater quantity and quality of information, from both verbal and nonverbal interactions, that contributes significantly to the development of knowledge-based and identification-based trust.

The sophistication and use of communication technology within the virtual team can mitigate some of these effects of distance on trust. Teams that make extensive use of audio and video conferencing systems, chat rooms, computer bulletin boards, e-mail, electronic whiteboards, and group project management software (Mittleman & Briggs, 1999) are more like to gather and exchange the kinds of information necessary for collective trust than more technologically deficient teams. Furthermore, the lack of technology can increase the rate of rumors and misinformation circulating in a group, causing mistrust of any received information as well as of its sources (Lipnack & Stamps (1997).

These barriers to trust in virtual teams can pose significant problems for organizational leaders. Leaders can address these problems, however, by fostering swift trust. Coutu (1998) noted that, contrary to the foregoing arguments, trust developed rather quickly in geographically dispersed teams. Meyerson, Weick, and Kramer (1996) argued that trust can develop quickly in temporary virtual teams that are formed in response to a crisis or an urgent change in an organization's operating environment. The risk engendered by exigencies facilitates calculative trust—the risks of unreliability and inconsistency are too great in a crisis. Meyerson et al. (1996) argued in essence that team members begin collaboration with a presumption of trust that is imported from other settings. Such trust makes use of category-driven or stereotype information, rather than evidence-driven information, about how team members are likely to behave in collective action.

Initial team trust is by nature fragile and begins to solidify through two processes. The first is what Coutu (1998) calls an "electronic courtship" in which team members exchange social-oriented electronic messages, creating a positive environment for growing team cohesion. Jarvenpaa and Leidner (1999) found in a series of descriptive case studies of global virtual teams that a lack of social introduction early in team communications resulted in low levels of initial trust, which were maintained through the history of each team. They found that teams with high levels of initial trust devoted almost half of their early communications during the first 2 weeks of the teams' existence to discussions of their families, hobbies, and weekend social activities. However, Jarvenpaa and Leidner noted that such communications were not sufficient to maintain trust. Instead, reflecting the second process, communications were more task-oriented. They contained what Meyerson et al. (1996) referred to as "a highly active, proactive, enthusiastic, generative style of action" (p. 180). Virtual teams that adopt such a style begin to confirm member expectations of team reliability under adversity. As these actions continue, team members accrue knowledge-based trust. Jarvenpaa et al. (1998) reported similar findings in a study of 75 global virtual teams.

Meyerson et al. (1996) also argued that swift trust in temporary teams develops when team members have clearly defined roles with specified and accurate behavioral expectations. Thus, virtual team interactions proceed from more stabilized social and normative systems. Indeed, Jarvenpaa and Leidner (1999) noted, "whereas traditional conceptualizations of trust are based strongly on interpersonal relationships, swift trust de-emphasizes the interpersonal dimensions and is based initially on broad categorical social structures, and later on action" (p. 794).

The influence of role-based structures, together with the importation of category-driven information at the initial formation of the virtual team, suggests that swift trust proceeds more readily from a strong professional climate, characterized by a rigid code of conduct, high ethical standards, and intensive training to codify and routinize role-based behaviors. Airplane and fire-fighting crews exemplify such climates. When virtual teams form with members having strong professional identities, then swift trust can emerge from stable role expectations and subsequent actions are likely to confirm these expectations, strengthening team trust.

Cohesion and Efficacy. Several of the aforementioned leadership processes suggested for virtual teams also enhance group cohesiveness, which in turn strengthens collective efficacy beliefs. Such leader actions have greater criticality because one of the most consistent findings in the virtual team literature is that members of virtual teams experience greater dissatisfaction and less cohesion than colocated or face-to-face teams (Hollingshead, McGrath, & O'Connor, 1993; Straus, 1996, 1997; Warkentin, Sayeed, & Hightower, 1997). The particular characteristics of virtual teams provide the rationale for these findings. The nature and degree of communication technology in the team can impair team interactions, making them more difficult. Straus (1996) compared 28 computer-mediated (CM) undergraduate teams with 26 face-to-face (FtF) teams on a decision task. She found that communication was slower and more inefficient in the CM teams than the FtF teams. Straus (1997) found in a study of 36 CM and 36 FtF undergraduate teams that CM teams recorded more disagreements and nonessential communications than FtF teams, resulting in lower cohesion and satisfaction. Both studies demonstrate impairments as a function of increased electronically mediated communication in teams.

Warkentin et al. (1997) reported similar decrements in virtual team member satisfaction and cohesion. They argued that physical distance and limitations of electronic communication impaired the formation of relational links that are associated with higher group cohesion. Such formation occurs through activities designed to support member and group well-being. These activities include "establishing position or group status of members, defining task roles of group members, and establishing norms for group interaction" (p. 979). Warkentin and his colleagues found in a study of 13 virtual and 11 traditional undergraduate teams that relational links and cohesion were weaker in the virtual teams.

Physical distance also impairs virtual team cohesion by increasing the number of competitors for team member attention and cognitive resources. When team members are located in different geographic spaces, local demands and distractions require attention. Thus, members are less committed to team action, impairing the team's task-based cohesion. Also, when distance translates into greater diversity in culture, climate, and social backgrounds (such as in global virtual teams), then an emphasis on individual identity can reduce cohesion. Walther (1997) manipulated the salience of group identity versus individual identity in 11 global undergraduate teams. He also varied groups on the length of their interactions (long vs. short term). He found that relational links were strongest in long-term virtual teams in which a group rather than individual identity was emphasized. This suggests that virtual teams that contain significant diversity as a function of distance and highlight that diversity are likely to suffer lower cohesion.

Walther (1997) demonstrated the deleterious effects of team impermanence on virtual team cohesion. He compared the communication content of face-to-face and computer-mediated undergraduate virtual teams. He also measured anticipations of future interactions (AFI). He found that AFI explained the effects of distance on relational links. Specifically, he found that CM teams reported lower AFI scores than FtF teams. Further, when team members anticipated future interactions, their communications were characterized by more immediacy and involvement, a greater focus on similarities, and greater receptivity, trust, composure, and relaxed tone. These findings suggest that when team formation is temporary, members will devote fewer resources and communications to the development of relationships that denote high group cohesion. This lack of development can have a corresponding deleterious effect on collective trust.

These conceptual arguments and empirical findings suggest that team building and cohesion development represent key leadership activities in virtual teams. The task of the virtual team leader becomes the development of "social presence," defined by Warkentin et al. (1997, p. 989) as "the extent to which a communication medium allows participants to experience each other as being psychologically close or present (Fulk & Boyd, 1991)." Leader–member exchange theory suggests that such closeness occurs when leaders maintain high levels of interaction with followers, grant them significant responsibilities, provide them with high levels of trust, support, and respect, and allow greater participation in team decision making. Indeed, Howell and Hall-Merenda (1999) found that physical distance in Canadian banking teams did not impair performance under conditions of high-quality leader–follower relationships—their performance levels matched those of their face-to-face counterparts.

Team Affective Processes

The affective climate within the team also influences team effectiveness. A positive mood among team members will foster more cooperation, more participation, less conflict, and stronger social cohesion (Carnevale & Isen, 1986; Rafaeli & Sutton, 1989). Collective negative moods result in more internal conflict and less willingness by team members to work with each other, that is, participate in team activities (Rhoades & O'Connor, 1995). The result is the impairment of motivational and coordination processes in teams and lower group performance (George, 1990). Affective climate also affects group information processing. Collective positive mood increases the amount of information that is processed in teams as well as the creativity of member contributions (Rhoades & O'Connor, 1995).

These observations are not meant to convey that conflict in groups is unproductive. A difference can be established between cognitive and affective conflict (Amason, 1986). The former refers to conflict among team members that "is generally task-oriented and focused on judgmental differences about how to best to achieve common objectives," whereas affective conflict "tends to be emotional and focused on personal incompatibilities or disputes" among team members (Amason, 1986, p. 127, 129). Amason found that cognitive conflict in 48 top management teams was positively associated with quality, understanding, and acceptance of team decisions; affective conflict impaired team decisions. Teams, then, need to establish the basis for constructive cognitive conflict, without fostering other more destructive forms of affective conflict.

As team environments become more aversive (i.e., more time-urgent, stressful, complex, ambiguous), team members obviously need to maintain a collective calm. If the team succumbs to stress, member interactions become more narrowly focused among a subset of the team, information becomes increasingly less shared among team members, decision alternatives are not fully explored, and decision-making accuracy declines (Argote, Turner, & Fichman, 1989; Gladstein & Reilly, 1985; Isenberg, 1981). Likewise, members become less committed to collective decisions (Frye & Stritch, 1964). Teams are not likely to be able to avoid environmental stressors; to be effective they need to develop collective coping mechanisms that foster continued effectiveness, even under stress.

Team Affective Processes and Leadership in Virtual Teams

The dispersion and communication technology features of virtual teams increase the difficulty for leaders to manage affective processes in their teams. Leaders need to be aware of changes in affect and particularly of increases in negative affect and stress. Such awareness follows from observation of nonverbal cues and interpretations of verbal communications. However, when team members are separated from leaders and connected only through electronic media, leaders lose nonverbal cues as an information source. Furthermore, physical distance and computer-mediated communications allow team members to hide their affect from one another and from their leader. Thus, leaders of virtual teams have a greater chance of missing affect spikes among their followers than do their face-to-face counterparts.

Computer-mediated communications increase the likelihood of misinterpreting affect in electronic messages. Leaders can mistake the tone of a message as overly negative or overly positive. Team members may also misinterpret communications, taking offense at a message that was intended to be innocuous. Such misinterpretations increase the likelihood of affective conflict in virtual groups.

There are few, if any, empirical studies of affective processes in virtual teams or of ways virtual team leaders can effectively manage such processes. This is unfortunate because many teams, such as military or fire teams and crews, are highly likely to be operating in very stressful and adverse circumstances. Their leaders will be tasked with the primary responsibility for managing the high affect such situations will engender. Thus, a greater understanding of these processes in virtual teams and how leaders manage them should be a priority for future leadership research.

Team Cognitive Processes

The motivational choices described earlier about what tasks to engage and how much resources to commit to team tasks (Kanfer & Ackerman, 1989) also reflect cognitive team regulation processes. Team members use, in part, their knowledge and understanding of the team situation to make choices about where to expend collective attention and effort (Zaccaro et al., 1997). Likewise, when teams adopt effective coordination patterns, these become encoded as part of "group memory." Thus, motivational choices as well as those related to team coordination are grounded in shared knowledge systems and individual mental models that arise through team experience (Hinsz et al., 1997; Klimoski & Mohammed, 1994). These attributes are vital to effective virtual team functioning and are covered in the next section.

Mental Models. Mental models have been defined as "mechanisms whereby humans are able to generate descriptions of system purpose and form, explanations of system functioning and observed system states, and predictions of future system states" (Rouse & Morris, 1986, p. 351). Mental models organize information about systems, the environments within which they operate, and the response patterns required of systems with respect to environmental dynamics (Veldhuyzen & Stassen, 1977). With respect to a team, such mental models developed by individual team members represent knowledge and understanding about the purpose of the team and its characteristics, the connections and linkages among team purposes, characteristics, and collective actions, and the various roles and behavior patterns required of individual members to successfully perform collective action. With well-developed team mental models, team members may be better able to anticipate each other's actions and reduce the amount of processing and communication required during team performance.

These characteristics of mental models have led several researchers to argue that effective team coordination depends upon the emergence of a *shared* mental model (Cannon-Bowers, Salas, & Converse, 1990, 1993; Klimoski & Mohammed, 1994). Shared mental models refer to common understanding established through experience among team members regarding expected collective behavior patterns during team action (Cannon-Bowers et al., 1990, 1993; Kleinman & Serfaty, 1989; Levine & Moreland, 1990). When such models are shared among team members, they may be better able to anticipate each other's actions and reduce the amount of processing and communication required during team performance.

Transactive Memory.   Another form of shared knowledge within teams is transactive memory. Teams are capable of maintaining large knowledge stores. However, each team member does not need to retain all of the team knowledge and expertise. Instead, for efficiency, team members need knowledge of what information or resources are possessed by which team member. Such knowledge distribution and sharing of information sources defines the transactive memory system of the team.

Wegner (1995) defined three components or processes of transactive memory. The first is *directory updating*, the process of identifying likely sources and repositories of particular knowledge among team members. The second is *information allocation*, the process of encoding, distributing, and storing information with team members whose types of expertise make them appropriate repositories of particular information. The third process, *retrieval coordination*, refers to the process of retrieving information from team members, given their distribution of expertise. Transactive memory develops through shared experiences among team members that result in the identification of particular forms of expertise among team members and the specification of who is the most efficient holder of particular kinds of knowledge. Such knowledge distribution maximizes the effective encoding and storage of collective information and therefore its utilization in collective information processing and problem solving.

Information Processing.   The collective information processing that occurs when teams confront tasks and problem situations represents the most proximal cognitive influence on team coordination and performance. Collective information processing actually occurs through several processes among team members (Hinsz et al., 1997). Although these processes are presented as occurring in steps or stages, they actually occur reciprocally, with team members moving back and forth across different processes. The first process is acquiring a shared awareness of a problem situation confronting a group. This involves developing a shared understanding of the team's problem parameters and processing objectives. The second process involves utilizing individual and shared knowledge structures to define solution alternatives. Shared mental models and transactive memory stores provide critical resources for solution identification. When solutions are not readily available, such knowledge stores are used to generate novel solutions. The third process concerns evaluating and reaching a threshold of agreement among team members on an acceptable solution. Team members share their concerns and ideas about particular alternatives and, it is hoped, narrow their choices to a selected one. The fourth and fifth processes in collective information processing involve, respectively, team planning and implementation of actions that form selected solutions and team monitoring of the implementation, outcomes, and consequences of selected solutions.

The success of team problem solving and decision making, then, depends upon how well individual members can integrate and share their own information processing activities. Each member has his or her own perspective of a team problem. The emergent team solution will depend upon the melding of these perspectives. Also, in complex team systems and problem scenarios, team members need to rely heavily on transactive memory, or their knowledge of who possesses what expertise. Thus, team members need to be ready to offer requisite information and participate in its collective analysis. Also, team members need to devote cognitive resources to monitoring solution implementation and, particularly, to participating in an after-action review of team processes and solution consequences. Team members then encode information from such a review in team mental models, shared knowledge stores, and transactive memory.

Team Cognitive Processes and Leadership in Virtual Teams

The main features of virtual teams, in particular geographically or temporally dispersed and electronic-mediated communication systems, can interfere significantly with team cognitive processes and collective information processing. Geographic distance inhibits the development of transactive memory and shared mental models. Hollingshead (1998) argued that transactive memory emerges from shared experiences and a common language and context. Griffith and Neale (2001) suggested that when team members are widely dispersed, they are likely to be variable in their expertise and perspectives, making transactive memory more difficult to establish (although, given the presence of greater diversity, the potential exists for richer knowledge stores; however, virtual team members will have more difficulty in identifying who knows what). They also argued that when great distances exist among team members, they will be less aware of visual and interpersonal cues that signal diversity in perspectives, leading them to perceive greater agreement and homogeneity in the team than is actually the case. Such misperceptions impair subsequent collective information processing.

Hinds (1999) compared the shared-task mental models of distributed versus colocated undergraduate teams. She found that mental models had fewer elements and relationships in common among virtual team members than among their counterparts in more traditional teams. Cramton (2001) used a case study analysis of 13 geographically dispersed undergraduate project teams to examine communication dynamics that contribute to lower levels of "mutual knowledge" in virtual teams (such knowledge would include both shared mental models and transactive memory). She reported five communications problems that were exacerbated by geographic dispersion and electronic mediation. One problem was a failure by team members to exchange and retain contextual information. Each member of a virtual team worked under different time constraints, deadlines, and work schedules. However, they often failed to share these differences with fellow team members. A second, related problem was the uneven distribution of information across team members. Thus, certain members had richer stores of information about team problems than other members; such narrowed communication inhibits the development of transactive memory and inherently impairs the development of shared mental models.

Cramton (2001) also reported problems from differences in the salience of information across virtual team members. That is, team members assumed that what information was important or salient to them would be equally salient to other team members. Nonverbal cues (e.g., body language, vocal tone, facial expressions) usually signal the salience or importance of information, and such cues are not present in mediated communication (Kiesler & Sproull, 1992; Sproull & Kiesler, 1986). Because mental models encode in their structures differential weight for different concepts, variation in information salience lessens the emergence of shared mental models in virtual teams.

Cramton (2001) also noted problems in virtual teams with differences in speed of information access and in interpretations of the meaning of silence. The level of technological sophistication can vary not only from team to team, but also from member to member in a widely dispersed global virtual team. Thus, some members had rapid access to shared information, whereas others had slow or limited access. This differential access slowed the rate of group information processing and inhibited the effective development of shared knowledge. Likewise, when team members did not respond to group requests or were uncommunicative in the face of team decisions, their silence was variously interpreted as agreement, disagreement, indifference, or unavailability. Such interpretations not only constrain mutual knowledge, they can also hurt team trust and cohesion.

These findings suggest that leaders of virtual teams need to facilitate the exchange, encoding, and storage of team information. By virtue of their central position in the communication network, leaders are likely to have the most access to all virtual team members. Thus, they are in a position to foster effective information exchange. In addition, by providing meaning to acquired information and facilitating discussion of such meaning, leaders can facilitate the emergence of shared mental models (Burke & Zaccaro, 2000; Marks, Zaccaro, & Mathieu, 2000).

Some research has identified how characteristics of virtual teams can impair collective information processing. Such information processing depends first upon the repository of shared information in the team. As noted in the foregoing, team dispersion and electronic communication interfere with the development of shared knowledge. In addition, virtual team members often fail to share all information relevant to a problem with other team members. Hightower and Sayeed (1994) defined this as "biased discussion." They noted,

> Biased discussion is the tendency of group members to introduce into discussion only part of the information they know. Biased discussion causes the group to discuss only information supporting the initial most popular position within the group. As the group moves toward a consensus, the relative proportion of arguments supporting that consensus increases. Thus, discussion fails to correct the group members' biased views of the information pool and the group's final choice is based on only a portion of the available information. (p. 35)

Biased discussion impairs several collective information processing steps. The lack of full information exchange results in narrow or inaccurate situational awareness, the identification of fewer solution alternatives, and the team's premature coalescence around potentially misguided solutions. Likewise, team monitoring of implemented solutions becomes stunted as members fail to share information about solution consequences.

Hightower and Sayeed (1995) argued that biased discussions occurred more frequently in virtual teams using mostly electronic communication. This effect emerges from the inefficiency and slowness of such communication, which causes members to include less information in their discussions. Biased discussions also occur because most electronic communications do not convey nonverbal cues that signal disagreement with emergent solutions. Hightower and Sayeed found support for these arguments in an experiment comparing computer-mediated and face-to-face undergraduate teams.

Team Boundary Spanning and Leadership

As teams become highly expert and effective, certain leadership functions may become increasingly shared across team members. However, in hierarchically organized teams, the designated leader will retain a major responsibility for team boundary spanning. The leader is the major, and often the only, link between the group and its strategic environment (Katz & Kahn, 1978). Thus, team leaders need to help their teams set performance objectives that are aligned with the strategic requirements operating in the team environment (Kozlowski, Gully, Salas, & Cannon-Bowers, 1996). They need to coordinate their team's acquisition of necessary resources (Fleishman et al., 1991). They also need to provide feedback and situation assessments to their teams so that team members can gauge the correspondence between their collective actions and changing environmental conditions (Kozlowski et al., 1996). Finally, team leaders need to represent the team's interests to external constituencies and stakeholders. As the internal processes of the team become more proficient and adaptive, these functions are increasingly likely to characterize the major portion of team leader responsibilities.

Summary

Virtual teams are likely to become an increasing reality in the operating environment of most organizations. The various dimensions described in this chapter—the degree of geographic and temporal dispersion, the anticipated duration of the team's existence, and the level of sophistication in the team's communication technology—will each be components of this operating environment. This chapter summarizes how each of these features can affect collective trust, group cohesion, and perceptions of collective efficacy in teams. Distance and electronic communication increase the difficulty for leaders to monitor and modulate the affective tone of the team. These features also inhibit the development of shared knowledge systems that are important for collective information processing. Finally, virtual teams contain more potential blocks to information processing than face-to-face and colocated teams. However, as noted, the degree of technological sophistication within the virtual team and frequent use of such technology can mitigate the deleterious effects of distance on collective trust, cohesion, and information processing.

The negative tone to these findings reflects the particular focus of the literature. Researchers have been concerned with identifying how the features of virtual teams, as compared with those of traditional teams, can impair critical team processes. However, little systematic research has sought to examine how the features of virtual teams and organizations improve overall organizational effectiveness and rate of adaptability. For example, team dispersion under conditions of enabling communication technology allows for greater participation of skilled participants in disconnected domains. This widens the pool of capabilities, skills, and knowledge potentially available to teams and organizations. The impermanence of some virtual teams also enables this outcome as organizations bring together for limited periods those individuals and units that can best contribute to a mission's success.

Greater dispersion coupled with effective use of communication technology can also increase the speed of response by units and organizations to rapidly shifting environmental contingencies. Furthermore, the ad hoc nature of some virtual teams can expose team members to a greater number of new perspectives, ideas, and experiences. This exposure can infuse them with additional knowledge, understanding, and social capital to apply to future missions and operations. Indeed, such tasks and assignments have been cited as critical dimensions of development work experiences that contribute to leader growth (McCauley, Ruderman, Ohlott, & Morrow, 1994; Van Velsor, McCauley, & Moxley, 1998).

The accrual of social capital may be a particularly important, albeit hidden, benefit of virtual teaming. Brass (2001) referred to social capital as

> social relationships that can potentially confer benefits to individuals and groups.... Social capital may be contrasted with human capital (personal attributes), financial capital (money) and physical capital (physical property such as land, buildings,

machinery). While human capital is an individual quality, social capital is an opportunity or potential benefit created by relationships with others. It is owned jointly by the parties in the relationship and is less easily transferred than physical, financial, human capital. (p. 133)

Successful virtual teaming can result in accrual of both human capital, because members can acquire more perspectives, experiences, and knowledge, and social capital when they develop trustworthy relationships with partners with whom they may team again in future operations.

Thus, whereas the literature on virtual teams documents mostly the potential process loss and ill effects of virtual teaming, recognition has also been granted to the potential benefits and advantages of virtual teams over more traditional forms (Kristof et al., 1995; Lipnack & Stamps, 1999). The key to unlocking such potential lies in the quality of virtual team leadership. Virtual team leadership in most organizational forms will need to have the capabilities to build trust and cohesion among dispersed and ad hoc team members, enable effective collective information processing across these members, modulate potentially extreme affective reactions to adversity, and maintain effective coordination over temporal and physical dispersion. The team members must be capable and comfortable with the sophisticated communication technology that facilitates other virtual and team leader capabilities.

Accordingly, this chapter suggests a number of *prescriptions* for leading virtual teams. These have been derived from a review of the sparse extant literature as well as deductively from several models of virtual team functioning. Table 11.2 summarizes these prescriptions. In line with the model in Fig. 11.2, these leadership actions are proposed as influencing team motivation, cognition, and coordination and thereby increasing the overall effectiveness of virtual teams. Certain processes are presumed to vary in criticality depending upon the presence or absence of virtual team characteristics. Thus, actions to foster quick trust are more critical in teams that are temporary. Greater geographic dispersion calls for more information management activities by team leaders. Further research is necessary to validate these prescriptions and identify the situations in which some leadership actions would be more critical than others.

LEADER COMPETENCIES AND LEADER DEVELOPMENT FOR VIRTUAL TEAMS

As organizational teams become more geographically dispersed and connected primarily through electronic channels, the nature of performance requirements that team leaders need to confront also shifts. Because the leader's operating environment in virtual teams expands to cover each geographic location for each dispersed member, the leader's boundary-spanning requirements become greater. In addition,

TABLE 11.2
Summary of Prescriptions for Leading Virtual Teams

Focus on the development of quick trust in virtual teams, especially when team membership and the team's existence is temporary.

Maximize technology enablement to foster greater interactions among geographically and temporally dispersed teams.

Routinize the use of e-mail, computer bulletin boards, chat rooms, and video and audio conferencing to monitor and record group action and progress.

Structure and facilitate social, enthusiastic supportive initial interactions among team members.

Provide clear role distinctions and role expectations among team members.

Provide a clear mission and purpose for group action.

Provide prompt and substantive verification of electronic communications and feedback on team actions.

Maintain a highly active and proactive action orientation in the team and through team communications.

Facilitate intensive and supportive interactions, face-to-face if possible, to address trust violations and repair broken trust.

Maintain frequent task-oriented communications, especially in physically distant teams.

Convey enthusiastic messages encouraging collective effort.

Keep an archive of team interactions and history to minimize disruptions of team cohesion by member turnover.

Emphasize a collective identity instead of an individualized identity among team members, especially in physically distant or culturally heterogeneous teams.

Develop electronic communication norms that emphasize mutual and minimize affective conflict.

Act as an information hub for the team, encouraging the exchange of information and the identification of distributed expertise among team members.

Encourage communication that confirms information receipt as well as provides information about local contextual constraints on team members.

Act as gatekeepers for all team members and avoid misinterpretations of silence and member nonresponsiveness.

Monitor and encourage full and complete information exchanges, and minimize biased discussions.

Facilitate continued searches for solution alternatives.

Prevent premature consensus on solution alternatives.

Make frequent requests of team members to report on solution implementation.

---

because team interaction can be almost entirely electronically mediated, leader communication requirements increase proportionately over such requirements in more traditional teams. Finally, because team management becomes increasingly more complex over electronically mediated team communication channels, the performance requirements of maintaining effective team interaction, minimizing conflict, and being aware of shifting social and emotional dynamics in the team also expand proportionately.

Changes in leader performance requirements mean alterations in the leader attributes, or the cognitive, personality, motives, skills, competencies, and knowledge, required for effective leadership. Zaccaro, Kemp, and Bader (2003) proposed two categories of leader attributes, those distal to leader effectiveness and those that are more proximal to performance (see also Ackerman & Humphreys, 1990;

Hough & Schneider, 1996; Kanfer, 1990, 1992). Distal leader attributes are less situationally bound and include cognitive capacities, personality, motives, and values. Proximal attributes reflect more situationally driven skills, competencies, expertise, and knowledge. That is, situational parameters in the leader's operating environment influence (a) the quality and appropriateness of certain leader skills and knowledge and (b) the appropriateness of particular leadership processes.

Because distal attributes are relatively immune to situational variations, the cognitive attributes, personality, motives, and values that promote leadership in traditional teams will also promote leadership in virtual teams. However, we suspect that because the virtual team environment represents a greater degree of complexity, certain attributes such as cognitive complexity, openness to new experiences, tolerance for ambiguity, and need for affiliation may also change somewhat in their degree of influence on leadership.

The significant shifts in requisite team leader attributes are more likely to occur among proximal skills and expertise. To be sure, the same competencies that foster team leader effectiveness in more traditional environments will apply as well to virtual environments. Some of these competencies are noted by Salas, Burke, and Stagl (chap. 13, this volume). However, in virtual team environments, leaders will need greater skills in, and understanding of, boundary-spanning and sense-making processes, communicating through electronic channels, conflict management, and emotion management (Zaccaro & Bader, 2002). Boundary-spanning skills will help the leader scan his or her expanded operating milieu more effectively, facilitating greater awareness of what is happening in the separated environments of each team member. Sense-making skills will help the leader understand the various parameters operating on the team across its disparate environment. The remaining three skills of communication, conflict resolution, and emotion management foster effective overall management of team interaction dynamics as team members become increasingly connected through electronic channels.

Because distal attributes are more stable and less susceptible to situational influences, short-term training effects and developmental interventions will not be effective in changing or growing such leader qualities. Accordingly, the development of cognitive capacities, personality orientation, motives, and values that contribute to effective virtual team leadership will correspond to the same kinds of long-term programs prescribed for traditional team leadership (see Day, 2000, and Mumford, Marks, Connelly, Zaccaro, & Reiter-Palmon, 2000, for descriptions of such programs).

The development of the proximal skills, competencies, and expertise that contribute to effective virtual team leadership can derive from a number of emerging team leader training and development strategies. Salas and his colleagues summarize many of these strategies (Salas, Burke, Fowlkes, & Wilson-Donnelly, chap. 12, this volume; Salas, Burke, & Stagl, chap. 13, this volume). We can consider these strategies also in terms of the three modes that typify most leader training and development—formal course instruction, developmental work assignments, and self-development activities (Salas, Burke, & Stagl, chap. 13, this volume; Sullivan, 1999). An essential principle that remains the same regardless of what mode of development is used, however, states that training and development needs to focus on the essential characteristics of virtual teams (as opposed to more traditional teams) and to have the leader experience how his or her operating environment changes in the virtual team setting. The argument for this kind of training corresponds to the one articulated by Salas, Burke, Fowlkes, and Wilson-Donnelly (chap. 12, this volume) for training multicultural teams—that training ought to focus on preparing the leader to effectively respond to and manage the process difficulties engendered by such teams. Indeed, given that many multicultural teams may also be virtual teams, the prescriptions outlined by Salas, Burke, Fowlkes, and Wilson-Donnelly (chap. 12, this volume) apply here as well.

Essentially, training for virtual team leadership should reflect the greater complexity afforded by such teams. Event-based training, described in detail by Salas, Burke, Fowlkes, and Wilson-Donnelly (chap. 12, this volume), offers a scenario-driven approach that can be used in formal instructional settings to present leaders with an array of virtual team situations. Such presentations can be crafted with key "trigger events" (Salas, Burke, Fowlkes, & Wilson-Donnelly, chap. 12, this volume) and structured feedback mechanisms that condition the development of leader knowledge structures, and the design and practice of potential responses. Such an approach, if set entirely within a computer-based program that is transportable and self-sustainable, may also be used as part of a self-development program.

Virtual team leaders can also grow the requisite skills through targeted developmental work experiences that capture some of the elements of virtual team leadership. Such assignments can include serving on the staff of other virtual team leaders or engaging in activities in traditional teams that require greater reliance on communication skills, boundary spanning, and conflict and emotion management. Ideally, such operational assignments ought to be paired with event-based formal course instruction or self-development exercises. In addition, developmental work assignments are more effective when experienced mentors and coaches guide the participants through the lessons learned (Zaccaro, 2001).

CONCLUSIONS

The nature of leadership in today's organizations has evolved to reflect the increasing global nature of organizational work and the extended reach and rapidity of communication technology. These organizational changes have altered the performance requirements of leaders by increasing their need to work with team members who are far-flung from the team's center. We described how the leader's activities could change as team members become increasingly more dispersed and connected primarily through electronic channels. We also outlined some potential leader competencies and corresponding leader development prescriptions that derive from these changes in leader performance requirements. However, leadership researchers and practitioners alike will need to focus more closely on the changing dynamics of virtual team leadership to continue conceptually modeling this domain and to develop effective tools and practices that can apply to such leadership. Indeed, as organizations continue to change, we suspect that virtual team leadership will become the norm (i.e., traditional) in our understanding of what is organizational leadership.

REFERENCES

Ackerman, P. L., & Humphreys, L. G. (1990). Individual differences in industrial and organizational psychology. In M. D. Dunnette & L. M. Hough (Eds.), *Handbook of industrial and organizational psychology* (2nd ed., vol. 1, pp. 223–282). Palo Alto, CA: Consulting Psychologists.

Amason, A. C. (1996). Distinguishing the effects of functional and dysfunctional conflict on strategic decision-making: Resolving a paradox for top management teams. *Academy of Management Journal, 39*, 123–148.

Argote, L., Turner, M. E., & Fichman, M. (1989). To centralize or not to centralize: The effects of uncertainty and threat on group structure and performance. *Organizational Behavior and Human Decision Processes, 42*, 58–74.

Bandura, A. (1986). *Social foundations of thought and action: A social cognitive theory*. Englewood Cliffs, NJ: Prentice-Hall.

Brass, D. J. (2001). Social capital and organizational leadership. In S. J. Zaccaro, & R. J. Klimoski (Eds.), *The nature of organizational leadership: Understanding the performance requirements confronting today's leaders*. San Francisco: Jossey-Bass.

Burke, C. S., & Zaccaro, S. J. (2003). *The influence of leader sense-making and sense-giving on team mental models and team adaptation*. (Unpublished manuscript.)

Cannon-Bowers, J. A., Salas, E., and Converse, S. A. (1990). Cognitive psychology and team training: Shared mental models in complex systems. *Human Factors Society Bulletin, 33*, 1–4.

Cannon-Bowers, J. A., Salas, E., & Converse, S. (1993). Shared mental models in expert team decision-making. In N. J. Castellan, Jr. (Ed.), *Current issues in individual and group decision-making*. Hillsdale, NJ: Lawrence Erlbaum Associates, Inc.

Carnevale, P. J. D., & Isen, A. M. (1986). The influence of positive effect and visual access on the discovery of integrative solutions in bilateral negotiations. *Organizational Behavior and Human Decision Processes, 37*, 1–13.

Cohen, S. G., & Mankin, D. (1999). Collaboration in the virtual organization. In C. L. Cooper, D. M. Rousseau (Eds.). *Trends in organizational behavior, Vol. 6: The virtual organization* (pp. 105–120). New York: John Wiley.

Coutu, D. L. (1998). Trust in virtual teams. *Harvard Business Review,* May–June, 20–21.

Cramton, C. D. (2001). The mutual knowledge problem and its consequences for dispersed collaboration. *Organization Science, 12*(3), 346–371.

Cummings, L. L., & Bromiley, P. (1996). The Organizational Trust Inventory (OTI). In R. M. Kramer, & T. R. Tyler (Eds.), *Trust in organizations: Frontiers of theory and research* (pp. 302–323). Thousand Oaks, CA: Sage.

Day, D. V. (2000). Leadership development: A review in context. *Leadership Quarterly, 11*(4), 581–613.

Fleishman, E. A., Mumford, M. D., Zaccaro, S. J., Levin, K. Y., Korotkin, A. L., & Hein, M. B. (1991). Taxonomic efforts in the description of leader behavior: A synthesis and functional interpretation. *Leadership Quarterly, 2*(4), 245–287.

Fleishman, E. A., & Zaccaro, S. J. (1992). Toward a taxonomy of team performance function. In R. W. Swezey & E. Salas (Eds.), *Teams: Their training and performance* (pp. 31–56). Westport, CT: Ablex.

Frye, R. L., & Stritch, T. M. (1964). Effect of timed vs. nontimed discussion upon measures of influence and change in small groups. *Journal of Social Psychology, 63*(1), 139–143.

Fulk, J., & Boyd, B. (1991). Emerging theories of communication in organizations. *Journal of Management, 17,* 407–446.

George J. M. (1990). Personality, affect, and behavior in groups. *Journal of Applied Psychology, 75,* 107–116.

Gladstein, D., & Reilly, N. (1985). Group decision making under threat: The tycoon game. *Academy of Management Journal, 28,* 613–627.

Griffith, T. L., & Neale, M. A. (2001). Information processing in traditional, hybrid, and virtual teams: From nascent knowledge to transactive memory. In B. Staw & R. Sutton (Eds.), *Research in organizational behavior* (Vol. 23, pp. 379–421). Stamford, CT: JAI Press.

Hackman, J. R. (1976). Group influence on individuals. In M. D. Dunnette (Ed.), *Handbook of industrial and organizational psychology* (pp. 1455–1525). Chicago: Rand-McNally.

Hackman, J. R., & Morris, C. G. (1975). Group tasks, group interaction process, and group performance effectiveness: A review and proposed integration. In L. Berkowitz (Ed.), *Advances in experimental social psychology* (vol. 8, pp. 45–99). New York: Academic.

Hightower, R., & Sayeed, L. (1994). The impact of computer-mediated communication systems on biased group discussion. *Computers in Human Behavior, 11,* 33–44.

Hinds, P. J. (1999). The curse of expertise: The effects of expertise and debiasing methods on prediction of novice performance. *Journal of Experimental Psychology: Applied, 5*(2), 205–221.

Hinsz, V. B., Tindale, R. S., & Vollrath, D. A. (1997). The emerging conceptualization of groups as information processors. *Psychological Bulletin, 121,* 43–64.

Hollingshead, A. B. (1998). Communication, learning, and retrieval in transactive memory systems. *Journal of Experimental Social Psychology, 34,* 423–442.

Hollingshead, A. B., McGrath, J. E., & O'Connor, K. M. (1993). Group task performance and communication technology: A longitudinal study of computer-mediated versus face-to-face work groups. *Small Group Research, 24*(3), 307–333.

Hough, L. M., & Schneider, R. J. (1996). Personality traits, taxonomies, and applications in organizations. In K. R. Murphy (Ed.), *Individual differences and behavior in organizations* (pp. 31–88). San Francisco, CA: Jossey-Bass.

Howell, J. M., & Hall-Merenda, K. E. (1999). The ties that bind: The impact of leader-member exchange, transformational and transactional leadership, and distance on predicting follower performance. *Journal of Applied Psychology, 84*(5), 680–694.

Isenberg, D. J. (1981). Some effects of time-pressures on vertical structure and decision-making accuracy in small groups. *Organizational Behavior and Human Performance, 27,* 119–134.

Jarvenpaa, S. L., Knoll, K., & Leidner, D. E. (1998). Is anyone out there? Antecedents of trust in global virtual teams. *Journal of Management Information Systems, 14,* 29–64.

Jarvenpaa, S. L., & Leidner, D. E. (1999). Communication and trust in global virtual teams. *Organization Science, 10,* 791–815.

Kanfer, R. (1990). Motivation and individual differences in learning: An integration of developmental, differential and cognitive perspectives. *Learning and Individual Differences, 2*(2), 221–239.

Kanfer, R. (1992). Work motivation: New directions in theory and research. In C. L. Cooper and I. T. Robertson (Eds.), *International review of industrial and organizational psychology* (Vol. 7, pp. 1–53). New York: Wiley.

Kanfer, R., & Ackerman, P. L. (1989). Motivational and cognitive abilities: An integrative/aptitude-treatment interaction approach to skill acquisition. *Journal of Applied Psychology, 74,* 657–690.

Katz, D., & Kahn, R. L. (1978). *The social psychology of organizations.* New York: Wiley.

Kiesler, S., & Sproull, L. (1992). Group decision making and communication technology. *Organizational Behavior and Human Decision Processes, 52*(1), 96–123.

Kleinman, D. L., & Serfaty. D. (1989). Team performance assessment in distributed decision-making. In R. Gibson, J. P. Kincaid, & B. Goldiez (Eds.), *Proceedings for interactive networked simulation for training conference* (pp. 22–27). Orlando, FL: Institute for Simulation and Training.

Klimoski, R., & Mohammed, S. (1994). Team mental model: Construct or metaphor? *Journal of Management, 20*, 403–437.

Kozlowski, S. W. J., Gully, S. M., Salas, E., & Cannon-Bowers, J. A. (1996). Team leadership and development: Theory, principles, and guidelines for training leaders and teams. In M. M. Beyerlein, D. Johnson, & S. T. Beyerlein (Eds.), *Advances in interdisciplinary studies of work teams: Vol. 3. Team leadership* (pp. 253–291). Greenwich, CT: JAI.

Kristof, A. L., Brown, K. G., Sims H. P., Jr., & Smith, K. A. (1995). The virtual team: A case study and inductive model. In M. M. Beyerlein, D. A. Johnson, & S. T. Beyerlein (Eds.), *Advances in Interdisciplinary studies of work Teams: Vol. 2. Knowledge work in teams* (pp. 229–253). Greenwich, CT: JAI.

Levine, J. M., & Moreland, R. L. (1990). Progress in small group research. *American Review of Psychology, 41*, 585–614.

Lewicki, R. J., & Bunker, B. B. (1996). Developing and maintaining trust in work relationships. In R. M. Kramer, & T. R. Tyler (Eds.), *Trust in organizations: Frontiers of theory and research* (pp. 114–139). Thousand Oaks, CA: Sage.

Lipnack, J., & Stamps, J. (1999). *Virtual Teams: People working across boundaries with technology.* New York: Wiley.

Marks, M., Zaccaro, S. J., & Mathieu, J. (2000). Performance implications of leader briefings and team interaction training for team adaptation to novel environments. *Journal of Applied Psychology.*

Mayer, R. C., Davis, J. H., & Schoorman, F. D. (1995). An integrated model of organizational trust. *Academy of Management Review, 20,* 709–734.

McCauley, C. D., Ruderman, M. N., Ohlott, P. J., & Morrow, J. E. (1994). Assessing the developmental components of managerial jobs. *Journal of Applied Psychology, 79*(4), 544–560.

Meyerson, D., Weick, K. E., & Kramer, R. (1996). Swift trust and temporary groups. In R. M. Kramer & T. R. Tyler (Eds.), *Trust in organizations: Frontiers of theory and research* (pp. 166–195). Thousand Oaks, CA: Sage.

Miles, R. E., & Snow, C. C. (1986). Organizations: New concepts for new forms. *California Management Review, 18*(3), 62–73.

Mittleman, D., & Briggs, R. O (1999). Communication technology for traditional and virtual teams. In E. Sundstrom (Ed.), *Supporting work team effectiveness* (pp. 246–270). San Francisco: Jossey-Bass.

Mumford, M. D., Marks, M. A., Connelly M. S., Zaccaro, S. J., & Reiter-Palmon, R. (2000). Development of leadership skills: Experience and timing. *Leadership Quarterly, 11*(1), 87–114.

Nieva, V. F., Fleishman, E. A., & Rieck, A. M. (1978). *Team dimensions: Their identity, their measurement, and their relationships.* Bethesda, MD: Advanced Research Resources Organization.

Oakley, J. G. (1998). Leadership processes in virtual teams and organizations. *Journal of Leadership Studies, 5*(3), 3–17.

Rafaeli, A., & Sutton R. I. (1989). The expression of emotional expression in organizational life. In B. M. Staw & L. L. Cummings (Eds.), *Research in organizational behavior* (vol. 11, pp. 1–42). Greenwich, CT: JAI.

Rhoades, J. A., & O'Connor, K. M. (1995). Affect in computer-mediated and face to face work groups: The construction and testing of a general model. *Computer Supported Cooperative Work, 4*, 203–228.

Rouse, W. B., & Morris, N. M. (1986). On looking into the black box: Prospects and limits in the search for mental models. *Psychological Bulletin, 100*, 350–363.

Salas, E., Dickinson, T. L., Converse, S., & Tannenbaum, S. I. (1992). Toward an understanding of team performance and training. In R. W. Swezey & E. Salas (Eds.), *Teams: Their training and performance* (pp. 3–29). Norwood, NJ: Ablex.

Sessa, V. I., Hansen, M. C., Prestridge, S., Kossler, M. E. (1999). *Geographically dispersed teams: An annotated bibliography.* Greensboro, NC: Center for Creative Leadership.

Shapiro, D. L., Sheppard, B. H., & Cheraskin, L. (1992). Business on a handshake. *Negotiation Journal,* *8*(4), 365–377.

Sproull, L., & Kiesler, S. (1986). Reducing social contact cues: Electronic mail in organizational communication. *Management Science, 32,* 1492–1512.

Straus, S. G. (1996). Getting a clue: The effects of communication media and information distribution on participation and performance in computer-mediated and face-to-face groups. *Small Group Research, 27,* 115–142.

Straus, S. (1997). Technology, group process, and group outcomes: Testing the connections in computer-mediated and face-to-face groups. *Human-Computer Interaction,* 12, 227–266.

Sullivan, G. (1999). Forword: From theory to practice. In J. G. Hunt, G. E. Dodge, & L. Wong (Eds.). *Out-of-the-box leadership: Transforming the twenty-first century army and other top performing organizations* (pp. xv–xxiii). Stamford, CT: JAI.

Townsend, A., DeMarie, S., & Hendrickson A. (1998). Virtual teams: Technology and the workplace of the future. *Academy of Management Executive, 12,* 17–29.

Van Velsor, E., McCauley, C. D., Moxley, R. S. (1998). Introduction: Our view of leadership development. In C. D. McCauley, R. S. Moxley, E. Van Velsor (Eds.), *Handbook of Leadership Development.* San Francisco: Jossey-Bass.

Veldhuyzen, W., & Stassen, H. G. (1977). The internal model concept: An application to modeling human control of large ships. *Human Factors, 19,* 367–380.

Walther, J. B. (1997). Group and interpersonal effects in international computer-mediated collaboration. *Human Communication Research, 23*(3), 342–369.

Warkentin, M. E., Sayeed, L., & Hightower, R. (1997). Virtual teams versus face-to-face teams: An exploratory study of a web-based conference system. *Decision Sciences, 28,* 975–996.

Wegner, D. M. (1995). A computer network model of human transactive memory. *Social Cognition, 13*(3), 319–339.

Weldon, E., & Weingart, L. R. (1993). Group goals and group performance. *British Journal of Social Psychology, 32*(4), 307–334.

Zaccaro, S. J., & Bader, P. (2002). E-leadership and the challenges of leading e-teams: Minimizing the bad and maximizing the good. *Organizational Dynamics,* 31, 377–387.

Zaccaro, S. J., Blair, V., Peterson, C., & Zazanis, M. (1995). Collective efficacy. In J. Maddux (Ed.), *Self-efficacy, adaptation, and adjustment* (pp. 305–328). New York: Plenum.

Zaccaro, S. J., Kemp, C., & Bader, P. (in press). Leader traits and attributs. In R. Sternberg, J. Antonakis, & A. Cianciolo (Eds.), *The nature of leadership.* Thousand Oaks, CA: Sage.

Zaccaro, S. J., & McCoy, M. C. (1988). The effects of task and interpersonal cohesiveness on performance of a disjunctive group task. *Journal of Applied Social Psychology, 18,* 837–851.

Zaccaro, S. J., Parker, C. W., Marks, M. A., Burke, C. S., Higgins, J. M., & Perez, R. S. (1997). *Team efficacy, communication and performance: Implications for collective regulatory processes.* Presented at the annual meeting of the Society for Industrial and Organizational Psychology, St. Louis.

Zaccaro, S. J., Rittman, A., & Marks, M. A. (2001). Team leadership. *Leadership Quarterly, 12,* 451–484.

12

Promoting Effective Leadership Within Multicultural Teams: An Event-Based Approach

Eduardo Salas, C. Shawn Burke, and
Katherine A. Wilson-Donnelly
University of Central Florida

Jennifer E. Fowlkes
CHI Systems, Inc.

Industry trends as well as a changing military environment are increasingly creating situations where individuals from two or more national cultures must interdependently and adaptively work together toward a common and valued goal (i.e., as a member of a multicultural work team). In terms of industry, Adler (1997) argued that over 10,000 American companies engage in business overseas. Similarly, in the military, cross-cultural forces are becoming increasingly common. Some have argued that mission-specific task forces composed of military personnel from different services and nations are becoming the norm (Meadows, 1995). Additionally, the role of the U.S. military is changing from a traditional war-fighting role to one in which stability and support operations require soldiers to work with (and among) different cultures (e.g., civilian populations, North Atlantic Treaty Organization teams).

Although it has been argued that multicultural teams can perform better over time than culturally homogeneous teams (Thomas, 1999; Watson, Kumar, & Michaelsen, 1993), more often members perceive these teams as being challenging and frustrating (Helmreich & Merritt, 1998). More specifically, multicultural teams initially tend to result in (a) process loss (Thomas, 1999), (b) lower levels of cohesion (Katz, Goldston, & Benjamin, 1958) and trust (Adler, 1997; Distefano

293

& Maznevski, 2000; Triandis, 2000), (c) misinterpretation and loss of communication (e.g., speech is less accurate, less information is transmitted, and much that is transmitted is lost; Adler, 1997; Li, 1999), and (d) an increased use of inappropriate stereotypes to assign attributions (Horenczyk & Berkerman, 1997). Due to the these process issues, these teams also initially tend to be less effective on complex tasks (Thomas, 1999) and result in higher levels of stress and tension (Adler, 1997). The bottom line is that cultural diversity may greatly increase the complexity of the processes that must occur for teams and organizations to reach their full potential. The following is an illustration of the complexity present within multicultural teams.

In 1990, Avianca Flight 52, a perfectly operational aircraft, crashed due to fuel exhaustion. Errors attributed to teamwork and national culture were cited as potential reasons for the crash, which resulted in the deaths of 73 passengers and crew (Helmreich, 1994). In terms of teamwork, failures in leadership, situation awareness, and assertiveness were cited as contributory causes. More specifically, Colombia, the flight's country of origin, is an example of a culture that ranks high in power distance (Hofstede, 1980), making it less likely that junior crew members would challenge the captain when he failed to make clear decisions. In addition, the captain's failure in leadership—neglecting to state an emergency—may have also been due to cultural factors. Finally, in terms of interaction between cultures, communication between American air traffic controllers and the Colombian aircrew resulted in a lack of understanding and consequently the crew focused on ensuring a clear understanding of its meaning to the neglect of information concerning the actual "state" of the aircraft.

Although multicultural teams pose additional challenges and are not always effective, the trend toward composing and managing multicultural teams to tackle global problems, conflicts, and obligations is only expected to increase. Therefore, it becomes of paramount concern to understand the challenges within these teams as well as the factors that distinguish effective multicultural teams from ineffective teams. One factor that has been argued to play a central role in the effectiveness of such teams is their leadership (Adler, 1997). Others have similarly argued for the important role that team leadership occupies within culturally homogeneous teams (Hackman, 2002; Stewart & Manz, 1995). Due to the complexity inherent within these teams, it has been argued that leadership within these teams poses additional challenges above and beyond those present within culturally homogeneous teams. However, when and if team leaders learn how to integrate and take advantage of a team's diversity, the wider range of human resources available to such teams allows them to often function more effectively than many homogeneous teams (Adler, 1997). Therefore, understanding the role of the team leader within multicultural teams as well as methods by which needed leader competencies can be developed would seem to be an efficient way to begin to explore the factors related to effective multicultural teams. Following from this, the purpose of this chapter is fourfold. First, some of the challenges that the leader may face in promoting effective team process and performance within multicultural teams are examined. In doing so, we briefly describe primary cultural dimensions as well as the basic tenets of team leadership. Second, based on these challenges, we describe a scenario-based instructional strategy for leader development (i.e., event-based approach to training, EBAT). In describing event-based training, we also illustrate its potential for enhancing our understanding of multicultural team training. Third, we integrate the leader challenges with event-based training to extract an initial set of team leader competencies that can be trained using EBAT and that are especially beneficial within multicultural teams. Finally, we note where we see holes within the literature.

TEAM LEADERSHIP

Although team leadership is a relatively young area of inquiry, it has been argued to have a considerable impact on the promotion of the dynamic processes (i.e., the knowledge, skills, and attitudes) involved in teamwork (e.g., Komaki, Desselles, & Bowman, 1989; Zaccaro, Rittman, & Marks, 2001) and has been argued to be increasingly important as complexity increases (Jacobs & Jaques, 1987). Because of the complex nature of multicultural teams, it would seem that leadership might be a key determinant of a team's success. Although it is important to understand this phenomenon, few, if any, talk about leadership within cross-cultural teams (i.e., impact on team process and teamwork). However, in beginning to understand this phenomenon, we can utilize the work on team leadership combined with that on cultural diversity to extract challenges, competency requirements, and instructional strategies.

Team Leadership Defined

As evidence of the young state of the literature, a universal definition of team leadership has yet to emerge. For the purposes of this chapter we draw from the functional approach to leadership (Salas, Burke, & Stagl, chap. 13, this volume) to define team leadership as encompassing both task and developmental roles. Within the task role, the leader serves as a boundary spanner to gather information and ensure that the team has the necessary material and personnel resources to accomplish the task at hand. Furthermore, team leaders adopting a task role also serve to dynamically structure and regulate team processes in order to meet shifting internal and external contingencies. Within the developmental role, the leader ensures that the team develops and maintains the requisite shared knowledges, affects, and behaviors that enable interdependent, coordinative, adaptive performance. Furthermore, team leadership is distinctly different from both individual and organizational leadership in that team leaders need to foster the requisite competencies (i.e., knowledges, skills, attitudes) that enable members to work *interdependently* and adaptively (see Salas et al., chap. 13, this volume).

THEORETICAL DRIVERS: TEAM LEADERSHIP WITHIN MULTICULTURAL TEAMS

Leadership Theories

Within the literature, there have been three leadership theories and approaches that have either been elevated to the team level (i.e., functional approach, leader–member exchange) or are especially relevant in that they have considered national culture (i.e., implicit leadership theory).

Functional Approach

Much of the work on team leadership has been conducted using the functional approach. The key assertion within this approach is that it is "the leader's job to do or get done whatever is not being adequately handled for group needs" (McGrath, 1962, as cited in Hackman & Walton, 1986, p. 75). This approach recognizes that there exists a generic set of leadership functions that can be tailored to fit the specific situation. In furthering the work on team leadership, several researchers have begun to delineate these functions (see Table 12.1). If one examines the functions listed in Table 12.1 along with the basic tenets of this approach (see Salas et al., chap. 13, this volume, for more information), it becomes apparent that team leaders en-act a powerful "sense-making" role for the team, a role especially important for multicultural teams. Specifically, sense making has been defined as (a) the place-ment of stimuli into some kind of framework (Starbuck & Milliken, 1988), (b) "the reciprocal interaction of information seeking, meaning ascription, and action" (Thomas, Clark, & Gioia, 1993, p. 240), and (c) "placement of items into frameworks, comprehending, redressing surprise, constructing meaning, interact-ing in the pursuit of mutual understanding and patterning" (Weick, 1995, p. 6). Additionally, although the definitions above primarily refer to sense making in terms of the interpretation of new cues, it also includes the process of recogniz-ing and singling out cues from ongoing experience (Weick, 1995). The functional approach is important in terms of the leadership of cross-cultural teams because (a) it recognizes the importance of context, (b) it recognizes the role team leaders occupy as problem solvers in which they develop and maintain shared behavior, cognition, and affect among team members, and (c) many of the functional behav-iors rely heavily on understanding and regulating member cognition in order to promote smooth, coordinated teamwork. Within cross-cultural teams, creating the underlying cognitive structures needed for effective teamwork and interpretation of meaning is predicted to be especially challenging.

TABLE 12.1
Illustration of Team Leader Functional Behaviors

McGrath (1962), as cited in Hackman and Walton, 1986, p. 75:

Diagnosing group deficiencies	Involves monitoring the activities internal to the team
Taking remedial action	Involves taking action to correct deficiencies that are identified while monitoring the internal action of the team
Forecasting impending changes	Involves monitoring the external environment that the team is operating within
Preventing harmful environmental changes or their effects	Involves taking action to mitigate harmful effects of environmental changes

Fleishman et al. (1991):

Searching and structuring information	Involves the systematic search, acquisition, evaluation, and organization of information regarding team goals and operations
Using information in problem solving	Involves using the information gained during the search and acquisition phase to arrive at and implement a problem solution; this process involves (a) precisely identifying the needs and requirements for problem solution, (b) planning and coordinating the implementation of the problem solution, and (c) communicating with others to obtain the requisite support for the proposed solution or influence attempt
Managing personnel resources	Managing and developing the individuals charged with accomplishing the task
Managing material resources	Managing and manipulating the material or physical resources needed to accomplish the task

Hackman and Walton (1986):

Providing clear, engaging direction	Involves providing direction that (a) is clear, but does not specify every detail, (b) provides meaningful goals, (c) provides members with opportunities for personal growth, and (d) holds members accountable
Creating of an enabling performance situation through coaching and process assistance	Involves ensuring that teams (a) exert sufficient effort to get the task completed in a timely manner, (b) possess the requisite competencies, and (c) use appropriate task strategies
Ensuring adequate material resources	Involves ensuring that teams have adequate task-related equipment and materials to get the job done

Leader–Member Exchange

Leader member exchange (LMX) is one of the few individual leadership theories that has recently been elevated to the team level and can provide some insight into leadership of multicultural teams. The central premise of this theory is that effective leadership occurs when the leader and followers are able to develop mature working relationships characterized by a high degree of mutual trust, respect, and obligation (Graen & Uhl-Bien, 1995). Moreover, this leadership theory recognizes that leaders may have differential relationships with subordinates (forming in and out-groups).

Most recently, the argument has been made that LMX should be viewed as a system of interdependent dyads where the focus is on examining how differentiated dyadic relationships combine and interact to form larger systems and affect outcomes (Tesluk & Gerstner, 2002). Within teams, we would argue that the formation of these types of relationships is crucial in order to form the shared cognitive structures (i.e., mental models) that allow meaning to be assigned to member actions (in terms of both the leader and members).

This leadership theory becomes relevant for cross-cultural teams in that it notes the importance of leader–subordinate relationships and the uniqueness of these relationships. Team leaders cannot treat all team members the same; it recognizes that relationships and actions will be differentially interpreted. Furthermore, it recognizes the dyadic influence that flows in both directions between team members and team leaders.

Implicit Leadership Theory

Implicit leadership theory represents the last theoretical driver that can be leveraged against, and although most of the work revolves around organizational and individual leadership, it represents some of the only work done on cross-cultural leadership. More specifically, the work originating within the GLOBE (Global Leader and Organizational Effectiveness) Research Program is relevant. The GLOBE research project examined implicit theories of leadership across cultures (i.e., individual perceptions of leadership effectiveness). Findings indicated that (a) charismatic value-based and team-orientated leadership styles are universally endorsed, (b) humane and participative styles are nearly universally endorsed, and (c) self-protective and autonomous styles are culturally contingent (House et al., 1999). These researchers also identified (a) 21 leader attributes and behaviors that are universally viewed as contributing to effective team leadership, many of them falling under the global dimension of charismatic leadership (Den Hartog, House, Hanges, & Ruiz-Quintanilla, 1999), (b) 8 attributes viewed as negative (e.g., loner, noncooperative, nonexplicit, dictatorial), and (c) 35 that were culturally contingent (e.g., cautious, risk taker, independent, formal, sensitive). Others have also found evidence for the idea that different cultures have various "prototypes" of what constitutes effective leadership (e.g., Bass, 1997; Sarros & Santora, 2001). Finally, it is important to note that even if a leadership style is culturally endorsed, the actual manifestation of that style may be different across cultures.

In terms of understanding how team leaders promote effective team processes and the corresponding performance within multicultural teams, the GLOBE work is important because at a broad level it provides guidance in terms of how a leader's behavior (i.e., leadership style) interacts with national culture to determine what a subordinate believes is "effective leadership." The implications here are that if leaders are not perceived as effective, members will be less willing to take direction from them or buy into their cognitive interpretations (i.e., mental models).

Summary

Synthesizing the aforementioned theories, we suggest that at a global level, team leadership can be described as involving two functional roles: sense making and sense giving. Leaders make sense out of dynamic circumstances by adopting a boundary-spanning role in which they gather information from their environment and encode the information into existing cognitive frameworks (i.e., mental models). Once the leader has encoded this information and assigned meaning to it, he or she then communicates this meaning to team members (i.e., sense giving) through a variety of mechanisms (e.g., clear direction, coaching and process assistance, feedback). It is at this point where leadership style and implicit leadership theories may come to bear. The cognitive frame that the leader has imparted to the team now serves to further aid in the interpretation of member actions as well as guide future actions. While this shared cognitive framework is being created, the leader simultaneously scans the environment so as to continue to dynamically provide sense to the team, thereby enacting his or her roles as sense maker and sense giver both within a task role, where the leader displays behavior related to task accomplishment, and within a developmental role. Finally, throughout this entire process, the assertions found within leader–member exchange are relevant for the leader's individual relationships with subordinates and affect the meanings assigned to member actions and help determine how sense giving should be provided.

So what makes sense making and sense giving a challenge within multicultural teams? Within multicultural teams, sense making is difficult for the leader, and team members are faced with trying to interpret environmental cues and member actions while operating from different cultural frameworks that comprise different beliefs, values, assumptions, preferences, and cognitive styles. To gain a better understanding of how this may evolve and what it means in terms of competencies that need to be trained, we turn to the literature on cultural diversity.

Cross-Cultural Dimensions

Culture has been defined as consisting of the shared norms, values, and practices of a nation (Helmreich, 2000). Others have argued that culture is the shared perception of the self and others, consisting not only of norms and behaviors, but also beliefs that serve to provide structure for member action (Dodd, 1991). Although many have argued and shown that national cultures differ in terms of their values and preferences for action and cognition, "researchers not only differ in which cultural patterns underlie culture, but also in their view as to how these cultural patterns define culture" (Straub, Loch, Evaristo, Karahanna, & Srite, 2002, p. 17). For example, some researchers have suggested that cultural dimensions cannot be examined in isolation (e.g., Parsons & Shils, 1951), whereas others have found this practice acceptable (e.g., Kluckhohn & Strodtbeck, 1961). Still others have suggested that no cultural dimension is an all-or-none situation, but that individuals have primary and secondary frames of reference (Trompenaars, 2002). These primary and secondary frames of reference can be used to explain the fact that individualists may not always act purely as individualists, but may have a secondary frame of reference as a collectivist depending on the situation. Therefore, we argue that the cross-cultural dimensions that appear in the literature should only serve as a starting point in understanding cross-cultural interactions (i.e., they are broad categorizations).

Although cultural values or attitudes have been perhaps the most commonly studied dimensions, cultural variables such as cognitive style and behavior also have been studied. A review of the cross-cultural literature reveals that although Hofstede's cultural value dimensions have been the most prevalently researched, researchers have proposed additional dimensions. Table 12.2 illustrates our initial categorization of cross-cultural dimensions based on definitions in the literature. It seems that dimensions predominantly fall within categories dealing with values, attitudes, or behaviors concerning human relations, power distribution, rules of behavior, orientation to time, rules for status ascription, expression of affect, orientation to nature, cognitive style, and norms regarding communication. We choose to focus on a subset of these cultural dimensions that we feel have the most impact on team processes and the leaders' structure and regulation of these processes.

PULLING IT ALL TOGETHER: PROPOSITIONS

So what does all this mean? It means that due to the inherent complexity within multicultural teams, effective leadership within these teams is a carefully leveraged balance beam. More specifically, when leaders can effectively integrate their functional roles as sense makers with the cultural diversity present within, their team's productivity is likely to be high and the experience rewarding, but when they cannot, results can be disastrous. What follows is an integration of the previously mentioned literatures and extraction of several propositions concerning effective team leadership within multicultural teams (see Fig. 12.1 for a guiding framework). These propositions will be divided into those focusing on sense making (i.e., gathering data, assigning meaning) and those that focus on sense giving or the communication of "sense" (i.e., providing clear direction, creating an enabling performance environment, and offering coaching and process assistance).

Sense Making: Gathering Data, Assigning Meaning

Proposition 1: A key responsibility of team leaders is to act as a boundary spanner and information gatherer; therefore leaders must realize that their own cultural frames will affect the cues that elicit their attention.

TABLE 12.2
Sampling of Key Cross-Cultural Dimensions by Grouping Variable

Cross-Cultural Dimension	Category	Definition
Individualism–collectivism (Hofstede, 1980)	Human relations	"A loosely knit social framework in which people are supposed to take care of themselves and of their immediate families only" (Hofstede, 1980, p. 45); a tight social framework "in which people distinguish between in-groups and out-groups, they expect their in-group to look out after them, and in exchange for that they feel they owe absolute loyalty to the in-group" (Hofstede, 1980, p. 45)
Individualism–communitarianism (Trompenaars & Hampden-Turner, 1998)	Human relations	How we relate to people; "Individualism encourages individual responsibility and freedom, communitarianism encourages individuals to work for consensus in the interests of the group" (Trompenaars & Hampden-Turner, 1998, p. 59)
Relational orientation (Kluckhohn & Strodtbeck, 1961)	Human relations	Modality of people's relationship to other people; can emphasize the lineal (submission to elders), collateral (agreement with group norms), or individualistic orientations
Self-orientation–collectivity orientation (Parsons & Shils, 1951)	Human relations	"Refers to the relation of an individual's pursuit of self versus collective interests" (Erez & Earley, 1993, p. 46)
Individualism–collectivism (Triandis, 1989, 2000)	Human relations	Individualism emerges in societies both loose and complex; collectivism in societies both simple and tight
Conservatism–autonomy (Schwartz, 1999)	Human relations	Conservatism is "a cultural emphasis on maintenance of the status quo, propriety, and restraint of actions or inclinations that might disrupt the solidarity group or the traditional order (social order, respect for tradition, family security, wisdom)" (Schwartz, 1999, p. 27); autonomy describes "cultures in which the person is viewed as an autonomous, bounded entity who finds meaning in his or her own uniqueness, who seeks to express his or her own internal attributes (preferences, traits, feelings, motives) and is encouraged to do so" (Schwartz, 1999, p. 27); intellectual autonomy is the extent to which individuals independently pursue their own ideas, whereas affective autonomy is the extent to which individuals independently pursue affectively positive experiences (Schwartz, 1999)

(Continued)

TABLE 12.2
(Continued)

Cross-Cultural Dimension	Category	Definition
Power distance (Hofstede, 1980)	Power relations	"The extent to which a society accepts the fact that power in institutions is distributed unequally" (Hofstede, 1980, p. 45); high-power-distance cultures accept this and social exchanges are based on this fact; low-power-distance cultures do not see a strict hierarchy among social exchanges
Universalism–particularism (Triandis, 1989, 2000)	Power relations	Universalist cultures try to treat others on the basis of universal criteria; particularist cultures treat others on the basis of who the other person is
Hierarchy–egalitarianism (Schwartz, 1999)	Power relations	Hierarchy involves "a cultural emphasis on the legitimacy of an unequal distribution of power, roles, and resources" (Schwartz, 1999, p. 27); egalitarianism involves an "emphasis on transcendence of selfish interests in favor of voluntary commitment to promoting the welfare of others (equality, social justice, freedom)" (Schwartz, 1999, p. 28)
Universalism–particularism (Trompenaars & Hampden-Turner, 1998)	Power relations	How we view rules and relationships; universalism refers to applying rules and procedures universally to ensure equity and equality throughout; particularism encourages flexibility by adapting rules and procedures to the context and circumstances
Vertical–horizontal (Triandis, 1989, 2000)	Power relations	Vertical cultures accept hierarchy as a given with those at the top having more power and privileges; horizontal cultures accept equality as a given
Uncertainty avoidance (Hofstede, 1980)	Rules orientation	"The extent to which a society feels threatened by uncertain and ambiguous situations and tries to avoid these situations by providing greater career stability, establishing more formal rules, not tolerating deviant ideas and behaviors, and believing in absolute truths and the attainment of expertise" (Hofstede, 1980, p. 45); ranges from high to low
Universalism–particularism (Trompenaars & Hampden-Turner, 1998)	Rules orientation	How we view rules and relationships; universalism refers to applying rules and procedures universally to ensure equity and equality throughout; particularism encourages flexibility by adapting rules and procedures to the context and circumstances

TABLE 12.2

(Continued)

Cross-Cultural Dimension	Category	Definition
Universalism–particularism (Parsons & Shils, 1951)	Rules orientation	"the role of general rules in guiding action" (Erez & Earley, 1993, p. 46); universalism refers to a broad set of rules and policies that guide actions; with particularism, individuals are guided by the unique aspects of the situation and its relevance to specific aspects of the actor
Tightness (Triandis, 1989, 2000)	Rules orientation	Tight cultures have many rules, norms, and ideas about what is correct behavior in each situation and conformity is high; loose cultures have fewer rules and norms, and people are tolerant of many deviations from normal behavior
Long- vs. short-term orientation (Hofstede, 2001)	Time orientation	"LTO [long-term orientation] stands for the fostering of virtues orientated towards future rewards, in particular perseverance and thrift"; "STO [short-term orientation] stands for the fostering of virtues related to the past and present, in particular respect for tradition, preservation of 'face' and fulfilling social orientations" (Hofstede, 2001, p. 359)
Sequential–synchronic (Trompenaars & Hampden-Turner, 1998)	Time orientation	Refers to relationship with time; extent to which time is viewed as a series of passing events (sequential) or viewed as synchronic, where past, present, and future are all considered and as such shape events
Past–future oriented (Hall & Hall, 1990)	Time orientation	Refers to the segments of time frame that are emphasized
Monochronic–polychronic (Hall & Hall, 1990)	Time orientation	Refers to the degree to which members of a culture pay attention to and do things one at a time (monochronic) versus being involved in many things at once (polychronic); within monochromic cultures, time is experienced and used in a linear way; segmented; compartmentalized (Hall and Hall, 1990)
Achievement–ascription (Trompenaars & Hampden-Turner, 1998)	Allocation of status	Relationship with power; The degree to which status is given based on one's achievements (doing) or based on personal characteristics (e.g., age, class, gender, education)
Ascription–achievement (Parsons & Shils, 1951)	Allocation of status	Refers to how an individual is judged in society; individuals in ascriptive cultures are judged by their attributes, those in achievement cultures are judged by their actions and performance
Neutral-emotional (Trompenaars & Hampden-Turner, 1998)	Affect	Degree to which people express affect.

(Continued)

TABLE 12.2
(Continued)

Cross-Cultural Dimension	Category	Definition
Affective–affective neutrality (Parsons & Shils, 1951)	Affect	"Extent to which it is acceptable for individuals to experience instant gratification" (Erez & Earley, 1993, p. 46)
Emotional expression–suppression (Triandis, 1989, 2000)	Affect	Refers to the degree to which people freely express their emotions no matter what the consequences (i.e., emotional expression); suppression refers to controlling the expression of emotion
Dionysian value (Morris)	Affect	"Indulgence of desires and overt expression of enjoyment" (Erez & Earley, 1993, p. 56)
Buddhistic value (Morris, 1956)	Affect	"Self-regulation and control as well as temperance of one's desires" (Erez & Earley, 1993, p. 56)
Inner–outer directed (Trompenaars & Hampden-Turner, 1998)	Orientation to nature	Refers to our relationship to nature; belief that society should control nature by imposing its will on it (inner directed) versus the belief that humanity is part of nature and must go along in harmony and forces with its laws (outer directed)
Man–nature orientation (Kluckhohn & Strodtbeck, 1961)	Orientation to nature	Can be a relationship involving subjugation (people accept the inevitable forces of nature, do not interfere), harmony, or mastery; what is a person's relationship with the external environment?
Active–passive (Triandis, 1989, 2000)	Orientation to nature	Active cultures try to change the environment to fit them; in passive cultures people change themselves to fit the environment (Diaz-Guerrero, 1979)
Promethean value (Morris, 1956)	Orientation to nature	"Tendency to actively shape the world and adapt it to man's interests" (Erez & Earley, 1993, p. 56)
Mastery–harmony (Schwartz, 1999)	Orientation to nature	Mastery involves "an emphasis on getting ahead through self-assertion," whereas harmony involves "emphasis on fitting in harmoniously into the environment (unity with nature)" (Schwartz, 1999, p. 28)
Analytic–holistic	Cognitive styles	Analytic cultures pay attention primarily to the object and the categories to which it belongs, and use rules and formal logic to understand its behavior; holistic cultures attend to the entire field and assign causality to interactions between the object and the field, making relatively little use of categories and formal logic; they rely on dialectical reasoning (Choi & Nisbett, 2000; Nisbett, Peng, Choi, & Norenzayan, 2001).

TABLE 12.2

(Continued)

Cross-Cultural Dimension	Category	Definition
Field dependence–independence	Cognitive styles	Field independence is a cognitive style exhibiting "the ability to highly differentiate between stimuli and to think analytically, whereas field dependence refers to lower levels of differentiation and global thinking" (Erez & Earley, 1993, p. 127); field-dependent people rely more on external social referents; field-independent people are less likely to be engaged in information-seeking behavior; field dependent people are more likely to have an interpersonal orientation
Specific–diffuse (Trompenaars & Hampden-Turner, 1998)	Context; how far we get involved	"Degree to which we engage people in specific areas of life and single levels of personality or diffusely in multiple areas of our lives and at several levels of personality at once" (Trompenaars & Hampden-Turner, 1998, p. 83)
Specific–diffuse (Parsons & Shils, 1951)	Context; how far we get involved	"The degree to which relations among actors and objects are limited"; in a diffuse culture, this relationship can be quite indirect; in a specific culture, the relationship is narrow and limited
Specific–diffuse (Triandis, 1989, 2000)	Context; how far we get involved	Diffuse cultures respond to the environment in a holistic manner; specific cultures discriminate different aspects of the stimulus complex
High–low context (Hall & Hall, 1990)	Context; how far we get involved	In high-context cultures, communication involves messages "in which most of the information is already in the person, while very little is in the coded, explicit, transmitted part of the message", whereas low-context cultures, the mass of the information is vested in explicit code (Hall & Hall, 1990, p. 6)
Masculinity–feminity (Hofstede, 1980)	Miscellaneous	"The extent to which the dominant values of society are 'masculine'—that is, assertiveness, the acquisition of money and things, and not caring for others, the quality of life, or people" (Hofstede, 1980, p. 45)
Space orientation (Kluckhohn & Strodtbeck, 1961)	Miscellaneous	Orientation toward the arrangement of organizational space; can emphasize private, public, or mixed
Space (Hall & Hall, 1990)	Miscellaneous	Boundaries of personal space and degree of territoriality
Activity orientation (Kluckhohn & Strodtbeck, 1961)	Miscellaneous	Modality of human activities may emphasize the being orientation, self-actualization (being-in-becoming), and doing (activity good for its own sake)

(Continued)

TABLE 12.2
(Continued)

Cross-Cultural Dimension	Category	Definition
Complexity (Triandis, 1989, 2000)	Miscellaneous	The degree to which culture is simple (individuals are in considerable agreement about beliefs and attitudes; have few jobs) or complex (subgroups with different beliefs, attitudes, etc.)
Monochronic–polychronic (Hall & Hall, 1990)	Miscellaneous	Monochronic time refers to paying attention to and doing only one thing at a time; time is linear, segmented, and compartmentalized; people do not like to be interrupted; polychronic culture means being involved in many things at once; characterized by the simultaneous occurrence of many things and by a great involvement with people; more emphasis on completing human transactions than on holding to schedules
Instrumental–expressive (Triandis, 1989, 2000)	Miscellaneous	Refers to the attributes that people within a culture pay attention to; those that are related to getting the job done (i.e., instrumental) or those regarding social relationships (i.e., expressive)
Information flow (Hall & Hall 1990)	Miscellaneous	Refers to the time it takes a message intended to produce an action to travel from one part of the organization to another and for that message to release the desired response (Hall & Hall, 1990, p. 22)

Most of the work on cross-cultural teams focuses on how the cultural composition of the team itself may affect team effectiveness. However, neglected here is the role that the leader's national culture plays during the sense-making process. More specifically, we argue that culture will influence the cues that elicit a leader's attention and the type of information he or she looks for within the environment. Uncertainty avoidance, high–low context, instrumental–expressive, field dependence–independence, and analytic–holistic reasoning are all cultural dimensions that could be argued to affect this process. For example, in terms of the information scanning process, the degree of uncertainty avoidance prevalent in their cultures may cause leaders to scan the environment differently. Harper and Rifkind (1995) found that in cultures that scored high on uncertainty avoidance (i.e., where workers are not comfortable with uncertainty), clear instruction, specialized careers, and cooperation among employees tend to be preferred. Taking this a step further, we suggest that within these cultures leaders may try to stay within their "comfort zone" and not attend to those cues that are felt to be more ambiguous when scanning the environment and acting within a boundary-spanning

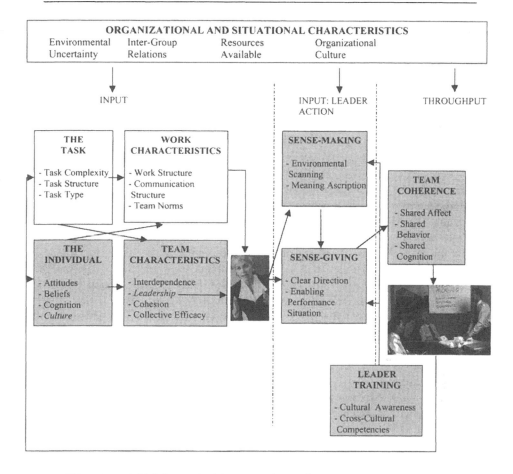

FIG. 12.1.   Initial theoretical framework used to guide the Propositions.

capacity. In line with this, it might be argued that team leaders coming from this type of culture may be more narrow in their search for information and less likely to accept information that does not conform to prior mental models.

The degree to which a team leader's cognitive style is field dependent or independent may also affect the ability of the leader to gather environmental cues. Specifically, field-dependent cultures tend to have lower levels of differentiation (Erez & Earley, 1993). Therefore, leaders that are field dependent may be less able to differentiate cues within the environment, leading to less effective information seeking and scanning behavior and fewer cues eliciting attention.

Additionally, cultural dimensions such as high–low context, instrumental–expressive, and holistic–analytic reasoning may affect the degree to which a leader attends to certain cues. For example, low-context cultures have been argued to seek data that emphasize personal or individual aspects as opposed to social or group aspects (Ting-Toomey, 1985). Similarly, cultures scoring high on the instrumental dimension primarily focus on attributes that are related to getting the job done as opposed to those regarding social relationships. Finally, cultures with a preference for holistic reasoning as opposed to analytic reasoning also tend to sample different types of cues (i.e., situational versus dispositional cues; see Choi & Nisbett, 2000).

Proposition 2:   Team leaders must be aware of the cultural bias inherent in their own cultural framework, because these biases will affect the meaning that is assigned to the environmental cues gathered during boundary spanning.

This proposition does not flow from any one cultural dimension, but from all combined. As stated earlier, culture has been defined as being composed of shared norms, values, and beliefs that exist within a nation, organization, or profession. These values and beliefs serve to form the basis of an individual's cognitive framework (i.e., mental model). In turn, mental models have been argued to contain internalized beliefs, assumptions, and perceptions (Klimoski & Mohammad, 1994) allowing individuals to generate descriptions of systems (e.g., equipment, people) as well as make predictions about future states (Rouse, Cannon-Bowers, & Salas, 1992). In assigning meaning to events, individuals compare new information to existing mental models and attempt to integrate the new information into their existing frameworks. In other words, meaning is assigned based on these frameworks. Information that does not conform to existing mental models may be disregarded or existing mental models may be updated. In either situation, the values and beliefs (e.g., cultural, task, team) flowing from mental models will serve to influence meaning assignment. In line with this thought, Klopf and Park (1982) argued that the encoding and decoding of information is highly culturally dependent.

Proposition 3:   Within multicultural teams, leaders must realize (as well as promote) the importance of nonverbal cues, as they may reveal hidden aspects of culture not revealed within verbal cues but are essential to the management and assignment of meaning to action.

One of the biggest problems that the team leader will face within multicultural teams revolves around communication and the assignment of meaning to communications and behaviors. Members from different cultural backgrounds are likely to exhibit very different styles of communication and action based on the values of their particular culture. For example, whereas individualist countries tend not to mind conflict among members, collectivist countries attempt to avoid conflict. As such, members in collectivist cultures most likely will not explicitly state an objection, especially if the person they are objecting to is of higher status. However, there may very well be nonverbal cues that will help members and the leader to realize the underlying meaning of what is being said as well as what is not being said.

Additionally, cultures vary in the degree to which they believe it is appropriate to express emotion or affect (i.e., emotional expression–suppression, neutral–emotional) and when emotion can be expressed. Therefore, nonverbal cues become increasingly important within these environments (Barnlund, 1989) and the team leader must educate members on the cultural differences in nonverbal cues, for they, too, can be misinterpreted. For example, in high-power-distance countries, members find it rude to maintain eye contact for long periods of time, whereas in low-power-distance countries, they tend to find this not only acceptable, but also important (Miller, Fields, Kumar, & Ortiz, 2000).

Proposition 4: Within multicultural teams, accurate shared team mental models may be more difficult to promote, but are essential, as they provide the basis for the assignment of meaning to member actions.

Team mental models have been argued to contain knowledge pertaining to the individual's role in the task as well as the role of other team members (Cannon-Bowers, Salas, & Converse, 1993). More specifically, these mental models contain the knowledge about team member characteristics, including their task knowledge, skills, abilities, and preferences. Although not explicitly stated, it would seem that this would also be the model that contains information regarding cultural differences among members (i.e., in the form of cultural preferences).

Within multicultural teams, it is important that the leader find a mechanism by which to structure team experiences so that all members, including the leader, possess accurate team mental models. Team members must learn upfront how cultural differences may affect teamwork processes, including communication, coordination, decision making, and feedback. Whereas some cultural differences are readily apparent in terms of visual cues, others may not stand out. In this situation, members may falsely assume that there are no differences. Moreover, building in correct knowledge pertaining to cultural values, which may influence interdependent actions, is important, for without this knowledge, team members will rely on stereotypes that may not be true. For example, Japanese individuals might consider Americans to be loud, boisterous, and rude due to their actions, but actually underlying these actions are the cultural dimensions of power distance and individualism–collectivism. The first step enabling multicultural teams to work together is their ability to recognize differences as well as similarities and building on both. In doing so, some have suggested that team leaders need to make a separate third culture—a hybrid culture (Earley & Mosakowski, 2000; Graen & Wakabayashi, 1994).

Sense Giving: Communication, Framing of Meaning

Once team leaders have perceived, attended to, and assigned meaning (i.e., integrated this information into existing cognitive frameworks) to environmental cues (both those internal and external to the team), this information must be effectively relayed to team members (i.e., sense giving).

Proposition 5:   In providing clear, engaging direction, team leaders must be careful to align this direction with team member cultural expectations.

Hackman (2002) argued that the direction provided to the team by the leader needs to be clear and engaging. Furthermore, it is argued that what is considered engaging will be determined, in part, by members' personal interests, values, and aspirations. Given this state of affairs, the leader must be careful to align directions to the team with cultural expectations. It is expected that the following cultural dimensions may be of relevance within this context: uncertainty avoidance, high–low context, time orientation, and individualism–collectivism. For example, uncertainty avoidance and high–low context may affect the degree to which directions are perceived as clear. It has been argued that cultures high in uncertainty avoidance prefer very clear instructions in that they provide a sense of control and order (Harper & Rifkind, 1995). Additional challenges are posed for the leader when teams comprise members from both high- and low-context cultures. If direction is given in a manner consistent with high-context cultures, members of low-context cultures are not likely to find the same message very clear because much of the meaning is context dependent and implicit. This is in direct contrast to the type of communication they prefer, in which messages are elaborated upon and highly specific.

In attempting to provide direction that is engaging, team leaders may also observe different perceptions of what is considered engaging, depending on culture. One aspect of engaging direction is the setting of goals. As much of the work on goal setting has been conducted within the United States, the rule of thumb is that goals should be (a) quantifiable, (b) specific, and (c) stretch the person to grow as a team member, but not be so hard that they are unattainable (Locke & Latham, 1994). Because cultures differ in terms of the degree to which they tolerate ambiguity and risk taking, it may be the case that, dependent on the level of uncertainty avoidance with which a culture is comfortable, goals need to be set differently. For example, whereas high-uncertainty-avoidance cultures are not comfortable with risk, the opposite is true of low-uncertainty-avoidance cultures. Therefore, challenging goals may not be motivating or engaging for those in low-uncertainty-avoidance cultures, but instead be perceived as threatening.

Proposition 6:   Team leaders must differentially structure feedback so that it is aligned with members' cultural lenses (i.e., feedback will be differentially interpreted).

Timely, constructive feedback that focuses on the task and not the person has been argued by many to be essential in creating and maintaining team coherence (i.e., shared affect, behavior, and cognition), which, in turn, leads to effective teamwork (Salas, Burke, & Cannon-Bowers, 2002). However, within cross-cultural teams, where the possibility of miscommunication is tremendous, a key challenge for the leader as well as team members is to ensure that feedback is interpreted in the manner in which it was intended. Cultural dimensions that may have an impact on this process include high–low context, neutral–emotional, achievement–ascription, and monochromic–polychromic orientation. For example, it has been argued that members from high–context cultures tend not to separate the person from the issue under consideration (Ting-Toomey, 1988), whereas low-context cultures encourage this type of separation in their communication. The implication for delivering feedback is that members of high-context cultures will be more likely to take the feedback personally even if it is focused on the task and not the person. Moreover, because there are differences (already covered) in the manner by which high- and low-context cultures format their communication, the leader also needs to take this into account when delivering feedback. Finally, low-context cultures seek interpersonal data emphasizing individual, personal aspects instead of social or group aspects (Ting-Toomey, 1988). This, in turn, will cause them to pay attention to different portions of the feedback and may also affect how valid they perceive feedback to be.

Additionally, the degree to which emotion is expressed in feedback must be aligned with cultural perceptions or else it may be misinterpreted. For example, Triandis (2000) cited a meeting between the foreign minister of Iraq and the secretary of state of the United States where communication was misinterpreted due to the foreign minister listening to how communication was stated as opposed to what was stated. The foreign minister reported the following back to Bagdad, "The Americans will not attack. They are weak. They are calm. They are not angry. They are only talking" (p. 145).

Finally, the validity and acceptance of feedback may be influenced by the degree to which cultures assign power based on achievement or ascription as well as the preference for monochromic or polychromic time orientation. Individuals within ascriptive cultures are judged and power assigned based on their attributes, whereas those within achievement cultures are judged based on their track record. Therefore, the feedback may be viewed as being more or less valid and important depending on who is delivering the feedback and how they came to be in that position. Similar arguments may be made for differences in power distance and its relation to the acceptance of feedback offered. More specifically, individuals in low-power-distance cultures may be more likely to question feedback received from a superior (especially if deemed as not valid) compared with individuals in high-power-distance cultures. Finally, because individuals within monochromic cultures prefer to compartmentalize their tasks and focus on only one aspect at a time, they may be less open to feedback from fellow team members while completing the task or when under time pressure. Conversely, individuals within polychromic cultures operate within a cultural framework where multiple things are happening at once, they do not mind being interrupted, and there exists more of an emphasis on human transactions than holding to schedules.

Proposition 7:   *The team leadership literature has argued that team leaders can create an enabling performance situation by promoting team self-correction behaviors. Some cultures may be more amenable to this process than others.*

There are many ways in which team leaders can intervene in order to help the team maintain team coherence. A recent instructional strategy that has proven to be effective is team self-correction training (Blickensderfer, Cannon-Bowers, & Salas, 1997). Team self-correction is a team-based instructional strategy that focuses on teaching team members how to provide developmental feedback and to self-critique one another. This process takes advantage of the team's natural tendency to review performance, but structures the process so that interaction is constructive and revolves around targeted team competencies (i.e., knowledge, attitudes, behavior). However, a key to this technique is that members must feel free to critique one another as well as themselves. Members who hold highly collectivistic values may have a very tough time offering criticism to those who are within their in-group. Research has shown that collectivists tend to be more favorable in their evaluations of in-group members (Gomez, Kirkman, & Shapiro, 2000). In addition, it may be harder to create a climate in which these members believe that it is safe and that they will not "lose face" during the feedback process.

The degree of complexity within a culture may also determine the degree to which members are comfortable with this process. Within simple cultures, members are often in considerable agreement about beliefs and attitudes, whereas in more complex cultures, subgroups exist within the larger group that have different beliefs and attitudes. Finally, although there is some structure to this technique, there is also a fair amount of ambiguity in that the exact nature of the feedback is dictated by the current situation and member contributions. Members from high-uncertainty-avoidance cultures may not be comfortable with this situation.

Proposition 8:   *Team leaders may have to intervene to recover team coherence more often within multicultural teams.*

Communication, back-up behavior and monitoring, member feedback, and adaptive behavior are several of the key processes that allow teams to capitalize on team synergy and perform better than the sum of their individual parts. However, within multinational teams, these processes may take more monitoring on the part of the team leader to ensure effectiveness. In terms of communication, the power distance that members are most comfortable with, will influence not only whom they are most likely to talk with, but also whom they are most likely to question and make eye contact with. For example, Conyne, Wilson, Tang, and Shi (1999) found that Chinese group members spoke directly to the group leader 33% of the time and to other members 14% of the time, whereas Americans directed communication to the leader 11% of the time and to fellow group members 34% of the time.

Back-up behavior may also be colored by cultural differences at several levels; we briefly focus on one. A key aspect of monitoring and back-up behavior is the ability to deliver constructive feedback once it is found that a team member is in trouble. Depending on members' national culture, they may be more or less willing to deliver information that may create conflict. More specifically, members from either high-uncertainty-avoidance cultures or those from collectivist nations will be more hesitant to create the conflict that feedback may create. Furthermore, the judged validity of the feedback may be differentially weighed by members depending on the source of the feedback (e.g., power distance) as well as the extent to which they trust the person delivering the feedback. Important to this process is that high- and low-context cultures look for different cues in calculating trust. A low-context person determines trust by looking for evidence about who individuals are, their worth, and competence, whereas a high-context person looks for evidence of group loyalty (Ting-Toomey, 1985).

Finally, communication may also be affected by culture in many ways, some of which have already been mentioned. However, the degree to which multicultural teams comprise members from individualistic-collectivist cultures may have an impact on group interaction as a whole in addition to the attributions made (Carpenter, 2000; Menon, Morris, Chiu, & Hong, 1999). Within collectivist cultures, there is a clear distinction between in-groups and out-groups, whereas this is less of a factor within individualistic cultures. Within a team context, this is important because if fellow team members are judged as being very dissimilar, members of collectivist cultures may place these members in the out-group. In turn, this may result in less interaction with these members, less value placed on their opinions, and differential evaluation of these team members as compared with in-group members. It becomes essential that early in the team development process the team leader emphasizes the similarities among members as well as the differences and attempts to find some common ground upon which members can begin to cohere. This, in turn, forms the foundation for group cohesion.

Finally, all of these team process dimensions combine to allow teams to be adaptive. However, certain cultural dimensions may limit a team's propensity to be adaptive. For example, tight cultures form many rules and norms. Therefore, conformity tends to be high within these cultures and deviations are not permitted. Unless norms are created that pertain to adaptive action, this tightness may inhibit members' ability to adapt to novel situations. Universalism may also reduce adaptability. Because universalist cultures tend to treat others on the basis of universal criteria instead of individual knowledges, skills, and attitudes, this may preclude adaptability, for individuals look for a standard set of operating procedures that can be applied across situations. Similar arguments can be made with Schwartz's conservatism–autonomy (intellective) dimension.

SCENARIO-BASED APPROACH
TO LEADER DEVELOPMENT

As the propositions illustrate, when compared to culturally homogeneous teams, multicultural teams present additional challenges in terms of effective team leadership, and little is known about how the various cultural dimensions combine and interact together. However, leaders can overcome these challenges if developed properly. Leader development has been defined as "occurring when individuals acquire experience and feedback; gain insights through reflection on their experiences and feedback and/or through instruction and other interventions; and, as a result, gain new skills, behavior, and knowledge that allow them to respond more effectively, flexibly, and proactively to changing environmental demands and opportunities" (Army Leader Development Working Session, 2002). Although there is a variety of cross-cultural training programs (i.e., cultural assimilator, lecture, experiential), most focus solely on promoting cultural awareness for expatriates and are designed for individuals. Whereas these programs have generally been shown to be effective and to tend to have a larger impact on cognition than behavior (Bhawuk & Brislin, 2000; Deshpande & Viswesvaran, 1992), few focus on the more specific topic of preparing team members to work as part of a multicultural team (interaction of culture with teamwork processes) and even fewer focus on preparing leaders to deal with the potential process difficulties within these types of teams. Furthermore, because most focus primarily on cultural awareness to the neglect of specific behavioral skills, it is not surprising that training has a larger impact on cognition. As evidenced by observations of a military unit preparing to deploy to Bosnia, where several training deficiencies in terms of content and a lack of diagnostic feedback were noted (Pierce, 2002), we do not yet have a good understanding of how to prepare teams or their leaders for operation within multicultural units.

In an effort to develop efficient, theoretically based training for those charged with leading multicultural teams as well as for the teams themselves, we propose to leverage against a proven instructional strategy known as event-based training. Event-based training is a scenario-based instructional approach that is relevant for training leaders of multicultural teams for several reasons. First, it has been used extensively within complex, dynamic environments such as those brought about by diversity (Fowlkes, Dwyer, Oser, & Salas, 1998). Second, its development is based on principles of human learning and the science of training. Third, it is a method by which some of the best aspects of existing multicultural training can be combined (i.e., it is very flexible). For example, it can be (a) embedded within various training formats (e.g., simulated environment, assessment center, on the job), (b) experientially based, (c) tailored to the stage of cultural assimilation, and (d) given almost any time and anywhere.

EVENT-BASED TRAINING

Event-based training (EBAT) is an instructional strategy in which the a priori defined scenarios that are embedded within training are themselves the training curriculum. The development of EBAT begins with the development of a skill inventory abstracted through the results of a job or task analysis or both. From this skill inventory, training objectives and competencies are identified. The next step is the translation of training objectives into learning objectives. These learning objectives serve to drive the development of the actual training scenarios and associated scripts. In crafting scenarios, a priori "trigger" events are embedded within the scenario at several points. Ideally, multiple events should be specified for each objective, vary in difficulty, and be introduced at several points during the exercise. These events serve as known opportunities for trainees to exhibit those competencies targeted in training. Once events and the associated scenarios are created, measurement instruments are developed for use in assessing task performance during each a priori defined event. Measurement tools are created that assess both process- and outcome-level feedback. Specifically, measurement should allow the assessment of whether targeted competencies are learned (i.e., outcome) along with why performance occurred as it did (i.e., process) by being tied to learning objectives and, more specifically, scenario events. Because this instructional strategy explicitly links learning objectives, exercise events, performance measures, and the associated feedback, it also standardizes measurement and training and reduces the workload for those in charge of observation and collection of performance data. Because performance measures are tied to previously defined events, the observer does not have to observe every instance of team behavior (reducing workload), and the form of the measurement instrument has also been argued to allow near real-time feedback to trainees. See Fig. 12.2 for a pictorial illustration of the life cycle of event-based training.

The use of this instructional strategy offers several benefits over instructional strategies currently used within cross-cultural training, including (a) standardization of training, (b) facilitation of diagnostic team assessment, (c) provision of known opportunities to practice targeted competencies, (d) simulation of dangerous or infrequently occurring cross-cultural situations, and (e) provision of performance measurement instruments (see TARGETS; Fowlkes, Lane, Salas, Franz, & Oser, 1994); in addition, when done well, scripts are transparent, giving the appearance of unscripted, free-flowing training.

EBAT is a flexible instructional strategy that can be used at a team or individual level, with colocated or distributed teams, across multiple formats, and for the teaching of a wide variety of competencies ranging from cultural awareness to actual strategy implementation. For example, within cross-cultural teams, members may be at different stages of awareness in terms of acculturation (Bennett, 1986). Training scenarios can be tailored based on the stage of awareness. In addition,

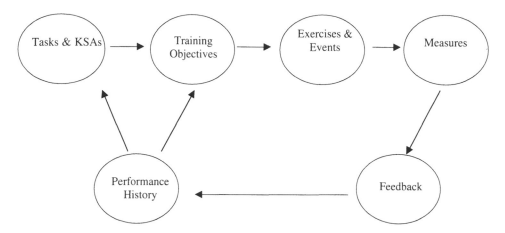

FIG. 12.2. The life cycle of scenario-based training. KSAs = knowledge, skills, and abilities. From "Advanced Technology in Scenario-Based Training," by J. A. Cannon-Bowers, J. J. Burns, E. Salas, and J. S. Pruitt, 1998, in *Making Decisions Under Stress: Implications for Individual and Team Training* (p. 366), edited by J. A. Cannon-Bowers and E. Salas, Washington, DC: American Psychological Association. Copyright 1998 by the American Psychological Association. Adapted with permission.

because multicultural teams are often ad hoc and have difficulty getting together for training (Pierce, 2002) EBAT's ability to be used for colocated or distributed teams offers a large benefit for these teams. Additional benefits include (a) the ability for experiential "lessons learned" to be turned into scenario events in an attempt to build tacit knowledge concerning leadership of multicultural teams and (b) the fact that training can be embedded into distributed simulation for use during downtime or as refresher training. Finally, although EBAT is often associated with simulation-based training, it can also be used to structure more traditional training venues. For example, it could be used to form the basis of traditional assessment center activities. The life cycle for development would be the same as described previously, with the caveat that instead of being embedded within a simulated environment, the scenarios would form the basis for the activities included in the assessment center.

Additionally, although EBAT has traditionally been used to train behavioral and attitudinal competencies, it could also be used to train cognitive skills needed within multicultural teams. For example, Fowlkes, Salas, Baker, Cannon-Bowers, and Stout (2000) used an event-based form of knowledge elicitation to capture information on situational awareness, which, with a few modifications, could be used as a training approach. Specifically, a series of scenarios was created and recorded on a video. The video included specific cue information pertaining to team interactions and flight situations, which were used to elicit experts' reactions.

Standardized points within the video provided opportunities for gathering knowledge such as participant's perception of the segment just viewed (as gathered via overview description), identification of the pertinent cues for maintaining situational awareness, identification of information that crew members should be sharing, and predictions for the next flight segment. More specifically, there were standardized points within the video where it was stopped and pilots responded to a priori defined questions. This technique was reported to have preliminary validity and could be modified for use in a training context by presenting trainees with a priori defined scenario sets targeted to key member cognitions regarding cross-cultural interactions. Then questions could be developed based on theory and research to elicit how trainees are thinking about the depicted cross-cultural interactions and the cognition that underlies their responses. Once participants have responded, diagnostic feedback can be given. This, in turn, serves to build knowledge competencies for cross-cultural teams. So what may these competencies be?

PRACTICAL APPLICATION OF EBAT FOR LEADER DEVELOPMENT

Up to this point, we have identified several challenges that leaders face in promoting effective teamwork within multicultural teams as well as argued for event-based training as a scenario-based instructional strategy that is theoretically based and has been successfully used within complex, dynamic environments (i.e., military command and control, military air wings). We have further argued that event-based training offers several advances over current multicultural training. Drawing from the proposed propositions, we next provide an illustration of how event-based training can be used to train a preliminary set of competencies needed by those leading multicultural teams. Specifically, we argue that event-based training should take three tracks: (a) scenarios that serve to illustrate the cultural biases inherent in the leader's own culture (own cultural awareness), (b) scenarios that serve to promote cultural awareness of broad cultural dimensions and how they may be manifested with regard to key leadership functions and teamwork, and (c) scenarios that develop the knowledge, skills, and attitudes that leaders need within these domains (essentially giving them strategies and opportunities to practice in a simulated context). Although many training programs teach cultural awareness, most do not tie it to how cultural dimensions may jointly interact to affect teamwork or the key functions that team leaders need to enact. Additionally, although understanding the concept and practice of culture is important, because this knowledge serves to trigger situational cues that might otherwise go unnoticed, Grahn and Swenson (2000) argued it is not enough—leaders must first understand their own culture and biases. Finally, the third track serves to take the awareness and knowledge gained from the first two tracks and ties behavioral skills to this knowledge.

Although all three of these tracks are important, we elaborate on only the third track due to space limitations. Initial guidance for the first two tracks can be found in the literature on cultural assimilators; however, it is difficult to offer explicit guidance concerning the second track because research has not yet examined how cultural dimensions may jointly interact to affect key leadership functions and the corresponding promotion of teamwork. The third track should focus on developing the knowledge, skills, and attitudes needed for effective leadership within cross-cultural teams. We suggest that leaders of multicultural teams need the following competencies as an initial set: metacognitive skills, social intelligence, communication skills, and flexible cognitive structures (i.e., mental models). It is important to note that this is only an initial set and is by no means intended to be inclusive—it represents a sampling of competencies that, based on the propositions offered earlier, we feel are important.

Metacognition

Metacognition has been investigated across many domains and can be described as an awareness of one's own cognitive processes and the ability to understand, control, and manipulate these processes (Davidson, Deuser, & Sternberg, 1994; Osman & Hannafin, 1992). Because much of culture has a cognitive basis, metacognitive skills are critical for team leaders to maintain an awareness of their own biases in interpretation and action. Furthermore, metacognition has been shown to have a substantial impact on (a) learning (Sternberg, 1998), (b) performing on complex team tasks (Ford, Smith, Weisshein, Gully, & Salas, 1998), and (c) social intelligence. Because cross-cultural teams represent a complex situation where members may be ad hoc, continuous learning is essential. This necessity also points to the importance of metacognitive skills.

Social Intelligence

Social intelligence has been defined as a complex process consisting of the ability to (a) perceive and accurately interpret critical situational contingencies and (b) use this information to derive, select, and implement the behavioral responses most appropriate for each situation (Zaccaro, 2002). This construct includes skills related to social perceptiveness and behavioral flexibility. Within cross-cultural teams, this skill is important because, in making and communicating sense to team members, team leaders may often have to perceive and understand subtle social cues. Furthermore, the subskill of behavioral flexibility is important because team leader's will have to have a flexible repertoire of behaviors and be able to see social situations from different frames of reference in order to tailor the actual manifestation of their leadership functions to cross-cultural interactions with team members.

Communication Skills

Communication has been defined as "the process by which information is clearly and accurately exchanged between two or more team members in the prescribed manner with the proper terminology; the ability to clarify or acknowledge the receipt of information" (Cannon-Bowers, Tannenbaum, Salas, & Volpe, 1995, p. 345). Whereas communication is often viewed in terms of verbal indices, within cross-cultural teams nonverbal communication is just as important, if not more so, For example, national cultures differ in the degree to which they openly express disagreement or affect. Team leaders need to be taught how to extract needed information from members of various cultures.

Communication skills are vital to the leader's role as a sense maker. Furthermore, it is through communication that leaders can create a hybrid third culture that takes advantage of the cultural diversity present within the team, which is then embedded within the shared mental models that underlie effective coordination. Team leaders must be taught how to attend to the sometimes subtle nonverbal cues that are offered by members. Furthermore, they must promote this skill within the team.

Flexible Cognitive Structures

Finally, within cross-cultural teams, leaders as well as team members need to form flexible cognitive structures that allow them to see situations from different perspectives and are malleable. Part of creating these knowledge structures is creating a team value in which cultural differences and similarities are valued and concerns and questions can be expressed.

Although we predict that the foregoing competencies will be important for leadership within cross-cultural teams, this should be verified based on a task analysis that captures both behavioral and cognitive data. Furthermore, lessons learned from soldiers stationed in Afghanistan, Somalia, and Bosnia can also serve as the basis for scenario development. Scenarios could be created in which events are embedded that would trigger the aforementioned behavioral skills as well as some of the more cognitive skills. The main difference would be that with the events that are to elicit the cognitive skills, the scenario might be interrupted or cued to stop so an assessment of cognition via a knowledge elicitation tool could be conducted. For the events that serve to elicit the behavioral or attitudinal competencies, assessment could be made with a measure such as TARGETS (Fowlkes et al., 1994). With such a measure, information can be captured as to whether a response was made as well as if it was correct. Additionally, more process-type information can be gathered by analyzing the data by the targeted teamwork dimensions; for example, the percentage of time that members correctly responded to an instance calling for behavioral flexibility can be examined. Once performance information is gathered, feedback can be given that contains what happened, trainee reaction, why it was appropriate or inappropriate, as well as what might be done to correct it in future situations. The feedback session should be very interactive and, in an effort to train behavioral flexibility as well as flexible cognitive structures, trainees should be presented with a variety of situations.

CONCLUDING COMMENTS

Whereas global conditions are making it imperative that researchers and practitioners alike understand the factors contributing to effective leadership of culturally diverse teams, there are few opportunities to leverage against existing work in terms of its effect on team process. However, we have leveraged against several literatures (e.g., team leadership, sense making, cultural diversity, team process) and provided connections where we saw appropriate. Furthermore, we have identified a need for training programs to go beyond cultural awareness to theoretically based training programs that impart skills along with knowledge. However, much remains to be done. More specifically, the propositions offered in this chapter and the initial proposed competencies are only a starting point and remain to be tested. Researchers also need to begin to examine truly cross-cultural teams so that knowledge can be gained concerning how the various cultural dimensions jointly interact to influence key leadership functions as well as teamwork.

REFERENCES

Adler, N. J. (1997). *International dimensions of organizational behavior* (3rd ed.). Cincinnati, OH: International Thomson.

Barnlund, D. C. (1989). *Communicative styles of Japanese and Americans: Images and realities.* Wadsworth.

Bass, B. M. (1997). Does the transactional–transformational leadership paradigm transcend organizational and national boundaries? *American Psychologist, 52*(2), 130–139.

Bennett, J. M. (1986). A developmental approach to training for intercultural sensitivity. *International Journal of Intercultural Relations, 10,* 179–196.

Bhawuk, D. P. S., & Brislin, R. W. (2000). Cross-cultural training: A review. *Applied Psychology: An International Review, 49*(1), 162–191.

Blickensderfer, E., Cannon-Bowers, J. A., & Salas, E. (1997). *Training teams to self-correct: An empirical investigation.* Paper presented at the 12th annual meeting of the Society for Industrial and Organizational Psychology, St. Louis, MO.

Cannon-Bowers, J. A., Burns, J. J., Salas, E., & Pruitt, J. S. (1998). Advanced technology in scenario-based training. In J. A. Cannon-Bowers & E. Salas (Eds.), *Making decisions under stress: Implications for individual and team training* (pp. 365–374). Washington, DC: American Psychological Association.

Cannon-Bowers, J. A., Salas, E., & Converse, S. A. (1993). Shared mental models in expert team decision-making. In N. J. Castellan, Jr. (Ed.), *Current issues in individual and group decision making* (pp. 221–246), Hillsdale, NJ: Lawrence Erlbaum Associates, Inc.

Cannon-Bowers, J. A., Tannenbaum, S. I., Salas, E., & Volpe, C. E. (1995). Defining team competencies and establishing team training requirements. In R. Guzzo, E. Salas, & Associates (Eds.), *Team effectiveness and decision making in organizations* (pp. 333–380). San Francisco: Jossey-Bass.

Carpenter, S. (2000). Effects of cultural tightness and collectivism on self-concept and causal attributions. *Cross-Cultural Research: The Journal of Comparative Social Science, 34*(1), 38–56.

Choi, I., & Nisbett, R. E. (2000). Cultural psychology of surprise: Holistic theories and recognition of contradiction. *Journal of Personality and Social Psychology, 79*(6), 890–905.

Conyne, R. K., Wilson, F. R., Tang, M., & Shi, K. (1999). Cultural similarities and differences and differences in group work: Pilot study of a U.S.–Chinese task group comparison. *Group Dynamics: Theory, Research, and Practice, 3*(1), 40–50.

Davidson, J. E., Deuser, R., & Sternberg, R. J. (1994). The role of metacognition in problem solving. In J. Metcalfe & A. P. Shimamura (Eds.), *Metacognitoin: Knowing about knowing* (pp. 207–226). Cambridge, MA: MIT Press.

Den Hartog, D. N., House, R. J., Hanges, P. J., & Ruiz-Quintanilla, S. A. (1999). Culture specific and cross-culturally generalizable implicit leadership theories: Are attributes of charismatic/transformational leadership universally endorsed? *Leadership Quarterly, 10*(2), 219–256.

Deshpande, S. P., & Viswesvaran, C. (1992). Is cross-cultural training of expatriate managers effective: A meta analysis. *International Journal of Intercultural Relations, 16*(3), 295–310.

Diaz-Guerrero, R. (1979). The development of coping style. *Human Development, 22*(5), 320–331.

Distefano, J. J., & Maznevski, M. L. (2000). Creating value with diverse teams in global management. *Organizational Dynamics, 29*(1), 45–63.

Dodd, C. H. (1991). *Dynamics of intercultural communication* (3rd ed.). Dubuque, IA: Brown.

Earley, P. C., & Mosakowski, E. (2000). Creating hybrid team cultures: An empirical test of transnational teams functioning. *Academy of Management Journal, 43*(1), 26–49.

Erez, M., & Earley, P. C. (1993). *Culture, self-identity, and work*. New York: Oxford University Press.

Fleishman, E. A., Mumford, M. D., Zaccaro, S. J., Kevin, K. Y., Korotkin, A. L., & Hein, M. B. (1991). Taxonomic efforts in the description of leader behavior: A synthesis and functional interpretation. *Leadership Quarterly, 2*(4), 245–287.

Ford, J. K., Smith, E. M., Weisshein, D. A., Gully, S. M., & Salas, E. (1998). Relationships of goal-orientation, metacognitive activities, and practice strategies with learning outcomes and transfer. *Journal of Applied Psychology, 83*, 218–233.

Fowlkes, J. E., Dwyer, D. Oser, R., & Salas, E. (1998). Event-based approach to training (EBAT). *International Journal of Aviation Psychology, 8*(3), 209–221.

Fowlkes, J. E., Lane, N. E., Salas, E., Franz, T., & Oser, R. (1994). Improving the measurement of team performance: The TARGETS methodology. *Military Psychology, 6*(1), 47–61.

Fowlkes, J. E., Salas, E., Baker, D. P., Cannon-Bowers, J. A., & Stout, R. J. (2000). The utility of event-based knowledge elicitation. *Human Factors, 42*(1), 24–35.

Gomez, C., Kirkman, B. L., & Shapiro, D. L. (2000). The impact of collectivism and in group/out-group membership on the evaluation generosity of team members. *Academy of Management Journal, 43*(6), 1097–1106.

Graen, G. B., & Uhl-Bien, M. (1995). Relationship-based approach to leadership: Development of leader-member exchange (LMX) theory of leadership over 25 years: Applying a multi-level multi-domain perspective. *Leadership Quarterly, 6*(2), 219–247.

Graen, G. B., & Wakabayashi, M. (1994). Cross-cultural leadership making: Bridging American and Japanese diversity for team advantage. In H. C. Triandis, M. D. Dunnette, & L. M. Hough (Eds.), *Handbook of industrial of organizational psychology* (2nd ed., vol. 4, pp. 415–446). Palo Alto, CA: Consulting Psychologists.

Grahn, J. L., & Swenson, D. X. (2000). Cross-cultural perspectives for quality training. *Cross cultural Management: An International Journal, 7*(3), 19–24.

Hackman, J. R. (2002). *Leading teams: Setting the stage for great performances*. Boston: Harvard Business School.

Hackman, J. R., & Walton, R. E. (1986). Leading groups in organizations. In P. S. Goodman and Associates (Eds.), *Designing effective work groups* (pp. 72–119). San Francisco: Jossey-Bass.

Hall, E. T., & Hall, M. R. (1990). *Understanding cultural differences.* Garden City, NY: Intercultural.

Harper, L. F., & Rifkind, L. J. (1995). Intercultural communication in the diversified quality workplace. In L. F. Harper & L. R. Rifkind (Eds.), *Cultural collision: Quality teamwork in the diverse workplace* (pp. 41–61). Dubuque, IA: Kendall/Hunt.

Helmreich, R. L. (1994). Anatomy of a system accident: The crash of Avianca Flight 052. *International Journal of Aviation Psychology, 4*(3), 265–284.

Helmreich, R. L., & Merritt, A. C. (1998). *Culture at work in aviation and medicine: National, organizational, and professional influences.* Aldershot, UK: Ashgate.

Hofstede, G. (1980). *Culture's consequences: International differences in work related values.* Beverly Hills, CA: Sage.

Hofstede, G. (2001). *Culture's consequences: Comparing values, behaviors, institutions, and organizations across nations.* Thousands Oaks, CA: Sage Publications.

Horenczyk, G., & Berkerman, Z. (1997). The effects of intercultural acquaintance and structured intergroup interaction on ingroup, outgroup, and reflected ingroup stereotypes. *International Journal of Intercultural Relations, 21*(1), 71–83.

House, R. J., et al. (1999). Cultural influences on leadership and organizations: Project GLOBE. In W. H. Mobley (Ed.), *Advances in global leadership* (vol. 1, pp. 171–233). Stamford, CT: JAI.

Jacobs, T.O., & Jaques, E. (1987). Leadership in complex systems. In J. A. Zeidner (Ed.), *Human productivity enhancement: Organizations, personnel and decision making* (p. 7–65). Orange, NJ: Greenwood Publishing Group.

Katz, I., Goldtson, J., & Benjamin, L. (1958). Behavior and productivity in biracial work groups. *Human Relations, 11,* 123–141.

Klimoski, R., & Mohammad, S. (1994). Team mental model: Construct or metaphor? *Journal of Management, 20,* 403–437.

Kluckhohn, F., & Strodtbeck, F. L. (1961). *Variations in value orientations.* Evanston, IL: Row, Peterson.

Komaki, J. L., Desselles, M. L., & Bowman, E. D. (1989). Definitely not a breeze: Extending an operant model of effective supervision to teams. *Journal of Applied Psychology, 74*(3), 522–529.

Li, H. Z. (1999). Communicating information in conversations: A cross-cultural comparison. *International Journal of Intercultural Relations, 56,* 1–23.

Locke, E. A., & Latham, G. P. (1994). Goal setting theory. In H. F. O'Neil, Jr., & M. Drillings (Eds.), *Motivation: Theory and research* (pp. 13–29). Hillsdale, NJ: Lawrence Erlbaum Associates, Inc.

Meadows, S. I. (1995). Multi-threat world dares U. S. to hatch new strategy. *National Defense, 80*(512), 12–13.

Menon, T., Morris, M. W., Chiu, C.-Y., & Hong, Y.-Y. (1999). Culture and the construal agency: Attribution to individual versus group disposition. *Journal of Personality and Social Psychology, 76*(5), 701–717.

Miller, M. D., Fields, R., Kumar, A., & Ortiz, R. (2000). Leadership and organizational vision in managing a multiethnic and multicultural project team. *Journal of Management in Engineering, 2000*(November/December), 18–22.

Morris, C. W. (1956). *Varieties of human value.* Chicago: University of Chicago Press.

Nisbett, R. E., Peng, K., Choi, I., & Norenzayan, A. (2001). Culture and systems of thought: Holistic versus analytic cognition. *Psychological Review, 108*(2), 291–310.

Osman, M. E., & Hannafin, M. J. (1992). Metacognition research and theory: Analysis and implications for instructional design. *Educational Technology Research and Development, 40,* 83–99.

Parsons, T., & Shils, E. (1951). *Toward a general theory of social action.* Cambridge, MA: Harvard University Press.

Pierce, L. G. (2002). Barriers to adaptability in a multinational team. In *Proceedings of the Human Factors Society 46th annual meeting* (pp. 225–229). Santa Monica, CA.

Rouse, W. B., Cannon-Bowers, J. A., & Salas, E. (1992). The role of mental models on team performance in complex systems. *IEEE Transactions on Systems, Man, and Cybernetics, 22,* 1296–1308.

Salas, E., Burke, C. S., & Cannon-Bowers, J. A. (2002). Tips and guidelines for designing and delivering team training. In K. Kraiger (Ed.), *Creating, implementing, and managing effective training and development: State-of-the-art lessons for practice* (pp. 234–259). San Francisco: Jossey-Bass.

Sarros, J. C., & Santora, J. C. (2001). Leaders and values: A cross-cultural study. *Leadership and Organizational Development Journal, 22*(5), 243–248.

Schwartz, S. H. (1999). A theory of cultural values and some implications for work. *Applied Psychology: An International Review, 48*(1), 23–47.

Starbuck, W. H., & Milliken, F. J. (1988). Executives' perceptual filters: What they notice and how they make sense. In D. C. Hambrick (Ed.), *The executive effect: Concepts and methods for studying top managers* (pp. 35–65). Greenwich, CT: JAI.

Sternberg, R. J. (1998). Metacognition, abilities, and developing expertise: What makes an expert student? *Instructional Science, 26,* 127–140.

Stewart, G. L., & Manz, C. C. (1995). Leadership for self-managing work teams: A typology and integrative model. *Human Relations, 48,* 747–770.

Straub, D. W., Loch, K. D., Evaristo, R., Karahanna, E., & Srite, M. (2002). Toward a theory-based measurement of culture. *Journal of Global Information Management, 10*(1), 13–23.

Tesluk, P. E., and Gerstner, C. R. (2002). Leading self-managing work groups: Effects on processes and performance. In J. C. Zeigert & K. Klein (Co-chairs), *Team leadership: Current theoretical and research perspectives.* Symposium conducted at the 17th annual meeting of the Society for Industrial and Organizational Psychology, Toronto, Canada.

Thomas, D. C. (1999). Cultural diversity and work group effectiveness. *Journal of Cross-cultural Psychology, 30*(2), 242–263.

Thomas, J. B., Clark, S. M., & Gioia, D. A. (1993). Strategic sensemaking and organizational performance: Linkages among scanning, interpretation, action, and outcomes. *Academy of Management Journal, 36*(2), 239–270.

Ting-Toomey, S. (1985). Toward a theory of conflict and culture. In W. B. Gudykunst, L. P., Stewart, and S. Ting-Toomey (Eds.), *Communication, culture, and organizational processes.* Newbury Park, CA: Sage.

Ting-Toomey, S. (1988). Intercultural conflict styles: A face negotiation theory. In Y. Y. Kim & W. B. Gudykunst (Eds.). *Theories in intercultural communication.* Newbury Park, CA: Sage.

Triandis, H. C. (1989). The self and behavior in different cultural contexts. *Psychological Review, 96,* 506–520.

Triandis, H. C. (2000). Culture and conflict. *International Journal of Psychology, 35*(2), 145–152.

Trompenaars, F. (2002). In V. Gupta & R. House (Chairs), *Building effective networks: Reconciling cultural dimensions of five international programs.* Symposium conducted at the annual meeting of the Academy of Management Conference, Denver, CO.

Trompenaars, F., & Hampden-Turner, C. (1998*). Riding the waves of culture: Understanding cultural diversity in global business.* New York: McGraw-Hill.

Watson, W. E., Kumar, K., & Michaelsen, L. K. (1993). Cultural diversity's impact on interaction process and performance: Comparing homogeneous and diverse task groups. *Academy of Management Journal, 36*(3), 590–602.

Weick, K. E. (1995). *Sensemaking in organizations.* Thousand Oaks, CA: Sage.

Zaccaro, S. J. (2002). Organizational leadership and social intelligence. In R. E. Riggio, S. E. Murphy, & F. J. Pirozzolo (Eds.), *Multiple intelligences and leadership* (pp. 29–54). Mahwah, NJ: Lawrence Erlbaum Associates, Inc.

Zaccaro, S. J., Rittman, A., & Marks, M. A. (2001). Team leadership. *Leadership Quarterly, 12,* 451–483.

13

Developing Teams and Team Leaders: Strategies and Principles

Eduardo Salas, C. Shawn Burke, and Kevin C. Stagl
University of Central Florida

One hundred ten miles off the coast of Scotland, the crew of Occidental's Piper Alpha oil rig were victims of a fiery explosion that occurred when the night crew activated a pump taken off line by the day crew for repairs. Amazingly, most survived the initial explosion, but breakdowns in teamwork following the emergency sealed the fate of the 167 who died. Following the explosion, failures in team leadership, crew communication, and situational awareness delayed evacuation and the shutting down of key operations that would have limited damage (Cullen, 1990).

On December 20, 1995, 160 passengers and crew of American Airlines Flight 965 perished just 38 miles short of their destination. At a time when the crew should have been discussing arrival and descent checklist procedures, the flight data recorder indicated that the final 30 min of conversation between the pilot and flight crew were dominated by a discussion of flight attendant duty schedules (Simmon, 1998). The breakdown in communication and a lack of situational awareness were cited as key contributory factors in the crash.

Thirty-seven sailors attached to the USS *Stark* were killed when their vessel was hit by incoming missiles fired from an Iraqi jet. Although the crew of the *Stark* had 2 min from missile launch detection until impact, no defensive maneuvers were attempted. Investigations suggested casualties could have been minimized if the crew had been able to overcome the intense pressure and stress to act in a coordinated, adaptive fashion (Anderson & Sandza, 1987).

Technological advances and a global economy are creating increasingly complex environmental contingencies, causing many industries to turn to teams as a key organizational strategy. However, teams are not always effective and teamwork is not an automatic consequence of placing people together (Salas, Cannon-Bowers, Rhodenizer, & Bowers, 1999). Thus, it is of paramount importance to understand the factors related to team effectiveness so that requisite competencies (i.e., knowledges, skills, and attitudes, KSAs) can be developed. Therefore, the purpose of this chapter is fourfold. First, the literature on teams is reviewed to extract a sample of the competencies needed for effective team performance. Second, based on the identified KSAs, instructional strategies that may be used to train targeted competencies are outlined. Third, because team leaders play a key role in determining a team's effectiveness, we examine the literature on team leadership to extract principles for guiding team leader development. Finally, where we see deficiencies in the literature, we highlight them, providing direction for future research initiatives.

TEAMS

Organizations are increasingly using teams as a mechanism by which to remain adaptive and competitive in a technologically advanced global market. Teams are complex, unique entities that have been characterized as (a) two or more individuals, (b) who interact socially, (c) adaptively, (d) have a shared or common goal, (e) hold meaningful task interdependencies, (f) are hierarchically structured, (g) have a limited life span, (h) whose expertise and roles are distributed, and (i) are embedded within an organizational and environmental context that influences their processes and outcomes (Salas, Dickinson, Converse, & Tannenbaum, 1992). Teams have boundaries; they are flexible and operate at multiple levels in the contextual space (e.g., vertical, horizontal, virtual). Teams evolve and mature; they are not static, but fluid and dynamic (Morgan, Salas, & Glickman, 1993). Teams are cyclical and perform in episodic events (Marks, Mathieu, & Zaccaro, 2001). Teams have members that think, do, and feel (Salas & Cannon-Bowers, 1997). Thus, teams are indeed complex social units. Furthermore, all teams are not created equal. Teams vary in size, function, capabilities, structure, and motivation. Sundstrom and colleagues suggested that team characteristics may also affect the importance of certain processes (Sundstrom, deMeuse, & Futrell, 1990; Sundstrom, McIntyre, Halfhill, & Richards, 2000). As a result of this, a number of typologies have appeared to help organize team types.

The team typology that is most commonly used is that of Sundstrom et al. (1990). This typology initially consisted of three team types, but was later refined to include six unique types of teams: (a) production, (b) service, (c) management,

TABLE 13.1
Team Typology

Team Type	Characteristics	Examples
Production	Low differentiation	Assembly teams
	High integration	Manufacturing crews
	Work cycles typically are repeated,	Flight attendant crews
	continuous processes that may be	Data processing groups
	shorter than team's life span	
Service	Low levels of team authority	Sales teams
	Low levels of team specialization	Human Resource teams
	Tight external linkages	
Executive management	High levels of authority	
	Tight external linkages	
	Varies within team specialization	
Project development	High specialization	Research groups
	Low integration	Planning teams
	Work cycles vary, depending on project	Development teams
		Task forces
Action	High differentiation	Sports teams
	High integration	Expeditions
	Operates in brief performance events	Negotiating teams
	of routine or novel nature	Surgery teams
		Cockpit crews
Parallel	Moderate differentiation	Quality circles
	Moderate integration	Employee involvement
		Selection committees
		Advisory groups

Note. Based on Sundstrom (1999).

(d) project, (e) action and performing, and (f) parallel (see Table 13.1) (Sundstrom, 1999). The primary distinguishing factors among these teams are the degree of differentiation (i.e., specialization, independence, autonomy from other work units) and integration (i.e., degree of integration or interaction with the larger system outside the team). Sundstrom's typology, and others like it, serves to organize team complexities, set boundaries that aid in result generalization, and raise issues to be dealt with during training.

TEAMS OPERATING IN COMPLEX ENVIRONMENTS

Of the several types of teams, this chapter is most relevant to action teams. Action teams comprise experts with specialized training, have extended life spans, and are synchronized with counterparts and support units. Thus, we argue that action teams hold the highest potential for meeting the demands within complex environments that are characterized by (a) rapidly evolving ambiguous situations, (b) high information overload, (c) severe time pressure and consequences of error, (d) adverse physical conditions, and (e) distributed multioperator problems (Orasanu & Salas, 1993). In what follows, we discuss a representative sample of actions teams within both industry and the military.

Commercial Aviation Teams

Examinations of accident reports have shown that the majority of aviation accidents can be attributed to human error, a large percentage of which is due to failures in coordination (Freeman & Simmon, 1991). There are several complexities within aviation teams that serve to make teamwork important, but challenging. First, teams operating within this context are most closely akin to ad hoc teams in that composition is often varied across flights, sometimes within and across different legs of the same flight. Due to the fluid nature of these teams, individual team members must learn transportable teamwork skills that can later be tailored to the particular situation (Cannon-Bowers, Tannenbaum, Salas, & Volpe, 1995). The short life span of some of these teams also necessitates that team competencies reach an asymptote in a compressed amount of time. Furthermore, because crew members may work together for a limited time, disband, and then come back together at a later date, standard operating procedures are exceedingly important because crews may not have the time to form the fully developed shared mental models that serve to guide coordination.

Medical Teams

Aviation is not the only industry working in mission critical, high-impact environments that has come to rely on the use of teams; the medical community is also increasingly using teams. In many ways, the current environment within the medical community is indicative of that within aviation before the implementation of team training and voluntary reporting systems. Specifically, the nature of medical teams is often such that members (a) may rotate in and out on an hourly basis, (b) represent different specialties, each of which has its own internal culture and norms, and (c) are expert in their own field but may know nothing about working as a team. Typically, clear lines of hierarchy in terms of who talks to whom and who can question others' actions also characterize these teams. Furthermore, these teams often operate in high-stress, life-threatening situations where neither the environment nor the situation is constant. For example, Edmondson (2002) found that operating rooms within the same hospital might comprise different equipment and configurations. Doctors and surgeons may even rotate from hospital to hospital, each with a different set of norms. Moreover, the culture within the medical community is one in which errors are infrequently admitted for fear of consequences. In turn, this makes it difficult to identify errors and develop training to help mitigate errors due to teamwork.

Command and Control Teams

The military has utilized teams for centuries and has heavily invested in their training. Command and control teams are examples of military action teams. At a general level, command and control teams comprise a commander, staff, and the C2 system (FM 3-0). The C2 system consists of three integrated components: communication systems, intelligence systems, and computer networks. Command and control team members utilize the C2 system to synchronize soldier action in order to meet the objectives of the commander's intent. Command and control team members are defined by their effort to reach common goals through specialized roles and their application of high levels of skill and ability to plan and replan strategic actions (Paris, Salas, & Cannon-Bowers, 2000). Another critical concern of command and control teams is the development, maintenance, and propagation of battlefield situational awareness. To reduce this concern, team members apply their multiple perceptual modalities to assess the environment and communicate their assessments to fellow members to promote shared situational awareness. Team members then act in a continuous manner to maintain and update situational awareness to improve lateral and vertical coordination. Complexities in the nature of the environments and situations encountered by command control team members serve to drive breakdowns in team processes such as decision making. Although illustrated separately here, command and control teams can also be distributed and will increasingly be so in future operations.

Distributed Decision-Making Teams

As witnessed in Afghanistan, digital warfare is waged via electronic connectivity at all levels of the Army and across all branches of the U.S. military (Shamir & Ben-Ari, 1999). It was once the case that the interdependent nature of teams required teammates to be colocated; today teams can be distributed. Members of distributed teams are connected via a computer network and thus can be located in different temporal, geographic, or virtual locations. Due to the fact that members can be located in different physical locations, distributed teams (a) are not limited by size constraints, (b) may comprise members with very different functional areas of expertise, and (c) often communicate through electronic, digital, or verbal media.

Distributed teams offer many benefits to organizations. For example, organizations can take advantage of the fact that the best combination of members for the job may not be located in close geographic proximity to one another. Furthermore, when distributed teams are used for training purposes, travel costs are saved. Distributed training and team interaction can occur any time and any place, provided the appropriate bandwidth capabilities are available. Despite their advantages, however, distributed teams also pose challenges in terms of both taskwork and teamwork. Outfitting soldiers with technology increases the need to institute training programs, which develop additional taskwork skills (e.g., basic computer skills, device-specific software skills). There are also significant teamwork obstacles to be overcome. For example, distributed teams pose challenges in terms of the establishment of trust (e.g., in technology, in other members) and the building of a group identity (Fisher, 1988). Also, even under the best circumstances, there are typically delays in communication. In addition, depending on the technology employed, many distributed teams are not physically able to see their teammates or are only able to see some of them. Consequently, there is a loss of environmental and social cues that traditional teams are able to utilize to help interpret the meaning of member communication, action, and responses. Townsend, DeMarie, and Hendrickson (1996) suggested that the loss of social and bodily cues makes it far more common for misunderstandings and miscommunications to occur. Furthermore, additional teamwork challenges are raised by the sheer quantity and complexity of information available on the digital battlefield. Markedly increasing access to real-time information may cognitively overwhelm and paralyze teams with indecision, thus reducing performance in situations that require team adaptability (Yukl, 1999).

Summary

Both industry and the military are increasingly utilizing teams to accomplish mission critical objectives. Commonalties exist between industry and military teams in that they consist of two or more interdependent members acting in a coordinated, adaptive fashion to achieve a shared goal. However, it is important to note that teams also differ on several dimensions: (a) the nature of their expertise, (b) the level of task interdependency, (c) their life span, (d) their degree of specialization, (e) their maturation level, and (f) the degree of interdependence with entities outside of the team. This suggests that to successfully overcome encountered challenges, each type of team must have a unique set of competencies at its disposal.

TEAM COMPETENCIES

Team performance can be described as a series of inputs, processes, and outputs (IPO) (Salas, Stagl, & Burke, in press). As the number of IPO models began to accrue, researchers noted the variability in the dimensions that different models proposed as constituting teamwork or team processes. In light of this, Salas, Cannon-Bowers, and colleagues began to systematically collect what was known about the competencies that contribute to successful team performance (Burke, Volpe, Cannon-Bowers, & Salas, 1993). This line of thinking sought to understand and improve team performance by both explicating principles to guide team interventions and proposing research questions to be tested in future endeavors. The results from this effort suggest that the skill competencies that constitute teamwork

TABLE 13.2

Team Skill Competencies

Process Skills	Definition
Adaptability and flexibility	Process by which a team utilizes information collected from the environment to adjust strategies
	Subsumes: Flexibility, compensatory behavior, and dynamic reallocation of functions
Shared situational awareness	Process by which team members develop shared models of the team's internal and external context
	Subsumes: Situational awareness, development of systems awareness, and shared problem model development
Performance monitoring, backup behavior, feedback	Capability of team members to give, seek, and receive task instructive feedback
	Subsumes: Intramember feedback, mutual performance monitoring, and procedure maintenance
Team leadership	Capability to direct and coordinate team members, assess team performance, allocate tasks, motivate subordinates, plan and organize, and maintain a positive team environment
	Subsumes: Task structuring, mission analysis, and motivation of others
Interpersonal relations	Capability to optimize the quality of team members' interactions
	Subsumes: Conflict resolution, cooperation, morale building, and boundary spanning
Coordination	Process by which team personnel resources, material resources, and responses are organized to ensure tasks are integrated, synchronized, and completed in time
	Subsumes: Task organization, task interaction, and timing and activity planning
Communication	Process via which information is clearly and accurately exchanged between two or more team members in the prescribed manner and with the proper terminology; also ability to clarify or acknowledge receipt of information
	Subsumes: Information exchange and consulting with others
Decision making	Capability to collect and integrate information, employ sound judgment, recognize alternatives, identify best solutions, and evaluate consequences
	Subsumes: Problem assessment and solving, planning, metacognition, and implementation

Note. Based on Cannon-Bowers, Tannenbaum, Salas, & Volpe (1995).

can be clustered into eight broad dimensions (Cannon-Bowers, Tannenbaum, Salas, & Volpe, 1995). The eight skill dimensions that promote effective teamwork are adaptability, shared situational awareness, performance monitoring and backup behavior, team leadership, interpersonal relations, coordination, communication, and decision making. These eight team skill dimensions, together with their definitions and component subskills, are illustrated in Table 13.2. Because

TABLE 13.3
Team Knowledge Competencies

Process Knowledges	Definition
Cue–strategy associations	Association of cues in the environment to appropriate coordination strategies
Task-specific teammate characteristics	Task-related competencies, preferences, tendencies, strengths, and weaknesses of teammates
Shared task models	Shared models of the situation and appropriate strategies for coping with task demands
Team mission, objectives, norms, and resources	Meaningful only for responding to a specific team and task; when one changes, knowledge must be adjusted to incorporate new team members and task demands
Task sequencing	Integrating task inputs according to team and task demands
Accurate task models	Team members must interpret task information and demands in a similar manner
Accurate problem models	Correct understanding of a problem including goals, information cues, strategies, and member roles
Team role interaction patterns	How teams communicate and arrive at decisions
Teamwork skills	Ability to comprehend the required skills and behaviors necessary for successful team performance
Boundary-spanning roles	Knowledge of how a team manages its interactions with other units and non-team members
Team orientation	Process by which information relevant to task accomplishment is generated and disseminated to team members

Note. Based on Salas and Cannon-Bowers (2000).

teamwork is thought to comprise knowledges, skills, and attitudes, later efforts served to delineate a set of common knowledge dimensions (see Table 13.3). Finally, building upon the work of Guzzo, Yost, Campbell, and Shea (1993), Salas and Cannon-Bowers (2000) listed seven attitudinal dimensions of teamwork (see Table 13.4).

While the work of Salas, Cannon-Bowers and colleagues has served to advance the field by making the argument for clear, concise definitions and consistency in operationalization of teamwork variables, another advance has recently been made. In light of many researchers arguing for the need to take into account the temporal dynamics that occur within teams, Marks et al. (2001) advanced an alternative team process taxonomy that proposes three classes of team processes (action, transition, and interpersonal), which are displayed in two recursive phases (action and transition) (see Table 13.5). The team action phase is marked by goal-directed task accomplishment behavior, whereas team members are concerned with evaluatory and planning activities in transition phases. Interpersonal processes occur throughout both action and transition phases and serve to support the specific processes occurring within these two phases.

TABLE 13.4
Team Attitude Competencies

Process Attitudes	Definition
Motivation	Process by which team objectives are defined and the team is energized to achieve the objectives
Collective efficacy and potency	Belief that the team can perform effectively as a unit when given specific task demands
Shared vision	Commonly held attitude regarding the direction, goals, and mission of a team
Team cohesion	Total field of forces that act on members to remain in a group; an attraction to the team as a means of task accomplishment
Mutual trust	An attitude held by team members regarding the aura, mood, or climate of the team's internal environment
Collective orientation	Belief that the team approach is better than the individual one
Importance of teamwork	The attitudes that the team members have toward working as a team

Note. Based on Salas and Cannon-Bowers (2000).

After reviewing the team process taxonomies (Tables 13.2–13.5), it is clear that there are more similarities than differences among the actual proposed processes. For example, several of the processes proposed by Salas et al. (2000), such as coordination and performance monitoring, have direct analogues in the model proposed by Marks et al. (2001). In addition, a majority of the other eight processes proposed by Marks et al. could be neatly classified as subskills and subsumed under the broad skill competency dimensions presented by Salas et al. (see Tables 13.2 and 13.5). Although the labels assigned to the competencies may differ at a surface level, the underlying teamwork processes are relatively identical. However, although the processes are indeed similar, there remain some fundamental differences between the two taxonomic initiatives. Perhaps the most important distinction between the two programs of research lies in the temporally anchored nature of Marks et al.'s model of team performance.

EMERGING TEAMWORK PRINCIPLES

As team members think, do, and feel (i.e., cognitions, behaviors, and attitudes) during task performance episodes, they dynamically apply their individual competencies to meet collective goals. After nearly two decades of systematically investigating teams, several key principles have emerged regarding what constitutes effective teamwork. For example, effective taskwork is an essential but not sufficient condition for team performance; teamwork skills are also needed (McIntyre & Salas, 1995). In addition, effective teams optimize resources as they develop

TABLE 13.5
Team Skill Competencies

Process Skills	Definition
Transition processes	
Mission analysis formulation and planning	Interpretation and evaluation of the team's mission, including identification of its main tasks as well as the operative environmental conditions and team resources available for mission execution
Goal specification	Identification and prioritization of goals and subgoals for mission accomplishment
Strategy formulation	Development of alternative courses of action for mission accomplishment
Action processes	
Monitoring progress toward goals	Tracking task and progress toward mission accomplishment, interpreting system information in terms of what needs to be accomplished for goal attainment, and transmitting progress to team members
Systems monitoring	Tracking team resources and environmental conditions as they relate to mission accomplishment, which involves (a) internal systems monitoring (tracking team resources such as personnel and equipment) and (b) environmental monitoring (tracking the environmental condition relevant to the team)
Team monitoring and backup behavior	Assisting team members to perform their tasks; assistance may occur by (a) providing a teammate verbal feedback or coaching, (b) helping a teammate behaviorally in carrying out actions, or (c) assuming and completing a task for a teammate
Coordination	Orchestrating the sequence and timing of interdependent actions
Interpersonal processes	
Conflict management	Preemptive conflict management involves establishing conditions to prevent, control, or guide team conflict before it occurs; reactive conflict management involves working through task and interpersonal disagreements among team members
Motivation and confidence building	Generating and preserving a sense of collective confidence, motivation, and task-based cohesion with regard to mission accomplishment
Affect management	Regulating member emotions during mission accomplishment, including (but not limited to) social cohesion, frustration, and excitement

Note. From "A Temporally Based Framework and Taxonomy of Team Process," by M. A. Marks, J. E. Mathieu, and S. J. Zaccaro, 2001, *Academy of Management Review, 26,* pp. 356–376. Copyright by Academy of Management. Adapted with permission.

and transform over time. Several of the most critical findings and principles are described in Table 13.6; we elaborate on a representative sample.

Principle 1. Teamwork is characterized by a set of flexible and adaptive behaviors, cognitions, and attitudes. This principle suggests team members actively gather and capitalize on information from their environment to adaptively alter what they are doing, thinking, and feeling. In a similar fashion, teamwork

TABLE 13.6
Teamwork Findings and Principles

Findings

Teamwork and taskwork are different components of team performance

Teamwork is affected by a number of external and internal factors

Effective teamwork requires that team members amass competencies for their specific team task before receiving training

There are a number of teamwork skills that are nonexclusive (generic)

Effective teams exhibit a strong feeling of "teamness"

Teams that are motivated and think about their efficacy will stretch themselves to attain what individuals would not contemplate as possible

Effective teams optimize resources

Teams develop and transform over time

Mature teams are composed of members who can foresee one another's needs

Mature teams depend less on overt communication to perform effectively

Because all teams are not equal, contextual factors as well as the task that is facing the team must be considered when deciding the importance of the various competencies needed within a particular team

Teams change over time

Principles

Teamwork is influenced by multiple environmental, situational, and input factors

Teamwork is characterized by a set of flexible and adaptive behaviors, cognitions, and attitudes

Teamwork requires that members monitor each other's behaviors and action and feel free to provide and accept feedback based on monitoring behavior

Teamwork is characterized by members being willing and able to back fellow members up during operations

Teamwork involves clear and concise communication

Teamwork requires coordination of collective and interdependent action

Teamwork requires leadership skills that enable the direction, planning, and coordination of activities

Teamwork implies that members provide feedback to and accept it from one another

Teamwork involves effective communication among members, which often involves closed-loop communication

Teamwork implies the willingness, preparedness, and proclivity to backup fellow members during operations

Teamwork involves group members' collectively viewing of themselves as a group whose success depends on their interaction

Teamwork means fostering within-team interdependence

Teamwork is characterized by a flexible repertoire of behavioral skills as a function of circumstances

Teamwork requires team member expectations and behavior to be driven by shared and accurate knowledge structures

Teamwork requires team members to actively manage conflict in order to create and maintain interpersonal and intrateam relationships

was defined as the "mechanism by which members are able to adapt and adjust the timing of action in order to meet the demands of other team members, thereby resulting in coordinated, synchronized collective action" (Salas et al., 2000, p. 344). Strategies for promoting the adaptive behaviors, cognitions, and attitudes that constitute teamwork are addressed in greater detail later in this chapter.

Principle 2.   Teamwork requires members to monitor each other's behavior and feel free about providing and accepting feedback based on this monitoring. This principle begets the need for teammates to continuously engage in mutual performance monitoring and use information gleaned from that process to provide targeted intramember feedback. Performance monitoring is critical to adaptive team performance and the reduction of catastrophic errors. Nowhere is this more salient and sobering than when the National Transportation Safety Board attributes airline fatalities to a lack of performance monitoring and intramember feedback.

Principle 3.   Effective teamwork requires members to engage in backup behavior. This principle suggests team members must have the willingness, capability, and preparedness to assume the duties of their fellow teammates. Teams that successfully engage in backup behavior will achieve a level of performance greater than the sum of its individual members. Information derived from mutual performance monitoring and environmental scanning drives the dynamic reallocation of resources and functions. For example, effective teams have members who opportunistically display compensatory behaviors such as providing and asking for assistance (Cannon-Bowers et al., 1995). Providing assistance to fellow team members can take on several forms (e.g., coaching, feedback, helping, assuming duties). Each of these behaviors serves to facilitate adaptive team performance. Furthermore, as technology fuels an accelerating rate of change, team member backup behavior will be even more critical for minimizing the process loss incurred from shifting contingencies and task overload.

Principle 4.   Teamwork involves clear and concise communication. Recent technological advances have vastly increased the capability of team members to engage in intrateam and interteam communication. There are severe negative consequences for organizations that fail to strategically manage team communication. For example, Salas et al. (2000) suggested that communication breakdowns are the second most frequently cited cause of teamwork failures and accidents. Furthermore, research evidence suggests teams can increase their effectiveness through the use of closed-looped communication (Bowers, Jentsch, Salas, & Braun, 1998; McIntyre & Salas, 1995). Closed-looped communication is built upon a strategy of verification that ensures that the message sent was received and interpreted as intended. The process of closed-looped communication is critical to team effectiveness in part because technological advances have increased (a) the number of communication media, (b) the volume of information, and (c) the complexity of the information being communicated between, within and across individual team members, teams, and multiteam systems.

Principle 5.   Teamwork requires the coordination of collective interdependent team member behavior. As illustrated by the examples offered at the opening of this chapter, team members' failure to act in a coordinated fashion can have devastating proximal and distal consequences. Team coordination was defined as the "process by which team resources, activities and responses are organized to ensure that tasks are integrated, synchronized and completed within established temporal constraints" (Cannon-Bowers et al., 1995, p. 344). A more recent and succinct definition of coordination described the team process as "orchestrating the sequence and timing of interdependent actions" (Marks et al., 2001). Accumulating empirical evidence suggests that coordination facilitates both team performance and effectiveness (Guzzo & Shea, 1992; Swezey & Salas, 1992). Furthermore, results suggest implicit coordination facilitates a team's capability to maintain high levels of performance, even when subjected to high levels of workload and stress (Kleinman & Sefarty, 1989). Implicit coordination occurs when team members dynamically reallocate resources among one another without being primed to do so by action plans or in reaction to explicit requests.

Principle 6. Teamwork requires team member expectations and behavior to be driven by shared and accurate knowledge structures. Teamwork is facilitated when team members develop compatible and accurate clusters of instantiated knowledge structures (i.e., shared mental models). There are many types of shared mental models (e.g., equipment, task, team, team interaction, and problem or situation). Each of these models contributes to what team members attend to in their environments and how they react to recognized environmental cues. Research suggests shared mental models serve to facilitate coordinated team action (Burke & Zaccaro, 2000; Heffner, Mathieu, & Goodwin, 1998). In addition to promoting team coordination, shared problem models may help facilitate the development of shared situational awareness. Shared situational awareness was defined as "the process by which team members develop compatible models of the team's internal and external environment" (Cannon-Bowers et al., 1995, p. 344).

Principle 7. Teamwork requires team members to actively manage conflict to create and maintain harmonious interpersonal and interteam relationships. This principle suggests that every team member must make a concerted effort to contribute to the collective social system within which team members operate. Specifically, team members must consciously manage interpersonal relationships because good relations can prompt the voicing of concerns, the giving of feedback, and the implementation of change. Interpersonal relations were defined as a team's "ability to optimize the quality of team members interactions through resolution of dissent, utilization of cooperative behaviors, or the use of motivational reinforcing statements" (Cannon-Bowers et al., 1995, p. 344). Similarly, the process of conflict management was also conceptualized by Marks et al. (2001) as either (1) preemptive, which involves "establishing conditions to prevent, control, or guide team conflict before it occurs," or (2) reactive, which involves "working through task and interpersonal disagreements amongst team members" (p. 363). Research also suggests that interpersonal skills such as conflict resolution facilitate team coordination (Cannon-Bowers & Salas, 1998).

Principle 8.   Teamwork is influenced by multiple environmental, situational, and input factors. This principle suggests that the relative contribution of any given competency to teamwork is contingent upon multiple factors such as team type and task characteristics. Essentially, both the nature of the team and the context within which the team is operating interactively drive the criticality of any given competency. Another perspective was advanced by Sundstrom (1999), who proposed that team type (e.g., action, parallel) affects team competency requirements. A third conceptualization suggests the specificity or generality of required team and task competencies drives their importance for teamwork (Cannon-Bowers et al., 1995).

Principle 9.   Teamwork requires leadership skill that enables the direction, planning and coordination of activities. Essentially this principle suggests that if teams are to create and sustain teamwork processes, strong leadership will have to guide the way. One way for team leaders to facilitate adaptive performance is by providing clear direction to team members. Specifically, leaders both provide clear communication and create enabling performance situations lending to the creation of team coherence (i.e., shared affect, behavior, and cognition). Clear direction is proposed to be an outcome of a leader's effort to structure and integrate his or her subordinates' tasks with the collective mission (Hackman & Walton, 1986). Successful integration of team member tasks with the collective mission facilitates the development of subordinate situational awareness.

TEAM TRAINING

As illustrated by the foregoing principles, "teamwork is the seamless integration of a number of KSAs" (Salas & Cannon-Bowers, 2000, p. 318), and we know that this integration does not occur automatically—teams need to be trained. Although historically the design and delivery of interventions to create and sustain effective teamwork have been guided more by art than by science, things are beginning to change. As efforts to systematically collect what is known about teams and team training increase, those responsible for designing team training are able to draw upon scientifically grounded theories (e.g., shared mental models) to support training initiatives.

The operationalization of team training has also been more clearly defined. For example, team training is not a location, single program, simulation, team building, individual training, or unguided practice. Team training is a set of theoretically derived tools and methodologies, which, when carefully blended with a set of required competencies and training objectives, forms an instructional strategy

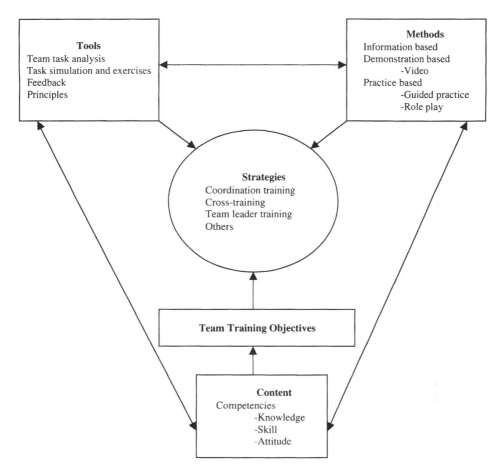

FIG. 13.1. Model of the structure of team training. Based on Salas and Cannon-Bowers (1997).

(see Fig. 13.1) (Salas & Cannon-Bowers, 1997). Team training targets team processes and outcomes by providing the opportunity to receive structured practice and feedback in a dynamic environment.

In addition to defining team training, recent research has resulted in empirically and theoretically grounded findings, tips, guidelines, and principles. Although tips and guidelines are important (Salas et al., 2002), we focus on a brief review of several general principles that serve to guide team training interventions (see Table 13.7). One of the most fundamental principles of team training states that training must include information presentation, demonstration of teamwork behaviors, practice, and feedback. Furthermore, teams should be provided with immediate feedback in the training environment. Another important principle suggests that to maximize transfer of training to performance environments, trainees should

TABLE 13.7
Team Training Principles

Team training must be skills based
Team leader training improves the team's ability to coordinate
Team training must focus on mutual dependency and interaction
Individual proficiency must precede team proficiency
Cross-training is effective in clarifying roles and building shared expectations
Stress exposure training is effective in teaching team members to manage stress
Team coordination training is effective in teaching team members to adjust their coordination
  strategies
Team training must facilitate information presentation, demonstration of teamwork behaviors,
  opportunities to practice, and diagnostic feedback

---

receive formal instruction on technical skills prior to developing teamwork skills. Researchers and practitioners alike have begun to apply these general principles to the design and implementation of team training. Next, we review some of the instructional strategies that are theoretically grounded in the principles of teamwork and team training.

Team Instructional Strategies

A variety of team training strategies exists (see Table 13.8), which target both individual-level phenomena (e.g., stress exposure, assertiveness, and metacognition) and team-level processes (e.g., situation-based training, team coordination, cross, team self-correction, on-the-job training). The choice and ultimate form of any given strategy are shaped by a number of factors such as available resources and technology, delivery mechanism, targeted competencies and stage of team development. Some of these instructional strategies are reviewed in greater detail next.

Team coordination training, also known as crew resource management training, has been widely applied in the aviation, medical, and military communities (Helmreich & Davies, 1997). This instructional strategy targets the development of teamwork through the creation of synchronization among team members. Multiple competencies can be targeted with team coordination training (e.g., adaptability, assertiveness, coordination, decision making, and leadership). This strategy typically combines the methods of lecture, demonstration, practice, and feedback. Team coordination training is typically delivered to trainees for up to 1 week and research supports its effectiveness in terms of positive trainee reactions, enhanced learning, and behavioral change (Salas, Burke, Bowers, & Wilson, 2001).

Scenario-based training is another common instructional strategy that has been utilized with teams operating in complex environments (Fowlkes, Dwyer, Oser, & Salas, 1998). Scenario-based training embeds trigger events into a priori

TABLE 13.8

Team Training Instructional Strategies

Instructional Strategy	Description
Cross-training	Teammates develop an understanding for the tasks, duties, and responsibilities of coworkers; strategy targets team members' interpositional knowledge and shared mental models for development; increases team coordination and reduces process loss from change
Team coordination training	Also known as crew resource management; focuses on teaching team members about basic process underlying teamwork; strategy widely applied in aviation, medical, and military communities; targets mutual performance monitoring and backup behavior
Team self-correction training	Team members are taught techniques for monitoring and then categorizing their own behaviors as to the degree of its effectiveness; this process generates instructive feedback so that team members can review performance episodes and correct deficiencies; additional knowledges, skills, and attitudes target initiative and communication
Team building	Targets role clarification, goal setting, problem solving, or interpersonal relations for improvement; however, recent meta-analytic evidence suggests team building only increases performance when targeting subjective criteria such as role clarification (Salas, Rozell, Mullen, & Driskell, 1999)
Assertiveness training	Utilizes behavioral modeling techniques to demonstrate both assertive and nonassertive behaviors; provides multiple practice and feedback opportunities for trainees
Metacognition training	Targets trainee's executive monitoring and self regulatory cognitive processes for development; training develops metacognitive skills, which serve to regulate cognitive abilities such as inductive and deductive reasoning
Stress exposure training	Targets trainee knowledge of both potential stressors and coping strategies; develops trainee insight into the link between stressors, perceived stress, and individual affect and performance
On-the-job training	Targets trainee psychomotor and procedurally based cognitive skills for development; training occurs on actual job as opposed to the typical artificial site
Scenario-based training	Scenario-based training incorporates trigger events that elicit targeted behavior in contextually rich environments; A product of this initiative is a framework that models the components of scenario-based training design; see Figure 13.2

defined scenarios. In turn, these trigger events serve to elicit targeted behaviors in a contextually rich environment. The first step in designing a scenario-based training intervention is to determine both the taskwork and teamwork competencies required by the trainee. The accumulated information then serves as a platform from which to derive training objectives. Training objectives in turn facilitate the creation of exercises and events, which are subsequently melded into an overall curriculum. The final step in this process illustrates how information collected from the measurement system is subsequently fed back to the trainee and his or her team.

Cross-training is an instructional strategy that has been demonstrated to promote coordination, communication, and team performance (Salas, Cannon-Bowers, & Johnston, 1997). Cross-training is built on the tenets of shared mental model theory. Shared mental model theory proposes that team members' shared knowledge structures serve to facilitate coordinated, adaptive performance. Training programs that utilize cross-training expose participants to other team member's roles, responsibilities, and task requirements to develop shared mental models. One intervention that is built on a platform of cross-training is the Team Model Trainer (TMT). The TMT can be utilized to train team leadership and is discussed in greater detail in the team leader training and development section.

TEAM LEADERSHIP

Although much is known about teams and team training, one area that has been relatively neglected within the team literature is the role of the team leader. Although it has been argued that leaders have considerable impact on individual, team, and organizational effectiveness (Klimoski & Jones, 1995; Tannenbaum, Salas, & Cannon-Bowers, 1996; Zaccaro, Rittman, & Marks, 2001), the functional role that leaders play within a team as well as the methods by which to train team leaders have remained relatively unexplored. In this section, we discuss both the underlying theory and the supporting research evidence relevant to how team leaders affect team affectiveness.

Team leaders are particularly important for promoting the dynamic throughput processes that constitute teamwork and facilitate adaptive performance (Entin, Sefarty, & Deckert, 1994; Kozlowski, Gully, Salas, & Cannon-Bowers, 1996). For example, team leaders drive team performance and effectiveness by communicating a clear direction, creating enabling performance environments, and providing process coaching (Hackman & Walton, 1986). Furthermore, team leaders serve to train and develop team members' individual and team-level competencies (Kozlowski et al., 1996). In addition, research suggests that the importance of leadership increases as the problems faced increase in complexity (Jacobs & Jaques, 1987). Perhaps this explains why such a wide variety of leadership theories exist (Bass, 1990).

Historically speaking, we know quite a lot about both leadership and teams, but have only recently begun to explore and understand team leadership. This is a problem because most current conceptualizations of leadership strictly describe how leaders go about managing their individual subordinates, ignoring in large part both teams and team processes. However, there are several important distinctions between leadership as it is traditionally described and the more recent concept of team leadership. For example, Kozlowski (2002) suggested leadership is typically fixed to a situation, whereas team leadership dynamically varies within the situation. In addition, leadership theories traditionally assume subordinate roles and linkages as loosely connected, whereas team leadership acknowledges the tight interdependencies and subsequent coordination requirements of team members. These differences in perspectives regarding task characteristics, member Linkages, and contingencies combine to impose distinctive emphases between the approaches. For example, the emphasis of traditional leadership theories has been on fitting the leader to the situation, task, or subordinates. This is markedly different from team leadership, where the emphasis is on structuring and regulating team processes to meet shifting internal and external contingencies.

Recently a consensus is beginning to form around conceptualizing team leadership from a functional perspective (Fleishman et al., 1991; Hackman, 2002; Zaccaro et al., 2001). Based upon both sociotechnical and open systems theory, the functional approach to leadership suggests that a team leader's primary directive is to "do, or get done, whatever is not being adequately handled for group needs" (McGrath, 1962, p. 5). Leadership from a functional perspective is a form of social problem solving that promotes coordinated, adaptive team performance by facilitating goal definition and attainment.

Under the functional perspective, team leadership can be described, at a general level, as a series of steps: problem identification and diagnosis, generation of solutions, and implementation of a chosen solution. This process is accomplished through the leader's generic responses to social problems. These generic responses are captured in four broad categories: (a) information search and structuring, (b) information use in problem solving, (c) managing personnel resources, and (d) managing material resources. The first of these four dimensions, information search and structuring, highlights the leader's role as a boundary spanner in his or her effort to seek out, acquire, evaluate, and organize goal-supporting information. The second dimension, information use in problem solving, describes a leader's application of a "best-fitting" solution to the problem at hand. As the team leader applies a chosen solution to a social problem, both personnel and material resources are called on and utilized in the process. Finally, team leaders dynamically manage both material and personnel resources. For example, a team leader manages material resources by ensuring the team has the proper equipment to accomplish the task. However, unless the team leader also acts to manage personnel resources by providing team members with appropriate training, team effectiveness will remain elusive.

These four dimensions and their corresponding 13 subdimensions (see Table 13.9) describe the behaviors that team leaders partake in to solve complex problems on the way to team goal attainment. The leader behaviors illustrate what needs to get done rather than what should get done to facilitate adaptive team performance. Each of the behaviors is sufficiently general enough to be applied sequentially and simultaneously to solve social problems in any team performance context.

TABLE 13.9
Functional Leadership Behaviors

Dimension	Subdimensions
Information search and structuring	Acquiring information
	Organizing and evaluating information
	Feedback and control
Information use in problem solving	Identifying needs and requirements
	Planning and coordinating
	Communicating information
Managing personnel resources	Obtaining and allocating personnel resources
	Developing personnel resources
	Motivating personnel resources
	Utilizing and monitoring personnel resources
Managing material resources	Obtaining and allocating material resources
	Maintaining material resources
	Utilizing and monitoring material resources

Summary

Synthesizing the foregoing theory and evidence suggests that at a global level, team leadership can be described in terms of two functional roles, task and developmental (Kozlowski, Gully, McHugh, Salas, & Cannon-Bowers, 1996). This suggests that team leaders either (a) display task accomplishment behavior or (b) serve to create an enabling performance environment for the development of team member KSAs. These two broad functional roles are proposed to subsume the four leadership behavior dimensions manifested in functional leadership theory. Specifically, three functional leader behavior dimensions (information search and structuring, information use in problem solving, and managing material resources) are conceptualized as functions leaders fill when adopting a task role, whereas the functional dimension of managing personnel resources is conceptualized as being filled when leaders adopt a developmental role. In essence, all of this can be interpreted as suggesting team leaders (a) foster successful within-team interdependence, (b) accept and value input from team members, (c) collect performance information and provide task feedback, (d) facilitate a collective mission focus, (e) explain the rationale for their decisions, actions, and thoughts, (f) plan future contingencies with team members, (g) help team members gain self-efficacy and mutual trust, (h) motivate team cohesion, (i) serve as a model of teamwork, (j) provide a supportive climate for teamwork, and (k) articulate clear and precise goals.

TEAM LEADER DEVELOPMENT

A majority of large organizations currently employ a three-pronged approach to training and developing their leaders. The training and development system typically consists of (a) formal institutional education, (b) operational assignments, and

(c) self-development. All of these three components are critical vehicles through which leaders develop KSAs (Sullivan, 1999) and thus each is described in greater detail in the following sections.

Team Leader Development Via Formal Training

Most organizational initiatives designed to target team leader competence rely upon formal training. Leaders participating in formal training can expect to experience a wide variety of instructional strategies, tools, and methods. For example, although cross-training is typically utilized to train team members, some programs, such as the TMT, can also be adopted for training team leadership skill. The TMT is a low-cost, personal computer-based simulator designed to target interpositional knowledge for development. Accumulating empirical research suggests the TMT and other interventions that utilize cross-training strategies promote the development of interpositional knowledge, which in turn facilitates coordination, communication, and team performance (Duncan, Cannon-Bowers, Johnston, & Salas, 1995; Marks, Sabella, Burke, & Zaccaro, 2002).

Leaders attempting to promote team adaptability will also need to be trained to display executive-level critical thinking skills such as metacognition. One conceptualization of metacognition defines it as the "executive functions that control the application and operation of cognitive abilities and skills" (e.g., inductive and deductive reasoning) (Zaccaro, 2001, p. 43). Leaders who engage in metacognitive processes have higher levels of performance on a variety of criteria (e.g., leadership and problem solving) (Kozlowski, 1998; Marshall et al., 2000). Recent empirical evidence suggests that leader metacognitive skill promotes adaptive team performance (Marsh, Kiechel-Koles, Boyce, & Zaccaro, 2001). In addition, leaders who promote collective team member metacognitive processing contribute to higher levels of team performance (Kozlowski, 1998; Tannenbaum, Smith-Jentsch, & Behson, 1998). Research also suggests that leader metacognition interacts with work experiences to predict tacit knowledge and social competency development (Banks, Bader, Fleming, Zaccaro, & Barber, 2001).

Leaders can be trained to effectively engage in metacognition and promote collective team metacognition (Cohen, Thompson, Adelman, Bresnick, & Riedel, 1999; Zaccaro et al., 2001). However, traditional training interventions are not typically designed to drive the development of either metacognitive or self-regulatory processes. Metacognitive training should focus on teaching leaders to increase their capability to engage in self-evaluation during both performance and transition episodes. The information delineated from self-monitoring and evaluation processes serves to facilitate the development and maintenance of leader mental models. This suggests metacognitive training can enhance adaptive performance both directly as well as indirectly, via its influence on the development of a leader's mental model(s), social intelligence, and tacit knowledge.

Recent theoretical conceptualizations of team leader training have focused on the importance of training leaders to promote continuous learning within teams. For example, Kozlowski et al. (1996) attempted to simultaneously model both the dynamic temporal processes that characterize team development and naturally occurring task variations. This approach to team leader training recognizes that teams operate within a temporally dynamic context that drives cyclical levels of high and low work loads and time pressure. An important implication of this framework is that it specifies multiple theoretically supported guidelines for the design and delivery of team leader training.

The framework of Kozlowski and colleagues implies that the formal training system may be viewed as a series of structured experiences embedded in multiple performance environments. Specifically, team leaders should integrate the team's learning cycle with both the stage of team development and natural cyclical variations in task performance requirements. In a similar fashion, there has been a growing interest in defining and understanding the key elements of a leader's work experiences so that operational assignments can be structured to maximally promote the development of leader KSAs. The process by which leaders develop KSAs outside the formal organizational training system is addressed in greater detail next.

Team Leader Development
Via Work Experiences

The formal organizational training system is one of three options that leaders can chose from to develop mission-critical KSAs. In addition to participating in traditional training interventions, leaders also need to use operational assignments to develop KSAs. This implies that leaders must proactively plan and manage their operational assignments to fully capitalize on available developmental opportunities. Operational assignments that are challenging and force a leader to stretch his or her self have been shown to create experiences that drive the development of requisite KSAs. Accumulating empirical evidence suggests that tacit knowledge derived from operational assignments is essential to leader learning and the subsequent development of KSAs (Banks et al., 2001; McCall, Lombardo, & Morrison, 1988; Tesluk, 1999; Tesluk, Dragoni, & Russell, 2002).

The experiential gain that leaders derive from operational assignments can be enhanced by creating career paths that include cross-unit rotation, expatriate assignments, and exposure to strategic competitor's and partner's business practices (Shamir & Ben Ari, 1999). Furthermore, Shamir and Ben Ari (1999) also suggest that organizations should implement a promotional system built on the concept of "boundary-spanning careers," whereby leaders circulate between several interorganizational branches and throughout other institutions. In addition, Yukl (1999) presented several strategies that can be employed to further maximize the amount of learning leaders derive from their work experiences, including special assignments, multirater feedback, developmental assessment centers, action learning, realistic field exercises, and after-action reviews. For example, action learning creates a linkage between formal training and experiences derived from operational work assignments. The process involves the target leader working on a project that calls for the application of KSAs learned in training. A coach or mentor who provides feedback and direction monitors progress on the project.

A final development lies within recent conceptualizations of challenging work experiences that have dichotomized the construct into those experiences that pose information complexity and those that pose social complexity (Bader, Fleming, Zaccaro, & Barber, 2002). Results from this research suggest these two types of experiences predict the development of unique sets of competencies. This implies that organizations must systematically link the KSAs they want to develop in leaders with specific types of operational experiences.

Team Leader Self-Development

Teams and team leaders operate in dynamic environments where success is contingent on implicit coordination and constant adaptation. Formal institutional training and operational assignments are necessary but insufficient components to achieving success in a global economy. As the rate of change accelerates, there is a growing impetus for team leaders to become the primary driver of their own development. The synergistic gains promised by teamwork can only be realized when both team members and team leaders opportunistically seek out, engage in, and actively craft their developmental experiences.

Conceptualizing team member and leader development in this fashion "blurs the distinction between training as a process separate from continuous learning within performance environments" (Kozlowski et al., 1996, p. 294). Essentially, this line of thinking suggests team leaders will need to engage in life-long learning in order to develop the KSAs required for adaptive performance and overall team effectiveness. This self-directed development agenda should serve to drive team leaders to seek out and participate in both formal institutional training programs and operational assignments that will provide specific opportunities for them to develop desired KSAs.

A technological revolution has created a set of circumstances where leaders can engage in "just-in-time" continuous self-development via Web-based distance learning. Certainly these Web-based training systems have tremendous potential, but caution is warranted because distance learning is not a panacea. For example, a number of questions have been raised regarding a process which is typically largely E electronic and devoid of the principles of learning. Furthermore, researchers have suggested that distributed performance and learning environments may lead to a sense of isolation (Driskell, Radtke, & Salas, in press) and or create obstacles to the development of social complexity (Day & Lance, chap. 3, this volume).

Throughout this chapter, we have repeatedly attempted to illustrate how technology is not an end in and of itself, and thus the design and delivery of Web-based training systems must be guided by the theories and principles delineated from the domains of distributive training, cognition, learning, and change. Fortunately, those concerned with delineating and applying theoretical grounded principles to enhance leader self-development have begun to illuminate the role of adult cognition in self-directed learning and growth (Halpern, chap. 6, this volume). Furthermore, empirical evidence suggests that providing trainees with adaptive guidance increases self-regulation, learning, and performance in complex contexts (Bell & Kozlowski, 2002).

Leaders pursuing self-development opportunities will increasingly need to engage in both self-regulatory and metacognitive processes. Specifically, leaders will have to fluidly monitor and adjust their use of cognitive abilities (e.g., critical reasoning) during learning and skill acquisition. Future training interventions should be constructed to promote metacognition by providing advanced organizers, learner control, and an environment that fosters learning goal orientations (Smith, Ford, & Kozlowski, 1997). Evidence suggests that embedded events can be utilized to trigger metacognitive monitoring and metacognitive control (Toney & Ford, 2001).

Summary

The rapidly changing nature of operating environments has created an impetus to rethink and reengineer our assumptions regarding both team and team leader training. All forms of training and development (e.g., institutional training, operational assignments, and self-development) will need to be increasingly coupled, coordinated, and proactively managed if leaders are to successfully develop all of the KSAs required for adaptive individual and team performance. In response to encountered economic and time pressures, organizations will continue to turn to technological solutions (e.g., distance learning and smart tutors) as a strategy for fulfilling the mantra of "better, faster, and cheaper." These ongoing changes raise questions that need to be addressed in future conceptual and empirical research endeavors. A sample of the most pertinent issues is illustrated in the next section.

KEY RESEARCH NEEDS AND FUTURE DIRECTIONS

Reflecting back on what is known about teams and team leadership, we believe that there are at least three central research needs that remain to be targeted within future initiatives: (a) the need to study team leadership "in the wild," (b) the need to design and test instructional strategies that will serve to develop team leader KSAs, and (c) the need to exploit developments in cognitive engineering, cognitive psychology, and naturalistic decision making for use in studying team leadership.

Research Need 1: Team Leadership Needs to Be Studied "in the Wild"

Although a relatively young field, much of what is known regarding team leadership is based on empirical studies conducted in laboratory settings using ad hoc teams. Although this line of research offers much to the study of team leadership, because due to the increasing fluidity of teams within complex environments, many teams operating in the wild can be conceptualized as ad hoc, there remains a need to study intact teams. For example, Kozlowski et al. (1996) proposed a conceptual framework that depicts leadership functions as differing across the life span of teams. Specifically, Kozlowski et al. proposed that team leaders occupy two primary functions (task and developmental) and that across the course of team development, leaders progress from mentor to instructor to coach and finally to facilitator. However, because most empirical studies of team leadership have been conducted with teams that have a relatively short life span (i.e., laboratory teams), this framework has yet to be empirically tested.

Additionally, although the laboratory serves as a leveraging block, experts use different decision strategies than novices. In essence, team leadership created within a laboratory is often at the level of a novice, whereas when team leadership is studied in the wild, there is more of an expertise flavor. Studying team leadership in the wild, can also lead to many other advantages, such as examining how the natural work environment can be used to facilitate adaptive team leaders. Further related questions are (a) how does team leadership manifest itself outside of a laboratory environment, (b) what is the effect of team leadership on team processes in the wild, (c) what factors facilitate or serve as barriers to team leadership within naturalistic settings (i.e., leadership in context), and (d) what are the differences in team leadership as one moves up the organizational hierarchy?

In addition, we need to extend what we have learned within the laboratory to "the wild." For example, whereas recent laboratory work (Marks et al., 2000) suggested how leaders affect the effectiveness of mission briefings, future research needs to examine how leaders can be trained to deliver effective mission briefings. In addition, research needs to examine how leaders can facilitate effective briefings during the natural variations in task cycle requirements that occur in performance environments.

Research Need 2: Instructional Strategies Are Needed That Promote Team Leader KSAs

The second need regards both refining current and creating new instructional strategies that can be utilized to promote the development of team leader KSAs. Specifically, we need to know more about how interventions such as on-the-job training, cognitive training, adaptability training, metacognition training, distance training, and simulation can be made maximally effective for developing team leaders.

One avenue that deserves immediate consideration regards how best to utilize event-based instructional strategies to promote the development of leader metacognition. Specifically, this approach would seek to blend what we know about both metacognition and event-based training into a unified, theoretically grounded instructional strategy. The objective of this research should focus on delineating principles and strategies that can later be utilized to guide the development and placement of embedded trigger events into training simulations for the purpose of eliciting trainee metacognition and subsequent self-regulation.

Another area that requires closer scrutiny concerns both the nature of and how to develop leadership in distributive environments (Zaccaro, Ardison, & Orvis, chap. 11, this volume). A technological revolution has created a situation within which team members no longer need to be colocated. Distributive teams afford a number of clear advantages to organizations and thus have experienced explosive popularity and growth. Leaders that are geographically dispersed will face considerable challenges to providing clear and engaging direction to subordinates. Furthermore, distributed team leaders will be hard pressed to create natural training opportunities for widely dispersed team members. At this time, it is not clear how leadership will evolve and be displayed in distributed environments. This suggests that in order to fully capitalize on the benefits that distributed teams offer, we need to develop a science of distributed team performance and training. A major thrust of this effort should be aimed at developing principles of distributive learning that can serve as a platform for the design and delivery of future training interventions.

Another related question concerns how best to structure complex simulation scenarios and measure performance within them (Dwyer, Fowlkes, Oser, Salas, & Lane, 1997). Whereas simulation is indeed a valuable tool for designers of team training, research is needed to investigate how current technologies can be integrated with instructional objectives and feedback to systematically facilitate skill development. Organizations seldom go the extra yard to conduct follow-up studies to determine whether newly acquired trainee KSAs transfer to the performance environment. This is a potential problem because organizations implementing training programs built around complex, networked simulations are often falsely assume that simulation in and of itself is equilavalent to training (Salas, Cannon-Bowers et al., 1999).

Research Need 3: Advances from Cognitive Psychology Need to Be Incorporated

There have been many advances made within the fields of cognitive engineering and cognitive psychology in terms of tools for knowledge elicitation and the measurement of knowledge structures. Team leadership already has a cognitive base, and knowledge structures have been shown to be a key driver of adaptive behavior. In fact, as operating environments become more complex and ambiguous, the role of cognitive competencies will increase in importance. Therefore, developments within cognitive engineering and psychology need to be extended to the study of team leadership. In addition, recent advances in decision-making theory (e.g., naturalistic decision making and recognition-primed decision making) need to be understood in terms of team leadership. For example, research has begun to indicate that when experts make decisions within complex, time-compressed situations, the rational model of decision making is not adhered to (Lipshitz, Klein, Orasanu, & Salas, 2001). The findings from this research need to be leveraged against to examine how team leaders' cognitive frameworks guide their decisions in naturalistic contexts.

CONCLUDING COMMENTS

The past two decades has shown a tremendous increase in the complexity of organizational environments and the use of teams as a key strategy by which to handle this complexity. The marked rise in the use of teams has inspired research to understand the factors and competencies related to team effectiveness and how to train these competencies. These efforts have resulted in theoretically sound and empirically based principles, guidelines, and tips for those responsible for team development and training.

Despite all of the advances made, the impact that team leaders can have on the promotion and maintenance of taskwork and teamwork competencies remains relatively unexplored. Although many have begun to argue for the importance of team leadership as a key determinant of team performance, we are only beginning to understand the functional roles and actions through which leaders promote the requisite shared behaviors, feelings, and cognitions needed for team effectiveness. Furthermore, even fewer investigatory initiatives have been undertaken to explore how to promote team leadership competencies through developmental experiences (e.g., formal training, work experiences, and self-development). This leaves many opportunities to explore within the relatively young area of team leadership. In doing so, it is vital that we leverage against what we know, expand our horizons to include concepts and methodologies from other domains (e.g., cognitive engineering, cognitive science, and decision making), and begin to examine team leadership in the wild.

REFERENCES

Anderson, H., & Sandza, R. (1987). A sting in the Gulf. Newsweek, *110*, 24–27.
Bader, P. K., Fleming, P. J., Zaccaro, S. J., & Barber, H. F. (April, 2002). *The developmental impact of work experiences on adaptability*. Presented at the 17th annual conference of the Society of Industrial Organizational Psychology, Toronto, Canada.

Banks, D., Bader, P., Fleming, P., Zaccaro, S., & Barber, H. (April, 2001). *Leader adaptability: The role of work experiences and leader attributes.* Paper presented at the 16th annual conference of the Society for Industrial and Organizational Psychology, San Diego, CA.

Bass, B. (1990). *Bass & Stodgill's handbook of leadership* (3rd ed.). New York: Free Press.

Bell, B. S., & Kozlowski, S. W. J. (2002). Adaptive guidance: Enhancing self-regulation, knowledge and performance in technology-based training. *Personnel Psychology, 55,* 267–306.

Bowers, C. A., Jentsch, F., Salas, E., & Braun, C. C. (1998). Analyzing communication sequences for team training needs assessment. *Human Factors, 40,* 672–679.

Burke, C. S., Volpe, C., Cannon-Bowers, J. A., & Salas, E. (1993). *So what is teamwork anyway? A synthesis of the team process literature.* Paper presented at the 39th annual meeting of the Southeastern Psychological Association, Atlanta, GA.

Burke, C. S., & Zaccaro, S. J. (2003). The influence of leader sense-making and sense-giving on team mental models and team adaptation (unpublished manuscript).

Cannon-Bowers, J. A., & Salas, E. (1998). Individual and team decision making under stress: Theoretical underpinnings. In J. A. Cannon-Bowers & E. Salas (Eds.), *Making decisions under stress: Implications for individual and team training* (pp. 17–38). Washington, DC: American Psychological Association.

Cannon-Bowers, J. A., Tannenbaum, S. I., Salas, E., & Volpe, C. E. (1995). Defining team competencies and establishing team training requirements. In R. A. Guzzo & E. Salas (Eds.), *Team effectiveness and decision making in organizations* (pp. 333–380). San Francisco, CA: Jossey

Cohen, M. S., Thompson, B. B., Adelman, L., Bresnick, T. A., & Riedel, S. L. (1999). *Training battlefield critical thinking and initiative.* Arlington, VA: Cognitive Technologies.

Cullen, D. (1990). The public inquiry into the Piper Alpha disaster. CM 1310, HMSo.

Driskell, J. E., Radtke, P. H., & Salas, E. (in press). *Virtual teams: Effects of technological mediation on team processes.* To appear in: Group Dynamics

Duncan, P. C., Cannon-Bowers, J. A., Johnston, J., & Salas, E. (June, 1995). *Using a simulated team to model teamwork skills: The team model trainer.* Presented at the World Conference on Educational Multimedia and Hypermedia, Graz, Austria.

Dwyer, D. J., Fowlkes, J. E., Oser, R. L., Salas, E., & Lane, N. E. (1997). Team performance measurement in distributed environments: TARGET's methodology. In M. T. Brannick, E. Salas, & C. Prince (Eds.), *Assessment and management of team performance: Theory, research and applications* (pp. 137–154). Mahwah, NJ: Lawrence Erlbaum Associates, Inc.

Edmondson, A. C. (April, 2002). *Leading for learning: How team leaders promote speaking up and learning in interdisciplinary action teams.* Symposium conducted at the 17th annual conference of the Society for Industrial and Organizational Psychology, Toronto, Canada.

Entin, E. E., Sefarty, D., & Deckert, J. C. (1994). *Team adaptation and coordination training* (Tech. Rep. No. 648-1). Burlington, MA: ALPHATECH.

Fisher, K. (1988). Leading self-directed work teams: A guide to developing leadership skills. Colombus, OH: McGraw Hill.

Fleishman, E. A., Mumford, M. D., Zaccaro, S. J., Levin, K. Y., Korotkin, A. L., & Hein, M. B. (1991). Taxonomic efforts in the description of leader behavior: A synthesis and functional interpretation. *Leadership Quarterly, 4,* 245–287.

Fowlkes, J. E., Dwyer, D. J., Oser, R. L., & Salas, E. (1998). Event-based approach to training (EBAT). *International Journal of Aviation Psychology, 8,* 218–233.

Freeman, C., & Simmon, D. A. (1991). Taxonomy of crew resource management: information processing domain. In R. S. Jensen (Ed.), *Proceeding of 6th Annual International Symposium on Aviation Psychology* (pp. 391–397). Colombus, OH.

Guzzo, R. A., & Shea, G. P. (1992). Group performance and intergroup relations in organizations. In M. D. Dunnette & L. M. Hough (Eds.), *Handbook of industrial and organizational psychology* (pp. 269–313). Palo Alto, CA: Consulting Psychologists.

Guzzo, R. A., Yost, P. R., Campbell, R. J., & Shea, G. P. (1993). Potency in groups: Articulating a construct. *British Journal of Social Psychology, 32,* 87–106.

Hackman, D. (2002). *Leading teams: Setting the stage for great performances.* Boston: Harvard Business School Press.

Hackman, J. R., & Walton, R. E. (1986). Leading groups in organizations. In Goodman & Associates (Eds.), *Designing effective work groups* (pp. 72–119). San Francisco. Jossey-Bass.

Heffner, J. S. Mathieu, J. E., & Goodwin, G. F. (1998). Teamtraining: the impact on shared mental models and performance. In K. Smith-Jentsch (chair). To be a team is to think like a team—A symposium presented at the 13th annual meeting of the Society for Industrial and Organizational Psychology, Dallas, TX.

Helmreich, R. L., & Davies, J. M. (1997). Anesthetic simulation and lessons to be learned from aviation. *Canadian Journal of Anesthesia, 44*, 907–912.

Jacobs, T. O., & Jaques, E. (1987). Leadership in complex systems. In J. Zeidner (Ed.), *Human productivity enhancement: Organizations, personnel and decision making.* (pp. 7–65). New York: Praeger.

Kleinman, D. L., & Sefarty, D. (1989). Team performance assessment in distributed decision making. In R. Gilson, J. P., Kincaid, & B. Goldiez (Eds.), *Proceedings of the Interactive Networked Simulation Training Conference* (pp. 22–27). Orlando, FL.

Klimoski, R., & Jones, R. G. (1995). Staffing for effective group decision making: Key issue in matching people and teams. In R. A. Guzzo & E. Salas (Eds.), *Team effectiveness and decision making in organizations* (pp. 291–332). San Francisco: Jossey-Bass.

Kozlowski, S. W. J. (1998). Training and developing adaptive teams: Theory, principles, and research. In J. A. Cannon-Bowers & E. Salas (Eds.), *Making decisions under stress: Implications for individual and team training* (pp. 115–153). Washington, DC: American Psychological Association.

Kozlowski, S. W. J. (2002). Discussant. In J. C. Ziegert & K. J. Klein (Chairs), *Team leadership: Current theoretical and research perspectives.* Symposium presented at the 17th annual conference of the Society for Industrial and Organizational Psychology, Toronto, Canada.

Kozlowski, S. W. J., Gully, S. M., McHugh, P. P., Salas, E., & Cannon-Bowers, J. A. (1996). A dynamic theory of leadership and team effectiveness: Developmental and task contingent leader roles. In G. R. Ferris (Ed.), *Research in personnel and human resources management* (vol. 14, pp. 253–305). Greenwich, CT: JAI.

Kozlowski, S. W. J., Gully, S. M., Salas, E., & Cannon-Bowers, J. A. (1996). Team leadership and development: Theory, principles, and guidelines for training leaders and teams. In M. Beyerlein, S. Beyerlein, & D. Johnson (Eds.), *Advances in interdisciplinary studies of work teams: Team leadership* (vol. 3, pp. 253–292). Greenwich, CT: JAI.

Lipshitz, R., Klein, G., Orasanu, J., & Salas, E. (2001). Focus article: Taking stock of naturalistic decision making. *Journal of Behavioral Decision Making, 14*, 331–352.

Marks, M. A., Mathieu, J. E., & Zaccaro, S. J. (2001). A temporally based framework and taxonomy of team processes. *Academy of Management Review, 26*, 356–376.

Marks, M. A., Sabella, M. J., Burke, C. S., & Zaccaro, S. J. (2002). The impact of cross-training on team effectiveness. *Journal of Applied Psychology, 87*, 3–13.

Marks, M. A., Zaccaro, S. J., & Mathieu, J. E. (2000). Performance implications of leader briefings and team interaction training for adaptation to novel environments. *Journal of Applied Psychology, 85*, 971–986.

Marsh, S. M., Kiechel-Koles, K. L., Boyce, L. A., & Zaccaro, S. J. (April, 2001). *Leader emergence and functional leadership: The role of leader traits and information provision in adaptive situations.* Paper presented at the 16th annual conference of the Society for Industrial and Organizational Psychology, San Diego, CA.

Marshall, J., Fleishman, E., Martin, J., Zaccaro, S., Baughman, W., & McGee, M. (2000). Development and evaluation of cognitive and metacognitive measures for predicting leadership potential. *Leadership Quarterly, 1*, 135–153.

McCall, M. W., Lombardo, M. M., & Morrison, A. M. (1988). *The lessons of experience: How successful executives develop on the job.* Lexington, MA: Lexington.

McGrath, J. E. (1962). *Leadership behavior: Requirements for leadership training.* Washington, DC: Prepared for U.S. Civil Service Commission Office of Career Development.

McIntyre, R. M., & Salas, E. (1995). Measuring and managing for team performance: Emerging principles from complex environments. In R. A. Guzzo & E. Salas (Eds.), *Team effectiveness and decision making in organizations* (pp. 149–203). San Francisco: Jossey-Bass.

Morgan, B., Salas, E., & Glickman, A. S. (1993). An analysis of team evolution and maturation. *Journal of General Psychology, 120,* 277–291.

Orasanu, J., & Salas, E. (1993). Team decision making in complex environment. In G. Klein, J. Orasanu, R. Calderwood, & C. E. Zsambok (Eds.), *Decision making in action: Models and methods* (pp. 327–345). Norwood, NJ: Ablex.

Paris, C. A., Salas, E., & Cannon-Bowers, J. A. (2000). Teamwork in multi-person systems: A review and analysis. *Ergonomics, 43,* 1052–1075.

Salas, E., Burke, C. S., Bowers, C. A., & Wilson, K. A. (2001). Team training in the skies: Does crew resource management (CRM) training work? *Human Factors, 43,* 641–674.

Salas, E., Burke, C. S., & Cannon-Bowers, J.A. (2000). What we know about designing and delivering team training: Tips and guidelines. In K. Kraiger (Ed.), *Creating, implementing, and managing effective training and development: State-of-the-art lessons for practice* (pp. 234–259). San Francisco.

Salas, E., & Cannon-Bowers, J. A. (1997). A framework for developing team performance measures in training. In M. T. Brannick, E. Salas, & C. Prince (Eds.), *Team performance assessment and measurement: Theory, methods, and applications* (pp. 45–62). Mahwah, NJ: Lawrence Erlbaum Associates, Inc.

Salas, E., & Cannon-Bowers, J. A. (2000). The anatomy of team training. In S. Tobias & J. D. Fletcher (Eds.), *Training and retraining: A handbook for business, industry, government, and the military* (pp. 312–335). New York: Macmillan.

Salas, E., Cannon-Bowers, J. A., & Johnston, J. H. (1997). How can you turn a team of experts into an expert team? Emerging training strategies. In C. E. Zsambok & G. Klein (Eds.), *Naturalistic decision making* (pp. 359–370). Mahwah, NJ: Lawrence Erlbaum Associates, Inc.

Salas, E., Cannon-Bowers, J. A., Rhodenizer, L., & Bowers, C. A. (1999). Training in organizations: Myths, misconceptions, and mistaken assumptions. *Personnel and Human Resources Management, 17,* 123–161.

Salas, E., Dickinson, T. L., Converse, S. A., & Tannenbaum, S. I. (1992). Toward an understanding of team performance and training. In R. J. Swezey & E. Salas (Eds.), *Teams: Their training and performance* (p. 3–29). Norwood, NJ: Ablex.

Salas, E., Rozell, D., Mullen, B., & Driskell, J. E. (1999). The effect of team building on performance. *Small Group Research, 30,* 309–329.

Salas, E., Stagl, K. C., & Burke, C. S. (in press). 25 years of team effectiveness in organizations: Research themes and emerging needs. To appear in C. L. Copper & I. T. Robertson (eds.), *International Review of Industrial and Organizational Psychology.* New York: John Willey.

Shamir, B., & Ben-Ari, E. (1999). Leadership in an open Army? Civilian connections, interorganizational frameworks and changes in military leadership. In J. G. Hunt, G. G. Dodge, & L. Wong (Eds.), *Out of the box leadership: Transforming the twenty-first century Army and other top-performing organizations* (pp. 15–40). Stamford, CT: JAI.

Simmon, D. A. (1998). Boeing 757 CFIT accident at Cali, Columbia, becomes focus of lessons learned. *Flight Safety Digest, 17,* 1–31.

Smith, E. M., Ford, J. K., & Kozlowski, S. W. J. (1997). Building adaptive expertise: Implications for training design strategies. In M. A. Quinones & A. Ehrenstein (Eds.), *Training for a rapidly changing workplace: Applications of psychological research* (89–118). Washington, DC: American Psychological Association.

Sullivan, G. (1999). Foreword: From theory to practice. In J. G. Hunt, G. G. Dodge, & L. Wong (Eds.), *Out of the box leadership: Transforming the twenty-first century Army and other top-performing organizations* (pp. 1–3). Stamford, CT: JAI.

Sundstrom, E. (1999). The challenges of supporting work team effectiveness. In E. Sundstrom & Associates (Eds.), *Supporting work team effectiveness* (pp. 3–23). San Francisco, CA: Jossey-Bass.

Sundstrom, E., deMeuse, K., & Futrell, D. (1990). Work teams: Applications and effectiveness. *American Psychologist, 45,* 120–133.

Sundstrom, E., McIntyre, M., Halfhill, T., & Richards, H. (2000). Work groups: From the Hawthorne studies to work teams of the 1990s and beyond. *Group Dynamics, 4,* 44–67.

Swezey, R. W., & Salas, E. (1992). Guidelines for use in team-training development. In R. W. Swezey & E. Salas (Eds.), *Teams: Their training and performance* (pp. 219–245). Norwood, NJ: Ablexo.

Tannenbaum, S.I., Salas, E., & Cannon-Bowers, J.A. (1996). Promoting team effectiveness. In M. A. West (Ed.), *Handbook of work group psychology* (pp. 503–529). Sussex, UK: Wiley.

Tannenbaum, S. I., Smith-Jentsch, K. K., & Behson, S. J. (1998). Training team leaders to facilitate team learning and performance. In J. A. Cannon-Bowers & E. Salas (Eds.), *Making decisions under stress: Implications for individual and team training* (pp. 247–270). Washington, DC: American

Tesluk, P. E. (April, 1999). *Theoretical issues in studying work experiences and implications for research and practice: On-the-job managerial experiences, manager characteristics, and managerial development and performance.* Presented at 14th annual conference of the Society for Industrial and Organizational Psychology, Atlanta, GA.

Tesluk, P. E., Dragoni, L., & Russell, J. A. (April 2002). *Growing management talent: Role of developmental work experiences, learning orientation, and access to opportunities in shaping managerial competencies and advancement potential.* Presented at 17th annual conference of the Society for Industrial and Organizational Psychology, Toronto, Canada.

Toney, R., & Ford, J. K. (2001). *Leveraging the capabilities of web based instruction to faster active learning.* Presented at the 16th Annual Conference of the Society of Industrial and Organizational Psychology, San Diego, CA.

Townsend, A. M., DeMarie, S. M. & Hendrickson, A. R. (1996). Are you ready for virtual teams? *HR Magazine, 1996;* 123–126.

U.S. Department of the Army (2001). FM 3-0 Operations (Document Version SS FM 100-5). Fort Leavenworth, KS.

Yukl, G. (1999). Leadership competencies required for the new Army and approaches for developing them. In J. G. Hunt, G. E. Dodge, & L. Wong (Ed.), *Out-of-the-box leadership: Transforming the twenty-first-century army and other top-performing organizations* (pp. 255–275). Stamford, CT: JAI.

Zaccaro, S. J. (2001). *Nature of executive leadership: Conceptual and empirical analysis of success.* Washington, DC: American Psychological Association.

Zaccaro, S. J., Rittman, A., & Marks, M. A. (2001). Team leadership. *Leadership Quarterly, 12,* 451–483.

VI

Conclusions and Implications

14

Leader Development and Change Over Time: A Conceptual Integration and Exploration of Research Challenges

Katherine J. Klein and Jonathan C. Ziegert
University of Maryland

Drawing attention to the importance of leader development, the chapters of this book highlight the knowledge and skills that leaders must acquire to be effective in transforming organizations. Leader development has been the object of surprisingly little empirical research within organizational behavior, industrial/organizational psychology, and related disciplines. Thus, the chapters of this book provide an important service to researchers and practitioners alike in addressing two fundamental questions about leader development: *What* knowledge and skills should leaders ideally acquire, over time, to excel in leading changing organizations? And, *how* do leaders develop over time?

The chapters of this book devote more attention to the first question than to the second. Accordingly, we focus on the second question in an effort to complement and extend the preceding chapters' contributions. Drawing on these chapters, the larger literature on organizational leadership, and related theory and research, we propose a preliminary conceptual model of the antecedents of leader development. As depicted in Fig. 14.1, our model outlines factors that may inflence the extent to which and the pace at which leaders change over time. Our hope is that this model serves as a useful heuristic in synthesizing what researchers, theorists, and practitioners know about the process of leader development. We propose the model not as a testable, structural model, but rather as a conceptual framework to highlight

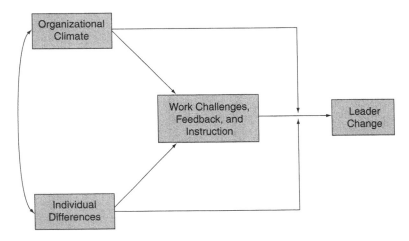

FIG. 14.1. Leader development conceptual model.

and explain the potential influence of work experiences, individual differences, and organizational climate on leader change.

We first present the central definitions and theoretical foundation upon which our model rests. We then present the elements of the model, drawing on the chapters in this book to illustrate these elements and the processes that link them. We conclude with a brief discussion of the remaining challenges that face researchers seeking to assess the antecedents of leader development over time.

DEFINITIONS

Scholars have proposed numerous definitions of leadership. As Bass (1990) noted, "there are almost as many different definitions of leadership as there are persons who have attempted to define the concept" (p. 11). Not surprisingly, then, the authors of the chapters in this book differ somewhat in their definitions of leadership. For example, Avolio (chap. 4, this volume) defines leadership in terms of the "full range model," including individualized consideration, idealized influence, and contingent reward. O'Neil and Fisher (chap. 5, this volume) adopt the Army's definition of leadership, highlighting leader values, skill, and actions. Day and Halpin (chap. 1, this volume) describe leadership as participative in nature and the outcome of social relationships and processes. McCauley and Van Velsor (2003) offered a general, summary definition of leadership that appears broad enough to encompass these and other definitions of leadership. According to those authors, leadership roles "are those that facilitate setting direction, creating alignment, and maintaining commitment, in groups of people who share common work." We adopt this generic definition in this chapter. In the interest of simplicity, we focus on leadership as demonstrated by a single individual who is a formally recognized supervisor, manager, or leader of an organizational entity—not shared leadership by a group of individuals, nor informal leadership by other group or organizational members. As the study of leader development grows over time, it will be important to expand the conceptualization of leader development to include the development of shared and informal leadership.

Formal definitions of leader development are rare, even in this book. Building on McCauley and Van Velsor's definition of leadership, we define *leader development* as the process whereby a leader gains knowledge or skills that enhance the leader's effectiveness in setting direction, creating alignment, and maintaining commitment in groups of people who share common work. In the introductory chapter to this volume, Day and Halpin suggest that leader development helps "individuals to better participate in the leadership tasks of their respective organizations." In a subsequent chapter, Day and Lance (chap. 3, this volume) suggest that leaders develop as they gain cognitive, behavioral, and social complexity (differentiation and integration). These conceptualizations and ours are entirely compatible, we believe. Our definition, however, offers a specificity that we find helpful in integrating prior theory and research on leader development and in setting the stage for further leader development theory and research.

Leader development, we caution, is a hypothesis—a hypothesis that leaders get better over time, that they gain behaviors, skills, attitudes, and knowledge that enhance their effectiveness. Yet we all know, of course, that leader development is not a foregone conclusion. All leaders do not get better over time. Some get worse. Some do not seem to change at all. And some get better more quickly than others. This is an obvious point, but an important one for leader development theory and research. Leader development is the fundamental hypothesis that leader development research must test. To circumvent the tautology inherent in this statement, we focus, in this chapter, on *leader change*, that is, the extent to which and the pace at which a leader's skills or knowledge change. Leader change, we predict, will ultimately influence a leader's effectiveness; one would expect (and hope) that increases or decreases in leader knowledge and skills would result in changes in leader effectiveness. Leader effectiveness, however, is both difficult to define and difficult to measure. Moreover, a number of factors may moderate the observed relationship between leader skills and knowledge and leader effectiveness. Accordingly, we limit our discussion in this chapter to leader change. In short, our outcome variable of interest is, in Day and Lance's terms—borrowed from latent growth modeling—the slope of leader skills or knowledge over time. That is, we are interested in explaining and predicting the nature and rate of leader change over time.

Two aspects of our definition of leader change bear mention. First, we make no assumptions about the nature or direction of leader change. Leader change, as we have defined it, is not necessarily an individual improvement process. Over time, a leader may hone *existing* skills and knowledge, gain *new* skills and knowledge, or even *lose*—that is, forget—earlier skills and knowledge. Thus, we accept the possibility that at least some of a leader's attributes may decline and worsen over time. What we have in mind here is not "unlearning"— the process whereby leaders and others replace skills and knowledge deemed to be wrong or inappropriate with new skills and knowledge deemed to be more appropriate and effective. We really do mean forgetting—the atrophy and loss of earlier skills and knowledge. Technical skills and knowledge are perhaps most likely to atrophy and decline over time. Consider, for example, a leader of a software design team who is promoted to general manager. The higher this individual climbs in the management hierarchy, the more likely his or her technical software skills and knowledge are to grow rusty and obsolete: Out of sight, out of demand—and ultimately, out of mind.

Second, we assume that leader change occurs across multiple dimensions simultaneously, such that a given leader may experience no change in one area of knowledge over time, great improvement in some behaviors over the same period of time, and a decline in still other skills during the same period. Figure 14.2 depicts this possibility. We have graphed the changes in a hypothetical leader's skills, behaviors, and knowledge over a 10-year period. As depicted in the figure, this leader's self-awareness developed slowly in the first half of the 10-year period, then increased dramatically in the fifth year, only to level off for the remaining years. The leader's charisma increased over the 10-year period, although not at a constant rate. Finally, the leader's technical knowledge and understanding of her subordinates' tasks declined, after a period of no change. (A leader might experience such a decline as he or she climbed the management hierarchy, as stated in the foregoing example.) Figure 14.2 is similar to Halpern's (chap. 6, this volume)

Leadership Competencies Over Time

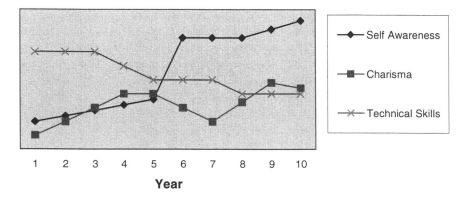

FIG. 14.2. Trajectory of four leadership competencies over a 10-year period.

Fig. 6.1, which illustrates different developmental trajectories for cognitive components. Like Halpern, we argue that development—or more specifically, leader change—may occur along multiple dimensions over time.

Day and Lance (chap. 3, this volume) make clear that we have the statistical tools to assess Fig. 14.1 and, more specifically, to test the antecedents of individuals' leadership trajectories over time. Needed now are the theoretical models—the conceptual tools—to guide hypothesis formation and data collection. Conceptual models may explain individual differences in the rate or the nature of leader change or both. In focusing on the *rate* of change, theorists and researchers ask, "Why do some individuals gain new knowledge and skills and/or hone their knowledge and skills over time, whereas other individuals experience no advances, or even declines over time?" In focusing on the nature of leader change, theorists and researchers ask, "Why do some individuals gain knowledge and skill in X, whereas other individuals gain knowledge and skill in Y?" We build on and extend prior research and theory, emphasizing predictors of the *rate* of leader change. As theoretical and empirical work on this topic advances, theorists and researchers may turn their attention to the predictors of the *nature* of leader change.

PRELIMINARY CONCEPTUAL MODEL
OF LEADER DEVELOPMENT

Theoretical Foundations: Self-Regulation Theory

Although our conceptual model, depicted in Fig. 14.1 summarizes and extends prior research and theory on leader development, it rests most fundamentally on self-regulation theory and research (e.g., Bandura, 2001; Carver & Scheier, 1981; Karoly, 1993; Wood & Bandura, 1989). Self-regulation theory is designed to explain and predict the processes and determinants of self-initiated learning and adaptation. A number of authors have proposed conceptual models of self-regulation (e.g., Tsui & Ashford, 1994; Wood & Bandura, 1989). These models differ in some respects, of course, but all converge around a fundamental, iterative sequence whereby individuals (a) regulate their attention and effort around self-set goals or assigned goals, (b) take action to achieve their goals, (c) obtain feedback that they use to interpret their progress toward their goals, (d) adapt their goals or their performance strategy, if necessary, to maintain or enhance their progress toward their goals, and (e) recommence the cycle. Tsui and Ashford's (1994) conceptual model of the effects of self-regulation on managerial effectiveness labels the first four of these steps (a) standard setting, (b) behavior, (c) discrepancy detection, and (d) discrepancy reduction. Drawing on self-regulation theory to examine the relationship of leadership and performance, Sosik, Potosky, and Jung (2002) noted that "individuals desire congruence between their own and

others' perceptions of their behavior, and, therefore, set and work toward goals
to reduce perceptual discrepancies, gain congruence, and improve their effectiveness" (p. 212). Adaptive self-regulation may, thus, they commented, "be viewed
as a social process in which managers attempt to understand and adapt to the role
and performance expectations of organizational constituents" (p. 212).

Self-regulation theory and research suggest that individuals are most motivated
to change their behavior when they perceive discrepancies between their performance and their goals or standards for performance. We argue that individuals are
most likely to experience such discrepancies when they tackle novel work challenges. Individuals who experience novel work challenges, we propose, are most
likely to perform, at least initially, below their standards and thus are likely to take
steps to enhance their performance by honing existing skills and knowledge or
by acquiring new skills and knowledge. Workplace feedback and instruction may
alert leaders that their performance is below standards or may inform leaders about
steps they may take to enhance their performance, reducing performance–goal
discrepancies. Accordingly, novel work challenge and workplace feedback and
instruction lie at the core of our model. Consistent with prior theory and research
on leader development (e.g., Day, 2001) as well as self-regulation (e.g., Wood &
Bandura, 1989; Tsui & Ashford, 1994), we propose that individual characteristics (e.g., learning orientation) and organizational characteristics (e.g., climate for
learning) may influence the extent to which leaders seek and respond adaptively to
novel work challenges and workplace feedback and instruction. We first describe
the proposed effects of novel work challenges, feedback, and instruction and then
consider the indirect and moderating influences of individual and organizational
differences on leader change.

From Work Experiences to Leader Change

Novel Work Challenges.   When leaders face novel work challenges, they are
likely, initially, to perform below standards, falling short of their own standards
or the standards and expectations of their peers, subordinates, or supervisors.
Indeed, if a leader excels immediately at a new task, the task—by definition—
is not challenging. New challenges—and, more specifically, performance–goal
discrepancies—inspire self-regulation. In the face of performance below standards,
leaders are likely to review their own performance, evaluate the importance and
appropriateness of their own and others' performance standards, and devise steps
to reduce performance–goal discrepancies (Tsui & Ashford, 1994). When a leader
strives to reduce performance–goal discrepancies by enhancing his or her existing
skills and knowledge or developing new skills and knowledge, the leader is likely
to experience positive change over time.

Of course, not all leaders experience positive change in response to novel work
challenges, but many do. This theme cuts across numerous chapters of the book.
Day and Lance (chap. 3, this volume), for example, suggest that the goal of leader

development is to use people's work itself (e.g., stretch assignments) to help them learn and develop. Avolio (chap. 4, this volume) argues that developmental trigger events foster leader development, enhancing a leader's enactment of transformational behaviors. Halpern (chap. 6, this volume) emphasizes the importance of work experiences as a teacher. Hall (chap. 7, this volume) highlights the influence of key workplace experiences and trigger events including status passages, formal initiation, and role transitions. Cianciolo, Antonakis, and Sternberg (chap. 9, this volume) describe the importance of experience in developing practical intelligence and suggest that experience can be a mentor, as evidenced by the title of their chapter. Salas, Burke, and Stagl (chap. 13, this volume) call for the use of challenging work—especially operational assignments—to enhance team leader development.

Recent theory and research, beyond the chapters of this book, echo these points. McCauley and Brutus (1998) emphasized the importance for leader development of "stretch" assignments—assignments that present unfamiliar responsibilities, require building or modifying relationships, and offer a great deal of responsibility and latitude. Others emphasize the long-term developmental benefits not just of stretching, but of hardship—stressful and disruptive experiences such as business mistakes, career setbacks, downsizing, and problem subordinates (McCall, Lombardo, & Morrison, 1988; Moxley, 1998). Hardships, these authors suggested, engender self-reflection, self-awareness, and adaptability. Indeed, McCauley and her colleagues (McCauley, Ruderman, Ohlott, & Morrow, 1994) found that challenging job assignments entailing unfamiliar responsibilities, such as responsibility for a start-up or turnaround venture, pressures to prove oneself, problem subordinates, and work overload, were associated with managers' self-reported learning and development on the job.

Workplace Feedback and Instruction.   We use the phrase "workplace feedback and instruction" to encompass a wide range of formal and informal interventions, activities, and relationships that offer leaders feedback regarding the quality of their performance or instruction regarding ways to enhance their performance. These include 360-degree feedback programs, performance appraisal interventions, formal training courses, executive coaching, mentoring, role modeling, and peer learning and exchange (e.g., through networks of practice). These interventions, activities, and relationships engender positive leader change by providing leaders with feedback and instruction. For example, a role model, mentor, peer, coach, or classroom instructor may either demonstrate or explicitly tell a focal leader the standards for his or her performance. Similarly, a role model, mentor, peer, coach, or classroom instructor may demonstrate or explicitly tell the focal leader how to overcome shortcomings in his or her performance. Feedback and instruction, we argue, are most likely to foster positive leader change if they alert leaders that their performance is below standards (discrepancy detection) and/or suggest to leaders ways in which they may meet performance standards (discrepancy reduction).

A number of the chapters of this book highlight the potential benefits of work-place feedback and instruction for leader development. Salas, Burke, and Stagl (chap. 13, this volume) emphasize the benefits of mentoring for leader development. Caruso and Wolfe (chap. 10, this volume) advocate formal training programs to enhance leaders' emotional intelligence. O'Neil and Fisher (chap. 5, this volume) describe the benefits of using computer games as a means of leader training. Cohen (chap. 8, this volume) highlights the potential benefits of critical thinking training. Finally, Salas, Burke, Fowlkes, and Wilson (chap. 12, this volume) describe an event-based approach of formal training for the development of multicultural leaders. Furthermore, related research on leader and professional development underscores the potential benefits of mentoring, role models, and leadership instruction (e.g., Dvir, Eden, Avolio, & Shamir, 2002; Higgins & Thomas, 2001; Ibarra, 1999).

Summary. Building on prior research and theory, we propose that novel work challenges foster positive changes in leader knowledge and skills. Furthermore, workplace feedback and instruction may also engender positive changes in leader knowledge and skills. However, some caution is warranted. The effects of novel work challenges may be curvilinear. The leader who experiences few work challenges may stagnate, exhibiting little or no growth in his or her knowledge and skills, whereas the leader who experiences work challenges grows in his or her knowledge and skills over time. However, extreme work challenges may frustrate and confuse a leader, causing anxiety, depression, or a loss of self-confidence rather than growth in leadership knowledge and skills.

Furthermore, we know of no published research on the effectiveness of some forms of feedback and instruction—most notably, executive coaching—in fostering positive leader change. Finally, recent research raises the possibility that feedback and instruction may not always enhance leader skills and knowledge. In a meta-analysis of the effects of performance feedback, Kluger and DeNisi (1996) found that in approximately one third of the studies they reviewed, individuals who received feedback subsequently performed worse than individuals who did not receive feedback. Perhaps the implication for leader development is that skills and knowledge may decline following feedback. However, skills and knowledge are not synonymous with performance. Moreover, feedback may engender an *immediate* decline in performance, followed by a *subsequent* increase in knowledge and skill. Still, Kluger and DeNisi's findings do suggest that the effects of feedback and instruction on leader development may not be uniformly positive. Perhaps individual and contextual differences may help to explain why some leaders respond more positively, evidencing more positive changes in their skills and knowledge in response to feedback (and also workplace instruction and novel work challenges) than do others. We next consider the influence of a number of individual and contextual (organizational) characteristics on leader change.

Individual Differences: Indirect and Moderating Influences on Leader Change

Individual differences, we argue, have both an indirect and a moderating effect on leader change. Individual differences have an *indirect* effect on leader change insofar as individual differences (specifically individual differences in self-monitoring, learning orientation, self-efficacy, and proactive behavior) may influence the extent to which a leader experiences work challenges and receives feedback and instruction. For example, a leader who is high in learning orientation is more likely than a leader who is low in learning orientation to seek and gain novel and challenging work assignments, feedback, and instruction. Individual differences may have a *moderating* influence on leader change insofar as they moderate, or condition, the effects of novel and challenging work, feedback, and instruction on leader change. For example, a leader who is high in self-monitoring is likely to respond more adaptively to workplace challenges, feedback, and instruction than is a leader who is low in these characteristics.

Although the chapters of this book devote more attention to the influence of work experiences on leader development than to the influence of individual differences, a number of chapters presage our observations. Halpern (chap. 6, this volume), for example, notes the influence of motivation to learn, self-efficacy, and need for cognition on individuals' willingness to seek and learn from new opportunities. Avolio (chap. 4, this volume) highlights the leadership consequences of individual "developmental readiness," a construct encompassing several factors including emotional self-awareness, metacognition, and goal orientation. Furthermore, Hall (chap. 7, this volume) suggests that self-awareness enhances a leader's ability to learn from experience, whereas Cianciola and her colleagues (chap. 9, this volume) propose that practical intelligence predicts a leader's ability to learn from experience. We next highlight the potential indirect and moderating effects of four individual characteristics: self-monitoring, goal orientation, self-efficacy, and proactive behavior.

Self-Monitoring.   Individuals who are high in self-monitoring (Snyder, 1979) tend to "monitor and control their self-expressions in social situations" (Mehra, Kilduff, & Brass, 2001, p. 124). They pay attention to situational cues regarding the most appropriate behaviors to demonstrate in a given setting and respond accordingly, endeavoring to adjust their behaviors to meet the standards and expectations of the social setting. In contrast, individuals who are low in self-monitoring are more oblivious to external cues regarding the appropriate behaviors to demonstrate in a given social setting. They are more likely to attend to internal cues, demonstrating relatively consistent behavior across settings. As Tsui and Ashford (1994) noted, high self-monitoring "almost definitionally implies an active participation in the adaptive self-regulation process" (p. 106).

Individuals who are high in self-monitoring are more likely both to seek out and respond adaptively to workplace feedback and instruction than are individuals who are low in self-monitoring. When high self-monitors experience new work challenges and thus, in all likelihood, experience performance–goal discrepancies as well, they are likely to seek feedback and instruction in an effort to comply quickly with the new standards for their performance. Furthermore, they are likely to be particularly receptive to feedback and instruction because high self-monitors are more sensitive to social cues and more effective in adapting their behavior in response to such cues than are low self-monitors. Indeed, these processes may help to explain why managers who are high in self-monitoring are more likely to be promoted than are managers who are low in self-monitoring (Kilduff & Day, 1994). In short, managers who are high in self-monitoring may develop leadership skills and knowledge more quickly than managers who are low in self-monitoring.

Goal Orientation.   Individuals differ in their prevailing or habitual responses to challenging situations, assignments, or tasks. Individuals who have a strong *learning goal orientation* welcome such challenges; they seek to develop their competence, acquire new skills, master new situations, and learn from experiences (VandeWalle, Cron, & Slocum, 2001). Others who have a strong *proving goal orientation* seek to demonstrate their competence and earn others' accolades (VandeWalle et al., 2001). Still others—those who are particularly high in *avoiding goal orientation*—eschew such challenges, seeking to avoid a show of incompetence.

Research on goal orientation (e.g., Dweck & Legett, 1988; Elliot & Harackiewicz, 1996; VandeWalle et al., 2001) has burgeoned in recent decades. This research suggests that leaders who are particularly high in learning goal orientation are more likely to seek and benefit from work challenges, feedback, and instruction than are individuals who are higher in either providing or avoiding goal orientation. Individuals who have a strong learning goal orientation value and seek work-related feedback more than individuals who are low in learning goal orientation do (VandeWalle, Ganesan, Challagalla, & Brown, 2000). Furthermore, learning goal orientation is positively associated with effort, self-efficacy, and goal-setting level (VandeWalle et al., 2001). In contrast, avoiding goal orientation is negatively related to self-efficacy and goal-setting level. Thus, leaders who are high in learning goal orientation appear likely to seek and welcome work challenges as opportunities from which they may learn new skills and gain new knowledge. Similarly, leaders who are high in learning goal orientation are likely to respond well to workplace feedback and instruction.

Self-Efficacy.   A wealth of theory and research suggests that individuals who are high in leadership self-efficacy—that is, individuals who believe they are capable of mobilizing the motivation, cognitive resources, and behaviors needed to perform well in leadership positions—are likely to evidence greater leader development than are individuals who question their leadership efficacy (e.g., Wood & Bandura, 1989). Leadership self-efficacy may influence leader development through a number of mechanisms. For example, Wood and Bandura (1989) suggested that people (a) "avoid activities and situations that they believe will exceed their coping capabilities, but they readily undertake challenging activities ... they judge themselves capable of managing" (p. 365); (b) "slacken their efforts or abort their efforts prematurely [if they question their efficacy, but] ... exert greater effort to master the effort [if they are high in self-efficacy]" (p. 365); (c) "experience stress, depression, and a lack of motivation in threatening or taxing situations if their self-efficacy for the given task is low, but not if their self-efficacy for the given task is high" (p. 366); and (d) "set low goals and visualize failure scenarios if their self-efficacy for a given task is low, but set high goals and visualize success if their self-efficacy for the task is high" (p. 366).

Accordingly, leaders who are high in leadership self-efficacy are likely to welcome work challenges and respond adaptively to workplace feedback and instruction. In response to performance–goal discrepancies, they are likely to redouble their efforts, and resist overwhelming stress and depression, to maintain or enhance their goals and visualize their success—all behaviors that appear likely to enhance leader development.

Proactive Behavior. Individuals exhibit proactive behavior when they take the initiative to improve current circumstances or create new ones (Crant, 2000). Proactive behavior "involves challenging the status quo rather than passively adapting to present conditions" (Crant, 2000, p. 436). In recent years, interest in proactive behavior at work has grown (e.g., Frese, Kring, Soose, & Zempel, 1996; Morrison & Phelps, 1999). Recent research suggests, for example, that individuals who have a strong proactive personality perform better at work, experience greater subjective career success, and are more highly rated as leaders (Crant, 1995; Crant & Bateman, 2000; Seibert, Crant, & Kraimer, 1999). Although the construct of proactive behavior remains new, it seems clear that individuals vary in proactive behavior and, furthermore, that individuals who are more proactive are more likely to seek and gain new, challenging work experiences, feedback, and instruction than are individuals who are less proactive.

Summary. Individuals who are high in self-monitoring, learning goal orientation, self-efficacy, and proactivity are most likely to seek, experience, and benefit from work challenges, feedback, and instruction. Individuals who are high in self-monitoring are likely to attend to social cues, note their performance–goal discrepancies, and take steps to modify their behavior accordingly. Individuals who are high in learning goal orientation are eager to learn from challenges, failures, and setbacks; they seek rather than eschew challenging assignments from which they may learn. Individuals who are high in leadership self-efficacy respond confidently to novel assignments, showing effort and persistence in the pursuit of ambitious goals. Finally, individuals who are proactive in their work behaviors actively seek work challenges and take steps to correct performance–goal discrepancies. Of course, the four personal traits are likely to be closely related. The individual who is high in all four is likely to show great leadership development over time.

The four traits are united by their contributions to individual learning. Individuals who are high in self-monitoring, learning goal orientation, self-efficacy, and proactivity are adept in learning the lessons of experience and maximizing the benefits of the feedback and instruction they receive. They embrace challenges, seek to acquire knowledge, and respond boldly to opportunities that might well daunt those lower in self-monitoring, learning goal orientation, self-efficacy, and proactivity.

Judge and his colleagues (Judge, Thoresen, Pucik, & Welbourne, 1999) recently reported research results suggesting that a number of personal traits (internal locus of control, generalized self-efficacy, self-esteem, positive affectivity, openness to experience, tolerance for ambiguity, and risk aversion) may influence managers' ability to "cope with organizational change." The ability to cope with organizational change differs notably, we believe, from the propensity to learn and develop in response to workplace challenges, feedback, and instruction. Surely organizational change may represent a workplace challenge. However, coping implies a relatively passive—although calm and measured—response to organizational challenges. Individuals cope by reducing, minimizing, or tolerating stressful events (Folkman, Lazarus, Gruen, & DeLongis, 1986). Accordingly, the personal traits that enhance managers' coping with organizational change may not lead to learning from organizational change. In short, we suspect that the personal characteristics that enhance managers' ability to cope with organizational change may well be positively related to the characteristics that we predict enhance leaders' eagerness for and learning from workplace challenges, feedback, and instruction, but not a substitute for these characteristics. (Only one characteristic is included in both our conceptual model and Judge et al.'s research: self-efficacy.) Ultimately, of course, research is needed to examine the relationships between managerial coping and leader development and the relationships among the characteristics specified in our model and in Judge et al.'s recent research.

Organizational Climate: Indirect and Moderating Influences on Leader Change

Like individual differences, organizational differences—specifically, differences in organizational climates—may have both an indirect and a moderating effect on leader change. An organization's climate may have an indirect effect on leader development by shaping the extent to which organizational leaders experience novel work challenges, feedback, and instruction. Furthermore, an organization's climate may have a moderating effect on leadership change by influencing the extent to which leaders gain new skills and knowledge as a result of the work challenges, feedback, and instruction they experience. Essentially, an organization's climate may strengthen or weaken leaders' motivation to learn from their work experiences, feedback, and instruction. This was shown in earlier research by Fleishman, which demonstrated the overriding influence of leadership climate on the effects of leadership training (Fleishman, 1953; Fleishman, Harris, & Burtt, 1955). We further explore these possibilities, focusing on two different, although related, kinds of organizational climate: climate for leader development and climate for learning. First, however, we offer a brief introduction to the construct of organizational climate.

The Organizational Climate Construct. Our conceptualization of organizational climate builds on the work of Schneider and his colleagues on the topic (e.g., Schneider & Gunnarson, 1990). Schneider (1990) defined *climate* as employees' "perceptions of the events, practices, and procedures and the kinds of behaviors that are rewarded, supported, and expected in a setting" (p. 384). Elaborating, Schneider and Bowen (1995) defined organizational climate as "the message employees get about what is important in the organization" as they "integrate hundreds, even thousands, of their [work] experiences into a theme" (p. 239). In a similar vein, Hofmann and Stetzer (1996) suggested that organizational climate develops "as individuals attach meanings to and interpret the environment within which they work. These meanings and perceptions then influence the way in which individuals behave within the organization through their attitudes, norms, and perceptions of behavior–outcome contingencies" (p. 314).

The organizational climate construct is similar and related to the construct of organizational culture (Denison, 1996; Schneider & Gunnarson, 1990). Both terms are used to describe "the internal social psychological environment of organizations and the relationship of that environment to individual meaning and organizational adaptation" (Denison, 1996, p. 625). The terms differ, however, in their roots (psychology or anthropology), their measurement (quantitative or qualitative), and their approach (etic or emic) (Denison, 1996). Perhaps most important for our chapter, the terms differ in specificity. Researchers and theorists commonly use the term organizational culture to refer to an organization's values, assumptions, and meanings as manifested in organizational symbols, stories, rituals, and other artifacts (e.g., Louis, 1985; Schein, 1985). In contrast, climate is commonly, although not always, used to describe an organization's policies, practices, rewards, rituals, values, and expectations *with respect to a specific strategic focus or outcome.* Recent research suggests that an organization's positive climate for a specific outcome may influence employee behaviors regarding that outcome. For example, climate for service predicts customer service (Schneider & Bowen, 1995; Schneider, White, & Paul, 1998), climate for transfer of training predicts training transfer (Rouiller & Goldstein, 1993; Tracey, Tannenbaum, & Kavanaugh, 1995), climate for technical updating predicts engineers' technical performance

(Kozlowski & Hults, 1987), and climate for technology implementation predicts manufacturing plants' use of a newly adopted technology (Klein, Conn, & Sorra, 2001).

Building on prior climate research, we consider the effects of an organization's climates for two different, but related strategic foci: leader development and learning. We know of little prior theory or research on climate for leader development and climate for learning per se. (Important exceptions to this general rule include Edmondson, 1999; Kozlowski & Hults, 1987; and Tetrick & Da Silva, 2003.) However, climate is an umbrella construct—useful for integrating past research and theory. In this sense, our conceptualization of organizational climate for leader development and organizational climate for learning is quite consistent with prior theory and research on leader development and organizational learning (e.g., Day, 2001; McCauley, 2001; Moxley & O'Connor Wilson, 1998). At the same time, our discussion of leader development climate and learning climate complements and extends the contributions of the preceding chapters of this book, because few chapters consider the influence of organizational context. Avolio (chap. 4, this volume) stands out in this regard, highlighting the influence of organizational culture on the effectiveness of any leader development program.

Organizational Climate for Leader Development. Organizational climate for leader development refers to employees'—specifically, leaders'—shared summary perceptions of the extent to which leader development is rewarded, supported, and expected within their organization. As Schneider's (1990; Schneider & Gunnarson, 1990) definitions of climate make clear, leaders' summary perceptions of the extent to which leader development is rewarded, supported, and expected derive from leaders' perceptions of development-related events, practices, procedures, policies, and statements within the organization. The more strongly and consistently an organization communicates to organizational leaders that their development as leaders is an organizational priority, the more positive is the organizational climate for leader development.

Many of the practices, procedures, and policies that communicate to organizational leaders that their development is an organizational priority also, of course, provide leaders with opportunities to acquire new skills and knowledge as leaders. Thus, the more developmental opportunities an organization offers leaders of the organization, the stronger is the organization's climate for leader development. For example, an organization that provides leaders with any or all of 360-degree feedback, executive coaching, a formal mentoring program for junior managers, leadership training, stretch assignments, and personal growth or action learning programs targeted to leaders (e.g., Day, 2001; Kozlowski & Hults, 1987; McCauley, 2001) is likely to have a more positive climate for leader development than an organization that does not offer leaders these opportunities. Furthermore, an organization that rewards leaders for their acquisition and refinement of leadership skills and knowledge has a more positive climate for leader development than does an organization that fails to offer such rewards.

Organizational climate for leader development has an indirect effect on leader development insofar as a positive climate for leader development supports (and reflects) the availability of novel work challenges, feedback, and instruction for developing leaders. Organizational climate for leader development has a moderating effect on the relationship between work challenges, feedback, and instruction and leader development insofar as a positive climate for leader development strengthens leaders' eagerness to learn all that they can from such experiences. A strong positive climate for leader development communicates to leaders that their development will be rewarded; leaders who acquire new leadership skills and knowledge will advance more rapidly within the organization than those who do not. Such rewards heighten leaders' sensitivity and openness to the lessons to be learned from 360-degree feedback, mentoring, leadership training, challenging work assignments, and other interventions. A strong climate for leader development makes development a leader's goal, enhancing and strengthening the attention the leader gives to development opportunities, the effort the leader makes to develop his or her skills and knowledge, and the persistence the leader shows in the face of leadership setbacks (Locke & Latham, 2002).

Two issues related to rewards of leader development bear mention. First, it may seem, at first blush, that all organizations would reward leader development. Don't all organizations reward and promote leaders who acquire valuable leadership skills and knowledge? We think not. Organizations present a continuum of rewards for leader development. At the low end of the continuum, organizations reward and promote leaders as a function of their seniority or connections, factors that may have little relation to leader skills and knowledge. At the high end of the continuum, organizations reward and promote leaders as a function of their participation in leadership development opportunities and programs and their growth in leadership skills and knowledge. In the middle of the continuum, perhaps, are organizations that reward and promote leaders as a function of the financial performance of the units they supervise. Although a unit's financial performance is likely to reflect the unit leader's leadership skills and knowledge, other factors, beyond the leader's immediate control or influence, may also prove influential.

Second, it may be possible for a climate for leader development to be "too positive." We are reminded of the adage, "Be careful what you wish for" and of cautions regarding the potential liabilities of strong goals. When a goal is very clear and strong, individuals may pursue that goal to the exclusion of other goals, distorting organizational priorities. Furthermore, if the rewards for leader development are very strong, competition among leaders may ensue as leaders strive to outshine other leaders in their display of leadership skills and knowledge. Although competition among leaders may be motivating, it may also reduce cooperation and knowledge sharing among leaders, important leadership outcomes not necessarily encapsulated by the construct of leader development. If an organization's climate for leadership may be too positive, perhaps a positive climate for organizational learning may prove more adaptive. We consider this possibility next.

Organizational Climate for Learning.   Organizational climate for learning refers to employees' shared summary perceptions of the extent to which their organization rewards, supports, and expects employee learning. In the past decade, the "learning organization" has received substantial attention—and plaudits—in both the academic and the popular business press. So, too, has "knowledge management." Both academic and popular writings on these topics suggest that some organizations excel in creating opportunities for employees to learn from experience, formal instruction, and one another (Argote, 1999; Davenport & Prusak, 1998; Garvin, 2000; Gupta & Govindarajan, 2000; Hansen, 2002; Hansen and von Oetinger, 2000; Pfeffer & Sutton, 2000). These organizations, we suggest, have a strong and positive climate for learning; in a variety of ways, these organizations reward, support, and expect employees to learn. The message employees receive is that they are expected and encouraged to acquire a broad array of skills and knowledge that may allow them to perform their jobs more effectively.

The focus of an organizational climate for learning is thus broader than that of an organizational climate for leader development. An organizational climate for learning supports and encourages employees (not just leaders) to acquire a broad array of skills and knowledge (not just leadership skills and knowledge) that may enhance their job performance and contribute to unit performance. Thus, the impact of a strong, positive climate for learning on leader development may be weaker than that of a strong, positive climate for leader development. However, the effects of a strong, positive climate for learning may be broader, influencing a wider spectrum of employees and uniting employees, including leaders, in a search for knowledge. Finally, an organization may have both a strong climate for learning and a strong climate for leader development; the two are compatible, not conflicting.

A climate for learning both supports and reflects organizational policies, practices, and procedures that promote and reward employee learning and knowledge sharing. For example, an organization may foster learning by requiring employees to participate in formal "after-action reviews" during which employees discuss the strengths and weaknesses of, and the lessons learned from, recently completed projects (Garvin, 2000). Furthermore, organizations may create and encourage experimentation, allowing employees to try new strategies, procedures, and projects and systematically evaluate their effectiveness (e.g., Garvin, 2000). Additionally, organizations may foster knowledge sharing among employees by creating mechanisms—informal or formal, technological or nontechnological—for employees to ask one another for advice and offer each other guidance (e.g., Hansen, Nohria, & Tierney, 1999). Knowledge-sharing mechanisms of this kind include job transfers between units; communities of practice linking geographically dispersed individuals who share technical or professional skills; repositories where employees may provide and access reports, presentations, and other documents that may be useful across positions and units; and employee directories that list employees' contact information and their areas of interest and expertise (e.g., Davenport & Prusak, 1998; Hansen et al., 1999). Finally, organizational reward systems may reward individuals not only for their individual performance, but also for the performance of their own team or unit, or even for the collective performance of multiple teams and units across the organization (e.g., Gupta & Govindarajan, 2000).

These kinds of policies, practices, and procedures present novel work challenges, feedback, and instruction to organizational leaders and other employees. Furthermore, these policies, practices, and procedures communicate to all organizational members that skill and knowledge development is supported, rewarded, and expected, enhancing all organizational members' motivation to learn. Accordingly, the more positive the organization's climate for learning, the more likely it is that all organizational members, including organizational leaders, will experience and benefit from novel work challenges, feedback, and instruction, engendering growth in employee skills and knowledge. In short, a strong, positive learning climate makes learning a goal for all employees, leaders included.

Summary.   The more positive an organization's climate for leader development and its climate for learning, the more likely organizational leaders are to show positive changes in their leadership skills and knowledge over time. In evoking the organizational climate construct, we highlight the influence of organizational context on leader development. The antecedents of leader development, we argue, transcend the leader's immediate work experiences (challenges, feedback, and instruction) and personal characteristics (self-monitoring, learning orientation, self-efficacy, and proactive behavior).

Organizational climate, we emphasize, is equifinal. Leader development climates of equal strength may ensue from quite different sets of policies and practices. For example, an organization may support and inspire leader development by offering leadership training, mentoring, 360-degree feedback, job rotation, or rewards for increases in leader skills and knowledge. An organization may support and inspire learning by creating cross-functional teams, offering extensive training, promoting knowledge sharing through technological and nontechnological channels, or rewarding collective performance. The climate construct thus pushes researchers away from the search for *the* critical determinants of leader development—training *or* rewards *or* feedback, for example—to the documentation of the cumulative influence of all of these on leader development. Climate—the cumulative and interactive effect of organizational policies, practices, procedures, rewards, and events—is key.

Organizational Climate and Individual Differences

An organization's climates both reflect and influence the characteristics of individual organizational members. Accordingly, Fig. 14.1 shows a reciprocal relationship between leader development climate and learning climate (organizational climate) on one hand, and leader self-monitoring, goal orientation, self-efficacy, and proactive behavior (individual differences) on the other. The link from individual characteristics to organizational climate reflects the attraction of leaders who are high in self-monitoring, learning goal orientation, self-efficacy, and proactivity to organizations that offer challenging work assignments and learning opportunities, as well as the collective influence of leaders who are high in these characteristics on the climates that emerge in their workplace (Schneider, 1987; Schneider, Goldstein, & Smith, 1995). The link from leader development climate and learning climate to leader characteristics highlights the influence of an organization's climates on organizational members' values, personalities, and behaviors. Individuals who work in an organization that supports, rewards, and expects leader development and learning are likely to internalize the values and norms that characterize their organization. Thus, strong, positive climates for leader development and learning may reinforce and enhance leaders' learning goal orientation, self-efficacy, and proactive behavior.

Summary: The Antecedents of Leader Development

In sum, leaders are likely to grow in their skills and knowledge as they experience work challenges, feedback, and instructions. These are the critical drivers, we predict, of leader development. Individual differences and organizational climate influence the extent to which leaders both experience and benefit from work challenges, feedback, and instruction. Individuals who are high in self-monitoring, learning goal orientation, self-efficacy, and proactive behavior are most likely to seek and benefit from work challenges, feedback, and instruction. Furthermore, organizational context is influential. When an organization's climates for leader development and for learning are strong and positive, leaders are challenged, stimulated, guided, and informed by work experiences, feedback, and instruction and eager to discern and apply the lessons to be learned from such experiences.

THE RESEARCH CHALLENGE: STUDYING LEADER DEVELOPMENT OVER TIME

The theoretical model presented in the preceding pages provides some guidance to researchers wishing to examine the antecedents of leader development over time. However, numerous challenges remain. First, we must caution that it would be nearly impossible to test our entire model at once. Instead, we present our framework in order to illustrate potential testable relationships between the components. Even with the identification of these potential relationships, to study leader development over time, a researcher must collect measures of specific individuals' knowledge and skills at multiple points over time. Not only does this necessitate tracking individuals over time—no small challenge—it also necessitates the collection of comparable measures of leader knowledge and skill both within leaders (over time) and across leaders. Thus, measures must be sensitive to changes in leader knowledge and skill over time, and must not be biased by a leader's (or other rater's) repeated exposure to the same, or essentially the same, measures. What knowledge and skills should researchers assess, how, and when? We consider each of these issues in turn.

What Knowledge and Skills Should Researchers Assess?

Researchers may choose generic measures—hypothesized to be broadly applicable across work contexts—or context-specific leadership skills and knowledge. Generic measures are likely to be derived from broad and basic leadership typologies. For example, one might use Avolio's full range model of leadership—specifically, the Multifactor Leadership Questionnaire—to assess the performance of leaders over time, examining the extent to which a leader provides intellectual stimulation, individualized consideration, inspirational motivation, and forms of leadership at different periods over time. Alternatively, a researcher might adopt Yukl's (2002) conceptualization of leader traits, skills, and knowledge, including planning operations, monitoring performance, contingent rewarding, coaching and mentoring, visioning, and more. Still further, a researcher might follow Van Velsor, McCauley, and Moxley's (1998) description of "the capacities . . . that leaders can, and even must, learn over time," which include self-awareness, self-confidence, the ability to view life from a broader, systemic point of view, and the ability to work in social systems, (pp. 17–19), among others. The obvious advantage of a generic approach is that it allows comparison of diverse leaders' performances over time, even if the leaders work in quite distinctive settings. A potential disadvantage is that generic measures may not be highly sensitive to the context-specific leader changes that are most likely to show over time.

Context-specific measures are tailored to the leaders' work settings and thus are likely to be particularly sensitive to leader changes over time. For example, one might build on the work of Salas, Burke, Fowlkes, & Wilson-Donnelly (chap. 12, this volume) regarding the leadership of multicultural teams to develop measures most appropriate for the leaders of such teams. In our research on emergency medical teams (shock trauma), we found it useful to develop context-specific measures of leadership, precisely because more generic models of leader knowledge and skills do not quite apply to the emergency medical context. (For example, we found little evidence that emergency team leader's valued or displayed vision or charisma. Patient injuries galvanize medical care givers, and inspirational leadership, via vision or charisma, is unnecessary.) Finally, context-specific measures of leaders' skills and knowledge seem more likely than generic measures to be sensitive to declines in leader skills and behaviors over time. For example, although leaders may not show marked declines over time in self-awareness, charisma, or individualized consideration, they may show marked declines in their specific technical skills—skills that may be critical for the close supervision of technical personnel, but less important for leaders as they climb the organizational hierarchy.

How Should Leaders' Knowledge and Skills Be Assessed?

Leaders' knowledge and skill may be assessed either objectively or subjectively. Objective performance would be ideal, eliminating the rating errors associated with subjective evaluation. Objective tests of leader knowledge might be feasible, although repeated exposure to the same tests would introduce measurement error over time. Furthermore, the results of knowledge tests may not generalize to leader behavior; leaders may know what to do, but not do it. Researchers might instead gather measures of the objective performance of each leader's unit over time. However, unit performance may reflect numerous factors beyond the performance of the unit's leaders. Furthermore, it may be difficult to compare multiple diverse units. These varied concerns call into some question the feasibility of objective measurement of leader knowledge and skills over time.

Subjective measures may be no less problematic, however. Clearly, self-serving biases call into question the value of self-ratings of performance. Subordinates' or supervisors' ratings of leader performance may be subjective and, perhaps more important, influenced by the passage of time. That is, an individual may use a different standard to rate a leader who has just gained a position of leadership than he or she uses to rate a leader who gained this position some time ago. Surely professors use different standards to rate the performance of a first-year graduate student and a fourth-year graduate student. The danger for those who wish to study leader development is that the individual who performed well at Time 1 (relative to others of comparable tenure and position) and who has grown tremendously over time may appear unchanged in his or her supervisor's ratings. He or she is still performing well relative to others of comparable tenure and position. However, he or she is performing extraordinarily well relative to his or her Time 1 performance—the effect that the researcher seeks, but may fail, to capture.

When Should Researchers Assess Leaders' Knowledge and Skills?

Mitchell and James (2001) argued that organizational theory and research would be enhanced by much more careful and explicit specification of when things happen.

A key consideration is the specification of how long things take. How long does it take X to influence Y, and how long do changes in Y persist? Mitchell and James' trenchant analysis is highly relevant to the study of leader development. How long does it take job challenges, or mentoring, or 360-degree feedback to alter a leader's skills and knowledge? How long do changes in a leader's skills and knowledge persist? Current theory and research provide very little guidance to researchers seeking to answer these questions and to fashion their research accordingly. In the absence of clear answers to these questions, researchers seeking to design studies of leader development can only guess at the most appropriate measurement intervals. This represents a real quandary and one unlikely to be addressed in the absence of exploratory research on the topic. Accordingly, we can offer little guidance to researchers struggling with this issue. We suspect that changes in context-specific leadership skills and knowledge may occur more quickly than do changes in generic leadership skills and knowledge. That is, relatively frequent measurement of context-specific leadership skills and knowledge (especially technical knowledge and skills) may be more appropriate and effective than equally frequent measurement of generic leadership skills and knowledge.

CONCLUSIONS

Although the study of leadership has a rich, lengthy, and voluminous history, empirical research regarding the content and process of leader development over time is quite limited. The very term "leader development" suggests that leaders get better over time, but this remains a largely untested hypothesis. In this chapter, we offered a preliminary theoretical framework designed to organize and reflect leadership theory and research and to provide, in combination with the other chapters of this volume, a foundation for new research. As the chapters of this book make abundantly clear, leader development is critical for organizational development, that is, for the development of flexible, adaptive organizations able to respond quickly, decisively, and effectively to changes in technology, demography, markets, customer and employee expectations, and global competition. We look forward to the new research and theory that will come in the next decades as researchers tackle the subject of leader development, further illuminating how, when, why, and in what ways leaders change over time.

REFERENCES

Argote, L. (1999). *Organizational learning: Creating, retaining, and transferring knowledge.* Norwell, MA: Kluwer.

Bandura, A. (2001). Social cognitive theory: An agentic perspective. *Annual Review of Psychology, 52,* 1–26.

Bass, B. M. (1990). *Bass & Stogdill's handbook of leadership: Theory, research and managerial applications* (3rd ed.). New York: Free Press.

Carver, C. S., & Scheier, M. F. (1981). *Attention and self-regulation: A control-theory approach to human behavior.* New York: Springer-Verlag.

Crant, J. M. (1995). The proactive personality scale and objective job performance among real estate agents. *Journal of Applied Psychology, 80,* 532–537.

Crant, J. M. (2000). Proactive behavior in organizations. *Journal of Management, 26,* 435–462.

Crant, J. M., & Bateman, T. S. (2000). Charismatic leadership viewed from above: The impact of proactive personality. *Journal of Organizational Behavior, 21,* 63–75.

Davenport, T. H., & Prusak, L. (1998). *Working knowledge: How organizations manage what they know.* Boston: Harvard Business School.

Day, D. V. (2001). Leadership development: A review in context. *Leadership Quarterly, 11,* 581–613.

Denison, D. R. (1996). What is the difference between organizational culture and organizational climate? A native's point of view on a decade of paradigm wars. *Academy of Management Review, 21,* 619–654.

Dvir, T., Eden, D., Avolio, B. J., & Shamir, B. (2002). Impact of transformational leadership on follower development and performance: A field experiment. *Academy of Management Journal, 45,* 735–744.

Dweck, C. S., & Leggett, E. L. (1988). A social–cognitive approach to motivation and personality. *Psychological Review, 95,* 256–273.

Edmondson, A. (1999). Psychological safety and learning behavior. *Administrative Science Quarterly, 44,* 350–383.

Elliott, A. J., & Harackiewicz, J. M. (1996). Approach and avoidance achievement goals and intrinsic motivation. *Journal of Personality and Social Psychology, 73,* 171–185.

Fleishman, E. A. (1953). Leadership climate, human relations training, and supervisory behavior. *Personnel Psychology, 6,* 205–222.

Fleishman, E. A., Harris, E. F., & Burtt, H. E. (1955). *Leadership and supervision in industry: An evaluation of a supervisory training program.* Columbus, OH: The Ohio State University Bureau of Educational Research.

Folkman, S., Lazarus, R. S., Gruen, R. J., & DeLongis, A. (1986). Appraisal, coping, health status, and psychological symptoms. *Journal of Personality and Social Psychology, 50,* 571–579.

Frese, M., Kring, W., Soose, A., & Zempel. (1996). Personal initiative at work: Differences between East and West Germany. *Academy of Management Journal, 39,* 37–63.

Garvin, D. A. (2000). *Learning in action: A guide to putting the learning organization to work.* Boston: Harvard Business School.

Gupta, A. K., & Govindarajan, V. (2000). Knowledge management's social dimension: Lessons from Nucor Steel. *Sloan Management Review, 2000,* 71–80.

Hansen, M. T. (2002). Knowledge networks: Explaining effective knowledge sharing in multi-unit companies. *Organization Science, 13,* 232–248.

Hansen, M. T., Nohria, N., & Tierney, T. (1999). What's your strategy for managing knowledge? *Harvard Business Review, 77,* 106–116.

Hansen, M. T., & von Oetinger, B. (2000). Introducing T-shaped managers: Knowledge management's next generation. *Harvard Business Review, 78,* 107–116.

Higgins, M. C., & Thomas, D. A. (2001). Constellations and careers. Toward understanding the effects of multiple developmental relationships. *Journal of Organizational Behavior, 22,* 223–247.

Hofmann, D. A., & Stetzer, A. (1996). A cross-level investigation of factors influencing unsafe behaviors and accidents. *Personnel Psychology, 49,* 307–339.

Ibarra, H. (1999). Provisional selves: Experimenting with image and identity in professional adaptation. *Administrative Science Quarterly, 44,* 764–791.

Judge, T. A., Thoresen, C. J., Pucik, V., & Welbourne, T. M. (1999). Managerial coping with organizational change: A dispositional perspective. *Journal of Applied Psychology, 84,* 107–122.

Karoly, P. (1993). Mechanisms of self-regulation: A systems review. *Annual Review of Psychology, 44,* 23–52.

Kilduff, M., & Day, D. V. (1994). Do chameleons get ahead? The effects of self-monitoring on managerial careers. *Academy of Management Journal, 37,* 1047–1060.

Klein, K. J., Conn, A. B., & Sorra, J. S. (2001). Implementing computerized technology: An organizational analysis. *Journal of Applied Psychology, 86,* 811–824.

Kluger, A. N., & DeNisi, A. (1996). The effects of feedback on performance: A historical review, a meta-analysis, and a preliminary feedback intervention. *Psychological Bulletin, 119,* 354–284.

Kozlowski, S. W. J., & Hults, B. M. (1987). An exploration of climates for technical updating and performance. *Personnel Psychology, 40,* 539–563.

Locke, E. A., & Latham, G. P. (2002). Building a practically useful theory of goal setting and task motivation: A 35 year odyssey. *American Psychologist, 57,* 705–717.

Louis, M. (1985). An investigator's guide to workplace culture. In P. Frost, L. Moore, M. Louis, C. Lundberg, & J. Martin (Eds.), *Organizational culture* (pp. 73–94). Beverly Hills, CA: Sage.

McCall, M. W., Jr., Lombardo, M. M., & Morrison, A. M. (1988). *The lessons of experience: How successful executives develop on the job.* San Francisco: New Lexington.

McCauley, C. D. (2001). Leader training and development. In S. J. Zaccaro & R. J. Klimoski (Eds.), *The nature of organizational leadership: Understanding the performance imperatives confronting today's leaders* (pp. 347–383). San Francisco: Jossey-Bass.

McCauley, C. D., & Brutus, S. (1998). *Management development through job experiences: An annotated bibliography.* Greensboro, NC: Center for Creative Leadership.

McCauley, C. D., Ruderman, M. N., Ohlott, P. J., & Morrow, J. E. (1994). Assessing the developmental components of managerial jobs. *Journal of Applied Psychology,* 544–560.

McCauley, C. D., & Van Velsor, E. (in press). *The Center for Creative Leadership handbook of leadership development* (2nd ed.). San Francisco: Jossey-Bass.

Mehra, A., Kilduff, M., & Brass, D. J. (2001). The social networks of high and low self-monitors: Implications for workplace performance. *Administrative Science Quarterly, 46,* 121–146.

Mitchell, T. R., & James, L. R. (2001). Building better theory: Time and the specification of when things happen. *Academy of Management Review, 26,* 530–548.

Morrison, E. W., & Phelps, C. C. (1999). Taking charge at work: Extra role efforts to initiate workplace change. *Academy of Management Journal, 42,* 403–419.

Moxley, R. S. (1998). Hardships. In C. D. McCauley, R. S. Moxley, & E. Van Velsor (Eds.), *The Center for Creative Leadership handbook of leadership development* (pp. 194–213). San Francisco: Jossey-Bass.

Moxley, R. S., & O'Connor Wilson, P. (1998). A systems approach to leadership development. In C. D. McCauley, R. S. Moxley, & E. Van Velsor (Eds.), *The Center for Creative Leadership handbook of leadership development* (pp. 217–241). San Francisco: Jossey-Bass.

Pfeffer, J., & Sutton, R. I. (2000). *The knowing–doing gap: How smart companies turn knowledge into action.* Boston: Harvard Business School.

Rouiller, J. Z., & Goldstein, I. L. (1993). The relationship between organizational transfer climate and positive transfer of training. *Human Resource Development Quarterly, 4,* 377–390.

Schein, E. (1985). *Organizational culture and leadership.* San Francisco: Jossey-Bass.

Schneider, B. (1987). The people make the place. *Personnel Psychology, 40,* 437–454.

Schneider, B. (1990). The climate for service: An application of the climate construct. In B. Schneider (Ed.), *Organizational climate and culture* (pp. 383–412). San Francisco: Jossey-Bass.

Schneider, B., & Bowen, D. E. (1995). *Winning the service game.* Boston: Harvard Business School.

Schneider, B., Goldstein, H. W., & Smith, D. B. (1995). The ASA framework: An update. *Personnel Psychology, 48,* 747–773.

Schneider, B., & Gunnarson, S. (1990). Organizational climate and culture: The psychology of the workplace. In J. W. Jones, B. D. Steffy, & D. Bray (Eds.), *Applying psychology in business: The manager's handbook* (pp. 542–551). Lexington, MA: Lexington.

Schneider, B., White, S., & Paul, M. C. (1998). Linking service climate and customer perceptions of service quality: Test of a causal model. *Journal of Applied Psychology, 83,* 150–163.

Seibert, S. E., Crant, J. M., & Kraimer, M. L. (1999). Proactive personality and career success. *Journal of Applied Psychology, 84,* 416–427.

Snyder, M. (1979). Self-monitoring processes. *Advances in experimental social psychology, 12,* 85–128.

Sosik, J. J., Potosky, D., & Jung, D. I. (2002). Adaptive self-regulation: Meeting others' expectations of leadership and performance. *Journal of Social Psychology, 142,* 211–232.

Tetrick, L. E., & Da Silva, N. (2003). Assessing the culture and climate for organizational learning. In S. E. Jackson, M. A. Hitt, & A. S. DeNisi (Eds.), *Managing knowledge for sustained competitive advantage* (pp. 333–359). San Francisco: Jossey-Bass.

Tracey, J. B., Tannenbaum, S. I., & Kavanagh, M. J. (1995). Applying trained skills on the job: The importance of the work environment. *Journal of Applied Psychology, 80,* 239–252.

Tsui, A. S., & Ashford, S. J. (1994). Adaptive self-regulation: A process view of managerial effectiveness. *Journal of Management, 20,* 93–121.

Van Velsor, E., McCauley, C. D., & Moxley, R. S. (1998). Introduction: Our view of leadership development. In C. D. McCauley, R. S. Moxley, & E. Van Velsor (Eds.), *The Center for Creative Leadership handbook of leadership development* (pp. 1–26). San Francisco: Jossey-Bass.

VandeWalle, D., Cron, W. L., & Slocum, J. W., Jr. (2001). The role of goal orientation following performance feedback. *Journal of Applied Psychology, 86,* 629–640.

VandeWalle, D., Ganesan, S., Challagalla, G. N., & Brown, S. P. (2000). An integrated model of feedback-seeking behavior: Disposition, context, and cognition. *Journal of Applied Psychology, 85,* 996–1003.

Wood, R., & Bandura, A. (1989). Social cognitive theory of organizational management. *Academy of Management Review, 14,* 361–384.

Yukl, G. A. (2002). *Leadership in organizations* (5th ed.). Upper Saddle River, NJ: Prentice-Hall.

15

Toward a Science
of Leader Development

David V. Day
Pennsylvania State University

Stephen J. Zaccaro
George Mason University

Across the various chapters and topics addressed in this book, myriad issues related to the *what,* the *how,* and the *why* of leader development have been addressed. The purpose of this final chapter is to briefly summarize key issues and contributions and, more important, to also synthesize themes and set a future direction for the science of leader development. The goal is not to provide a single, testable model of leader development (too premature) or even to outline some version of a grand unified theory of leader development (too presumptuous). Instead, our purpose is to highlight what we see as the primary contributions of this book in furthering a nascent science of leader development.

One issue that needs to be addressed immediately is why a science of leader development is needed. The simple answer might be because we do not have one, although a more reasoned response requires some historical perspective. Until fairly recently, practice has "owned" the topic of leader development. This may be due in large part to lucrative business drivers (e.g., financial incentives associated with designing and delivering development programs) that made the topic of leader development the purveyance of consultants and other providers. This might be an overly cynical appraisal (or partial appraisal) of the situation because there were other reasons why scholarly researchers devoted so little attention to leader development. In particular, there have been major obstacles and challenges to studying leader development from a scientific perspective. Some of these challenges remain, whereas there are others in which important advances have been made. We discuss seven of what we see as the most important challenges, past and present, and also briefly discuss the relevant conceptual, theoretical, and methodological advances that make the present an ideal time to initiate serious scientific efforts in the area of leader development.

CHALLENGE 1: CONCEPTUALIZING AND MEASURING CHANGE

At the heart of leader development is the concept of change. Indeed, change is foundational for much of the behavioral sciences in general. Despite its core importance, change has often been conceptualized as a simple difference between two states and operationalized as a simple difference score. There are numerous methodological shortcomings with this approach (discussed later). Equally limiting has been the relatively scant attention paid to conceptualizing and explaining the processes underlying change. What is typically measured or observed by social scientists is the proverbial "tip of the iceberg" in terms of change. Underlying relatively macro-level changes in behavior or thinking are likely to be micro-level processes that are no doubt less amenable to direct measurement, at least without some sort of implicit or indirect techniques.

Day and Lance (chap. 3, this volume) propose that observable changes in leader behavior (e.g., self-awareness and adaptation) are due to deeper, more micro changes in complexity (cognitive, behavioral, and social; also see Hooijberg, Hunt, & Dodge, 1997), which are the result of ongoing processes associated with differentiation and integration. Thus, conceptualizing change requires some attention to the appropriate level of analysis. What is expected to change and when depend on the particular level of analysis that is relevant for the study at hand (Mitchell & James, 2001). Researchers should give careful attention to linking specific measures with theory to better understand and predict the change processes that underlie development.

A classic article in the field of psychology questioned whether researchers could or even should try to measure change (Cronbach & Furby, 1971). The ability to effectively and accurately model change has progressed dramatically over the last decade. Our knowledge of multilevel growth models (e.g., Little, Schnable, & Baumert, 2000) and similar techniques such as latent growth models (e.g., Day & Lance, chap. 3, this volume) and random coefficient growth curve models allow researchers to model within- and between-person change over time. Such models can also incorporate complex error structures that are associated with longitudinal analyses (e.g., first-order autoregression, heterogeneous variances), but cannot be handled by less sophisticated techniques such as multiple regression analyses or analysis of variance. Longitudinal growth curve models are flexible, powerful, and accessible; thus, there is every reason to adopt these methods in the modeling of leader development. Despite these many advantages, few researchers have availed themselves of these powerful modeling techniques. A recent notable exception examined how project team leaders adapted to their role responsibilities over time (Ployhart, Holtz, & Bliese, 2002). This is an especially fitting example given the focus on the theoretically relevant criterion of leader adaptability. We strongly encourage researchers to consider these methodological tools in their work. More widespread use would likely add considerable value to building a science of leader development.

CHALLENGE 2: CRITERION DEVELOPMENT

Better clarity is needed regarding the most appropriate criteria to model in leader development. Because our focus is on leader development, it makes sense that the criterion of interest should be development. Too often, however, there is a tendency to substitute individual, team, or even organizational performance as criteria. Development and performance are not equivalent constructs. As part of a personal challenge to do things differently or to use underdeveloped abilities, there would likely be initial performance declines as development unfolds. Thus, evaluating developmental efforts by means of a performance criterion would likely result in erroneous conclusions about the intervention, especially if the timing of the evaluation is premature. There is a need for greater theoretical as well as empirical attention to criterion development efforts.

A first step in such efforts would be to "unpack" the development construct. As mentioned, Day and Lance (chap. 3, this volume) propose a multilevel framework in which the processes of differentiation and integration contribute to the development of enhanced complexity and more macro-level leader competencies. This is one approach to criterion development, but it is not the only one. In a recent longitudinal field experiment (Dvir, Eden, Avolio, & Shamir, 2002), researchers operationalized a multifaceted development construct. Specifically, the focus was on the effects of transformational leadership training on follower development, as measured by follower (a) self-actualization, (b) extra effort, (c) internalization of organizational moral values, (d) collectivist orientation, (e) critical thinking, (f) active engagement, and (g) self-efficacy. The study was carefully designed to test theoretically grounded hypotheses regarding how transformational leaders might enhance follower development, transforming them and ultimately transforming the organization. In addition, Avolio (chap. 4, this volume) reviews the theory and research behind the full range leadership model. The work of Avolio and colleagues offers an established and validated conceptual model that can be used to guide criterion development efforts. Despite these recent advances in criterion development, the noted challenge is not completely removed. To advance a science of leader development, researchers and theorists need to keep a collective eye on the importance of aligning theory with appropriate outcomes.

CHALLENGE 3: RESEARCH METHODS

The rigorous scientific study of leader development will require research methods that may be difficult to implement. Given that leader development reflects a process of change, its causes and most efficacious drivers will need to be identified through longitudinal methodologies that track and control for extraneous or random effects. Thus, to effectively study leader development, scientists would identify and assess a priori conditions, note the nature of particular modes of change, then observe and assess the short- and long-term effects on selected criteria of leader development. Scientists will also need to incorporate multiple control groups and covariate measures. Such methodological approaches will be difficult to implement and fraught with potential biases and systematic sources of variance that can mitigate the drawing of unambiguous conclusions.

Such approaches are used relatively infrequently in leadership research and are almost nonexistent in the leader development literature. Such research approaches have occurred in studies of leader advancement and promotion and can provide a model for longitudinal studies of leader development (e.g., Bentz, 1967, 1990; Boyatzis, 1982; McClelland, 1985; Moses, 1985; Sparks, 1990). The most ambitious and comprehensive of these were the AT&T assessment center studies (Bray, 1982; Bray, Campbell, & Grant, 1974; Howard & Bray, 1988, 1990). Bray and colleagues used a 3-day assessment center to collect measures of cognitive, motivation, personality, and managerial skills in organizational managers. They followed these initial assessments with subsequent assessments 8 and 20 years later. They also conducted interviews with the managers' supervisors during the years between assessments. They found that attributes reflecting advancement motivation, interpersonal skills, intellectual ability, and administrative skills predicted attained managerial level 20 years after initial assessments. This study, although fairly comprehensive, did not specifically look at the drivers of leader development in the 20-year history of their study. However, some of the motivational attributes studied by Bray and colleagues, such as advancement motivation and an orientation toward achievement, may be strong candidates as developmental drivers.

We hasten to add that longitudinal methods are not the only way to draw rigorous scientific conclusions about leader development. Indeed, if one is interested in the long-term effects of organizational context on development, a necessary research requirement may be participants who stay with the same organization over a long period of time, an increasing rarity in today's organizations (Allred, Snow, & Miles, 1996). The U.S. military branches are examples of such organizations, where senior leaders obviously come from within. Perhaps for this fundamental reason, the military branches devote considerable resources to the study and practice of leadership over an officer's career span. We suspect that the most appropriate leader development research program will incorporate different research methods and include a rigorous longitudinal component.

CHALLENGE 4: DEVELOPMENTAL THEORY

As discussed, development is a form of change. It is impossible to develop without some type of change occurring. In the context of leader development, learning drives change and development. Learning is typically defined as the acquisition of a relatively permanent change in a person due to practice or experience—but a change in what? It has been noted that learning has been defined historically by two very different traditions (Hogan & Warrenfeltz, 2003). The more customary definition approaches learning as a relatively permanent change in *behavior* following experience. This perspective is grounded in behaviorism, and may help to explain the previously noted tendency to evaluate development efforts in terms of changes in performance.

In most managerial applications, performance is measured using behaviorally based ratings due to the complexity of the performance domain (i.e., it does not lend itself well to objective measures). Although there is an inferential leap involved (probably implicit), it can probably be assumed that researchers incorporating performance-based criteria in their developmental frameworks are looking at performance as a proxy for behavior. This may—or may not—be a reasonable inference. A very different tradition, however, conceptualizes learning as a change in or the construction of new mental models. This tradition is based on Gestalt psychology, and by that virtue takes a more holistic and cognitive–perceptual approach to learning. New or improved mental models contribute to more sophisticated ways of making sense of experience.

Although based in very different traditions, Hogan and Warrenfeltz (2003) make an excellent point that the behaviorist and Gestalt traditions articulate complementary processes rather than competing theoretical explanations for learning. A relevant maxim from social psychology is that thinking is for doing, and doing causes thinking. Development therefore consists in changing mental models and adding new behaviors, in the belief that these forms of learning are reciprocal. Nonetheless, there has been relatively little attention to some of the more Gestalt-oriented models from the adult development literature. For example, the reflective judgment model (Kitchener, 1986; Kitchener & King, 1990) postulates a stage model conceptualizing a series of changes that occur in the way that adults understand the process of knowing. Models of postformal and postautonomous ego development (Cook-Greuter, 1990, 1999) examine the level of individual conceptual competence through the content and structure of language production. Level of functioning (i.e., complexity of mental models) can be assessed using the

Washington University Sentence Completion Test (Hy & Loevinger, 1996; Loevinger, 1998). A constructivist developmental stage model proposes various levels of consciousness or complexity in thinking (Kegan, 1994) by examining the number and type of knowledge principles (i.e., differentiation) and their interconnections (i.e., integration). Individuals at higher consciousness levels use greater numbers of knowledge principles to make sense of their experiences and make more interconnections among these principles, which contributes to a broader and more inclusive perspective.

These are just a few relevant theories that are devoted to explaining changes in the construction of new mental models (i.e., learning from a Gestalt tradition). Although there are certainly other learning-based approaches that focus on the cognitive changes underlying skill acquisition (Kanfer & Ackerman, 1989), there has been almost no attention given to the Gestalt-based theories of learning. Given that a hallmark of science is theory testing, greater attention to and inclusion of theories from the adult development literature will contribute to the goal of establishing a leader development science.

CHALLENGE 5: CONTEXT

A hallmark of science is the scientific method, in which tightly controlled experiments are designed to eliminate or greatly minimize extraneous effects on the outcome of interest. True experiments allow strong causal inferences to be drawn between experimental manipulations and measured outcomes. As such, they serve as the gold standard of science. However, leadership is a highly contextualized construct (Hollander & Julian, 1969) involving complex interactions among leaders, followers, and situations. In addition, the most potent forces for leader development often occur in the context of ongoing work rather than in a highly controlled environment like a laboratory or a classroom (McCall, Lombardo, & Morrison, 1988). Stated in a somewhat different manner, the state-of-the-art in leader development is helping leaders learn from the challenges presented in their ongoing work rather than removing them from their work to learn (Moxley & O'Connor Wilson, 1998). Most true experiments strive to control those very "extraneous" contextual factors that are critically important for leader learning and development.

It is possible to study leader development scientifically (Dvir et al., 2002), but doing so also requires a firm understanding of the context. One important context for leader development is the interpersonal one associated with teams. Part V of this book is devoted to articulating contextual issues related to virtual teams (Zaccaro, Ardison, & Orvis, chap. 11, this volume), multicultural issues (Salas, Burke, Fowlkes, & Wilson-Donnelly, chap. 12, this volume), and in developing teams and team leaders (Salas, Burke, & Stagl, chap. 13, this volume). This does not mean that the context issue is solved. Rather, understanding team contexts in this case helps to identify what kinds of things leaders need to do and how to prepare (i.e., develop) them to be successful as team leaders. As mentioned, context in the form of situationally embedded factors can be a potent driver of development, especially by enhancing learning (London & Maurer, in press). A science of leader development cannot advance by ignoring or controlling the context in which leadership occurs. Instead, this science needs to recognize contextual factors as important forces in the ongoing development of leaders.

CHALLENGE 6: MODE OF DEVELOPMENT

Scientific models of leader development will need to consider the different processes that are reflected in alternate modes of development. Leaders can grow through formal, structured instruction, developmental work experiences, and self-initiated learning. Most formal instruction is of relatively short duration and likely to be most effective at targeting skills and knowledge that can be developed fairly quickly. This mode of leader development is likely to be less effective if one is attempting to grow attributes that are slow to change, such as dispositional orientation and cognitive abilities. Also, research on aptitude-by-treatment interactions in training suggests that more formalized and structured learning contexts are more likely to benefit individuals of relatively modest cognitive ability. Although structured, noncomplex instruction has been found to increase the learning and motivation of low-ability learners, such instruction has the opposite effect on high-ability learners (Snow, 1989a, 1989b; Snow & Lohman, 1984). Snow (1989a) noted, for example, that

> High structure appears to help less able learners but often seems to hurt more able learners, relative to less structure. It is noteworthy that students of high ability placed in a high structured condition, when interviewed, often gave evidence of both cognitive and conative problems; they say they experience cognitive interference or motivational turn-off trying to conform to a structured treatment that prevents them from learning in their own way. (p. 441)

Formal classroom instruction, then, is likely to foster a relatively narrower range of leader attributes and is likely to driven by different motivational and cognitive dynamics than other forms of leadership development.

Developmental work experiences provide challenging work assignments to budding leaders that push them to construct new understandings of their more complex operating environment. McCauley, Eastman, and Ohlott (1995) identified five categories of developmental experiences: *transitions, creating change, high level of responsibility, nonauthority relationships,* and *obstacles.* The common elements across these experiences include granting leaders greater job scope, responsibility, and autonomy and placing them in positions requiring them to develop different kinds of relationships than the ones that characterized their prior work environments. Also, stretch assignments foster the development of new and more complex frames of reference, or mental models, of a leader's operating environment. McCauley et al. (1995) noted that "successfully dealing with obstacles deepens a manager's understanding of problematic situations and increases confidence in facing challenges again" (p. 98).

The success of developmental work experiences is likely to be driven by attributes that only partially overlap with those that foster success in formal developmental exercises. For example, it has been argued that individuals with high levels of certain characteristics or abilities are more likely to receive certain assignments and experiences (Tesluk & Jacobs, 1998). Also, individuals can select, shape, or define the nature of their work experiences, thereby increasing or decreasing their developmental potential. Formal classroom instruction offers less control to the learner. Finally, certain attributes will lead different individuals to draw different lessons from the same experience. Along these lines, Banks, Bader, Fleming, Zaccaro, and Barber (2001) showed that developmental work experiences resulted in tacit knowledge gains in Army officers only when they had the requisite metacognitive skills and cognitive complexity to interpret the lessons offered by such experiences.

Leader self-development efforts are typically the least systematic and organized of these three modes of development because they are the ones most dependent upon the learner's own behavior in structuring the learning experience. In a conceptual review of Army leader self development, Bryant (1994) noted that too much has been asked of self-development within the contemporary context. As a result, self-development has become the residual category for any sort of professional education that does not fit within institutional training, or operational assignments. This has diluted both the meaning and effectiveness of self-development.

Compounding the issues raised by Bryant (1994) are the kinds of self-biases and "self-distortions" that may hinder the effectiveness of even well-designed and well-supported leader self-development programs. Various literatures on social cognition and the self are replete with references to biases and motives that contort how individuals perceive and evaluate their selves and their behavior (e.g., Bradley, 1978; Fiske & Taylor, 1991; Miller & Ross, 1975; Snyder, Stephan, & Rosenfield, 1978; Weary, 1980). Effective self-development begins with an accurate and realistic appraisal of one's own strengths and weaknesses. When such appraisals are distorted by self-defensive or self-enhancement biases, subsequent efforts cannot be very effective and indeed may be counterproductive. Thus, more than other forms of leader development, self-development is likely to be more firmly grounded in self-regulation processes and the attributes that foster the effective utilization of such processes.

The differences outlined here (briefly) point to the need for scientific models of leader development that specify clearly how the processes and drivers of change vary across the different modes of learning. Different learning processes likely produce strong outcomes in each mode. Also, the sets of individual attributes that provide the foundations for success in each mode only partially overlap. We also suspect rather strongly that different modes of leader development will be more effective for different targeted leader attributes. Thus, mode of development will likely prove to be a crucial moderator of processes and models specified by scientists of leader development.

CHALLENGE 7: LEADERS AND LEADERSHIP

As mentioned in the introduction to this book (Day & Halpin, chap. 1, this volume), the choice of leader development as the focus of this book was deliberate. There is longstanding conceptual confusion regarding the differences between leader development and leadership development (Day, 2000). Most approaches and practices focus on the development of individual-level knowledge, skills, and abilities (i.e., human capital). Human capital adds value to organizations in similar ways that financial capital and physical capital (e.g., tools, machines, and other equipment) add value (Becker, 1964; Schultz, 1961). However, creating human capital through effective leader development does not guarantee that better leadership will result. In a similar vein, developing more leaders does not guarantee that more leadership will happen. Leadership occurs in a social context and is a direct function of the relationships or connections among individuals in a given situation. From this perspective, leadership is embedded in social structures and processes (Salancik, Calder, Rowland, Leblebici, & Conway, 1975) and drawn out through interaction. Some researchers have labeled those resources that are embedded in networked relationships among participants as social capital (e.g., Nahapiet & Ghoshal, 1998). The emerging area of social capital research has focused on identifying those properties of relationships that make them valuable to individuals and organizations (e.g., Burt, 1992, 1997; Seibert, Kraimer, & Liden, 2001; Tsai & Ghoshal, 1998). Put simply, relationships add value to organizations. In this way, the development of leadership is more closely related to the creation of relational resources in a collective than the development of individual skills or abilities.

There is a reciprocal relationship between the creation of human and social capital. Developing intrapersonal skills in the form of human capital can contribute to the effectiveness of how individual leaders create and manage relationships. Based on leader–member exchange (LMX) theory, those leaders who have the ability to take the perspective of their direct reports are more likely to negotiate high-quality exchanges with them than leaders who cannot take followers' perspectives (Graen, Novak, & Sommerkamp, 1982). Research has shown that high exchange quality is associated with better follower performance, career advancement, and job satisfaction and lower turnover (Gerstner & Day, 1997). Thus, helping leaders develop or enhance their emotional intelligence (Caruso & Wolfe, chap. 10, this volume) could translate into better relationship-management skills for building high-quality exchanges with followers. Of course, it does not guarantee that those skills will be used effectively, but it does provide the basic human capital that is necessary to better understand others and to take their perspective. In this manner, human capital development offers the raw material to be used in the developing social capital.

As mentioned, this is a reciprocal relationship: Social capital can also create human capital. Social capital within a team, business unit, or organization can provide access to leaders' human capital (Coleman, 1988). Access to human capital resources outside of the team, unit, or organization can be enhanced through a leader who occupies a structural hole (i.e., connects otherwise unconnected networks; Burt, 1992). In this manner, the social capital embedded in a network of relationships can provide the resources or opportunities to develop human capital.

An ongoing challenge with regard to developing a science of leader development is the tendency to equate leaders with leadership. As noted by Hollander and Julian (1969) many years ago, a major element of confusion in the study of leadership is the failure to distinguish it as a process from the leader as a person who occupies a central role in that process. The most highly developed leader in the world will impart absolutely no leadership if stranded alone on a desert island. Effective leaders can act with followers to draw out leadership that is a function of the quality and type of relationships that constitute a network. Rather than debating whether leader or leadership development is appropriate, organizations should focus on how to bridge the two. Given the noted reciprocal relationships between the creation of human and social capital, there is likely a mutually reinforcing process between leader and leadership development. Likewise, a systematic perspective on leader(ship) development may require a focus as well on effective *followership* processes and dynamics, which are part of the broader system of leadership relationships. Understanding this bridge and how it is constructed and maintained will be a key piece in building a comprehensive science of leader development.

CONTRIBUTIONS TOWARD A LEADER DEVELOPMENT SCIENCE

The chapters in this book all contribute in some way to addressing or removing the noted obstacles toward the goal of building a science of leader development. Many of the chapters highlight potential areas for making strategic investments in the process ("how) or content ("what") of leader development. The chapters in Part I, however, mainly articulate the "why" of leader development. Maj. Gen. Maggart (chap. 2, this volume) discusses the origins of the Army's transformational efforts to an Objective Force that will be capable of defending the nation in times of great uncertainly and unpredictability. He makes the point that many of the same kinds of threats now faced by the Army are very similar to threats faced in the corporate environment (e.g., rapid deployment, getting the job done in an ambiguous environment, adjusting to radical change). Day and Halpin (chap. 1, this volume) also articulate ways in which organizational landscapes have become increasingly complex, requiring more complex leaders and new ways of constructing leadership across all organizational levels. They also make the point that leader development is a necessary and useful tool to transform organizations. Leader development is needed not only because organizations are transforming, but also because it is a primary driver of that transformational process.

The chapters in Part II (Accelerating Leader Development) offer different perspectives on how to better understand and facilitate the process of leader development, from conceptualizing and modeling change (Day & Lance, chap. 3, this volume) to summarizing a validated model of leadership model to guide the selection of what areas need to be developed and ways to measure those areas in assessing change (Avolio, chap. 4, this volume), to using computer technology as a catalyst for leader development (O'Neil & Fisher, chap. 5, this volume). The chapters in Part III (Cognitive Skills Development) and Part IV (Developing Practical and Emotional Intelligence) offer different perspectives on the important skills needed for developing leaders. What may not be apparent immediately are some of the connections among these various perspectives.

Halpern (chap. 6, this volume) discusses the role of adult cognition from a developmental perspective, and Cohen (chap. 8, this volume) examines how dialogue and language underpin the leadership that emerges among leaders and followers. Both of these approaches can be seen from the Gestalt tradition of learning in terms of the acquisition of new mental models. The reflective judgment model of adult development (Kitchener, 1983) is based on an epistemology of learning that guides how adults understand the process of knowing, which is discussed by Halpern as a basic principle of cognitive development. Ego development models of adult development (e.g., Cook-Greuter, 1990) are grounded in the assumption that the content and structure of individuals' language production can be taken as an indicator of individuals' respective level of conceptual competence. Cohen illustrates how the dialogue among leaders and followers can be used to make inferences about the nature and quality of leadership that exists in a dyad or larger social structure. All of these approaches inform on the relative level of leader cognitive complexity (Day & Lance, chap. 3, this volume) and, as such, can be used as important diagnostic indicators of complexity and can also be used in criterion development efforts. Measuring changes in cognition and complexity through changes in epistemologies of knowing and changes in language and dialogue could be relevant and important indicators of leader development.

Also in Part III, Hall (chap. 7, this volume) explores the relevance of identity and self-awareness to leader development. The connections to other chapters may be evident, but are probably worth stating explicitly. Identity changes across the life span are inextricably bound with growth in self-awareness. As Day and Lance (chap. 3, this volume) propose, self-awareness along with adaptability are important attributes of contemporary leaders, which are developed through posi- tive changes in complexity (cognitive, behavioral, and social). It is not much of a stretch to imagine how practical and emotional intelligence (see Part IV) play a role in the development of what Hall calls the "metacompetence" of self-awareness.

The chapters in Part IV dealing with practical and emotional intelligence have in common an emphasis on the social aspects of being an effective leader. Both approaches could be seen as relevant to the development of social complexity in leaders. The importance of social complexity is evident because of the interpersonal environment in which leaders operate. Social complexity acknowledges that an understanding of the demands and intricacies of various social situations is required in order to develop appropriate situation-based behaviors (Zaccaro, 1999).

The kinds of tacit knowledge and practical intelligence that are important for managers and military leaders (Cianciolo, Antonakis, & Sternberg, chap. 9, this volume) appear to be strongly associated with social complexity. Indeed, Cian- ciolo et al. make the point that the problem-solving expertise that is acquired through experience and held as tacit knowledge is different from cognitive abil- ity or traditional general mental ability. The measures that have been developed (see Figs. 9.3 and 9.4 in their chapter for examples) involve situations in which the focal problems are socially based. Both examples that are provided in their chapter deal with subordinates not completing assigned work. Understanding the problem and constructing cognitive and behavioral strategies for dealing with the poor-performing subordinates is likely a function of the social complexity of the leader. Those leaders with greater levels of social complexity are likely to be able to generate multiple perspectives on the problem situation that provide greater insight into possible causes—and solutions—of the presenting problem. Those leaders at a relatively simple level of social complexity will likely con- struct the situation in relatively simple terms such as a failure to follow directives or even insubordination. The types of actions that are generated are also likely to be simple and direct (e.g., disciplining the follower), but may not shed much light on the cause of the problem or be an effective long-term solution. In terms of the relevance for leader development, directly trying to enhance or teach tacit knowledge and practical intelligence may not be appropriate given the purported implicit nature of the construct. Indeed, attempting to make explicit and convey things that are by definition implicitly held does not appear to make a great deal of sense. However, by focusing on directly and explicitly developing social com- plexity through experience and feedback, it is likely that gains in tacit knowledge and practical intelligence will follow.

Caruso and Wolfe (chap. 10, this volume) expound on the role of emotional in- telligence in organizations, and, more specifically, in leadership contexts. They take an ability-based perspective, in which emotional intelligence is denoted through the relative level of four interrelated abilities: (a) accurately identifying emo- tions, (b) generating emotions and using them emotions to help with thinking, (c) understanding the causes of emotion, and (d) being able to blend emotional and rational information in ways that lead to effective and adaptive outcomes (Mayer & Salovey, 1997). They point out that the abilities composing emotional intelligence, such as emotional identification and emotional regulation, rest on a foundation of cognitive, behavioral, and social complexity. Although Caruso and Wolfe are equivocal about whether emotional intelligence can be directly improved, there is little doubt that emotionally related complexity can be developed. Key to doing this successfully would be to link possible developmental interventions with the processes of differentiation and integration that contribute to enhanced cognitive, behavioral, and social complexity relevant to emotional identification and regulation.

The chapters in Part V delve into various aspects of team leadership and leader development in team contexts. As discussed, a science of leader development must be concerned with context because leadership is a highly contextualized construct. One particular facet of the leadership context that is becoming increasingly more common is the virtual nature of teams. Zaccaro, Ardison, and Orvis (chap. 11, this volume) provide an overview of some of the more important aspects of a virtual context and link these context attributes with desired leader competencies and their development. In this way, Zaccaro et al. contribute to a better understanding of the developmental content for leaders of virtual teams. Skills such as communication, conflict resolution, and emotion management are all consistent with earlier themes regarding the "what" of leader development.

Salas, Burke, Fowlkes, and Wilson-Donnelly (chap. 12, this volume) further elaborate on the evolving context of team leadership. These authors explore a number of issues related to the multicultural context within many teams and how an event-based approach can help develop leaders who will be effective in these contexts. Specifically, events are embedded within presented scenarios that serve as trigger points for demonstrating certain behavioral competencies. This is consistent with Avolio's discussion (chap. 4, this volume) of how planned trigger events can enhance self-regulatory behavior and facilitate leader development. Both of these approaches are in line with what Kegan (1994) proposed in terms of offering opportunities to get "in over our heads" in a relatively safe environment, that is, try out new ways of thinking and new behaviors as a means of encouraging development. Kegan described the process as ensuring that a developmental bridge is anchored firmly on both ends before expecting anyone to traverse it.

Salas, Burke, and Stagl (chap. 13, this volume) outline what they see as important team competencies needed for success in increasingly complex and dynamic environments. As with individual leader development, increased adaptability is a critical concern. One message of this chapter is that a high degree of team interdependence is needed to adapt successfully to the complex challenges faced by many teams. Indeed, many of the role requirements of effective team members are much the same as those expected of team leaders. The line that differentiates a team leader from an "ordinary" team member is becoming increasingly fuzzy. As noted by Day and Halpin (chap. 1, this volume), there is a pervasive need for people in every function and at every level to participate in the leadership process, not just those who are designated as the formal leader. No single leader can possibly have all the answers to every problem, especially if those problems are in the form of adaptive challenges that are novel and complex. Because of these contextual demands, all organizational members need to be leaders and all leaders need to be better prepared to participate in leadership.

Klein and Ziegert (chap. 14, this volume) offer another perspective on context. In addition to considering individual differences in the willingness or ability to engage in leader development, an organization's climate for learning and development is a critical part of the leader development context. Without some shared summary perceptions that leader development is rewarded, supported, and expected within an organization, all other efforts are potentially futile. This reinforces the important point that leader development is a contextually embedded process, and the context must be more than merely neutral. In order for individuals to learn from their experiences in a manner that encourages ongoing development, the context should support and nurture such efforts and not just tolerate them.

CONCLUSIONS

The title of this book is *Leader Development for Transforming Organizations.* However, much more has been written about the leader development aspects than those related to organizational transformation per se. If readers expected a detailed treatment of how to restructure organizations to bring about transformation, then they likely will have been sorely disappointed. Such readers will also have missed an important point. Focusing solely on structure as the way to transform organizations is akin to rearranging deck chairs on the *Titanic.* Profound organizational transformation occurs through transforming individuals, for, as Ben Schneider (1987) pointed out, the people make the place. It is certainly the case that structure can provide an obstacle and ongoing challenge to transformation, especially if it deters individual development. However, if true and lasting change is desired, transformation must be tackled by investing in those most valuable of organizational resources—people.

REFERENCES

Allred, B. B., Snow, C. C., & Miles, R. E. (1996). Characteristics of managerial careers of the 21st century. *Academy of Management Executive, 10,* 17–27.
Banks, D., Bader, P., Fleming, P., Zaccaro, S. J., & Barber, H. (2001, April). *Leader adaptability: The role of work experiences and individual differences.* Paper presented at the 16th annual meeting of the Society for Industrial and Organizational Psychology, San Diego, CA.
Becker, G. S. (1964). *Human capital.* New York: Columbia University.

Bentz, V. J. (1967). The Sears experience in the investigation, description, and prediction of executive behavior. In F. R. Wickert & D. E. McFarland (Eds.), *Measuring executive effectiveness* (pp. 147–206). New York: Appleton-Century-Crofts.

Bentz, V. J. (1990). Contextual issues in predicting high-level leadership performance: Contextual richness as a criterion consideration in personality research with executives. In K. E. Clark & M. B. Clark (Eds.), *Measures of leadership* (pp. 131–143). Greensboro, NC: Center for Creative Leadership.

Boyatzis, R. R. (1982). *The competent manager: A model for effective performance.* New York: Wiley.

Bradley, G. W. (1978). Self-serving biases in the attribution process: A re-examination of the fact or fiction question. *Journal of Personality and Social Psychology, 4,* 121–156.

Bray, D. W. (1982). The assessment center and the study of lives. *American Psychologist, 37,* 180–189.

Bray, D. W., Campbell, R. J., & Grant, D. L. (1974). *Formative years in business: A long-term AT&T study of managerial lives.* New York: Wiley.

Bryant, C. D. (1994). *Strategies for augmentation initiatives for leadership self-development program* (Res. Note 94-29; DTIC ADA285307). Alexandria, VA: U.S. Army Research Institute for the Behavioral and Social Sciences.

Burt, R. S. (1992). *Structural holes: The social structure of competition.* Cambridge, MA: Harvard University Press.

Burt, R. S. (1997). The contingent value of social capital. *Administrative Science Quarterly, 42,* 339–365.

Coleman, J. S. (1988). Social capital in the creation of human capital. *American Journal of Sociology, 94*(Supplement), S95–S120.

Cook-Greuter, S. R. (1990). Maps for living: Ego-development stages from symbiosis to conscious universal embeddedness. In M. L. Commons, C. Armon, L. Kohlberg, F. A. Richards, T. A. Grotzer, & J. D. Sinnott (Eds.), *Adult development: Models and methods in the study of adolescent and adult thought* (vol. 2, pp. 79–103). New York: Praeger.

Cook-Greuter, S. R. (1999). *Postautonomous ego development: A study of its nature and measurement.* Unpublished dissertation, Harvard University, Cambridge, MA.

Cronbach, L. J., & Furby, L. (1971). How should we measure "change"— Or should we? *Psychological Bulletin, 74,* 68–80.

Day, D. V. (2000). Leadership development: A review in context. *Leadership Quarterly, 11,* 581–613.

Dvir, T., Eden, D., Avolio, B. J., & Shamir, B. (2002). Impact of transformational leadership on follower development and performance: A field experiment. *Academy of Management Journal, 45,* 735–744.

Fiske, S. T., & Taylor, S. E. (1991). *Social cognition* (2nd ed.). New York: McGraw-Hill.

Gerstner, C. R., & Day, D. V. (1997). Meta-analytic review of leader–member exchange theory: Correlates and construct issues. *Journal of Applied Psychology, 82,* 827–844.

Graen, G. B., Novak, M., & Sommerkamp, P. (1982). The effects of leader–member exchange and job design on productivity and satisfaction: Testing a dual attachment model. *Organizational Behavior and Human Performance, 30,* 109–131.

Hogan, R., & Warrenfeltz, R. (2003). Educating the modern manager. *Academy of Management Learning and Education, 2,* 74–84.

Hollander, E. P., & Julian, J. W. (1969). Contemporary trends in the analysis of leadership processes. *Psychological Bulletin, 71,* 387–397.

Hooijberg, R., Hunt, J. G., & Dodge, G. E. (1997). Leadership complexity and development of the leaderplex model. *Journal of Management, 23,* 375–408.

Howard, A., & Bray, D. W. (1988). *Managerial lives in transition: Advancing age and changeing times.* New York: Guilford.

Howard, A., & Bray, D.W. (1990). Predictions of managerial success over long periods of time: Lessons from the Management Progress Study. In K. E. Clark & M. B. Clark (Eds.), *Measures of leadership* (pp. 113–130). West Orange, NJ: Leadership Library of America.

Hy, L. X., & Loevinger, J. (1996). *Measuring ego development* (2nd ed.). Mahwah, NJ: Lawrence Erlbaum Associates, Inc.

Kanfer, R., & Ackerman, P. L. (1989). Motivation and cognitive abilities: An integrative/aptitude–treatment interaction approach to skill acquisition. *Journal of Applied Psychology Monographs, 74,* 657–690.

Kegan, R. (1994). *In over our heads: The mental demands of modern life.* Cambridge, MA: Harvard University.

Kitchener, K. S. (1983). Cognition, metacognition, and epistemic knowledge: A three-level model of cognitive processing. *Human Development, 4,* 222–232.

Kitchener, K. S. (1986). The reflective judgment model: Characteristics, evidence, and measurement. In R. A. Mines & K. S. Kitchener (Eds.), *Adult cognitive development: Methods and models* (pp. 76–91). New York: Praeger.

Kitchener, K. S., & King, P. M. (1990). The reflective judgment model: Ten years of research. In M. L. Commons, C. Armon, L. Kohlberg, F. A. Richards, T. A. Grotzer, & J. D. Sinnott (Eds.), *Adult development: Models and methods in the study of adolescent and adult thought* (vol. 2, pp. 63–78). New York: Praeger.

Little, T. D., Schnable, K. U., & Baumert, J. (Eds.). (2000). *Modeling longitudinal and multilevel data: Practical issues, applied approaches, and specific examples.* Mahwah, NJ: Lawrence Erlbaum Associates, Inc.

Loevinger, J. (Ed.). (1998). *Technical foundations for measuring ego development: The Washington University Sentence Completion Test.* Mahwah, NJ: Lawrence Erlbaum Associates, Inc.

London, M., & Maurer, T. J. (in press). Leadership development: A diagnostic model for continuous learning in organizations. In R. J. Sternberg, J. Antonakis, & A. T. Cianciolo (Eds.), *The nature of leadership.* Thousand Oaks, CA: Sage.

Mayer, J. D., & Salovey, P. (1997). What is emotional intelligence? In P. Salovey & D. Sluyter (Eds.), *Emotional development and emotional intelligence: Implications for educators* (pp. 3–31). New York: Basic Books.

McCall, M. W., Lombardo, M. M., & Morrison, A. M. (1988). *The lessons of experience: How successful executives develop on the job.* Lexington, MA: Lexington.

McCauley, C. D., Eastman, L. J., & Ohlott, P. J. (1995). Linking management selection and development through stretch assignments. *Human Resource Management, 34,* 93–115.

McClelland, D. C. (1985). *Human motivation.* Glenview, IL: Scott Foresman.

Miller, D. T., & Ross, M. (1975). Self-serving biases in the attribution of causality: Fact or fiction. *Psychological Bulletin, 82,* 213–225.

Mitchell, T. R., & James, L. R. (2001). Building better theory: Time and the specification of when things happen. *Academy of Management Review, 26,* 530–547.

Moses, J. L. (1985). Using clinical methods in a high level management assessment center. In H. J. Bernardin & D. A. Bownas (Eds.), *Personality assessment in organizations* (pp. 177–192). New York: Praeger.

Moxley, R. S., & O'Connor Wilson, P. (1998). A systems approach to leadership development. In C. D. McCauley, R. S. Moxley, & E. Van Velsor (Eds.), *The Center for Creative Leadership handbook of leadership development* (pp. 217–241). San Francisco: Jossey-Bass.

Nahapiet, J., & Ghoshal, S. (1998). Social capital, intellectual capital, and the organizational advantage. *Academy of Management Review, 23,* 242–266.

Ployhart, R. E., Holtz, B. C., & Bliese, P. D. (2002). Longitudinal data analysis: Applications of random coefficients modeling to leadership research. *Leadership Quarterly, 13,* 455–486.

Salancik, G. R., Calder, B. J., Rowland, K. M., Leblebici, H., & Conway, M. (1975). Leadership as an outcome of social structure and process: A multidimensional analysis. In J. G. Hunt & L. L. Larson (Eds.), *Leadership frontiers* (pp. 81–101). Kent, OH: Kent State University.

Schneider, B. (1987). The people make the place. *Personnel Psychology, 40,* 437–453.

Schultz, T. W. (1961). Investment in human capital. *American Economic Review, 51,* 1–17.

Seibert, S. E., Kraimer, M. L., & Liden, R. C. (2001). A social capital theory of career success. *Academy of Management Journal, 44*, 219–237.

Snow, R. E. (1989a). Aptitude–treatment interaction as a framework of research in individual differences in learning. In R. Kanfer, P. L. Ackerman, & R. Cudeck (Eds.), *Abilities, motivation, and methodology* (pp. 435–474). Hillsdale, NJ: Lawrence Erlbaum Associates, Inc.

Snow, R. E. (1989b). Cognitive–conative aptitude interactions in learning. In P. L. Ackerman, R. J. Sternberg, & R. Glaser (Eds.), *Learning and individual differences: Advances in theory and research* (pp. 13–59). New York: Freeman.

Snow, R. E., & Lohman, D. F. (1984). Toward a theory of cognitive aptitude for learning from instruction. *Journal of Educational Psychology, 76*, 347–376.

Snyder, M. L., Stephan, W. G., & Rosenfield, D. (1978). Attributional egotism. In J. H. Harvey, W. Icjkes, & R. F. Kidd (Eds.), *New directions in attribution theory* (vol. 2, pp. 91–120). Hillsdale, NJ: Lawrence Erlbaum Associates, Inc.

Sparks, C. P. (1990). Testing for management potential. In K. E. Clark & M. B. Clark (Eds.), *Measures of leadership* (pp. 103–112). Greensboro, NC: Center for Creative Leadership.

Tesluk, P. E., & Jacobs, R. R. (1998). Toward an integrated model of work experience. *Personnel Psychology, 51*, 321–355.

Tsai, W., & Ghoshal, S. (1998). Social capital and value creation: The role of intrafirm networks. *Academy of Management Journal, 41*, 464–476.

Weary, G. (1980). Examination of affect and egotism as mediators of bias in causal attributions. *Journal of Personality and Social Psychology, 38*, 348–357.

Zaccaro, S. J. (1999). Social complexity and the competencies required for effective military leadership. In J. G. Hunt, G. E. Dodge, & L. Wong (Eds.), *Out-of-the-box leadership: Transforming the twenty-first army and other top-performing organizations* (pp. 131–151). Stamford, CT: JAI.

Author Index

A

Abedi, J., 100, 107, 119
Ackerman, P. L., 137, 150, 272, 279, 286, 289, 290, 388, 398
Adams, C., 106, 117
Adams, P. C., 104, 109, 117
Adelman, L., 179, 192, 195, 197, 199, 207, 345, 352
Aditya, R. N., 82, 97, 213, 214, 235
Adler, N. J., 293, 294, 320
Aguinis, H., 11, 21
Alderfer, C. P., 157, 176
Alessi, S. M., 104, 113, 117
Allen, J. S., 77, 96
Alliger, G. M., 213, 235
Allred, B. B., 386, 396
Amabile, T., 147, 150
Amason, A. C., 278, 289
Amory, A., 106, 117
Anderson, H., 326, 351
Anderson, L.W., 117
Andrews, D., 104, 119
Antonakis, J., 73, 78, 79, 96, 216, 217, 223, 226, 227, 228, 232, 234
Antonietti, A., 107, 117
Argote, L., 278, 289, 374, 379
Argyris, C., 232, 234
Arthur, M., 75, 98
Arthur, W., Jr., 108, 117
Ashburner, J., 128, 151
Ashby, F. G., 244, 260
Ashford, S. J., 363, 364, 367, 382
Ashforth, B., 154, 157, 160, 164, 171, 173
Ashforth, B. E., 252, 260
Ashkanasy, N. M., 253, 260

Atwater, D., 86, 96
Atwater, L. A., 84, 86, 96, 96
Austin, J., 185, 206
Avolio, B. J., 4, 13, 21, 71, 72, 73, 76, 78, 79, 80, 81, 83, 87, 91, 95, 96, 97, 98, 253, 261, 366, 380, 385, 388, 397

B

Baddeley, A. D., 144, 150
Bader, P., 286, 287, 292, 345, 346, 352, 390, 396
Bader, P. K., 347, 351
Baker, D. P., 316, 321
Baker, E. L., 113, 115, 117, 119
Bales, R. F., 21
Baltes, P. B., 41, 67, 129, 131, 150, 150
Bandura, A., 134, 150, 172, 173, 273, 289, 363, 364, 369, 379, 382
Banks, D., 345, 346, 352, 390, 396
Barach, J. A., 251, 260
Barber, H., 345, 346, 352, 390, 396
Barber, H. F., 347, 351
Bareket, T., 108, 118
Barge, J. K., 178, 179, 206
Barley, S., 164, 173
Barling, J., 13, 22, 77, 81, 82, 96, 98
Barnlund, D. C., 309, 320
Bar-On, R., 241, 261
Barrett, L. F., 245, 260
Barsade, S. G., 252, 261
Barton, N., 115, 119
Bass, B., 342, 352
Bass, B. M., 4, 21, 71, 72, 73, 74, 75, 77, 78, 80, 81, 82, 96, 98, 177, 207, 214, 234, 253, 261, 298, 320, 360, 379

Bateman, T. S., 369, 380
Battaglia, D. A., 113, 115, 120
Battista, M., 171, 174
Baughman, W., 345, 353
Baughman, W. A., 228, 235
Baumeister, R. F., 154, 174
Baumert, J., 384, 398
Becker, G. S., 391, 396
Becker, H., 164, 173
Begley, I. J., 114, 117
Behson, S. J., 345, 355
Beier, M. E., 137, 150
Bell, B. S., 348, 352
Bell, E. L., 158, 171, 174
Ben-Ari, E., 329, 346, 354
Benjamin, A. S., 141, 151
Benjamin, B., 5, 21
Benjamin, L., 293, 322
Bennett, J. M., 315, 320
Bennett, W. R., 53, 68
Bennis, W. G., 5, 22
Bentz, V. J., 386, 397
Berkerman, Z., 294, 322
Berlew, D. E., 167, 174
Betz, J. A., 108, 117
Bewley, W., 103, 117
Beyer, J. M., 72, 96
Bhawuk, D. P. S., 314, 320
Billingsley, K., 54, 67
Birnbaum, D., 240, 263
Bjork, R. A., 140, 141, 142, 143, 150
Blair, V., 273, 292
Blanchard, K. H., 252, 262
Blickensderfer, E., 312, 320
Bliese, P. D., 385, 398
Blumer, R., 178, 207
Bohm, D., 206, 207
Bollen, K. A., 59, 67
Boodoo, G., 242, 246, 262
Bouchard, T. J., 242, 246, 262
Bowen, D. E., 371, 381
Bowen, K. R., 137, 150
Bower, G. H., 240, 261
Bowers, C. A., 326, 336, 340, 350, 352, 354, 354
Bowman, E. D., 295, 322
Boyatzis, R. E., 241, 261
Boyatzis, R. R., 386, 397
Boyce, L. A., 345, 353
Boyd, B., 277, 290
Boykin, A. W., 242, 246, 262

Bradford, L. P., 5, 21
Bradley, G. W., 390, 397
Braithwaite, J., 108, 121
Bransford, J., 138, 150
Brass, D. J., 284, 289, 367, 381
Bratman, M. E., 189, 207
Braun, C. C., 336, 352
Braverman, E. P., 213*nd214, 223, 235
Bray, D. W., 386, 397
Breinin, E., 76, 98
Bresnick, T., 179, 192, 195, 197, 199, 207
Bresnick, T. A., 345, 352
Brett, J., 84, 96
Brett, J. M., 53, 67
Brewer, M. B., 15, 21
Bridges, W., 158, 174
Briggs, R. O., 269, 270, 275, 291
Brim, O., 161, 174
Briscoe, J. P., 47, 67, 153, 174
Brislin, R. W., 314, 320
Brody, N., 242, 246, 262
Bromiley, P., 273, 289
Brooks, F. P., Jr., 115, 117
Brown, A., 138, 150
Brown, B. R., 114, 117
Brown, D. J., 15, 22, 93, 97
Brown, F., 100, 117
Brown, J. D., 246, 263
Brown, K. G., 269, 270, 285, 291
Brown, P., 179, 181, 193, 207
Brown, S. P., 368, 382
Brownlee, J., 107*nd108, 120
Bruning, R. H., 107, 117
Brutus, S., 50, 68, 365, 381
Bryant, C. D., 390, 397
Bullis, R. C., 216, 223, 227, 235
Bundy, D. A., 217, 227, 236
Bunker, B. B., 274, 291
Burke, C. S., 279, 282, 289, 292, 310, 323, 330, 331, 333, 335, 336, 337, 340, 345, 352, 354
Burns, J. J., 320
Burns, J. M., 72, 74, 96
Burt, R. S., 391, 392, 397
Burtt, 5
Burtt, H. E., 371, 380
Butcher, V., 13, 22, 77, 98
Bycio, P., 77, 96
Byrne, R. W., 179, 208

C

Cacioppo, J. T., 136, 150
Calder, B. J., 7, 12, 22, 391, 398
Campbell, D. P., 156, 174
Campbell, R. J., 332, 352, 386, 397
Campion, M. A., 213*nd214, 223, 235
Cannon-Bowers, 346, 347, 355
Cannon-Bowers, J. A., 106, 108, 120, 280, 283,
    289, 291, 308, 309, 310, 312, 316, 319, 320,
    321, 321, 323, 326, 328, 329, 330, 331, 332,
    333, 335, 336, 337, 338, 339, 342, 344,
    346, 347, 349, 350, 352, 352, 353, 354, 355
Carey, J. O., 113, 118
Carey, L., 113, 118
Carlston, D. E., 15, 21, 45, 67
Carnevale, P. J. D., 278, 289
Carpenter, S., 313, 321
Carroll, J. B., 242, 246, 255, 261
Carter, G. W., 223, 235
Cartier, F., 86, 96
Caruso, D. R., 242, 243, 247, 250, 255, 261, 262
Carver, C. S., 363, 380
Casella, D. F., 253, 261
Ceci, S. J., 242, 246, 262
Challagalla, G. N., 368, 382
Chambers, C., 104, 109, 117
Chan, D., 52, 56, 57, 62, 63, 67
Chan, K. Y., 136, 150
Cheraskin, L., 274, 292
Chinnappan, M., 142, 151
Chiu, C.-Y., 313, 322
Choi, I., 304, 308, 321, 322
Christopher, E. M., 105, 117
Church, A. H., 251, 261
Cianciolo, A. T., 217, 227, 228, 229, 232, 233,
    234
Clark, R. E., 103, 117, 120
Clark, S. M., 296, 323
Clifton, T. C., 76, 98
Clore, G. L., 256, 262
Cocking, R., 138, 150
Cohen, M., 189, 190, 206, 207
Cohen, M. S., 113, 115, 117, 179, 187, 190, 192,
    195, 197, 198, 206, 207, 345, 352
Cohen, S. G., 269, 289
Coleman, J. S., 392, 397
Collaer, M. L., 144, 151
Collins, A., 256, 262
Colquitt, J. A., 133, 134, 150
Conger, J. A., 5, 21

Conn, A. B., 372, 381
Connelly, M. S., 76, 98, 212, 234, 236, 287,
    291
Converse, S., 268, 280, 289, 291
Converse, S. A., 280, 289, 309, 320, 326, 354
Conway, M., 7, 12, 22, 391, 398
Conyne, R. K., 312, 321
Cook-Greuter, S. R., 387, 393, 397
Coons, A. E., 4, 22
Costa, P. T., Jr., 136, 152
Coutu, D. L., 275, 289
Crafts, J. L., 213, 235
Cramton, C. D., 281, 282, 289
Crant, J. M., 369, 380, 382
Crisafulli, L., 107, 117
Cron, W. L., 368, 382
Cronbach, L. J., 52, 67, 384, 397
Cropanzano, R., 253, 263
Cross, T. C., 80, 96
Csikszentmihalyi, M., 9, 21
Cull, W. L., 142, 150
Cullen, D., 325, 352
Cummings, L. L., 273, 289

D

Da Silva, N., 372, 382
Damasio, A. R., 240, 261
Dansereau, D. F., 144, 150
Darrow, C. N., 161, 175
Daudelin, M. W., 170, 175
Davenport, T. H., 374, 380
Davidow, 269
Davidson, J. E., 318, 321
Davies, J. M., 340, 353
Davis, J. H., 274, 291
Day, D., 102, 117
Day, D. V., 6, 9, 21, 45, 50, 51, 65, 67, 79, 85,
    86, 96, 218, 234, 240, 245, 287, 261, 289,
    364, 368, 372, 380, 381, 391, 397
De Vader, C. L., 213, 235
Deaux, K., 171, 174
Deci, E. L., 106, 118
Deckert, J. C., 342, 352
Dees, S. M., 144, 150
DeGroot, T., 80, 96
Delongis, A., 370, 380
DeMarie, S., 268, 269, 270, 292
DeMarie, S. M., 330, 355
deMeuse, K., 326, 355

Den Hartog, D. N., 298, 321
DeNisi, A., 51, 68, 134, 151, 366, 381
Denison, D. R., 45, 46, 67, 371, 380
Dennis, M., 216, 223, 227, 235
DeSanctis, G., 91, 96
Deshpande, S. P., 314, 321
DeSmet, A. L., 245, 262
Desselles, M. L., 295, 322
Deuser, R., 318, 321
DeWinstanley, P., 107, 118
deWinstanley, P. A., 140, 143, 150
Diamond, M. A., 99, 119
Diaz-Guerrero, R., 304, 321
Dick, W., 113, 118
Dickinson, T. L., 268, 291, 326, 354
Distefano, J. J., 293*nd294, 321
Dixon, N. M., 10, 21, 49, 67
Dobroth, K. M., 246, 261
Dodd, C. H., 299, 321
Dodge, G., 91, 96
Dodge, G. E., 12, 13, 21, 42, 46, 47, 67, 212,
     215, 235, 384, 397
Donchin, E., 104, 118
Doohar, M. S., 5, 21
Doolittle, J. H., 107, 118
Downton, J. V., 72, 74, 96
Doyle, M., 126, 149, 151
Dragoni, L., 346, 355
Drasgow, F., 136, 150
Drath, W., 4, 14, 21, 44, 67, 90, 97
Drath, W. H., 11, 21, 44, 67
Drebot, M., 227, 228, 229, 232, 233
Drew, P., 178, 207
Driskell, J. E., 105, 118, 341, 347, 352, 354
Driver, M. J., 42, 68
Drucker, P. F., 16, 21
Druckman, D., 141, 142, 150
Dumdum, R., 80, 81, 97
Duncan, P. C., 345, 352
Duncan, S. C., 57, 67
Duncan, S. E., 57, 67
Duncan, T. E., 57, 67
Dunlosky, J., 148, 152
Dunnette, M. D., 223, 235
Dutton, J. E., 9, 22, 255, 261
Dvir, T., 81, 97, 366, 380, 385, 388, 397
Dweck, C. S., 84, 97, 134, 139, 150, 368, 380
Dwyer, D., 314, 321
Dwyer, D. J., 105, 118, 340, 350, 352

E

Earley, P. C., 301, 303, 304, 305, 307, 309, 321
Eastman, L. J., 389, 390, 398
Eccles, 275
Eckhardt, D. R., 251, 260
Eden, D., 4, 21, 81, 97, 366, 380, 385, 388, 397
Edmondson, A., 372, 380
Edmondson, A. C., 328, 352
Ekman, P., 256, 261
Elliott, A. J., 368, 380
Endsley, M. R., 113, 115, 118, 120
Engelbrecht, S. E., 49, 68
Entin, E. E., 342, 352
Epitropaki, O., 13, 22, 77, 98
Erez, M., 301, 303, 304, 305, 307, 321
Erikson, E. H., 157, 174
Evaristo, 299, 323

F

Facteau, C. L., 86, 97
Facteau, J. D., 86, 97
Faria, A. J., 104, 105, 118, 118
Fehr, B., 181, 207
Feinstein, J. A., 136, 150
Feldon, D., 100, 118
Fery, Y. A., 108, 118
Fichman, M., 278, 289
Fiedler, F. E., 6, 21
Fields, R., 309, 322
Finnegan, E. B., 213*nd214, 223, 235
Fiol, C. M., 11, 21
Fisher, C. D., 160, 174
Fisher, J. Y. C., 113, 115, 119
Fisher, K., 330, 352
Fiske, S. T., 15, 21, 49, 67, 390, 397
Fleenor, J., 13, 22
Fleishman, E., 345, 353
Fleishman, E. A., 5, 21, 212, 228, 235, 235, 268,
     283, 289, 290, 291, 297, 321, 343, 371, 380
Fleming, P., 345, 346, 352, 390, 396
Fleming, P. J., 347, 351
Fletcher, J., 166, 174
Folkman, S., 370, 380
Fong, G. T., 148, 151
Ford, J. K., 135, 152, 318, 321, 348, 354, 355
Forgas, J. P., 240, 261
Forsythe, G. B., 213, 214, 216, 223, 227, 227,
     228, 232, 235, 236

Foshay, W. R., 113, 120
Foster, L. W., 172, 174
Foti, R. J., 213, 214, 235, 236
Fowlkes, J. E., 314, 315, 316, 319, 321, 340, 350, 352
Frackowiak, R. S., 128, 151
Frackowiak, R. S. J., 128, 151
Franz, T., 315, 319, 321
Freeman, C., 328, 352
Freeman, J. T., 113, 115, 117, 189, 190, 206, 207
Freiberg, S. J., 15, 22
French, J .R., 11, 21
Frensch, P. A., 107, 119
Frese, M., 369, 380
Frieberg, S. J., 93, 97
Friedman, H. S., 253, 261
Frith, C. D., 128, 151
Frost, P. J., 255, 261
Frye, R. L., 278, 290
Fulk, J., 277, 290
Fulmer, R. M., 5, 22
Funder, D. C., 246, 261
Furby, L., 52, 67, 384, 397
Futrell, D., 326, 355

G

Gadian, D. G., 128, 151
Ganasen, S., 368, 382
Gardner, H., 242, 261
Gardner, W., 15, 21
Garland, D. J., 113, 115, 118
Garvin, D. A., 374, 380
Gaspar, R., 80, 97
Geer, B., 164, 173
Geis, M., 181, 182, 187, 189, 207
Geissler, P. W., 217, 227, 236
George, J. M., 250, 253, 261, 278, 290
Gerlock, D. L., 114, 117
Gerstner, C. R., 298, 323, 391, 397
Gessner, T. L., 76, 98
Getels, J. W., 9, 21
Gharajedaghi, J., 42, 67
Ghatala, E. S., 148, 152
Ghoshal, S., 391, 398, 399
Gibbons, T. C., 72, 76, 96
Gibson, D. E., 240, 243, 252, 261
Gibson, J. J., 217, 235
Gil, G., 227, 228, 229, 232, 233, 234
Gilbert, J. A., 49, 50, 69, 212, 234, 236

Gioia, D. A., 296, 323
Gladstein, D., 278, 290
Glickman, A. S., 326, 354
Godfrey, P. A., 160, 176
Goldstein, H. W., 13, 22, 376, 381
Goldstein, I. L., 371, 381
Goldston, J., 293, 322
Goleman, D., 83, 97, 99, 118, 155, 174, 241, 261
Golembiewski, R. T., 54, 67
Gomez, C., 312, 321
Good, C. D., 128, 151
Goodheim, L., 253, 261
Goodwin, F. K., 256, 261
Goodwin, J. F., 337, 353
Goodwin, V. L., 74, 75, 78, 97
Gopher, D., 108, 118
Gosen, J., 104, 120
Govindarajan, V., 374, 375, 380
Graen, G. B., 297, 309, 321, 391, 397
Graesser, A. C., 140, 151
Graham, S. E., 113, 115, 118
Grahn, J. L., 317, 321
Grandey, A. A., 245, 261
Grant, D. L., 386, 397
Greenfield, P. M., 107, 118
Greenhouse, J. B., 143, 151
Grice, P., 183, 184, 186, 207
Griffith, T. L., 268, 270, 271, 281, 290
Grigorenko, E. L., 213, 214, 217, 223, 227, 228, 229, 232, 233, 234, 236
Grolnic, S., 140, 151
Grootendorst, R., 182, 189, 197, 208
Gross, J. J., 256, 261
Grosz, B. J., 189, 207
Gruen, R. J., 370, 380
Guastello, S. J., 54, 67
Gulley, S. M., 135, 151
Gully, S. M., 283, 291, 318, 321, 342, 344, 346, 347, 349, 353
Gunnarson, S., 371, 372, 381
Gupta, A. K., 374, 375, 380
Guzzo, R. A., 332, 337, 352

H

Hackett, R. D., 77, 96
Hackman, D., 343, 353
Hackman, J. R., 273, 290, 294, 296, 297, 310, 321, 322, 338, 342, 353

Hakel, M., 137, 149, 151
Halfhill, T., 326, 355
Hall, D. T., 47, 67, 153, 155, 157, 158, 160, 166, 167, 170, 172, 174, 175
Hall, E. T., 303, 305, 306, 322
Hall, F. S., 172, 174
Hall, M. R., 303, 305, 306, 322
Hall-Merenda, K. E., 277, 290
Halpern, D. F., 106, 118, 137, 144, 146, 149, 151, 242, 246, 262
Halpin, S. M., 50, 51, 67, 102, 117
Hamblin, C. H., 182, 207
Hampden-Turner, C., 301, 302, 303, 304, 305, 323
Hanges, P. J., 298, 321
Hannafin, M. J., 318, 322
Hansen, M. C., 268, 291
Hansen, M. T., 374, 380
Hanson, M. A., 213, 235
Harackiewicz, J. M., 368, 380
Harding, F. D., 212, 235
Hargan, C. S., 104, 120
Harper, L. F., 306, 310, 322
Harris, 5
Harris, E. F., 371, 380
Harter, J. K., 93, 97
Harvey, O. J., 42, 67
Harville, D. L., 53, 68
Hastie, R., 189, 207
Hayes, J. R., 107, 118
Hayes, T. L., 93, 97
Heckhausen, J., 132, 151
Hedlund, J., 213, 214, 216, 217, 223, 226, 227, 228, 232, 234, 235, 236
Heffner, J. S., 337, 353
Heifetz, R., 4, 21
Hein, M. B., 283, 289, 297, 321, 343, 352
Helmreich, R. L., 293, 294, 299, 322, 340, 353
Hendrickson, A., 268, 269, 270, 292
Hendrickson, A. R., 330, 355
Heritage, J., 178, 207
Hersey, P., 252, 262
Hertzog, C., 84, 97
Higgins, J. M., 279, 292
Higgins, M. C., 165, 166, 175, 366, 380
Highhouse, S., 5, 21
Hightower, R., 276, 277, 283, 290, 292
Hill, L. A., 164, 171, 175
Hinds, P. J., 281, 290
Hinsz, V. B., 268, 272, 279, 280, 290

Hoang, T., 99, 120
Hochschild, A. R., 245, 262
Hochwarter, W. A., 136, 151
Hofmann, D. A., 371, 380
Hofstede, G., 294, 301, 302, 303, 305, 322
Hogan, R., 387, 397
Holder, L. D., 113, 118
Hollander, E. P., 388, 392, 397
Hollenbeck, G. P., 160, 175
Hollingshead, A. B., 276, 281, 290
Holtz, B. C., 385, 398
Hong, E., 100, 118
Hong, Y.-Y., 313, 322
Hooijberg, R., 12, 13, 21, 42, 45, 46, 47, 67, 212, 215, 235, 384, 397
Hopwood, D., 104, 120
Horenczyk, G., 294, 322
Horn, J. L., 63, 67, 125, 151
Horvath, J. A., 213, 214, 216, 223, 227, 228, 232, 235, 236
Hough, L. M., 287, 290
House, R. J., 72, 75, 82, 97, 98, 213, 214, 215, 235, 298, 321, 322
Howard, A., 386, 397
Howell, J. M., 277, 290
Howell, J. P., 76, 97
Hu, X., 140, 151
Hughes, E., 164, 173
Hults, B. M., 372, 381
Hultsch, D., 84, 97
Humphreys, L. G., 286, 289
Humphreys, R. H., 252, 260
Hunt, D. E., 42, 67
Hunt, J. G., 12, 13, 21, 42, 46, 47, 67, 77, 97, 212, 215, 235, 384, 397
Hunter, J. E., 232, 235
Hutchins, E., 179, 193, 207
Hy, L. X., 388, 398

I

Ibarra, H., 164, 165, 175, 366, 380
Institute for Creative Technologies, 112, 118
Isaacs, W., 206, 207
Isen, A. M., 240, 244, 260, 262, 278, 289
Isenberg, D. J., 278, 290
Ives, 269
Izard, C. E., 242, 262

J

Jackson, S., 182, 197, 208
Jacobs, R. R., 390, 399
Jacobs, S., 182, 197, 208
Jacobs, T. O., 212, 235, 295, 322, 342, 353
James, L. R., 53, 67, 378, 381, 384, 398
Jamison, K. R., 256, 261
Jaques, E., 295, 322, 342, 353
Jarvenpaa, S. L., 268, 269, 270, 273, 274, 275, 276, 290
Jarvin, L., 227, 228, 229, 232, 233, 234
Jarvis, W. B. G., 136, 150
Jentsch, F., 336, 352
Jepson, C., 148, 151
Johansen, 269, 275
Johnson, W. B., 149, 151
Johnson-Laird, P. N., 198, 207
Johnsrude, I. S., 128, 151
Johnston, J., 345, 352
Johnston, J. H., 342, 354
Jones, C., 214, 223, 236
Jones, R. G., 342, 353
Jordan, J. A., 108, 117
Judge, T. A., 9, 12, 21, 370, 380
Julian, J. W., 388, 392, 397
Jung, D. I., 73, 78, 96, 363, 382

K

Kacmar, K. M., 136, 151
Kahai, S. S., 91, 96
Kahn, R. L., 16, 22, 42, 68, 283, 290
Kanfer, R., 137, 150, 272, 279, 287, 290, 388, 398
Kanov, J. M., 255, 261
Karahanna, 299, 323
Kark, R., 76, 97
Karoly, P., 363, 380
Kasermann, M., 200, 201, 207
Katz, D., 16, 22, 42, 68, 283, 290
Katz, I., 293, 322
Kavanaugh, M. J., 371, 382
Kaye, D., 107, 118
Kegan, J., 76, 97
Kegan, R., 42, 43, 44, 45, 50, 65, 68, 154, 155, 161, 162, 163, 169, 175, 388, 395, 398
Keith, W. H., 115, 119
Kelloway, E. K., 81, 82, 96
Kelly, G., 46, 47, 68

Kemp, C., 286, 292
Kenny, D. A., 214, 236
Keppler, A., 183, 207
Kevin, K. Y., 297, 321, 343
Kiechel-Koles, K. L., 345, 353
Kiel, F., 126, 149, 151
Kiesler, S., 282, 290, 292
Kiker, D. S., 80, 96
Kilduff, M., 367, 368, 381
Kilpatrick, H., 107, 118
King, P. M., 387, 398
Kirkman, B. L., 312, 321
Kitchener, K. S., 387, 393, 398
Klein, E. B., 161, 175
Klein, G., 113, 115, 119, 120, 351, 353
Klein, K. J., 72, 97, 372, 381
Kleinman, D. L., 280, 291, 337, 353
Klimoski, R., 279, 280, 291, 308, 322, 342, 353
Klopf, 308
Kluckhohn, F., 299, 301, 304, 305, 322
Kluger, A. N., 51, 68, 134, 151, 366, 381
Knoblauch, H., 183, 207
Knoll, K., 269, 273, 275, 290
Koles, K. L. K., 135, 151
Komaki, J. L., 295, 322
Korotkin, A. L., 283, 289, 297, 321, 343, 352
Kosman, G., 103, 117
Kossler, M. E., 268, 291
Kouzes, J. M., 169, 175
Kozlowski, S. W. J., 135, 152, 283, 291, 342, 343, 344, 345, 346, 347, 348, 349, 352, 353, 354, 372, 381
Kraimer, M. L., 369, 382, 391, 399
Kram, K. E., 165, 166, 167, 175
Kramer, R., 275, 276, 291
Krantz, D. H., 148, 151
Krathwhol, D. R., 117
Kring, W., 369, 380
Kristof, A. L., 269, 270, 285, 291
Kroeck, K. G., 80, 81, 97
Kucik, P., III, 104, 109, 117
Kuhnert, K. W., 76, 97
Kumar, A., 309, 322
Kumar, K., 293, 323

L

Lahey, L. L., 163, 175
Laird, J. E., 104, 111, 119, 119
Lance, C. E., 52, 53, 54, 56, 57, 59, 63, 68, 69

Lane, N. E., 315, 319, 321, 350, 352
Latham, G. P., 310, 322, 373, 381
Lave, J., 179, 208
Lawson, M. J., 142, 151
Lazarus, R. S., 370, 380
Leblebici, H., 7, 12, 22, 391, 398
Legett, E. L., 368, 380
Legless Productions, 112, 119
Leibrecht, B. C., 113, 118
Leidner, D. E., 268, 269, 270, 273, 274, 275, 276, 290
Lepper, M. R., 104, 106, 119
Lepsinger, R., 250, 263
Lev, B., 91, 97
Leviathan, U., 4, 21
Levin, K. Y., 283, 289
Levine, J. M., 280, 291
Levinson, D. J., 161, 162, 175
Levinson, M. H., 161, 175
Levinson, S. C., 179, 180, 181, 193, 207
Lewicki, R. J., 274, 291
Lewis, P., 76, 97
Li, H. Z., 294, 322
Liden, R. C., 391, 399
Lilius, J. M., 255, 261
Lindenberger, U., 129, 131, 150
Lindley, S., 120
Linell, P., 200, 207
Linville, P. W., 46, 48, 68
Lipnack, J., 269, 273, 285, 291, 291
Lipshitz, R., 351, 353
Little, T. D., 384, 398
Loch, 299, 323
Locke, E. A., 310, 322, 373, 381
Loehlin, J. C., 242, 246, 262
Loevinger, J., 388, 398
Lohman, D. F., 389, 399
Lombardo, M., 158, 175
Lombardo, M. M., 4, 22, 212, 235, 346, 353, 365, 381, 388, 398
London, M., 85, 87, 97, 389, 398
Lord, R. G., 4, 15, 22, 93, 97, 213, 235
Louis, M., 371, 381
Loukopoulos, L. D., 49, 68
Lovett, M. C., 143, 151
Lowe, K., 80, 81, 97
Lowe, K. B., 80, 81, 97
Luckman, T., 200, 207
Luckmann, T., 183, 207
Luthans, F., 83, 98
Lysy, D. C., 246, 262

M

Macredie, R., 104, 106, 120
Mael, F., 154, 173
Magill, R. A., 108, 119
Maguire, E. A., 128, 151
Maher, K. J., 4, 22
Maki, R. H., 139, 151
Malone, 269
Malone, T. W., 104, 106, 119
Mankin, D., 269, 289
Manz, C. C., 294, 323
Mark, M. M., 240, 263
Marks, M., 282, 291
Marks, M. A., 212, 234, 236, 268, 271, 279, 287, 291, 292, 295, 323, 326, 332, 333, 334, 337, 342, 343, 345, 349, 353, 355
Markus, H., 75, 87*nd88, 98
Markus, H. R., 88, 98
Marquis, V., 5, 21
Marsh, S. M., 345, 353
Marshall, J., 345, 353
Marshall-Mies, J. C., 228, 235
Martin, J., 345, 353
Martin, J. A., 228, 235
Marvin, F., 179, 192, 195, 197, 199, 207
Marx, R. D., 53, 68
Mason, R., 179, 180, 181, 201, 207
Matarazzo, J. D., 240, 262
Mathieu, J., 282, 291
Mathieu, J. E., 326, 332, 333, 334, 337, 349, 353
Matthews, M. D., 113, 115, 118, 120
Maurer, T. J., 389, 398
Mayer, J. D., 83, 98, 241, 242, 243, 246, 247, 250, 255, 261, 262, 263, 395, 398
Mayer, R. C., 274, 291
Mayer, R. E., 107, 113, 117, 119, 144, 151
Maznevski, M. L., 293*nd294, 321
McArdle, J. J., 57, 62, 63, 67, 68
McCall, M. W., 4, 22, 212, 235, 346, 353, 388, 398
McCall, M. W., Jr., 158, 173, 175, 365, 381
McCauley, C. D., 5, 22, 45, 49, 50, 68, 149, 152, 284, 291, 292, 360, 365, 372, 377, 381, 382, 389, 390, 398
McClain, T. M., 256, 263
McClelland, D. C., 386, 398
McCloskey, M. J., 113, 115, 120
McCoy, M. C., 273, 292
McCrae, R. R., 136, 152

McDaniel, M. A., 213, 213*nd214, 214, 222, 223, 227, 235
McDermott, P. L., 113, 115, 120
McGee, M., 345, 353
McGee, M. L., 228, 235
McGrath, J. E., 276, 290, 343, 354
McHugh, P. P., 344, 347, 353
McIntyre, M., 326, 355
McIntyre, R. M., 333, 336, 354
McKee, B., 161, 175
Mead, A. W., 52
Meade, A. W., 52, 56, 57, 68
Meadows, S. I., 293, 322
Mehra, A., 367, 381
Meliza, L. L., 113, 114, 117, 119
Menon, T., 313, 322
Meredith, W., 57, 68
Merritt, A. C., 293, 322
Meulenbroek, R. G. J., 49, 68
Meyerson, D., 275, 276, 291
Michaelsen, L. K., 293, 323
Miles, G., 102, 121
Miles, R. E., 269, 270, 291, 386, 396
Miller, D. T., 390, 398
Miller, J., 100, 119
Miller, M. D., 309, 322
Milliken, F. J., 296, 323
Milner, C., 13, 22, 77, 98
Mirvis, P. H., 172, 174
Mischel, W., 245, 262
Mitchell, T. R., 72, 97, 378, 381, 384, 398
Mittleman, D., 269, 270, 275, 291
Mohammed, S., 279, 280, 291, 308, 322
Moore, M. R., 99, 119
Moran, L., 260, 262
Moreland, R. L., 280, 291
Morgan, B., 326, 354
Morgeson, F. P., 213*nd214, 223, 235
Morreall, J., 244, 262
Morris, C. G., 273, 290
Morris, C. W., 304, 322
Morris, M. W., 313, 322
Morris, N. M., 279, 291
Morrison, A., 158, 175
Morrison, A. M., 4, 22, 212, 235, 346, 353, 365, 381, 388, 398
Morrison, E. W., 369, 381
Morrison, J. E., 113, 119
Morrison, R. H., 153, 175
Morrow, J. E., 149, 152, 284, 291, 365, 381
Mosakowski, E., 309, 321

Moses, J. L., 386, 398
Moss, M. T., 249, 262
Motowidlo, S. J., 213, 223, 235
Mowshowitz, 269
Moxley, R. S., 5, 22, 45, 49, 68, 85, 98, 284, 292, 365, 372, 377, 381, 382, 388, 398
MSG. W., 230, 235
Mulaik, S. A., 53, 60, 67, 68
Mullen, B., 341, 354
Mumford, M. D., 49, 50, 69, 76, 98, 212, 234, 235, 236, 283, 287, 289, 291, 297, 321, 343
Muthn, B. O., 62, 68

N

Nadler, D. A., 54, 68
Nahapiet, J., 391, 398
Naicker, K., 106, 117
National Research Council, 112, 119
Neale, M. A., 268, 269, 270, 271, 281, 290
Neisser, U., 226, 235, 242, 246, 262
Newman, J. R., 256, 263
Nguyen, N. T., 213, 214, 222, 223, 227, 235
Nicholson, N., 160, 175
Nieva, V. F., 268, 291
Nisbett, R. E., 146, 148, 151, 152, 304, 308, 321, 322
Nkomo, S. M., 171, 174
Nohria, 275
Nohria, N., 374, 380
Nokes, C., 217, 227, 236
Nordyke, J. W., 114, 117
Norenzayan, A., 304, 322
Northhouse, P. G., 178, 207
Novak, M., 391, 397
Nurius, P., 75, 87*nd88, 98
Nygren, H. T., 160, 175

O

Oakley, J. G., 269, 270, 291
O'Conner, 278
O'Conner, J., 76, 98
O'Conner, K. M., 276, 290, 291
O'Connor, E. J., 11, 21
O'Connor Wilson, P., 372, 381, 388, 398
O'Hara-Devreaux, 269, 275
Ohlott, P. J., 149, 152, 284, 291, 365, 381, 389, 390, 398

Okagaki, L., 107, 119, 227, 230, 231, 236
Okatcha, F., 217, 227, 236
O'Neil, H. F., Jr., 100, 103, 104, 107, 113, 115,
    117, 118, 119
Orasanu, J., 328, 351, 353, 354
Ortiz, R., 309, 322
Ortony, A., 256, 262
Oser, R., 314, 315, 319, 321
Oser, R. L., 340, 350, 352
Osman, M. E., 318, 322

P

Pagonis, W. G., 254, 262
Palfai, T. P., 256, 262
Palus, C. J., 11, 21, 44, 67
Pandemic Studios, 112, 119
Paris, A. H., 107, 119
Paris, C. A., 329, 354
Paris, S. G., 107, 119
Parisi, A. G., 53, 68
Park, 308
Parker, C. W., 279, 292
Parmalee, P. A., 52, 56
Parsons, T., 299, 301, 303, 304, 305, 322
Paul, M. C., 371, 381
Paulhus, D. L., 246, 262
Payne, S. C., 135, 151
Peace, W. H., 257, 258, 259, 262
Pelletier, L. G., 106, 118
Peng, K., 146, 152, 304, 322
Pennebaker, J. W., 256, 262, 263
Pennington, N., 189, 207
Peregoy, P. L., 54, 69
Perez, R. S., 279, 292
Perloff, R., 242, 246, 262
Person, N. K., 140, 151
Peterson, C., 273, 292
Petty, R. E., 109, 120, 136, 150
Pfeffer, J., 374, 381
Phelps, C. C., 369, 381
Phillips, J., 113, 115, 120
Piaget, J., 125, 152
Pierce, L. G., 314, 316, 322
Pillay, H. K., 107*nd108, 120
Pleban, R. J., 113, 115, 120
Ployhart, R. E., 385, 398
Pomerantz, A., 181, 207
Ponserre, S., 108, 118
Poole, M. S., 91, 96

Popper, M., 76, 98
Posner, B. Z., 169, 175
Poteet, M. L., 86, 97
Potosky, D., 363, 382
Pratt, M. G., 171, 175
Pressley, M., 148, 152
Prestridge, S., 268, 291
Pretz, J. E., 216, 217, 223, 226, 227, 228, 232,
    234
Priester, J. R., 109, 120
Prince, R., 217, 227, 236
Pruitt, J. S., 320
Prusak, L., 374, 380
Pucik, V., 9, 12, 21, 370, 380

Q

Quicksilver Software, 112, 120
Quinn, C. N., 107, 120
Quinn, R. E., 45, 46, 67
Quinones, M. A., 134, 152

R

Radtke, P. H., 347, 352
Rafaeli, A., 278, 291
Ramsberger, P. F., 104, 120
Rao, C. R., 57, 68
Rashotte, C. A., 216, 227, 228, 236
Raven, B. H., 11, 21
Rawson, K. A., 148, 152
Regian, J. W., 108, 117
Reidel, S., 179, 192, 198, 207
Reidel, S. L., 345, 352
Reilly, N., 278, 290
Reiter-Palmon, R., 287, 291
Rescher, N., 182, 208
Rhee, K. S., 241, 261
Rhoades, J. A., 278, 291
Rhodenizer, L., 326, 350, 354
Ricci, K. E., 106, 108, 120
Richards, H., 326, 355
Richter, J., 172, 175
Rieck, A. M., 268, 291
Riedel, S., 195, 197, 199
Rifkind, L. J., 306, 310, 322
Riggio, R. E., 253, 261
Rimmer, E., 126, 149, 151

Rittman, A., 268, 271, 292, 295, 323, 342, 343, 345, 355
Roediger, H. L., 142, 152
Rogoff, B., 179, 208
Rommetveit, R., 200, 208
Ronning, R. R., 107, 117
Rosenbaum, D. A., 49, 68
Rosenberg, M., 171, 175
Rosenfield, D., 390, 399
Ross, M., 390, 398
Rouiller, J. Z., 371, 381
Rouse, W. B., 279, 291, 308, 323
Rowland, K. M., 7, 12, 22, 391, 398
Rozell, D., 341, 354
Ruben, B. D., 104, 120
Ruderman, M. N., 149, 152, 284, 291, 365, 381
Ruiz-Quintanilla, S. A., 298, 321
Russell, J. A., 346, 355
Russell, J. E., 86, 97
Ruvolo, A. P., 88, 98
Ryan, R. M., 106, 118

S

Sabella, M. J., 345, 353
Sacks, H., 181, 184, 193, 194, 195, 196, 197, 199, 208
Saks, A. M., 160, 173
Salancik, G. R., 7, 12, 22, 391, 398
Salas, E., 106, 108, 120, 179, 192, 195, 197, 198, 199, 207, 268, 280, 283, 289, 291, 308, 309, 310, 312, 314, 315, 316, 318, 319, 320, 321, 323, 326, 328, 329, 330, 331, 332, 333, 335, 336, 337, 338, 339, 340, 341, 342, 344, 345, 346, 347, 349, 350, 351, 353, 354, 355,
Sale, K., 45, 68
Salovey, P., 83, 98, 240, 241, 242, 243, 245, 246, 247, 250, 255, 256, 260, 261, 262, 263, 395, 398
Sandelands, L. E., 9, 22
Sandza, R., 326, 351
Santora, J. C., 298, 323
Sarros, J. C., 298, 323
Sashkin, M., 212, 235
Sayeed, L., 276, 277, 283, 290, 292
Sayer, A. G., 57, 62, 69
Scarr, S., 246, 263
Schank, R. C., 189, 208
Scheier, M. F., 363, 380

Schein, E., 371, 381
Schein, E. H., 5, 22, 165, 166, 175
Schmidt, F. L., 93, 97, 232, 235
Schmidt, J. A., 91, 98
Schnable, K. U., 384, 398
Schneider, B., 11, 13, 22, 160, 175, 371, 372, 376, 381, 396, 398
Schneider, R. J., 287, 290
Schoel, L., 86, 97
Schon, D., 89, 98
Schn, D. A., 221, 235
Schoorman, F. D., 274, 291
Schraw, G. J., 107, 117
Schroder, H. M., 42, 67, 68
Schultz, T. W., 391, 398
Schwartz, B. L., 141, 150
Schwartz, S. H., 301, 302, 304, 323
Schwarz, N., 256, 263
Searle, J. R., 185, 186, 189, 208
Sefarty, D., 337, 342, 352, 353
Seibert, K. W., 170, 175
Seibert, S. E., 369, 382, 391, 399
Self, R. M., 54, 57, 68
Senge, P. M., 66, 68
Serfaty, D., 280, 291
Sessa, V. I., 268, 291
Shaffer, D. R., 52, 56
Shamir, B., 75, 76, 81, 97, 98, 329, 346, 354, 366, 380, 385, 388, 397
Shapiro, D. L., 274, 292, 312, 321
Shay, J., 203, 208
Shea, G. P., 332, 337, 352
Shebilske, W. L., 108, 117
Shedden, K., 62, 68
Sheppard, B. H., 274, 292
Sheridan, J. E., 54, 69
Sherlock, T. D., 104, 109, 117
Shi, K., 312, 321
Shils, E., 299, 301, 303, 304, 305, 322
Sidner, C. L., 189, 207
Silverman, D., 182, 208
Simmering, M. J., 133, 134, 150
Simmon, D. A., 325, 328, 352, 354
Sims, H. P., Jr., 269, 270, 285, 291
Sims, V. K., 107, 119
Sinclair, R. C., 240, 263
Sindell, M., 99, 120
Sitarenios, G., 243, 262
Sivasubramaniam, N., 78, 79, 80, 81, 96, 97
Slocum, J. W., Jr., 368, 382
Sluyter, D., 255, 263

Smith, B. D., 13, 22
Smith, D. B., 376, 381
Smith, E. M., 135, 152, 318, 321, 348, 354
Smith, J. A., 213, 235
Smith, K. A., 269, 270, 285, 291
Smith, L., 24, 38
Smith-Jentsch, K. K., 345, 355
Snook, S., 216, 223, 235
Snook, S. A., 213, 214, 223, 227, 228, 232, 236
Snow, C. C., 269, 270, 291, 386, 396
Snow, R. E., 389, 399
Snyder, M., 367, 382
Snyder, M. L., 390, 399
Sommerkamp, P., 391, 397
Soose, A., 369, 380
Sorra, J. S., 372, 381
Sosik, J. J., 363, 382
Sparks, C. P., 386, 399
Sperber, D., 179, 181, 182, 183, 186, 187, 190,
    208
Sproull, L., 282, 290, 292
Srite, 299, 323
Stagl, K. C., 330, 354
Stamford, 271
Stamps, J., 269, 273, 275, 285, 291, 291
Starbuck, W. H., 296, 323
Starks, J. L., 120
Stassen, H. G., 279, 292
Staudinger, U. M., 129, 131, 150
Staw, B. M., 9, 22
Stephan, W. G., 390, 399
Sternberg, R. J., 212, 213, 214, 216, 217, 223,
    226, 227, 228, 229, 230, 231, 232, 233,
    234, 235, 236, 242, 246, 259, 262, 263,
    318, 321, 323
Stetzer, A., 371, 380
Stewart, G. L., 294, 323
Stewart, I. N., 54, 69
Stewart, R. W., 107, 121
Stogdill, R. M., 4, 22
Stoolmiller, M., 57, 67
Stout, R. J., 316, 321
Strater, L. D., 113, 115, 120
Straub, 299, 323
Straus, S., 276, 292
Straus, S. G., 276, 276, 292
Strauss, A., 164, 173, 175
Straw, B., 271
Streufert, S., 42, 68
Stritch, T. M., 278, 290
Strodtbeck, F. L., 299, 301, 304, 305, 322

Strong, M. H., 108, 117
Sugrue, B., 103, 120
Sujan, H., 216, 227, 228, 236
Sujan, M., 216, 227, 228, 236
Sullivan, G., 288, 292, 345, 354
Sundstrom, E., 326, 327, 338, 355
Super, D. E., 154, 155, 175
Sutton, 271
Sutton, R. I., 245, 263, 374, 381
Sutton, R. L., 278, 291
Swenson, D. X., 317, 321
Swezey, R. W., 337, 355

                            T

Tang, M., 312, 321
Tannenbaum, S. I., 268, 291, 319, 321, 326, 328,
    336, 337, 338, 342, 345, 352, 354, 355,
    371, 382
Taylor, S., 13, 22
Taylor, S. E., 390, 397
Taylor, S. F., 246, 263
Teachout, M. S., 53, 68
Tennyson, R. D., 113, 120
Tesluk, P. E., 298, 323, 346, 355, 390, 399
Tetrick, L. E., 372, 382
Thayer, R. E., 256, 263
Thiede, K. W., 148, 152
Thomas, D. A., 157, 176, 366, 380
Thomas, D. C., 293, 294, 323
Thomas, J. B., 296, 323
Thomas, P., 104, 106, 120
Thompson, B., 113, 115, 117
Thompson, B. B., 187, 189, 190, 206, 207, 345,
    352
Thor, K. K., 49, 50, 69
Thordsen, M. L., 113, 115, 120
Thoresen, C. J., 370, 380
Thorensen, C. J., 9, 12, 21
ThoughtLink, 115, 120
Threlfall, K. V., 212, 234
Thurow, L. C., 8, 22
Tierney, T., 374, 380
Tindale, R. S., 268, 272, 279, 280, 290
Ting-Toomey, S., 308, 311, 313, 323
Tisak, J., 57, 68
Toney, R., 348, 355
Townsend, A., 268, 269, 270, 292
Townsend, A. M., 330, 355
Tracey, J. B., 371, 382

Triandis, H. C., 294, 301, 302, 303, 304, 305, 306, 311, 323
Trollip, S. R., 104, 117
Trompenaars, F., 300, 301, 302, 303, 304, 305, 323
Tsai, W., 391, 399
Tse, B., 253, 260
Tsui, A. S., 363, 364, 367, 382
Turken, A. U., 244, 260
Turner, M. E., 278, 289
Turner, N., 13, 22, 77, 98
Turner, M., 179, 208
Tushman, M. L., 54, 68

U

Uhl-Bien, M., 297, 321
Underhill, W. G., 104, 120
University of Michigan, 129, 152
Unsworth, K., 9, 22
Urbina, S., 242, 246, 262
U.S. Department of Labor, Bureau of Labor Statistics, 133, 146, 149, 152
U.S. Department of the Army, 7, 22, 100, 102, 109, 120, 231, 236, 250, 254, 263, 355

V

Vallerand, R. J., 106, 118
van Dijk, T. A., 178, 208
van Eemeren, F. H., 182, 189, 197, 208
Van Gennep, A., 158, 176
van Lent, M., 104, 111, 113, 119, 119, 120
Van Maanen, J., 160, 176
Van Velsor, E., 5, 22, 45, 49, 68, 284, 292, 360, 377, 381, 382
Vandenberg, R. J., 54, 57, 59, 63, 68, 69
VandeWall, D., 368, 382
Vaughan, J., 49, 68
Veldhuyzen, W., 279, 292
Vicere, A. A., 5, 22
Vincent, J., 106, 117
Visweswaran, C., 314, 321
Vitello-Cicciu, J. M., 249, 263
Vollrath, D. A., 268, 272, 279, 280, 290
Volpe, C., 330, 352
Volpe, C. E., 319, 321, 328, 336, 337, 338, 352
von Oetinger, B., 374, 380
Vroom, V., 213, 236

W

Wagner, R. K., 213, 214, 216, 223, 223, 227, 228, 229, 230, 231, 232, 236
Wakabayashi, M., 309, 321
Waldman, D. A., 86, 96
Wall, S., 250, 263
Walther, J. B., 277, 292
Walton, D. N., 182, 199, 208
Walton, R. E., 296, 297, 322, 338, 342, 353
Wampler, R. L., 113, 118
Warkentin, M. E., 276, 277, 292
Warrenfeltz, R., 387, 397
Washbush, J., 104, 120
Wasielewski, P. L., 253, 263
Watson, W. E., 293, 323
Weary, G., 390, 399
Weber, M., 72, 98
Weber, T., 81, 82, 96
Weekley, J. A., 214, 223, 236
Wegener, D. T., 109, 120
Wegner, D. M., 280, 292
Weick, K., 177, 204, 208
Weick, K. E., 10, 15, 22, 49, 69, 275, 276, 291, 296, 323
Weil, M., 108, 118
Weingart, L. R., 273, 292
Weiss, H. A., 253, 263
Weisshein, D. A., 318, 321
Welbourne, T. M., 9, 12, 21, 370, 380
Weldon, E., 273, 292
Welles, M. L., 53, 68
West, M. A., 160, 175
Westbrook, J. I., 108, 121
Wheeler, M. A., 142, 152
Whetten, D. A., 160, 176
White, S., 371, 381
Whiteman, J. A. K., 135, 151
Whitten, A., 179, 208
Whittington, J. L., 74, 75, 78, 97
Wiggins, S. L., 113, 115, 120
Willet, J. B., 57, 62, 69
Williams, K., 126, 149, 151
Williams, W. M., 213, 214, 216, 223, 227, 228, 232, 235, 236
Williamson, G. M., 52, 56, 57, 68
Williamson, J. E., 108, 117
Wilson, D. A., 181, 182, 183, 186, 187, 190, 208
Wilson, F. R., 312, 321
Wilson, K. A., 340, 354
Wilss, L., 107, 108, 120

Witt, L. A., 136, 151
Wittrock, M. C., 113, 119, 142, 152
Wofford, J. C., 74, 75, 78, 97
Wolfe, C. J., 257, 263
Wood, L. W., 107, 121
Wood, R., 363, 364, 369, 382
Woodworth, R. S., 240, 263
Woolfolk, A. E., 106, 121
Worline, M. C., 255, 261

Y

Yammarino, F. J., 74, 98
Yankelovich, D., 206, 208

Yeager, S., 54, 67
Yearout, S., 102, 121
Yik, M. S. M., 246, 262
Yost, P. R., 332, 352
Young, P. T., 240, 263
Yukl, G., 47, 69, 72, 76, 98, 177, 206, 208, 212, 231, 233, 236, 330, 346, 355
Yukl, G. A., 250, 258, 259, 263, 377, 382

Z

Zaccaro, S., 345, 345, 346, 352, 353
Zaccaro, S. J., 46, 48, 49, 50, 69, 212, 214, 228, 234, 235, 2

Subject Index

A

Ability(ies)
  cognitive explanation for, 218–222, 219 (fig), 220 (fig)
  to facilitate thought
    employment of, 251–252
    teaching of, 256
  to identify emotions
    employment of, 251
    teaching of, 256
  to manage emotions
    employment of, 252–253
    teaching of, 256
  to measure emotions, 246–247
  to understand emotions
    employment of, 252
    teaching of, 256
  to use emotions
    instruction in, 256
Ability model of emotional intelligence, 243–245, 244 (fig)
  as framework for development, 257 (tab)
Accessibility, in conversations among leaders, 183
Accuracy of self perceptions, description of, 168
Accurate problem models competency, definition of, 332 (tab)
Accurate task models competency, definition of, 332 (tab)
Action
  determining and taking, 221–222
  identifying conditions for, 220–221
Adaptability
  competence and, 18
  in leadership complexity, 49–50

Adaptability competency, definition of, 331 (tab)
Adjacency pairs, in conversations among leaders, 195
Adjustment, in role transitions, 160
Adult cognition, development of
  acceleration of learning in, 145
  adulthood and, 125
  basic learning principles in, 138–145
  cognitive abilities and, 137
  errors and, 135
  expectancy models of, 134
  feedback in, 134–135
  future research recommendations for, 146–150
  human development and, 127
  individual differences and, 135–137
  intelligence as developed expertise and, 132–133
  interests and, 137
  lifelong learning and, 126–127
  mental aging in adulthood and, 128–129, 129 (fig), 130 (fig), 131
  motivation to learn and, 133–135
  motivational traits and, 137
  personality variables and, 137
  understanding developmental trajectories and, 131–132
Adult development
  relational influences on, 166–167
  stages of identity evolution in, 161–167
    Daniel Levinson model of, 161–162
    Robert Kegan model of, 162–163
Adulthood, mental aging in, 128–129, 129 (fig), 130 (fig), 131
Affect management competency, definition of, 334 (tab)

Alpha change, definition of, 54
Ambiguous environment, knowledge vs
    understanding in, 29–33
Appropriation, in leadership
    development, 91–92
Armed Services Vocational Aptitude
    Battery (ASVAB), 226
Army. *See also* Military
    in ambiguous environment
        knowledge/understanding vs
        doing/getting job done, 29–33
    leader development defined by, 102, 103 (fig)
    leadership challenges for future in, 23–27
        changing patterns of operations, 34
        deployment and combat operations in new
            arena, 27–29
        seeing and understanding the battlefield,
            33–34
    leadership definition of, 100, 101 (fig)
    leadership doctrine of, 7
    logistics of, 35
    Objective Force of, 23
    support in ongoing operations in, 35
    transformation and, 8
Army leader development model, 103 (fig)
Assertions, in conversations among leaders, 185
Assertiveness training, description of, 341 (tab)
Assessment
    of intelligent use of learned information, 146
    of leaders knowledge and skills, 377–379
ASVAB. *See* Armed Services Vocational
    Aptitude Battery
Attitudes, computer games and, 109
Avoiding goal orientation, leader change
    and, 368

                                    B

Backup behavior competency, definition of,
    331 (tab), 334 (tab)
Battle-command, computer games designed for,
    109, 110–111 (tab), 112–113
Battlefield dominance, in Army applications, 26
Beginnings, in identity change, 159
Behavior, proactive, leader change and, 369
Behavioral complexity, 46–47
Behavioral differentiation, 47
Behavioral repertoire, 47
Behvaioral complexity, in leadership
    development, 253

Beliefs, adult cognition development and,
    138
Beta change, definition of, 54
Between-groups differences change and,
    52 (tab), 55
Biculturalism, definition of, 158
Boundary-spanning roles competency, definition
    of, 332 (tab)
Business arena, new, challenges on entering into,
    27–29
Business changes, adjusting to, 34
Business environment, appreciation of,
    33–34

                                    C

Calculus-based trust, motivational team
    processes and, 274
Career anchors
    definition of, 165
    Schein's research on, 165–166
Career growth, defining and measuring of,
    172–173
Career identity, 168
Cattell Culture Fair Test, 226
Challenge-defend transaction
    in conversations among leaders, 197–199
    dialogue mental model for, 198 (fig)
Change
    alpha, 54
    beta, 54
    between-groups differences and, 52 (tab), 55
    concomitant, 52 (tab), 55
    continuous vs discontinuous, 52 (tab), 53–54
    gamma, 54
    growth and, 41–42
    individual differences in, 52 (tab), 54–55
    individual-level vs group-level, 52 (tab), 54
    longitudinal, latent growth models of, 57–61,
        58 (fig), 59 (fig), 60 (fig), 61 (fig),
        63 (fig)
    measurement of
        efficacy of approaches to, 55, 56 (tab), 57
        issues in, 51–55, 52 (tab)
    qualitative vs quantitative, 52 (tab), 54
    random vs systematic, 52 (tab), 53
    reversible vs irreversible, 52 (tab), 53
    unitary vs multipath, 52 (tab), 53
Change over time, leader development and,
    359–360, 360 (fig)

Cognition. *See also* Adult cognition
  definition of, 127–128
  need for, 136
Cognitive abilities, adult cognition
    development and, 137
Cognitive complexity, definition of, 46
Cognitive dialogue theory, 178
  definition of leadership, 179
  items in, 189
  leader development and, 204–206
  sources of
    conversation analysis, 181–182
    dialogue theory, 182
    pragmatics, 180–181
Cognitive differentiation, definition of, 46
Cognitive integration, 46
Cognitive intent(ion), in conversations
    among leaders, 182–183, 189
Cognitive structures, flexible, in
    event-based training, 319–320
Cognitive-communicative interaction, leadership
    as, 177–179
Cohesion,
  in motivational team processes, 273, 276–277
Collective efficacy
  definition of, 333 (tab)
  motivational team processes and, 272–273
Collective orientation competency,
    definition of, 333 (tab)
Combat operations, on entry, 27–29
Command and control teams, 329
Commercial aviatiion teams, 328
Communication competency, definition of,
    331 (tab)
Communication skills, in event-based
    approach training, 319
Communications, ubiquitous, 94–95
Communicative intent, in conversations
    among leaders, 183, 184–185, 189
Complexity
  change and, 42
  core components of, 17
  as developmental imperative, 45
  measurement of, 47 (note)
Computer games
  attitudes and, 109
  benefits of, 104
  characteristics of, 104–105
  components of, 105
  design of

  for battle-command, 109, 110–111 (tab),
      112–113
  for military training, 113–114
  evaluation of, 110–111(tab) 115–116
  knowledge and, 108–109
  metacognition and, 107–108
  motivation and, 106–107
  power and potential of, 104
  search for, 105–106, 105 (tab)
  skills and, 108–109
  thinking skills and, 107
Computer video games. *See* Computer games
Conceptual ideals, in leadership development, 73
Conceptual skills, in U.S. Army
    leadership doctrine, 7
Concomitant change, 52 (tab), 55
Confidence building, definition of, 334 (tab)
Conflict management competency, definition of,
    334 (tab)
Contingent reward, for transactional
    leadership, 74
Continuous change, discontinuous vs, 52 (tab),
    53–54
Control, in conversations among leaders,
    199–201
Controlling the floor, in conversations among
    leaders, 195–197
Conversation
  illustrating leadership skills, 180 (tab)
  among leaders
    communicating intent, 184–185
    controlling the floor, 195–197
    expressing emotion, 184
    failing to cooperate, 201–203
    negotiating dialogue roles, 192–197
    protecting face, 193–195
    relying on cooperation, 185–187
    sense making, 203–204
    sharing control, 199–201
    showing facts, 182–184
    thinking critically, 197–199, 198 (fig)
    transacting conversational business,
        187–192, 188 (fig)
  violating expectations, 181 (tab)
Conversation analysis, cognitive dialogue theory
    and, 181–182
Conversational business transaction, among
    leaders, 187–192, 188 (fig)
Cooperation, among leaders
  failing in, 201–203
  relying on, 185–187

Coordination competency, definition of,
    331 (tab), 334 (tab)
Correction invitation, in conversations
    among leaders, 196
Critical discussion, among leaders, 197
Critical thinking
    in conversations among leaders, 197–199,
        198 (fig)
    importance of, 148–149
Cross-cultural dimensions, within
    multicultural teams, 299–300, 301–306
    (tab)
Cross-training, description of, 341 (tab)
Cue-strategy associations competency,
    definition of, 332 (tab)

D

Decision making competency, definition of,
    331 (tab)
Deployment operations, on entry, 27–29
Development
    definition of, 42, 128
    difference betweem training and, 10
    mode of, 389–391
Developmental framework, Kegan's, 43–45
Developmental imperative, complexity as, 45
Developmental readiness, 83
Developmental theory, 387–388
Developmental trajectories, 131–132
Developmental trigger events, self-awareness
    and, 84–86
Dialogue
    description of, 186, 187
    relational, 44–45
Dialogue roles, among leaders, 192–197
Dialogue theory, 182
Differences
    in change, 52 (tab), 54–55
    in developing adult cognition, 135–136
Differentiation
    complexity and, 42
    as core of complexity, 17
Direct speech act, in conversations
    among leaders, 185
Directory updating, definition of, 280
Discontinuous change
    continuous vs, 52 (tab), 53–54
Dissemination, importance of, 149
Distance learning, in leader development, 65–66

Distributed decision-making teams, 329–330
Dominance, personal, 44
Dual effect, by transformational leaders, 76

E

EBAT. See Event-based approach
    training
ECI. See Emotional Competence
    Inventory
Efficacy, as team motivational process,
    276–277
EI. See Emotional intelligence
Emotion(s)
    expression of, 184
    identification of, 243
        instruction in, 256
        by leaders, 251
    management of, 245
        instruction in, 256
        by leaders, 252–253
    measurement of
        by informants, 246
        by performance, 246–247, 248 (fig), 249
        by self-report, 245–246
    understanding of, 244–245
        instruction in, 256
        by leaders, 252
    use of, 243–244
    at work, 240
Emotional Competence Inventory (ECI),
    241–242
Emotional intelligence (EI)
    ability model of, 243–245, 244 (fig)
        foundation of, 240–241
    as framework for development, 257 (tab)
    within framework of leadership, 250
    definition of, 19
    description of, 241–242
    existence of, 242–243
    in leadership, 249–253, 251 (tab)
    in leadership development, 237–240
        empathy, 254–255
        morale, 254
        social and behavioral complexity, 253
    Mayer-Salovey ability model of, 244 (fig)
Emotional knowledge, teaching of, 255–256
Emotional skills, teaching of, 255–256
Emotionally intelligent leaders, 249–250
Empathy, development of, 254–255

Employee engagement, definition of, 93
Encounter, in role transitions, 160
Ending, in identity change, 159
Engagement, in leadership development, 93–94
Environment(s)
    ambiguous, knowledge vs understanding in, 29–33
    business, appreciation of, 33–34
    complex, teams operating in, 327–330
Errors, as motivation for learning, 135
Ethnicity, social identity and, 157–158
Evaluation, in leadership development, 93
Event-based approach training (EBAT)
    within multicultural team leadership, 315–317, 316 (fig)
    practical application of
        communication skills, 319
        flexible cognitive structures, 319–320
        for leader development, 317–320
        metacognition, 318
        social intelligence, 318
Expectancy models
    influence of, 146–147
    as motivation to learn, 134
Expectation(s), conversation violating, 181 (tab)
Expected results, in conversations among leaders, 190
Experience, in adult cognition development, 138
Expertise
    aging and, 147
    intelligence as, 132–133
Explicit contracting, in transformational leadership, 75

F

Face threats, in conversations among leaders, 193
Failing to cooperate, in conversations among leaders, 201–203
Family identity, 168
Feedback
    effects of, in motivation for learning, 134–135
    influence of, 147
    in leader development, 64–65
Feedback competency, definition of, 331 (tab)
Field manuals, after World War II, 31

Flexibility competency, definition of, 331 (tab)
Flexible cognitive structures
    in event-based approach training, 319–320
FRL. See Full Range Leadership
Full Range Leadership (FRL)
    development of, 82
    hierarchical model of, 80–81
Full Range Leadership (FRL) developemnt
    definition of, 71–72
    causal links for, 81–82
    hierarchical model of, 78–79, 78 (fig)
Full Range Leadership (FRL) model
    components of, 73–77
        measurement of, 77–78, 78 (fig)
        conceptualization of, 72–73
        efficacy of, 79–82
Functional approach
    to multicultural team leadership, 296
    to team leader behavior, 297 (tab)
Functional behavior(s), of team leader, 297 (tab)

G

Games. See Computer games
Gamma change, definition of, 54
Gender, social identity and, 157–158
Germany, return of forces to, in Gulf War, 27–28. See also REFORGER
Global positioning system (GPS), in Gulf War, 27–28
Globalization, team diversity and, 20
Goal orientation, leader change and, 368
Goal specification competency, definition of, 334 (tab)
GPS. See Global positioning system
Group-level vs individual-level change, individual-level vs, 52 (tab), 54
Growth, change and, 41–42
Gulf War, 27–29
    preparation for, 28–29

H

Hierachical model of leadership, 78 (fig)
    performance impact and, 80–81
Hierarchical linear modeling (HLM), 57 (note)
Hill's research, on managerial identity development, 164

HLM. *See* Hierarchical linear modeling
Holding environment, 163
Human development, uneven course
    of, 127

I

Ibarra's research, on identity change,
    164–165
Identification-based trust, motivational team
    processes and, 274
Identity. *See also* Self-awareness
    career, 168
    competence and, 18
    description of, 154
    dimensions of, 167–169
    family, 168
    motivation and, 171
    organizational, 168
    personal, 168
    questions about, 171–173
    social, 168, 171–172
    socialization and, 160–161
    use of term, 154 (note)
    work, 168
Identity change(s)
    Ibarra's research on, 164–165
    rapid role changes and, 171
    stages in, 159
Identity clarity
    personal, 168
    promotion of, 169–170
Identity development, occupational
    studies of *see also* Identity
    evolution
    Hill's research, 164
    Ibarra's research, 164–165
    Schein's research, 165–166
    at University of Chicago, 163–164
Identity evolution *see also* Identity
    development
    Daniel Levinson model of, 161–162
    Robert Kegan model of, 162–163
    stages of, in adult development, 161–167
Identity learning ability, 168–169
Implicit contracting, in transformational
    leadership, 75
Implicit leadership theory, 298–299
Importance of teamwork competency, definition
    of, 333 (tab)

In-depth understanding, adult cognition
    development and, 141–142
Indirect speech act, in conversations among
    leaders, 185
Individual differences
    in change, 52 (tab), 54–55
    in developing adult cognition, 135–136
    leader change and, 367–370
    organizational climate and, 375–376
Individual utterances, in conversations among
    leaders, 187–188
Individualized consideration, in transactional
    and transformational leadership, 75
Individual-level vs group-level change, 52 (tab),
    54
Influence, interpersonal, 44
Informants, in measuring emotions, 246
Information, learned, intelligent use of, 146
Information allocation, definition of, 280
Information processing, as team cognitive
    process, 280–281
Initiative-response analysis, in conversations
    among leaders, 200
Insertion sequence, in conversations among
    leaders, 197
Inspirational leadership, 75
Instruction, in conversations among leaders, 183
Integration
    complexity and, 42
    as core of complexity, 17
Intelligence
    criteria for, 242–243
    as developed expertise, 132–133
    emotional, 19
    practical
        definition of, 214
        description of, 212–213
        leadership and, 211–214
    social, in event-based training, 318
    successful, definition of, 212
    tests of, 226
Interaction, leadership in, 179–180,
    180 (tab), 181 (tab)
Interactional dominance, in conversations
    among leaders, 200
Interests, adult cognition development and, 137
Interpersonal influence, leadership through, 44
Interpersonal relations competency, definition
    of, 331 (tab)
Irreversible vs reversible change, 52 (tab), 53

K

Kegan's developmental framework of leadership
    complexity, 43–45
Kegan's model of identity evolution, 162
Knowledge
    in adult cognition development, 138
    in army applications, 24
    computer games and, 108–109
    understanding vs, 29–33
Knowledge Post, 230
Knowledge-based trust, motivational team
    processes and, 274

L

Latent growth models (LGM)
    of longitudinal change, 57–61, 58 (fig), 59
        (fig), 60 (fig), 61 (tab)
    extensions to, 61–64, 63 (fig)
    in understanding leader development
        distance learning, 65–66
        feedback, 64–65
        simulations, 66
Leader(s)
    emotional intelligence abilities
        displayed by, 250–253, 251 (tab)
    facilitation of thought by, 251–252
    identification of emotions by, 251
    management of emotions by, 252–253
    understanding of emotions by, 252
Leader change
    definition of, 361–362
    individual differences and, 367–370
    organizational climate and, 370–375
    from work experiences to, 364–366
Leader competency, for virtual teams, 285–288
Leader development, 6–7, 391–392
    antecedents of, 376
    Army's definition of, 102, 103 (fig)
    change over time and, 359–360
    cognitive dialogue theory and, 204–206
    conceptual model of, 360 (fig)
    context for, 86–87
    definition of, 361
    knowledge and skills assessment in, 377–379
    latent growth modeling and, 64–66
    novel work challenges and, 364–365
    organizational climate for, 372–373
    organizational transformation through, 12–16

practical event-based training for, 317–320
rapid, implications for, 229–232
scenario-based approach to, 314
toward science of, 383–384
    conceptualizing and measuring change,
        384–385
    context, 388–389
    contributions, 392–396
    criterion development, 385–386
    developmental theory, 387–388
    leaders and leadership, 391–392
    mode of development, 389–391
    research methods, 386–387
    self-awareness and, 158–161
    self-regulation theory of, 363–364
    technologies for, military, 102–104
    for virtual teams, 285–288
    from work experiences, 364–366
    workplace feedback and instruction in,
        365–366
Leader development science, 392–396
Leader member exchange (LMX), within
    multicultural teams, 297–298
Leaderplex model of leadership complexity,
    46–47
Leadership. See also Team leadership
    in Army applications, 26–27
    Army's definition of, 100
    cognitive diaglogue theory definition of, 179
    as cognitive-communicative interaction,
        177–179
    hierachical model of, 78 (fig)
    in interaction, 179–180, 180 (tab), 181 (tab)
    motivation and, 75–76
    within multicultural teams, 293–295
        application of EBAT, 317–320
        event-based training, 315–317
        propositions, 300, 306–313, 307 (fig)
        scenario-based approach, 314
        team leader functional behavior, 297 (tab)
        team leadership, 295–296
        theoretical drivers, 296–300
    multiple views of, 99–100, 101 (fig) 102
    practical intelligence and, 211–214
    purpose of, 100
    relational dialogue approach to, 44–45
    styles of, 99–100, 101 (fig), 102
    team boundary spanning and, 283
    in terms of personal dominance, 44
    through interpersonal influence, 44
    time frame issue for, 100, 102

Leadership (*Cont.*)
  in virtual teams, 267–268
    team affective processes, 277–279
    team cognitive processes, 281–283
    team motivational processes, 274–277
Leadership competencies over time, 362–363,
      362 (fig)
Leadership complexity development, 41–42,
      50–51
  of adaptability, 49–50
  complexity and, 45
  issues in, 51–55, 52 (tab)
  Kegan's developmental framework, 43–45
  latent growth models, 57–61, 58 (fig), 59 (fig),
      60 (fig), 61 (tab)
    extensions to, 63 (fig) 64
  leaderplex model of, 46–47
  measurement of change in, 55, 56 (tab), 57
  proposed model of, 48, 48 (fig)
  reconceptualization of, 47–50
  self-awareness and, 48–49
Leadership development, 6–7, 391–392
  ability model of emotional
      intelligence and, 256–259
  advancement of, 90–91
  appropriation in, 91–92
  considerations in, 91–94
  context for, 86–87
  emotional intelligence and, 237–240, 253–255
    empathy, 254–255
    morale, 254
    social and behavioral complexity, 253
  engagement in, 93–94
  evaluation in, 93
  framework for, 256–259
  moving toward ubiquitous strategies in, 94–95
  new directions in, 91–94
  self-awareness and, 86–87
  self-regulation and, 87
  sustaining conditions for, 88–90
  ubiquitous communications and, 94–95
Leadership functions, emotional intelligence
      processes and, 251 (tab)
Leadership potential, developing full range
      of, 82
Leadership skills
  conversation illustrating, 180 (tab)
  of U.S. Army leadership doctrine, 7
Leadership subidentity growth, 156 (fig)
Leadership theories, with multicultural teams,
      296–299

Leader-team relations, virtual team
      characteristics and, 272 (fig)
Learned information, intelligent use of, 146
Learning
  acceleration of, 145
  basic principles in, 138–145
    beliefs, 138
    experience, 138
    in-depth understanding, 141–142
    lectures, 140–141
    long-term retrieval, 143–144
    planning, 139–140
    practice at retrieval, 142–143
    prior knowledge, 138
    remembering, 141
    re-representing, 144–145
    theories, 139
  definition of, 127
  distance, 65–66
  lifelong, 126–127
  motivation for, 133–135
  organizational climate for, 374–375
  self-awareness and, 84
  theories about, 139
Learning goal orientation
  leader change and, 368
  self-awareness and, 84
Learning opportunities, comparison of, 149
Learning research, funding needed for, 146
Lectures, in adult cognition development,
      140–141
Levinson's model of identity evolution, 161–162
LGM. *See* Latent growth models
Lifelong learning, 126–127
LMX. *See* Leader member exchange
Logistics, in support of ongoing operations, 35
Longitudinal change, latent growth models of,
      57–61, 58 (fig), 59 (fig), 60 (fig), 61 (tab)
    extensions to, 61–64, 63 (fig)
Longitudinal research, lack of, concerning
      identity, 171
Long-term retention, teaching for, 145
Long-term retrieval, in adult cognition
      development, 143–144

                              M

Managerial identity development, Hill's research
      on, 164

Managers, tacit knowledge inventory for, 224 (fig)

Market arena, new, challenges on entering into, 27–29

Market changes, adjusting to, 34

Mayer, Salovey, Caruso Emotional Intelligence Test (MSCEIT), 247, 248 (fig), 249

Mayer-Salovey ability model of emotional intelligence, 244 (fig)

Means, in conversations among leaders, 189

Measurement ideals, in leadership development, 73

Medical teams, 328

Mental aging, in adulthood, 128–129, 129 (fig), 130 (fig), 131

Mental models, as team cognitive process, 279–280

Metacognition
computer games and, 107–108
in event-based approach training, 318

Metacognition training, 341 (tab)

Military, technologies for leader development in, 102–104. See also Army

Military leadership, tacit knowledge for, 225 (fig)

Military training, computer games designed for, 113–114. See also Training

Mission analysis formulation and planning competency, definition of, 334 (tab)

MLQ. See Multi-factor Leadership Questionnaire

Monitoring progress toward goals competency, definition of, 334 (tab)

Morale, development of, 254

Motivation
computer games and, 106–107
leadership and, 75–76
to learn, 133–135
importance of, 147
unstudied links between identity and, 171

Motivation building competency, definition of, 334 (tab)

Motivation competency, definition of, 333 (tab)

Motivational team processes. See Team motivational processes

Motivational traits, adult cognition development and, 137

Motive, in conversations among leaders, 189

MSCEIT. See Mayer, Salovey, Caruso Emotional Intelligence Test

Multicultural teams, leadership within, 293–295. See also Teams
cross-cultural dimensions, 299–300, 301–306 (tab)
event-based training, 315–317, 316 (fig)
functional approach, 296–297
functional behaviors, 297 (tab)
implicit leadership theory, 298–299
leader-member exchange, 297–298
leadership theories, 296–299
propositions, 300, 306–313, 307 (fig)
sense giving, 309–313
sense making, 300, 306–309

Multi-factor Leadership Questionnaire (MLQ), 77

Multilevel model of self-leadership development, 82–83, 83 (fig)
developmental readiness in, 83–84
developmental trigger events in, 84–86

Multipath vs unitary change, 52 (tab), 53

Mutual trust competency, definition of, 333 (tab)

N

National Training Center (NTC)
in Gulf War, 27
review of, 24–25

Negative face threats, in conversations among leaders, 193

Negotiation of dialogue roles, 192–197

Neutral zone, in identity change, 159

Norms competency, definition of, 332 (tab)

Novel work challenges, 364–365

NTC. See National Training Center

O

Objective Force
description of, 23
important areas of, 37
transformation toward, 8

Objectives competency, definition of, 332 (tab)

On-the-job training, 341 (tab)

Opportunity, in conversations among leaders, 189

Organization(s)
continuous change in, 8–12
transformation of, 12–16
uncertainty in, 8

Organizational climate
    individual differences and, 375–376
    leader change and, 370–375
    for leader development, 372–373
    for learning, 374–375
Organizational climate construct, leader change
    and, 371–372
Organizational identity, 168

                            P

PC games. *See* Computer games
Peace, transition to war from, 27–29
Performance goal orientation, self- awareness
    and, 84
Performance measures of emotions, 246–247
Performance monitoring competency, definition
    of, 331 (tab)
Personal dominance, leadership in terms of, 44
Personal identity
    description of, 168
    social identity and, 155
        unclear links between, 171–172
    subidentities and, 155–157, 156 (fig)
Personal identity clarity, 168
Personality variables, adult cognition
    development and, 137
Personalized charismatic leaders, 76
Planning, adult cognition development and,
    139–140
Politeness theory, 193–195
Positive face threats, in conversations among
    leaders, 193
Potency competency, definition of, 333 (tab)
Practical intelligence, 212–213
    definition of, 214
    detailed model of, 220 (fig)
    leadership and, 211–214
    measurement of, research support for,
        227–228
    tacit knowledge and, 218–222, 219 (fig), 220
        (fig)
        conceptual model of, 219 (fig)
        measure of, 222–223, 224 (fig), 225 (fig),
            226–227
Practical intelligence tests, 226–227
Practical intelligence theory, 214–218
    future research directions and, 232–233
Practice at retrieval, in adult cognition
    development, 142–143

Pragmatics, cognitive dialogue theory and,
    180–181
Preparation, in role transitions, 160
Proactive behavior, leader change and, 369
Propositions. *See* Sense making propositions
Protecting face, in conversations among leaders,
    193–195
Proximal skills, development of, 287–288

                            Q

Qualitative vs quantitative change, 52 (tab), 54
Quantitative vs qualitative change, 52 (tab), 54
Quantitative dominance, in conversations among
    leaders, 200

                            R

Race, social identity and, 157–158
Random vs systematic change, 52 (tab), 53
Rapid role changes, identity changes and, 171
Readiness. *See* Developmental readiness
Recognition vs reward type items, 74
REFORGER, in Gulf War, 27–28
Relational dialogue approach to leadership,
    44–45
Relational influences, on adult development,
    166–167
Relevance theory, in conversations among
    leaders, 186–187
Remembering, in adult cognition development,
    141
Request-offer transaction, in conversations
    among leaders, 188–189
    dialogue mental model for, 188 (fig)
Requests, in conversations among leaders, 185
Re-representation, in adult cognition
    development, 144–145
Resources competency, definition of, 332 (tab)
Retention, long-term, teaching for, 145
Retrieval, in adult cognition development
    long-term, 143–144
    practice at, 142–143
Retrieval context, effect of, 143
Retrieval coordination, definition of, 280
Retrieval intervals, spacing of, 142–143
Reversible vs irreversible change, 52 (tab), 53
Reward type items, for transactional leadership,
    74

Role Concept Repertoire Test, 47 (note)
Role transitions, effects of, 160

S

Scenario-based training
    description of, 341 (tab)
    life cycle of, 316 (fig)
Schein's research on career anchors,
        165–166
See through, description of, 43
Sees with, description of, 43
Selective combination, 216
Selective comparison, 216
Selective encoding, 216
Self, use of term, 154 (note)
Self-assessments, adult learning and, 148
Self-awareness
    as aspect of emotional intelligence, 241
    competence and, 18
    description of, 154–155
    everyday changes in, 172
    leader development and
        effects of change, 158–161
        role transitions, 160
        socialization, 160–161
        status passage, 158–160
    in leadership complexity, 48–49
    leadership development and, 86–87
    measurement issues concerning, 171
    promotion of, 169–170
    protean career contract and, 172
    role transitions and, 160
Self-complexity, 46
Self-concept, use of term, 154 (note)
Self-development, as team leader, 347–348
Self-efficacy, leader change and, 368–369
Self-leadership development
    developmental readiness in, 83–84
    multilevel model of, 82–83, 83 (fig)
    supporting components of, 87–90
    trigger events in, 84–86
Self-management, emotional intelligence and,
        241–242
Self-monitoring, leader change and, 367–368
Self-perceptions, accuracy of, 168
Self-regulation, leadership development and, 87
Self-regulation theory of leader development,
        363–364
Self-report, in measuring emotions, 245–246

Semantic dominance, in conversations among
        leaders, 200
Sense giving propositions, within multicultural
        team leadership, 309–313
Sense making, in conversations among leaders,
        203–204
Sense making propositions
    within multicultural team leadership, 300,
        306–309
    theoretical framework for, 307
Sequences of utterances, in conversations among
        leaders, 187–188
Shared situational awareness competency,
        definition of, 331 (tab)
Shared task models competency, definition of,
        332 (tab)
Shared vision competency, definition of,
        333 (tab)
Sharing control, in conversations among leaders,
        199–201
Showing facts, in conversations among leaders,
        182–184
Simulations, in leader development, 66
SIT. See Social identity theory
Situational awareness, in Army applications,
        25–26
Situational awareness competency, definition of,
        331 (tab)
Situational understanding. See Situational
        awareness
Skills, computer games and, 108–109. See also
        specific skills; Thinking skills
Smiling, in conversations among leaders,
        184
Social awareness, as aspect of emotional
        intelligence, 242
Social complexity, 46–47
    in leadership development, 253
Social differentiation, 46
Social identity, 168
    personal identity and, 155
    unclear links between, 171–172
Social identity theory (SIT), 155
    description of, 157–158
Social integration, 46
Social intelligence, in event-based approach
        training, 318
Social skills, as aspect of emotional intelligence,
        242
Social smiling, in conversations among leaders,
        184

Socialization
    dimensions of, 161
    effects of, on identity, 160–161
Socialized charismatic leaders, 76
Speech acts, in conversations among leaders,
    185
Stabilization, in role transitions, 160
Status passage, leader development and,
    158–160
Strategy formulation competency, definition of,
    334 (tab)
Stress exposure training, 341 (tab)
Subidentities, personal identity and, 155–157,
    156 (fig)
Subject-object relations, process of, 163
Successful intelligence, definition of, 212
Successful intelligence theory, 213
Symbology, in knowledge vs understanding,
    29–30
Systematic vs random change, 52 (tab), 53
Systems monitoring competency,
    definition of, 334 (tab)

T

Tacit knowledge
    incorrect, 221
    for military leadership, 225 (fig)
    practical intelligence, 218–222, 220 (fig)
        conceptual model of, 219 (fig)
        measure of, 222–223, 224 (fig), 225 (fig),
        226–228
Tacit knowledge inventory, 224 (fig)
Tactical skills, of U.S. Army leadership doctrine,
    7
Task sequencing competency, definition of,
    332 (tab)
Task-specific teammate characteristics
    competency, definition of, 332 (tab)
Team affective processes, 277–279
    leadership in virtual teams and, 278–279
Team attitude competencies, definition of,
    333 (tab)
Team boundary spanning, leadership and, 283
Team building, 341 (tab)
Team cognitive processes, 279–283
    information processing, 280–281
    leadership in virtual teams and, 281–283
    mental models, 279–280

transactive memory, 280
Team cohesion competency, definition of,
    333 (tab)
Team competencies, 330–333
    attitude, 333 (tab)
    knowledge, 332 (tab)
    skill, 331 (tab)
Team coordination, defintion of, 337
Team coordination training, description of,
    341 (tab)
Team knowledge competencies, definitions of,
    332 (tab)
Team leader development, 344–345
    by formal training, 345–346
    scenario-based approach to, 314
    by self-development, 347–348
    by work experiences, 346–347
Team leaders, functional behaviors of, 297 (tab),
    344 (tab)
Team leadership, 342–343. See also
    Leadership
    definition of, 295–296
    functional leadership behaviors, 297 (tab),
    344 (tab)
    within multicultural teams
        cross-cultural dimensions, 299–300
        leadership theories, 296–299, 297 (tab)
    research needs and future directions of,
        349–351
Team leadership competency, definition of, 331
    (tab)
Team mission competency, definition of, 332
    (tab)
Team monitoring competency, definition of, 334
    (tab)
Team motivational processes, 272–277
    leadership and, 274–276
Team orientation competency, definition of, 332
    (tab)
Team role interaction patterns
    competency, definition of, 332 (tab)
Team self-correction training, 341 (tab)
Team skill competencies, definitions of, 334
    (tab)
Team skill competency, definitions of, 331 (tab)
Team training, 338–340
    instructional strategies for, 340–342,
        341 (tab)
    principles of, 340 (tab)
    structure of, 339 (fig)

Team typology, 326–327, 327 (tab)
Teams. *See also* Multicultural teams;
  Virtual teams
  command and control, 329
  commercial aviation, 328
  distributed decision-making, 329–330
  medical, 328
  operating in complex environments,
    327–330
Teamwork competency, definition of, 332 (tab)
Teamwork findings and principles, 335 (tab)
Technical skills, of U.S. Army leadership
    doctrine, 7
Technology(ies)
  advances in, team diversity and, 20
  in Army applications, 25
  broad definition of, 99
  for military leader development,
    102–104
Terrorism, as unpredictability, 8
Testing effect, 142
Theory(ies), about learning, adult
    cognition development and, 139
Thinking critically, in conversations
    among leaders, 197–199, 198 (fig)
Thinking skills, computer games and, 107.
    See also Skills
Thought, facilitation of, 256
  by leaders, 251–252
Training
  difference between development and, 10
  military, computer games designed for,
    113–114
Transactional leadership, rewards for, 74
Transactive memory, as team cognitive process,
    280
Transfer, teaching for, 145
Transformation
  toward an Objective Force, 8
  organizational, through leader
    development, 12–16
  of organizations, 8–12
  U.S. Army's efforts regarding, 8
Transformational leaders, dual effect by, 76
Transformational leadership, 75
Transition, identity change and, 160
Trigger events. *See* Developmental trigger
    events
Trust as team motivational process, 273–276
Turbulence, in organizational domain, 8

U

Ubiquitous communications, leadership
    development and, 94–95
Uncertainty, in organizational domain, 8
Understanding
  in conversations among leaders, 185
  in-depth, adult cognition development and,
    141–142
  knowledge vs, 29–33
Unitary vs multipath change, 52 (tab) 53
University of Chicago study, of identity
    development, 163–1164
Unpredictability, in organizational domain, 8
Utterances, in conversations among leaders,
    187–188

V

Values, as deminsion of identity, 168
Video games. *See* Computer games
Vietnam War, 27
Virtual teams. *See also* Multicultural teams;
    Teams
  characteristics of, 272 (fig)
  definition of, 268–271, 269 (tab)
  dimensions of, 271 (fig)
  leadership in, 267–268
    leader competencies, 285–288
    team motivational processes, 274–277
  prescriptions for, 286 (tab)
  processes in, 271–272
    affective, 277–279
    cognitive, 279–283
    coordination, 272
    motivational, 272–277

W

War, transition from peace to, 27–29
Work experiences, to leader change, 364–366
Work identity, 168
  description of, 168
Workplace feedback and instruction, 365–366
World War II, field manuals following, 31
  description of, 168
Workplace feedback and instruction, 365–366
World War II,

Printed in the USA/Agawam, MA
March 7, 2013

573435.010